Principles of Taxation

Principles of Taxation

for Business and Investment Planning   2013 Edition

Sally M. Jones
Professor Emeritus of Accounting
McIntire School of Commerce
University of Virginia

Shelley C. Rhoades-Catanach
Associate Professor of Accountancy
School of Business
Villanova University

McGraw-Hill Irwin

McGraw-Hill Irwin

PRINCIPLES OF TAXATION FOR BUSINESS AND INVESTMENT PLANNING: 2013 EDITION

Published by McGraw-Hill, a business unit of The McGraw-Hill Companies, Inc., 1221 Avenue of the Americas, New York, NY 10020. Copyright © 2013 by The McGraw-Hill Companies, Inc. All rights reserved. Printed in the United States of America. Previous editions © 2012, 2011 and 2010. No part of this publication may be reproduced or distributed in any form or by any means, or stored in a database or retrieval system, without the prior written consent of The McGraw-Hill Companies, Inc., including, but not limited to, in any network or other electronic storage or transmission, or broadcast for distance learning.

Some ancillaries, including electronic and print components, may not be available to customers outside the United States.

This book is printed on acid-free paper.

1 2 3 4 5 6 7 8 9 0 QDB/QDB 1 0 9 8 7 6 5 4 3 2

ISBN 978-0-07-802548-8
MHID 0-07-802548-6
ISSN 1099-5587

VP, General Manager, Products & Markets: *Brent Gordon*
Vice President of Specialized Publishing: *Janice M. Roerig-Blong*
Publisher: *Tim Vertovec*
Sponsoring Editor: *Donna Dillon*
Marketing Manager: *Dean Karampelas*
Editorial Coordinator: *Jessica Wiley*
Lead Project Manager: *Jane Mohr*
Design Coordinator: *Brenda A. Rolwes*
Cover Designer: *Matthew Baldwin*
Buyer: *Nicole Baumgartner*
Media Project Manager: *Prashanthi Nadipalli*
Compositor: *MPS Limited*
Typeface: *10/12 Times New Roman*
Printer: *Quad/Graphics*

All credits appearing on page or at the end of the book are considered to be an extension of the copyright page.

To Zane and Tony

About the Authors

Sally M. Jones is professor emeritus of accounting at the McIntire School of Commerce, University of Virginia, where she continues to teach graduate tax courses. Before joining the Virginia faculty in 1992, Professor Jones spent 14 years on the faculty of the Graduate School of Business, University of Texas at Austin. She received her undergraduate degree from Augusta College, her MPA from the University of Texas, and her Ph.D. from the University of Houston. She is also a CPA. Professor Jones was the first editor of *Advances in Taxation* (JAI Press) and the *PriceWaterhouse Case Studies in Taxation.* She has published numerous articles in the *Journal of Taxation, The Tax Adviser,* and the *Journal of the American Taxation Association.* Professor Jones is a frequent speaker at tax conferences and symposia, a past president of the American Taxation Association, and the 2000 recipient of the Ray M. Sommerfeld Outstanding Tax Educator Award.

Shelley Rhoades-Catanach is an associate professor of accountancy at Villanova University and a CPA. She teaches a variety of tax courses in Villanova's undergraduate, masters of accounting, and graduate tax programs. Before joining the Villanova faculty in 1998, Professor Rhoades-Catanach spent four years on the faculty of Washington University in St. Louis. She has also served as a visiting faculty member at the Darden Graduate School, University of Virginia, and at INSEAD, an international MBA program in Fontainebleau, France. She received her undergraduate degree in accounting from the University of Nebraska at Lincoln and her Ph.D. from the University of Texas at Austin. Professor Rhoades-Catanach has published articles in numerous journals, including the *Journal of the American Taxation Association,* the *Accounting Review, Issues in Accounting Education,* the *Journal of Accounting Education,* and *Review of Accounting Studies.* She has served as president, vice president, and trustee of the American Taxation Association and on the editorial boards of the *Journal of the American Taxation Association* and the *Journal of International Accounting, Auditing and Taxation.* Professor Rhoades-Catanach is the 2010 recipient of the Ray M. Sommerfeld Outstanding Tax Educator Award.

Brief Contents

A Note from the Authors   xiv
Introduction to Students   xxvi

PART ONE
Exploring the Tax Environment

1 Taxes and Taxing Jurisdictions   3

2 Policy Standards for a Good Tax   21

PART TWO
Fundamentals of Tax Planning

3 Taxes as Transaction Costs   47

4 Maxims of Income Tax Planning   69

5 Tax Research   93

PART THREE
The Measurement of Taxable Income

6 Taxable Income from Business Operations   117

7 Property Acquisitions and Cost Recovery Deductions   157

   Appendix 7–A Midquarter Convention Tables   195

8 Property Dispositions   199

9 Nontaxable Exchanges   241

PART FOUR
The Taxation of Business Income

10 Sole Proprietorships, Partnerships, LLCs, and S Corporations   271

11 The Corporate Taxpayer   309

   Appendix 11–A Schedule M-3 for Reconciling Book and Taxable Income   341

12 The Choice of Business Entity   345

13 Jurisdictional Issues in Business Taxation   371

PART FIVE
The Individual Taxpayer

14 The Individual Tax Formula   407

15 Compensation and Retirement Planning   441

16 Investment and Personal Financial Planning   485

   Appendix 16–A Comprehensive Schedule D Problem   529

17 Tax Consequences of Personal Activities   535

   Appendix 17–A Social Security Worksheet (Adapted from IRS Publication 915)   566

PART SIX
The Tax Compliance Process

18 The Tax Compliance Process   569

APPENDIXES

A Present Value of $1   **593**
B Present Value of Annuity of $1   **594**
C 2012 Income Tax Rates   **595**

GLOSSARY   597

INDEX   609

Contents

A Note from the Authors   xiv
Introduction to Students   xxvi

PART ONE
EXPLORING THE TAX ENVIRONMENT

Chapter 1
Taxes and Taxing Jurisdictions   3

Some Basic Terminology   4
  The Relationship between Base, Rate,
  and Revenue   5
  Transaction- or Activity-Based Taxes   6
  Earmarked Taxes   6
The Pervasive Nature of Taxation   6
  Local Taxes   7
  State Taxes   8
  Federal Taxes   10
  Taxes Imposed by Foreign Jurisdictions   12
  Jurisdictional Competition   12
Dynamic Nature of Taxation   13
  Tax Base Changes   13
  Taxes and the Political Process   14
Sources of Federal Tax Law   14
  Statutory Authority   15
  Administrative Authority   15
  Judicial Authority   16
Conclusion   16
Key Terms   16
Questions and Problems for Discussion   17
Application Problems   18
Issue Recognition Problems   19
Research Problems   20
Tax Planning Cases   20

Chapter 2
Policy Standards for a Good Tax   21

Standards for a Good Tax   22
Taxes Should be Sufficient   22
  The National Debt   23
  How to Increase Tax Revenues   23
  Static versus Dynamic Forecasting   23
  Behavioral Responses to Rate Changes   25

Taxes Should be Convenient   28
Taxes Should be Efficient   28
  The Classical Standard of Efficiency   29
  Taxes as an Instrument of Fiscal Policy   29
  Taxes and Behavior Modification   30
Taxes Should be Fair   32
  Ability to Pay   32
  Horizontal Equity   32
  Vertical Equity   33
  Distributive Justice   36
  The Perception of Inequity   38
Conclusion   38
Key Terms   39
Questions and Problems for Discussion   39
Application Problems   40
Issue Recognition Problems   42
Research Problems   43
Tax Planning Case   43

PART TWO
FUNDAMENTALS OF TAX PLANNING

Chapter 3
Taxes as Transaction Costs   47

The Role of Net Present Value in
Decision Making   48
  Quantifying Cash Flows   48
  The Concept of Present Value   48
  The Issue of Risk   50
  A Net Present Value Example   51
Taxes and Cash Flows   51
  The Significance of Marginal Tax Rate   52
  Net Present Value Example Revisited   53
  The Uncertainty of Tax Consequences   55
Structuring Transactions to Reduce Taxes   57
  An Important Caveat   58
  Transactional Markets   58
Conclusion   62
Key Terms   63
Questions and Problems for Discussion   63
Application Problems   63
Issue Recognition Problems   67
Tax Planning Cases   68

Chapter 4
Maxims of Income Tax Planning 69

Tax Avoidance—Not Evasion 70
What Makes Income Tax Planning
Possible? 70
The Entity Variable 71
 Income Shifting 72
 Deduction Shifting 72
 Constraints on Income Shifting 73
The Time Period Variable 73
 Income Deferral and Opportunity Costs 75
 Income Deferral and Rate Changes 76
The Jurisdiction Variable 77
The Character Variable 77
 Determining the Value of Preferential Rates 78
 Constraints on Conversion 79
 Implicit Taxes 79
Developing Tax Planning Strategies 80
 Additional Strategic Considerations 81
 Tax Legal Doctrines 83
Conclusion 84
Key Terms 85
Questions and Problems for Discussion 85
Application Problems 86
Issue Recognition Problems 89
Research Problems 90
Tax Planning Cases 90

Chapter 5
Tax Research 93

Developing Tax Research Skills 93
 The Tax Research Process 94
Step 1: Get the Facts 95
Step 2: Identify the Issues 96
Step 3: Locate Authority 97
 Primary Authorities 97
 Secondary Authorities 99
 Strategies for Locating Relevant Authority 100
Step 4: Analyze Authority 103
Step 5: Repeat Steps 1 through 4 105
Step 6: Communicate your Conclusions 106
Conclusion 108
Key Terms 109
Questions and Problems for Discussion 109
Application Problems 110
Issue Recognition Problems 112
Research Problems 113
Tax Planning Cases 113

PART THREE
THE MEASUREMENT OF TAXABLE INCOME

Chapter 6
Taxable Income from Business Operations 117

Business Profit as Taxable Income 118
The Taxable Year 119
 Changing a Taxable Year 120
 Annualizing Income on a Short-Period Return 120
Methods of Accounting 122
 Tax Policy Objectives 123
The Cash Method 125
 Constructive Receipt 126
 Prepaid Expenses and Interest 127
 Merchandise Inventories 128
 Limitations on Use of the Cash Method by Corporations 129
The Accrual Method 129
 Contrasting Perspectives on Income Measurement 130
 Permanent versus Temporary Differences 130
 Tax Expense versus Tax Payable 132
 Temporary Book/Tax Accounting Differences 133
Net Operating Losses 139
 The Problem of Excess Deductions 139
 Solution: The NOL Deduction 140
 Valuing an NOL Deduction 141
 Giving Up an NOL Carryback 142
 Accounting for NOLs 143
Conclusion 143
Sources of Book/Tax Differences 144
Key Terms 144
Questions and Problems for Discussion 144
Application Problems 145
Issue Recognition Problems 152
Research Problems 154
Tax Planning Cases 154

Chapter 7
Property Acquisitions and Cost Recovery Deductions 157

Deductible Expense or Capitalized Cost? 158
 Repairs and Cleanup Costs 159
 Deductions of Capital Expenditures as Subsidies 160
The Critical Role of Tax Basis 161
 Basis, Cost Recovery, and Cash Flow 162
 Cost Basis 163

Introduction to Cost Recovery Methods   164
Inventories and Cost of Goods Sold   165
  The Unicap Rules   *165*
  Computing Cost of Goods Sold   *166*
Depreciation of Tangible Business Assets   166
  Book and Tax Concepts of Depreciation   *166*
  The MACRS Framework   *167*
  Limited Depreciation for Passenger Automobiles   *173*
  Section 179 Expensing Election   *174*
  Bonus Depreciation   *176*
  Purchase versus Leasing Decision   *177*
Amortization of Intangible Assets   178
  Organizational and Start-Up Costs   *178*
  Leasehold Costs and Improvements   *180*
  Business Acquisition Intangibles   *180*
  Comprehensive Example of a Lump-Sum Purchase   *182*
Depletion of Natural Resources   182
  Percentage Depletion   *183*
Conclusion   184
Sources of Book/Tax Differences   185
Key Terms   185
Questions and Problems for Discussion   185
Application Problems   186
Issue Recognition Problems   192
Research Problems   192
Tax Planning Cases   193
Appendix 7–A Midquarter Convention Tables   195

Chapter 8
Property Dispositions   199

Computation of Gain or Loss Recognized   200
  Sales and Exchanges   *201*
  Seller-Financed Sales   *203*
  Disallowed Losses on Related Party Sales   *206*
Tax Character of Gains and Losses   208
  Capital Asset Defined   *208*
  Capital Loss Limitation   *209*
  Taxation of Capital Gains   *211*
  Capital Asset Definition Revisited   *211*
Dispositions of Noncapital Assets   212
  Inventory   *212*
  Business Accounts Receivable and Supplies   *213*
  Section 1231 Assets   *214*
  Depreciation Recapture   *216*
  Comprehensive Example   *220*
Other Property Dispositions   222
  Abandonment and Worthlessness   *222*
  Foreclosures   *224*
  Casualties and Thefts   *224*

Conclusion   225
Sources of Book/Tax Differences   225
Key Terms   225
Questions and Problems for Discussion   226
Application Problems   227
Issue Recognition Problems   236
Research Problems   237
Tax Planning Cases   237
CPA Exam Simulation   239

Chapter 9
Nontaxable Exchanges   241

Tax Neutrality for Asset Exchanges   241
A Generic Nontaxable Exchange   242
  Exchanges of Qualifying Property   *242*
  The Substituted Basis Rule   *243*
  The Effect of Boot   *244*
  Book/Tax Difference from Nontaxable Exchange   *245*
  Summary   *246*
Like-Kind Exchanges   246
  Exchanges of Mortgaged Properties   *249*
Involuntary Conversions   251
Formations of Business Entities   252
  Corporate Formations   *252*
  Partnership Formations   *254*
Wash Sales   255
Conclusion   255
Sources of Book/Tax Differences   256
Key Terms   256
Questions and Problems for Discussion   256
Application Problems   257
Issue Recognition Problems   263
Research Problems   264
Tax Planning Cases   265
Comprehensive Problems for Part Three   266

PART FOUR
THE TAXATION OF BUSINESS INCOME

Chapter 10
Sole Proprietorships, Partnerships, LLCs, and S Corporations   271

Sole Proprietorships   272
  Overview of Schedule C   *272*
  Employment Taxes   *276*
  Self-Employment Tax   *278*
Partnerships   279
  Forming a Partnership   *279*

Partnership Reporting Requirements   281
Tax Consequences to Partners   284
*Adjusting the Basis of a Partnership
Interest   287*
Limited Liability Companies   290
Subchapter S Corporations   291
Eligible Corporations   293
Tax Consequences to Shareholders   295
*Adjusting the Basis of S Corporation
Stock   297*
Conclusion   298
Key Terms   299
Questions and Problems for Discussion   299
Application Problems   300
Issue Recognition Problems   304
Research Problems   306
Tax Planning Cases   306
CPA Exam Simulation   308

Chapter 11
The Corporate Taxpayer   309

Legal Characteristics of Corporations   310
Affiliated Groups   310
Nonprofit Corporations   312
Computing Corporate Taxable Income   312
The Dividends-Received Deduction   314
Reconciling Book Income and Taxable Income   315
Computing the Regular Corporate Tax   316
Personal Service Corporations   318
Reduced Tax Burden on Domestic Manufacturers   318
Tax Credits   319
Rehabilitation Credit   320
Alternative Minimum Tax   321
Alternative Minimum Taxable Income   322
Calculating AMT   324
Minimum Tax Credit   325
Payment and Filing Requirements   326
Distributions of Profits to Investors   327
Alternatives to Double Taxation   328
Incidence of the Corporate Tax   329
Conclusion   330
Sources of Book/Tax Differences   330
Key Terms   330
Questions and Problems for Discussion   330
Application Problems   331
Issue Recognition Problems   337
Research Problems   338
Tax Planning Cases   339
CPA Exam Simulation   340

Appendix 11–A Schedule M-3 for Reconciling
Book and Taxable Income   341

Chapter 12
The Choice of Business Entity   345

Tax Planning with Passthrough Entities   346
Tax Benefit of Start-Up Losses   346
Avoiding a Double Tax on Business Income   347
Income Shifting among Family Members   348
Partnership or S Corporation?   351
Contrasting Characteristics   351
Two Planning Cases   353
Tax Planning with Closely Held Corporations   354
Getting Cash out of the Corporation   354
Decline of the Corporate Tax Shelter   357
Penalty Taxes on Corporate Accumulations   358
Controlled Corporate Groups   360
Conclusion   361
Key Terms   361
Questions and Problems for Discussion   361
Application Problems   363
Issue Recognition Problems   366
Research Problems   368
Tax Planning Cases   369

Chapter 13
Jurisdictional Issues in Business
Taxation   371

State and Local Taxation   372
Constitutional Restrictions on State Jurisdiction   372
Apportionment of Business Income   374
Tax Planning Implications   376
Gross Receipts Taxes   377
Tax Consequences of International Business
Operations   378
Income Tax Treaties   378
U.S. Jurisdiction to Tax Global Income   379
Foreign Tax Credit   379
Limitation on the Annual Credit   380
Organizational Forms for Overseas Operations   383
Branch Offices and Foreign Partnerships   383
Domestic Subsidiaries   383
Foreign Subsidiaries   384
Deferral of U.S. Tax on Foreign Source Income   386
Controlled Foreign Corporations   388
Transfer Pricing and Section 482   391
Book/Tax Differences Related to Foreign Operations   392
Conclusion   392

Sources of Book/Tax Differences   393
Key Terms   393
Questions and Problems for Discussion   393
Application Problems   394
Issue Recognition Problems   399
Research Problems   400
Tax Planning Cases   401
Comprehensive Problems for Part Four   402

PART FIVE
THE INDIVIDUAL TAXPAYER

Chapter 14
The Individual Tax Formula   407

Filing Status for Individuals   408
Married Individuals and Surviving Spouses   408
Unmarried Individuals   409
Overview of the Taxable Income Computation   409
The Four-Step Procedure   409
Step 1: Calculate Total Income   410
Step 2: Calculate Adjusted Gross Income   410
Step 3: Subtract Standard Deduction or Itemized Deductions   410
Step 4: Subtract Exemption Amount   415
The Taxable Income Formula   418
Computing Individual Tax   419
The Marriage Penalty Dilemma   421
The Elusive Marginal Tax Rate   422
Individual Tax Credits   424
Child Credit   424
Dependent Care Credit   425
Earned Income Credit   425
Excess Social Security Tax Withholding Credit   426
Alternative Minimum Tax   427
The AMT Trap   429
Payment and Filing Requirements   429
Conclusion   431
Key Terms   432
Questions and Problems for Discussion   432
Application Problems   433
Issue Recognition Problems   438
Research Problems   439
Tax Planning Cases   440

Chapter 15
Compensation and Retirement Planning   441

The Compensation Transaction   442
Employee or Independent Contractor?   442

Tax Consequences of Worker Classification   442
Worker Classification Controversy   443
Wage and Salary Payments   445
Reasonable Compensation   445
Foreign Earned Income Exclusion   448
Employee Fringe Benefits   449
Fringe Benefits and Self-Employed Individuals   450
Compensation Planning with Fringe Benefits   451
Employee Stock Options   452
Book/Tax Difference   454
Incentive Stock Options   454
Employment-Related Expenses   456
Moving Expenses   456
Retirement Planning   457
Tax Advantages of Qualified Retirement Plans   457
Premature Withdrawals   459
Types of Qualified Plans   460
Employer-Provided Plans   460
Keogh Plans for Self-Employed Individuals   464
Individual Retirement Accounts   465
Contribution Limits   465
Deduction of IRA Contributions   466
Withdrawals from IRAs   468
Rollovers to IRAs   470
Conclusion   472
Sources of Book/Tax Differences   472
Key Terms   472
Questions and Problems for Discussion   472
Application Problems   473
Issue Recognition Problems   479
Research Problems   481
Tax Planning Cases   482

Chapter 16
Investment and Personal Financial Planning   485

Business Versus Investment Activities   486
Investments in Financial Assets   486
Dividend and Interest Income   486
Tax-Exempt Interest   488
Deferred Interest Income   490
Life Insurance Policies and Annuity Contracts   492
Gains and Losses from Security Transactions   494
Computing Gains and Losses   494
Tax Consequences of Capital Gains and Losses   497
Netting Capital Gains and Losses   497
Preferential Rates on Long-Term Capital Gains   500

Policy Reasons for a Preferential Rate *501*
Capital Loss Limitation *502*
Investments in Small Corporate Businesses 503
Qualified Small Business Stock *503*
Section 1244 Stock *504*
Investment Expenses 504
Investment Interest Expense *505*
Investments in Real Property 506
Undeveloped Land *506*
Rental Real Estate *507*
Investments in Passive Activities 508
Passive Activity Loss Limitation *509*
Planning with Passive Activity Losses *511*
Unearned Income Medicare Contribution Tax 512
Wealth Transfer Planning 512
The Transfer Tax System *513*
The Gift Tax *513*
The Estate Tax *515*
Conclusion 518
Key Terms 518
Questions and Problems for Discussion 518
Application Problems 519
Issue Recognition Problems 525
Research Problems 526
Tax Planning Cases 527
Appendix 16–A Comprehensive Schedule D
Problem 529

Chapter 17
**Tax Consequences of Personal
Activities 535**

Gross Income From Whatever Source Derived 535
Personal Receipts *536*
Legal Settlements *537*
Government Transfer Payments *538*
Gains on Sales of Personal Assets *540*
Personal Expenses 541
Medical Expenses *541*
Local, State, and Foreign Tax Payments *542*
Charitable Contributions *543*
Tax Subsidies for Education *544*
Personal Losses 545
Losses on Sales of Personal Assets *545*
Casualty and Theft Losses *546*
Hobby and Gambling Losses *547*
Tax Consequences of Home Ownership 548
Home Mortgage Interest Deduction *549*
Vacation Homes *550*
Exclusion of Gain on Sale of Principal Residence *550*

Itemized Deductions as AMT Adjustments 551
Conclusion 553
Key Terms 553
Questions and Problems for Discussion 553
Application Problems 554
Issue Recognition Problems 560
Research Problems 561
Tax Planning Cases 562
Comprehensive Problems for Part Five 563
CPA Exam Simulations 564
Appendix 17–A Social Security Worksheet (Adapted
from IRS Publication 915) 566

PART SIX
THE TAX COMPLIANCE PROCESS

Chapter 18
The Tax Compliance Process 569

Filing and Payment Requirements 570
Late-Filing and Late-Payment Penalty *571*
Return Processing *572*
The Audit Process 573
Your Rights as a Taxpayer *574*
Noncompliance Penalties *575*
Tax Return Preparer Penalties *578*
Contesting the Result of an Audit 578
Litigation *579*
A Case History: Lori Williams *v.* United States *580*
Making the Legal System More Taxpayer Friendly *581*
IRS Collection Procedures *582*
The Innocent Spouse Rule *583*
Conclusion 584
Key Terms 584
Questions and Problems for Discussion 584
Application Problems 586
Issue Recognition Problems 588
Research Problems 589
Tax Planning Cases 589

Appendix A **Present Value of $1 593**

Appendix B **Present Value of
Annuity of $1 594**

Appendix C **2012 Income Tax Rates 595**

Glossary 597

Index 609

A Note from the Authors

Principles of Taxation for Business and Investment Planning is a unique approach to the subject of taxation. This text is designed for use in introductory tax courses included in either undergraduate or graduate business programs. Its objective is to teach students to recognize the major tax issues inherent in business and financial transactions. The text focuses on fundamental concepts, the mastery of which provides a permanent frame of reference for future study of advanced tax topics. Unlike traditional introductory texts, *Principles of Taxation for Business and Investment Planning* downplays the technical detail that makes the study of taxation such a nightmare for business students. Traditional texts are heavily compliance oriented and convince many students that the tax law is too complex and specialized to be relevant to their future careers. This text attempts to do just the opposite by convincing students that an understanding of taxation is not only relevant but critical to their success in the business world.

Principles of Taxation for Business and Investment Planning has its origin in the 1989 White Paper entitled *Perspectives on Education: Capabilities for Success in the Accounting Profession,* published jointly by the Big Eight public accounting firms. The White Paper expressed disenchantment with the narrow technical focus of undergraduate accounting curricula and called for scholastic emphasis on a broad set of business skills necessary for professional success. The Accounting Education Change Commission (AECC), operating under the aegis of the American Accounting Association, embraced the philosophy reflected in the White Paper. In September 1990, the AECC published its Position Statement No. One, entitled *Objectives of Education for Accountants.* This statement reiterated that an undergraduate business education should provide a base for lifelong learning.

Despite these calls for reform, many undergraduate tax courses are taught in a traditional manner based on a paradigm developed a half-century ago. In the modern (postwar) era of business education, the first generation of tax teachers were practitioners: accountants or attorneys hired as adjunct faculty to initiate students into the mysteries of the newly enacted Internal Revenue Code of 1954. These practitioners taught their students in the same way they trained their employees. In doing so, they created a compliance-oriented paradigm. In today's world, this traditional paradigm is an anachronism. Business students don't need to learn how to generate tax information. Instead, they must learn how to use tax information to make good business and financial decisions.

A New Paradigm for the Introductory Tax Course

Principles of Taxation for Business and Investment Planning provides a paradigm for meeting the educational needs of tax students in the twenty-first century. This paradigm is based on three postulates:

- **Postulate 1: Students should learn the tax law as an integrated component of a complex economic environment.** They should be aware of the role taxes play in financial decision making and should understand how taxes motivate people and institutions to engage in certain transactions.

- **Postulate 2: Students should comprehend the tax law as an organic whole rather than as a fragmented collection of rules and regulations.** They should learn general tax rules rather than the myriad of exceptions that confuse rather than clarify the general rules. They should appreciate how the general rules apply to all taxpaying entities before they learn how specialized rules apply to only certain entities. Finally, they should learn how the law applies to broad categories of transactions rather than to a particular transaction.

- **Postulate 3: Students who learn fundamental concepts have a permanent frame of reference into which they can integrate the constant changes in the technical minutiae of the law.** The rapid evolution of the tax law results in a short shelf life for much of the detailed information contained in undergraduate tax texts. Yet the key elements of the law—the statutory and judicial bedrock—do not change with each new revenue act. Students who master these key elements truly are prepared for a lifetime of learning.

The authors know that traditional paradigms die hard and educational reform is difficult. Nevertheless, we also believe that change in the way college and university professors teach tax is both inevitable and worthwhile. Our responsibility to our students is to prepare them to cope in a business world with little tolerance for outdated skills or irrelevant knowledge. Our hope is that *Principles of Taxation for Business and Investment Planning* is a tool that can help us fulfill that responsibility.

Using This Text in a First-Semester Tax Course

Principles of Taxation for Business and Investment Planning is designed for use in a one-semester (15-week) introductory tax course. Instructors can choose which of the 18 chapters deserve a full week's coverage and which can be covered in less than a week. Instructors may even decide to omit chapters that seem less relevant to the educational needs of their students. Business students who complete a one-semester course based on this text will be well prepared to function in the modern tax environment. If they are required (or may elect) to take a second tax course, they will have a solid, theoretical foundation on which to build.

This is the sixteenth annual edition of *Principles of Taxation for Business and Investment Planning*. We've been students of the tax law far too long to believe that this edition is free from technical error or includes every relevant topic. Adopters of the text will certainly have many excellent suggestions to improve the next edition. We welcome any and all comments and encourage fellow teachers to e-mail us (smj7q@virginia.edu and shelley.rhoades@villanova.edu) with their input.

Sally M. Jones
Shelley C. Rhoades-Catanach

Key Features

The content and organization of this text are highly compatible with the Model Tax Curriculum proposed by the American Institute of Certified Public Accountants. According to the AICPA, the introductory tax course should expose students to a broad range of tax concepts and emphasize the role of taxation in the business decision-making process. Under the model curriculum, students first learn to measure the taxable income from business and property transactions. They are then introduced to the different types of business entities and the tax considerations unique to each type. Individual taxation should be one of the last topics covered, rather than the primary focus of the course. Because *Principles of Taxation for Business and Investment Planning* reflects this recommended pedagogical approach, the text is ideal for courses based on the AICPA Model Tax Curriculum.

Part One consists of two chapters that familiarize students with the global tax environment. Chapter 1 describes the environment in terms of the legal relationship between taxes, taxpayers, and governments. Definitions of key terms are developed, and the major taxes are identified. Chapter 2 considers the tax environment from a normative perspective by asking the question: "What are the characteristics of a good tax?" Students are introduced to the notions of tax efficiency and tax equity and learn how contrasting political beliefs about efficiency and equity continue to shape the tax environment.

Part Two concentrates on developing a methodology for incorporating tax factors into business decisions. Chapter 3 introduces the pivotal role of net present value of cash flows in evaluating financial alternatives. Students learn how to compute tax costs and tax savings and how to interpret them as cash flows. Chapter 4 covers the maxims of income tax planning. The characteristics of the tax law that create planning opportunities are explained, and the generic techniques for taking advantage of those opportunities are analyzed. Chapter 5 provides a succinct overview of the tax research process and prepares students to solve the research problems included at the end of each chapter. The chapter explains the six steps in the tax research process and contains a cumulative example of the application of each step to a research case.

PART ONE
Exploring the Tax Environment

1 Taxes and Taxing Jurisdictions   3
2 Policy Standards for a Good Tax   21

PART TWO
Fundamentals of Tax Planning

3 Taxes as Transaction Costs   47
4 Maxims of Income Tax Planning   69
5 Tax Research   93

PART THREE

The Measurement of Taxable Income

6 Taxable Income from Business Operations   117

7 Property Acquisitions and Cost Recovery Deductions   157

8 Property Dispositions   199

9 Nontaxable Exchanges   241

PART FOUR

The Taxation of Business Income

10 Sole Proprietorships, Partnerships, LLCs, and S Corporations   271

11 The Corporate Taxpayer   309

12 The Choice of Business Entity   345

13 Jurisdictional Issues in Business Taxation   371

PART FIVE

The Individual Taxpayer

14 The Individual Tax Formula   407

15 Compensation and Retirement Planning   441

16 Investment and Personal Financial Planning   485

17 Tax Consequences of Personal Activities   535

PART SIX

The Tax Compliance Process

18 The Tax Compliance Process   569

Appendix A   Present Value of $1   593

Appendix B   Present Value of Annuity of $1   594

Appendix C   2012 Income Tax Rates   595

Part Three focuses on the quantification of business taxable income. Chapter 6 covers the computation of income or loss from ongoing commercial activities, with special emphasis on differences between taxable income and net income for financial statement purposes. Chapters 7 and 8 explore the tax implications of acquisitions and dispositions of business property, while Chapter 9 is devoted to nontaxable exchanges.

Part Four teaches students how to calculate the tax on business income. Chapter 10 describes the function of sole proprietorships, partnerships, LLCs, and S corporations as conduits of income, while Chapter 11 discusses corporations as taxable entities in their own right. Chapter 12 builds on the preceding two chapters by exploring the tax planning implications of the choice of business entity. Chapter 13 broadens the discussion by considering the special problems of businesses operating in more than one tax jurisdiction. This chapter introduces both multistate and international tax planning strategies.

Part Five concentrates on the tax rules and regulations unique to individuals. Chapter 14 presents the individual tax formula and acquaints students with the complexities of computing individual taxable income. Chapter 15 covers compensation and retirement planning. Chapter 16 covers investment and rental activities and introduces wealth transfer planning. Finally, Chapter 17 analyzes the tax consequences of personal activities, with particular emphasis on home ownership.

Part Six consists of Chapter 18, which presents the important procedural and administrative issues confronting taxpayers. It covers the basic rules for paying tax and filing returns, as well as the penalties on taxpayers who violate the rules. Chapter 18 also describes the judicial process through which taxpayers and the IRS resolve their differences.

Key Learning Tools

Learning Objectives

The chapters begin with learning objectives that preview the technical content and alert students to the important concepts to be mastered. These objectives appear again as marginal notations marking the place in the chapter where each learning objective is addressed.

Learning Objectives

After studying this chapter, you should be able to:

1. Differentiate between tax avoidance and tax evasion.
2. List the four variables that determine the tax consequences of a transaction.
3. Explain why an income shift or a deduction shift can improve NPV.
4. Explain how the assignment of income doctrine constrains income-shifting strategies.
5. Identify the circumstances in which a tax deferral strategy may not improve NPV.
6. Contrast the tax character of ordinary income and capital gain.

Objective 4
Explain how the assignment of income doctrine constrains income-shifting strategies.

Assignment of Income Doctrine

The federal courts have consistently held that our income tax system cannot tol- cial shifts of income from one taxpayer to another. Over 75 years ago, the Sup decided that income must be taxed to the person who earns it, even if another p legal right to the wealth represented by the income.[5] Thus, a business owner w a $10,000 check in payment for services rendered to a client can't avoid reporti income by simply endorsing the check over to his daughter. In the picturesque the Court, the tax law must disregard arrangements "by which the fruits are att different tree from that on which they grew."

The Supreme Court elaborated on this theme in the case of a father who ne gotiable interest coupons from corporate bonds and gave the coupons to his so

Examples and Cases

The chapters contain numerous examples and cases illustrating or demonstrating the topic under discussion.

Conflicting Maxims

Firm MN operates as two separate taxable entities, Entity M and Entity N. The firm ating a transaction that will generate $25,000 cash in year 0 and $60,000 cash in Entity M undertakes the transaction, taxable income will correspond to cash flow (M will report $25,000 and $60,000 taxable income in years 0 and 1). If Entity N u the transaction, it must report the entire $85,000 taxable income in year 0. Entit 30 percent marginal tax rate while Entity N has a 25 percent marginal tax rate. Firm a 9 percent discount rate to compute NPV.

	Entity M	Entity
Year 0:		
Before-tax cash flow	$25,000	
Taxable income	$25,000	$85,000

Tax Talk

Each chapter includes items of "Tax Talk." These items highlight new tax planning strategies, tax facts, legislative proposals, or innovative transactions with interesting tax implications reported in the business press.

Tax Talk
The Irish rock band U2 transferred part of its publishing company, U2 Limited, out of Ireland to a Dutch financial management company because royalty income is taxed by Ireland but is virtually tax-exempt in the Netherlands.

come. Firm Y operates in State Y, which imposes a flat 4 percent tax on busine Firm Z operates in State Z, which imposes a flat 10 percent tax on business in federal purposes, state income tax payments are deductible in the computation income.[8] Both firms face a 39 percent federal tax rate. Under these facts, Firm have the following after-tax cash flows.

	Firm Y	Firm Z
Before-tax cash/income	$5,000	$5,000
State income tax cost	(200)	(500)
Federal taxable income	$4,800	$4,500
Federal tax cost (Taxable income × 39%)	(1,872)	(1,755)
After-tax cash flow	$2,928	$2,745

End-of-Chapter Material

Key Terms

Key terms are indicated in boldface in the text. A list of key terms is also supplied at the end of the chapter with page references for easy review. Definitions of key terms from all the chapters are compiled in a Glossary for the text.

Key Terms

accrual method of accounting *129*
all-events test *134*
allowance method *138*
annualized income *121*
calendar year *119*
cash method of accounting *125*
constructive receipt *126*
deferred tax asset *132*
deferred tax liability *132*

economic performance *135*
fiscal year *119*
generally accepted accounting principles (GAAP) *129*
gross income *118*
hybrid method of accounting *128*
key-person life insurance policies *124*
method of ac   *122*

NOL carryf
payment liab
permanent d
personal ser
corporatio
prepaid inco
realization
recognition
recurring ite
exception
short-period

Sources of Book/Tax Differences

Chapters 6, 7, 8, 9, 11, 13, and 15 provide a list of the sources of book/tax differences introduced in the chapter.

Sources of Book/Tax Differences

Permanent
- Interest on state and local bonds
- Key-person life insurance proceeds and premiums
- Fines and penalties
- Political contributions and lobbying expense
- Meals and entertainment expense
- Dom   duction activities

Temporary
- Prepaid income
- Bad debts
- Accrued expenses failing all-events test
- Compensation accruals
- Related party accruals
- NOL carryforwards

Questions and Problems for Discussion

Challenge students to think critically about conceptual and technical issues covered in the chapter. These problems tend to be open-ended and are designed to engage students in debate. Many problems require students to integrate material from previous chapters in formulating their responses.

Questions and Problems for Discussion

1. Discuss the choice of a taxable year for the following businesses.
   a. Retail plant and garden center.
   b. French bakery.
   c. Chimney cleaning business.
   d. Moving and transport business.
   e. Software consulting business.
2. Corporation DB operates three different lines of business. Can the cor different overall method of accounting for each line or must the corpor overall method?
3. Firm LK bought a warehouse of used furniture to equip several of its An employee discovered a cache of gold coins in a desk drawer. A loca Firm LK the rightful owner of the coins, which have a $72,000 FMV

Application Problems

Give students practice in applying the technical material covered in the chapter. Most of the problems are quantitative and require calculations to derive a numeric solution.

Issue Recognition Problems

Develop students' ability to recognize the tax issues suggested by a set of facts and to state those issues as questions. The technical issues buried in these problems typically are *not* discussed in the chapter. Consequently, students must rely on their understanding of basic principles to analyze the problem, spot the tax concern or opportunity, and formulate the question to be resolved. In short, students must take the first steps in the tax research process.

Research Problems

Provide further opportunity for students to develop their analytic skills. These problems consist of short scenarios that suggest one or more tax issues. The scenarios conclude with explicit research questions for the students to answer. To find the answers, they need access to either a traditional or an electronic tax library.

Tax Planning Cases

Give students an opportunity to integrate their tax knowledge into a business planning framework. Most cases involve taxpayers who must decide whether to undertake a certain transaction or who must choose between alternative transactions. Students must assume the role of tax adviser by recommending a course of action to maximize the after-tax value of the transaction.

Tax Planning Cases

1. Firm NS owns 90 percent of Corporation T's outstanding stock. NS also realty that T needs for use in its business. The FMV of the realty is NS's adjusted basis is $5.6 million. Both NS and T are in the 35 perce bracket. Discuss the tax implications of each of the following course decide which course you would recommend to NS.

   a. NS could exchange the realty for newly issued shares of T stock wo

   b. NS could sell the realty to T for $4 million cash.

   c. NS could lease the realty to T for its annual fair rental value of $60

2. Firm K, a noncorporate taxpayer, has owned investment land with a $6 four years. Two unrelated parties want to acquire the land from K. Part $770,000 cash, and Party B has offered another tract of land with a $7 K accepts Party B's offer, it would hold the new land for no more than t selling it. The FMV of this land should appreciate 10 percent annually capital gain is 15 percent, and it uses a 7 percent discount rate to comp offer should K accept to maximize the NPV of the transaction?

   tion EE decides to outmoded busines

CPA Exam Simulations

Prepare students to sit for the computerized CPA exam by working tax problems in a web-based interface identical to that used in the exam. Chapters 8, 10, 11, and 17 include directions to new Kaplan CPA Review simulations. Give your students a competitive edge by familiarizing them with the content and structure of tax questions as well as the software by which the CPA exam is administered.

KAPLAN

CPA REVIEW

CPA Exam Simulation

Please visit the text website for the online CPA simulation: mhhe.com/s

Miller, Smith and Tucker decided to form a partnership to perform engine The new entity, MST Consulting Services, LLP, began operations on Januar uses the calendar year for reporting purposes. The partners expect to wo MST, and each contributed cash and other property to the partnership su mence operations.

Topics covered in the simulation:

- Basis of contributed property
- Depreciation of contributed property

Supplements

Instructor's Manual

An **Instructor's Manual** includes a course outline, topics for class discussion, and teaching hints for a one-semester introductory tax course. The Instructor's Manual also provides suggested solutions to all end-of-chapter problems and cases.

Test Bank

A **Test Bank** contains true/false, multiple-choice, and application problems in a Windows platform.

These resource supplements are located on the Instructor site on the Online Learning Center.

Online Learning Center

A **web page** (www.mhhe.com/sjones2013) includes valuable material for both instructors and students. These include PowerPoint slides and online quizzes for students with solutions and their rationales. All web page materials are produced by the authors. This Online Learning Center (OLC) can be delivered in multiple ways—professors and students can access it directly through the textbook website, through PageOut, or within a course management system (i.e., WebCT, Blackboard, TopClass, or eCollege).

Changes in *Principles of Taxation*, 2013 edition

Chapter 1

- Added new Tax Talk and new example.

Chapter 2

- Updated federal deficit and national debt data.
- Updated several examples.
- Added several new Tax Talks.

Chapter 4

- Substantially revised discussion of Tax Legal Doctrines beginning on page 83 to include recent codification of the economic substance doctrine in Section 7701(o).

Chapter 5

- Added several additional examples demonstrating steps in the research process.
- Added new Application Problems and a new Tax Planning Case.

Chapter 6

- Expanded definition of ordinary and necessary business expenses.

Chapter 7

- Updated for law changes related to bonus depreciation and the Section 179 deduction.
- Updated passenger automobile limitations.
- Added new Tax Talk and new examples related to depreciation.
- Added discussion of capital loss deduction for individuals.

Chapter 8

- Added new Kaplan CPA Exam Simulation covering tax research and capital loss limitations.

Chapter 9

- Added new Tax Talk.

Chapter 10

- Updated Schedule C, Form 1065, Form 1120-S, and Schedule K-1s to 2011 versions.
- Updated discussion of payroll and self-employment taxes to reflect extension of payroll tax reduction and changes to inflation-adjusted Social Security tax threshold.
- Added new Kaplan CPA Exam Simulation covering basis of contributed property and depreciation of contributed property.

Chapter 11

- Updated filing statistics in Tax Talks throughout.
- Updated Form 1120 and Schedule M-3 to 2011 versions.
- Revised discussion of Tax Freedom Day to reflect current statistics.

- Added new Kaplan CPA Exam Simulation covering charitable contribution limitations, payments to owners for services rendered, payments for health insurance for owners, and business meals and entertainment expenses.

Chapter 13

- Added discussion of trend toward state gross receipts taxes, with specific references to the Ohio CAT, Texas Margin, and Washington B&O taxes.
- Added new example that reviews the ongoing saga of state tax changes in Michigan over the past five years.

Chapter 14

- Updated coverage of standard deduction, exemption amount, individual tax rates, and earned income credit to reflect 2012 inflation adjustments.
- Updated Volpe family examples throughout chapter to include 2011 Form 1040 (pages 1 and 2 and Schedule A).
- Deleted discussion of making work pay credit.
- Replaced Tax Planning Case 3 with updated version.

Chapter 15

- Updated a few examples to include 2011 Form W-2 and Form 1099-MISC.
- Updated coverage of Employer-Provided Plans to reflect 2012 inflation adjustments.
- Updated coverage of Individual Retirement Accounts to reflect 2012 inflation adjustments.
- Added two new Tax Talks.

Chapter 16

- Updated Mr. and Mrs. David examples to include 2011 Form 1040, Schedule B and Schedule E.
- Substantially revised coverage of Netting Capital Gains and Losses to include new Form 8949 and 2011 version of Form 1040, Schedule D.
- Added a new topic, UNEARNED INCOME MEDICARE CONTRIBUTION TAX, that includes two new shaded examples.
- Deleted discussion of 2010 transition rules for the federal estate tax.
- Revised Appendix 16-A to include new Form 8949 and 2011 version of Form 1040, Schedule D.

Chapter 17

- Added a new shaded example of gross income inclusion.
- Substantially revised coverage of Gains on Sales of Personal Assets and added a new shaded example.
- Replaced Issue Recognition Problem 10 with a new problem.
- Added new Kaplan CPA Exam Simulations covering several topics including mortgage points, casualty loss definition, and insurance reimbursements.

Chapter 18

- Updated audit coverage data in example.
- Added new Tax Talk.
- Replace shaded example with new example.

Acknowledgments

We want to thank the many friends and colleagues who continue to share their ideas for this textbook. We particularly want to acknowledge the contribution of Professor Pat Wilkie (University of Virginia) and Professor Jim Young (Northern Illinois University). Their article entitled "Teaching the Introductory Tax Course: A Template of the Federal Income Tax Formula, Taxpayer Activities, and Taxpayer Entities" in the *Journal of the American Taxation Association* (Fall 1997) profoundly influenced the organization of this book. Thanks also to the individuals who reviewed the 2012 edition of the text. Their expert comments were invaluable, and this edition is significantly improved because of their involvement:

Brad Cripe, *Northern Illinois University*

John Dorocak, *California State University–San Bernadino*

Jack Lachman, *City University of New York–Brooklyn College*

Robert Lin, *California State University–East Bay*

Sandra Owen, *Indiana University–Bloomington*

Susan Porter, *University of Virginia*

Paul Recupero, *Newbury College*

Leigh Rosenthal, *Florida Atlantic University*

Donald Samelson, *Colorado State University*

A.J. Stagliano, *Saint Joseph's University*

James Trebby, *Marquette University*

Jennifer Williams, *Assumption College*

Jennifer Wright, *Drexel University*

Lorraine Wright, *North Carolina State University*

We are grateful to the entire McGraw-Hill/Irwin team for their professional support. In particular, we want to acknowledge Tim Vertovec, Donna Dillon, Jessica Wiley, Jane Mohr, Dean Karampelas, Matthew Baldwin, Debra Sylvester, and Prashanthi Nadipalli.

Sally M. Jones
University of Virginia

Shelley C. Rhoades-Catanach
Villanova University

Introduction to Students

Principles of Taxation for Business and Investment Planning explores the role that taxes play in modern life. The book is written for business students who have completed introductory courses in accounting and finance and are familiar with basic business concepts. Those of you who fit this description, regardless of your future career path, will make decisions in which you must evaluate the effect of taxes. At the most fundamental level, all business decisions have the same economic objective: maximization of long-term wealth through cash flow enhancement. The cash flow from any transaction depends on the tax consequences. Therefore, business men and women must appreciate the role of taxes before they can make intelligent decisions, whether on behalf of their firm or on their personal behalf.

Taxes as Business Costs

When businesspeople are asked to identify the common goal of all business decisions, their immediate response tends to be that the goal is to increase profits. When prompted to think past the current year, most eventually conclude that the long-term goal of business decisions is to maximize the value of the firm. In this text, a **firm** is a generic business organization. Firms include sole proprietorships, partnerships, limited liability companies, subchapter S and regular corporations, and any other arrangement through which people carry on a profit-motivated activity. Firm managers know that short-term profits and long-term value are enhanced when operating costs, including taxes, are controlled. Experienced managers never regard taxes as fixed or unavoidable costs. As you will soon discover, opportunities abound for controlling the tax cost of doing business.

The preceding paragraph suggests that tax planning means reducing tax costs to maximize the value of the firm. Firms can reduce taxes by any number of strategies. However, tax cost is only one variable that managers must consider in making business decisions. A strategy that reduces taxes may also have undesirable consequences, such as reducing revenues or increasing nontax costs. Because of nontax variables, the strategy with the least tax cost may not be the best strategy. Therefore, tax minimization in and of itself may be a short-sighted objective. This point is so elementary yet so important: *Effective tax planning must take into account both tax and nontax factors*. When faced with competing strategies, managers should implement the strategy that maximizes firm value, even when that strategy has a higher tax cost than the alternatives. In other words, managers should never let the tax tail wag the business dog.

Taxes as Household Expenditures

Principles of Taxation for Business and Investment Planning concentrates on the income taxation of business activities and organizations. This does not mean that the tax rules applying to individuals are ignored. Quite to the contrary. For income tax purposes, individuals and the profit-making activities in which they engage are entwined. As we will observe over and over again, the ultimate taxpayers in every business are the people who own and operate that business.

As you study this text, consider your own role as a lifelong taxpayer. Regardless of who you are, where you live, or how you earn and spend your money, you will pay taxes on a regular basis to any number of governments. In fact, in the United States, taxes are the single largest household expenditure. The pie chart on page xxvii shows that a person working an eight-hour day spends almost three hours working to pay local, state, and federal taxes.

**Tax Bite in the
Eight-Hour Day**

Source: Tax Foundation.

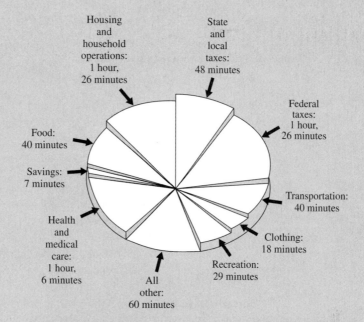

People who are clueless about taxes must take a passive role, participating in a tax system they don't understand and over which they exercise no control. In contrast, if you understand how taxes relate to your life, you can take an active role. You can take positive steps to minimize your personal tax to the fullest extent allowed by law. You can make informed financial decisions to take advantage of tax-saving opportunities. You can draw rational conclusions about the efficiency and fairness of existing tax laws and can assess the merit of competing tax reform proposals. Finally, you can change the tax system by participating as a voter in the democratic process.

The Text's Objectives

Principles of Taxation for Business and Investment Planning has three objectives that motivate the overall design of the text, the selection and ordering of topics, and the development of each topic.

Introducing Tax Policy Issues

The first objective is to acquaint you with the economic and social policy implications of the tax systems by which governments raise revenues. Most of the subject matter of the text pertains to today's tax environment and how successful businesses adapt to and take advantage of that environment. But the text also raises normative issues concerning the efficiency and equity of many features of the tax environment. You will learn how certain provisions of the tax law are intended to further the government's fiscal policy goals. You are invited to evaluate these goals and to question whether the tax system is an appropriate mechanism for accomplishing the goals.

The text identifies potentially negative aspects of the tax environment. It explains how taxes may adversely affect individual behavior or cause unintended and undesirable outcomes. You will be asked to consider whether certain provisions of the tax law favor one group of taxpayers over another and whether such favoritism is justifiable on any ethical grounds. After probing both the strengths and weaknesses of the current tax system, you can draw your own conclusions as to how the system can be improved.

Bridging the Gap between Finance and Tax

The second objective of the text is to bridge the academic gap between the study of financial theory and the study of tax law. Finance courses teach students how to make decisions on the basis of after-tax cash flows. However, these courses give only rudimentary instruction on determining the tax consequences of transactions and overlook the possibilities for controlling tax costs to maximize cash flows. In extreme cases, financial models simply ignore tax consequences by assuming that business decisions are made in a tax-free environment.

Traditional tax law courses err in the opposite direction. These courses teach students to apply statutory rules to well-defined, closed-fact situations to determine the tax consequences. Correct application of the rule is the learning objective. Students are not required to integrate the tax consequences of transactions into a business decision-making framework. In other words, they don't translate tax outcomes into cash flows. Traditional law courses may fail to encourage students to consider how closed-fact situations can be restructured to change the tax outcome and improve financial results. Consequently, students often develop the habit of analyzing transactions from a backward-looking *compliance* perspective rather than a forward-looking *planning* perspective.

The focus of *Principles of Taxation for Business and Investment Planning* is the common ground shared by financial theory and tax law. The connecting links between the two disciplines are stressed throughout the text. You will learn how effective business planning depends on an accurate assessment of relevant tax factors. Tax rules and regulations are presented and illustrated in the context of a decision-making framework. Admittedly, these rules and regulations are tough to master. Two observations should give you reassurance. First, while the tax law is extremely technical and complex, the application of its underlying principles to business decision making is relatively straightforward. Second, you can learn to appreciate tax planning strategies without becoming a tax-compliance expert.

Teaching the Framework of the Income Tax

The third objective of *Principles of Taxation for Business and Investment Planning* is to teach the framework of the federal income tax, the dominant feature of the modern tax environment. This framework has been remarkably stable over time, even though the details of the law change every year. Students who learn the framework needn't worry that their knowledge will be outdated when Congress enacts its next revenue bill.

The federal income tax system has a bad reputation as an impenetrable, intractable body of law. While the income tax law is every bit as complicated as its critics suggest, its framework consists of a manageable number of basic principles. The principles are internally consistent and underlie many technical provisions. By concentrating on these principles, you can attain a sufficient level of tax knowledge in a single introductory course. You will not be a tax expert, but you will be tax literate. You may not be capable of implementing sophisticated tax planning strategies, but you will appreciate how those strategies can improve cash flows and maximize wealth.

Because this text takes a conceptual approach to the tax law, narrowly drawn provisions, exceptions, limitations, and special cases are deemphasized. Details with the potential to confuse rather than clarify tax principles are usually relegated to footnotes. When we do examine a detailed provision of the law, the detail should illuminate an underlying concept. Or we may discuss a thorny technical rule just to emphasize the practical difficulties encountered by tax professionals who don't have the luxury of dealing with concepts.

The conceptual approach should sensitize you to the tax implications of transactions and cultivate your ability to ask good tax questions. This approach downplays the importance of the answers to these questions. Knowing the answers or, more precisely, *finding* the answers to tax questions is the job of accountants and attorneys who devote long hours in their research libraries to that end. A tax-sensitive business manager knows when to consult these experts and can help formulate the tax issues for the expert to resolve. The text's emphasis on issue recognition rather than issue resolution is reflected in the problems at the end of each chapter. Many of these problems ask you to analyze a fact situation and simply identify any tax concerns or opportunities. Other problems present you with facts suggesting tax issues with no correct solution.

A Word to Accounting Majors

Principles of Taxation for Business and Investment Planning is an ideal introductory text for those of you who are concentrating in accounting and who may even plan to specialize in taxation. You will benefit enormously from mastering the framework of the income tax as the first step in your professional education. This mastery will be the foundation for the future study of advanced topics. You will gain a command of basic principles on which to rely as you develop an instinct for your subject—a facility for diagnosing the tax issues suggested by unfamiliar and unusual transactions.

The conceptual approach is appropriate for the first tax course because it concentrates on broad issues concerning most taxpayers instead of narrow problems encountered by only a few taxpayers. If you learn these issues, you will be well prepared to expand and deepen your tax knowledge through professional experience. You will understand that taxes are only one aspect of the economic decision-making process. Because of this understanding, those of you who become tax professionals will be equipped to serve your clients not just as tax specialists but as business advisers.

CPA Exam Preparation

This text provides excellent preparation for the computer-based CPA exam. The text covers approximately 90 percent of the specified federal tax content of the Regulation portion of the exam. The 10 percent remaining content consists of advanced topics usually covered in a second-semester undergraduate tax course.

The CPA exam includes a variety of interactive problems designed to test your knowledge of the tax law and your ability to apply the law in realistic situations. Many of the problems are in the form of *simulations:* short cases in which you must demonstrate your tax research and analytic skills. These are the exact skills that you will learn, practice, and refine as you work your way through *Principles of Taxation for Business and Investment Planning*.

Conclusion

The authors hope this introduction has conveyed the message that people who decide on a particular course of action without considering the tax outcomes are making an uninformed, and possibly incorrect, decision. By proceeding with the course of study contained in this text, you will learn to recognize the tax implications of a whole spectrum of transactions. On entering the business world, you will be prepared to make decisions incorporating this knowledge. You will spot tax problems as they arise and will call in a tax professional before, rather than after, a transaction with profound tax consequences. Finally, you will understand that effective tax planning can save more money than the most diligent tax compliance.

Part **One**

Exploring the
Tax Environment

1 Taxes and Taxing Jurisdictions

2 Policy Standards for a Good Tax

Chapter **One**

Taxes and Taxing Jurisdictions

Learning Objectives

After studying this chapter, you should be able to:

1. Define the terms *tax, taxpayer, incidence,* and *jurisdiction.*

2. Express the relationship between tax base, rate, and revenue as a formula.

3. Describe the taxes levied by local governments, state governments, and the federal government.

4. Explain why different jurisdictions compete for revenues from the same taxpayer.

5. Identify the reasons why governments modify their tax systems.

6. Describe the three primary sources of federal tax law.

An explorer planning a journey through unknown territory prepares by inspecting a map of the territory. The explorer becomes familiar with topographic features such as major highways, mountain ranges, lakes and rivers, and population centers, and gathers information about the climate of the region and the language and customs of its inhabitants. This preliminary knowledge helps the explorer chart the course and reduces the danger that progress will be impeded by unforeseen circumstances.

For students who are just beginning their study of taxation, the tax environment in which individuals and organizations must function is unknown territory. Chapter 1 serves as a map of this territory. The chapter begins by describing the environment in terms of the basic relationship among taxes, taxpayers, and governments. It identifies the major types of taxes that businesses routinely encounter and examines how governments with overlapping jurisdictions compete for tax revenues. By reading the chapter, you will gain a familiarity with the tax environment that will help you understand the role of taxes in the business decision-making process.

The chapter should alert you to two important features of the tax environment. First, taxes are *pervasive* because they are so widespread, come in so many varieties, and affect virtually every aspect of modern life. Second, taxes are *dynamic* because the tax laws change so frequently. The rate of change reflects the fact that the economic and political assumptions on which tax structures are based are constantly evolving. While these two features make the tax environment a challenging one for business managers, they also create a vitality that makes the study of tax planning so fascinating.

SOME BASIC TERMINOLOGY

Objective 1

Define the terms *tax, taxpayer, incidence,* and *jurisdiction.*

Before beginning our exploration of the tax environment, we must define some basic terminology. A **tax** can be defined as a payment to support the cost of government. A tax differs from a fine or penalty imposed by a government because a tax is not intended to deter or punish unacceptable behavior. On the other hand, taxes are compulsory rather than voluntary on the part of the payer. A tax differs from a user's fee because the payment of a tax does not entitle the payer to a specific good or service in return. In the abstract, citizens receive any number of government benefits for their tax dollars. Nevertheless, the value of government benefits received by any particular person is not correlated to the tax that person must pay. As the Supreme Court explained:

> A tax is not an assessment of benefits. It is . . . a means of distributing the burden of the cost of government. The only benefit to which the taxpayer is constitutionally entitled is that derived from his enjoyment of the privileges of living in an organized society, established and safeguarded by the devotion of taxes to public purposes.[1]

A **taxpayer** is any person or organization required by law to pay a tax to a governmental authority. In the United States, the term *person* refers to both natural persons (individuals) and corporations. Corporations are entities organized under the laws of one of the 50 states or the District of Columbia. These corporate entities generally enjoy the same legal rights, privileges, and protections as individuals. The taxing jurisdictions in this country uniformly regard corporations as entities separate and distinct from their shareholders. Consequently, corporations are taxpayers in their own right.

The **incidence** of a tax refers to the ultimate economic burden represented by the tax. Most people jump to the conclusion that the person or organization that makes a direct tax payment to the government bears the incidence of such tax. But in some cases, the payer can shift the incidence to a third party. Consider the following examples.

Income Tax Incidence	Government G imposes a new tax on corporate business profits. A manufacturing corporation with a monopoly on a product in great demand by the public responds to the new tax by increasing the retail price at which it sells the product. In this case, the corporation is nominally the taxpayer and must remit the new tax to the government. The economic burden of the tax falls on the corporation's customers who are indirectly paying the tax in the form of a higher price for the same product.

Property Tax Incidence	Mr. Blaire owns an eight-unit apartment building. Currently, the tenants living in each unit pay $9,600 annual rent. The local government notifies Mr. Blaire that his property tax on the apartment building will increase by $5,400 for the next year. Mr. Blaire reacts by informing his tenants that their rent for the next year will increase by $675. Consequently, Mr. Blaire's total revenue will increase by $5,400. Although Mr. Blaire is the taxpayer who must remit the property tax to the government, the incidence of the tax increase is on the tenants who will indirectly pay the tax through higher rent.

The right of a government to levy tax on a specific person or organization is referred to as **jurisdiction.** Jurisdiction exists because of some rational linkage between the government and the taxpayer. For instance, our federal government has jurisdiction to tax any

[1] *Carmichael v. Southern Coal & Coke Co.,* 301 U.S. 495, 522 (1937).

individual who is a U.S. citizen or who permanently resides in this country. The government also claims jurisdiction to tax individuals who are neither U.S. citizens nor residents (nonresident aliens) but who earn income from a source within the United States.

U.S. Jurisdiction over Nonresident Aliens	Mr. Kohala is a citizen of Spain and resides in Madrid. He owns an interest in a partnership formed under Florida law that conducts a business within the state. Even though Mr. Kohala is a nonresident alien, the United States claims jurisdiction to tax him on his share of the partnership income because the income was earned in this country.

The Relationship between Base, Rate, and Revenue

Objective 2
Express the relationship between tax base, rate, and revenue as a formula.

Taxes are usually characterized by reference to their base. A **tax base** is an item, occurrence, transaction, or activity with respect to which a tax is levied. Tax bases are usually expressed in monetary terms.[2] For instance, real property taxes are levied on the ownership of land and buildings, and the dollar value of the property is the tax base. When designing a tax, governments try to identify tax bases that taxpayers cannot easily avoid or conceal. In this respect, real property is an excellent tax base because it cannot be moved or hidden, and its ownership is a matter of public record.

The dollar amount of a tax is calculated by multiplying the base by a tax rate, which is usually expressed as a percentage. This relationship is reflected in the following formula.

$$\text{Tax (T)} = \text{Rate (r)} \times \text{Base (B)}$$

A single percentage that applies to the entire tax base is described as a **flat rate.** Many types of taxes use a **graduated rate** structure consisting of multiple percentages that apply to specified portions or **brackets** of the tax base.

Graduated Rate Structure	Jurisdiction J imposes a tax on real property located within the jurisdiction. The tax is based on the market value of the real property and consists of three rate brackets.

Percentage Rate	Bracket
1%	Value from –0– to $100,000
2%	Value from $100,001 to $225,000
3%	Value in excess of $225,000

Company C owns a tract of real property worth $500,000. The tax on this property is $11,750.

1% of $100,000 (first bracket of base)	$ 1,000
2% of $125,000 (second bracket of base)	2,500
3% of $275,000 (third bracket of base)	8,250
Total tax on $500,000 base	$11,750

The term **revenue** refers to the total tax collected by the government and available for public use. Note that in the equation $T = r \times B$, the tax is a function of both the rate and the base. This mathematical relationship suggests that governments can increase revenues by increasing either of these two variables in the design of their tax systems.

---

[2] A per capita, or head, tax requires each person subject to the tax to pay the same amount to the government. This antiquated type of tax does not have a monetary base.

Transaction- or Activity-Based Taxes

Taxes can be characterized by the frequency with which they are levied. A tax can be **event or transaction based** so that the tax is triggered only when an event occurs or a transaction takes place. A familiar example is a sales tax levied on the purchase of retail goods and services. A second example is an estate tax levied on the transfer of property from a decedent to the decedent's heirs. Taxpayers may have some degree of control over the payment of these types of taxes. By avoiding the event or transaction on which the tax is based, a person avoids the tax. With certain taxes, such as excise taxes levied on the purchase of liquor and cigarettes, people have total discretion as to whether they ever pay the tax. By choosing not to drink alcoholic beverages or not to smoke, they are also choosing not to pay the excise tax. In contrast, no individual can avoid an estate or inheritance tax levied on the transfer of property at death by indefinitely postponing the event that triggers the tax!

A tax can be described as **activity based** when it is imposed on the cumulative result of an ongoing activity. Taxpayers must maintain records of the activity, summarize the result at periodic intervals, and pay tax accordingly. An annual income tax is a prime example of an activity-based tax.

An **income tax** is imposed on the periodic inflow of wealth resulting from a person's economic activities. For persons who engage in a limited number or variety of economic transactions, the measurement of taxable income is relatively simple. For persons who engage in complex activities involving many economic transactions, the measurement of taxable income can be a challenging process.

Earmarked Taxes

Still another way to characterize taxes is to link them to government expenditures. The revenues from some taxes are **earmarked** to finance designated projects. For instance, revenues from local real property taxes are typically earmarked to support public school systems. Revenues generated by the federal payroll and self-employment taxes fund the Social Security system (Old-Age, Survivors, and Disability Insurance Trust Fund) and Medicare (Hospital and Supplementary Medical Insurance Trust Funds). Revenues from so-called environmental excise taxes on businesses are appropriated to the Environmental Protection Agency's Hazardous Substance Superfund, which subsidizes the cleanup and disposal of toxic wastes. In contrast to these earmarked taxes, revenues from taxes that pour into a general fund may be spent for any public purpose authorized by the government.

THE PERVASIVE NATURE OF TAXATION

Supreme Court Justice Potter Stewart perfectly described the U.S. tax environment by observing:

> Virtually all persons or objects in this country . . . may have tax problems. Every day the economy generates thousands of sales, loans, gifts, purchases, leases, wills and the like, which suggest the possibility of tax problems for somebody. Our economy is "tax relevant" in almost every detail.[3]

Why are taxes so pervasive in our modern world? One reason is the multiplicity of jurisdictions in which people conduct business. Every firm operates in some geographic location within the taxing jurisdiction of one or more local governments. Local governments include townships, cities, municipalities, counties, and school districts, all of which have operating budgets financed by tax revenues. Local governments are subject to the authority of state governments, and state constitutions or statutes typically regulate the nature and extent of local taxation.

[3] *United States v. Bisceglia,* 420 U.S. 141, 154 (1975).

The governments of each of the 50 states and the District of Columbia levy taxes on firms conducting business within their geographic territory. In turn, the states' taxing jurisdiction is subject to federal constitutional and statutory constraints. The federal government represents still another jurisdiction that taxes business activities conducted within the United States. Consequently, even the smallest domestic enterprise is usually required to pay taxes to support at least three different levels of government. If a domestic enterprise conducts any business in a foreign country, the number of potential taxing jurisdictions is even higher.

Business managers who want to control tax costs must be aware of any local, state, federal, or foreign tax for which the firm is, or might become, liable. In the next section of Chapter 1, we will survey the types of taxes levied by different jurisdictions to finance their governments.

Local Taxes

Objective 3
Describe the taxes levied by local governments.

Local governments depend heavily on real property taxes and personal property taxes, which are frequently referred to as **ad valorem taxes.** According to the most recent census data, these two taxes account for more than 70 percent of local government tax revenues.[4]

Real Property Taxes

All 50 states allow local jurisdictions to tax the ownership of real property sited within the jurisdiction. Real property or **realty** is defined as land and whatever is erected or growing on the land or permanently affixed to it. This definition encompasses any subsurface features such as mineral deposits

Real property taxes are levied annually and are based on the market value of the property as determined by the local government. Elected or appointed officials called **tax assessors** are responsible for deriving the value of realty and informing the owners of the assessed value. Property owners who disagree with the assessed value may challenge the assessment in an administrative or judicial proceeding. A unique feature of real property taxes is that the tax rate is determined annually, based on the jurisdiction's need for revenue for that particular budget year.

Property Tax Rates	Springfield's city council decides that the city must raise $12 million of real property tax revenues during its next fiscal year. Because Springfield's tax assessor determines that the total value of real property located within the city limits is currently $230 million, the council sets the tax rate for the upcoming year at 5.22 percent ($12 million ÷ $230 million). This rate can be adjusted each year, depending on Springfield's future revenue needs and the fluctuating value of its real property tax base.

Local governments may establish different tax rates for different classifications of property. For instance, a township may choose to tax commercial realty at a higher rate than residential realty, or a county might tax land used for agricultural purposes at a higher rate than land maintained for scenic purposes. Governments may grant permanent tax-exempt status to realty owned by charitable, religious, or educational organizations and publicly owned realty. They may also grant temporary tax exemptions called **abatements** for limited periods of time. Governments usually grant abatements to lure commercial enterprises into their jurisdiction, thereby creating jobs and benefiting the local economy. From a business manager's point of view, the tax savings obtained through abatements can be significant. Consequently, firms contemplating expansion into new jurisdictions frequently negotiate for property tax abatements before acquiring or beginning construction of realty within the jurisdiction.

[4] These and subsequent data are obtained from *Quarterly Summaries of Federal, State, and Local Tax Revenues,* Bureau of the Census, U.S. Department of Commerce.

Local Tax Abatements	Late in 2004, computer maker Dell Inc. announced plans to build a manufacturing plant in North Carolina. The announcement prompted a bidding war among North Carolina cities and counties to entice Dell to locate within their jurisdiction. Winston-Salem, along with Forsyth County, won by offering Dell a package of tax abatements worth $37 million.

Personal Property Taxes

Most states permit localities to tax the ownership of **personalty,** defined as any asset that is not realty. Like real property taxes, personal property taxes are based on the value of the asset subject to tax. However, such value is not usually assessed by a government official. Instead, individuals and organizations must determine the value of their taxable personalty and render (i.e., report) the value to the tax assessor.

There are three general classes of taxable personalty: household tangibles, business tangibles, and intangibles.[5] Household tangibles commonly subject to tax include automobiles and recreational vehicles, pleasure boats, and private airplanes. Taxable business tangibles include inventory, furniture and fixtures, machinery, and equipment. The most common intangible assets subject to personal property tax are marketable securities (stocks and bonds).

During the last century, personal property taxation has declined steadily as a revenue source. One reason for the decline is that this tax is much more difficult to enforce than other taxes. Personalty is characterized by its mobility; owners can easily hide their assets or move them to another jurisdiction. Any governmental attempt to actively search for personalty, particularly household tangibles, could violate individual privacy rights. Governments have responded to these practical problems by linking the payment of personal property tax to asset registration or licensing requirements.

State Taxes

Objective 3
Describe the taxes levied by state governments.

In the aggregate, state governments rely in almost equal measure on sales taxes and income taxes as major sources of funds. These two kinds of taxes account for approximately 90 percent of total state tax revenues.

Retail Sales, Use, and Excise Taxes

Forty-five states and the District of Columbia impose a tax on in-state sales of tangible personal property and selected services. (The exceptions are Alaska, Delaware, Montana, New Hampshire, and Oregon.) Moreover, 33 states allow local governments to levy additional sales taxes. Sales taxes have been the great growth taxes of state governments during the past century.[6] In 1930, only two states had a general sales tax. During the depression era, revenue-starved states began enacting temporary sales taxes as an emergency measure. These taxes proved to be both simple and effective and soon became a permanent feature of state tax systems. Sales taxes produce about $250 billion of annual revenue, about one-third of all state tax collections. Sales taxes also have become an important revenue source for local governments, although property taxes remain their primary revenue source.

A **sales tax** is typically based on the retail price of tangible personalty. State tax rates range from 2.9 percent of the dollar amount in Colorado to 7.25 percent in California. Sales taxes are broad based and apply to most types of consumer goods and even to selected

---

[5] Tangible property has physical substance that can be perceived by sight or touch. Intangible property has no physical substance.

[6] Jerome Hellerstein and Walter Hellerstein, *State Taxation,* vol. II (Boston: Warren, Gorham & Lamont, 1993), p. 12–1.

Tax Talk

New Jersey residents bear the heaviest state and local tax burden (12.2 cents of every dollar of income) while Alaska residents bear the lightest (6.3 cents of every dollar of income). The national average state and local tax burden is 9.8 cents of every dollar of income.

consumer services, such as telephone or cable television service.[7] The tax may take the form of a business tax levied on the seller or, more commonly, a consumption tax levied on the purchaser. Regardless of the form, the seller is responsible for collecting the tax at point of sale and remitting it to the state government.

Every state with a sales tax imposes a complementary **use tax** on the ownership, possession, or consumption of tangible goods within the state. The use tax applies only if the owner of the goods did not pay the state's sales tax when the goods were purchased. A use tax acts as a backstop to a sales tax by discouraging residents from purchasing products in neighboring jurisdictions with lower sales tax rates. The one-two punch of a sales and use tax theoretically ensures that state residents are taxed on all purchases of consumer goods, regardless of where the purchase occurred. As a result, merchants operating in high-tax states are not at a competitive disadvantage with respect to merchants operating in low-tax states.

As a general rule, consumers may take a credit for out-of-state sales taxes against their in-state use tax liability.

Use Tax Calculation	Ms. Goode is a resident of New Jersey, which has a 7 percent sales and use tax. While on vacation in Hawaii, Ms. Goode purchased a diamond bracelet for $7,600 and paid $304 (4 percent) Hawaiian sales tax. Because Ms. Goode did not pay her own state's sales tax on the purchase, she owes $228 use tax to New Jersey. The use tax equals $532 (7 percent of $7,600) minus a $304 credit for the Hawaiian sales tax. If Ms. Goode had vacationed in California and paid that state's 7.25 percent sales tax on her jewelry purchase, she would not owe any New Jersey use tax.

Tax Talk

According to the Campaign for Tobacco-Free Kids, states are losing $1 billion annual revenue from excise taxes on tobacco because of untaxed Internet sales and cigarette smuggling.

Millions of people are unaware of their responsibility for paying use tax on goods purchased out of state or through mail-order catalogs, or they ignore their self-assessment responsibility. States have recently become much more aggressive in collecting use taxes directly from their residents and have entered into cooperative agreements to share sales and use tax audit information. Twenty-three states have added lines to their personal income tax returns on which individuals are instructed to report the use tax due on their out-of-state and catalog purchases for the year.

An **excise tax** is imposed on the retail sale of specific goods, such as gasoline, cigarettes, or alcoholic beverages, or on specific services, such as hotel or motel accommodations. States may impose an excise tax in addition to or instead of the general sales tax on a particular good or service. In either case, the seller is responsible for collecting and remitting the excise tax. Excise taxes can be extremely heavy. Washington levies a 37.5-cent excise tax on each gallon of gasoline, Rhode Island levies a $3.46 excise tax on one pack of cigarettes, and Alaska levies a $12.80 excise tax per gallon of distilled liquor.

Personal Income Taxes

Forty-three states and the District of Columbia levy some form of personal income tax on individuals who reside in the state and nonresidents who earn income within the state. (The exceptions are Alaska, Florida, Nevada, South Dakota, Texas, Washington, and Wyoming.) The technical details of the computation of taxable income vary considerably from state to state, but the tax rates are uniformly modest. Currently, the maximum rates range from 3.07 percent in Pennsylvania to 11 percent in Hawaii and Oregon.

Corporate Income Taxes

Forty-six states and the District of Columbia tax corporations on their net income attributable to the state. (The exceptions are Nevada, South Dakota, Washington, and Wyoming.)

---

[7] Many states provide sales tax exemptions for items considered necessities of life, such as food and prescription drugs.

Many states allow their cities and counties to tax either the gross receipts or net income of both incorporated and unincorporated businesses operating within the locality.

The computation of corporate taxable income is prescribed by state law. Conceptually, each state could have its own unique set of computational rules, so that one corporation operating in all 46 taxing jurisdictions would be required to make 46 different calculations of taxable income. Fortunately for corporate America, differences in the computations are the exception rather than the rule. All 46 jurisdictions refer to the *federal* definition of taxable income as the starting point for calculating state taxable income. "The outstanding characteristic of State corporate net income measures is their broad conformity to the measure of the Federal corporation income tax."[8]

The major advantage of state conformity to federal income tax law is simplicity. State legislatures do not have to reinvent the wheel by enacting a comprehensive income tax statute. State agencies responsible for administering their state's income tax can refer to regulatory and judicial interpretations of the federal law. A second advantage is that state conformity to federal tax law eases the compliance burdens of corporate taxpayers. The major disadvantage is the states' lack of control over their corporate income tax revenues. Each time the U.S. Congress changes the federal definition of taxable income, the income tax base of conforming states is increased or decreased.

Corporate income tax rates vary from state to state. The majority of states use a flat rate, while the remainder use a mildly progressive graduated rate structure. Currently, the maximum rates range from 4.63 percent in Colorado to 12 percent in Iowa.

Federal Taxes

Objective 3
Describe the taxes levied by the federal government.

The U.S. government depends almost exclusively on the income tax as a source of general revenues. The federal income tax applies to both individuals and corporations, as well as trusts and estates. The structure and operation of the federal income tax are discussed in considerable detail in Parts Three, Four, and Five of this text. At this point, suffice it to say that the federal income tax predominates in the business environment.

History of the Income Tax

The modern income tax does not have a particularly long history in this country. The federal government enacted the first personal income tax in 1861 to raise money to support the Union armies during the Civil War. Even though Congress allowed the tax to expire in 1872, its revenue-generating capability made a lasting impression on the legislative memory. In 1894, Congress needed a permanent source of funds and decided to resurrect the personal income tax. However, in the landmark case of *Pollock* v. *Farmers' Loan and Trust Company*,[9] the Supreme Court held that the U.S. Constitution did not authorize the federal government to levy a national income tax. Determined to have its way, Congress launched a campaign to change the Constitution, a campaign that ended victoriously on February 25, 1913, when Wyoming became the 36th state to ratify the Sixteenth Amendment:

> The Congress shall have the power to lay and collect taxes on incomes from whatever source derived, without apportionment among the several states, and without regard to any census or enumeration.

Congress immediately exercised its new power by passing the Revenue Act of 1913, and the income tax became a permanent feature of American life. In 1939, Congress organized all of the federal tax laws then in effect (income and otherwise) into the first Internal Revenue Code. This compilation was substantially revised as the Internal Revenue Code of 1954 and again as the Internal Revenue Code of 1986. Although Congress has not changed the title of the Internal

---

[8] Hellerstein and Hellerstein, *State Taxation*, p. 7–3.
[9] 157 U.S. 429 (1895).

Tax Talk
The IRS is spearheading an effort to allow corporations to file combined electronic federal and state tax returns. Officials anticipate a flood of returns from corporations taking advantage of the simplicity of joint e-filing.

Revenue Code since 1986, it enacts new legislation each year to amend the Code. For example, in 2010, Congress enacted over a dozen bills that changed the statutory fabric of the tax law.

The Sixteenth Amendment: Pro and Con	Supporters of the Sixteenth Amendment praised the new income tax because it applied only to the very wealthy and forced "the Carnegies, the Vanderbilts, the Morgans, and the Rockefellers" to pay while sparing the middle class from pain. But opponents of the tax warned that "When men get into the habit of helping themselves to the property of others, they cannot easily be cured of it."[10]

Employment and Unemployment Taxes

The two largest programs sponsored by the federal government are the Social Security system, which provides monthly old-age, survivors, and disability benefits to qualifying citizens and residents, and Medicare, which provides hospital insurance for the elderly and disabled. These programs are not funded from the general revenues of the income tax. Instead, the revenues from the federal **employment taxes** are earmarked to pay for Social Security and Medicare. These taxes are based on annual wages and salaries paid by employers to their employees and on the net income earned by self-employed individuals. The details of these important taxes are discussed in Chapter 10.

The federal and state governments act in coordination to provide monetary benefits to individuals who are temporarily unemployed through no fault of their own. This national unemployment insurance system is administered by the states and financed by federal and state taxes imposed directly on employers. These **unemployment taxes** are based on the annual compensation paid to employees. Virtually every business in this country pays unemployment taxes with respect to its workforce, and significant planning opportunities do exist for controlling this particular cost. Nevertheless, because of the narrow scope of the unemployment taxes, we will not discuss them further in this text.

Other Federal Taxes

Tax Talk
In 1934, excise taxes raised 46 percent of federal revenues.

The federal government raises general revenues from excise taxes imposed on the retail purchase of specific goods and services such as tobacco products, luxury automobiles, and firearms. The federal **transfer taxes,** which are based on the value of an individual's wealth transferred by gift or at death, are also a source of general revenues. Transfer taxes play a key role in family tax planning and are described in detail in Chapter 16. As Exhibit 1.1 shows, these two types of taxes are a minor source of federal funds. In fiscal year 2010, excise taxes accounted for only 2.4 percent of federal tax revenues, while transfer taxes accounted for just 1.0 percent.

EXHIBIT 1.1
Fiscal Year 2010
Federal Tax Revenues

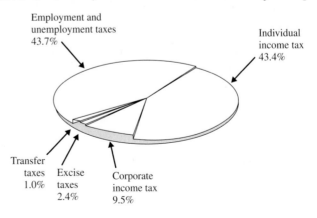

Employment and unemployment taxes 43.7%

Individual income tax 43.4%

Transfer taxes 1.0%

Excise taxes 2.4%

Corporate income tax 9.5%

[10] "Unleashing America's Potential: A Pro-Growth, Pro-Family Tax System for the 21st Century," National Commission on Economic Growth and Tax Reform, 70 *Tax Notes* 413, 418.

Taxes Imposed by Foreign Jurisdictions

The types of foreign taxes that firms encounter when expanding from domestic to international operations are as varied as the languages, politics, and cultures characterizing the global environment. Many foreign taxes have a familiar structure. National governments and their political subdivisions the world over levy income taxes, property taxes, and retail sales taxes. Other taxes have no counterpart in the United States and are therefore less familiar to domestic companies operating abroad. For instance, many industrialized nations depend heavily on some type of **value-added tax (VAT)** as a revenue source. Value-added taxes are levied on firms engaged in any phase of the production of goods and are based on the incremental value that the firm adds to the goods.

Value-Added Tax	Firm M and Firm W operate in a jurisdiction that imposes a 5 percent VAT. Firm M manufactures small electronic appliances. M's material cost per unit is $40, and M sells each unit to Firm W, a regional wholesaler, for $46. The $6 difference represents the incremental value that M added to the production process. Therefore, M must pay a 30-cent VAT (5 percent of $6) for each unit sold. Firm W sells the appliances purchased from Firm M to various unrelated retailers for $50 per unit. Firm W's $4 gross profit on the sale of each unit represents the incremental value that W added to the production process by providing distribution services. Consequently, Firm W must pay a 20-cent VAT (5 percent of $4) for each unit sold.

This example is extremely simplistic because it ignores the possibility that both Firm M and Firm W can shift the economic incidence of the VAT by increasing the price at which they sell their product to the next business in the production sequence. To the extent that a VAT is shifted along the entire production sequence to the final purchaser (the customer who buys the product for personal consumption), the VAT resembles a retail sales tax.

Jurisdictional Competition

Objective 4
Explain why different jurisdictions compete for revenues from the same taxpayer.

Domestic businesses pay tax to state and local governments, as well as to the federal government. International businesses pay tax to any number of foreign jurisdictions. Governments understand that their taxing jurisdictions overlap and that, as a result, they are competing for revenues from the same businesses. They also understand that taxpayers are mobile, and that business managers make location decisions with an eye on comparative tax costs. Thus, jurisdictional competition creates an interesting tension. On the one hand, a government that fails to protect its jurisdictional turf may lose revenues to more assertive taxing authorities. On the other hand, a government that is overly aggressive may drive businesses away from its jurisdiction.

In the United States, the competing levels of government have traditionally accommodated each other by relying on different taxes as their primary source of funding. As we learned earlier in the chapter, property taxes are the mainstay of local governments, while retail sales taxes are used almost exclusively by state governments. Our federal government does not levy either property taxes or a national sales tax, but instead relies on income and employment taxes for its revenues.

Ready for a National Sales Tax?	A group of business executives organized as Americans for Fair Taxation are publicly campaigning to replace the federal income tax, Social Security and Medicare employment taxes, and transfer taxes with a 23 percent national sales tax. The tax would apply to retail purchases of all goods and services, including food, medicine, and housing. According to AFT, this new tax would raise the same federal revenue as existing taxes, while stimulating economic growth.

Corporations conducting business in more than one state face particularly difficult problems of duplicative taxation. The jurisdictional concerns of corporations engaged in interstate commerce are discussed more fully in Chapter 13. Of course, the potential for jurisdictional conflict is greatest when corporations operate on a global scale. Industrialized nations assume that it is in their self-interest to promote the growth of international business operations. These nations understand that if they fail to adapt their tax systems to the needs of the worldwide marketplace, their economies will be at a competitive disadvantage. Consequently, the industrialized nations have created a network of bilateral and multilateral tax treaties to minimize friction among their respective tax systems and to reduce duplicative taxation of international businesses. The role of these treaties and other unique features of international tax planning are covered in Chapter 13.

DYNAMIC NATURE OF TAXATION

Objective 5
Identify the reasons why governments modify their tax systems.

Business managers must understand not only that taxes are pervasive in the modern world but that tax systems are in a constant state of flux. Tax systems are dynamic because they must be attuned to the fiscal condition of their respective jurisdictions. In every jurisdiction, individual citizens and organizations continually reevaluate the nature and level of services they want from their governments. Governments, in turn, must reassess the tax systems that pay for those services.

Tax Base Changes

Any government dependent on a tax system that no longer raises sufficient revenues will sooner or later be forced to change the system. The loss of revenue-generating power is often attributable to an eroding tax base. For instance, cities that depend on real property taxes experience a decline in revenues when their populations decrease. As families and businesses move away from urban areas, residential and commercial properties located within the city lose value. Owners can no longer afford to maintain the properties and, in extreme cases, they may simply abandon them. Cities only worsen this cycle of deterioration if they raise their property tax rates. The only solution may be to identify an alternative tax base or a source of nontax revenue.

Tax Talk
States often devote gambling revenues to popular public services. A congressman boasted that Oregon residents "are gambling for education, salmon restoration, parks, and economic activity. It's an amazing phenomenon."

Legalized Gambling

One controversial source of nontax revenue is legalized gambling. About 40 years ago, a few states experimented with lotteries as a means of raising money. Lotteries proved so lucrative that 43 states and the District of Columbia are now sponsoring these betting games. In the late 1980s, states in the Midwest and the South decided to shore up their tax bases by going into the casino business and gave private gambling corporations legal monopolies to operate within the state. Today, casinos are legal in more than half the states, and all but two states (Hawaii and Utah) depend on some form of gambling as a source of revenue.

A Gambler's Worst Bet

According to a report by the National Gambling Impact Study Commission, state lotteries pay back only 50 percent of the money received from ticket sales—the smallest share of the take of any legal gambling game. In contrast, slot machines, which offer the worst odds of any private casino game, pay back 85 percent of the money fed into them.

Sales Tax Expansion

State and local governments are aggressive in exploiting new tax bases that develop in the economy. Historically, state sales taxes applied to retail purchases of tangible property but not to purchases of retail services. Because of the dramatic growth in the service sector over the last several decades, an increasing number of states are adding selected services, such as utilities, cable television, parking, and theater tickets, to their sales tax base. Currently, Hawaii and New Mexico are the most aggressive in taxing services. According to a recent survey, Hawaii's broad-based sales tax applies to 160 different services, while New Mexico's tax applies to 158 different services.

States are trying to find a way to force mail-order and Internet companies to collect tax on sales made to residents. Millions of consumers have discovered the ease of shopping by catalog and online. Quite naturally, states take the position that their residents who do so should bear the same tax burden as residents who patronize retail stores located within the state. In 1992, the Supreme Court ruled that state laws requiring companies with no *physical* presence in a state to collect sales tax were unconstitutional, regardless of the volume of business in the state.[11] State governments were infuriated with this decision and have been lobbying Congress ever since to enact federal legislation permitting states to require sales tax collection on mail-order and Internet transactions.

Tax Talk
Internet giant Amazon collects sales tax only in the five states in which it maintains stores or offices: Kansas, Kentucky, New York, North Dakota, and Washington.

Taxes and the Political Process

The political process by which tax law is made contributes to the dynamic nature of taxes. In this country, local, state, and federal tax laws are the result of democratic systems in which elected or appointed representatives decide on the appropriate tax structure. These representatives are naturally sensitive to the political climates of their respective constituencies. As these climates change over time, representatives may decide that the tax structure should change as well. Many of these changes have little to do with revenues. Instead, the changes are philosophic in nature, reflecting a shift in the public attitude concerning the proper role of taxes in society.

Tax Talk
According to Otto von Bismarck, the "Iron Chancellor" of nineteenth-century Germany, "The less people know about how sausages and laws are made, the better they'll sleep at night."

Special interest groups have a significant effect on the tax legislative process. Thousands of organizations have pet provisions in the existing law or wish lists of proposals for new provisions. These organizations use their own emissaries or hire professional lobbyists to communicate their point of view to government officials. The constant pressure from powerful organizations with competing and even conflicting political objectives certainly adds to the vibrant nature of the tax law.

People do not enjoy paying tax and are willing to devote considerable money and effort to avoid doing so. Each time taxpayers or their advisers devise a new tactic to reduce their tax burdens, governments respond by enacting a new rule to render the tactic ineffective. This constant gamesmanship is yet another reason why the tax environment is dynamic. As humorist Dave Barry explains, "[Tax laws] are constantly changing as our elected representatives seek new ways to ensure that whatever tax advice we receive is incorrect."

SOURCES OF FEDERAL TAX LAW

Objective 6
Describe the three primary sources of federal tax law.

Throughout this text, we will constantly refer to the **tax law.** For modern tax systems, this term encompasses three basic sources of authority: statutory law, administrative pronouncements, and judicial decisions. In combination, these sources provide the rules of the game by which both taxpayers and governments must abide. This final section of Chapter 1 describes the primary sources of authority that comprise our federal tax law. In subsequent chapters of the text, you will encounter much technical information originating from this body of law. You should have a much easier time understanding this information if you are familiar with the underlying sources from which the information is derived.

---

[11] *Quill Corporation v. North Dakota*, 504 U.S. 298 (1992).

Statutory Authority

In its narrowest sense, federal tax law means the **Internal Revenue Code of 1986,** the voluminous compilation of statutory rules enacted by Congress. The Internal Revenue Code itself is a dynamic document; at least once a year, Congress passes legislation that adds to, deletes from, or modifies its provisions.

The Vanishing Tax Act	President Bush signed the Economic Growth and Tax Relief Reconciliation Act into law on June 7, 2001. This act, which made hundreds of changes to the tax system, is a nightmare of complexity because many of the changes are phased in over a number of years. Perhaps the most controversial feature of the 2001 act is its "sunset provision" under which the entire act was scheduled to expire on December 31, 2010. At the last minute, Congress voted to extend the 2011 act for two more years with a revised expiration date of December 31, 2012.

The Internal Revenue Code consists of numerically ordered **sections,** beginning with Section 1 and ending (at last count) with Section 9833. Each section contains an operational, definitional, or procedural rule relating to one of the federal taxes. Code section numbers have become the language in which tax experts communicate, and accountants and lawyers have incorporated many of them into their professional jargon. (Bob, I think our client has a real Section 469 problem.) Sections are divided into subsections, paragraphs, subparagraphs, and so on. In the footnotes to the text, a reference such as §469(f)(3)(B) is citing the precise statutory rule under discussion.

Administrative Authority

The Department of the Treasury is responsible for writing regulations to interpret and illustrate the rules contained in the Internal Revenue Code. These **Treasury regulations** provide tremendous guidance to taxpayers and their advisers. The Treasury regularly publishes new regulations or amends existing regulations to keep abreast of legislative developments. While Treasury regulations carry great authority as the government's official explanation of the law, they are not laws in and of themselves. On rare occasions, taxpayers have convinced the federal courts that a regulation was an incorrect interpretation of statute and was therefore invalid.[12]

The citation to a Treasury regulation consists of a sequence of numbers, the first of which identifies the type of federal tax under consideration. For instance, a regulation beginning with 1 is an income tax regulation. The next number identifies the Code section to which the regulation relates. The last number in the sequence is the number of the regulation itself. The cite Reg. §1.469-4 refers to the fourth Treasury regulation relating to Section 469 of the Internal Revenue Code. Some sections have only one regulation while others have dozens, and some Code sections have no interpretive regulations at all!

The **Internal Revenue Service (IRS),** the subdivision of the Treasury responsible for the enforcement of the law and collection of tax, provides still more guidance in the form of revenue rulings and revenue procedures. A **revenue ruling** explains how the IRS applies the tax law to a particular set of facts. A **revenue procedure** advises taxpayers how to comply with IRS procedural or administrative matters. While these pronouncements carry much less authority than the Code and regulations, they do represent the IRS's official position and provide valuable insight on specific issues. Rulings and procedures are published in weekly **Internal Revenue Bulletins (IRBs)** that are compiled into semiannual **Cumulative Bulletins (CBs)**. Footnote references such as Rev. Rul. 2011-13, 2011-23 IRB 841, or Rev. Proc. 89-17, 1989-1 CB 118, are citing these sources of authority.

---

[12] The Internal Revenue Code occasionally empowers the Treasury to write regulations that have the force and effect of law. These so-called legislative regulations have the same authority as statutory law.

Goodbye to the Penny	In one of the first revenue rulings published after Congress enacted the Internal Revenue Code of 1954, the IRS authorized taxpayers to eliminate the penny from their bookkeeping by rounding numbers up or down to the nearest dollar.

Judicial Authority

The third primary source of tax law is the federal judicial system. Taxpayers who disagree with the IRS's interpretation of the law as it applies to their own situations may take their cases to federal court. The hundreds of legal decisions handed down every year clarify the correct implementation of the tax law. The weight of authority of a particular case depends on the court that rendered the verdict. Trial court verdicts have less authority than verdicts by an appellate court. A Supreme Court verdict is the equivalent of law and becomes the final word in any tax dispute. Chapter 18 discusses the process by which a federal judge or jury resolves a controversy between a taxpayer and the IRS. When this text refers to a judicial decision, an accompanying footnote provides the complete legal cite. You can use the cite to locate the decision in any law library or commercial tax service.

Conclusion

Business managers engaged in effective tax planning take into account the variety of taxes existing in the modern economic environment. When making strategic decisions, managers must consider their firm's total tax burden rather than any tax in isolation. A strategy that decreases the cost of one tax could easily increase the cost of another. The primary focus of this text is the federal income tax; as a result, other taxes that affect business and investment decisions will be mentioned only occasionally. Even so, many income tax planning strategies are valid in other tax contexts. Decision makers should remember that every tax represents a controllable cost of conducting business.

As greater numbers of U.S. firms expand their operations across national boundaries, jurisdictional tax planning becomes crucial. Managers must decide which tax systems are attractive and which systems are inhospitable to foreign investors. They must be aware of differences between competing tax regimes and how those differences can be exploited to the firm's advantage. In today's tax environment, successful tax planning must be conducted on a global scale.

Key Terms

abatements *7*	income tax *6*	sales tax *8*
activity-based tax *6*	Internal Revenue Bulletins	section *15*
ad valorem tax *7*	(IRBs) *15*	tax *4*
brackets *5*	Internal Revenue Code of	tax assessors *7*
Cumulative Bulletins	1986 *15*	tax base *5*
(CBs) *15*	Internal Revenue Service	tax law *14*
earmarked tax *6*	(IRS) *15*	taxpayer *4*
employment taxes *11*	jurisdiction *4*	transfer taxes *11*
event- or transaction-based	personalty *8*	Treasury regulations *15*
tax *6*	real property taxes *7*	unemployment tax *11*
excise tax *9*	realty *7*	use tax *9*
flat rate *5*	revenue *5*	value-added tax (VAT) *12*
graduated rate *5*	revenue procedure *15*	
incidence *4*	revenue ruling *15*	

Questions and Problems for Discussion

1. How do tax payments differ from other payments that people or organizations make to governmental agencies?

2. The Green River, which is heavily polluted by industrial waste, flows through State S. Eighty-five companies operate manufacturing facilities that border the river. State S recently enacted legislation requiring each company to pay $50,000 annually into a special fund to clean up Green River. Does this payment meet the definition of a tax?

3. Custer County is considering raising revenues by imposing a $25 fee on couples who obtain a marriage license within the county. Does this fee meet the definition of a transaction-based tax?

4. Mr. P owns a residential apartment complex in a suburban area. This year, the local jurisdiction increased the property tax rate on the apartment complex. To offset this additional cost, Mr. P decreased the amount he usually spends on maintaining the exterior of the building and the landscaping. Who bears the incidence of the increased property tax?

5. Mr. and Mrs. K pay $18,000 annual tuition to a private school for their three children. They also pay $2,300 property tax on their personal residence to support the local public school system. Should Mr. and Mrs. K be exempt from this property tax?

6. A local government imposed a new 2 percent tax on the gross receipts of businesses operating within its jurisdiction. XYZ Company, which manufactures soap and other toiletries, responded to the tax by reducing the size of its bars of soap and purchasing a cheaper grade of ingredients. By making these changes, XYZ maintained its before tax level of profits. Who bears the incidence of the new gross receipts tax?

7. Why is real property a better tax base than personal property?

8. Many local jurisdictions apply a low property tax rate to land owned by privately operated golf courses. What is the economic justification for such a preferential rate?

9. University K is located in a small town that depends on real property taxes for revenue. Over the past decade, University K has expanded by purchasing a number of commercial buildings and personal residences and converting them to classrooms and dormitories. In what way could this expansion result in a decline in the town's revenues?

10. Why can people avoid paying an excise tax more readily than they can avoid paying a sales tax?

11. The Internal Revenue Code and Treasury regulations are two major sources of federal tax law. Differentiate between the Code and the regulations in terms of their relative weight of authority.

12. A city government increased its local sales tax from 1 percent to 2 percent of the dollar value of consumer goods purchased in the city. However, the city's sales tax revenues increased by only 30 percent after the doubling of the tax rate. What factors might account for this result?

13. Both the federal government and many states impose so-called sin taxes: excise taxes levied on the retail sale of liquor and cigarettes. Discuss the reasons why sales of these particular items make a good tax base.

14. Does the federal income tax or the federal payroll tax have the broader tax base?

15. Differentiate between a property tax and a transfer tax.

16. One way for the federal government to increase tax revenues would be to enact either a VAT or a national retail sales tax. The U.S. sales tax could be collected in the same manner and at the same time as state and local sales taxes. Which tax would be less costly for the federal government to implement and administer? Which tax would be less likely to cause jurisdictional conflict?

Application Problems

1. Mr. JK, a U.S. citizen and resident of Vermont, owns 100 percent of the stock of JK Services, which is incorporated under Vermont law and conducts business in four counties in the state. JK Services owns 100 percent of the stock of JK Realty, which is incorporated under Massachusetts law and conducts business in Boston.

   a. How many taxpayers are identified in the above statement of facts?

   b. Identify the governments with jurisdiction to tax each of these taxpayers.

2. In each of the following cases, determine whether the United States has jurisdiction to tax Mrs. CM.

   a. Mrs. CM is a citizen of Brazil but is a permanent resident of Orlando, Florida.

   b. Mrs. CM is a citizen and resident of Brazil. She owns Manhattan real estate that generates $100,000 net rental income annually.

   c. Mrs. CM is a citizen and resident of Brazil. She owns no property and conducts no business in the United States.

   d. Mrs. CM is a U.S. citizen but is a permanent resident of São Paulo, Brazil.

3. The city of Springvale levies a tax on the value of real property located within its city limits. The tax equals 2 percent of the property's assessed value up to $500,000 plus 4 percent of the value in excess of $500,000.

   a. Compute the tax on real property valued at $415,000.

   b. Compute the tax on real property valued at $725,000.

4. This year, Company LI built a light industrial facility in County G. The assessed property tax value of the facility is $20 million. To convince Company LI to locate within its jurisdiction, the county abated its 4 percent property tax for the year. Because of the local economic boom created by the new facility, the aggregate assessed value of County G's property tax base (including the LI facility) increased by $23 million. Calculate the net effect on County G's current year tax revenue from the abatement.

5. This year, Jurisdiction A raised revenues by increasing its general sales tax rate from 5 percent to 6 percent. Because of the increase, the volume of taxable sales declined from $800 million to $710 million. In contrast, Jurisdiction Z raised revenues from its 5 percent sales tax by expanding the tax base to include certain retail services. The volume of services subject to tax was $50 million. Compute the additional revenue raised by Jurisdiction A and by Jurisdiction Z.

6. Firm H operates its business in Jurisdiction H, which levies a 6 percent sales and use tax. This year, the firm purchased a $600,000 item of tangible property in Jurisdiction K and paid $18,000 sales tax to the jurisdiction. It also purchased a $750,000 item of tangible property in Jurisdiction L and paid $48,750 sales tax to the jurisdiction. Firm H transported both items of property into Jurisdiction H for use in its business.

   a. Compute the use tax that Firm H owes to Jurisdiction H for the property purchased in Jurisdiction K.

   b. Compute the use tax that Firm H owes to Jurisdiction H for the property purchased in Jurisdiction L.

7. Mrs. DK, a resident of Pennsylvania, traveled to Delaware to purchase an oil painting from a local artist. The cost of the painting was $9,400. Pennsylvania has a 7 percent sales and use tax, while Delaware has no sales and use tax.

   a. How much Pennsylvania use tax does Mrs. DK owe on the purchase she made in Delaware?

   b. How much Pennsylvania use tax would Mrs. DK owe if she purchased the painting from a gallery in New York City and paid New York's 8.75 percent tax on the transaction?

    c. How much Pennsylvania use tax would Mrs. DK owe if she purchased the painting from a dealer in Richmond and paid Virginia's 5 percent tax on the transaction?

8. Firm L, which operates a mail-order clothing business, is located in State L. This year, the firm shipped $18 million of merchandise to customers in State R. State R imposes a 6 percent sales and use tax on the purchase and consumption of retail goods within the state.

    a. Do State R residents who purchased Firm L merchandise owe use tax on their purchases?

    b. If State R could legally require Firm L to collect a 6 percent tax on mail-order sales made to residents of the state, how much additional revenue would the state collect? Explain the reasoning behind your answer.

9. Mr. and Mrs. CS operate a hardware store in a jurisdiction that levies both a sales tax on retail sales of tangible personalty and an annual personal property tax on business tangibles. The personal property tax is based on book value as of December 31. This year, Mr. and Mrs. CS purchased $840,000 of inventory for their store.

    a. Are Mr. and Mrs. CS required to pay sales tax on the purchase of the inventory?

    b. How can Mr. and Mrs. CS minimize their personal property tax by controlling the timing of their inventory purchases?

10. Firm Q and Firm R conduct business in a jurisdiction that imposes a 3 percent VAT. Firm Q produces entertainment videos at a $6 cost per unit and sells the videos to Firm R for $9 per unit. Firm R sells the videos at retail for $10 per unit. This year, the combined efforts of Firm Q and Firm R resulted in sales of 12.4 million videos to the public. Compute the VAT for each firm.

Issue Recognition Problems

Identify the tax issue or issues suggested by the following situations, and state each issue in the form of a question.

1. A local government levies an annual real property tax on the personal residence located at 123 Maple Drive. This tax is assessed on a calendar year basis, and the homeowner must pay the tax before December 31. In November, Mr. and Mrs. J received the annual tax bill for $2,900. The couple purchased the home on October 6.

2. Company F operates in a jurisdiction that levies real property tax but no personal property tax. This year, the company spent $6 million to add an exterior lighting system and security fences to the parking lot adjacent to its corporate headquarters.

3. Company B, which has offices in six states, owns an airplane that company executives use to travel from office to office. When the plane is not in use, it is stored in a hangar located in a jurisdiction that does not levy a personal property tax on business tangibles. When the plane is in use, it is stored on a temporary basis in hangars located in jurisdictions that tax business tangibles.

4. For the past 22 years, Mrs. O contributed part of her salary to a retirement plan sponsored by her corporate employer. Under federal law, Mrs. O did not pay tax on the income so contributed. She will, however, pay federal income tax on the distributions from the plan when she retires. Mrs. O has resided in State A for her entire life. Because State A's personal income tax is based on taxable income for federal purposes, Mrs. O never paid State A tax on her retirement contributions. This year, Mrs. O retires and moves to State K, which has no personal income tax.

5. Business Q orders $500,000 of office furniture from Vendor V, which ships the furniture by rail from its manufacturing facility in State V to Business Q's corporate headquarters in State Q. State V imposes a 6.5 percent sales tax while State Q imposes only a 4 percent sales tax.

6. Acme Corporation was formed under the laws of State X and has its corporate headquarters in that state. Acme operates a manufacturing plant in State Y and sells goods to customers in States X, Y, and Z. All three states have a corporate income tax. This year, Acme's net profit from its tristate operation was $14 million.

7. Mr. W is a professional golfer who played 23 tournaments in 14 different states and earned $893,000 total prize money for the year. When he is not traveling, Mr. W lives with his family in Tucson, Arizona.

8. Eighteen months ago, BBB Company opened a manufacturing facility in County K. As an incentive for BBB to locate within its jurisdiction, County K abated all local property taxes for the first two years of operation. BBB recently announced that it will shut down the facility before the end of the year.

9. Dempsey Corporation is organized under Canadian law and has its corporate headquarters in Montreal. This year, Dempsey sold $28 million of goods to customers who live in the United States. However, Dempsey does not maintain any type of office in the United States.

10. Mr. KW, age 72, has lived in Los Angeles his entire life. His net worth is estimated at $95 million. Mr. KW is considering renouncing his U.S. citizenship, selling his home in Los Angeles, and permanently relocating to the Cayman Islands. The Cayman Islands impose no tax of any sort on their residents.

Research Problems

1. Visit the website for the Federation of Tax Administrators (**www.taxadmin.org**) to find out if your state has either an individual or a corporate income tax. If so, what is the maximum tax rate?

2. Visit the website for the Internal Revenue Service (**www.irs.gov**). What is the name of the Commissioner of the IRS, and how many employees work for the IRS?

3. Conduct a search on the Internet to find a brief description of the flat tax. Write a short paragraph describing the flat tax and explaining how it differs from the federal individual income tax.

4. The next time you buy groceries in a supermarket, study your receipt. Which items that you purchased were subject to your state's sales tax, and which items were exempt from sales tax?

Tax Planning Cases

1. The management of WP Company must decide between locating a new branch office in foreign Jurisdiction F or foreign Jurisdiction G. Regardless of location, the branch operation will use tangible property (plant and equipment) worth $10 million and should generate annual gross receipts of $2 million. Jurisdiction F imposes an annual property tax of 4 percent of the value of business property and a 15 percent gross receipts tax. Jurisdiction G imposes no property tax but imposes a 30 percent gross receipts tax. Solely on the basis of these facts, should WP locate its new branch in Jurisdiction F or Jurisdiction G?

2. KTR Company earns a $10 profit on each unit of manufactured goods, and it sells 20 million units each year. KTR's income tax rate is 20 percent. However, the jurisdiction in which KTR operates just increased the tax rate to 22 percent for next year. KTR's owners are considering two alternatives. They could simply accept the $4 million tax increase as a reduction in their after-tax profit, or they could raise the price of each unit by 20 cents, thereby increasing the profit per unit to $10.20. However, the marketing department estimates that the price increase could reduce annual sales to 19 million units. Which alternative is better for KTR's owners?

Chapter Two

Policy Standards for a Good Tax

Learning Objectives

After studying this chapter, you should be able to:

1. Explain the concept of sufficiency of a good tax.

2. Differentiate between the income effect and the substitution effect.

3. Describe the characteristics of a convenient tax.

4. Contrast the classical and the modern concepts of tax efficiency.

5. Define horizontal and vertical equity.

6. Differentiate among regressive, proportionate, and progressive rate structures.

7. Explain the difference between marginal and average tax rates.

8. Discuss distributive justice as a tax policy objective.

In Chapter 1, we identified the various taxes that characterize the modern tax environment. In this chapter, we will consider a more qualitative dimension of the environment as we identify the *normative* standards by which politicians, economists, social scientists, and individual taxpayers evaluate the merit of a tax.

Governments are cognizant of and influenced by these standards as they formulate tax policy. **Tax policy** can be defined as a government's attitude, objectives, and actions with respect to its tax system. Presumably, tax policy reflects the normative standards that the government deems most important. After reading this chapter, you can draw your own conclusions as to the relative importance of the standards by which tax systems are judged. You will be able to evaluate the current federal tax system in light of these standards. When you are asked as a voter to choose between competing tax policy proposals, the material covered in this chapter will help you make an informed decision.

Business managers and their tax advisers share a keen interest in tax policy. They know that many complex rules in the Internal Revenue Code have an underlying policy rationale. If they can understand this rationale, the rule itself is easier to interpret and apply. Moreover, business managers know that today's policy issues shape tomorrow's tax environment. By paying close attention to the current policy debate, managers can anticipate developments that might affect their firm's long-term strategies. Their familiarity with policy issues helps them assess the probability of changes in the tax law and develop contingent strategies to deal with such changes.

STANDARDS FOR A GOOD TAX

The American jurist Oliver Wendell Holmes is quoted as saying, "I like to pay taxes. With them I buy civilization." Few people in modern society seem to share this sentiment. In fact, many people regard taxes as a necessary evil and consider the notion of a good tax as a contradiction in terms. Nonetheless, theorists maintain that every tax can and should be evaluated on certain basic standards.[1] These standards can be summarized as follows:

- A good tax should be sufficient to raise the necessary government revenues.
- A good tax should be convenient for the government to administer and for people to pay.
- A good tax should be efficient in economic terms.
- A good tax should be fair.

In Chapter 2, we will discuss these four standards in detail. We will also identify the reasons why standards that are easy to describe in the abstract can be so difficult to put into practice.

TAXES SHOULD BE SUFFICIENT

Objective 1
Explain the concept of sufficiency of a good tax.

The first standard by which to evaluate a tax is its **sufficiency** as a revenue raiser. A tax is sufficient if it generates enough funds to pay for the public goods and services provided by the government. After all, the reason that governments tax their citizens in the first place is to raise revenues needed for specific purposes. If a tax (or combination of taxes) is sufficient, a government can balance its budget. Tax revenues equal government spending, and the government has no need to raise additional funds.

What is the consequence of an insufficient tax system? The government must make up its revenue shortfall (the excess of current spending over tax receipts) from some other source. In Chapter 1, we learned that state governments now depend heavily on legalized gambling as an alternative source of funds. Governments may own assets or property rights that they can lease or sell to raise money. For example, the U.S. government raises minuscule revenues by selling energy generated by federally owned dams and mineral and timber rights with respect to federal lands.

Another option is for governments to borrow money to finance their operating deficits. In the United States, the federal, state, and local governments sell debt obligations in the capital markets. By selling both short-term instruments (such as U.S. Treasury bills) and long-term bonds, governments with insufficient tax systems can make ends meet. Debt financing is not a permanent solution to an insufficient tax system. Like other debtors, governments must pay interest on borrowed funds. As the public debt increases, so does the annual interest burden. At some point, a government may find itself in the untenable position of borrowing new money not to provide more public goods and services but merely to pay the interest on existing debt.

In a worst-case scenario, a government may be forced to default on its debt obligations, damaging its credibility and creating havoc in its capital markets.

Tax Talk
The Brookings Institution released a study describing three different strategies for balancing the federal budget by 2014. All three include tax increases, and one calls for raising tax revenues by $629 billion over 10 years. The study warns that deficit spending is "out of control" and that "there is no end in sight to this tide of red ink."

[1] Adam Smith, author of *The Wealth of Nations,* was one of the first economists to suggest such standards. Smith's four canons were that a good tax should be equitable, certain in application, convenient for people to pay, and economical for the government to collect.

The National Debt

According to Congressional Budget Office data, the federal government operated at a deficit for every fiscal year from 1970 through 1999. After generating small surpluses in 2000 and 2001, the government returned to chronic deficit spending in 2002. In 1970, the national debt was about $380 billion and interest payments totaled $14 billion. In 2011, the debt exceeded $14.9 trillion and interest payments on this debt totaled $454 billion.

These data suggest that our federal tax system is insufficient to support the level of government spending. Yet politicians continue to tell their constituencies that taxes are too high, and few people seem inclined to disagree. But the arithmetic is inescapable. If we want to pay less tax and at the same time curb the growth of the national debt, the federal government must cut spending. If we want our government to maintain its level of spending without incurring additional debt, we should be prepared to pay the necessary federal tax.[2]

How Much Deficit?	For fiscal year 2011, the federal government operated at a $1,315 billion deficit. This deficit, however, included a $62 billion Social Security Trust Fund surplus, which is earmarked to fund retirement benefits to future Social Security recipients. If Social Security is excluded from the budget, the 2011 operating deficit was $1,377 billion.

How to Increase Tax Revenues

Taxing jurisdictions can attempt to increase revenues in at least three ways. One way is to exploit a new tax base. For instance, the legislature of one of the seven states without a personal income tax could enact such a tax. Another way is to increase the rate of an existing tax. A jurisdiction with a 5 percent corporate income tax could increase the rate to 7 percent. Still a third way is to enlarge an existing tax base. A jurisdiction with a retail sales tax applying to tangible goods could expand the tax to apply to selected personal services, such as haircuts or dry cleaning. A jurisdiction that exempts land owned by private charities from real property tax could simply eliminate the exemption.

From a pragmatic perspective, the enactment of a tax on a new base is the most radical and politically sensitive way to increase revenues. Consequently, elected officials tend to favor the less drastic alternative of enhancing the revenue-raising capability of a tax that people are accustomed to paying. In this situation, an increase in the percentage rate is the more obvious strategy and therefore is likely to anger the greatest number of voters. In contrast, an expansion of the tax base is more subtle and less likely to attract public attention. It is hardly surprising that many significant tax increases in recent years have been accomplished through the base-expansion method.

Social Security Tax Increases	The 6.2 percent rate for the federal Social Security payroll tax has not increased since 1990. However, the tax base (the annual amount of wages or salary subject to tax) increases every year. In 1990, this wage base was $51,300. In 2012, the base is $110,100. In 1990, an employee with a $120,000 salary paid $3,181 Social Security tax (6.2 percent of $51,300). In 2012, that employee would pay $6,826 Social Security tax (6.2 percent of $110,100).

Static versus Dynamic Forecasting

In Chapter 1, we expressed the amount of tax as an arithmetic function of the tax rate and base: $T = r \times B$. This equation suggests that an increase in the rate should increase government

---

[2] As another author so eloquently describes the situation, "Elected representatives must eventually confront the political reality of an electorate with an apparently insatiable appetite for 'public goods' that at the same time harbors a deep-rooted intolerance for the levels of taxation sufficient to support its own proclivities." Sheldon D. Pollack, "The Failure of U.S. Tax Policy: Revenue and Politics," 73 *Tax Notes* 341, 348.

revenues by a proportionate amount. For instance, if the tax rate is 5 percent and the base is $500,000, a rate increase of one percentage point should generate $5,000 additional tax. This straightforward math represents a **static forecast** of the incremental revenue resulting from a change in the rate structure. The forecast is static because it assumes that B, the base variable in the equation, is independent of r, the rate variable. Accordingly, a change in the rate has no effect on the tax base.

Economic theory suggests that in many cases the two variables in the equation $T = r \times B$ are correlated. In other words, a change in the rate actually causes a change in the base.

Effect of a Rate Change on Base

For the last 10 years, the city of Fairview has levied a hotel occupancy tax equal to 10 percent of the price of a room. In the prior fiscal year, this tax yielded $800,000 revenue.

Total annual hotel receipts subject to tax	$8,000,000
Prior year rate	.10
Prior year revenue	$ 800,000

At the beginning of the fiscal year, the city increased the tax rate to 12 percent. On the basis of a static forecast, the city expected revenue to increase to $960,000.

Forecasted hotel receipts subject to tax	$8,000,000
Current year rate	.12
Forecasted current year revenue	$ 960,000

Unfortunately, business travelers and tourists reacted to the additional cost represented by the higher room tax by purchasing fewer accommodations from Fairview hotels. Occupancy rates fell, and annual hotel receipts declined by $500,000. Consequently, the room tax yielded only $900,000 current year revenue.

Actual hotel receipts subject to tax	$7,500,000
Current year rate	.12
Actual current year revenue	$ 900,000

In the above example, the increase in the tax rate caused a decrease in the tax base. Because Fairview failed to anticipate this effect, it overestimated the incremental revenue from the rate increase.

If a jurisdiction can predict the extent to which a change in tax rates will affect the tax base, it can incorporate the effect into its revenue projections. These projections, which assume a correlation between rate and base, are called **dynamic forecasts.** The accuracy of dynamic forecasts depends on the accuracy of the assumptions about the correlation. In a complex economic environment, a change in tax rates may be only one of many factors contributing to an expansion or contraction of the tax base. Economists may be unable to isolate the effect of the rate change or to test their assumptions empirically. Consequently, governments usually rely on static forecasting to estimate the revenues gained or lost because of a tax rate change.

Behavioral Responses to Rate Changes

Objective 2
Differentiate between the income effect and the substitution effect.

In the case of an income tax, the incremental revenue generated by a rate increase depends on whether (and to what extent) the increase affects the aggregate amount of income subject to tax. Specifically, the increment depends on the ways that individuals modify their economic behavior in response to higher tax rates.

Income Effect

An increase in income tax rates might induce people to engage in more income-producing activities. Consider the case of Mr. Spivey, who earns $25,000 a year as a factory worker and pays 20 percent of that income ($5,000) in tax. Mr. Spivey spends every penny of his $20,000 after-tax income to make ends meet. How might Mr. Spivey react if the government increases the tax rate to 30 percent, thereby reducing his disposable income to $17,500? He might decide to work more hours or even take a second job to increase his before-tax income to at least $28,600. Under the new rate structure, Mr. Spivey will pay $8,580 tax on this income, leaving him with $20,020 and the same disposable income he enjoyed before the rate increase. This reaction (akin to running faster just to stay in the same place) has been labeled the **income effect** of a rate increase.[3]

If Mr. Spivey responds to the higher tax rate by working longer to generate more income, the government will enjoy a revenue windfall. A static forecast indicates that the government should collect an additional $2,500 revenue from Mr. Spivey because of the 10 percent rate increase.

Static Forecast	
Revenue after rate increase	
(30% × $25,000 base)	$7,500
Revenue before rate increase	
(20% × $25,000 base)	(5,000)
Additional revenue from Mr. Spivey	$2,500

However, if Mr. Spivey reacts by increasing his income from $25,000 to $28,600, the government will actually collect $3,580 additional revenue.

Income Effect	
Revenue after rate increase	
(30% × $28,600 base)	$8,580
Revenue before rate increase	
(20% × $25,000 base)	(5,000)
Additional revenue from Mr. Spivey	$3,580

Substitution Effect

If we change the financial circumstances of our hypothetical taxpayer, we might expect a different behavioral response to an income tax rate increase. Assume Ms. Hoover works

---

[3] Richard A. Musgrave and Peggy B. Musgrave, *Public Finance in Theory and Practice,* 5th ed. (New York: McGraw-Hill, 1989), p. 663.

60 hours a week as a self-employed management consultant, earning $350,000 annual income. At a 20 percent tax rate, her after-tax income is $280,000—more than enough to support her comfortable lifestyle. If the government increases the tax rate to 30 percent, Ms. Hoover may devote less time and effort to her income-producing activity. Such a reaction makes sense if the after-tax value of an hour of additional labor is now worth less to her than an additional hour of leisure. This behavioral reaction to a rate increase is called the **substitution effect.**[4]

If Ms. Hoover responds to the higher tax rate by working fewer hours and generating less income, the government will suffer a revenue shortfall. On the basis of a static forecast, the government is anticipating an additional $35,000 revenue from Ms. Hoover.

Base does not change

Static Forecast	
Revenue after rate increase (30% × $350,000 base)	$105,000
Revenue before rate increase (20% × $350,000 base)	(70,000)
Additional revenue from Ms. Hoover	$ 35,000

If Ms. Hoover's income falls to $325,000 because the tax increase dampened her entrepreneurial spirit, the additional revenue from Ms. Hoover will be only $27,500.

Base Changes

Substitution Effect	
Revenue after rate increase (30% × $325,000 base)	$97,500
Revenue before rate increase (20% × $350,000 base)	(70,000)
Additional revenue from Ms. Hoover	$27,500

The probability of a substitution effect varies across taxpayers. The degree of personal control that individuals exercise over their careers determines the extent to which they can replace an hour of work with an hour of relaxation. Consequently, the substitution effect is more potent for self-employed persons than for salaried employees with rigid 9 A.M. to 5 P.M. schedules. The financial flexibility necessary to curtail work effort is more characteristic of a family's secondary wage earner than of the primary wage earner. Finally, ambitious career-oriented people who are highly motivated by nonmonetary incentives such as prestige and power may be impervious to the substitution effect.

Whether an income tax will goad a person to extra effort or whether it will be a disincentive to work depends on that person's economic circumstances. Theoretically, the income effect is most powerful for lower-income taxpayers who may already be at a subsistence standard of living and don't have the luxury of choosing leisure over labor. The substitution effect becomes stronger as an individual's disposable income rises and the

[4] Ibid.

financial significance of each additional dollar declines. From a macroeconomic view-point, these contradictory behavioral reactions have important tax policy implications. Conventional wisdom suggests that governments needing more revenue should increase the tax rate on people with the highest incomes. But if the tax rate climbs too high, the substitution effect may become so strong that the projected revenues never materialize as more and more people are discouraged from working because the after-tax return on their labor is too small.

Supply-Side Economics

Faith in the substitution effect is the foundation for **supply-side economic theory,** which holds that a decrease in the highest income tax rates should ultimately result in an increase in government revenues. The logic underlying this theory is that a rate cut increases the value of income-generating activities (work and investment) relative to the value of non-income-generating activities (leisure and consumption). Accordingly, people who benefit directly from the rate reduction will invest their tax windfall in new commercial ventures rather than simply spend it. This influx of private capital will stimulate economic growth and job creation. An expanding economy will result in prosperity across the board so that everyone, regardless of income level, indirectly benefits from the tax rate reduction. People will earn more income for the government to tax, and revenues attributable to this enlarged tax base will swell.

Does this supply-side theory hold true? In 1981, the Reagan administration, acting on its belief in the theory, convinced Congress to enact the Economic Recovery Tax Act. This legislation lowered the highest marginal individual tax rates from 70 percent to 50 percent on ordinary income and from 28 percent to 20 percent on capital gains. The Tax Reform Act of 1986 went even further by reducing the highest marginal rate for individuals to 28 percent. These deep rate cuts were just one of many dramatic factors affecting the U.S. economy during the 1980s. The price of oil dropped by half, and the double-digit inflation of the late 1970s fell to less than 4 percent. Federal spending on many domestic programs declined, but defense spending soared. Congress increased the federal payroll tax rates significantly to keep pace with the explosive growth in Social Security and Medicare outlays. The government borrowed money at an unprecedented rate, creating deficits of record peacetime magnitude.[5]

Supply-side economics fell out of favor during the Clinton administration when Congress raised the highest individual tax rate to 39.6 percent. However, the spirit of "Reaganomics" was revived in George W. Bush's first term by the Economic Growth and Tax Relief Reconciliation Act of 2001. This legislation decreased the highest individual rate on ordinary income to 35 percent. The next year, Congress followed up by reducing the individual rate on capital gains and dividend income to 15 percent. Theoretically, the stimulative effect of these tax cuts should have increased federal revenues and reduced the federal deficit. But the economic convulsion following the September 11, 2001, terrorist attacks and the unanticipated cost of the wars in Afghanistan and Iraq pushed annual deficits to ever-higher levels. The 2008 collapse of the housing industry and the meltdown of global financial markets forced the Bush and Obama administrations to spend enormous sums to stave off a depression. Once again, a complex tangle of events made it impossible to prove or disprove the efficacy of supply-side economic theory.

Tax Talk

In January 2001, the Congressional Budget Office (CBO) projected a decade of annual government surpluses, and the Bush administration and Congress responded by cutting income taxes by $1.7 trillion. When tax revenues plummeted, the federal government was forced to wage the Afghanistan and Iraq wars with borrowed money. With the Bush tax cuts still in place, the CBO is now projecting huge deficits "essentially forever."

---

[5] Isabel V. Sawhill, "Reaganomics in Retrospect: Lessons for a New Administration," *Challenge,* May–June 1989, p. 57.

TAXES SHOULD BE CONVENIENT

Objective 3
Describe the
characteristics of
a convenient tax.

Our second standard for evaluating a tax is **convenience.** From the government's viewpoint, a good tax should be convenient to administer. Specifically, the government should have a method for collecting the tax that most taxpayers understand and with which they routinely cooperate. The collection method should not overly intrude on individual privacy but should offer minimal opportunity for noncompliance. States that levy retail sales taxes use a collection method under which sellers are responsible for collecting the tax from buyers at point of sale and remitting the tax to the state. This method is effortless for buyers and offers them no opportunity to evade the tax. States can concentrate their enforcement efforts on retail businesses, which are much easier to audit than individual consumers. In contrast, states have yet to develop a workable collection mechanism for use taxes; consequently, these taxes generate almost no revenue.

A good tax should be economical for the government. The administrative cost of collecting and enforcing the tax should be reasonable in comparison with the total revenue generated. At the federal level, the Internal Revenue Service (IRS) is the agency responsible for administering the income, payroll, excise, and transfer taxes. For its 2010 fiscal year, the IRS operated at a cost of $12.35 billion and collected $2,345 billion tax revenue. Thus, the federal government's cost of collecting $100 tax was a modest 53 cents.[6]

From the taxpayer's viewpoint, a good tax should be convenient to pay. The convenience standard suggests that people can compute their tax with reasonable certainty. Moreover, they do not have to devote undue time or incur undue costs in complying with the tax law. A retail sales tax receives high marks when judged by these criteria. People can easily compute the sales tax on a purchase and can pay the tax as part of the purchase price with no effort whatsoever!

In contrast, the federal income tax is denounced as both uncertain and costly. Because the income tax laws are so complex and change with such frequency, even tax professionals are often unsure how the law should apply to a particular transaction. Millions of Americans are bewildered by the income tax and have no confidence in their ability to compute the amount they owe. As a result, the majority pay someone else to prepare their income tax returns. By any measure, the cost to society of complying with the federal tax law is high; according to IRS estimates, taxpayers devote almost 6 billion hours each year to this inconvenient task. In dollar terms, the annual private sector cost of federal tax compliance is estimated at $400 billion.[7]

Tax Talk
*The Internal
Revenue Code
contains over
3.5 million words
and the Treasury
Regulations contain
another 8 million.
Together, they are
12 times the length
of Shakespeare's
complete works and
15 times the length
of the King James
Bible.*

TAXES SHOULD BE EFFICIENT

Our third standard for a good tax is economic **efficiency.** Tax policymakers use the term *efficiency* in two different ways. Sometimes the term describes a tax that does not interfere with or influence taxpayers' economic behavior. At other times, policymakers describe a tax as efficient when individuals or organizations react to the tax by deliberately changing their economic behavior. In this section of the chapter, we will compare these two competing concepts of efficiency.

[6] IRS 2010 Data Book, Table 29.
[7] "The Rising Cost of Complying with the Federal Income Tax," The Tax Foundation Special Report, January 10, 2006.

The Classical Standard of Efficiency

Objective 4
Contrast the classical and the modern concepts of tax efficiency.

Policymakers who believe that competitive markets result in the optimal allocation of scarce resources within a society define an efficient tax as one that is *neutral* in its effect on the free market. From this perspective, a tax that causes people to modify their economic behavior is inefficient because it distorts the market and may result in suboptimal allocations of goods and services.

The classical economist Adam Smith believed that taxes should have as little effect as possible on the economy. In his 1776 masterwork, *The Wealth of Nations,* Smith concluded the following:

> A tax . . . may obstruct the industry of the people, and discourage them from applying to certain branches of business which might give maintenance and employment to great multitudes. While it obliges the people to pay, it may thus diminish, or perhaps destroy, some of the funds which might enable them more easily to do so.

The laissez-faire system favored by Adam Smith theoretically creates a level playing field on which individuals and organizations, operating in their own self-interest, freely compete. When governments interfere with the system by taxing certain economic activities, the playing field tilts against the competitors engaging in those activities. The capitalistic game is disrupted, and the outcome may no longer be the best for society.

Of course, every modern economy has a tax system, and firms functioning within the economy must adapt to that system. Business managers become familiar with the existing tax laws and make decisions based on those laws. To return to the sports metaphor, these managers have adjusted their game plan to suit the present contours of the economic playing field.

When governments change their tax structures, firms are forced to reevaluate their tax situations in light of the change. Some may find that they benefit from the change, while others may conclude that the new tax structure puts them at a competitive disadvantage. Managers must reassess how the tax laws affect their particular business operations. They may discover that traditional planning strategies no longer work, while the efficacy of new strategies is uncertain. In short, every time the government changes its tax structure, the contours of the economic playing field shift. Because these shifts are both costly and unsettling to the business community, many economists conclude that "an old tax is a good tax."

Taxes as an Instrument of Fiscal Policy

Tax Talk
According to John Maynard Keynes, "Capitalism is the astounding belief that the most wickedest of men will do the most wickedest of things for the greatest good of everyone."

The British economist John Maynard Keynes disagreed with the classical notion that a good tax should be neutral. Keynes believed that free markets are effective in organizing production and allocating scarce resources but lack adequate self-regulating mechanisms for maintaining economic stability.[8] According to Keynes, governments should protect their citizens and institutions against the inherent instability of capitalism. Historically, this instability caused cycles of high unemployment, severe fluctuations in prices (inflation or deflation), and uneven economic growth. Lord Keynes believed that governments could counteract these problems through *fiscal policies* to promote full employment, price-level stability, and a steady rate of economic growth.

In the Keynesian schema, tax systems are a primary tool of fiscal policy. Rather than trying to design a neutral tax system, governments should deliberately use taxes to move the economy in the desired direction. If an economy is suffering from sluggish growth and high unemployment, the government could reduce taxes to transfer funds from the public to the private sector. The tax cut should both stimulate demand for consumer goods and

[8] John Maynard Keynes, *The General Theory of Employment, Interest and Money* (New York: Harcourt, Brace, 1936).

services and increase private investment. As a result, the economy should expand and new jobs should be created. Conversely, if an economy is overheated so that wages and prices are in an inflationary spiral, the government could raise taxes. People will have less money to spend, the demand for consumer and investment goods should weaken, and the upward pressure on wages and prices should be relieved.

The U.S. government formally embraced its fiscal policy responsibilities when Congress enacted the Employment Act of 1946. This legislation charged the Executive Branch with promoting full employment and a stable dollar and resulted in the formation of the President's Council of Economic Advisers. Since 1946, both political parties have regarded the federal income tax as a legitimate instrument of fiscal policy and have advocated changes in that system to further their respective economic agendas. Changes that have the intended macroeconomic effect are touted as enhancing the efficiency of the tax system, while changes that have no effect on the national economy are branded as inefficient. Certainly, this Keynesian concept of efficiency is far removed from the classic concept of economic neutrality.

Economic Booster Shot	On February 17, 2009, President Obama signed the American Recovery and Reinvestment Act of 2009. This massive stimulus package appropriated $787 billion for "job preservation and creation, infrastructure investment, energy efficiency and science, assistance to the unemployed, and State and local fiscal stabilization." The package included $288 billion in tax cuts for middle- and lower-middle-class individuals.

Taxes and Behavior Modification

Modern governments use their tax systems to address not only macroeconomic concerns but also social problems. Many such problems could be reduced if people or organizations could be persuaded to alter their behavior. Governments can promote behavioral change by writing tax laws to penalize undesirable behavior or reward desirable behavior. The penalty takes the form of a higher tax burden, while the reward is some type of tax relief.

Some of the social problems that the federal income tax system tries to remedy are by-products of the free enterprise system. Economists refer to these by-products as **negative externalities.** One of the most widely recognized is environmental pollution. The tax system contains provisions that either pressure or entice companies to clean up their act, so to speak. One example of a provision that discourages environmentally unfriendly behavior is the excise tax on ozone-depleting chemicals manufactured in or exported into the United States.[9] An example of a provision that encourages the private sector to be more environmentally responsible is the lucrative tax break for the construction of pollution control facilities such as wastewater purification plants.[10]

Disposable Bag Tax	Washington, D.C., has banned the use of nonrecyclable disposable carryout bags and charges consumers a five-cent-per-bag tax on recyclable disposable plastic and paper bags. According to the city's chief financial officer, the bag tax should result in an 80 percent reduction in the use of disposable bags by 2013.

Tax systems may also promote activities that are undervalued by the free market but that the government believes are socially desirable. By bestowing a tax benefit on the activity, the government is providing a financial "carrot." This carrot should induce more taxpayers to engage in the activity and thus result in a greater level of the activity across society. An example of an activity that the federal government promotes is the rehabilitation of historic buildings. The law allows firms to reduce their annual tax bill by a percentage of the cost

[9] §4681.
[10] §169.

of renovating a certified historic structure.[11] Without this tax break, firms might find it cheaper to build or purchase modern buildings than to invest in historic structures requiring extensive renovation. At the margin, the tax break could make the investment in the historic structure the more cost-effective business decision.

Governments use tax breaks to subsidize targeted activities, thereby making those activities less costly or more profitable. An excellent example of such a subsidy is the provision in the Internal Revenue Code making the interest paid on state and local debt obligations nontaxable.[12] Because investors pay no tax on the income generated by these tax-exempt bonds, they are willing to accept a lower before-tax interest rate than if the interest was taxable. Consequently, state and local governments can pay less interest than other debtors and still compete in the financial markets. By providing this tax break, the federal government subsidizes state and local governments by reducing their cost of borrowed capital.

Income Tax Preferences

Provisions in the federal income tax system designed as incentives for certain behaviors or as subsidies for targeted activities are described as **tax preferences.** These provisions do not contribute to the accurate measurement of the tax base or the correct calculation of the tax. Tax preferences do not support the primary function of the law, which is to raise revenues. In fact, tax preferences do just the opposite. Because they allow certain persons or organizations to pay less tax, preferences lose money for the Treasury. In this respect, preferences are indirect government expenditures.

Like any other government outlay, a tax preference is justifiable only if the intended result has merit and deserves public support. But a tax preference should be subject to a second level of scrutiny: Is a tax incentive the best way to accomplish the intended result, or would direct government support be more effective? This question can be hard to answer in any objective manner. Preferences are based on assumptions about how taxpayers react to the law. In a complex economy consisting of well over 100 million taxpayers, measuring the aggregate reaction to a tax preference is extremely difficult.

A Call for Tax Neutrality	On November 1, 2005, the President's Advisory Panel on Federal Tax Reform released its 271-page report recommending an overhaul of the Internal Revenue Code. The report proposes repealing many tax preferences that benefit only certain persons or organizations. Supporters of the report are enthusiastic about a return to a level playing field: "The whole idea behind tax reform is getting the government out of the business of encouraging or discouraging any activity, however worthwhile. To the extent that this 'tax neutrality' hurts anyone, the pain consists of losing the right to continue picking the pockets of other taxpayers."[13]

The Tax Expenditures Budget

Opponents of tax preferences maintain that they are too well hidden within the Internal Revenue Code and, as a result, their cost to the government is easily overlooked. In response to this criticism, the Congressional Joint Committee on Taxation publishes an annual **Tax Expenditures Budget** that quantifies the revenue loss from each major tax preference.[14] For example, the government loses about $95 billion each year because individuals can deduct their home mortgage interest payments and another $18 billion

---

[11] §47.

[12] §103.

[13] Steven Pearlstein, "Tax Reform That's Bold and Beautiful," *The Washington Post,* November 4, 2005.

[14] A tax expenditure is measured by the difference between tax liability under present law and the tax liability that would result from a recomputation of tax without benefit of the tax expenditure. This measurement is static because taxpayer behavior is assumed to remain unchanged for tax expenditure estimate purposes.

because they can deduct their medical expenses. The total revenue loss from tax expenditures exceeds $1 trillion annually.

The Tax Expenditures Budget sheds light on the cost of specific preferences and their aggregate cost to the government. However, tax expenditures are not included in the calculation of any federal operating deficit. Another troubling aspect of tax preferences is that they add enormously to the length and complexity of the tax law. If the Internal Revenue Code could be stripped of every provision that is not strictly necessary to measure taxable income and compute tax, it would be far simpler to understand and apply.

TAXES SHOULD BE FAIR

The fourth standard by which to evaluate a tax is whether the tax is fair to the people who must pay it. While no economist, social scientist, or politician would ever argue against fairness as a norm, there is precious little agreement as to the exact nature of tax equity. Many people believe that their tax burden is too heavy, while everyone else's burden is too light. As former U.S. Senator Russell Long expressed it, the attitude of the man on the street about tax equity is "Don't tax you, don't tax me; tax the fellow behind the tree." Clearly any meaningful discussion of the standard of fairness must rise above this sentiment.

Ability to Pay

A useful way to begin our discussion of equity is with the proposition that each person's contribution to the support of government should reflect that person's **ability to pay.** In the tax policy literature, ability to pay refers to the economic resources under a person's control. Each of the major taxes used in this country is based on some dimension of ability to pay. For instance, income taxes are based on a person's inflow of economic resources during the year. Sales and excise taxes are based on a different dimension of ability to pay: a person's consumption of resources represented by the purchase of goods and services. Real and personal property taxes complement income and sales taxes by focusing on a third dimension of ability to pay: a person's accumulation of resources in the form of property. Transfer taxes capture a fourth dimension: the accumulated wealth that a person gives to others during life or at death.

Horizontal Equity

Objective 5
Define horizontal equity.

If a tax is designed so that persons with the same ability to pay (as measured by the tax base) owe the same amount of tax, that system can be described as horizontally equitable. This standard of **horizontal equity** is consistent with the principle of equal protection under the law guaranteed by the U.S. Constitution. In the federal income tax system, the tax base is annual taxable income. Consequently, the income tax is horizontally equitable if the taxable income calculation accurately reflects ability to pay. Let's explore this notion in more depth by comparing two people, Ms. Buell and Mr. Deetz, both unmarried, both earning a $65,000 annual salary. Neither has any additional inflows of economic resources. Do Ms. Buell and Mr. Deetz have the same ability to pay an income tax? If we consider only their identical marital status and salaries, the answer must be yes, and the two should pay an equal tax.

But what additional facts might be relevant in measuring ability to pay? Suppose that Ms. Buell suffers from a chronic illness and has $7,000 of uninsured medical expenses each year while Mr. Deetz is in perfect health. Suppose that Mr. Deetz pays $3,850 annual alimony to a former spouse while Ms. Buell has no such legal obligation. On the basis of this new evidence, should we still conclude that Ms. Buell and Mr. Deetz have the same ability to pay an income tax? To ask the question another way, should medical expenses and alimony enter into the computation of taxable income? Certainly our two individuals would argue that it is only fair to consider these variables.

The horizontal equity of the income tax is enhanced by refining the calculation of taxable income to include the significant variables affecting a person's economic circumstances. But refining the tax base has its price: Every refinement adds another page to the Internal Revenue Code. Increased precision in the measurement of ability to pay may improve the horizontal equity of the income tax, but it also increases the complexity of the law.

Annual versus Lifetime Horizontal Equity

Federal taxable income is computed on a 12-month basis. This annual measurement of ability to pay may bear little or no relationship to a person's lifetime ability to pay.

Annual versus Lifetime Equity	This year, a blue-collar laborer wins a $300,000 lottery jackpot and, as a result, has the same taxable income as the scion of a wealthy family who lives off the interest and dividends from a trust fund. Prior to his lucky year and for the rest of his working life, the laborer's taxable income averages $35,000 while the trust fund beneficiary's income averages $300,000. Nevertheless, both individuals owe the same tax this year.

Tax Preferences and Horizontal Equity

In the previous section of this chapter, we introduced the concept of tax preferences. These income tax provisions are designed as incentives or subsidies and favor people who arrange their affairs to take advantage of the preference. Consequently, the tax benefit represented by preferences is not distributed impartially across taxpayers.

Preferences and Equity	Two unrelated individuals, Mr. Malone and Ms. Olaf, invested in two different businesses this year. Both businesses earned a $20,000 profit for their respective investors. Mr. Malone's business qualifies for several tax preferences. As a result, Mr. Malone must report only $14,000 of the profit on his income tax return. In contrast, Ms. Olaf must report her entire profit. Their businesses increased our two individuals' economic ability to pay by $20,000. But because of the tax preferences with respect to his business, Mr. Malone's taxable income is $6,000 less than Ms. Olaf's.

This example suggests that tax preferences can distort the horizontal equity of the income tax. Certainly the public perception is that the law is riddled with preferences that allow a privileged few to avoid paying their fair share of tax. We will examine the validity of this perception in later chapters of the text. Even if the perception is false and preferences do not undermine horizontal equity, the perception nonetheless erodes civic confidence in the fairness of the income tax system.

Vertical Equity

Objective 5
Define vertical equity.

A tax system is vertically equitable if persons with a greater ability to pay owe more tax than persons with a lesser ability to pay. While horizontal equity is concerned with a rational and impartial measurement of the tax base, **vertical equity** is concerned with a fair rate structure by which to calculate the tax.

Horizontal and Vertical Equity	A local government enacted a real property tax and established a board of assessors to determine the market values of the properties in its jurisdiction. The board completes its task in a conscientious manner so that each resident's tax base (assessed value of their real property) is fairly measured. The property tax system has a two-bracket rate structure.

Percentage Rate	Bracket
2%	Assessed value from –0– to $1 million
1%	Assessed value in excess of $1 million

Mr. Foley owns real property with an assessed value of $500,000; his property tax is $10,000 (2 percent of $500,000). Ms. Lennon owns real property with an assessed value of $1.5 million; her property tax is $25,000 (2 percent of $1 million + 1 percent of $500,000).

This property tax is horizontally equitable because the base is fairly measured, and taxpayers with equal bases (assessed value) bear an equal tax burden. The tax is also vertically equitable because taxpayers with a greater base (such as Ms. Lennon) owe more tax than taxpayers with a lesser base (such as Mr. Foley).

Regressive Taxes

Objective 6
Differentiate among regressive, proportionate, and progressive rate structures.

The property tax described in the preceding example meets a strict definition of vertical equity because Mr. Foley pays less tax than Ms. Lennon: his $10,000 to her $25,000. However, Mr. Foley's average tax rate of 2 percent ($10,000 tax ÷ $500,000 base) is *more than* Ms. Lennon's average tax rate of 1.667 percent ($25,000 tax ÷ $1,500,000 base).

This inversion in average rates occurs because the property tax has a **regressive rate structure:** graduated rates that decrease as the base increases. Tax policymakers agree that regressive rates are inequitable because they place a proportionally greater tax burden on persons with smaller tax bases. However, the regressive nature of a tax is not always obvious from its rate structure.

Retail sales taxes consist of only a single rate and therefore are not explicitly regressive. Even so, many economists criticize these taxes as regressive in operation, bearing most heavily on people with the least economic resources.

Regressive Sales Tax Rates

Mr. James and Mr. Kim live in Maryland, which has a 5 percent sales tax on all retail purchases. Mr. James earns $20,000 annual disposable income and spends this entire amount on taxable purchases. Mr. James pays $1,000 sales tax, and his average tax rate (with respect to disposable income) is 5 percent.

$1,000 tax ÷ $20,000 base = 5% average tax rate

In contrast, Mr. Kim earns $100,000 annual disposable income, spends only $75,000, and invests the remaining $25,000. Mr. Kim pays $3,750 sales tax, and his average tax rate is 3.75 percent.

$3,750 tax ÷ $100,000 base = 3.75% average tax rate

According to a 2009 study, "Sales and excise taxes are very regressive. Poor families pay almost eight times more of their incomes in these taxes than the best-off families, and middle-income families pay more than four times the rate of the wealthy."[15] The majority of states mitigate the regressivity of sales taxes by legislating broad exemptions for groceries purchased for home consumption, prescription medicines, and residential utilities.

Income Tax Rate Structures

In an income tax system, the simplest rate structure consists of a single rate applied to taxable income. To illustrate this **proportionate rate structure,** consider a group of three

[15] *Who Pays? A Distributional Analysis of the Tax Systems in All 50 States, 3rd edition,* Institute on Taxation and Economic Policy, November 2009, p. 4.

individuals, A, B, and C, who have respective incomes of $20,000, $45,000, and $100,000. A proportionate 10 percent income tax results in the following tax for each individual.

Proportionate Rate (10%)		
	Taxable Income	**Tax**
Taxpayer A	$ 20,000	$ 2,000
Taxpayer B	45,000	4,500
Taxpayer C	100,000	10,000
		$16,500

Tax Talk
Adam Smith wrote in The Wealth of Nations: *"The necessaries of life occasion the great expense of the poor. . . . The luxuries and vanities of life occasion the principal expense of the rich. It is not very unreasonable that the rich should contribute to the public expense, not only in proportion to their revenue, but something more than in that proportion."*

Under this rate structure, individual C, who has the most taxable income and presumably the greatest ability to pay, owes the most tax, while B, who has more income than A, owes more tax than A. Despite this result, many theorists believe that a single rate fails to fairly apportion the tax burden across people with different incomes. They argue that the 10 percent tax is relatively less of a hardship on C than on A and B. Although the tax rate is proportionate, the economic sacrifice is disproportionate.

This argument is based on the theory of the **declining marginal utility of income.** This theory presumes that the financial importance of each dollar of income diminishes as total income increases. In other words, people value the subsistence income spent on necessities, such as food and shelter, more than they value incremental income spent on luxury items. According to this theory, a **progressive rate structure** in which the rates increase as income increases results in an equality of sacrifice across taxpayers.[16]

Assume that our individuals A, B, and C compute their income tax under a progressive rate structure consisting of three rate brackets.

Percentage Rate	Bracket
5%	Income from –0– to $20,000
10%	Income from $20,001 to $50,000
16%	Income in excess of $50,000

This rate structure results in the following.

Progressive Rates			
	Taxable Income	**Tax Computation**	**Tax**
Taxpayer A	$ 20,000	5% of 20,000	$ 1,000
Taxpayer B	45,000	5% of 20,000 +10% of 25,000	3,500
Taxpayer C	100,000	5% of 20,000 +10% of 30,000 +16% of 50,000	12,000
			$16,500

[16] See Walter J. Blum and Harry Kalven, Jr., *The Uneasy Case for Progressive Taxation* (Chicago: University of Chicago Press, 1953), for a provocative analysis of the arguments for and against progressive tax rates.

Note that this rate structure raises the same $16,500 revenue as the 10 percent proportionate rate structure, and the aggregate tax burden is unchanged. However, A and B are paying fewer dollars while C's tax has increased by $2,000.

Is the proportionate or the progressive rate structure the more equitable for our three individuals? If the progressive rate structure seems fairer than the proportionate structure, would a more progressive structure—perhaps with a top rate of 25 percent—be even fairer? There are no objective answers to these questions. Progressivity has an intuitive appeal to many people, and the U.S. income tax has always used a progressive rate structure. Nonetheless, while it may be plausible that individuals value income less as their economic resources increase, this proposition cannot be tested empirically. To refer back to our illustration, the taxing authorities have no idea how A, B, or C personally values income, or whether the economic sacrifices each makes by paying tax are even remotely comparable. Until economists discover how to measure the utility of income and to compare utilities across individuals, the extent to which any progressive rate structure achieves equality of sacrifice is a matter of opinion.

Objective 7
Explain the difference between marginal and average tax rates.

Marginal and Average Tax Rates

Before leaving the subject of income tax rate structures, we must distinguish between marginal and average tax rates. The **marginal rate** is the rate that applies to the *next* dollar of income. In the progressive rate structure in our example, individual C with $100,000 taxable income owed $12,000 tax. If C earns one more dollar, that dollar is subject to a 16 percent tax rate. Nevertheless, the fact that C is in the 16 percent marginal tax bracket does not mean she is paying 16 percent of her income to the government. Her $12,000 tax divided by $100,000 taxable income is an **average rate** of only 12 percent. Similarly, individual B has a 10 percent marginal rate, but her average rate is 7.8 percent ($3,500 tax divided by $45,000 taxable income).

Under a proportionate rate structure, the marginal and average rates are the same for all levels of taxable income. Under a progressive rate structure, the marginal rate is higher than the average rate for incomes in excess of the first rate bracket. The graphs in Exhibit 2.1 illustrate the relationship between marginal and average rate for the proportionate and progressive tax structures in our examples. In both graphs, the marginal rate is represented by a solid line, and the average rate is represented by a broken line.

Objective 8
Discuss distributive justice as a tax policy objective.

Distributive Justice

In a social sense, a tax is equitable if it redresses inequities existing in a capitalistic system. A vastly uneven distribution of private wealth across households, characterized by extremes of poverty and affluence, is one such inequity. By definition, taxes appropriate private wealth for public use, and they appropriate more from the rich than from the poor. Consequently, taxes become mechanisms for the redistribution of wealth across society. Wealth transfer taxes, such as the federal estate and gift taxes, are prime examples of taxes with strong distributional implications. These taxes were enacted early in this century to allow the government to tap into the immense personal fortunes amassed during America's "gilded age." Some policymakers believe that the justification for a progressive income tax is its potential for rectifying distributive inequity. "The case for drastic progression in taxation must be rested on the case against inequality—on the ethical or aesthetic judgment that the prevailing distribution of wealth and income reveals a degree (and/or kind) of inequality that is distinctly evil or unlovely."[17]

---

[17] Henry Simons, *Personal Income Taxation* (Chicago: University of Chicago Press, 1938), pp. 18–19.

EXHIBIT 2.1A
Marginal and
Average Tax Rates
under Proportionate
Rate Structure

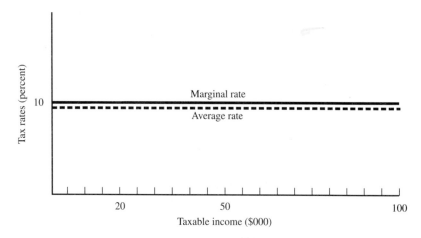

EXHIBIT 2.1B
Marginal and
Average Tax Rates
under Progressive
Rate Structure

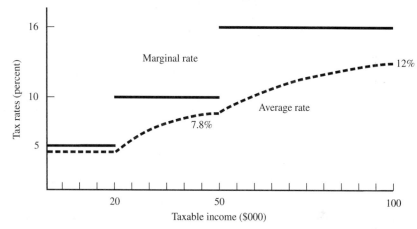

Share of Income/
Share of Taxes

In 2009, the top 1 percent of U.S. taxpayers (with incomes in excess of $343,927) accounted for 16.9 percent of the total income reported on all individual tax returns filed for that year. This highest income group also accounted for 36.7 percent of the total individual tax paid in 2009.

In contrast, the bottom 50 percent of U.S. taxpayers (with incomes less than $32,396) accounted for just 13.5 percent of total income reported. However, this lowest income group accounted for only 2.3 percent of the total tax paid.

Many social commentators view the current distribution of wealth across American households as unjust.[18] These commentators suggest that the federal government could combat this injustice by making the income tax rate structure more progressive. But once again the question arises: How much more progressivity is desirable? Only the most fanatic egalitarian would argue that the tax system should result in a perfectly equal distribution of wealth across households. Although many people agree (to a greater or lesser extent) with the concept of distributive justice, many also oppose the notion of Uncle Sam playing Robin Hood. In the final analysis, the degree of progressivity in the income tax system remains a matter of political taste.

[18] In 2007, the richest 1 percent of Americans owned 34.6 percent of the national wealth, the richest 20 percent owned 85 percent of the wealth, and the poorest 40 percent owned 0.2 percent of the wealth. Edward N. Wolff, *Recent Trends in Household Wealth in the United States: Rising Debt and the Middle-Class Squeeze—an Update to 2007* (The Levy Economics Institute, March 2010).

The Perception of Inequity

The most widespread complaint against the federal income tax system is that it is unfair. Of course, no government has been or ever will be capable of designing a tax that people enjoy paying. As Edmund Burke, the English parliamentarian and social scientist, observed, "To tax and to please, no more than to love and be wise, is not given to man." Nevertheless, the public perception that the federal income tax is unfair has increased in recent decades.

This perception of inequity has many negative consequences. Research has shown that individuals who believe that the income tax system is unfair are more likely to deliberately underreport their incomes than individuals who believe the system is fair. This result suggests that as public confidence in the equity of the federal tax system erodes, the level of compliance will decline. As greater numbers of citizens regard tax evasion as acceptable, and even rational, behavior, the tax system will place an increasingly unfair burden on the honest remainder who comply with the law.

> Taxpayer morale ultimately depends on the belief that taxes are fair. If the basis for this belief comes under suspicion, voluntary compliance with the tax laws is jeopardized. Thus, the perceived lack of fairness of the income tax may be as important as actual complexities, economic distortions, and inequities.[19]

Many individuals believe that the income tax system is unfair because it is so complicated. They are convinced that the system is full of exotic loopholes benefitting only the rich who can afford expert legal advice. As you will learn, this conviction is unfounded. Many of the complexities of the law were designed to ensure that high-income taxpayers *cannot* manipulate the system to unwarranted advantage. Affluent individuals undeniably use the tax planning strategies discussed throughout this text on a routine basis to maximize the net present value of their business and investment transactions. However, most of these strategies derive from commonplace features of the law rather than from closely guarded secrets known only to tax professionals.

Conclusion

Jack Kemp, the 1996 Republican vice-presidential candidate, provided this summary description of a good tax.

> Surely, a tax code which is simple and fair must generate sufficient revenue so that the federal government may carry out its legitimate tasks. Second, it must not place a tax burden on those members of society least able to bear one. And, perhaps most important of all, it must not restrict the innovative and entrepreneurial capacities of Americans upon which rising living standards and our general prosperity so greatly depend.[20]

This summary touches on the four normative standards discussed in Chapter 2: sufficiency, convenience, efficiency, and equity. In our discussions, we learned that people interpret these standards in different ways and hold different opinions as to how each should be achieved.

The standards for a good tax are not necessarily in harmony, and reconciling them can be a tricky proposition. A government's attempt to improve the sufficiency of its tax system by raising rates or expanding the base could make the tax less efficient in terms of its economic effect. The introduction of a preferential rule to enhance economic efficiency might damage the equity of the tax. Conversely, the enactment of a provision making a tax more fair may create complexity that makes it more difficult to administer. Tax policymakers are well aware of the frictions between the standards for a good tax. They know that trade-offs may be necessary in the design and implementation of the tax system that best serves the needs of their governments.

[19] Department of the Treasury, *Tax Reform for Fairness, Simplicity, and Economic Growth*, vol. 1 (Washington, D.C.: U.S. Government Printing Office, 1984), p. 9.

[20] "Unleashing America's Potential: A Pro-Growth, Pro-Family Tax System for the 21st Century," National Commission on Economic Growth and Tax Reform, 70 *Tax Notes* 413, 415.

Key Terms

ability to pay *32*	marginal rate *36*	substitution effect *26*
average rate *36*	negative externality *30*	sufficiency *22*
convenience *28*	progressive rate	supply-side economic
declining marginal utility	structure *35*	theory *27*
of income *35*	proportionate rate	Tax Expenditures
dynamic forecast *24*	structure *34*	Budget *31*
efficiency *28*	regressive rate	tax policy *21*
horizontal equity *32*	structure *34*	tax preferences *31*
income effect *25*	static forecast *24*	vertical equity *33*

Questions and Problems for Discussion

1. Identify the tax policy issue that you believe is the most important in today's society.

2. What evidence suggests that the federal tax system receives a low grade when evaluated on the standard of sufficiency?

3. Identify three ways that governments can alter their tax system to increase revenues.

4. National governments have the authority to print their own currency. Why might governments be reluctant to finance an operating deficit (excess of spending over revenues) simply by printing more money?

5. In each of the following cases, discuss how the taxpayers might respond to a tax rate increase in a manner consistent with the income effect.

   a. Mr. E earns $32,000 a year as an employee, and Mrs. E doesn't work.

   b. Mr. F earns $22,000 a year as an employee, and Mrs. F earns $10,000 a year as a self-employed worker.

   c. Mr. G earns $22,000 a year as an employee, and Mrs. G earns $10,000 a year as an employee.

6. In each of the following cases, discuss how the taxpayers might respond to a tax rate increase in a manner consistent with the substitution effect.

   a. Mr. H earns $195,000 a year as a salaried employee, and Mrs. H doesn't work.

   b. Mr. J earns $195,000 a year as a salaried employee, and Mrs. J earns $38,000 a year as a salaried employee.

   c. Ms. K is single and earns $195,000 a year as a self-employed consultant.

7. Ms. V resides in a jurisdiction with a 35 percent income tax. Ms. V has $40,000 that she could invest in bonds paying 8 percent annual interest. She is also considering spending the $40,000 on a new luxury automobile. Ms. V is having a hard time deciding between these two alternatives. Why might her decision be easier if the jurisdiction increases its income tax rate to 50 percent?

8. What nonmonetary incentives affect the amount of time and energy people devote to income-generating activities?

9. The U.S. Congress has occasionally considered enacting a federal tax on the sale of consumer goods and services. This national sales tax would be in addition to any state and local sales tax. Would this new source of federal revenue affect the revenues of state and local governments?

10. The federal government levies a gift tax on the value of property that people give away during their life and an estate tax on the value of property that people transfer at death. From the government's perspective, which tax is more convenient?

11. Discuss the tax policy implications of the saying "an old tax is a good tax."

12. Jurisdiction R and Jurisdiction S both impose a personal income tax on their residents. Under Jurisdiction R's system, employers are required to withhold income tax

from their employees' paychecks and remit the tax to the government. Jurisdiction S's system has no such withholding requirement. Instead, residents must compute their income tax and pay the tax directly on a monthly basis. Which tax system is more convenient for the government and for the taxpayer?

13. The federal income tax is criticized as being both inequitable across individuals and overly complicated. Discuss why equity and simplicity can be considered conflicting tax policy goals.

14. Jurisdiction W has decided to enact a personal income tax on its residents. Policymakers are considering the following alternatives.

    a. No tax on income up to $35,000, and a 15 percent tax on all income in excess of $35,000.

    b. A 10 percent tax on all income.

    c. A 15 percent tax on all income up to $80,000, and no tax on any income in excess of $80,000.

    Identify the rate structure of each of the three alternatives.

15. Corporation R and Corporation T conduct business in Jurisdiction Q. The corporations' financial records for last year show the following.

	Corporation R	Corporation T
Gross receipts from sales	$5,000,000	$5,000,000
Cost of goods sold	(3,200,000)	(3,670,000)
Gross profit	$1,800,000	$1,330,000
Annual operating expenses	(1,000,000)	(400,000)
Charitable contributions	–0–	(300,000)
Net profit	$ 800,000	$ 630,000

Jurisdiction Q decided to enact a tax on corporations conducting business within its jurisdiction but has not decided on the tax base. Identify four different tax bases suggested by the corporations' financial records and discuss each base in terms of horizontal equity.

16. Jurisdiction E spends approximately $7 million each winter on snow removal. The jurisdiction is considering adding a new income tax provision that would allow people to deduct the cost of snow removal equipment purchased during the year.

    a. Does this proposed change in Jurisdiction E's tax law meet the definition of a tax preference? Explain briefly.

    b. Jurisdiction E forecasts that the proposed change will decrease its annual tax revenues by $250,000 but will improve the jurisdiction's financial condition by $300,000. On what assumptions is this forecast based?

17. Ms. P is considering investing $20,000 in a new business. She projects that this investment should generate $3,000 income each year. In estimating her tax on this future income stream, should Ms. P use her marginal or her average tax rate?

Application Problems

1. Country M levies a 10 percent excise tax on the retail price of any automobile purchased in the country. This year, the aggregate purchase price subject to tax was $8 million, so current year revenue was $800,000. Country M plans to increase the tax rate next year to 11 percent. Compute next year's excise tax revenue assuming:

    a. Next year's tax base equals the current year base.

    b. Next year's tax base increases to $9.3 million.

    c. Next year's tax base decreases to $7 million.

2. The city of Lakeland levies a 2 percent tax on the value of all restaurant meals served to the public within the city limits. This year, the aggregate value subject to tax was $29.4 million, so current year revenue was $588,000. Lakeland plans to decrease the tax rate next year to 1.5 percent. Compute next year's restaurant tax revenue assuming:

   a. Next year's tax base equals the current year base.

   b. Next year's tax base increases to $36 million.

   c. Next year's tax base increases to $41 million.

3. Mrs. K, a single taxpayer, earns a $42,000 annual salary and pays 15 percent in state and federal income tax. If tax rates increase so that Mrs. K's annual tax rate is 20 percent, how much additional income must she earn to maintain her after-tax standard of living?

4. Mr. and Mrs. J own a dry cleaning business that generates $125,000 taxable income each year. For the past few years, the couple's federal tax rate on this income has been 32 percent. Congress recently increased the tax rate for next year to 40 percent.

   a. Based on a static forecast, how much additional revenue will the federal government collect from Mr. and Mrs. J next year?

   b. How much additional revenue will the government collect if Mr. and Mrs. J respond to the rate increase by working harder and earning $140,000 next year?

   c. How much additional revenue will the government collect if Mr. and Mrs. J respond to the rate increase by working less and earning only $110,000 next year?

5. Jurisdiction B levies a flat 7 percent tax on the first $5 million of annual corporate income.

   a. Jersey Inc. generated $3.9 million income this year. Compute Jersey's income tax and determine its average and marginal tax rate on total income.

   b. Leray Inc. generated $9.6 million income this year. Compute Leray's income tax and determine Leray's average and marginal tax rate on total income.

   c. What type of rate structure does Jurisdiction B use for its corporate income tax?

6. Jurisdiction X levies a flat 14 percent tax on individual income in excess of $35,000 per year. Individuals who earn $35,000 or less pay no income tax.

   a. Mr. Hill earned $98,750 income this year. Compute his income tax and determine his average and marginal tax rate.

   b. Ms. Lui earned $47,900 income this year. Compute her income tax and determine her average and marginal tax rate.

   c. Ms. Archer earned $34,100 income this year and paid no income tax. Describe her average and marginal tax rate.

   d. What type of rate structure does Jurisdiction X use for its individual income tax?

7. Government G levies an income tax with the following rate structure.

Percentage Rate	Bracket
6%	Income from –0– to $30,000
10	Income from $30,001 to $70,000
20	Income from $70,001 to $200,000
28	Income in excess of $200,000

   a. Taxpayer A's annual income is $119,400. Compute A's tax and average tax rate. What is A's marginal tax rate?

   b. Taxpayer B's annual income is $383,900. Compute B's tax and average tax rate. What is B's marginal tax rate?

8. Refer to Government G's rate structure described in the preceding problem. Taxpayer O earns $50,000 annually during years 1 through 10. Taxpayer P earns $20,000 annually during years 1 through 5 and $80,000 annually during years 6 through 10.

   a. How much total income does each taxpayer earn over the 10-year period?

   b. Compute each taxpayer's average tax rate for the 10-year period.

9. Jurisdiction Z levies an excise tax on retail purchases of jewelry and watches. The tax equals 3 percent of the first $1,000 of the purchase price plus 1 percent of the purchase price in excess of $1,000.

   a. Individual C purchases a watch for $500. Compute C's excise tax and average excise tax rate.

   b. Individual D purchases a watch for $5,000. Compute D's excise tax and average excise tax rate.

   c. Is Jurisdiction Z's excise tax vertically equitable? Explain briefly.

Issue Recognition Problems

Identify the tax issue or issues suggested by the following situations, and state each issue in the form of a question.

1. County M imposes a 1 percent tax on the gross receipts earned by firms operating within its jurisdiction. For the last year, gross receipts subject to tax totaled $400 million. The county government is considering raising the tax rate to 2 percent because it needs $400,000 additional revenue to improve its road system.

2. Mrs. K is completely blind, while Mr. L is paralyzed from the waist down. Both individuals have the same income. The Internal Revenue Code provides a preferential deduction for individuals who are blind, and as a result, Mrs. K's income tax liability is less than Mr. L's income tax liability.

3. Four years ago, the citizens of Country C complained that the national tax system was too uncertain because the government changed the tax laws so frequently. In response to this criticism, the government enacted a 10-year moratorium on change: No existing tax law can be modified and no new tax law can be enacted for a decade. This year, Country C is experiencing a severe recession. Economic growth is at a standstill, and the national unemployment rate is 18 percent.

4. Two years ago, the government of State P decided to improve the horizontal equity of its individual income tax by allowing families to deduct the cost of heating and air conditioning their homes. This modification necessitated an additional tax form and three additional pages of instructions. For the past two years, only one-third of the families eligible for the deduction actually claimed it on their returns.

5. Jurisdiction J decides to clean up its streets, parks, and waterways by providing a tax break for businesses that assign employees to pick up trash for a minimum number of hours each month. The annual revenue loss from this tax break is $1.9 million.

6. Country O imposes just two taxes on its citizens. The first tax is a 20 percent excise tax on motor fuel and motor oil. This tax is earmarked for Country O's Highway Improvement Trust Fund, and the revenues cannot be spent for any other purpose. The second tax is a 10 percent general sales tax on consumer goods and services (excluding retail purchases of motor fuel and motor oil). Sales tax revenues can be spent for any authorized public purpose. This year, Country O collected $185 million in excise tax and spent only $77 million from the Highway Improvement Trust Fund. It collected $718 million in sales tax and spent $800 million for public purposes.

Research Problems

1. Visit the website for the Congressional Budget Office (**www.cbo.gov**), follow the link to Budget and Economic Information, and look up the most current Monthly Budget Review. What is the CBO's estimate of the U.S. government's total budget surplus or deficit for fiscal year 2012? Does this estimate include or exclude the surplus in the Social Security Trust Fund?

2. Visit the website for the Tax Foundation (**www.taxfoundation.org**). Select the link "About Us" to read the organization's mission statement. Select the link "Tax Freedom Day" to research the following:

   a. What and when was Tax Freedom Day in 2011?

   b. How many additional days would Americans have to work to pay off the 2011 federal budget deficit?

3. Visit the U.S. Treasury's Public Debt website (**www.publicdebt.treas.gov**) to find out today's total national debt to the penny!

Tax Planning Case

Jurisdiction B's tax system consists of a 6.5 percent general sales tax on retail goods and selected services. Over the past decade, the average annual volume of sales subject to this tax was $500 million. The jurisdiction needs to increase its tax revenues by approximately $5 million each year to finance its spending programs. The taxing authorities are considering two alternatives: a 1 percent increase in the sales tax rate or a new 2 percent tax on the net income of corporations doing business in the jurisdiction. Based on recent economic data, the annual net income subject to the new tax would be $275 million. However, the jurisdiction would have to create a new agency responsible for enforcing and collecting the income tax. The estimated annual cost of the agency is $500,000. Jurisdiction B borders four other taxing jurisdictions, all of which have a general sales tax and two of which have a corporate income tax.

1. Based on a static forecast, how much incremental revenue would Jurisdiction B raise under each alternative?

2. Assume that the taxing authorities in Jurisdiction B want a dynamic forecast of the incremental revenues under each alternative. What additional facts would be important in making such a forecast and why?

Fundamentals
of Tax Planning

3 Taxes as Transaction Costs

4 Maxims of Income Tax Planning

5 Tax Research

Taxes as Transaction Costs

Learning Objectives

After studying this chapter, you should be able to:

1. Compute the tax cost of an income item and the tax savings from a deduction.

2. Integrate tax costs and savings into NPV calculations.

3. Identify the uncertainties concerning future tax costs and savings.

4. Explain why tax minimization may not be the optimal business strategy.

5. Explain why bilateral tax planning is important in private market transactions.

6. Distinguish between arm's-length and related party transactions.

In the introduction to *Principles of Taxation for Business and Investment Planning,* we established the premise that the overall objective of business decisions is to maximize the value of the firm. The premise is relevant to managers who are employed to make decisions on behalf of the owners of the firm. Managers who make good decisions that increase the value of owners' equity can expect to be well compensated for their success. Managers who make bad decisions that decrease value can expect to lose their jobs. A variation of the premise holds true for individuals acting in their own economic self-interest. Individuals want to make personal financial decisions that further their goal of wealth maximization.

In Chapter 3, we will explore the business decision-making process. The chapter begins with a review of the concept of net present value of cash flows as the cornerstone of this process. The chapter then focuses on how the tax consequences of business transactions affect net present value and how these consequences must be integrated into the decision-making framework. We will consider how managers can structure transactions to control tax consequences and maximize net present value. The chapter concludes by discussing the extent to which the various parties to a business transaction can negotiate to reduce the tax burden on the transaction and to share the tax savings among themselves.

THE ROLE OF NET PRESENT VALUE IN DECISION MAKING

Every business activity consists of a series of transactions intended to generate profit and create value. Business managers need a method for evaluating whether an isolated transaction or an integrated sequence of transactions will contribute to or detract from the profitability of the activity. The method should be useful to managers who must choose between alternative transactions that accomplish the same result for the firm.

Quantifying Cash Flows

Financial theorists agree that the first step in evaluating a business transaction is to quantify the cash flows from the transaction. Some transactions result in the receipt of cash by the firm. The sale of merchandise to a customer and the rental of property to a lessee are examples of transactions generating cash inflows. Other transactions require the firm to disburse cash. The purchase of business assets and the hiring of employees are common transactions requiring cash outflows. Of course, many transactions involve both inflows and outflows and must be evaluated on the basis of **net cash flow** (the difference between cash received and cash disbursed).

The various revenue-generating transactions in which firms engage typically result in positive net cash flows that increase the value of the firm. If managers must choose between alternative revenue-generating opportunities, they should choose the opportunity with the greatest positive net cash flow. The various costs that firms incur can be expressed as negative net cash flows. Viewed in isolation, negative net cash flows decrease the value of the firm. However, costs are essential components of an integrated business activity and contribute to short-term and long-term profitability. If managers conclude that a particular cost is unnecessary because it does not enhance profitability, the cost should be eliminated. If a cost is justified, managers should reduce the negative net cash flow associated with the cost as much as possible.

In summary, managers want to make decisions that enhance profitability by increasing revenues and controlling costs. More precisely, *managers want to make decisions that maximize the value of the firm by maximizing positive cash flow or minimizing negative cash flow.*

The Concept of Present Value

When cash flows from a transaction occur at different times, the quantification of net cash flow should take into account the **time value of money.** Time value refers to the fact that a dollar available today is worth more than a dollar available tomorrow because the current dollar can be invested to start earning interest immediately.[1] A dollar available today has a present value of a dollar. The present value of a dollar available in the future is based on a **discount rate**—the after-tax rate of interest on invested funds for the deferral period. A transaction's **net present value (NPV)** is the sum of the present values of cash inflows and outflows from the transaction.

The next several paragraphs review the mathematical derivation of present value. If you are already familiar with this material, please feel free to jump ahead to the issue of risk on page 50.

---

[1] This proposition is the first basic principle of finance. Richard A. Brealey and Stewart C. Myers, *Principles of Corporate Finance,* 5th ed. (New York: McGraw-Hill, 1996).

Present Value

The algebraic expression of the present value (PV) of a dollar available at the end of one period based on the discount rate (r) for that period is:

$$PV(\$1) = \frac{1}{1 + r}$$

PV Calculation	At an annual 10 percent discount rate, the present value of $1 to be received at the end of one year is $.9091. $$\$.9091 = \frac{1}{1.10}$$

If the availability of the dollar is deferred for a number of periods (n) over which the discount rate is constant, the algebraic expression of present value is:

$$PV(\$1) = \frac{1}{(1 + r)^n}$$

PV Calculation	At an annual 10 percent discount rate, the present value of $1 to be received at the end of three years is $.7513. $$\$.7513 = \frac{1}{1.331} = \frac{1}{(1.10)^3}$$ In other words, $.7513 invested today to earn 10 percent compounded annually will accumulate to $1 at the end of three years.

Present Value of an Annuity

A cash flow consisting of a constant dollar amount available at the end of the period for a specific number of periods is called an **annuity.** Examples include monthly rent payments over the term of a lease agreement and equal annual payments to retire the principal of an outstanding loan. The algebraic expression of the present value (PV) of an annuity of one dollar for a number of periods (n) based on the discount rate (r) over the period is:

$$PV(\$1 \text{ for n periods}) = \frac{1}{r} - \frac{1}{r(1 + r)^n}$$

PV of an Annuity	At a 10 percent annual discount rate, the present value of $1 to be received at the end of years 1 through 4 is $3.1699. $$PV(\$1 \text{ for 4 years}) = \frac{1}{.10} - \frac{1}{.10(1.10)^4}$$ $$PV(\$1 \text{ for 4 years}) = 10 - \frac{1}{.10(1.4641)}$$ $$\$3.1699 = 10 - 6.8301$$ The present value of the annuity is the sum of the present values of the four $1 payments. Note that this formula works only for a series of *equal* payments.

Present Value Tables

The algebraic formulas in the preceding paragraphs can be used to derive tables of discount factors for computing the present value of cash receipts or payments deferred for any given number of periods. Appendix A of this text is a table of discount factors for computing the present value of $1 available at the end of 1 through 20 years at annual discount rates ranging from 3 percent to 20 percent. Appendix B is a table of discount factors for computing the present value of a $1 annuity for a period of 1 through 20 years at annual discount rates ranging from 3 percent to 20 percent. Throughout the text, computations of the net present value of cash flows are based on factors from these tables.

The net present value of cash flows can also be computed by using a financial calculator or a spreadsheet computer program such as Microsoft Excel. Remember that discount factor tables, calculators, and electronic spreadsheets are all means to the same end. Business managers can use whichever tool is the most convenient for computing net present value.

The Issue of Risk

The quantification of cash flows and calculation of their net present value are based on assumptions concerning future events. In projecting the cash inflows and outflows from a proposed transaction, business managers research pertinent industry and economic data, consult professionals who have expertise relevant to the transaction, and rely on their experience with past transactions of a similar nature. Nonetheless, even the most carefully developed projections can be inaccurate, and unexpected events can alter the actual cash flows from a transaction.

Financial forecasters must accept the possibility that one or more of the assumptions on which their cash flow projections are based will be wrong. Of course, some assumptions are more certain than others. The assumption that the U.S. government will pay the interest on its debt obligations is more certain than the assumption that the value of an initial public offering (IPO) of stock will double in value over the next 12 months. This difference in certainty makes a decision to invest in U.S. Treasury bills less risky than a decision to invest in the IPO.

Business managers must be sensitive to the uncertainties and the resultant degree of risk inherent in any transaction. When calculating net present value, they should invoke the financial principle that a safe dollar is worth more than a risky dollar. In other words, the present value of a highly speculative future dollar should be based on a higher discount rate than the present value of a guaranteed future dollar.

High Risk and Low Risk	Firm Z has the opportunity to invest $200,000 in a new business venture. The promoters of the venture provide Firm Z with a 10-year projection of net cash flows. Firm Z determines that the venture has a high degree of risk and therefore decides to use a 15 percent discount rate to calculate the net present value of the projected cash flows. With the high discount rate, the net present value is a *negative* number. Consequently, Firm Z decides not to make the investment. In contrast, assume that Firm Z determines that the venture has a low degree of risk and uses a 7 percent discount rate to calculate net present value. With the lower discount rate, the net present value is a positive number and Firm Z decides to make the investment.

Because this text concentrates on the tax aspects of business decisions, the cash flow examples throughout the text incorporate two simplifying assumptions about financial risk. First, they assume that the discount rate in the example accurately reflects the risk of the transaction under consideration. Second, the examples assume that such risk is stable over time so that the appropriate discount rate does not change from period to period.

A Net Present Value Example

Let's summarize our discussion of net present value and its role in business decision making by working through a simple example. Suppose a consulting firm must decide between two engagements, either of which would require the firm's complete attention for two years. Engagement 1 will generate $150,000 of revenues in each of the two years. The firm estimates that this engagement will require $90,000 of expenses in the current year and $10,000 of expenses in the next year. Engagement 2 will generate $200,000 of revenues in the current year and $125,000 of revenues in the next year. The firm estimates that Engagement 2 will require $65,000 of annual expenses. Based on a 10 percent discount rate and *without considering the effect of any type of tax,* the net present values of the competing engagements are computed as follows.

	Engagement 1	Engagement 2
Current year:		
Cash revenues	$150,000	$200,000
Cash expenses	(90,000)	(65,000)
Net cash flow	$ 60,000	$135,000
Next year:		
Cash revenues	$150,000	$125,000
Cash expenses	(10,000)	(65,000)
Net cash flow	$140,000	$ 60,000
Present value of current year cash flow	$ 60,000	$135,000
Present value of next year cash flow		
(cash flow $\times$ .909 discount factor)	127,260	54,540
NPV	$187,260	$189,540

The firm now has a rational basis for choosing between the two consulting opportunities. It should accept Engagement 2 because Engagement 2 has a greater net present value than Engagement 1.

In the above example, the net cash flow received in the current year was not discounted, and the net cash received in the next year was discounted for one period. This treatment is based on an assumption that cash flows attributable to the current year (year 0) are available immediately and are not discounted. Cash flows attributable to the next year (year 1) are available one year hence and are discounted for one period, and so forth. *This assumption is used consistently throughout the NPV examples in the text and for the solutions to the problems and cases at the end of each chapter.*

TAXES AND CASH FLOWS

Calculations of net present value must reflect all cash flows including any tax costs or tax savings resulting from the transaction. In the business decision-making process, cash flows *before* tax have no relevance.

Words of Wisdom   Legendary investor Warren Buffet made the following observation. "What is one really trying to do in the investment world? Not pay the least taxes, although that may be a factor to be considered in achieving the end. Means and end should not be confused, however, and the end is to come away with the largest after-tax rate of compound."

Objective 1
Compute the tax cost of an income item and the tax savings from a deduction.

Tax Costs

If a transaction results in an increase in any tax for any period, the increase (**tax cost**) is a cash outflow. A tax cost may be incremental to a nontax cost. For instance, a firm that purchases machinery may pay a sales tax; the cash outflow from the transaction includes both the purchase price and the tax. In the context of an income tax, tax cost can be a direct result of the receipt of taxable income; the cash outflow represented by the tax is linked to any cash inflow represented by the income item.

Income Tax Cost	Firm F sells a unit of inventory for $50 cash. If the unit cost was $40, the sales transaction generates $10 taxable income. If the firm is subject to a 30 percent income tax, the tax cost of the transaction is $3. The sales transaction generates both $50 cash inflow and $3 cash outflow, resulting in positive net cash flow of $47.

Tax Savings

If a transaction results in a decrease in any tax for any period, the decrease (**tax savings**) is a cash inflow. In the income tax system, tax liability is based on net business profits rather than gross revenues. Accordingly, many business expenditures can be subtracted, or deducted, in the computation of taxable income. The **deduction** reduces taxable income and causes a corresponding reduction in tax. Hence, the deductible expenditure results in a tax savings.[2]

Income Tax Savings	Firm F leases office space for $1,000 monthly rent. Each $1,000 expenditure is deductible in computing the firm's taxable income; in other words, the expenditure shields $1,000 income from tax. If the firm is subject to a 30 percent tax rate, the deduction causes a $300 tax savings. The monthly rent transaction involves both a $1,000 cash outflow and a $300 cash inflow, resulting in negative net cash flow of $700.

Note that in both of the above examples, the tax cost or tax savings from a transaction is treated as a cash flow *in the year that the transaction occurs*. This timing of the cash flow reflects the reality that taxpayers must pay the tax on their current income *during the current year* and not when they file their tax return in the following year. (The tax payment requirements for corporations are discussed in Chapter 11, and the tax payment requirements for individuals are discussed in Chapter 14.) If a taxpayer engages in a transaction with tax consequences in 2012, the taxpayer's tax cost or savings is a 2012 cash flow.

The Significance of Marginal Tax Rate

The income tax cost or savings from a transaction is a function of the firm's marginal tax rate. In Chapter 2, we defined marginal rate as the rate that applies to the next dollar of taxable income. In an analysis of transactions that either increase or decrease taxable income, the marginal rate is the rate at which the increase or decrease would be taxed. If this rate is constant over the increase or decrease, the computation of the tax cost or savings from the transaction is simple.

Constant Marginal Rate	Firm F is subject to a progressive income tax consisting of two rates: 15 percent on the first $50,000 taxable income and 30 percent on taxable income in excess of $50,000. The firm's taxable income to date is $100,000. If Firm F engages in a transaction that generates $10,000 additional income, the entire increment is subject to a 30 percent tax rate. Therefore, the transaction has a $3,000 tax cost.

---

[2] In the accounting and finance literature, the tax savings from deductible business expenditures are often described as *tax shields*.

The computation of tax cost or savings is more complex if the marginal tax rate is not constant over the change in taxable income.

Changing Marginal Rate	Firm G is subject to a progressive income tax consisting of two rates: 15 percent on the first $50,000 taxable income and 30 percent on taxable income in excess of $50,000. The firm's taxable income to date is $44,000. If Firm G engages in a transaction that generates $10,000 additional income, the marginal rate on the first $6,000 increment is 15 percent and on the next $4,000 increment is 30 percent. Thus, the transaction has a $2,100 tax cost. If Firm G engages in a transaction that generates a $10,000 deduction, the marginal tax rate on the entire income shielded by the deduction is 15 percent. Thus, the transaction results in a $1,500 tax savings.

Obviously, managers must know their firm's marginal tax rate to compute the tax cost or savings from a transaction.

Net Present Value Example Revisited

Objective 2
Integrate tax costs and savings into NPV calculations.

Let's integrate income tax consequences into the net present value example developed earlier in the chapter. Remember that our consulting firm must choose between two engagements with different revenues and expenses over a two-year period. Now assume that the revenues are taxable, the expenses are deductible, and the income tax rate is 40 percent. Based on these assumptions, the net present values of the competing engagements are computed as follows.

	Engagement 1	Engagement 2
Current year:		
Taxable revenues	$150,000	$200,000
Deductible expenses	(90,000)	(65,000)
Before-tax cash flow/taxable income	$ 60,000	$135,000
Income tax cost at 40%	(24,000)	(54,000)
After-tax cash flow	$ 36,000	$ 81,000
Next year:		
Taxable revenues	$150,000	$125,000
Deductible expenses	(10,000)	(65,000)
Before-tax cash flow/taxable income	$140,000	$ 60,000
Income tax cost at 40%	(56,000)	(24,000)
After-tax cash flow	$ 84,000	$ 36,000
Present value of current year cash flow	$ 36,000	$ 81,000
Present value of next year cash flow		
(after-tax cash flow × .909 discount factor)	76,356	32,724
NPV	$112,356	$113,724

(handwritten annotations) $6\,0000 \times (1-t)$; $60,000(1-.40)$; $60,000 \times .60$

The introduction of an income tax reduced the NPV of each engagement but did not change the proportionate difference between the values. With or without the tax, the NPV of Engagement 1 is only 98.80 percent of the NPV of Engagement 2. Because the income tax applies in the same manner to each engagement and because the marginal rate doesn't

change over the two-year period, the tax is neutral. In other words, income tax consequences are not a factor affecting the decision as to which engagement to accept. Now let's
consider two examples in which the income tax consequences become an important factor
in the decision-making process.

Different Tax Treatments across Transactions

Tax costs are not neutral if the income tax law applies differentially to the two engage-
ments. Assume that the law allows the firm to deduct 100 percent of the expenses of
Engagement 1 but only 75 percent of the expenses of Engagement 2. Observe how the
NPV computations change:

	Engagement 1	Engagement 2
Current year:		
Taxable revenues		$150,000	$200,000
Deductible expenses		(90,000)	(48,750)
Nondeductible expenses		–0–	(16,250)
Before-tax cash flow		$ 60,000	$135,000
Income tax cost:		
Taxable income	$ 60,000	$151,250
	.40	.40
Tax cost	(24,000)	(60,500)
After-tax cash flow	$ 36,000	$ 74,500
Next year:		
Taxable revenues		$150,000	$125,000
Deductible expenses		(10,000)	(48,750)
Nondeductible expenses		–0–	(16,250)
Before-tax cash flow		$140,000	$ 60,000
Income tax cost:		
Taxable income	$140,000	$ 76,250
	.40	.40
Tax cost	(56,000)	(30,500)
After-tax cash flow	$ 84,000	$ 29,500
Present value of current year cash flow	$ 36,000	$ 74,500
Present value of next year cash flow		
(after-tax cash flow × .909 discount factor)	76,356	26,816
NPV	$112,356	$101,316

The fact that the tax law limits the deduction for the Engagement 2 expenses increases
the tax cost of the engagement and decreases after-tax cash flow. As a result, the NPV of
Engagement 2 is less than that of Engagement 1, and Engagement 1 is the superior opportunity. In this case, tax consequences are a factor in the decision.

Different Tax Rates over Time

Calculations of net present value are sensitive to changes in tax rates over time. To illustrate
this point, modify the example again by returning to the initial assumption that the firm can
deduct 100 percent of the expenses of both engagements. But now assume that Congress

recently enacted legislation reducing the income tax rate from 40 percent in the current year to 25 percent in the next year.

	Engagement 1	Engagement 2
Current year:		
Taxable revenues	$150,000	$200,000
Deductible expenses	(90,000)	(65,000)
Before-tax cash flow/taxable income	$ 60,000	$135,000
Income tax cost at 40%	(24,000)	(54,000)
After-tax cash flow	$ 36,000	$ 81,000
Next year:		
Taxable revenues	$150,000	$125,000
Deductible expenses	(10,000)	(65,000)
Before-tax cash flow/taxable income	$140,000	$ 60,000
Income tax cost at 25%	(35,000)	(15,000)
After-tax cash flow	$105,000	$ 45,000
Present value of current year cash flow	$ 36,000	$ 81,000
Present value of next year cash flow		
(after-tax cash flow × .909 discount factor)	95,445	40,905
NPV	$131,445	$121,905

The fact that a lower tax rate applies next year decreases the tax cost for that year relative to the tax cost for the current year. Engagement 1 generates more of its taxable income in the next year than Engagement 2. Consequently, Engagement 1 has a lower overall tax cost and a greater NPV than Engagement 2 and is the superior opportunity.

The Uncertainty of Tax Consequences

Objective 3
Identify the uncertainties concerning future tax costs and savings.

A net present value calculation is incomplete unless it includes cash flows attributable to the current and future tax consequences of the proposed transaction. However, assumptions concerning tax consequences have their own unique uncertainties.

Audit Risk

Oftentimes the correct application of the tax law to a proposed transaction is unclear or unresolved. In such case, business managers must decide on the most probable tax consequences to incorporate into their net present value calculations. Whenever a firm enters into a transaction involving ambiguous tax issues, it runs the risk that the Internal Revenue Service (or state and local tax authorities) will challenge the tax treatment on audit. The IRS may conclude that the transaction resulted in a greater tax cost or a smaller tax savings than the manager originally projected. The firm can dispute the unfavorable result of the audit in court.[3] But even if the firm wins its case, the cost of litigation can be substantial.

---

[3] Historically, the burden of proof in a federal tax case was on the taxpayer, not the government. In other words, taxpayers had to convince the court that the IRS was wrong in its conclusions. In the IRS Reform and Restructuring Act of 1998, Congress modified this long-standing rule. Section 7491(a) provides that the burden of proof with *respect to any factual issue* shifts to the IRS if the taxpayer introduces credible evidence concerning the facts, meets any statutory substantiation requirements, and has cooperated with the IRS in establishing the facts of the case. Corporations, trusts, and partnerships with net worth in excess of $7 million are ineligible for the benefits of the burden-shifting provision.

Accordingly, actual cash flows from a contested transaction may vary from the estimated cash flows in the NPV calculation.

Managers can reduce the risk of an IRS challenge by engaging a tax professional, such as a CPA or an attorney, to analyze questionable transactions and render an expert opinion as to the proper tax treatment. Managers can even ask the IRS to analyze a proposed transaction and to conclude how the tax law should be applied. The IRS will communicate its conclusion in the form of a **private letter ruling (PLR)** to the firm. Obtaining a private letter ruling can be expensive; firms typically require professional help in drafting a ruling request, and the IRS currently charges an $18,000 fee for a ruling.[4] Despite the cost, a private letter ruling can be invaluable when thousands or even millions of tax dollars are at stake. If a firm reports the tax consequences of a transaction in accordance with a private letter ruling, it has a guarantee that the consequences will not be challenged by the IRS upon subsequent audit.[5]

Tax Law Uncertainty

A second source of uncertainty is the possibility that tax laws may change during the time period of the NPV computation. Of course, the potential for change varies greatly with the particular tax under consideration. The federal income tax system is notorious for the frequency with which Congress changes the rules of the game. But even within this volatile tax system, some provisions are quite stable. The tax consequences of a proposed transaction to which a stable tax provision applies are more predictable than the consequences of a transaction subject to a provision that Congress modifies every year. As a result, the NPV of the former transaction can be calculated with greater certainty than the NPV of the latter.

Stable and Unstable Tax Provisions	The Internal Revenue Code allows firms to deduct "all interest paid or accrued within the taxable year on indebtedness." This provision was included in the Internal Revenue Code of 1939 and has been substantially unchanged for almost 70 years. In contrast, the provision requiring taxpayers to pay an alternative minimum tax in addition to regular income tax was added to the Internal Revenue Code in 1986, then amended in 1988, 1993, 1996, 1998, 2001, 2003, and 2010.

Marginal Rate Uncertainty

The estimated tax cost or savings from a transaction are a function of the firm's projected marginal tax rate. This marginal rate may change in future years because the government changes the statutory rates for all taxpayers. The marginal rate may also change because of a change in the firm's circumstances. In the income tax context, marginal rate depends on the amount of annual taxable income. If taxable income for a future year is significantly more or less than anticipated, the actual marginal rate for that year may vary from the projected rate. If the actual rate is higher than projected, the tax cost or savings in that year will be more than expected. Conversely, if the rate is lower than projected, the tax cost or savings will be less than expected.

---

[4] Rev. Proc. 2012-1, Appendix A, 2012-1 IRB 1.

[5] A taxpayer may rely on a ruling unless the ruling request misstated or omitted material facts concerning the proposed transaction or the actual transaction differs substantially from the proposed transaction. No taxpayer may rely on a ruling issued to another taxpayer. Rev. Proc. 2012-1, Section 11, 2012-1 IRB 1.

Marginal Rate *Increase*	Last year, Company N had to choose between two business opportunities in different tax jurisdictions. The company projected that Opportunity 1 would generate $100,000 income taxed at 30 percent, while Opportunity 2 would generate $90,000 income taxed at 20 percent. Company N chose Opportunity 2 because its $72,000 projected after-tax income ($90,000 − $18,000 tax) exceeded the $70,000 projected after-tax income ($100,000 − $30,000 tax) from Opportunity 1. Because of an unexpected change in circumstances, the marginal tax rate on the income from Opportunity 2 increased to 25 percent this year. As a result, Company N's after-tax income was only $67,500 ($90,000 − $22,500), and in retrospect, Opportunity 2 was the wrong choice.

STRUCTURING TRANSACTIONS TO REDUCE TAXES

The tax consequences of business transactions depend on the legal and financial structure of the transaction. Firms often can change the tax consequences by changing the structure. For instance, a firm that needs an additional worker to perform a certain task could hire a part-time employee. As a result of this employment transaction, the firm is liable for federal and state payroll taxes on the salary paid to the employee.[6] Alternatively, the firm could engage an independent contractor to perform the same task. The firm is not liable for payroll taxes on the fee paid to the independent contractor. Thus, by changing the legal structure of the transaction, the firm eliminates the payroll tax cost of adding personnel.

Let's add some numbers to compute the after-tax cost of each alternative.

Cost of *Employee*	Firm W plans on hiring an employee to perform a certain task. The firm would pay a $15,000 salary and $1,250 payroll tax on the salary. Both the salary and the payroll tax are deductible in computing taxable income. If the firm's marginal income tax rate is 35 percent, the after-tax cost of the transaction is $10,562.

Cash flows:	
Salary	$(15,000)
Payroll tax cost	(1,250)
Income tax savings ($16,250 × 35%)	5,688
Net cash flow	$(10,562)

Cost of *Independent* *Contractor*	If Firm W engages an independent contractor to perform the task and pays the contractor a $15,000 fee, the after-tax cost of the transaction is only $9,750.

Cash flows:	
Fee	$(15,000)
Income tax savings ($15,000 × 35%)	5,250
Net cash flow	$ (9,750)

[6] An independent contractor is a self-employed individual who performs services for compensation. Unlike an employee, an independent contractor significantly controls the manner in which the services are performed.

In this simple example, Firm W can eliminate the payroll tax cost without affecting any nontax cash flow. The income tax applies in the same manner to both alternatives and thus is a neutral consideration. Consequently, Firm W can minimize the after-tax cost of the transaction by engaging an independent contractor instead of hiring an employee.

An Important Caveat

Objective 4
Explain why tax minimization may not be the optimal business strategy.

Business managers who decide to change the structure of a transaction to reduce tax costs must consider the effect of the change on nontax factors. If a change that saves tax dollars adversely affects other factors, the change may be a bad idea. In financial terms, a strategy that minimizes the tax cost of a transaction may not maximize net present value and may not be the optimal strategy for the firm.

To demonstrate this important point, reconsider the example in which Firm W can either hire an employee or engage an independent contractor to perform a task. The firm can hire the employee for a $15,000 salary and a $10,562 after-tax cost. But what if the independent contractor demands a $17,500 fee to do the job?

Cost of Independent Contractor	If Firm W engages an independent contractor to perform the task and pays the contractor a $17,500 fee, the after-tax cost of the transaction is $11,375.

Cash flows:	
Fee	$(17,500)
Income tax savings ($17,500 × 35%)	6,125
Net cash flow	$(11,375)

Now the alternative that eliminates the payroll tax cost increases the compensation that Firm W must pay. As a result, the after-tax cost of engaging an independent contractor ($11,375) exceeds the after-tax cost of hiring an employee ($10,562). Firm W should hire the employee, even though this alternative does not minimize the payroll tax cost of the transaction.

Transactional Markets

The extent to which managers can control the tax consequences of transactions depends on the nature of the market in which the transaction occurs. A **market** is a forum for commercial interaction between two or more parties for the purpose of exchanging goods or services. One or both parties may want to customize the terms of the exchange to obtain a certain tax result. Their ability to do so depends on the flexibility of the particular market.

Private Market Transactions

Objective 5
Explain why bilateral tax planning is important in private market transactions.

Many business transactions involve private parties who deal directly with each other. The parties have flexibility in designing a transaction that accommodates the needs of both. The legal and financial characteristics of the transaction are specified in the contract to which both parties finally agree. In negotiating such **private market** transactions, each party can evaluate the tax consequences not only to itself but also to the other party. By doing so, the parties can work together to minimize the aggregate tax cost of the transaction and share the tax savings between them.

To illustrate this bilateral approach to tax planning, consider the case of Firm M and key employee Mr. Grant, and their negotiation of a new employment contract. For simplicity's sake, the case disregards payroll tax costs and focuses on the income tax consequences of the contract. Firm M and Mr. Grant have respective marginal income tax rates of 35 percent and 30 percent. Salary payments are deductible by Firm M and taxable to Mr. Grant.

Initial Compensation Package	Firm M and Mr. Grant begin their negotiation by analyzing the consequences of a $120,000 salary payment. The firm's after-tax cost of the $120,000 payment would be $78,000.

Cash flows:	
Salary	$(120,000)
Income tax savings	
($120,000 × 35%)	42,000
Net cash flow	$ (78,000)

Mr. Grant's after-tax cash flow would be $84,000.

Cash flows:	
Salary	$120,000
Income tax cost	
($120,000 × 30%)	(36,000)
Net cash flow	$ 84,000

Both parties know that Mr. Grant spends $10,000 each year to pay the premiums on his family's health insurance policy. Mr. Grant can't deduct this expense in computing taxable income; therefore, the premium payments don't result in any tax savings to him.[7] After this expense, Mr. Grant's after-tax cash flow is only $74,000.

Health Insurance Factor	Cash flows:	
	Salary	$120,000
	Income tax cost	
	($120,000 × 30%)	(36,000)
	Insurance premium	(10,000)
	Net cash flow	$ 74,000

Both parties also know that Firm M could pay a $5,000 premium for comparable health insurance for Mr. Grant under its group plan. Moreover, Firm M could deduct the premium payment. The compensatory fringe benefit (employer-provided health insurance) would be nontaxable to Mr. Grant.[8] On the basis of this mutual knowledge, the parties agree to a final compensation package.

[7] The tax consequences of an individual's personal expenses are discussed in Chapter 17.
[8] Nontaxable employee fringe benefits are discussed in Chapter 15.

Final Compensation Package

Firm M agrees to pay Mr. Grant a $110,000 salary and provide health insurance coverage under its group plan. The firm's after-tax cost of this compensation package is $74,750.

Cash flows:	
Salary	$(110,000)
Insurance premium	(5,000)
Income tax savings	
($115,000 × 35%)	40,250
Net cash flow	$ (74,750)

Based on this compensation package, Mr. Grant's after-tax cash flow is $77,000.

Cash flows:	
Salary	$110,000
Income tax cost	
($110,000 × 30%)	(33,000)
Insurance premium	–0–
Net cash flow	$ 77,000

By considering the tax consequences to both parties, Firm M and Mr. Grant structured their contract to improve both their after-tax positions. Specifically, Firm M decreased the after-tax cost of employing Mr. Grant by $3,250, and Mr. Grant increased his after-tax cash flow by $3,000.

The Arm's-Length Presumption

An important presumption about market transactions is that the parties are negotiating at arm's length. In other words, each party is dealing in its own economic self-interest, trying to obtain the most advantageous terms possible from the other party. In an **arm's-length transaction,** the parties' consideration of the mutual tax consequences is just one element of their bargaining strategy. If one party suggests a modification to the transaction that directly improves its tax outcome, the other party may not agree unless it can indirectly capture some part of the tax benefit for itself. To do so, the other party might demand more favorable terms with respect to another aspect of the transaction.

This *quid pro quo* is exemplified in the employment contract between Firm M and Mr. Grant. The fact that Mr. Grant's compensation package includes a nontaxable fringe benefit (the insurance coverage) results in a direct tax savings to him. However, the firm captures part of this tax savings by paying less salary to Mr. Grant. In the final analysis, Firm M agreed to a compensation package that includes the fringe benefit because the package minimizes its after-tax cost, not because the package saves income tax for Mr. Grant.

The only interested party worse off because of the final terms of the employment contract is the federal government. The inclusion of a nontaxable fringe benefit in the compensation package costs the Treasury $1,250 in revenue.

Tax Cost to Government		Initial Compensation Package	Final Compensation Package	Increase (Decrease) in Tax Revenue
	Firm M's tax savings	$42,000	$40,250	$ 1,750
	Mr. Grant's tax cost	36,000	33,000	(3,000)
	Net decrease in tax revenue			$(1,250)

In spite of potential revenue loss, the IRS (and state and local tax authorities) generally accepts the tax consequences of arm's-length transactions because those consequences reflect economic reality. The IRS understands that parties negotiate to further their respective business objectives and that any favorable tax outcomes are legitimate by-products of these negotiations.

Public Market Transactions

Some business transactions occur in **public markets** that are too large, too impersonal, or too regulated to allow parties to communicate privately and to customize their transactions. Firms entering such markets must accept the terms dictated by the market. For instance, if a firm decides to invest excess working capital in short-term U.S. government bonds, it must purchase the bonds through a federal bank for the prevailing market price. The firm can't negotiate with the selling party (the government) to buy the bonds at a different price. Similarly, the financial characteristics of the bonds such as the interest rate and maturity date are nonnegotiable.

Firms have limited flexibility in tailoring public market transactions to control the tax results. Because buyers and sellers are not involved in direct negotiation, they can't develop a bilateral strategy to improve their joint tax consequences. Any tax planning that does occur must be one-sided.

Fictitious Markets: Related Party Transactions

Objective 6
Distinguish between arm's-length and related party transactions.

The arm's-length presumption is unreliable for transactions between related parties, such as family members or subsidiary corporations owned by the same controlling parent corporation. **Related party transactions** lack the economic tension characteristic of transactions between unrelated parties. In commercial dealings, unrelated parties typically have competing objectives; related parties may have compatible objectives or even share a single objective. Unrelated parties are motivated by self-interest to drive the hardest possible bargain; related parties may be eager to accommodate each other in their negotiations.

If related parties are not dealing at arm's length, no true market exists, and any transaction between them may not reflect economic reality. In this fictitious market setting, related parties are unconstrained by many of the financial considerations that normally drive arm's-length transactions. As a result, they enjoy significant flexibility in controlling the tax consequences of their transactions. The IRS is well aware that related party transactions lack arm's-length rigor and regards the tax consequences with suspicion. If the IRS concludes that a transaction is bogus, it may disallow any favorable tax outcome claimed by the related parties.

Let's examine a related party transaction with a favorable tax outcome.

Related Party Transaction	Mr. and Mrs. Bowen are business owners with a 35 percent marginal tax rate. The couple has a 17-year-old son who is interested in taking over the business at some future date. Mr. and Mrs. Bowen decide to give their son some experience by hiring him as a full-time employee. If Mr. and Mrs. Bowen pay their son a $20,000 annual salary, this deductible payment saves them $7,000 a year in federal income tax.[9] Because the son has so little taxable income, his marginal tax rate is only 10 percent. Consequently, his tax cost of the salary is only $2,000. As a result of this related party transaction, the Bowen family saves $5,000 income tax.

While the federal tax laws don't explicitly prohibit Mr. and Mrs. Bowen from deducting the salary payment to their son, the IRS will carefully scrutinize the employment transaction if it audits the parents' tax return. The familial relationship of the transacting parties suggests that the salary was not negotiated at arm's length. If the IRS examines all the relevant facts, it may discover that the son did not actually perform any valuable services whatsoever for his parents' business. In this extreme case, the employment transaction had no purpose other than tax avoidance, and the IRS may recast the $20,000 payment from parents to child as a gift.[10] Consequently, Mr. and Mrs. Bowen lose their $20,000 tax deduction, the son has no salary income, and the family's anticipated income tax savings disappear.

On the other hand, the relevant facts may indicate that the son is a genuine employee and that his salary is comparable to the salary an unrelated person could have negotiated at arm's length. In this case, the IRS should respect the transaction and accept the favorable tax consequences of the $20,000 salary payment. Whatever the outcome, the lesson from this example should be clear. Whenever related parties transact, they must be aware that the tax authorities may challenge the validity of the transaction. If the related parties can't offer convincing evidence that the terms of the transaction approximate an arm's-length standard, they may forfeit control of the tax consequences altogether.

Conclusion

Estimating cash flows and calculating the net present value of those cash flows are central to the business decision-making process. A manager's ability to determine after-tax cash flows depends on his or her skill in quantifying the tax cost or savings from the transaction. Managers must be familiar with current tax law and must be prepared to make informed assumptions concerning how that law might change in future periods. Managers involved in business negotiations should evaluate the tax implications for all parties to the transaction in formulating an optimal tax strategy.

While managers should view all business taxes as controllable costs, they should understand that the transaction with the least tax cost may not maximize net present value. Business transactions consist of any number of interrelated tax and nontax variables, all of which must be considered in the decision-making process. In the next chapter, we will concentrate on strategies that manipulate the income tax variable. But as we focus on tax planning ideas, remember the basic lesson of this chapter. Cash flows can't be analyzed in a meaningful way until they are stated as after-tax numbers.

---

[9] Federal payroll taxes are not an issue in this example because such taxes are not levied on wages paid by parents to their children under age 18. §3121(b)(3)(A).

[10] When a related party transaction is a blatant tax avoidance scheme, the IRS may impose monetary penalties on the taxpayers. See the discussion of taxpayer negligence and fraud in Chapter 18.

Key Terms

annuity *49*	net cash flow *48*	public market *61*
arm's-length transaction *60*	net present value (NPV) *48*	related party transaction *61*
deduction *52*	private letter ruling	tax cost *52*
discount rate *48*	(PLR) *56*	tax savings *52*
market *58*	private market *58*	time value of money *48*

Questions and Problems for Discussion

1. Does the NPV of future cash flows increase or decrease as the discount rate increases?
2. Explain the relationship between the degree of financial risk associated with future cash flows and the discount rate used to compute NPV.
3. Does the after-tax cost of a deductible expense increase or decrease as the taxpayer's marginal income tax rate increases?
4. Firm A and Firm Z are in the same business. Both firms considered spending $10,000 for the exact same reason. The expenditure would be deductible for both firms. Firm A decided that the expenditure was worthwhile and spent the money, but Firm Z rejected the expenditure. Can you provide a tax reason to explain these apparently inconsistent decisions?
5. In what circumstance is the before-tax cost of an expenditure equal to its after-tax cost?
6. Corporation N must decide between two opportunities that will generate different cash flows over a five-year period. Describe the circumstances in which the tax cost of the opportunities is a neutral factor in the corporation's decision-making process.
7. Which assumption about the tax consequences of a future transaction is more uncertain: an assumption based on a provision that has been in the Internal Revenue Code for 25 years or an assumption based on a provision that Congress added to the Code two years ago?
8. Which type of tax law provision should be more stable and less uncertain as to its future application: a provision relating to the proper measurement of taxable income or a provision designed to encourage individual taxpayers to engage in a certain economic behavior?
9. In the U.S. system of criminal justice, a person is innocent until proven guilty. Does this general rule apply to disputes between a taxpayer and the IRS?
10. Identify two reasons why a firm's actual marginal tax rate for a year could differ from the projected marginal tax rate for that year.
11. Firm F is negotiating to purchase a multimillion-dollar computer system from the manufacturer. Under applicable state law, Firm F is exempt from sales tax on the purchase. Because the manufacturer discovered this fact, it increased its selling price for the system by $25,000. Is this transaction taking place in a private or a public market?
12. Corporation P owns 85 percent of the outstanding stock of Corporation R. This year, employees of Corporation R performed extensive management services for Corporation P. In return for the services, Corporation P paid a $250,000 fee to Corporation R, which Corporation P reported as a deductible business expense.
    a. Is the consulting arrangement an arm's-length transaction?
    b. If the IRS challenges the validity of Corporation P's deduction, what facts might the corporation offer as evidence of the validity of the payment?

Application Problems

1. Use the present value tables in Appendix A and Appendix B to compute the NPV of each of the following cash inflows.
   a. $18,300 received at the end of 15 years. The discount rate is 5 percent.
   b. $5,800 received at the end of four years and $11,600 received at the end of eight years. The discount rate is 7 percent.

  c. $1,300 received annually at the end of each of the next seven years. The discount rate is 6 percent.

  d. $40,000 received annually at the end of each of the next three years and $65,000 received at the end of the fourth year. The discount rate is 9 percent.

2. Use the present value tables in Appendix A and Appendix B to compute the NPV of each of the following cash inflows.

  a. $89,000 received at the end of six years. The discount rate is 12 percent.

  b. $3,400 received annually at the end of each of the next 15 years. The discount rate is 9 percent.

  c. A 10-year annuity of $5,000 per annum. The first $5,000 payment is due immediately. The discount rate is 6 percent.

  d. $20,000 received annually at the end of years 1 through 5 followed by $13,000 received annually at the end of years 6 through 10. The discount rate is 15 percent.

3. Use a 10 percent discount rate to compute the NPV of each of the following series of cash receipts and payments.

  a. $6,200 received now (year 0), $1,890 paid in year 3, and $4,000 paid in year 5.

  b. $10,000 paid now (year 0), $12,690 paid in year 2, and $31,000 received in year 8.

  c. $20,000 received now (year 0), $13,500 paid in year 5, and $7,500 paid in year 10.

4. Company N will receive $100,000 of taxable revenue from a client. Compute the NPV of the $100,000 in each of the following cases.

  a. Company N will receive $50,000 now (year 0) and $50,000 in year 1. The company's marginal tax rate is 30 percent, and it uses a 6 percent discount rate.

  b. Company N will receive $50,000 in year 1 and $50,000 in year 2. The company's marginal tax rate is 40 percent, and it uses a 4 percent discount rate.

  c. Company N will receive $20,000 now (year 0) and $20,000 in years 1, 2, 3, and 4. The company's marginal tax rate is 10 percent, and it uses a 9 percent discount rate.

5. Taxpayer Y, who has a 30 percent marginal tax rate, invested $65,000 in a bond that pays 8 percent annual interest. Compute Y's annual net cash flow from this investment assuming that:

  a. The interest is tax-exempt income.

  b. The interest is taxable income.

6. Investor B has $100,000 in an investment paying 9 percent taxable interest per annum. Each year B incurs $825 of expenses relating to this investment. Compute B's annual net cash flow assuming the following.

  a. B's marginal tax rate is 10 percent, and the annual expense is not deductible.

  b. B's marginal tax rate is 35 percent, and the annual expense is deductible.

  c. B's marginal tax rate is 25 percent, and the annual expense is not deductible.

  d. B's marginal tax rate is 40 percent, and only $500 of the annual expense is deductible.

7. Firm E must choose between two alternative transactions. Transaction 1 requires a $9,000 cash outlay that would be nondeductible in the computation of taxable income. Transaction 2 requires a $13,500 cash outlay that would be a deductible expense. Determine which transaction has the lesser after-tax cost, assuming that:

  a. Firm E's marginal tax rate is 20 percent.

  b. Firm E's marginal tax rate is 40 percent.

8. Firm Q is about to engage in a transaction with the following cash flows over a three-year period.

	Year 0	Year 1	Year 2
Taxable revenue	$13,000	$16,250	$23,400
Deductible expenses	(3,900)	(6,000)	(8,100)
Nondeductible expenses	(350)	(2,000)	–0–

If the firm's marginal tax rate over the three-year period is 30 percent and its discount rate is 6 percent, compute the NPV of the transaction.

9. Corporation ABC invested in a project that will generate $60,000 annual after-tax cash flow in years 0 and 1 and $40,000 annual after-tax cash flow in years 2, 3, and 4. Compute the NPV of these cash flows assuming that:

   a. ABC uses a 10 percent discount rate.

   b. ABC uses a 7 percent discount rate.

   c. ABC uses a 4 percent discount rate.

10. Firm W has the opportunity to invest $150,000 in a new venture. The projected cash flows from the venture are as follows.

	Year 0	Year 1	Year 2	Year 3
Initial investment	$(150,000)			
After-tax cash flow		$11,000	$16,000	$ 18,000
Return of investment				150,000
Net cash flow	$(150,000)	$11,000	$16,000	$168,000

Determine if Firm W should make the investment, assuming that:

   a. It uses a 15 percent discount rate to compute NPV.

   b. It uses a 9 percent discount rate to compute NPV.

11. Investor W has the opportunity to invest $500,000 in a new venture. The projected cash flows from the venture are as follows.

	Year 0	Year 1	Year 2	Year 3	Year 4
Initial investment	$(500,000)				
Taxable revenue		$ 62,500	$ 57,500	$ 47,500	$ 42,500
Deductible expenses		(10,000)	(10,000)	(12,000)	(12,000)
Return of investment					500,000
Before-tax net cash flow	$(500,000)	$ 52,500	$ 47,500	$ 35,500	$530,500

Investor W uses a 7 percent discount rate to compute NPV. Determine if she should make this investment assuming that:

   a. Her marginal tax rate over the life of the investment is 15 percent.

   b. Her marginal tax rate over the life of the investment is 20 percent.

   c. Her marginal tax rate in years 1 and 2 is 10 percent and in years 3 and 4 is 25 percent.

12. Firm X has the opportunity to invest $200,000 in a new venture. The projected cash flows from the venture are as follows.

	Year 0	Year 1	Year 2	Year 3
Initial investment	$(200,000)			
Revenues		$40,000	$40,000	$40,000
Expenses		(25,000)	(7,000)	(7,000)
Return of investment				200,000
Before-tax net cash flow	$(200,000)	$15,000	$33,000	$233,000

Firm X uses an 8 percent discount rate to compute NPV, and its marginal tax rate over the life of the venture will be 35 percent. Determine if Firm X should make the investment, assuming that:

a. The revenues are taxable income, and the expenses are deductible.

b. The revenues are taxable income, but the expenses are nondeductible.

13. Business J operates in a jurisdiction that levies an income tax with the following rate structure.

Percentage Rate	Bracket
7%	Income from –0– to $75,000
10	Income from $75,001 to $150,000
15	Income in excess of $150,000

Business J has the opportunity to invest in a project that should generate $35,000 additional taxable income for the year. Compute the tax cost of this additional income assuming that:

a. Business J's taxable income before considering the additional income is $92,000.

b. Business J's taxable income before considering the additional income is $400,000.

c. Business J has a $16,000 loss before considering the additional income.

14. Refer to the income tax rate structure in the preceding problem. Company K incurs a $22,000 deductible expense. Compute the current year tax savings from the deduction assuming that:

a. Company K's taxable income before considering the additional deduction is $65,000.

b. Company K's taxable income before considering the additional deduction is $168,000.

c. Company K has a $4,000 loss before considering the additional deduction.

15. Company DL must choose between two business opportunities. Opportunity 1 will generate $14,000 before-tax cash in years 0 through 3. The annual tax cost of Opportunity 1 is $2,500 in years 0 and 1 and $1,800 in years 2 and 3. Opportunity 2 will generate $14,000 before-tax cash in year 0, $20,000 before-tax cash in years 1 and 2, and $10,000 before-tax cash in year 3. The annual tax cost of Opportunity 2 is $4,000 in years 0 through 3. Which opportunity should Company DL choose if it uses a 10 percent discount rate to compute NPV?

16. Firm E must choose between two business opportunities. Opportunity 1 will generate an $8,000 deductible loss in year 0, $5,000 taxable income in year 1, and $20,000 taxable income in year 2. Opportunity 2 will generate $5,000 taxable income in years 0 through 2. The income and loss reflect before-tax cash inflow and outflow. Firm E uses a 12 percent discount rate to compute NPV and has a 40 percent marginal tax rate over the three-year period.

    a. Which opportunity should Firm E choose?

    b. Would your answer change if Firm E's marginal tax rate over the three-year period is 15 percent?

    c. Would your answer change if Firm E's marginal tax rate is 40 percent in year 0 but only 15 percent in years 1 and 2?

Issue Recognition Problems

Identify the tax issue or issues suggested by the following situations, and state each issue in the form of a question.

1. Mr. and Mrs. J's taxable income from their business has been stable for the last five years, and their average federal income tax rate has ranged between 22 and 24 percent. Because of a boom in the local economy, the couple estimates that their business will generate an additional $100,000 taxable income next year. In making their cash flow projections, they estimate that their federal income tax cost with respect to this incremental income will be $24,000.

2. Firm V must choose between two alternative investment opportunities. On the basis of current tax law, the firm projects that the NPV of Opportunity 1 is significantly less than the NPV of Opportunity 2. The provisions in the tax law governing the tax consequences of Opportunity 1 have been stable for many years. In contrast, the provisions governing the tax consequences of Opportunity 2 are extremely complicated and have been modified by Congress several times during the last five years.

3. Company WB is evaluating a business opportunity with uncertain tax consequences. If the company takes a conservative approach by assuming the least beneficial tax consequences, the tax cost is $95,000. If the company takes an aggressive approach by assuming the most beneficial tax consequences, the tax cost is only $86,000. If the company takes the aggressive approach, the IRS will certainly challenge the approach on audit.

4. Refer to the facts in problem 3. Company WB is considering engaging a CPA to prepare a request for a private letter ruling from the IRS concerning the tax consequences of the business opportunity.

5. Ms. O is the chief financial officer for Firm XYZ. The marketing department requested approval for an $80,000 cash expenditure. The request points out that the expenditure would be deductible. Therefore, the marketing department concludes that Ms. O should approve the expenditure because it would reduce XYZ's tax cost.

6. Earlier in the year, Mrs. G, a business manager for Company RW, evaluated a prospective opportunity that could generate $20,000 additional taxable income. Mrs. G determined that the company's marginal tax rate on this income would be 25 percent. Later in the year, a different manager evaluated another opportunity that could generate $100,000 additional taxable income. This manager referred to Mrs. G's earlier evaluation and used the same 25 percent marginal rate in his analysis of after-tax cash flows.

7. Firm UW is about to enter into a venture that will generate taxable income for the next six to eight years. The director of tax has come up with an idea to restructure the venture in a way that will reduce tax costs by at least 5 percent.

8. DLT's chief operating officer is negotiating the acquisition of a controlling interest in the stock of AA Inc. from Mr. and Mrs. A. The director of tax suggested that the acquisition be structured as a nontaxable transaction to Mr. and Mrs. A. The CEO rejected the suggestion by saying, "Since DLT is the purchaser, our negotiating team doesn't really care if the structure of the acquisition saves taxes for the seller."

9. Ms. S is the sole shareholder and chief executive officer of SMJ Corporation. Ms. S's college roommate recently lost her job, is in financial difficulty, and has asked Ms. S for a loan. Instead of a loan, Ms. S offered the roommate a job with SMJ at a $35,000 annual salary.

Tax Planning Cases

1. Firm B wants to hire Mrs. X to manage its advertising department. The firm offered Mrs. X a three-year employment contract under which it will pay her an $80,000 annual salary in years 0, 1, and 2. Mrs. X projects that her salary will be taxed at a 25 percent rate in year 0 and a 40 percent rate in years 1 and 2. Firm B's tax rate for the three-year period is 34 percent.

   a. Assuming an 8 percent discount rate for both Firm B and Mrs. X, compute the NPV of Mrs. X's after-tax cash flow from the employment contract and Firm B's after-tax cost of the employment contract.

   b. To reduce her tax cost, Mrs. X requests that the salary payment for year 0 be increased to $140,000 and the salary payments for years 1 and 2 be reduced to $50,000. How would this revision in the timing of the payments change your NPV computation for both parties?

   c. Firm B responds to Mrs. X's request with a counterproposal. It will pay her $140,000 in year 0 but only $45,000 in years 1 and 2. Compute the NPV of Firm B's after-tax cost under this proposal. From the firm's perspective, is this proposal superior to its original offer ($80,000 annually for three years)?

   d. Should Mrs. X accept the original offer or the counterproposal? Support your conclusion with a comparison of the NPV of each offer.

2. Firm D is considering investing $400,000 cash in a three-year project with the following cash flows.

	Year 0	Year 1	Year 2
Investment/ return of investment	$(400,000)	–0–	$400,000
Revenues	80,000	$ 65,000	35,000
Expenses	(25,000)	(25,000)	(10,000)
Before-tax net cash flow	$(345,000)	$ 40,000	$425,000

   Under each of the following assumptions, determine if Firm D should make the investment. In each case, use a 10 percent discount rate to compute NPV.

   a. The revenue is taxable, the expenses are deductible, and the marginal tax rate is 15 percent.

   b. The revenue is taxable, the expenses are deductible, and the marginal tax rate is 40 percent.

   c. The revenue is taxable, only one-half the expenses are deductible, and the marginal tax rate is 15 percent.

   d. Firm D can deduct the expenses in the year paid (against other sources of income) but can defer recognizing the $180,000 total income until year 2. (It will *collect* the revenues as indicated in years 0, 1, and 2 so that before-tax cash flows do not change.) The marginal tax rate is 40 percent.

Maxims of Income Tax Planning

Learning Objectives

After studying this chapter, you should be able to:

1. Differentiate between tax avoidance and tax evasion.

2. List the four variables that determine the tax consequences of a transaction.

3. Explain why an income shift or a deduction shift can improve NPV.

4. Explain how the assignment of income doctrine constrains income-shifting strategies.

5. Identify the circumstances in which a tax deferral strategy may not improve NPV.

6. Contrast the tax character of ordinary income and capital gain.

7. Distinguish between an explicit tax and an implicit tax.

8. Summarize the four tax planning maxims.

9. Describe the legal doctrines that the IRS uses to challenge tax planning strategies.

In Chapter 3, we learned that the concept of net present value (NPV) plays a key role in the business decision-making process and that the computation of NPV incorporates tax costs as cash outflows and tax savings as cash inflows. With these lessons in mind, we begin Chapter 4 by defining **tax planning** as the structuring of transactions to reduce tax costs or increase tax savings to maximize the NPV of the transaction.

Why does the structure of a transaction matter in the tax planning process? Specifically, what are the variables that determine the tax outcome of the transaction? These questions are addressed in the first section of the chapter. Our study of the variables leads to the development of *income tax planning maxims*—basic principles that are the foundation for many planning techniques discussed in subsequent chapters. We will analyze how these maxims improve the tax outcomes of transactions. We will also identify the limitations on their use in the planning process. In the final section of the chapter, we will consider how managers use the maxims to develop tax strategies for their firms and why managers must be cognizant of how the Internal Revenue Service (IRS) may react to their strategies.

$(345,000)$

$(51,750$

TAX AVOIDANCE—NOT EVASION

Objective 1
Differentiate between tax avoidance and tax evasion.

Our discussion in this and subsequent chapters is restricted to tax planning ideas that are entirely legal. Legitimate means of reducing taxes are described as **tax avoidance;** illegal means to the same end constitute **tax evasion.** Tax evasion is a federal crime—a felony offense punishable by severe monetary fines and imprisonment.[1] The qualitative difference between avoidance and evasion is in the eye of the beholder. Many aggressive tax plans involve major questions of judgment. Taxpayers eager to implement these plans run the risk that the IRS will conclude that the plan crosses the line between a good faith effort to reduce tax and a willful attempt to defraud the U.S. government. Business managers should always exercise caution and consult a tax professional before engaging in any transaction with profound tax consequences.

Even if tax avoidance strategies are legal, are they ethical? In 1947, federal judge Learned Hand answered this question in the following way:

> Over and over again courts have said that there is nothing sinister in so arranging one's affairs as to keep taxes as low as possible. Everybody does so, rich or poor; and all do right, for nobody owes any public duty to pay more than the law demands: taxes are enforced exactions, not voluntary contributions. To demand more in the name of morals is mere cant.[2]

This spirited defense of planning makes the point that every person has the civic responsibility of paying the legally required tax and not a penny more. Business managers should be reassured that when they engage in effective tax planning, they are engaging in proper behavior from the perspective of their firm, their government, and society.

WHAT MAKES INCOME TAX PLANNING POSSIBLE?

The federal income tax system applies to every entity conducting business in the United States. If the tax law applied uniformly to every transaction by every entity in every time period, it would be neutral and therefore irrelevant in the business decision-making process. However, as we will observe over and over again, the income tax is anything but neutral. The tax system is replete with rules affecting only particular transactions, entities, or time periods. In every case in which the law applies differentially to a certain dollar of business profit or cost, a planning opportunity is born.

Tax Planning Driver	According to former New York State Tax Commissioner James W. Wetzler, "tax planning is driven by the fact that under a nonneutral tax law, transactions or arrangements whose economic differences are minor can have significantly different tax consequences."

The tax consequences of a transaction depend on the interaction of four variables common to all transactions.

Objective 2
List the four variables that determine the tax consequences of a transaction.

1. The entity variable: Which entity undertakes the transaction?
2. The time period variable: During which tax year or years does the transaction occur?
3. The jurisdiction variable: In which tax jurisdiction does the transaction occur?
4. The character variable: What is the tax character of the income from the transaction?

We will focus on each variable in turn to learn why the variable matters and how it can be manipulated to change the tax outcome of the transaction.

---

[1] The civil and criminal penalties for tax evasion are discussed in Chapter 18.

[2] *Commissioner v. Newman*, 159 F.2d 848, 850 (CA-2, 1947).

THE ENTITY VARIABLE

In the federal tax system, individuals and corporations are the two entities that pay tax on business income. While trusts and estates are also taxable entities, they don't routinely engage in the active conduct of a business. For this reason, this text doesn't address the specialized rules governing the income taxation of trusts and estates. Businesses can be organized as sole proprietorships, partnerships, LLCs, or S corporations, but these organizational forms are not taxable entities. Income generated by a proprietorship, partnership, LLC, or S corporation is taxed to the proprietor, partners, members, or shareholders. The operation of these passthrough entities is examined in detail in Chapter 10.

For the most part, the provisions in the Internal Revenue Code governing the computation of taxable income apply uniformly across organizational forms.[3] In other words, the *amount of taxable income* from a business activity does not depend on the type of entity conducting the business; the tax law is essentially neutral across entities with respect to the tax base. So why do the tax consequences of business transactions depend on which entity undertakes the transaction? The answer lies in the potential difference between applicable *tax rates*.

Section 1 of the Internal Revenue Code provides the tax rate structure for individuals, which currently consists of six income brackets with rates ranging from 10 percent to 35 percent. Section 11 provides a completely different rate structure for corporations; the corporate rates range from 15 percent to 39 percent. (The rates for both individuals and corporations are provided in Appendix C.) Both the individual and corporate rate structures are progressive, so that the tax on a given dollar of income depends on the marginal rate of the entity earning that dollar.[4] An entity with a lower marginal rate will pay less tax on a dollar of income than an entity with a higher marginal rate. Consequently, the after-tax value of the dollar is greater to the low-tax entity than to the high-tax entity.

Tax Rate Differential	Entity H has a 39 percent marginal tax rate while Entity L has a 15 percent marginal tax rate. Both receive $100 cash that represents taxable income. The after-tax cash available to each entity is computed as follows.

	Entity H	Entity L
Cash received	$100	$100
Tax cost ($100 income × marginal rate)	(39)	(15)
After-tax cash	$ 61	$ 85

A comparison of the tax consequences to Entities H and L suggests our first income tax planning maxim: *Tax costs decrease (and cash flows increase) when income is generated by an entity subject to a low tax rate.*

This maxim is especially important when entrepreneurs are starting a new venture and must decide which organizational form to adopt. The choice of organizational form determines whether the business income will be taxed at the individual rates or the corporate rates. Chapter 12 provides an in-depth discussion of the tax implications of the choice of organizational form for new businesses.

[3] The few special provisions applying only to businesses operated in the corporate form are discussed in Chapter 11.

[4] A complete discussion of the intricacies of the corporate rate structure is included in Chapter 11.

Income Shifting

Objective 3

Explain why an income shift or a deduction shift can improve NPV.

The first maxim implies that the tax on business income can be reduced if that income is shifted from an entity with a high tax rate to an entity with a low tax rate. Assume that Entity H in the previous example could redirect its $100 cash receipt (and the income represented by the cash) to Entity L.

Income Shift

Entity H and Entity L both expect to receive $100 cash that represents taxable income. Entity H arranges to shift its $100 to Entity L. The after-tax cash available to each entity is computed as follows.

	Entity H	Entity L
Cash received	–0–	$200
Tax cost (taxable income × marginal rate)	–0–	(30)
After-tax cash	–0–	$170

This income shift reduces the tax on the shifted $100 from $39 to $15 and increases the after-tax cash from $61 to $85. However, that after-tax cash now belongs to Entity L rather than to Entity H. From Entity H's perspective, the income shift *reduces* its after-tax cash flow from $61 to zero. On the presumption that Entity H makes rational decisions, this transaction makes sense only if Entity H controls, enjoys, or benefits from the shifted cash in some manner. One possible explanation is that Entity L is a corporation and Entity H is its sole shareholder. In such case, any cash shifted from Shareholder H to Corporation L increases the value of Corporation L's stock and still belongs indirectly to Shareholder H. Although Shareholder H holds less cash, Shareholder H's wealth (which includes the value of Corporation L stock) increases by the $24 tax savings from the income shift.

Deduction Shifting

Entities with different marginal rates can save tax not only by shifting income but also by shifting deductible expenses. To illustrate a deduction shift, let's use Entities H and L again.

Deduction Shift

Entity L expects to pay an $80 expense that is fully deductible in computing taxable income. Because Entity L is in a 15 percent marginal tax bracket, the $80 deduction would save $12 in tax, and the after-tax cost of the payment is $68.

Cash expended by Entity L	$(80)
Tax savings ($80 deduction × 15%)	12
After-tax cost	$(68)

If Entity H could make the $80 payment on behalf of Entity L and claim the $80 deduction on its own tax return, the tax savings would increase to $31 and the after-tax cost would decrease to $49.

Cash expended by Entity H	$(80)
Tax savings ($80 deduction × 39%)	31
After-tax cost	$(49)

Because the deduction is shifted from the entity with the low tax rate to the entity with the high tax rate, the cash outflow with respect to the expense decreases by $19. But the shift actually increases Entity H's cash outflow by $49. Entity H would never agree to this strategy unless it derives some indirect economic benefit from the tax savings.

Constraints on Income Shifting

Because income-shifting transactions involve transfers of value from one party to another, they usually occur between related parties. After the income shift, the parties *in the aggregate* are financially better off by the tax savings from the transaction. Congress has long recognized that income-shifting techniques lose revenue for the Treasury. Many effective techniques that were once widely used by related parties have been abolished by legislation; in subsequent chapters, we will consider a number of powerful statutory restrictions on income shifting. The IRS is vigilant in policing related party transactions involving beneficial income shifts. If a transaction serves no genuine purpose besides tax avoidance, the IRS may disallow the tax consequences intended by the parties.

Objective 4
Explain how the assignment of income doctrine constrains income-shifting strategies.

Assignment of Income Doctrine

The federal courts have consistently held that our income tax system cannot tolerate artificial shifts of income from one taxpayer to another. Over 75 years ago, the Supreme Court decided that income must be taxed to the person who earns it, even if another person has a legal right to the wealth represented by the income.[5] Thus, a business owner who receives a $10,000 check in payment for services rendered to a client can't avoid reporting $10,000 income by simply endorsing the check over to his daughter. In the picturesque language of the Court, the tax law must disregard arrangements "by which the fruits are attributed to a different tree from that on which they grew."

The Supreme Court elaborated on this theme in the case of a father who detached negotiable interest coupons from corporate bonds and gave the coupons to his son as a gift.[6] When the coupons matured, the son collected the interest and reported it as income on his own tax return. The Court concluded that the interest income was taxable to the father because he continued to own the underlying asset (the bonds) that created the right to the interest payments. The holdings in these two cases have melded into the **assignment of income doctrine:** Income must be taxed to the entity that renders the service or owns the capital with respect to which the income is paid. Over the years, the IRS has frustrated many creative income-shifting schemes by invoking this simple, but potent, doctrine.

THE TIME PERIOD VARIABLE

Because both federal and state income taxes are imposed annually, the tax costs or savings from a transaction depend on the year in which the transaction occurs. In Chapter 3, we learned that these costs and savings are a function of the firm's marginal tax rate. If that rate changes from one year to the next, the tax costs and savings fluctuate accordingly. We've also discussed the fact that the technical details of the federal and state income tax systems change periodically. A tax benefit available in one year may disappear in the next. Conversely, a statutory restriction causing a tax problem this year may be lifted in the future. Managers must be aware of annual changes in the tax laws pertaining to their business operations. By controlling the timing of transactions, they may reduce the tax cost or increase the tax savings for their firm.

[5] *Lucas v. Earl*, 281 U.S. 111 (1930).
[6] *Helvering v. Horst*, 311 U.S. 112 (1940).

Even if marginal tax rates and the tax law were absolutely stable over time, the tax costs and savings from transactions would still vary with the time period during which the transaction occurs. This variation is because of the time value of money. In present value terms, a tax dollar paid this year costs more than a tax dollar paid in a future year. Conversely, a tax dollar saved this year is worth more than a tax dollar saved in the future.

Consider a transaction that takes place over two taxable years. In the first year (year 0), Firm R receives $120 revenues and pays $40 expenses. In the next year (year 1), it receives $180 revenues and pays $80 expenses. If the revenues are taxable when received and the expenses are deductible when paid, Firm R has $80 taxable income in the first year and $100 taxable income in the next year. If it has a 35 percent tax rate for the two-year period and uses a 12 percent discount rate, the NPV of the cash flows is $110.

		Year 0	Year 1
Revenues		$120	$180
Expenses		(40)	(80)
Income tax cost:			
Taxable income	$80		$100
	.35		.35
Tax cost		(28)	(35)
After-tax net cash flow		$ 52	$ 65
Present value of year 0 cash flow		$ 52	
Present value of year 1 cash flow			
($65 × .893 discount factor)		58	
NPV		$110	

Now assume that Firm R could restructure the transaction in a way that *doesn't affect before-tax cash flows* but allows it to report the entire $180 taxable income (and pay the $63 tax thereon) in year 1.[7]

		Year 0	Year 1
Revenues		$120	$180
Expenses		(40)	(80)
Income tax cost:			
Taxable income	–0–		$180
			.35
Tax cost		–0–	(63)
After-tax net cash flow		$ 80	$ 37
Present value of year 0 cash flow		$ 80	
Present value of year 1 cash flow			
($37 × .893 discount factor)		33	
NPV		$113	

---

[7] For purposes of computing NPV, before-tax cash flows, tax costs, and tax savings in the same taxable year are assumed to occur at the same point in time.

The NPV of Firm R's restructured transaction is $3 more than that of the original transaction. This entire increase is attributable to the deferral of a $28 tax cost for one year. The only difference in the transactions is one of timing. This observation suggests our second income tax planning maxim: *In present value terms, tax costs decrease (and cash flows increase) when a tax is deferred until a later taxable year.*

Income Deferral and Opportunity Costs

The restructured transaction in the preceding example represents an ideal situation in which a firm defers the payment of tax without affecting before-tax cash flows. Realistically, firms can defer tax only by deferring the taxable income generated by the transaction, which may be difficult to do without affecting cash flows. A tax deferral strategy that does affect before-tax cash flows may not improve NPV. To illustrate this possibility, assume that Firm R avoids taxable income in year 0 by delaying the receipt of $80 of revenue until year 1. Let's recompute the NPV of the transaction based on this assumption.

	Year 0	Year 1
Revenues	$ 40	$260
Expenses	(40)	(80)
Income tax cost:		
Taxable income	–0–	$180
		.35
Tax cost	–0–	(63)
After-tax net cash flow	–0–	$117
Present value of year 0 cash flow	–0–	
Present value of year 1 cash flow		
($117 × .893 discount factor)	$104	
NPV	$104	

In this transaction, the NPV is $6 *less* than that of the original transaction. While Firm R defers a $28 tax cost for one year, it also delays the receipt of $80 cash. The net result is that Firm R loses the use of $52 for one year at an opportunity cost of $6 [$52 − ($52 × .893 discount factor)].

Instead of delaying the receipt of revenues, what if Firm R could defer taxable income by paying all the expenses in the first year?

	Year 0	Year 1
Revenues	$120	$180
Expenses	(120)	–0–
Income tax cost:		
Taxable income	–0–	$180
		.35
Tax cost	–0–	(63)
After-tax net cash flow	–0–	$117
Present value of year 0 cash flow	–0–	
Present value of year 1 cash flow		
($117 × .893 discount factor)	$104	
NPV	$104	

Tax Talk

Congress enacted a special law to allow individuals who donated cash for the relief of victims of the January 12, 2010, Haiti earthquake to deduct the donation in 2009 if they paid the donation before March 1, 2010. This timing rule accelerated the tax savings from the deduction by one year.

This alternative method for deferring taxable income has exactly the same negative effect on NPV. By deferring a $28 tax cost and accelerating the payment of $80 of expenses, Firm R deprives itself of the use of $52 for one year at an opportunity cost of $6. In both transactions, the advantage of tax deferral is overwhelmed by a disadvantageous change in before-tax cash flows. Consequently, we can conclude that our second tax planning maxim holds true only when a tax payment can be deferred independently of before-tax cash flows or when the value of the deferral exceeds any opportunity cost of a coinciding change in before-tax cash flows.

Income Deferral and Rate Changes

Objective 5
Identify the circumstances in which a tax deferral strategy may not improve NPV.

The deferral of taxable income into future years creates uncertainty as to the marginal rate that will apply to that income. The value of the deferral could be reduced if Congress were to increase the statutory rates or if the firm were to move unexpectedly into a higher tax bracket. The risk that deferred income will be taxed at a higher rate escalates with the length of the deferral period. To illustrate this problem, assume that Firm N, which is in a 35 percent marginal tax bracket, generates $30,000 profit on a transaction. It has the choice of reporting the entire profit as current year income or reporting the profit as income ratably over the next three years at no opportunity cost. Firm N chooses the deferral strategy based on the following projection (which uses a 9 percent discount rate).

	Year 0	Year 1	Year 2	Year 3
Without deferral:				
Taxable income	$30,000	–0–	–0–	–0–
Tax cost at 35%	$10,500	–0–	–0–	–0–
NPV of tax costs	$10,500			
With deferral:				
Taxable income	–0–	$10,000	$10,000	$10,000
Tax cost at 35%	–0–	$ 3,500	$ 3,500	$ 3,500
Discount factors		.917	.842	.772
		$ 3,210	$ 2,947	$ 2,702
NPV of tax costs	$ 8,859			

Now assume that Firm N's marginal tax rate in years 1 through 3 jumps to 45 percent because of a change in the tax law. As a result, the tax costs in years 1 through 3 are much higher than projected.

	Year 0	Year 1	Year 2	Year 3
Taxable income	–0–	$10,000	$10,000	$10,000
Tax cost at 45%	–0–	$ 4,500	$ 4,500	$ 4,500
Discount factors		.917	.842	.772
		$ 4,127	$ 3,789	$ 3,474
Actual NPV of tax costs	$11,390			

Because the value of deferring the tax cost is insufficient to compensate for the higher rate at which the deferred income is taxed, Firm N's choice to defer the income *increased* the tax cost of the transaction by $890 in present value terms.

Actual NPV of tax costs	$ 11,390
NPV of tax cost without deferral	(10,500)
	$ 890

THE JURISDICTION VARIABLE

Every domestic business is subject to the tax jurisdiction of the federal government. Therefore, the geographic location of a firm within the United States is a neutral factor in the computation of its federal income tax. However, most states and the District of Columbia also tax business income. Because of the differences in state tax systems, a firm's aggregate income tax liability (federal, state, and local) is very much a function of the jurisdictions in which it conducts business.

Consider two domestic firms that each receive $5,000 cash, all of which is taxable income. Firm Y operates in State Y, which imposes a flat 4 percent tax on business income. Firm Z operates in State Z, which imposes a flat 10 percent tax on business income. For federal purposes, state income tax payments are deductible in the computation of taxable income.[8] Both firms face a 39 percent federal tax rate. Under these facts, Firms Y and Z have the following after-tax cash flows.

> **Tax Talk**
>
> *The Irish rock band U2 transferred part of its publishing company, U2 Limited, out of Ireland to a Dutch financial management company because royalty income is taxed by Ireland but is virtually tax-exempt in the Netherlands.*

	Firm Y	Firm Z
Before-tax cash/income	$5,000	$5,000
State income tax cost	(200)	(500)
Federal taxable income	$4,800	$4,500
Federal tax cost (Taxable income × 39%)	(1,872)	(1,755)
After-tax cash flow	$2,928	$2,745

A comparison of these after-tax cash flows gives us our third income tax planning maxim: *Tax costs decrease (and cash flows increase) when income is generated in a jurisdiction with a low tax rate.*

The comparison between the after-tax cash flows of Firms Y and Z would be more complex if these firms operate in any foreign country that taxes business income. Clearly, managers must be aware of the income tax laws of every locality in which their firm operates or plans to operate in the future. Managers should appreciate that they can often minimize the total tax burden by conducting business in jurisdictions with favorable tax climates. The intricacies of tax planning in a multijurisdictional setting are the subject of Chapter 13.

> *Global Tax Costs*
>
> The accounting firm KPMG has indexed the tax costs imposed by 10 industrialized countries on businesses operating within the country's jurisdiction. This Total Tax Index uses the U.S. tax cost as its baseline of 100 against which other countries are scored. Mexico's score of 59.9 represents the lowest tax cost compared to the United States, while France's score of 181.4 represents the highest tax cost.

THE CHARACTER VARIABLE

The fourth variable that determines the tax consequences of transactions is the tax character of the income generated by the transaction. The tax character of any item of income is determined strictly by law; it is not intuitive and may bear no relationship to any financial or economic attribute of the income. In addition, the character of income and the ramifications

---

[8] §164(a).

of that characterization can change with each new tax bill passed by Congress or each new regulation published by the Treasury. Because the character variable is artificial, it is the hardest one to discuss in a generalized manner.

Objective 6

Contrast the tax character of ordinary income and capital gain.

Every item of income is ultimately characterized for tax purposes as either **ordinary income** or **capital gain.** The income generated by routine sales of goods or services to customers or clients is ordinary income. The yield on invested capital, such as interest, dividends, and rents, is also ordinary in character. As the label implies, most ordinary income is taxed at the regular individual or corporate rates. The sale or exchange of certain types of property, referred to as capital assets, gives rise to capital gain. The term *capital asset* is defined in detail in Chapter 8. Historically, capital gain has enjoyed favorable treatment under the federal tax law, usually in the form of a preferential tax rate. Currently, individuals (but not corporations) pay tax on their capital gains at a 28, 25, 15, or zero percent rate.[9]

Many items of ordinary income and capital gain have additional characteristics that affect the tax on the income. For instance, the ordinary income earned by a U.S. firm conducting business both in the United States and foreign countries is characterized as either U.S. source income or foreign source income. As we will discuss in Chapter 13, this characterization is crucial in determining how much federal income tax the firm must pay on its ordinary income.

To demonstrate the effect of the character variable, let's compare the cash flow consequences of three different items of income received by Mr. Thompson, who has a 35 percent regular marginal tax rate. Each item consists of $1,000 cash. The first item is ordinary income with no other special characteristic; the second item is capital gain eligible for the 15 percent rate; and the third item is interest on a bond issued by the City of New York. While interest generically is ordinary income, municipal bond interest has a very special characteristic—it is exempt from federal income tax. In other words, municipal bond interest is taxed at a preferential rate of zero.

	Ordinary Income	Capital Gain	Tax-Exempt Income
Before-tax cash/income	$1,000	$1,000	$1,000
Tax cost	(350)	(150)	–0–
After-tax cash flow	$ 650	$ 850	$1,000

The fact that the character of income determines whether the income is taxed at the regular rate or at a special rate suggests our fourth tax planning maxim: *Tax costs decrease (and cash flows increase) when income is taxed at a preferential rate because of its character.*

Determining the Value of Preferential Rates

The value of a preferential rate to a particular taxpayer can be quantified only by reference to that taxpayer's regular marginal rate. In the above example, the $200 difference between the after-tax cash flow from the ordinary income and the capital gain is due to the 20 percentage point spread between Mr. Thompson's 35 percent regular tax rate and the 15 percent preferential rate on the capital gain. If Mr. Thompson's marginal rate on

[9] The preferential rates apply only to long-term capital gains. Chapter 16 includes a detailed discussion of the individual preferential rates.

ordinary income is only 28 percent, the 13 percentage point spread between the regular rate and the preferential rate results in only a $130 difference in after-tax cash flow.

	Ordinary Income	Capital Gain
Before-tax cash/income	$1,000	$1,000
Tax cost (28% regular rate)	(280)	(150)
After-tax cash flow	$ 720	$ 850

Constraints on Conversion

For many years, taxpayers and their advisers have heeded the fourth tax planning maxim by structuring transactions to result in capital gain rather than ordinary income. The more aggressive have devised ingenious techniques for converting the potential ordinary income from a transaction to capital gain. In response, Congress has worked hard to protect the integrity of the distinction between the two types of income. The Internal Revenue Code contains dozens of prohibitions against artificial conversions of ordinary income into capital gain, many of which we will examine in later chapters. In fact, the preferential treatment of capital gains is responsible for more complexity in the federal income tax system than any other feature. Why then does Congress persist in maintaining the capital gains preference? This tax policy question is addressed in Chapter 16.

Implicit Taxes

Objective 7
Distinguish between an explicit tax and an implicit tax.

The decision to engage in a transaction generating income taxed at a preferential rate should be based on the NPV of the transaction rather than the fact of the preferential rate. The tax cost may not be the only cash flow affected by the tax-favored character of the income. Suppose that Ms. Crowe has $20,000 to invest in either a tax-exempt municipal bond or a corporate bond of identical risk. The interest from the latter would be ordinary income taxed at 33 percent. Let's make an initial assumption that both bonds pay 10 percent interest per annum. A comparison of the annual after-tax cash flows indicates that the municipal bond is the superior investment.

	Corporate Bond Interest	Municipal Bond Interest
Before-tax cash/income	$2,000	$2,000
Tax cost	(660)	–0–
After-tax cash flow	$1,340	$2,000

The assumption that the two bonds offer identical before-tax yields is unrealistic. State and local governments take advantage of the tax-exempt status of their debt obligations by offering lower interest rates than their competitors in the capital markets. They know that many investors will accept the lower rate because of the tax-favored status of the bonds. Let's change our example by assuming that the municipal bond would pay only 8 percent interest on Ms. Crowe's $20,000 investment.

	Corporate Bond Interest	Municipal Bond Interest
Before-tax cash/income	$2,000	$1,600
Tax cost	(660)	–0–
After-tax cash flow	$ 1,340	$1,600

While the municipal bond is still a better investment than the corporate bond, the value of the preferential tax rate to Ms. Crowe has decreased because of the difference in the bonds' respective before-tax yields. While Ms. Crowe would pay no direct **explicit tax** on the interest from the municipal bond, she must accept a reduced market rate of return to take advantage of the tax preference. In the tax literature, this reduction is referred to as an **implicit tax.**[10]

What if the municipal bond would pay only 6.5 percent interest on the $20,000 investment?

	Corporate Bond Interest	Municipal Bond Interest
Before-tax cash/income	$2,000	$1,300
Tax cost	(660)	–0–
After-tax cash flow	$ 1,340	$1,300

Now the $700 implicit tax that Ms. Crowe would incur by purchasing the municipal bond (the reduction in the before-tax yield) is greater than the $660 explicit tax on the interest from the corporate bond. Consequently, the after-tax cash generated by the corporate bond exceeds the after-tax cash generated by the tax-favored municipal bond, and Ms. Crowe should invest accordingly.

Municipal bond interest has no inherent financial characteristic that creates a natural immunity to taxation.[11] Congress granted tax-exempt status to this type of income to help state and local governments compete in the capital markets. The loss in revenues attributable to the tax preference represents an indirect federal subsidy to these governments. Whether this tax preference (or any other preference) is worth anything to a given investor depends on the investor's marginal tax rate and any implicit tax on the investment.

DEVELOPING TAX PLANNING STRATEGIES

Our analysis of the variables that determine the tax consequences of transactions resulted in the following maxims.

Objective 8
Summarize the four tax planning maxims.

- *Tax costs decrease (and cash flows increase) when income is generated by an entity subject to a low tax rate.*
- *In present value terms, tax costs decrease (and cash flows increase) when a tax is deferred until a later taxable year.*

[10] This term was popularized by Myron S. Scholes and Mark A. Wolfson in *Taxes and Business Strategy: A Planning Approach* (Englewood Cliffs, N.J.: Prentice Hall, 1992).

[11] For state income tax purposes, interest on state and local bonds is generally taxable.

- *Tax costs decrease (and cash flows increase) when income is generated in a jurisdiction with a low tax rate.*
- *Tax costs decrease (and cash flows increase) when income is taxed at a preferential rate because of its character.*

Tax planning strategies that enhance cash flows typically reflect at least one of these maxims. Many strategies combine two or more maxims working together to minimize taxes. Other strategies may adhere to one maxim but violate another. In such cases, business managers must carefully assess the overall tax consequences to determine if the strategy improves NPV. The following example demonstrates the problem of conflicting maxims.

Conflicting Maxims

Firm MN operates as two separate taxable entities, Entity M and Entity N. The firm is negotiating a transaction that will generate $25,000 cash in year 0 and $60,000 cash in year 1. If Entity M undertakes the transaction, taxable income will correspond to cash flow (i.e., Entity M will report $25,000 and $60,000 taxable income in years 0 and 1). If Entity N undertakes the transaction, it must report the entire $85,000 taxable income in year 0. Entity M has a 30 percent marginal tax rate while Entity N has a 25 percent marginal tax rate. Firm MN uses a 9 percent discount rate to compute NPV.

	Entity M		Entity N	
Year 0:				
Before-tax cash flow		$25,000		$25,000
Taxable income	$25,000		$85,000	
	.30		.25	
Tax cost		(7,500)		(21,250)
After-tax cash flow		$17,500		$ 3,750
Year 1:				
Before-tax cash flow		$60,000		$60,000
Taxable income	$60,000		–0–	
	.30			
Tax cost		(18,000)		–0–
After-tax cash flow		$42,000		$60,000
Present value of year 0 cash flow		$17,500		$ 3,750
Present value of year 1 cash flow (.917 discount factor)		38,514		55,020
NPV		$56,014		$58,770

On the basis of an NPV comparison, Firm MN should undertake the transaction through Entity N. This strategy adheres to the tax planning maxim that cash flows increase when income is generated by an entity with a low tax rate. However, the strategy accelerates the entire tax on the transaction into year 0, thus violating the maxim that calls for tax deferral.

Additional Strategic Considerations

The four tax planning maxims offer general guidance to the tax planning process. Like all generalizations, each one is subject to conditions, limitations, and exceptions depending on the specific tax strategy under consideration. Even though the maxims focus on the reduction of tax costs, managers should remember that their strategic goal is not tax minimization per se but NPV maximization. Consequently, they must consider key factors other than tax costs in formulating a winning strategy. One obvious factor is the expense of implementing the strategy. Firms may require professional advice in designing, executing, and monitoring a sophisticated tax plan, and the cost of the advice must be weighed against the potential tax savings from the strategy.

Tax Savings versus Additional Costs	Firm B has a choice between two strategies for reducing its tax with respect to a line of business. The simpler of the two strategies would reduce the annual tax by $50,000 and would not cost anything to implement. The more complex of the two strategies would reduce the annual tax by $70,000 but would require additional legal and accounting fees with an after-tax cost of $25,000. Firm B should choose the simpler strategy because it has the greater value even though it saves less tax.

Managers must consider the economic consequences of tax strategies to all parties. In Chapter 3, we learned that firms negotiating in private markets can work together to maximize the after-tax value of the transaction to both parties. A manager intent on implementing a unilateral tax strategy may miss an opportunity for effective multilateral planning. Even worse, if a manager fails to consider the repercussions of a strategy on other interested parties, those parties might retaliate in ways that diminish the overall value of the strategy to the firm.

Multilateral Planning	Corporation F and Corporation D plan to form a joint venture to conduct a new business. Corporation F's tax cost would be minimized if the business is conducted in Germany. Corporation D's tax cost would be minimized if the business is conducted in the United States. Corporation F agrees to locate the business in the United States, provided that it receives 60 percent of the profit and Corporation D receives only 40 percent. This compromise increases Corporation F's tax cost and decreases Corporation D's before-tax profit. Nevertheless, the corporations agree to the compromise because it maximizes the after-tax value of the joint venture to both corporations.

Tax strategies must be evaluated on the basis of flexibility: the extent to which the strategy can be adapted to unforeseen circumstances. Every strategy's anticipated effect on cash flows is based on assumptions about the future. The more uncertain the assumptions, the greater the risk that the strategy could backfire and have a detrimental effect on cash flows. If the firm can quickly modify or even reverse a failed strategy at minimal cost, this risk may be slight. But if the strategy is irreversible or would be expensive to fix, the cost of potential failure may outweigh the benefit of success.

The Flexibility Factor	Four years ago, Firm D formed a Brazilian corporation to operate its business in South America. Firm D selected the corporate form to take advantage of generous tax preferences available only to Brazilian corporations. This year, Brazil repealed the preferences and substantially increased its corporate tax rate. If Firm D had not formed the corporation, it could easily avoid the tax increase by restructuring its South American operation. But Firm D cannot dissolve the Brazilian corporation without incurring prohibitively high legal and political costs. With hindsight, Firm D would have maximized the after-tax value of its South American operation by choosing a more flexible tax strategy.

Tax Legal Doctrines

Objective 9
Describe the legal doctrines that the IRS uses to challenge tax planning strategies.

Managers must be confident that they have identified the correct tax consequences of the strategies implemented by their firm. If a manager makes a technical error in applying the tax law and the IRS discovers the error on audit, the planning strategy could unravel, with disastrous effects on cash flows. Even when managers believe that a strategy is technically sound, they must consider the government's reaction to the overall propriety of the strategy. Over the years, both the IRS and the federal courts have made taxpayers adhere not only to the letter but also to the spirit of the law. Consequently, four important common law doctrines have evolved in the tax planning area. The IRS can invoke these doctrines when a firm seems to be bending the rules to gain an unjustified tax advantage.

The **economic substance doctrine** holds that a transaction that doesn't change the taxpayer's economic situation except by the tax savings from the transaction can be disregarded by the IRS. This doctrine is closely aligned with the **business purpose doctrine** that a transaction should not be effective for tax purposes unless it has a business purpose other than tax avoidance. In 2010, Congress codified these common law doctrines by enacting Section 7701(o) of the Internal Revenue Code. This new subsection states that a transaction has economic substance only if it "changes in a meaningful way (apart from Federal income tax effects) the taxpayer's economic position, and the taxpayer has a substantial purpose (apart from Federal income tax effects) for entering into such transaction." A transaction that is devoid of economic substance will not be respected for tax purposes.[12]

Lack of Economic Substance	Mr. Early planned to sell developed real estate held in his own name to raise cash to fund a new investment opportunity. The proposed sale would generate a substantial gain, which would be taxed to Mr. Early at a 25 percent rate. Instead of selling the real estate directly, Mr. Early contributed the real estate to a corporation in which he was the sole shareholder. The corporation sold the real estate, paid tax on the gain at a much lower rate, then made an interest-free loan of the after-tax cash proceeds to Mr. Early. If the IRS concludes that Mr. Early's contribution of the real estate to the corporation had no economic effect or business purpose other than reducing the tax cost of the sale, it could disregard the transaction and require Mr. Early to pay tax on the gain at his 25 percent rate.[13]

The **substance over form doctrine** holds that the IRS can look through the legal formalities to determine the economic substance (if any) of a transaction. If the substance differs from the form, the IRS will base the tax consequences of the transaction on the reality rather than the illusion.[14]

Substance over Form	The sole shareholder and president of Corporation JKL negotiated a leasing contract with a local businessman. Under the terms of the contract, JKL paid $35,000 for the use of equipment for one year and deducted this payment as a business expense. The revenue agent who audited JKL's tax return uncovered two additional facts. First, the local businessman who received the $35,000 was a candidate for state political office and was enthusiastically endorsed by JKL's owner. Second, the corporation had no apparent need for the leased equipment. If these facts convince the agent that the substance of the leasing arrangement was a disguised political contribution (which is completely nondeductible), JKL may lose its $35,000 deduction and the tax savings therefrom.

[12] These doctrines originated with the case of *Gregory* v. *Helvering,* 293 U.S. 465 (1935).
[13] This example is based on the facts in *Paymer* v. *Commissioner,* 150 F.2d 334 (CA-2, 1945).
[14] *Commissioner* v. *Danielson,* 378 F.2d 771 (CA-3, 1967), *cert. denied* 389 U.S. 858 (1967).

The **step transaction doctrine** allows the IRS to collapse a series of intermediate transactions into a single transaction to determine the tax consequences of the arrangement in its entirety.[15] The IRS applies the doctrine when transactions are so obviously interdependent that the parties involved would not have initiated the first transaction without anticipating that the whole series of transactions would occur. Transactions occurring within a short period of time are more vulnerable to the step transaction doctrine than those occurring over a longer interval. As a rule of thumb, the IRS considers transactions occurring within a 12-month period as suspect.[16] Transactions separated in time by more than 12 months are presumed to be independent. In tax parlance, the first transaction is "old and cold" with no connection to the second transaction.

Potential Step Transactions	ABC Corporation sells property to an unrelated purchaser who subsequently resells the property to ABC's wholly owned subsidiary. If these two sales occur within the same month, the IRS would certainly question their autonomy. Unless ABC could present evidence to the contrary, the IRS could collapse the two transactions into a direct sale of property from ABC to its subsidiary and recast the tax consequences of this related party transaction. On the other hand, if the first sale occurs five years before the second sale, the substantial length of time between the sales should make them immune to the step transaction doctrine.

There is considerable overlap in the scope of the common law doctrines, and the IRS frequently uses them in combination to challenge an offending transaction. Of course, the courts may or may not uphold the IRS's challenge. Judges or juries may side with the taxpayer by concluding that a transaction has economic substance that matches its legal form. Business managers should understand that the doctrines seem to be the exclusive property of the IRS; taxpayers can't invoke them to undo the consequences of their own ill-fated tax strategies.[17] Managers should be aware that the IRS's application of these doctrines is subjective. Given the threat of these doctrines, managers can never be absolutely certain that a creative tax plan will work, even if it seems to comply with the letter of the law.

Conclusion

Tax planning is the structuring of transactions to reduce tax costs or increase tax savings to maximize NPV. Chapter 4 introduced the four structural variables (entity, time period, jurisdiction, and income character) that affect the tax consequences of transactions. To the extent that taxpayers can control these variables, they can structure transactions to achieve the most advantageous tax outcome. But before taxpayers can properly structure their transactions, they must understand exactly how the tax law pertains to the facts and circumstances of the transaction. Each transaction is unique and may raise any number of tax questions that must be answered before the final outcome of the transaction can be determined with certainty. The art of asking and answering tax questions is called *tax research,* which is the subject of the next chapter.

---

[15] *Helvering v. Alabama Asphaltic Limestone Co.,* 315 U.S. 179 (1942).

[16] Reg. §1.368-2(c).

[17] *Durkin,* TC Memo 1992-325.

Key Terms

assignment of income
    doctrine *73*
business purpose
    doctrine *83*
capital gain *78*
economic substance
    doctrine *83*

explicit tax *80*
implicit tax *80*
ordinary income *78*
step transaction
    doctrine *84*
substance over form
    doctrine *83*

tax avoidance *70*
tax evasion *70*
tax planning *69*

Questions and Problems for Discussion

1. For each of the following situations, discuss whether the individual is engaging in tax avoidance or tax evasion.

   a. Mr. L performed minor construction work for a number of people who paid him in cash. Because Mr. L knows that there is almost no chance that the IRS could learn of these payments, he reports only half the payments as income on his federal tax return. EVASION

   b. Mr. P, who is in the 35 percent tax bracket, recently had the opportunity to invest $50,000 in a new business that should yield an annual return of at least 17 percent. Rather than invest himself, Mr. P gave $50,000 cash to his son, who then made the investment. The son's marginal tax rate is only 15 percent. AVOIDENCE

   c. Mrs. Q sold an asset during January. Her $12,000 profit on the sale is ordinary income. After preparing her income tax return for the prior year, Mrs. Q realized that her marginal tax rate for that year was 28 percent. She also realized that her marginal rate for this year will be 35 percent. Mrs. Q decides to report the profit on her prior year return to take advantage of the lower tax rate Can't Shift Income to Avoid Taxes

2. Assume that Congress amends the tax law to provide for a maximum 18 percent rate on rental income generated by single-family residences. What effect might this preferential rate have on the market value of this category of real estate?

3. Tax planners often tell their clients that "a tax delayed is a tax not paid." Can you provide a more formal explanation of this bit of wisdom?

4. Mrs. K is about to begin a new business activity and asks you if she can reduce taxable income by operating the activity as a corporation rather than as a sole proprietorship. How do you answer Mrs. K?

5. Is every business organization a taxable entity for federal income tax purposes? Explain briefly.

6. On the basis of the rates schedules in Appendix C, determine the marginal tax rate for:

   a. A corporation with $23,000 taxable income.

   b. A corporation with $250,000 taxable income.

   c. A single (unmarried) individual with $53,000 taxable income.

   d. A single (unmarried) individual with $625,000 taxable income.

7. Assume that the U.S. Congress replaces the current individual and corporate income tax rate structures with a proportionate rate that applies to both types of taxpayers. Discuss the effect of this change in the federal law on tax strategies based on:

   a. The entity variable.

   b. The time period variable.

   c. The jurisdiction variable.

   d. The character variable.

8. Compare the potential tax savings of an income shift from one entity to another if the entities are subject to:

    a. A progressive income tax system with rates from 5 percent to 19 percent.

    b. A progressive income tax system with rates from 10 percent to 50 percent.

    c. A 20 percent proportionate income tax system.

9. Why do income shifts and deduction shifts usually occur between taxpayers who are related parties?

10. Corporation P owns a controlling stock interest in Subsidiary S and Subsidiary T. Corporation P's marginal tax rate is 25 percent. It engages in one transaction that shifts $10,000 income to Subsidiary S and a second transaction that shifts a $15,000 deduction to Subsidiary T. Based on these facts, what conclusions can you draw about marginal tax rates of the two subsidiaries?

11. Firm A expects to receive a $25,000 item of income in August and a second $25,000 item of income in December. The firm could delay the receipt of both items until January. As a result, it would defer the payment of tax on $50,000 income for one full year. Firm A decides to receive the August payment this year (and pay current tax on $25,000 income) but delay the receipt of the December payment. Can you offer an explanation for this decision?

12. Identify the reasons why managers should evaluate the flexibility of a tax planning strategy before implementing the strategy.

13. In June, Congress enacts legislation that increases income tax rates for all entities effective for the next calendar year.

    a. Why might such legislation result in an increase in federal tax revenues for this year?

    b. In what way would this legislation create a conflict between tax planning maxims?

14. Mr. T is considering a strategy to defer $10,000 income for five years with no significant opportunity cost. Discuss the strategic implications of the following independent assumptions.

    a. Mr. T is age 24. He graduated from law school last month and accepted a position with a prominent firm of attorneys.

    b. Mr. T is age 63. He plans to retire from business at the end of this year and devote his time to volunteer work and sailing.

Application Problems

1. Refer to the corporate rate schedule in Appendix C.

    a. What are the tax liability, the marginal tax rate, and the average tax rate for a corporation with $48,300 taxable income?

    b. What are the tax liability, the marginal tax rate, and the average tax rate for a corporation with $615,800 taxable income?

    c. What are the tax liability, the marginal tax rate, and the average tax rate for a corporation with $16,010,000 taxable income?

    d. What are the tax liability, the marginal tax rate, and the average tax rate for a corporation with $39,253,000 taxable income?

2. Refer to the individual rate schedules in Appendix C.

    a. What are the tax liability, the marginal tax rate, and the average tax rate for a married couple filing jointly with $51,900 taxable income?

   b. What are the tax liability, the marginal tax rate, and the average tax rate for a single individual with $197,200 taxable income?

   c. What are the tax liability, the marginal tax rate, and the average tax rate for a head of household with $446,300 taxable income?

3. Ms. JK recently made a gift to her 19-year-old daughter, Alison. Ms. JK's marginal income tax rate is 35 percent, and Alison's marginal income tax rate is 15 percent. In each of the following cases, compute the annual income tax savings resulting from the gift.

   a. The gift consisted of rental property generating $19,100 annual rental income to its owner.

   b. The gift consisted of a $4,625 interest coupon from a corporate bond owned by Ms. JK.

   c. The gift consisted of a $2,200 rent check written by the tenants who lease rental property owned by Ms. JK.

   d. The gift consisted of a corporate bond paying $5,900 annual interest to its owner.

4. Firm A has a 15 percent marginal tax rate, and Firm Z has a 28 percent marginal tax rate. Firm A owns a controlling interest in Firm Z. The owners of Firm A decide to incur a $9,500 deductible expense that will benefit both firms. Compute the after-tax cost of the expense assuming that:

   a. Firm A incurs the expense.

   b. Firm Z incurs the expense.

5. Company G, which has a 30 percent marginal tax rate, owns a controlling interest in Company J, which has a 12 percent marginal tax rate. Both companies perform engineering services. Company G is negotiating a contract to provide services for a client. Upon satisfactory completion of the services, the client will pay $85,000 cash. Compute the after-tax cash from the contract assuming that:

   a. Company G is the party to the contract and provides the services to the client.

   b. Company J is the party to the contract and provides the services to the client.

   c. Company J is the party to the contract but Company G actually provides the services to the client.

6. BPK Inc. and OPK Inc. are owned by the same family. BPK's marginal tax rate is 25 percent, and OPK's marginal tax rate is 40 percent. BPK is about to incur a $72,000 deductible expense that would benefit both corporations. OPK could obtain the same mutual benefit by incurring a $92,500 deductible expense. Which corporation should incur the expense?

7. Firm M and Firm N are related parties. For the past several years, Firm M's marginal tax rate has been 34 percent, and Firm N's marginal tax rate has been 25 percent. Firm M is evaluating a transaction that will generate $10,000 income in each of the next three years. Firm M could restructure the transaction so that the income would shift to Firm N. Because of the restructuring, the annual income would decrease to $9,000. Should Firm M restructure the transaction?

8. Company K has a 30 percent marginal tax rate and uses a 7 percent discount rate to compute NPV. The company started a venture that will yield the following before-tax cash flows: year 0, $12,000; year 1, $21,000; year 2, $24,000; year 3, $17,600.

   a. If the before-tax cash flows represent taxable income in the year received, compute the NPV of the cash flows.

   b. Compute the NPV if Company K can defer the receipt of years 0 and 1 cash flows/income until year 2. (It would receive no cash in years 0 and 1 and would receive $57,000 cash in year 2.)

    c. Compute the NPV if Company K can defer paying tax on years 0 and 1 cash flows until year 2. (It would receive $24,000 cash in year 2 but would pay tax on $57,000 income.)

9. Firm H has the opportunity to engage in a transaction that will generate $100,000 cash flow (and taxable income) in year 0. How does the NPV of the transaction change if the firm could restructure the transaction in a way that does not change before-tax cash flow but results in no taxable income in year 0, $50,000 taxable income in year 1, and the remaining $50,000 taxable income in year 2? Assume a 10 percent discount rate and a 34 percent marginal tax rate for the three-year period.

10. What is the effect on the NPV of the restructured transaction in the preceding problem if Firm H's marginal tax rate in year 2 increases to 39 percent?

11. Corporation R signed a contract to undertake a transaction that will generate $360,000 total cash to the corporation. The cash will represent income in the year received and will be taxed at 35 percent. Corporation R will receive $200,000 in year 0 and $160,000 in year 1. The other party to the contract now wants to restructure the transaction in a way that would increase the total cash to $375,000 ($215,000 received in year 0 and $160,000 received in year 1). However, Corporation R would recognize the entire $375,000 taxable income in year 0. If Corporation R uses an 8 percent discount rate to compute NPV, should it agree to restructure the transaction?

12. Company EJ plans to build a new plant to manufacture bicycles. EJ sells its bicycles in the world market for $400 per bike. It could locate the plant in Province P, which levies a 20 percent tax on business income. On the basis of the cost of materials and labor in Province P, EJ estimates that its manufacturing cost per bike would be $212. Alternatively, EJ could locate the plant in Province W, which levies a 16 percent tax on business income. On the basis of the cost of materials and labor in Province W, EJ estimates that its manufacturing cost per bike would be $230. In which province should Company EJ build its new plant?

13. Moto Inc. pays state income tax at a 6 percent rate and federal income tax at a 34 percent rate. Moto recently engaged in a transaction in Country N, which levied a $97,300 tax on the transaction. This year, Moto generated $2.738 million net income before consideration of any tax. Compute Moto's total tax burden (federal, state, and foreign) assuming that:

    a. The tax paid to Country N is deductible for both state and federal tax purposes.

    b. The tax paid to Country N is not deductible for state tax purposes but is deductible for federal tax purposes.

    c. The tax paid to Country N is not deductible for either state or federal tax purposes.

14. Mr. G has $15,000 to invest. He is undecided about putting the money into tax-exempt municipal bonds paying 7 percent annual interest or corporate bonds paying 9.5 percent annual interest. The two investments have the same risk.

    a. Which investment should Mr. G make if his marginal tax rate is 33 percent?

    b. Would your conclusion change if Mr. G's marginal tax rate is only 15 percent?

15. At the beginning of the year, Mr. L put $50,000 cash into an investment. At the end of the year, he received a check for $5,000, representing his annual return on the investment. Mr. L's marginal tax rate on ordinary income is 28 percent. However, his return on this particular investment is a capital gain taxed at 15 percent. Compute the value of the preferential rate to Mr. L.

16. Refer to the facts in the preceding problem. At the beginning of the year, Mr. L could have invested his $50,000 in a business with a 12 percent annual return. However, this return would have been ordinary income rather than capital gain.

a. Considering the fact that Mr. L could have invested in this business, how much implicit tax did he pay with respect to the investment described in the preceding problem?

b. Did Mr. L make the correct investment decision?

17. Assume that Congress amends the tax law to provide for a maximum 20 percent rate on royalty income. Calculate the annual tax savings from this new preferential rate to each of the following taxpayers.

   a. Ms. A, who is in a 35 percent marginal tax bracket and receives $8,000 royalty income each year.

   b. Mr. B, who is in a 33 percent marginal tax bracket and receives $15,000 royalty income each year.

   c. Mr. C, who is in a 10 percent marginal tax bracket and receives $3,000 royalty income each year.

   d. Mrs. D, who is in a 28 percent marginal tax bracket and receives $70,000 royalty income each year.

18. Firm L has $500,000 to invest and is considering two alternatives. Investment A would pay 13 percent ($65,000 annual before-tax cash flow). Investment B would pay 9.5 percent ($47,500 annual before-tax cash flow). The return on Investment A is taxable, while the return on Investment B is tax exempt. Firm L forecasts that its 35 percent marginal tax rate will be stable for the foreseeable future.

   a. Compute the explicit tax and implicit tax that Firm L will pay with respect to Investment A and Investment B.

   b. Which investment results in the greater annual after-tax cash flow?

19. Firm W, which has a 34 percent marginal tax rate, plans to operate a new business that should generate $40,000 annual cash flow/ordinary income for three years (years 0, 1, and 2). Alternatively, Firm W could form a new taxable entity (Entity N) to operate the business. Entity N would pay tax on the three-year income stream at a 25 percent rate. The nondeductible cost of forming Entity N would be $5,000. If Firm W uses a 6 percent discount rate, should it operate the new business directly or form Entity N to operate the business?

Issue Recognition Problems

Identify the tax issue or issues suggested by the following situations, and state each issue in the form of a question.

1. Mr. and Mrs. TR own an investment yielding a 7.2 percent after-tax return. Their friend Ms. K is encouraging them to sell this investment and invest the proceeds in her business, which takes advantage of several favorable tax preferences. Consequently, Ms. K's after-tax return from this business is 8.4 percent.

2. Company QP must decide whether to build a new manufacturing plant in Country B or Country C. Country B has no income tax. However, its political regime is unstable and its currency has been devalued four times in three years. Country C has both a 20 percent income tax and a stable democratic government.

3. Dr. P is a physician with his own medical practice. For the last several years, his marginal income tax rate has been 35 percent. Dr. P's daughter, who is a college student, has no taxable income. During the last two months of the year, Dr. P instructs his patients to remit their payments for his services directly to his daughter.

4. Mrs. Y owns 1,800 shares of Acme common stock, which she purchased for $10 per share in 2002. In October, she decides to sell her Acme stock for the market price of

$27 per share, the highest price at which the stock has traded in the last 22 months. A friend advises her to hold the Acme stock until next January so that her gain from the sale will be taxed next year rather than this year.

5. In November, Corporation Q negotiated to sell a tract of land to an unrelated buyer. The buyer refused to close the sale until February. Corporation Q wanted to close the sale by year-end so that the gain would be taxed at its current 25 percent rate. Corporation Q's rate for next year will be 39 percent. In December, Corporation Q sold the land to its wholly owned subsidiary. In February, the subsidiary sold the land to the unrelated buyer.

6. Mr. and Mrs. K own rental property that generates $4,000 monthly revenue. The couple is in the highest marginal tax bracket. For Christmas, Mr. and Mrs. K give the uncashed rent checks for October, November, and December to their 19-year-old grandson as a gift.

7. Firm Z is considering implementing a long-term tax strategy to accelerate the deduction of certain business expenses. The strategy has an opportunity cost because it decreases before-tax cash flows, but the tax savings from the strategy should be greater than this opportunity cost. The strategy is aggressive, and the IRS might disallow the intended tax outcome if it audits Firm Z's tax returns.

8. Ms. LG plans to structure a transaction as a legal sale of property, even though the economic substance of the transaction is a lease of the property. In her current position, the tax consequences of a sale are much more favorable than those of a lease. Ms. LG believes that if her position unexpectedly changes so that she would prefer a lease to a sale, she can ignore the legal formalities and report the transaction as a lease.

9. Firm HR is about to implement an aggressive long-term strategy consisting of three phases. It is crucial to the success of the strategy that the IRS accepts Firm HR's interpretation of the tax consequences of each distinct phase. The firm could implement the first phase in November 2012 and the second phase in August 2013. Alternatively, it could delay the second phase until January 2014.

Research Problems

1. Using an electronic library such as Checkpoint, CCH Internet Tax Research NetWork, or LexisNexis, determine how many federal tax cases decided in 2011 contain the phrase *step transaction*.

2. Select a case that discusses the step transaction doctrine in the opinion and prepare a written summary (brief) of the case.

3. Using an electronic library such as Checkpoint, CCH Internet Tax Research NetWork, or LexisNexis, find a federal tax case in which the taxpayer is found guilty of tax evasion. After reading the case, list the behaviors of the taxpayer that convinced the court that the taxpayer was evading (rather than legally avoiding) tax.

Tax Planning Cases

1. Ms. Z has decided to invest $75,000 in state bonds. She could invest in State A bonds paying 5 percent annual interest or in State R bonds paying 5.4 percent annual interest. The bonds have the same risk, and the interest from both is exempt from federal income tax. Because Ms. Z is a resident of State A, she would not pay State A's 8.5 percent personal income tax on the State A bond interest, but she would pay this tax on the State R bond interest. Ms. Z can deduct any state tax payments in the computation of her federal taxable income, and her federal marginal rate is 33 percent. Should Ms. Z invest in the State A or the State R bonds?

2. Firm DFG plans to open a foreign subsidiary through which to sell its manufactured goods in the European market. It must decide between locating the subsidiary in Country X or Country Z. If the subsidiary operates in Country X, its gross receipts from sales will be subject to a 3 percent gross receipts tax. If the subsidiary operates in Country Z, its net profits will be subject to a 42 percent income tax. However, Country Z's tax law has a special provision to attract foreign investors: No foreign subsidiary is subject to the income tax for the first three years of operations.

   DFG projects the following annual operating results for the two locations (in thousands of dollars).

	Country X	Country Z
Gross receipts from sales	$110,000	$110,000
Cost of sales	(60,000)	(60,000)
Operating expenses	(22,000)	(15,000)
Net profit	$ 28,000	$ 35,000

   DFG projects that it will operate the foreign subsidiary for 10 years (years 0 through 9) and that the terminal value of the operation at the end of this period will be the same regardless of location. Assuming a 10 percent discount rate, determine which location maximizes the NPV of the foreign operation.

3. Mr. A, who is in a 35 percent marginal tax bracket, must decide between two investment opportunities, both of which require a $50,000 initial cash outlay in year 0. Investment 1 will yield $8,000 before-tax cash flow in years 1, 2, and 3. This cash represents ordinary taxable income. In year 3, Mr. A can liquidate the investment and recover his $50,000 cash outlay. He must pay a nondeductible $200 annual fee (in years 1, 2, and 3) to maintain Investment 1.

   Investment 2 will not yield any before-tax cash flow during the period over which Mr. A will hold the investment. In year 3, he can sell Investment 2 for $75,000 cash. His $25,000 profit on the sale will be capital gain taxed at 15 percent.

   Assuming a 9 percent discount rate, determine which investment has the greater NPV.

4. Mrs. O is negotiating to purchase a tract of land from DC Company, which is a calendar year taxpayer. DC bought this land six years ago for $480,000. According to a recent appraisal, the land is worth $800,000 in the current real estate market. According to DC's director of tax, the company's profit on the sale will be taxed at 30 percent if the sale occurs this year. However, this tax rate will definitely increase to 40 percent if the sale occurs next year. Mrs. O is aware of DC's need for haste and offers to pay $785,000 for the land with a guarantee that the sale will close by December 31. Should DC accept Mrs. O's offer?

Tax Research

Learning Objectives

After studying this chapter, you should be able to:

1. Understand and apply the six steps of the tax research process.

2. Identify primary sources of tax law.

3. Utilize secondary sources of tax law to locate primary authorities.

Tax Talk

The AICPA Core Competency Framework defines research skill *as the ability "to access relevant guidance or other information, understand it, and apply it."*

Tax research is the process of determining the most probable tax consequences of a course of action undertaken by an individual or organization. Because of the complexity of state, local, and federal tax laws, most taxpayers are unable to conduct research on their own behalf. Consequently, they engage professionals such as certified public accountants (CPAs) or attorneys to investigate the tax consequences of their business, investment, and financial transactions. Taxpayers expect to receive fair value in return for the substantial fees paid to their tax advisers. Specifically, they expect their advisers to provide accurate, useful, and complete tax information on a timely basis.

A client may engage a tax adviser to research a transaction (or series of transactions) that has already occurred. In such case, the adviser must identify the consequences of the transaction and the proper reporting of the transaction on the client's tax return. Because the transaction is complete, the facts surrounding the transaction are a matter of record and are no longer subject to the client's control. The tax consequences of such a closed-fact transaction can't be changed, even if they are not to the client's liking. Thus, the adviser is limited to providing a tax compliance service to the client.

Alternatively, a client may engage a tax adviser to research a transaction that the client proposes to undertake at some future date. In this case, the adviser not only can determine the tax consequences of the prospective transaction but also can suggest ways in which the transaction can be modified to result in a more favorable outcome. The facts surrounding a prospective transaction have yet to be established and, therefore, are subject to the client's control. In such an open-fact transaction, the adviser can help the client create facts that will influence the tax consequences. Clearly, this tax planning service can be extremely valuable to clients who want to maximize the after-tax value of their transactions.

DEVELOPING TAX RESEARCH SKILLS

Tax research is an intellectual skill that is developed through both education and experience. Men and women who enter the tax profession have completed many hours of formal study as part of their undergraduate and graduate education. During their careers, they will devote many more hours to maintaining the currency of their technical tax knowledge. Tax professionals also learn by doing. As with any skill, proficiency comes with practice, and tax professionals become more proficient with every research project they undertake.

Students enrolled in an introductory tax class are struggling to learn the rudiments of the tax law. Their knowledge of the subject is limited and they have no professional experience on which to draw. Nonetheless, even beginning tax students can benefit from an introduction to the tax research process. By studying this process, students gain insight into the nature of the work performed by tax professionals. They learn how CPAs and attorneys identify tax problems, solve those problems, and communicate the solutions to their clients. They gain an appreciation of the expertise necessary to perform these tasks. Finally, students start to develop their own analytic framework for determining the tax consequences of business, investment, and financial transactions.

Several textbooks are devoted entirely to tax research. Most graduate accounting and law programs offer a course on the subject. Obviously, this chapter provides only a brief discussion of the fundamentals of a complex subject. However, after reading this chapter, students should be ready to try their hand at solving the Research Problems provided at the end of the subsequent chapters. Students who do so will enjoy an intellectual challenge that will increase their understanding of the fascinating subject of taxation.

The Tax Research Process

Objective 1
Understand and apply the six steps of the tax research process.

The tax research process can be broken down into six steps. This chapter provides a description of each research step, followed by an example of the application of the step to a research case. Students who are just starting to develop their research skills should focus on and complete each distinct step in sequence. By doing so, students will establish good research habits. As they become more proficient, students will gradually integrate the steps into a seamless research process. Those students who become accomplished researchers will automatically perform the six steps for every research project they undertake.

The six steps of the tax research process are presented in summary form in Exhibit 5.1, and listed on page 95.

EXHIBIT 5.1
The Tax Research Process

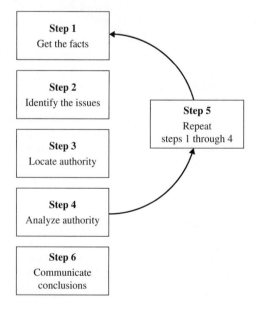

1. Understand the client's transaction and get the facts.
2. Identify the tax issues, problems, or opportunities suggested by the facts and formulate specific research questions.
3. Locate relevant tax law authority.
4. Analyze relevant authority and answer the research questions.
5. Repeat steps 1 through 4 as many times as necessary.
6. Document your research and communicate your conclusions.

STEP 1: GET THE FACTS

Before a researcher can analyze the tax consequences of a transaction, she must thoroughly understand the transaction itself. Specifically, the researcher should discuss the details of the transaction with her client to ascertain the client's motivation. What are the client's economic objectives in undertaking the transaction? What does the client foresee as the desired outcome? What risks has the client identified? By asking these types of questions, the researcher acquaints herself with the nontax features of the transaction before considering any tax implications.

The researcher must discover all the facts concerning the client's transaction. Like a newspaper reporter, the researcher should question the client about the precise "who, when, where, why, and how" of the transaction. The researcher should not assume that the client's initial summary of the transaction is factually accurate and complete. Perhaps the client hasn't determined all the facts that the researcher needs. Or the client may have discounted the significance of certain facts and omitted them from the initial summary. The researcher should encourage the client to be objective in stating the facts. Oftentimes a client will unwittingly present the researcher with the client's subjective conclusions about the facts rather than with the facts themselves.

When a researcher is working with a client to uncover the relevant facts, the researcher must take into account the level of the client's tax knowledge. If the client has some knowledge of the tax law, the researcher can ask questions that presume such knowledge. On the other hand, if the client is unsophisticated in tax matters, the researcher should ask only questions that the client can answer without reference to the tax law.

Applying Step 1	Sara Colter, a professional photographer, is a new client who has engaged your accounting firm to determine the tax consequences of a proposed transaction: Sara's sale of a 12-acre tract of land to CCM Inc. Sara provides the following facts in her initial summary of the transaction. • Sara purchased the land from Mr. and Mrs. Bianca in 2004 for $400,000 cash. • Sara and CCM Inc. have reached a tentative agreement under which CCM will pay $325,000 cash for the land and will pay all transaction expenses. As a tax professional, you know that the tax consequences of a transaction may depend on whether the parties involved are "related parties" for federal tax purposes. You also know that the tax consequences of the sale of an asset depend on the classification of the asset as capital or noncapital. Because Sara is unsophisticated in tax matters, you cannot ask her directly if she and CCM Inc. are related parties. Nor can you ask Sara if the land is a capital asset. Because of her lack of tax knowledge, such questions would be meaningless to your client. Accordingly, you decide to ask Sara the following series of questions. • Do you have any personal relationship with Mr. and Mrs. Bianca? Did you know them in any capacity other than as the sellers of the land that you purchased in 2004?

- What was your reason for purchasing the land? Have you made any improvements to the land since 2004? Have you purchased or sold any other real estate during the last 10 years?
- How did you and CCM Inc. reach an agreement that the land is worth only $325,000? Why has the land declined in value since you purchased it?
- Do you own any stock in CCM Inc.? Who are CCM Inc.'s stockholders?

In response to your questions, Sara provides the following additional facts.

- She has no personal relationship with the Biancas and did not know them prior to her purchase of their land. The purchase was arranged through a professional real estate broker.
- She purchased the land because she thought that its value would increase over time and she could eventually sell it at a profit. She has not made any improvements to the land; it is in exactly the same condition today as the day she purchased it. She has never purchased nor sold any other real estate other than her personal residence.
- Two months ago, Sara obtained two independent appraisals of the value of the land. The appraisals both concluded that the current market value of the land is $325,000. CCM Inc. performed its own appraisal that confirmed this value. The $75,000 decline in value is attributable to local zoning restrictions on the land that were put in place in 2007.
- Sara does not own any CCM Inc. stock. Twenty-four individual stockholders own the 1,000 outstanding CCM shares. Two of these stockholders are Sara's brother Jack and Jack's son Robert. Sara is not acquainted with any of the other stockholders.

STEP 2: IDENTIFY THE ISSUES

After a researcher is satisfied that she understands her client's transaction and knows all the relevant facts, she can proceed to the second step in the research process. In this step, the researcher identifies the tax issue or issues suggested by the transaction. The ability to recognize tax issues is the product of technical education and professional experience. Consequently, this step is usually the most challenging for students in an introductory tax course.

The identification of issues leads to the formulation of tax research questions. The tax researcher should be as precise as possible in formulating questions. A precise question is narrowly stated and provides clear parameters for the remaining steps in the research process. An imprecise question that is vague or overly broad in scope may provide insufficient parameters and result in wasted time and effort.

If the tax issues suggested by a transaction lead to multiple research questions, the researcher must determine the order in which the questions should be answered. In our complex tax system, the answer to a question often depends on the answer to one or more preliminary questions. Tax researchers who understand the hierarchy of their research questions can address each question in the right order and conduct their research with maximum efficiency.

Applying Step 2	After studying the facts, you conclude that Sara's proposed transaction involves one basic tax issue: Will Sara's sale of the land to CCM Inc. result in a loss that she can deduct on her individual income tax return? This issue suggests four research questions, which you decide to address in the following order. Will Sara realize a loss on the sale of her land to CCM Inc.? Can Sara recognize her realized loss? What is the character of any recognized loss? Given the character of the loss, to what extent can Sara deduct the loss in the computation of taxable income for the year of sale?

Students should note that the research problems provided at the end of the chapters do not require students to perform the first two steps in the tax research process. These problems are deliberately written to contain all the facts necessary to solve the problem. Moreover, the problems provide the specific research question or questions for students to answer. Such is the nature (and weakness) of textbook research problems! But in the real world of tax practice, the first two tasks are not performed by anyone but the researcher. If the researcher fails to get the key facts, identify the important issues, and ask the right questions, all her subsequent efforts are futile.

STEP 3: LOCATE AUTHORITY

As the third step in the research process, the researcher heads for a tax library. Her mission is to locate authority providing answers to the research questions. Traditional libraries consist of shelves filled with books, loose-leaf binders, magazines, and other published materials containing all the technical minutiae of the tax law. Today, traditional libraries are disappearing as professional tax advisers gain access to the electronic libraries available on CD-ROM or the Internet. One obvious advantage of electronic libraries is the speed at which researchers can access sources of authority and move among the sources. A second advantage is the ease with which electronic databases can be updated to include current developments. A third advantage is that an electronic library is portable. A tax researcher with a laptop computer can access the library at any time and from any location.

Regardless of whether a tax researcher is working in a traditional or electronic library, she must be knowledgeable about the content and organization of the reference materials in that library. The researcher must know how to locate references pertaining to the problem at hand. The researcher must also be able to distinguish between the two main categories of reference materials: **primary authorities** and **secondary authorities.**

Primary Authorities

Objective 2
Identify primary sources of tax law.

Chapter 1 introduced the three sources of authority that comprise the federal tax law: statutory authority, administrative authority, and judicial authority. Recall that statutory tax rules enacted by Congress are compiled in the **Internal Revenue Code of 1986.** Administrative authority is provided by the Treasury Department in the form of written **Treasury regulations** interpreting the Internal Revenue Code.

The Internal Revenue Service provides additional administrative guidance in a variety of forms. **Revenue rulings** and **revenue procedures** were introduced in Chapter 1. The IRS also issues two types of administrative guidance that are authoritative only for the specific taxpayer to whom they are issued and cannot be relied on as authority by any other taxpayer. A taxpayer may request a **private letter ruling (PLR)** from the IRS regarding the appropriate tax treatment of a proposed transaction or a completed transaction for which a tax return has not yet been filed. The request must detail all relevant facts surrounding the transaction and requires the payment of a user's fee that could be as high as several thousand dollars. The PLR controls the tax treatment of the transaction for that taxpayer if it is completed in the manner described in the ruling request. A revenue agent or appeals officer can request a **technical advice memorandum (TAM)** during the examination or appeal of a taxpayer's return. The TAM represents the IRS position on a disputed item in the return and applies only to the taxpayer for whom it was issued.

When conflicts between taxpayers and the IRS cannot be resolved administratively, federal courts often hear tax cases. Their decisions represent judicial authority that interprets the tax law and often expands it beyond the narrow language of the Code. For researchers,

Tax Talk
IRS Tax Trails *offer interactive question and answer sessions to determine the solution to a variety of common tax questions. Find a list of* Trails *at http://www.irs .gov/ita/article/ 0,,id=219874,00 .html.*

the decisions rendered by these courts are important sources of primary authority in addition to the Code and the administrative pronouncements of the IRS and Treasury.

In federal tax matters, one of three trial courts has original jurisdiction. A taxpayer may refuse to pay the deficiency determined by the IRS and file a petition with the **U.S. Tax Court** to hear the case. Alternatively, the taxpayer may pay the deficiency, then immediately sue the government for a refund in either the local **U.S. District Court** or the **U.S. Court of Federal Claims** located in Washington, D.C. The losing party at the trial court level (taxpayer or government) may appeal the verdict to one of 13 **U.S. Circuit Courts of Appeals.** The geographic location of the trial court determines which appellate court has jurisdiction. These courts generally do not review findings of fact by a lower court, but they will consider if the lower court properly applied the relevant law to the facts. After the appellate court has either affirmed or reversed the trial court's decision, the losing party may appeal the case to the **U.S. Supreme Court.** This Court may agree to hear the case (*grant certiorari*) or refuse to hear it (*deny certiorari*). When the Supreme Court denies certiorari, the decision of the appellate court is final. During an average term, the Supreme Court hears no more than a dozen federal tax cases, which are selected either because the Court believes that the case involves a significant principle of law or because two or more appellate courts have rendered conflicting opinions on the proper resolution of a tax issue.

Evaluating Related Judicial Decisions	The legal decision rendered by a trial court or circuit court of appeals may be invalidated if a subsequent appeal reverses that decision. For example, consider the case of *Frank Lyons Co. v. U.S.* Lyons entered into a transaction involving the sale and leaseback of real estate. The company deducted depreciation on the real estate as the owner and lessor of the building. The IRS disallowed the deduction, asserting that under the substance over form doctrine depreciation should be taken by the lessee because it was the true owner of the building. The trial court in this case, the District Court for Eastern Arkansas (36 AFTR 2d 75-5154 [DC AR, 6/11/1975]), ruled in favor of the taxpayer. The IRS appealed the decision, and the 8th Circuit Court of Appeals (38 AFTR 2d 76-5060 [CA8, 5/26/1976]) reversed the District Court decision, ruling in favor of the government. Lyons appealed to the U.S. Supreme Court (41 AFTR 2d 78-1142 [US, 4/18/1978]), which reversed the 8th Circuit Court's decision, finally ruling in favor of the taxpayer. A tax researcher should only rely on the final decision in this sequence as valid legal authority. However, it might be necessary to read all three decisions in order to fully understand the facts and reasoning of the courts.

Exhibit 5.2 provides examples of citations to each type of statutory, administrative, and judicial authority discussed above. Because court cases are published in several different sources, multiple citations are possible for a single case. The exhibit lists alternative citations to sample decisions and the reporters in which they are published.

EXHIBIT 5.2
Sample Citations to Primary Authorities

Type of Authority	Citation(s)	Explanation
Internal Revenue Code	Section 1250(d)(1) Sec. 1250(d)(1) § 1250(d)(1)	Three alternative citations to the first paragraph, subsection d of Section 1250.
Treasury Regulations	Reg. Sec. 1.267-5(b) Reg. 1.267-5(b) Reg. § 1.267-5(b)	Three alternative citations to the fifth subpart of the regulations under Section 267.

(Continued)

Revenue Rulings	Rev. Rul. 89-257, 1989-1 C.B. 221	Citation to the 257th revenue ruling issued in 1989, appearing in the first volume of the 1989 cumulative bulletin, page 221.
Revenue Procedures	Rev. Proc. 2002-32, 2002-1 C.B. 959	Citation to the 32nd revenue procedure issued in 2002, appearing in the first volume of the 2002 cumulative bulletin, page 959.
U.S. Tax Court memorandum decisions	*Jack D. Carr*, T.C. Memo 1985-19 *Jack D. Carr*, PH TCM ¶85019 *Jack D. Carr*, 49 TCM 507.	Three alternative citations to a Tax Court memorandum decision. The first is published by the U.S. government, the second by Thomson Reuters (formerly RIA) and the third by CCH.
U.S. Tax Court regular decisions	*Teleservice Co. of Wyoming Valley*, 27 T.C. 722 (1957)	Citation to a regular Tax Court decision, published by the U.S. government.
U.S. District Court decisions	*Montgomery Engineering Co.* v. *U.S.*, 64-2 USTC ¶9618 (D.Ct. N.J., 1964) *Montgomery Engineering Co.* v. *U.S.*, 13 AFTR2d 1747 (D.Ct. N.J., 1964) *Montgomery Engineering Co.* v. *U.S.*, 230 F. Supp. 838 (D.Ct. N.J., 1964)	Three alternative citations to a 1964 district court case for New Jersey. The first is published by CCH, the second by Thomson Reuters, and the third by West.
U.S. Courts of Appeals	*Lengsfield* v. *Comm.*, 57-1 USTC ¶9437 (CA-5, 1957) *Lengsfield* v. *Comm.*, 50 AFTR 1683 (CA-5, 1957) *Lengsfield* v. *Comm.*, 241 F.2d 508 (CA-5, 1957)	Three alternative citations to a 1957 case before the Fifth Circuit Court of Appeals. The first is published by CCH, the second by Thomson Reuters, and the third by West.
U.S. Supreme Court	*U.S.* v. *Donruss Co.*, 69-1 USTC ¶9167 (USSC, 1969) *U.S.* v. *Donruss Co.*, 23 AFTR2d 69-418 (USSC, 1969) *U.S.* v. *Donruss Co.*, 89 S.Ct. 501 (USSC, 1969)	Three alternative citations to a 1969 case before the Supreme Court. The first is published by CCH, the second by Thomson Reuters, and the third by West.

Secondary Authorities

While primary authorities are required to adequately support tax conclusions and recommendations, they are written in detailed legal and technical language and are often difficult to understand and interpret. Secondary authorities, such as textbooks, treatises, professional journals, and commercial tax services, attempt to explain and interpret the tax law. Commercial tax services also organize information about primary authorities in a manner that facilitates tax research. While these resources are an excellent starting point in the tax research process, the researcher should always ensure that any conclusions drawn from secondary resources are adequately supported by the underlying primary authority. Our discussion of secondary authorities will focus on describing the content of the more popular commercial tax services. In the next section, we'll explore how these services can be used to guide the tax research process.

Traditionally, tax services are multivolume publications in looseleaf form, containing a wealth of tax information. Most services are now also available electronically, either on CD-ROM or over the Internet. While each service has its own organizational format and special features, there are commonalities in the type and scope of information presented. In paper format, tax services are organized either topically or by Code section. The popular Code-arranged tax services are *United States Tax Reporter* (published by Thomson Reuters) and *Standard Federal Tax Reporter* (published by CCH). The popular topically arranged tax services are *Federal Tax Coordinator 2d* (published by Thomson Reuters), *CCH Federal Tax Service* (published by CCH), *Law of Federal Income Taxation* (also called Mertens, published by West), and *Tax Management Portfolios* (published by BNA). In electronic format, each type of information is contained in a separate database, with the ability to search multiple databases and with frequent hyperlinks from items in one database to related items in other databases. The Checkpoint online tax research service includes both the *United States Tax Reporter* and *Federal Tax Coordinator 2d.* The CCH Internet Tax Research Network includes both *Standard Federal Tax Reporter* and *CCH Federal Tax Service.*

Although the format differs, the Thomson Reuters and CCH Code–arranged services contain similar information. These services reproduce the text of each Code section and related Treasury regulations. Each service also provides some legislative history for each Code section. Following each Code section and its regulations is an editorial explanation written by the publisher. The explanation attempts to clarify application of the Code section. While these editorial explanations are often helpful to researchers in locating primary authority, they do not themselves constitute primary authority and should not be cited. Following the editorial explanation, each service provides a citation listing and brief summary of court cases, revenue rulings, and other primary authorities relevant to the Code section under discussion. These summaries are helpful to the researcher in locating primary authority. Each service also contains a detailed topical index that can be searched for relevant keywords as a means to locate useful material. Finally, each service attempts to highlight current developments and incorporates new information into the text of the service on at least a monthly basis (more frequently in the online versions).

The topically oriented services are organized according to major topic areas, with more extensive editorial explanation of the application of tax law to specific topics. These services also provide citations to court cases, revenue rulings, and other primary authority related to the topics under discussion. The organization and content of the major topically oriented services differ considerably; experience working with a particular service will increase the researcher's efficiency in finding useful material.

Strategies for Locating Relevant Authority

Objective 3
Utilize secondary sources of tax law to locate primary authorities.

The materials used for tax research will depend on both the nature of the research question and the experience level of the researcher. Skilled researchers tend to rely on those materials they can use most efficiently to find answers to their questions in minimal time. They may bypass many of the steps suggested below as they find a research approach that works best for them. The novice researcher will tend to examine more materials in a methodical manner, so as to maximize her opportunities to find all relevant information. The strategies suggested below are just that—suggestions!

Let's suppose you have completed steps 1 and 2 of the research process, as described above, and are now ready to identify relevant authority. One option would be to go directly to the Internal Revenue Code and use the topical index for the Code to find the relevant

Code section. For some research questions, this approach may be sufficient to answer the question. However, what if this approach does not uncover a clear solution? In some cases, more than one Code section may seem to apply. In other cases, the Code may be very general, and the researcher may wish to find other authority that seems to match the specific facts at hand and more clearly support the research conclusions. To do so, the researcher may turn to one of the commercial tax services and adopt one or more of the following approaches: (1) Use the topical index, (2) use the table of contents, or (3) in an electronic service, use a keyword search.

Using the Topical Index

Each service provides a detailed topical index, listing hundreds of tax-related terms alphabetically. As with any index, a single term will appear in multiple places within the service; thus it may be necessary to check several referenced locations before the relevant use of the term is located. The researcher should also try several different wordings or related terms to ensure complete coverage of topics related to the issue being researched.

To illustrate this approach, suppose you are researching an issue related to the deductibility of losses incurred by an individual taxpayer related to a horse-breeding activity. You know from your study of taxation that such losses should be deductible if the activity is considered a trade or business rather than a hobby. A review of the topical index for the *United States Tax Reporter* under the letter "H" reveals the topic "Hobby losses and expenses." This topic heading lists four references for the general topic and also provides eight subtopics, including "horse ranching." Four additional references are listed for this subtopic. The researcher would turn to each of these references in the search for additional information.

Using the Table of Contents

A researcher may also wish to begin the search for authorities by scanning the table of contents of a tax service to locate an area of discussion that appears relevant. This approach is particularly useful with topically oriented services. For the novice researcher, this alternative has the additional benefit of helping the researcher become familiar with the organization of the service.

To illustrate this approach, let's reconsider our example involving horse breeding. The table of contents to the *Federal Tax Coordinator 2d* lists "Chapter M, Deductions: Losses, Bad Debts." Further examination of the table of contents reveals the following subchapter within Chapter M: "M-5800 Activities Not Engaged in for Profit—Hobby Losses." This portion of the service would seem a useful starting point in the search for information relevant to the research question.

Keyword Searching

In an electronic service, the researcher has the option of searching the entire database or a specified portion of the database for user-defined keywords. This type of search is similar to using a topical index but allows the researcher to combine words and phrases to target the search. While keyword searching can be very efficient, the researcher must take care to ensure that important information is not missed because the keywords were defined too narrowly.

Keyword Search Options	Checkpoint (and other online research databases) now offers two types of keyword searching: Terms & Connectors and Natural Language. The Natural Language search method uses regular language phrases to generate search results. For example, you could enter:
	Can I deduct utility costs for my home office?

> The Terms & Connectors method lets you search for documents by specifying words and phrases that describe your search. Specialized search connectors allow you to customize the search for more specific results. For example, you could enter:
>
> Utilities & "home office"

Tax Talk

TaxAlmanac is a source of free online tax research resources, offering access to statutory, administrative, and judicial authorities, as well as a variety of secondary resources, at http:// www.taxalmanac.org.

To return to our horse-breeding example, a Terms & Connectors keyword search could combine the phrase "hobby loss" and the word "horse" to narrow the identification of potential authorities relative to the material found via use of the topical index or table of contents entries regarding the hobby loss rules. Using the keyword search function in Checkpoint, the search *"hobby loss" & horse* identifies 74 documents within the federal income tax database in which the phrase "hobby loss" and the word "horse" appear. Each of these documents can then be examined by the researcher to determine their usefulness in answering the research question.

Once a promising starting point is located, via the topical index, table of contents, or a keyword search, the researcher can examine related material in the service. For example, if the search term is found within an editorial explanation, the researcher should read the related Code section, scan the regulations, and examine any references to court cases or other primary authorities to determine whether that material addresses the tax issue at hand. Cross-references within the material initially examined can also lead the researcher in promising directions for further exploration. When primary authorities have been identified that appear relevant, the researcher should read those sources carefully.

To return to our horse-breeding example, a review of the documents identified in the Checkpoint keyword search uncovers a reference to a U.S. Tax Court memorandum decision *Herbert C. Sanderson,* T.C. Memo 1964-284. In this case, a doctor and his wife were allowed a deduction for losses incurred in breeding, raising, showing, racing, and selling horses. This case should be examined further as possible authority to support a deduction for horse-breeding expenses.

Before relying on a judicial opinion to support research conclusions, one final step is needed to ensure that the opinion remains a valid interpretation of the law. In particular, has the decision been appealed and, if so, what was the result? The researcher might also wish to determine whether other courts have supported the conclusion of the court in the opinion in question. These issues can be assessed using an important resource called the **Citator.** The Citator may be used to determine the status of tax judicial decisions, Revenue Rulings, and Revenue Procedures. Citators are published by Thomson Reuters, CCH, and Shepard's and are also available through the major computerized tax services. For each case reported, the Citator provides a list of subsequent rulings that have referenced the case and a brief indication of the nature of the subsequent reference. For example, a review of the Thomson Reuters Citator listing for *Herbert C. Sanderson,* T.C. Memo 1964-284 reveals that the case was not appealed (no appellate court decision is listed), the case has been cited favorably in four subsequent cases, and the case has been distinguished (the cited case is distinguished either in law or on the facts) in one subsequent case. The Citator listing provides complete citations to each of these subsequent cases, which the researcher may wish to examine further.

If the first application of the process described above fails to provide an answer to the tax research question, additional iterations will be necessary. The researcher might proceed by trying other search terms, defining the search either more broadly or more narrowly, and combining use of the topical index, table of contents, and various keywords to discover useful information. The researcher may also wish to consult more than one service.

Applying Step 3	Return to the example involving Sara Colter's sale of land on pages 95 and 96. To begin your search for authority, you turn to the table of contents of the *Federal Tax Coordinator 2d*. You locate "Chapter I, Sales and Exchanges, Capital Gains and Losses, Cost Recovery Recapture, Depreciation Recapture." Within this chapter, Subchapter I-2500, "Amount of Gain or Loss on Sale or Exchange," refers you to Section 1001 of the Internal Revenue Code. When you examine this section, you determine that subsections (a) and (c) seem relevant.

> Section 1001. Determination of amount of and recognition of gain or loss
>
> (a) Computation of gain or loss
> The gain from the sale or other disposition of property shall be the excess of the amount realized therefrom over the adjusted basis provided in section 1011 for determining gain, and the loss shall be the excess of the adjusted basis provided in such section for determining loss over the amount realized.
>
> (c) Recognition of gain or loss
> Except as otherwise provided in this subtitle, the entire amount of the gain or loss, determined under this section, on the sale or exchange of property shall be recognized.

Section 1001(c) reminds you that gain or loss realized on a sale or exchange is not always recognized. Further examination of the subchapters of Chapter I in the *Federal Tax Coordinator 2d* reveals I-3500, "Losses Resulting from Sales and Exchanges between Related Taxpayers." This subchapter points you to Section 267, which provides that a taxpayer cannot recognize a loss realized on a sale to a related party.

STEP 4: ANALYZE AUTHORITY

Regardless of whether a researcher is reading from a printed page or a computer screen, she must have the skill to interpret and evaluate the authority at hand. In some cases, the authority may provide an unambiguous answer to the researcher's question. In other cases, the answer may be equivocal because the authority is inconclusive or subject to interpretation. Or perhaps different sources of authority provide conflicting answers. In these cases, the researcher must bring her judgment to bear in analyzing the authority and answering the question.

As part of the analytic process, the researcher should decide if the authority requires her to make a factual judgment or an evaluative judgment. In making a factual judgment, the researcher compares the authority to a set of facts. Assuming that the facts are complete and accurate, the researcher can provide a definitive answer to the research question. For example, consider the following research problem.

> Mr. Johnson provides 100 percent of the financial support for his 12-year-old granddaughter Cassie, who has lived in Mr. Johnson's home since 2004. Does Cassie qualify as Mr. Johnson's dependent?

Section 152 provides the relevant statutory authority for this research question.

> Section 152 Dependent defined
>
> (a) In general
> For purposes of this subtitle, the term "dependent" means—
> (1) a qualifying child, or
> (2) a qualifying relative.
>
> (c) qualifying child. For purposes of this section—
> (1) In general
> The term "qualifying child" means, with respect to any taxpayer for any taxable year, an individual—
> (A) who bears a relationship to the taxpayer described in paragraph (2),

(B) who has the same principal place of abode as the taxpayer for more than one-half of such taxable year,

(C) who meets the age requirements of paragraph (3), and

(D) who has not provided over one-half of such individual's own support for the calendar year in which the taxable year of the taxpayer begins.

(2) Relationship

For purposes of paragraph (1)(A), an individual bears a relationship to the taxpayer described in this paragraph if such individual is—

(A) a child of the taxpayer or a descendant of such a child, or

(B) a brother, sister, stepbrother, or stepsister of the taxpayer or a descendant of any such relative.

(3) Age requirements

(A) In general. For purposes of paragraph (1)(C), an individual meets the requirements of this paragraph if such individual—

(i) has not attained the age of 19 as of the close of the calendar year in which the taxable year of the taxpayer begins, or

(ii) is a student who has not attained the age of 24 as of the close of such calendar year.

By comparing the facts of this research problem to the relevant authority, a researcher can conclude that Cassie qualifies as Mr. Johnson's dependent. Therefore, the answer to the research questions is an unqualified yes.

Researchers are required to make evaluative judgments when the relevant authority relates to a conclusion inferred from a set of facts, rather than to the facts themselves. By definition, conclusions are subjective; different observers may draw different conclusions from the same facts. A researcher who must draw a conclusion to complete a research project can never be sure that such conclusion will go unchallenged by the IRS. Therefore, the researcher should never give an unqualified answer to a research question requiring an evaluative judgment. This point is illustrated by the following research problem.

Mrs. Clancy operates a business as sole proprietorship. Last week, she traveled to New York for an important meeting with a major client. Mrs. Clancy paid $2,615 for a first-class airline ticket and paid $340 per night for her hotel room. Can Mrs. Clancy deduct these business expenses on her Schedule C, Form 1040?

Section 162 provides the relevant statutory authority for this research question.

Sec. 162. Trade or business expenses

(a) In general

There shall be allowed as a deduction all the ordinary and necessary expenses paid or incurred during the taxable year in carrying on any trade or business, including—

(1) a reasonable allowance for salaries or other compensation for personal services actually rendered;

(2) traveling expenses (including amounts expended for meals and lodging other than amounts which are lavish or extravagant under the circumstances) while away from home in the pursuit of a trade or business.

This authority requires the researcher to evaluate the circumstances surrounding Mrs. Clancy's travel expenses. If the expenses were not lavish and extravagant, the entire amount is deductible. However, if some amount was lavish or extravagant, such amount is nondeductible. Note that the term "lavish or extravagant" is a matter of opinion, and reasonable persons might disagree as to whether the term describes Mrs. Clancy's expenses. If the researcher believes that the facts and circumstances support a conclusion that the travel expenses were not lavish or extravagant, the researcher could advise Mrs. Clancy to deduct the expenses. But the researcher should qualify this advice by explaining the risk that an IRS agent might draw the opposite conclusion and disallow the deduction.

*Applying
Step 4*

Return to the example involving Sara Colter's sale of land on pages 95, 96, and 103. On the basis of your reading of Section 1001(a), you determine that Sara will realize a $75,000 loss if she sells her land to CCM Inc. for $325,000 cash. According to the general rule of Section 1001(c), realized losses are recognized "except as otherwise provided in this subtitle." Therefore, Sara can recognize the loss and report it on her tax return for the year of sale unless Section 267 disallows the loss. The portions of Section 267 that seem applicable to Sara's case read as follows:

Sec. 267. Losses, expenses, and interest with respect to transactions between related taxpayers

(a) In general

(1) Deduction for losses disallowed
No deduction shall be allowed in respect of any loss from the sale or exchange of property, directly or indirectly, between persons specified in any of the paragraphs of subsection (b).

(b) Relationships
The persons referred to in subsection (a) are:

(2) An individual and a corporation more than 50 percent in value of the outstanding stock of which is owned, directly or indirectly, by or for such individual;

(c) Constructive ownership of stock
For purposes of determining, in applying subsection (b), the ownership of stock—

(3) An individual shall be considered as owning the stock owned, directly or indirectly, by or for his family;

(4) The family of an individual shall include only his brothers and sisters (whether by the whole or half blood), spouse, ancestors, and lineal descendants; and

(5) . . . stock constructively owned by an individual by reason of the application of paragraph (2) or (3) shall not be treated as owned by him for the purpose of again applying either of such paragraphs in order to make another the constructive owner of such stock.

According to Section 267(a)(1), Sara cannot recognize her realized loss if she and CCM Inc. are related parties. According to Section 267(b)(2), Sara and CCM Inc. are related parties if Sara directly or indirectly owns more than 50 percent in value of CCM's outstanding stock. You know that Sara does not own any CCM stock directly, but you are uncertain as to whether she owns any stock indirectly. Section 267(c)(2) provides that Sara is considered to own any CCM stock owned by her "family." When you refer to the facts you established during your first meeting with Sara, you discover that you do not know how many shares of CCM stock are owned by Sara's brother Jack and nephew Robert.

STEP 5: REPEAT STEPS 1 THROUGH 4

At some point in the research process, even an expert may discover that she failed to ascertain all the facts necessary to complete the analysis of the client's transaction. In such case, the researcher must repeat Step 1 by obtaining additional information from the client. Oftentimes the additional information suggests additional tax issues and research questions that the researcher must address. A researcher may have to repeat steps 1 through 4 several times before she is satisfied with the analysis.

*Applying
Step 5*

You contact Sara to ask one more question: How many shares of CCM stock do Jack and Robert each own? She replies that Jack owns 350 shares and Robert owns 200 shares of the 1,000 outstanding shares of CCM stock. With this additional fact, you can complete your analysis of Section 267 as it applies to Sara's proposed sale.

According to Section 267(c)(2), Sara's family includes her brother Jack but does not include her nephew Robert. Therefore, Sara indirectly owns the 350 CCM shares directly owned by Jack. However, Jack also indirectly owns the 200 CCM shares owned by his son Robert.

Section 267(c)(5) states that Jack's indirect ownership of these shares is disregarded for the purpose of determining Sara's ownership. On the basis of these statutory rules, you conclude that Sara directly and indirectly owns only 350 (35 percent) of CCM's 1,000 outstanding shares of stock. Thus, she and CCM Inc. are not related parties, Section 267(a) will not apply to her sale of the land to the corporation, and Sara can recognize her $75,000 realized loss.

You continue to analyze sources of information and sources of authority that pertain to your last two research questions. Sara's recognized loss is considered a capital loss if the land is considered a capital asset under Section 1221. The land is not a capital asset if it is considered property held for sale to customers under Section 1221(a)(1). This determination has been the topic of numerous judicial decisions. One recent case, *James E. Zurcher Jr.* v. *Commissioner*, T.C. Memo 1997-203, states in part:

> Whether the Property is a capital asset or was instead held primarily for sale in the ordinary course of petitioner's business is a factual determination. . . . Courts have developed the following nonexclusive factors to assist in this determination: (1) The nature of the taxpayer's business; (2) the taxpayer's purpose in acquiring and holding the property; (3) subdivision, platting, and other improvements tending to make the property more marketable; (4) the frequency, number, and continuity of sales; (5) the extent to which the taxpayer engaged in the sales activity; (6) the length of time the property was held; (7) the substantiality of income derived from the sales, and what percentage the income was of the taxpayer's total income; (8) the extent of advertising and other promotional activities; and (9) whether the property was listed directly or through brokers.

> Sara's stated purpose in acquiring the land was to hold it as a long-term investment. She has made no improvements to the property, engaged in no other real estate sales (other than of her personal residence), does not derive a substantial portion of her income from such sales, and does not advertise or promote real estate activities. On the basis of these facts, you conclude that Sara did not hold the land for sale in the ordinary course of business and thus the land is a capital asset and her loss is a long-term capital loss. She can deduct this loss in the year of sale to the extent of any capital gains recognized during the year. If the capital loss exceeds her capital gains, Sara is allowed to deduct $3,000 of the excess in the computation of adjusted gross income. Any nondeductible loss becomes a long-term capital loss carryforward into subsequent taxable years.

STEP 6: COMMUNICATE YOUR CONCLUSIONS

The tax researcher's task is to find an accurate, useful, and complete answer to the research question(s) concerning the client's situation. This task is not finished until the researcher documents her work by preparing a written summary of the research process. Such summary usually takes the form of a research memo that includes (1) a statement of the pertinent facts, (2) a statement of the research issue or issues, (3) an analysis of the relevant sources of authority, (4) an explanation of the researcher's conclusions, and (5) the details of any advice given to the client as part of the research engagement. While the content of a tax research memo is fairly standard, the order in which such content is presented can vary. For example, some researchers prefer to present their research conclusions immediately following statement of the issues and before the detailed analysis of legal authorities. This memo becomes a permanent record of the research process—a record to which the researcher (or any other professional) can refer at a future date.

The researcher also must communicate her conclusions to the client. Typically, the researcher writes a client letter containing information similar to that in the research memo.

In writing the letter, the researcher should tailor both the contents and the writing style to accommodate the client. For example, a letter to a client who has extensive tax knowledge may contain technical references that would be inappropriate in a letter to a client with minimal tax knowledge. Similarly, a letter to an individual who has been both a client and friend for many years may be written in an informal style that would be inappropriate for a letter to the chief financial officer of a new corporate client.

Applying Step 6	You write the following research memo for your permanent record.

March 5, 2011

TAX FILE MEMORANDUM

From: Bridget McGuffin
Subject: Sara Colter
              Engagement Research Conclusions

Summary of Facts

Sara Colter is considering a sale of 12 acres of undeveloped land to CCM Inc. at a proposed price of $325,000. The land was purchased in 2004 for $400,000 as a long-term investment from unrelated sellers, Mr. and Mrs. Bianca. Ms. Colter has made no improvements to the land since the date of purchase and has neither purchased nor sold any real estate with the exception of her personal residence. CCM Inc. is a closely held corporation with 1,000 shares of stock outstanding. Ms. Colter is not a shareholder of CCM; however, her brother Jack Colter and his son Robert Colter own 350 and 200 shares, respectively. Ms. Colter is not acquainted with any other CCM shareholders.

Research Issue

Is Ms. Colter entitled to recognize any realized loss on sale of the land?

Law and Analysis

Under Section 1001 of the Internal Revenue Code of 1986, Ms. Colter will realize a $75,000 loss on the proposed sale of the land equal to the excess of her adjusted basis in the land ($400,000 purchase price) over the amount realized on the sale ($325,000 proposed sales price). However, Section 267(a)(1) provides that no deduction is allowed for a loss from the sale or exchange of property between related parties, as defined in subsection (b) of Section 267. For this purpose, related parties include an individual and a corporation more than 50 percent in value of the outstanding stock of which is owned, directly or indirectly, by or for such individual. Although Ms. Colter does not directly own any stock in CCM Inc., we must consider whether ownership of CCM stock by her brother and nephew constitutes indirect ownership of more than 50 percent of the value of CCM stock.

Section 267(c)(2) provides that, in determining indirect ownership for purposes of Section 267(b), an individual is considered as owning the stock owned, directly or indirectly, by or for his family. Under Section 267(c)(4), family includes an individual's brothers, sisters, spouse, ancestors, and lineal descendants. Thus, Sara Colter is considered to own indirectly the stock owned by her brother Jack Colter, but not the stock owned by her nephew, Robert Colter. Note that Jack Colter would be considered to indirectly own the stock owned by his son, Robert Colter. However, under Section 267(c)(5), Jack's indirect ownership of these shares is disregarded in determining Sara's ownership. Thus, Sara Colter indirectly owns 350 shares of CCM Inc., equaling 35 percent of its 1,000 outstanding shares of stock. Because Ms. Colter's ownership of CCM is less than 50 percent, the related party loss disallowance rule of Section 267(a) does not apply.

Ms. Colter's recognized loss is considered a capital loss if the land is considered a capital asset under Section 1221. The land is not a capital asset if it is considered property held for sale to customers (Section 1221(a)(1)). This determination has been the topic of numerous judicial decisions. One recent case, *James E. Zurcher Jr. v. Commissioner*, T.C. Memo 1997-203, states in part:

> Whether the Property is a capital asset or was instead held primarily for sale in the ordinary course of petitioner's business is a factual determination. . . . Courts have developed the following nonexclusive factors to assist in this determination: (1) The nature of the taxpayer's business; (2) the taxpayer's purpose in acquiring and holding the property; (3) subdivision, platting, and other improvements tending to make the property more marketable; (4) the frequency, number, and continuity of sales; (5) the extent to which the

taxpayer engaged in the sales activity; (6) the length of time the property was held; (7) the substantiality of income derived from the sales, and what percentage the income was of the taxpayer's total income; (8) the extent of advertising and other promotional activities; and (9) whether the property was listed directly or through brokers.

Ms. Colter's stated purpose in acquiring the land was to hold it as a long-term investment. She has made no improvements to the property, engaged in no other real estate sales (other than of her personal residence), does not derive a substantial portion of her income from such sales, and does not advertise or promote real estate activities. These facts support the conclusion that Ms. Colter did not hold the land for sale in the ordinary course of business and thus the land is a capital asset.

Conclusions

Ms. Colter will recognize a $75,000 capital loss. Because she held the land for more than one year, the loss will be a long-term capital loss. If the loss exceeds any recognized capital gains, under Section 1211(b) she may deduct $3,000 of the excess in computing adjusted gross income. Any nondeductible loss may be carried forward into subsequent taxable years.

You also write the following letter to Sara Colter.

March 5, 2011

Ms. Sara Colter
1812 Riverbend Place
Kirkwood, Missouri 62119

Dear Ms. Colter:

This letter is in response to your inquiry concerning the tax consequences of a proposed sale of 12 acres of undeveloped land to CCM Inc. Before stating my conclusions, I'd like to summarize the facts of your case. You purchased the land in 2004 as a long-term investment. The purchase price was $400,000 and the sellers of the property, Mr. and Mrs. Bianca, are unrelated to you. You have not improved the land in any way since date of purchase and have neither purchased nor sold any other real estate with the exception of your personal residence. CCM Inc. is a closely held corporation with 1,000 shares of outstanding stock. Although you do not own any shares, your brother Jack Colter and his son Robert Colter own 350 and 200 shares, respectively. You are not acquainted with any other CCM stockholders. The accuracy of my conclusions depends entirely on my understanding of these facts. Consequently, if the statement of facts is in any way incorrect or incomplete, please notify me immediately.

If you sell your land to CCM Inc. for the proposed contract price of $325,000, you will realize a $75,000 loss. This loss equals the excess of your $400,000 investment in the land over the $325,000 cash you will receive at closing. You are allowed to report this loss on your individual tax return in the year of sale unless you and CCM Inc. are "related parties" within the meaning of the tax law. According to my research, you and CCM Inc. do not meet the statutory definition of "related parties," even though your brother and nephew own an aggregate 55 percent interest in CCM Inc. Therefore, you can report your $75,000 loss for tax purposes. Because you held the land for investment and owned it for more than one year, the loss is classified as a long-term capital loss. You can deduct a long-term capital loss to the extent of your capital gains for the year. If your capital loss exceeds your capital gains, you can deduct only $3,000 of the excess loss against other sources of income.

Thank you for giving my firm the opportunity to advise you in this matter. If you have any questions about my conclusions, please don't hesitate to call me. If you proceed with your plans to sell the land, I would be glad to meet with you to develop a strategy to maximize your deduction for the projected $75,000 capital loss.

Sincerely,

Bridget McGuffin

Conclusion

Given the length and complexity of existing tax law, tax research is a critical skill for the tax practitioner. Tax research often occurs as part of tax compliance and is also important to the tax planning process by allowing the researcher to identify and explore the tax consequences of alternative investment and business choices. The six steps reviewed in this chapter provide a guide to the novice tax researcher in formulating research questions, identifying and analyzing relevant authority, and communicating research results. As the tax researcher gains experience and familiarity with the variety of legal resources available, the tax research process will become a natural part of strategic tax planning.

Now that you've completed Part Two of *Principles of Taxation for Business and Investment Planning,* you should appreciate how tax planning strategies can reduce costs and increase the NPV of business transactions. In addition, you have learned the basics of tax research necessary to analyze the tax consequences of tax planning alternatives. The framework for a thorough understanding of the tax planning process is in place. Parts Three and Four of the text build on this framework by presenting the basics of the income tax law: how firms compute annual taxable income and the federal tax on that income. As you integrate this legal knowledge into your understanding of taxes as financial costs, your appreciation of the tax planning process will progress from the abstract to the specific.

Key Terms

Citator *102*
Internal Revenue Code of
  1986 *97*
primary authorities *97*
private letter ruling
  (PLR) *97*
revenue procedures *97*

revenue rulings *97*
secondary authorities *97*
technical advice
  memorandum (TAM) *97*
Treasury regulations *97*
U.S. Circuit Courts of
  Appeals *98*

U.S. Court of Federal
  Claims *98*
U.S. District Court *98*
U.S. Supreme Court *98*
U.S. Tax Court *98*

Questions and Problems for Discussion

1. Why is tax research necessary? In other words, why is it not possible for experienced tax professionals to answer all tax questions without performing tax research?

2. Why is it important for a tax researcher to understand the client's motivation in undertaking a transaction? How will this knowledge assist the tax professional in serving her client?

3. Explain the difference between a tax issue and a research question.

4. Explain the difference between primary and secondary authorities as sources of tax information. On which type of authority should professional tax research conclusions be based?

5. Discuss why and how a researcher might use secondary authorities in performing tax research.

6. If a trial court decision has been appealed and the appellate court reversed the trial court's decision, which of the two court decisions is considered authoritative? Briefly explain your answer.

7. Explain why a researcher should consult the Citator before relying on a judicial opinion to support research conclusions.

8. Describe two alternative strategies for using a tax service to locate primary authorities.

9. Explain why, in the course of tax research, it may be necessary for the researcher to gather more facts.

10. Discuss potential differences in content and style between a research memo and a client letter communicating research results.

Application Problems

1. As discussed in Chapter 3, the IRS carefully scrutinizes transactions between related parties. Several different code sections define which taxpayers are considered related parties. Suppose that Marsha and Jan are sisters. Are they considered family members and, therefore, related parties under Section 318(a)(1)? How about under Section 267(b)(1)?

2. One of your clients is planning to sell a piece of raw land and expects to incur a substantial gain on the sale. He has asked you to determine whether this gain will be considered capital gain or ordinary income. List five specific questions you should ask your client to gather more information prior to beginning your research.

3. One of your clients is planning to start a business. She has incurred costs to investigate potential locations for the business and hired a consultant to conduct a feasibility study. She wishes to know whether such costs will be currently deductible. List five specific questions you should ask your client to gather more information prior to beginning your research.

4. Find and provide a citation for the IRC section that defines taxable income. Be precise in your reference (e.g., Section 61(a)(1), not Section 61).

5. Find and provide a citation for the IRC section that provides an exclusion from gross income for interest earned on investments in state and local bonds. Be precise in your reference (e.g., Section 61(a)(1), not Section 61).

6. Find and provide a citation for the IRC section that defines a capital asset. Be precise in your reference (e.g., Section 61(a)(1), not Section 61).

7. Find Rev. Rul. 72-542, 1972-2 CB 37, and answer the following questions. The purpose of these questions is to enhance your skills in reading and interpreting authorities that you locate while doing tax research.

   a. What are the basic tax issues addressed in the revenue ruling?

   b. Which of the basic tax legal doctrines discussed in Chapter 4 is applied in this ruling?

   c. From the ruling, identify the IRC section defining gross income.

   d. From the ruling, identify the IRC section permitting a charitable contribution deduction.

   e. Has this ruling been cited in other rulings or cases? If so, how many times?

8. Find a 2006 10th Circuit Court of Appeals decision involving *Roger L. Watkins* and answer the following questions. The purpose of these questions is to enhance your skills in reading and interpreting authorities that you locate while doing tax research.

   a. What is the complete citation to the case?

   b. What is the citation to the original trial court decision to which this appeal relates?

   c. In your own words, explain the basic tax issues addressed in the case.

   d. Which of the four basic tax planning variables described in Chapter 4 is at issue in this case?

   e. Has this case been cited in other cases? If so, how many times?

9. Cameron owns an antique car that she inherited from her father. She is planning to sell it over the Internet and is wondering about the tax consequences of such a sale. If you were to research this question using a keyword search in an electronic library, what keywords would you use? Propose three distinct keyword searches that could get you started researching this issue.

10. Refer to the facts in question 7. Using an electronic research database such as Checkpoint, CCH Tax Research NetWork, or LexisNexis, run the keyword searches

you proposed in question 7. Include both primary sources and editorial materials in your search. How many documents did each search locate? Explain which of your searches you feel would be most useful in researching this issue.

11. Using an electronic research database such as Checkpoint, CCH Tax Research Network, or LexisNexis, do a keyword search that includes both the phrase *capital gain* and the keyword *livestock*. Include both primary sources and editorial materials in your search.

    a. How many documents did your search find that meet these search criteria?

    b. Of the documents found, how many represent primary authorities and how many are secondary authorities?

    c. Of the documents found, provide citations to two primary authorities and two secondary authorities.

12. IRC Section 117 provides that qualified educational scholarships are not taxable in certain circumstances. Included in this exclusion are both scholarships and fellowship grants.

    a. Use Section 117 and the related regulations to find definitions of the terms *scholarship* and *fellowship grant* and provide precise citations to the code and/or regulation sections containing these definitions.

    b. In your own words, explain the distinction between a scholarship and a fellowship grant.

13. Find the IRS Revenue Procedure that gives the standard deduction amounts for the 2009 tax year. Typically the Revenue Procedure is released in the fourth quarter of the previous year. Prepare a table reporting the standard deduction amounts and their associated filing statuses. Also report the full citation for your source, in the form of the following example: Rev. Proc. 98-1, 1998-1 C.B. 7.

14. Using an electronic research database such as Checkpoint, CCH Tax Research NetWork, or LexisNexis, do a keyword search on the phrase *hobby loss* to find secondary authorities discussing the tax treatment of losses incurred in pursuing activities as a hobby.

    a. Provide citations to three of the secondary authorities you located.

    b. Provide citations to three primary authorities referenced in the secondary authorities found in your search, including the IRC section that addresses the tax treatment of hobby losses.

    c. Does the IRC section identified in part (b) contain the phrase *hobby loss*? What phrase does the IRC section use to refer to activities considered a hobby?

15. In researching a tax issue, you locate the case *Stern, Sidney B. & Vera L.*, 77 T.C. 614 which seems relevant to your issue. However, before completing your research you check the Citator for subsequent information about the case. What do you find in the Citator for this case that indicates you should not rely on it as judicial authority?

16. Find a tax glossary on any freely accessible website and provide the URL. Also find and provide a citation for the IRC section that defines a long-term capital gain.

    a. What is the tax glossary's definition of a long-term capital gain?

    b. How does the IRC define a long-term capital gain?

    c. Of the two definitions, which would a taxpayer without extensive tax knowledge find easier to understand? Why?

    d. Which of the two definitions is relevant for a tax researcher? Why?

17. Find Revenue Ruling 83-163, 1983-2 CB 26, and answer the following questions. The purpose of these questions is to enhance your skills in reading and interpreting authorities that you locate while doing research.

    a. To which Code section(s) does this revenue ruling relate?

    b. *In your own words*, briefly explain why the taxpayers were required to include the value of barter club services received in their gross incomes.

    c. Find the most recent court case citing this revenue ruling and provide the citation to the case.

18. Using an electronic research database such as Checkpoint, CCH Tax Research NetWork, or LexisNexis, find the case *Mortex Manufacturing Co., Inc.*, T.C. Memo 1994-110, and answer the following questions. The purpose of these questions is to enhance your skills in reading and interpreting authorities that you locate while doing research.

    a. What is the general controversy being litigated in this case?

    b. Which party—the taxpayer or the government—won the case?

    c. What is the relationship between Max Deason, the founder of the business, and Carlene Deason, the vice president?

    d. For the 1988 and 1989 tax years, how much salary did Carlene Deason receive from the corporation? What did the court decide was a reasonable amount of compensation for her for those years?

    e. Why did the court conclude that the salary paid to Carlene Deason was excessive?

    f. Was this case appealed? How did you determine your answer?

19. Using an electronic research database such as Checkpoint, CCH Tax Research NetWork, or LexisNexis, find the case *Thomas A. Curtis, M.D., Inc., 1994 TC Memo ¶94,015*, and answer the following questions. The purpose of these questions is to enhance your skills in reading and interpreting authorities that you locate while doing research.

    a. What is the general controversy being litigated in this case?

    b. Which party—the taxpayer or the government—won the case?

    c. Why is the plaintiff the corporation instead of Dr. and/or Mrs. Curtis?

    d. What is the relationship between Ellen Barnett Curtis and Dr. Thomas A. Curtis?

    e. For the fiscal year ended in 1989, how much salary did Ms. Curtis receive from the corporation? What did the court decide was a reasonable amount of compensation for her for that year?

    f. Was this case appealed? How did you determine your answer?

Issue Recognition Problems

Identify the tax issue or issues suggested by the following situations and state each issue in the form of a question.

1. In researching the taxability of noncash compensation, a tax researcher identifies a judicial decision that seems to address the issue at hand. However, the decision was rendered in 1975, and the researcher knows that the tax law has changed many times in the last 36 years.

2. Guenther is researching a tax issue involving the deductibility of costs to remodel an office building. He has found several authorities permitting such costs to be deducted, and several others requiring that remodeling costs be capitalized and depreciated for tax purposes.

3. Marvin is researching the tax rules related to Individual Retirement Accounts. He is very confused by the information he has found in the IRC and Treasury regulations

regarding deductibility of IRA contributions. However, he has found an IRS publication on the IRS website that provides a much clearer explanation of the rules.

4. Allison works full time as a dental hygienist. She devotes her spare time to designing and creating stained glass pieces. During the past year, she has sold 10 of her pieces at local craft fairs and was recently commissioned to create three stained glass windows for the home of a new customer. She has incurred a number of expenses for taking stained glass classes, purchasing materials and tools, and participating in craft fairs.

5. John is a dentist. His neighbor Wade is a carpenter. John has agreed to perform dental work for Wade and his wife in exchange for Wade's installing a new laminate floor in John's dental office.

6. Marybeth works as a financial analyst at a brokerage firm. At night, she is taking courses to complete her MBA degree. Her firm pays 50 percent of her tuition cost for these courses, and Marybeth pays the remainder personally.

7. Argonaut Corporation sustained considerable damage to one of its warehouses during a recent hurricane. It expects to pay $200,000 to replace the roof of the building and repair other damage. It is unclear at this point whether any of the loss will be compensated by insurance.

8. Natalie appeared on a game show last year and won a car valued at $30,000. After driving it for six months, she sold it for $24,000.

Research Problems

1. Find the IRS website and locate the following items:
   a. Find the IRS publication dealing with moving expenses. What is its publication number?
   b. Find the IRS publication providing tax information relevant to divorced or separated individuals. What is its publication number?
   c. Find the IRS publication dealing with charitable contributions. What is its publication number?
   d. Find the tax form for reporting depreciation deductions for business assets. What is the form number?
   e. Find form 4626. What is the title of this form?

2. Find the Internal Revenue Code on any freely accessible website and provide the URL. Do you consider the site reliable? Why or why not? What assurance, if any, does the site provide that its information is accurate and up to date?

3. Find the website for the U.S. Treasury Department and report its URL. Who is the current secretary of the Treasury? Find the equivalent of the U.S. Treasury Department for one of the following countries: Western Australia, Germany, Japan, or Spain. Report that URL. If you have difficulty finding the foreign countries, start at *The Tax and Accounting Sites Directory* found at http://www.taxsites.com/international.html.

Tax Planning Cases

1. Art likes to invest his spare cash in the stock market. In the past, he has focused on growth stocks and long-term value, to take advantage of the preferential tax rate on long-term capital gains. He recently learned that this rate is also available for dividend income. However, he is confused by his brokerage statement, which lists both qualifying dividends and nonqualifying dividends.

   For Art's benefit, investigate the requirements under which dividends qualify for the preferential tax rate. Write a letter to Art communicating the results of your research.

2. Lance Strongarm, a recently retired professional athlete, is writing his memoirs. He intends to direct any royalties received on the book to his favorite charitable organization. He has not yet signed a contract with a publisher.

   Will the future royalties be included in Lance's taxable gross income? Why or why not? If your answer is yes, is any alternative arrangement available that Lance might make to avoid gross income recognition? Prepare a written memorandum stating the research issue(s), your conclusions concerning the issues(s), and the specific statutory, regulatory, or judicial authority supporting your conclusions.

3. Lucille is an avid boater living near Gotham City. Gotham has recently created a harbor improvement special assessment district to oversee renovations to the public boat docks and boardwalk area surrounding the city harbor. The special assessment district plans to issue bonds to fund a portion of the planned improvements. Lucille is considering an investment in these bonds, but is unsure whether the interest income she would earn qualifies for tax exemption. Prepare a written memorandum stating the research issue(s), your conclusions concerning the issues(s), and the specific statutory, regulatory, or judicial authority supporting your conclusions.

The Measurement of Taxable Income

6 Taxable Income from Business Operations

7 Property Acquisitions and Cost Recovery Deductions

8 Property Dispositions

9 Nontaxable Exchanges

Taxable Income from Business Operations

Learning Objectives

After studying this chapter, you should be able to:

1. Describe the relationship between business operating cycle and taxable year.

2. Identify the permissible methods of accounting for tax purposes.

3. Explain why tax policy objectives affect the taxable income computation.

4. Apply the cash method of accounting to compute taxable income.

5. Contrast the principles of conservatism reflected by GAAP and by the tax law.

6. Differentiate between a permanent and a temporary book/tax difference.

7. Explain the difference between tax expense per books and tax payable.

8. Apply the tax accounting rules for prepaid income and accrued expenses.

9. Explain how the NOL deduction smooths taxable income over time.

The keynote of the text to this point has been the role of taxes in the business decision-making process. We've been concerned with income and deductions only in the generic sense and have worked through a series of hypothetical transactions demonstrating how income and deductions result in tax costs and tax savings. We have incorporated these costs and savings into cash flow models for computing the net present value (NPV) of the transactions.

In Part Three, our attention turns to the statutory, regulatory, and judicial rules governing the measurement of taxable income. Chapter 6 examines the effect of a firm's choice of a taxable year and a method of accounting on the measurement process, with emphasis on the differences between the computation of financial statement income and taxable income. In contrast to earlier chapters, this chapter contains numerous references to the Internal Revenue Code, Treasury regulations, and court cases pertaining to the computation of taxable income. We will analyze this new technical material in terms of its effect on cash flows and its relevance to the tax planning process. In doing so, we will accomplish one of the main objectives of *Principles of Taxation for Business and Investment Planning*—bridging the gap between finance courses that assume knowledge of the tax law and traditional law courses that ignore the role of taxes in the larger context of financial decision making.

BUSINESS PROFIT AS TAXABLE INCOME

[handwritten margin notes:]
Gross Income
Taxable Incom
Gross Income
— allowable deductions
Taxable Incom

The base for the federal income tax is **taxable income,** defined as gross income minus allowable deductions.[1] The Internal Revenue Code defines **gross income** by stating that "gross income means all income from whatever source derived."[2] In a business context, gross income consists primarily of revenues from the sale of goods or performance of services in the regular course of a commercial activity. Gross income from the sale of tangible goods by a manufacturer, wholesaler, or retailer equals gross receipts less cost of goods sold.[3] Gross income from the performance of services includes all charges, fees, commissions, and bonuses received as compensation. Gross income also includes rents received for the occupancy of real estate or the use of tangible personalty, royalties received for the use of intellectual properties (copyrights, trademarks, formulas, patents, and software), and interest and dividends received as a return on invested capital.

Gross Income	
Calzo Company sells lighting and plumbing fixtures to wholesale and retail customers and provides installation and repair services for its products. Calzo owns a warehouse and sublets surplus space to another company. It invests its excess working capital in a money market account. This year, Calzo derived the following items of gross income from its commercial activities.	

Gross receipts from sales	$2,436,100	
Cost of goods sold	(1,606,400)	
Gross income from sales		$ 829,700
Gross receipts from services		512,900
Rent revenue		38,100
Interest on money market account		1,010
Gross income from commercial activities		$1,381,710

The federal courts have consistently ruled that the concept of gross income *from whatever source derived* is broad enough to include any accession to wealth or increase in net worth.[4] Consequently, firms may derive gross income from events or transactions occurring outside the course of their routine commercial activities.

Discharge of Debt Income	
Calzo Company had an $18,000 overdue account payable to a major supplier. The supplier needed to settle the account as quickly and as advantageously as possible. After some negotiation, Calzo paid $14,000 cash to the supplier in full settlement of the account payable. Because Calzo extinguished an $18,000 liability with only $14,000 of assets, its net worth increased by $4,000, an increase that Calzo must include in gross income.[5]	

[1] §63(a).

[2] §61(a).

[3] Reg. §1.61-3(a).

[4] *Commissioner* v. *Glenshaw Glass Co.,* 348 U.S. 426 (1955).

[5] §61(a)(12).

The Internal Revenue Code allows a deduction for "all the ordinary and necessary expenses paid or incurred during the taxable year in carrying on any trade or business."[6] According to judicial interpretation, an expense is ordinary if it is customary for a particular type of trade or business and is commonly or frequently incurred. An expense is necessary if it is appropriate and helpful for the development of the business and the generation of revenue.[7] Because of this broad authorization, firms can deduct most routine operating expenses in the computation of taxable income. They can also deduct the various state, local, and foreign taxes incurred in carrying on their business activities.[8] Firms can even deduct the cost of assets acquired for long-term use in their business; these cost recovery deductions (such as depreciation) are typically spread over some extended period of years. Cost recovery deductions are discussed in detail in Chapter 7. Because the tax law allows firms to deduct expenses and costs incurred in revenue-generating activities, the federal income tax is imposed on *net profit* rather than gross receipts.

Necessary Ordinary expenses (handwritten margin note)

Taxable Income

This year, Calzo Company incurred $722,900 deductible operating expenses and was allowed a $30,114 depreciation deduction. Consequently, Calzo's taxable income was $632,696.

Gross income from commercial activities	$1,381,710
Gross income from discharge of debt	4,000
Deductible operating expenses	(722,900)
Depreciation deduction	(30,114)
Taxable income	$ 632,696

THE TAXABLE YEAR

A firm must measure its taxable income every year and pay tax on an annual basis. Firms have considerable latitude with respect to the 12-month period over which to measure income. A firm's taxable year generally corresponds to its annual accounting period for financial statement purposes.[9] If a firm keeps its financial books and records on a **calendar year,** it measures taxable income over the same January through December period. If a firm keeps its financial records on a **fiscal year** (any 12-month period ending on the last day of any month except December), it uses this fiscal year as its taxable year.[10]

Objective 1
Describe the relationship between business operating cycle and taxable year.

The choice of a calendar or fiscal year is usually dictated by the firm's operating cycle; firms want to close their books and calculate their profit at the end of a natural cycle of business activity. A retail clothing store might find that a February 28 fiscal year-end most accurately reflects an operating cycle that peaks during the holiday season and reaches its lowest point before the beginning of the spring season. A ski resort might use a May 31 fiscal year-end so that its financial statements reflect the profit from an operating cycle that ends when the snow finally melts off the slopes.

---

[6] §162(a).

[7] *Daniel E. Fuhrman,* TC Memo 2011-236.

[8] §164(a). Firms may forgo a deduction for foreign income taxes paid to claim a credit for these taxes against their federal income tax liability. The foreign tax credit is discussed in Chapter 13.

[9] §441(b) and (c).

[10] Firms may also use a 52–53-week year for financial statement and tax return purposes. A 52–53-week year is an annual period that is either 52 or 53 weeks long and that always ends on the same day of the week. §441(f).

Changing a Taxable Year

As a general rule, a new business entity establishes its taxable year by filing an initial tax return on the basis of such year.[11] The initial return reflects taxable income or loss from the date business began until the end of the year. As a result, an initial return typically reflects a short period of less than 12 months. After establishing a taxable year, a firm can't change its year unless it formally requests and receives permission to do so from the IRS.[12] This requirement has particular significance when an individual begins a new business as a sole proprietor and wants to keep records on a fiscal year basis. In all likelihood, the individual has always filed a calendar year tax return. Although the business itself is new, the taxable entity (the owner) is already established as a calendar year taxpayer. Consequently, the individual must request permission from the IRS to change to a fiscal year conforming to the sole proprietorship's accounting records.

When a firm has a convincing reason for changing its annual accounting period, the IRS usually grants permission for the firm to change its taxable year. If the firm lacks a convincing reason, the IRS may withhold permission for the change. In those cases in which the IRS grants permission, the firm files a **short-period return** to accomplish the change.

Changing a Taxable Year

Corporation B, a calendar year taxpayer since 1985, recently developed a new line of business with an annual operating cycle ending in midsummer. The corporation requests and receives permission from the IRS to change to a fiscal year ending July 31. To move from a calendar year to a fiscal year, the corporation files a return for the seven-month period from January 1 through July 31. Corporation B's returns for future years will reflect a 12-month taxable year from August 1 through July 31. This change in taxable years is illustrated by the following time line.

Annualizing Income on a Short-Period Return

Because a short-period return reflects less than a full year of income, the tax on that income might be abnormally low. To demonstrate this possibility, assume that Corporation B in the previous example generates $10,000 monthly income. In a 12-month year, the corporation's average tax rate is 25.04 percent. However, in a taxable year consisting of only seven months, the average tax rate falls to 17.86 percent.

---

[11] Reg. §1.441-1(c)(1).

[12] §442. Rev. Proc. 2006-45, 2006-45 IRB 851, provides that certain corporations that have not changed their taxable year within a 48-month period ending with the close of the proposed year can change their year without IRS approval.

	12-Month Year	7-Month Year
Taxable income	$120,000	$70,000
Tax on:		
First $50,000 at 15%	$ 7,500	$ 7,500
Next $25,000 at 25%	6,250	5,000
Next $25,000 at 34%	8,500	
Next $20,000 at 39%	7,800	
Total tax	$ 30,050	$12,500

12-month year: $30,050 tax ÷ $120,000 taxable income = 25.04%
7-month year: $12,500 tax ÷ $ 70,000 taxable income = 17.86%

The 7.18 percent rate reduction would result in a $5,026 permanent tax savings ($70,000 × 7.18 percent) to Corporation B. The savings results from the application of progressive rates to a truncated tax base.

The federal tax law prevents this result when a firm files a short-period return to change its taxable year. The taxable income reported on the return must be **annualized**—mathematically inflated to reflect 12 months of operations.[13] The tax is calculated on the inflated base, then deflated to reflect the actual number of months covered by the return. Let's annualize Corporation B's taxable income on its short-period return and see what happens.

	7-Month Year
Taxable income	$ 70,000
Multiplied by inflation factor (12 months ÷ 7 months)	1.7143
Annualized income	$120,000
Tax on annualized income	$ 30,050
Multiplied by deflation factor (7 months ÷ 12 months)	.5833
Total tax	$ 17,528

$17,528 tax ÷ $70,000 taxable income = 25.04%

Corporation B's average tax rate on the short-period return is 25.04 percent, the same rate at which it pays tax on a normal 12-month basis. Because of the annualization requirement, firms reap no tax benefit when they file a short-period return because of a change in their taxable year. The requirement is inapplicable to short-period returns filed because the taxable entity was *in existence* for only a portion of a taxable year.[14] Accordingly, the short-period income reported on the first return filed by a new business entity or the last return filed by an entity going out of business may be taxed at a bargain rate.

[13] §443(b).
[14] Reg. §1.443-1(a)(2).

No Annualization Required	Corporation W, a calendar year taxpayer since 1988, ceased operations and dissolved under state law on March 31. For the last 25 years, the corporation's average tax rate on annual income was 34 percent. On its last federal tax return, Corporation W reported $96,200 taxable income earned from January 1 through March 31. Because it was in existence for only three months, the corporation was not required to compute its tax on an annualized basis, and its tax on the short-period return was $20,958.

Tax on:	
First $50,000 at 15%	$ 7,500
Next $25,000 at 25%	6,250
Next $21,200 at 34%	7,208
Total tax	$20,958

Consequently, Corporation W's average tax rate for its last year was only 21.79 percent ($20,958 tax ÷ $96,200 taxable income).

METHODS OF ACCOUNTING

Objective 2
Identify the permissible methods of accounting for tax purposes.

After establishing its taxable year, a firm must assign the items of income and deduction from its transactions to a particular year. To do this, the firm must adopt a **method of accounting:** a consistent system for determining the point in time at which items of income and deduction are *recognized* (taken into account) for tax purposes. The Internal Revenue Code permits firms to use the cash receipts and disbursements (cash) method, the accrual method, or a combined (hybrid) method as their overall method of computing taxable income.[15] We will discuss each of these three methods later in the chapter. The Code also provides specialized methods of accounting that apply only to particular transactions. For example, firms that contract to manufacture an item of property that will take more than 12 months to complete (an oceangoing oil tanker, for example) must use the Section 460 percentage-of-completion method of accounting to measure the annual taxable income from the contract.

The tax law acknowledges that "no uniform method of accounting can be prescribed for all taxpayers. Each taxpayer shall adopt such forms and systems as are, in his judgment, best suited to his needs."[16] Moreover, a taxpayer engaged in more than one business may use a different method of accounting for each business.[17] This permissive attitude is tempered by a caveat: "No method of accounting is acceptable unless, in the opinion of the Commissioner [of the IRS], it clearly reflects income."[18] Thus, the IRS has the right to satisfy itself that a firm's method of income **recognition** accurately measures its ability to pay federal tax.

Tax Talk
Pharmaceutical giant Glaxo paid $3.4 billion to the IRS to settle a two-decade-long Section 482 dispute over the accounting method used to allocate income between the British parent corporation and its American subsidiary.

When related parties enter into business transactions, the IRS has particular reason to scrutinize the methods of accounting used to report the tax consequences, and it has broad authority to challenge these methods. Section 482 of the Internal Revenue Code states that in the case of two or more businesses under common ownership or control, the IRS may "distribute, apportion, or allocate gross income, deduction, credits, or allowances" among the businesses to clearly reflect the income of each.

[15] §446(c).
[16] Reg. §1.446-1(a)(2).
[17] §446(d).
[18] Reg. §1.446-1(a)(2).

The IRS typically invokes Section 482 when a method of accounting results in a beneficial shift of income between related parties. The following example illustrates this situation.

Using an Accounting Method to Shift Income	ABC Inc. and XYZ Inc. are owned by the same group of investors. ABC operates a manufacturing business, and XYZ is a regional wholesaler that purchases its inventory from a number of suppliers, including ABC. ABC's marginal tax rate is 35 percent, and XYZ's marginal tax rate is only 15 percent. As a result, the owners have an incentive to shift income from ABC to XYZ. They accomplish this shift by having ABC sell its product to XYZ at cost instead of the market price charged to unrelated wholesalers. When XYZ sells ABC's product to its customers, the entire profit with respect to the manufacture and sale of the product is included in XYZ's income.

In the above example, ABC's method of accounting for sales to XYZ distorts the taxable income of both corporations. If a revenue agent discovers the questionable accounting method during an audit, the IRS could use its Section 482 authority to allocate income from XYZ to ABC to correct the distortion.

Section 482 Allocation	During its audit of ABC Inc.'s 2010 tax return, the IRS determined that ABC would have recognized $670,000 more gross income if it had charged an arm's-length market price for the inventory sold to XYZ Inc. Accordingly, the IRS allocated $670,000 gross income from XYZ to ABC to accurately measure the 2010 taxable income of both corporations.

Once a firm adopts a method of accounting, it may not change the method unless it formally requests and receives permission to do so from the IRS.[19] The request must state the reason why the firm wants to change and provide a detailed description of its present and proposed method of accounting. The IRS does not rubber-stamp these requests. When the IRS does grant permission, it carefully monitors the change to make sure that the firm does not omit income or duplicate deductions in the year of conversion to the new method of accounting.[20]

A Request Denied	In 1987, American Express requested the IRS's permission to change its method of accounting for the annual fees received from credit card holders. Until 1987, American Express recorded these fees as income in the month that they were billed. It requested a change to a "ratable inclusion" method under which fees would be recorded as income in equal monthly portions over the 12-month period beginning on the date of billing. The IRS took the position that the proposed method did not clearly reflect the corporation's taxable income and denied permission to make the change. American Express took its case to federal court, but after 14 years of litigation, the U.S. Court of Appeals held for the government. As a result, American Express incurred $199 million additional tax in 1987.[21]

Tax Policy Objectives

Objective 3
Explain why tax policy objectives affect the taxable income computation.

The accurate measurement of income is not the sole objective of the tax law. Congress wants the law to be consistent with public policy and political concerns, and the tax rules that achieve this consistency have nothing to do with income measurement. For instance, contributions to political parties or candidates for public office and federal or

---

[19] §446(e). Firms must file Form 3115 Application for Change in Accounting Method during the tax year for which the change is requested.

[20] §481(a).

[21] *American Express Company v. United States,* 262 F.3d 1376 (CA FC, 2001), *aff'm* 47 Fed Cl 127 (2000).

Tax Talk

Congress wants to expand the definition of nondeductible penalties to include payments to settle civil lawsuits. According to Senator Charles Grassley, "A civil settlement is supposed to sting like a bee, not annoy like a gnat. Letting companies deduct settlement payments from their income taxes takes away from the sting."

state lobbying expenses are not deductible.[22] Firms must record these expenses in their accounting records, but because Congress does not want to subsidize political activities, these expenses do not reduce taxable income. Similarly, firms cannot deduct illegal bribes or kickbacks or fines or penalties paid to any government for a violation of law because Congress does not want to subsidize bad behavior with a tax deduction.[23]

The tax treatment of meals and entertainment expenses is intended to make the law more equitable. Many firms incur these expenses to improve their relationships with customers, clients, investors, and employees. While these expenses may have a good business purpose, they may also result in personal enjoyment for the participants. The "three-martini lunch" has become a catchphrase for lavish meals and entertainment that involve more pleasure than business. In response to criticism that the tax law should not underwrite such activities, Congress allows firms to deduct only 50 percent of most meal and entertainment expenses.[24]

Nondeductible Expenses	Firm PLW operates a manufacturing business. This year, PLW paid a $2,000 fine to the city of Memphis for violating a local zoning law, contributed $3,500 to a candidate for state office, and spent $8,200 on meals and entertainment. While these items were recorded as expenses on PLW's books, the fine and political contribution were nondeductible and only $4,100 of the meals and entertainment expense was deductible.

Tax Preferences

The tax law contains many provisions to encourage certain economic behaviors or activities. In Chapter 4, we learned that the interest paid on state and local debt obligations is exempt from federal income tax. Firms that earn tax-exempt interest record it as revenue on their books but do not recognize it as gross income for tax purposes. The law provides a similar preference for the proceeds of life insurance policies: The proceeds are excluded from the recipient's gross income.[25] Many firms insure the lives of their officers and top-level management to protect against business disruption if one of these essential personnel dies. The firm itself (rather than the insured employee's family) is the beneficiary of such **key-person life insurance policies.** When a key person dies and the firm receives payment from the insurance company, the payment is recorded as revenue but is not taxable.

A corollary to the tax-exempt status of municipal bond interest and key-person life insurance proceeds is that expenses related to these income items are nondeductible. Accordingly, a firm can't deduct the interest paid on a debt if the borrowed funds were used to purchase or carry tax-exempt bonds.[26] Nor can a firm deduct the annual premiums paid on key-person life insurance policies.[27]

---

[22] §276 and §162(e).

[23] §162(c) and (f).

[24] §274(n). Section 274 includes many complicated restrictions on the deduction of business travel and entertainment expenses.

[25] §101(a).

[26] §265(a)(2).

[27] §264(a).

Key-Person Life Insurance	OKD owns insurance policies on the lives of its CEO and five other corporate officers and paid $14,300 premiums on these policies this year. In November, the CEO was killed in a boating accident, and OKD received $750,000 of insurance proceeds. OKD cannot deduct the $14,300 premium expense, and it does not include the $750,000 proceeds in gross income.

As part of the American Jobs Creation Act of 2004, Congress enacted a major tax preference: the deduction for income attributable to domestic production activities.[28] This deduction generally equals **9 percent** of a firm's net income derived from sales of property "manufactured, produced, grown, or extracted" within the United States. Here is a simple example.

Domestic Production Activities Deduction	Firm K earned the following manufacturing income this year.

Net income from U.S. manufacturing	$500,000
Net income from foreign manufacturing	600,000

Its domestic production activities deduction is $45,000 (9 percent × $500,000 net income from U.S. manufacturing). Thus, Firm K's taxable income from its U.S. manufacturing operation is only $455,000.

According to Congress, this **domestic production activities deduction** indirectly reduces the tax rate on *domestic* manufacturing income. The policy objectives of this preferential rate are to help U.S. businesses compete in the global marketplace, encourage investment in domestic manufacturing facilities, and create and preserve U.S. manufacturing jobs. The deduction is discussed in greater detail in Chapter 11.

THE CASH METHOD

Objective 4
Apply the cash method of accounting to compute taxable income.

Under the **cash method of accounting,** firms record revenue from the sale of goods or the performance of services in the year that payment is received, regardless of when the sale occurred or the services were performed.

Cash Method for Revenues	Firm CM, a calendar year, cash basis consulting business, completed an engagement late in the year. On December 12, the firm mailed a bill to the client for its $20,000 consulting fee. If CM does not receive a check in payment before year-end, it does not record revenue for the year, even though the services were performed during the year. CM will record $20,000 revenue when it receives payment in the following year.

Under the cash method, firms record expenses in the year the expense is paid, regardless of when the liability for the expense was incurred.

Cash Method for Expenses	Firm CM hired a temporary employee to help the secretarial staff with year-end paperwork. The temp completed the assignment on December 28, but CM didn't issue his $950 paycheck until January 15. CM incurred the $950 liability when the employee completed the job in a satisfactory manner. Even so, it will record the $950 expense when it makes payment in the following year.

[28] §199.

The Cash Method and Cash Flows

The term *cash method* should not be taken too literally. In the first place, the receipt of noncash forms of payment creates revenue equal to the value of the payment. The fact that no money is received is irrelevant.

Noncash Receipts	Firm CM billed a client for a $12,000 consulting fee, and the client settled the bill by transferring $12,000 worth of marketable securities to the firm. CM records $12,000 revenue on the receipt of the securities, even though the transaction did not involve the receipt of money.

As this example suggests, the net income computed under the cash method does not equate to net cash flows. In other words, the terms *income* and *cash* are not synonymous, even for a cash-basis taxpayer.

Income and Cash Flow	Firm CM lends $25,000 to an unrelated party at a 10 percent annual interest rate. Three years later, the debtor pays $33,275 ($25,000 principal + $8,275 interest) to CM in satisfaction of the debt. CM's income, expense, and cash flow from this transaction are as follows.

	Income/Expense	Cash Flow
Year of loan	–0–	$(25,000)
Year of repayment	$8,275	33,275

Constructive Receipt

Under the cash method of accounting, income is received when a person has unrestricted access to and control of the income, even if it is not in the person's actual possession. Treasury regulations state that this doctrine of **constructive receipt** applies when income is credited to a taxpayer's account, set apart for him, or otherwise made available so the taxpayer can draw on it during the taxable year.[29] For instance, interest accumulating in a savings account is constructively received on the day the owner has the right to withdraw the interest. The owner doesn't avoid income recognition merely because she declines to make the withdrawal.

In litigation between cash basis firms and the IRS, the courts have generally concluded that constructive receipt occurred if no substantial barrier to the firm's control and possession of the income existed. In other words, a calendar year, cash basis firm can't defer income from one year to the next by holding the checks received from its customers in December and cashing the checks the following January.[30]

The Lost Check	Horace and Donna Walter used the cash method to account for the income from their cattle ranch. During an audit of the Walter's 1996 tax records, an IRS agent found the top half of a business document indicating that Mr. Walter sold 115 steers to a customer for $77,442. The document apparently had been attached to a check from the customer. However, the Walter's bank records did not show a deposit of $77,442 during 1996. Mr. Walter contacted the customer, who advised him that the check issued in 1996 had never been cashed. The customer then issued a new check, which Mr. Walter received and deposited in 1998. The

---

[29] Reg. §1.451-2(a).
[30] *C. F. Kahler*, 18 T.C. 31 (1952).

Walters argued that they were not in constructive receipt of the income represented by the original check in 1996 because they had obviously lost the check instead of cashing it. The IRS contended that the fact that the Walters failed to cash the check was irrelevant, and they must include the $77,442 payment in 1996 income. The federal court that decided the case agreed with the IRS, stating, "Losing the check was a restriction on collection imposed by the Walters, the payees. No tax case has recognized an exception to the rule that receipt of a check is constructive receipt of the income when the restrictions on the disposition of the proceeds were the payees' own."[31]

Prepaid Expenses and Interest

Under the cash method of accounting, an expense is recorded in the year when payment is made. Cash basis firms can accelerate a deduction by paying an expense before the year in which the expense contributes to the generation of revenues. If the tax savings from the deduction is greater than the opportunity cost of the early payment, the firm has implemented a successful tax-planning strategy. This strategy is limited by the well-established principle that any business expenditure creating a benefit with a useful life extending substantially beyond the close of the year is not deductible but must be capitalized and amortized over its useful life.[32] The tax law provides a "12-month rule" for determining whether an expenditure is currently deductible or must be capitalized to an intangible asset account. If the expenditure results in a benefit with a duration of 12 months or less *and* that benefit does not extend beyond the end of the taxable year *following* the year of payment, the expenditure is deductible in the year of payment. If the expenditure results in a benefit with a duration of more than 12 months, it must be capitalized.[33]

Prepaid Insurance	On November 28, 2011, Firm L, a calendar year taxpayer, paid a $9,930 premium to acquire a casualty insurance policy on its business equipment.

- If the insurance policy has a one-year term from December 1, 2011, through November 30, 2012, its benefit has a duration of only 12 months and does not extend beyond 2012. Therefore, Firm L can deduct the $9,930 premium in 2011.
- If the insurance policy has a one-year term from February 1, 2012, through January 31, 2013, its benefit has a duration of only 12 months, but this benefit extends beyond 2012. Therefore, Firm L must capitalize the $9,930 premium. It can amortize and deduct $9,103 (11/12 × $9,930) of the cost in 2012 and $827 (1/12 × $9,930) of the cost in 2013.
- If the insurance policy has a three-year term from January 1, 2012, through December 31, 2014, its benefit has a three-year duration. Therefore, Firm L must capitalize the $9,930 premium and can amortize and deduct $3,310 (1/3 × $9,930) of the cost in 2012, 2013, and 2014.

For many years, cash basis firms with excess liquidity toward the end of the year could generate a deduction by prepaying interest expense to cooperative creditors. Congress forestalled this planning technique by enacting a statutory requirement that prepaid interest be capitalized and deducted in the future year or years for which the interest is actually charged.[34]

---

[31] *Walter v. United States,* 148 F.3d 1027 (CA-8, 1996).

[32] *Welch v. Helvering,* 290 U.S. 111 (1933).

[33] Reg. §1.263(a)-4(f). This 12-month rule applies to both cash and accrual basis taxpayers.

[34] §461(g).

Prepaid Interest	On October 1, Firm W, a calendar year, cash basis taxpayer, borrowed $100,000 from a local bank at 8.2 percent interest per annum. On December 19, the firm paid $8,200 to the bank for the first year's interest on the loan. Even though Firm W is a cash basis taxpayer, it can deduct only $2,050 (the interest for October, November, and December). The $6,150 interest for January 1 through September 30 of the following year is deductible in the following year.

Merchandise Inventories

Firms that sell merchandise to their customers must use the accrual method to account for purchases and sales of the merchandise.[35] In other words, they must capitalize the cost of merchandise as an inventory asset and can expense only the cost of inventory sold during the year. Moreover, they must record revenue from the sale of inventory when the sale occurs instead of when payment is received. Firms that sell merchandise can use an overall **hybrid method of accounting** in which they account for purchases and sales of inventories under the accrual method and all other transactions under the cash method.

Hybrid Method of Accounting	LWT Company, a retail sporting goods store, uses a hybrid method of accounting under which it accounts for all transactions that don't involve inventory under the cash method. It accounts for inventory transactions under the accrual method by capitalizing all merchandise purchases to inventory, performing a physical count at year-end to determine ending inventory and cost of goods sold, and recording revenues from inventory sales when the sales occur.

Many firms that provide services to clients may also sell tangible products as a *secondary component* of their principal service activity. For example, landscaping companies usually provide both design services and the plant materials necessary to implement the designs. Plumbing contractors usually provide both installation and repair services and any plumbing parts and fixtures incidental to the services. These firms may have inventories of the products sold in conjunction with their service activities. Under the general rule for inventories, they must account for purchases and sales of these products under the accrual method. However, the law provides a simplified cash method of accounting for service firms with average annual gross receipts of $10 million or less. These small businesses do not have to use the accrual method to account for their sales of products. However, they must account for their product inventory on hand at year-end as an asset.[36]

Small Service Business Exception	Jamestown Animal Hospital's principal business activity is the provision of veterinarian services, but it also sells pet supplies to its patients' owners. Jamestown's average annual gross receipts are $3 million. Consequently, it can use the cash method to account for its sales of both services and supplies. During the last month of this taxable year, Jamestown purchased $6,580 of pet supplies to restock its shelves. At year-end, it had $4,110 of these supplies on hand, so it could deduct only $2,470 of the cost this year. Jamestown can deduct the $4,110 capitalized cost in the year when it sells the supplies.

[35] Regs. §1.446-1(a)(4)(i) and §1.471-1.
[36] Rev. Proc. 2002-28, 2002-1 CB 815.

Limitations on Use of the Cash Method by Corporations

The cash method of accounting is both simple and objective because the measurement of income is based on cash receipts (bank deposits) and disbursements (checks written). The cash method also provides some control over the timing of income recognition.

Year-End Tax Planning under the Cash Method	Firm E is a calendar year, cash basis service business. At the end of each year, the firm delays billing its clients for work performed in December until the following January to defer taxable income. It also prepays as many expenses as possible to accelerate tax deductions.

Because the cash method can be manipulated to defer income and accelerate deductions, the tax law limits its use by large corporations. Corporations that average more than $5 million annual gross receipts cannot use the cash method for tax purposes.[37] This prohibition extends to partnerships with corporate partners. However, it does not apply to **personal service corporations,** defined as corporations that offer professional services (medical, legal, accounting, etc.) performed by individual shareholder/employees for the corporate clients. Any corporation, no matter how large, that is a personal service corporation can use the cash method to compute taxable income.

Goodbye to the Cash Method	Walsham Partnership, which operates a construction business, has 18 individual partners. The partnership has used the cash method of accounting since it was organized in 1996. Since its organization, Walsham's annual gross receipts have averaged $20 million a year. For compelling legal reasons, the partners have decided to incorporate their partnership. Once Walsham is converted to a taxable corporation, it must switch to the accrual method of accounting for tax purposes.

THE ACCRUAL METHOD

According to **generally accepted accounting principles (GAAP),** only the accrual method of accounting correctly measures annual income.[38] Firms that provide audited financial statements to external users are typically required to use the accrual method. The Security and Exchange Commission (SEC) requires every publicly held corporation to prepare accrual basis financial statements in accordance with GAAP.

Under the **accrual method of accounting,** firms record revenue when the revenue is realized. **Realization** occurs when the earnings process with respect to the provision of goods or services is complete, regardless of when payment for the goods or services is received.

Accrual Method for Revenues	Firm ADM, a calendar year, accrual basis consulting business, performed client services during October and November and billed the client for $9,200 on December 8. ADM recorded a $9,200 account receivable and $9,200 revenue even though it did not receive payment from the client until January 10 of the following year.

Accrual basis firms match expenses against revenue in the year the liability for the expense is incurred, regardless of when payment of the expense is made.

---

[37] §448.

[38] Generally accepted accounting principles are developed by the Financial Accounting Standards Board (FASB) and adhered to by the public accounting profession.

Accrual Method for Expenses	Firm ADM hired a plumber to repair some leaky pipes in the executive washroom. The plumber completed his repairs on December 19 and submitted his bill for $550. ADM recorded a $550 account payable and a $550 expense even though it did not pay the bill until January 20 of the following year.

If a firm uses the accrual method for both financial accounting (book) purposes and tax purposes, doesn't its annual income per books equal its taxable income? The answer to this question is usually no. For most accrual basis firms, book income and taxable income are different numbers. Discrepancies between the two income computations occur because certain transactions are treated one way under GAAP and another way for tax accounting purposes. One explanation for the inconsistent treatment is the contrast in perspectives on income measurement that shape financial accounting principles and the tax law.

Contrasting Perspectives on Income Measurement

Objective 5
Contrast the principles of conservatism reflected by GAAP and by the tax law.

Business managers have one attitude toward income measurement for financial statement purposes and a different attitude toward income measurement for tax purposes. Managers have incentives to report as much book income as possible. Their compensation and even their job security may depend on the level of earnings reported to existing and potential investors. However, GAAP is based on a principle of conservatism: When in doubt, financial statements should delay the realization of income and accelerate the realization of losses. In theory at least, GAAP curbs any tendency of management to *inflate* book income by overstating revenues or understating expenses.

In contrast to their expansive attitude toward book income, managers want to *deflate* the taxable income (and resultant tax cost) reported to the government. Congress and the Treasury are well aware of this measurement bias. Consequently, the federal tax law also embraces a principle of conservatism, but one that operates to prevent managers from understating gross income and overstating deductions. The contrasting principles of conservatism reflected by GAAP and the federal tax law lead to many of the book/tax differences described in Part Three of the text. To help readers keep track, a list of the sources of book/tax differences introduced in each chapter is provided at the end of the chapter.

Different Goals and Responsibilities	According to the Supreme Court, "The primary goal of financial accounting is to provide useful information to management, shareholders, creditors, and others properly interested; the major responsibility of the accountant is to protect these parties from being misled. The primary goal of the income tax system, in contrast, is the equitable collection of revenue; the major responsibility of the Internal Revenue Service is to protect the public fisc."[39]

Permanent versus Temporary Differences

Objective 6
Differentiate between a permanent and a temporary book/tax difference.

Differences between book income and taxable income are either permanent or temporary. A **permanent difference** results when income or gain is realized for book purposes but *never* recognized for tax purposes. Tax-exempt interest is an example of this type of permanent difference. Permanent differences also result when an expense or loss is realized for book purposes but *never* recognized for tax purposes. Nondeductible fines and penalties are good examples. Finally, permanent differences result when the tax law provides for a deduction that *never* corresponds to a book expense or loss. The domestic production activities deduction described earlier in this chapter and the dividends-received deduction that we will study in Chapter 11 are prime examples. Firms that have permanent book/tax differences never recoup the tax cost or repay the tax savings attributable to the differences.

[39] *Thor Power Tool Co. v. Comm.*, 439 U.S. 522 (1979).

Permanent Book/Tax Differences

Kalvoni Inc. earned $114,000 tax-exempt interest, incurred $386,400 nondeductible expenses, and was allowed a $767,000 domestic production activities deduction this year. If these were Kalvoni's only book/tax differences and its book income before tax was $4,712,000, its taxable income is computed as follows:

Book income before tax	$4,712,000
Income never recognized	(114,000)
Expenses never deducted	386,400
Deduction never expensed	(767,000)
Taxable income	$4,217,400

(handwritten annotations: "Tax Exempt Come Over" next to "Income never recognized"; "This was in Bod Inc°" next to $4,712,000; "This was def in Books" next to 386,400; "This was in book Income" next to (767,000))

Kalvoni's $494,600 permanent excess of book income over taxable income represents a $168,164 permanent tax saving ($494,600 excess × 34 percent) for the corporation.

A permanent book/tax difference affects only the year in which it occurs. Consequently, income tax expense *for financial statement purposes* is based on book income adjusted for all permanent differences.

Tax Expense per Books

Kalvoni's audited financial statements must include its federal income tax expense for the year. The tax expense per books is based on Kalvoni's book income adjusted for its permanent book/tax differences.

Book income before tax	$4,712,000
Income never recognized	(114,000)
Expenses never deducted	386,400
Deduction never expensed	(767,000)
Adjusted book income	$4,217,400
Tax rate	.34
Tax expense per books	$1,433,916

Temporary differences occur when an item of income, gain, expense, or loss is taken into account in a different year (or years) for book purposes than for tax purposes. Any excess of taxable income over book income from a temporary difference turns around to become an excess of book income over taxable income in some future year, and vice versa. The tax cost or tax savings from temporary differences are recouped or repaid in the future year in which the difference reverses.

Reversal of Temporary Book/Tax Difference

In year 1, Corporation QZ engages in a transaction that generates $100,000 income for financial accounting purposes. For tax purposes, the transaction generates $60,000 income in year 1, $35,000 income in year 2, and $5,000 income in year 3. The following table shows the computation of the book/tax difference each year and the tax savings (cost) at a 34 percent rate.

	Book Income	Taxable Income	Difference	Tax Savings (Cost)
Year 1	$100,000	$ 60,000	$40,000	$13,600
Year 2	–0–	35,000	(35,000)	(11,900)
Year 3	–0–	5,000	(5,000)	(1,700)
Total	$100,000	$100,000	–0–	–0–

Objective 7
Explain the difference between tax expense per books and tax payable.

Tax Expense versus Tax Payable

Firms compute tax expense for financial statement purposes based on book income adjusted for permanent book/tax differences. In contrast, temporary book/tax differences do not affect tax expense per books. According to GAAP, the tax effects of temporary differences are captured as deferred tax assets or liabilities on the balance sheet.

A temporary difference between book income and taxable income generates either a deferred tax asset or a deferred tax liability equal to the difference multiplied by the firm's tax rate. A temporary excess of taxable income over book income generates a **deferred tax asset.**[40] Because a deferred tax asset is analogous to a prepaid tax, temporary differences generating deferred tax assets are described as *unfavorable.* A temporary excess of book income over taxable income generates a **deferred tax liability.** Because a deferred tax liability is analogous to a delayed tax, temporary differences generating deferred tax liabilities are described as *favorable.*

Deferred Tax Asset

In year 1, Holmes Inc. engaged in a transaction resulting in a $19,000 expense but only an $11,500 tax deduction. This $7,500 unfavorable book/tax difference generated a $2,625 deferred tax asset ($7,500 × 35 percent) on Holmes's balance sheet. This difference reversed in year 4 when Holmes reported a $7,500 tax deduction and no book expense. To account for this reversal, Holmes reduced the deferred tax asset from the original transaction to zero.

Deferred Tax Liability

In year 1, Holmes Inc. engaged in a second transaction generating $50,000 book income but only $27,200 taxable income. This $22,800 favorable book/tax difference generated a $7,980 deferred tax liability ($22,800 × 35 percent) on Holmes's balance sheet. This difference partially reversed in year 2 when Holmes reported $10,000 taxable income but no book income. To account for this partial reversal, Holmes reduced the deferred tax liability from the original transaction to $4,480 [$7,980 − ($10,000 × 35 percent)].

Firms compute their federal tax payable based on their taxable income, which reflects both permanent and temporary differences from book income. Let's conclude our discussion of tax expense versus tax payable with a comprehensive example.

Permanent and Temporary Differences

Corporation XYZ engages in many transactions that result in permanent and temporary differences between book income and taxable income. This year, XYZ's financial records show the following.

Book income before tax	$712,000
Net permanent differences	(19,000)
Net temporary differences	63,000
Taxable income	$756,000

XYZ's tax expense for financial statement purposes is $235,620.

[40] If the realization of a deferred tax asset is questionable, the asset may be reduced by a valuation allowance on the balance sheet.

Tax expense [handwritten]
BI Adj for permm [handwritten]

Book income before tax	$712,000
Permanent differences	(19,000)
	$693,000
Tax rate	.34
Tax expense per books	$235,620

XYZ's tax payable is $257,040.

Taxable income	$756,000
Tax rate	.34
Tax payable	$257,040

The $21,420 excess of tax payable over tax expense equals 34 percent of XYZ's $63,000 net temporary book/tax difference. This unfavorable difference results in a $21,420 net increase in XYZ's deferred tax assets.

Temporary Book/Tax Accounting Differences

Prepaid Income

Objective 8
Apply the tax accounting rules for prepaid income and accrued expenses.

According to GAAP, income from the sale of goods or performance of services is realized in the year the goods and services are provided to customers and clients and the earnings process is complete. This rule applies even if customers or clients pay for the goods and services in advance. For tax purposes, income is recognized when all events have occurred that fix the taxpayer's right to receive the income and the amount of income can be determined with reasonable accuracy. According to the IRS, a taxpayer's right to receive income generally is fixed when the earnings process is complete *or* when the taxpayer receives payment, *whichever happens first*. Because of this tax accounting rule, accrual basis firms must recognize many types of **prepaid income** in the year of receipt.[41]

Prepaid Rent Income

Firm CRO leases real estate to a tenant for $30,000 annual rent. At the beginning of the year, CRO received a $90,000 payment from the tenant for three years' rent. For financial statement purposes, it reported $30,000 rent revenue on its income statement and $60,000 unearned revenue as a liability on its balance sheet. For tax purposes, CRO must recognize the entire $90,000 prepayment as income. The $60,000 excess of taxable income over book income is a temporary difference that will reverse over the next two years.[42]

Accrual basis firms that receive prepayments for *services* to be performed for clients or customers may recognize income under a one-year deferral method authorized by the IRS. Under this special method of accounting, only the portion of the prepayment allocable to services performed in the year of receipt is included in taxable income for such year. The remaining prepayment is included in taxable income for the following year.[43]

[41] Reg. §1.451-1(a). See also Rev. Rul. 84-31, 1984-1 CB 127.
[42] Reg. §1.61-8(b).
[43] Rev. Proc. 2004-34, 2004-1 CB 991.

Prepaid Service Income	SueLee Company, a calendar year taxpayer, offers ballroom dancing lessons to its clients. In October 2011, SueLee entered into a contract that entitles Ms. Jax to take 60 lessons over the next 36 months. Each lesson costs $40, and Ms. Jax was required to prepay the entire $2,400 contract price. By the end of 2011, Ms. Jax had taken nine lessons.
	Under the one-year deferral method, SueLee includes $360 of the $2,400 prepayment (nine lessons × $40) in 2011 income. SueLee must include the $2,040 remaining prepayment in 2012 income, *regardless* of when Ms. Jax takes the 51 lessons remaining under the contract.

A major exception to the general rule regarding prepaid income applies to advanced payments received for future sales of inventory. Firms can elect to include such advanced payments in taxable income either in the year of receipt or in the year in which the payments are included in income for financial reporting purposes.[44]

Advanced Payment for Inventory	Unsler Products, a calendar year taxpayer, manufactures and sells paper products. On November 16, 2012, Unsler received a $75,000 advanced payment from a customer for an order of paper that Unsler shipped from its warehouse on February 20, 2013. For financial statement purposes, Unsler reports advanced payments for inventory as revenue when the inventory is shipped. Consequently, Unsler can elect to include the $75,000 payment in taxable income in 2013, the year in which it is included in book income.

Accrued Expenses

At the close of the year, GAAP requires firms to identify any liability for an unpaid expense and accrue both the expense and the liability on the firm's financial statements. According to GAAP, this requirement results in a proper match of the accrued expense against current year revenue. Even so, the tax law does not allow a deduction for the expense unless the accrual satisfies the **all-events test.**[45] This test consists of three requirements. First, the liability for the unpaid expense must be *fixed* because all events establishing the fact of the liability have occurred. Second, the amount of the liability must be *determinable* with reasonable accuracy. Third, *economic performance* with respect to the liability has occurred. Let's begin our discussion of the all-events test by looking at some examples of the first two requirements.

Fixed and Determinable Liability	MQP, a calendar year taxpayer, hired 113 temporary employees to work during the last two weeks of December 2012, but did not receive a bill for their services from the employment agency before year-end. On the basis of its record of hours worked, MQP calculated that the bill would be $121,500. Consequently, MQP accrued a $121,500 expense and a $121,500 liability for temp services payable for financial statement purposes. Because MQP's liability to pay for the services is *fixed* and the amount is *determinable* with reasonable accuracy, the accrual satisfies the first two requirements of the all-events test.

Liability Not Fixed and Determinable	SFL Inc. provides a medical reimbursement plan for its 4,800 employees. At the end of each year, SFL estimates the reimbursable expenses incurred during the year for which employees have not yet filed written claims. On the basis of this estimate, SFL accrues a medical reimbursement expense and a corresponding liability for financial statement purposes. Because SFL's liability for a claim is not fixed until the written claim is filed, the accrual fails the all-events test.[46]

[44] Reg. §1.451-5.

[45] §461(h)(1) and (4).

[46] *United States* v. *General Dynamics Corp.*, 481 U.S. 239 (1987).

Liability Not Fixed and Determinable	SkyHigh Airlines issues travel vouchers to customers who voluntarily surrender their reserved seats on overbooked flights. The vouchers are for a stated dollar amount and can be used to purchase future tickets. The vouchers are valid for only one year, and many expire without being used. At the end of each year, SkyHigh accrues an unused travel voucher expense and a corresponding liability for financial statement purposes. Because SkyHigh's liability for a voucher is not fixed until the customer uses it to purchase a ticket, the accrual fails the all-events test.[47]

Even when the liability for an accrued expense is fixed and determinable, the expense is not deductible until **economic performance** with respect to the liability has occurred. If a liability relates to the provision of services, property, or the use of property *to* the taxpayer *by* another party, economic performance occurs when the other party provides the services, property, or the use of property.

Provision of Services to Taxpayer	Refer to the previous example in which MQP accrued a $121,500 expense for temp services. MQP's liability to pay for the services is fixed and determinable, and the employees provided the services to MQP in December 2012. Therefore, economic performance occurred in December, and the accrual meets the three requirements of the all-events test. As a result, MQP can deduct the $121,500 accrued expense in 2012.

Provision of Property to Taxpayer	On November 18, 2012, MQP ordered $4,400 of supplies from a vendor, which delivered the supplies on December 4. MQP did not pay the vendor before year-end. Consequently, MQP accrued a $4,400 expense and a $4,400 liability for supplies payable for financial statement purposes. The liability is fixed and determinable, and economic performance occurred on December 4. Because the accrual meets the three requirements of the all-events test, MQP can deduct the $4,400 accrued expense in 2012.

If a liability relates to the provision of services or property *by* the taxpayer *to* another party, economic performance occurs when the taxpayer provides the services or property.

Provision of Services by Taxpayer	Bearden Inc., a calendar year corporation, sells tractors under a three-year warranty obligating Bearden to repair the tractors during the warranty period. In 2012, Bearden sold 218 tractors with warranty periods extending into 2015. At the end of 2012, Bearden accrued a $60,000 expense and a $60,000 liability for future warranty costs. This liability is fixed and determinable with reasonable accuracy. However, economic performance has not occurred because Bearden has not provided the repair service. Consequently, the accrued liability fails the all-events test and the $60,000 accrued expense is not deductible in 2012. Bearden can deduct its warranty cost in any future year in which it does provide the service.[48]

In the case of a few specific liabilities, economic performance occurs only when the taxpayer makes payment to the person to whom the liability is owed. These so-called **payment liabilities** include liabilities arising under any workers compensation act or out of a tort, breach of contract, or violation of law; liabilities for customer rebates or refunds; liabilities for awards, prizes, or jackpots; and liabilities for taxes imposed by a governmental authority.[49]

[47] IRS Letter Ruling 200203004 (January 18, 2002).
[48] Reg. §1.461-4(d)(7), Example 2.
[49] Reg. §1.461-4(g).

Payment Liability	Solange Inc., a calendar year taxpayer, was sued in 2010 by a customer who was injured on Solange's premises because of the corporation's alleged negligence. Solange accrued a $2 million estimated settlement expense and a $2 million contingent liability for 2010 financial statement purposes. In 2011, Solange and the customer agreed to a $1.5 million out-of-court settlement. Solange actually paid $1.5 million to the customer on April 6, 2012. Solange could not deduct any settlement expense in 2010 when the liability was accrued or in 2011 when the liability became fixed and determinable. Solange could deduct the $1.5 million settlement in 2012 because it made payment to the customer.

The tax law moderates the effect of the economic performance requirement on standard accounting practices by providing a **recurring item exception.**[50] Taxpayers may adopt this exception as a method of accounting for liabilities regularly incurred from year to year and properly accrued at year-end under GAAP. Under this exception, if economic performance occurs within eight and one-half months after the close of the year, the business can deduct the corresponding expense in the year of accrual.

Recurring Item Exception	Omero Company, a calendar year taxpayer, sells digital cameras. Omero refunds the full purchase price of a camera to any customer who requests the refund in writing within 90 days of purchase. At the end of 2012, Omero accrued a $17,600 expense and a $17,600 liability for refunds payable with respect to 88 refund requests received but unpaid. Omero paid all of these requests by September 15, 2013. If Omero has not adopted the recurring item exception as its method of accounting for refunds, economic performance (payment) occurred in 2013, and the $17,600 expense is deductible in 2013. If Omero has adopted this method of accounting, it can deduct the $17,600 accrued expense in 2012.[51]

Recurring Item Exception	Refer to the previous example in which Bearden Inc. sold 218 tractors with warranty periods extending into 2015. At the end of 2012, Bearden accrued a $60,000 warranty expense. By September 15, 2013, Bearden had provided $9,045 worth of repairs under its 2012 warranties. If Bearden has adopted the recurring item exception as its method of accounting for warranty costs, it can deduct $9,045 of the accrued warranty expense in 2012.

Compensation Accruals

The tax law includes a particular rule governing the timing of an employer's deduction for employee compensation. The deduction is allowed in the employer's taxable year in which the compensation is included in the employee's gross income.[52] In other words, compensation is deductible in the year of payment to cash basis employees. Consequently, an accrued expense for compensation payable is not deductible in the year of accrual but in the year the liability is paid. There is an important exception to this timing rule: An accrued compensation expense is deductible if payment is made to the employee within two and one-half months after the close of the employer's taxable year.[53]

---

[50] §461(h)(3). The recurring item exception does not apply to liabilities for workers compensation, tort, breach of contract, or violation of law. Reg. §1.461-5(c).

[51] Reg. §1.461-5(e), Example 1.

[52] §404(a)(5) and (b)(1). According to Reg. §1.461-4(d)(2)(iii), the economic performance requirement is satisfied to the extent an employee benefit is deductible under Section 404.

[53] Reg. §1.404(b)-1T, Q&A 2.

Compensation Accruals	Panok, a calendar year corporation, pays its employees on a monthly basis and distributes paychecks on the fourth business day after the close of each month. At the end of 2012, Panok accrued a $639,200 expense and a $639,200 liability for December wages payable. Panok paid these wages on January 6, 2013. Because payment occurred by March 15, 2013, Panok could deduct the $639,200 accrued expense in 2012.
	On December 28, Panok's board of directors authorized a $15,000 year-end bonus for each of six corporate executives. Consequently, Panok accrued a $90,000 expense and a $90,000 liability for bonuses payable. Because of cash flow problems, Panok was unable to pay these bonuses until April 3, 2013. Consequently, Panok could not deduct the $90,000 accrued expense in 2012 but could deduct the payment in 2013.
	Panok's employees are compensated with two to six weeks of paid vacation each year. Employees accumulate any unused vacation indefinitely. At the end of 2012, Panok accrued a $144,900 expense and a $144,900 liability for vacation pay accumulated by its employees for the year. Panok paid $28,700 of this liability to employees who took vacation between January 1 and March 15, 2013. Consequently, Panok could deduct $28,700 of its accrued vacation pay expense in 2012. Panok will deduct the remaining expense in the year of payment.

Related Party Accruals

The two parties to a transaction may use different methods to account for the tax consequences of the transaction. As a result, the two sides of the transaction may be reported in different years.

Different Accounting Methods: Arm's-Length Transaction	Company AB, an accrual basis taxpayer, hires Firm CB, a cash basis taxpayer, to provide professional services. Firm CB performs the services in year 1 and bills Company AB for $10,000. Company AB pays this bill in year 2. For financial statement purposes, the two parties record the following.

	Year 1	Year 2
Company AB's accrued expense	$(10,000)	–0–
Firm CB's realized income	–0–	$10,000

If Company AB and Firm CB are not related parties, the tax consequences of the transaction are consistent with the financial accounting treatment. Company AB reaps the tax savings from a $10,000 deduction in year 1, while Firm CB bears the tax cost of $10,000 income in year 2. In present value terms, the tax savings exceed the tax cost, even if both parties have the same marginal tax rate. Although the Treasury is being whipsawed because of the difference in the parties' accounting methods, the tax law tolerates the result because it arises from an arm's-length transaction.

Now assume that Firm CB owns a controlling interest in Company AB. Because the transaction occurs between related parties, the tax law does not allow Company AB to deduct the accrued expense in year 1. Instead, Company AB must defer the $10,000 deduction until year 2 when Firm CB recognizes $10,000 income from the transaction.[54]

---

[54] §267(a)(2). Under this section, a controlling interest is generally more than a 50 percent ownership interest.

Different Accounting Methods: Related Parties	If Company AB and Firm CB are related parties, Company AB accrues the $10,000 expense in year 1 but reports a $10,000 deduction in year 2.

	Year 1	Year 2
Company AB's:		
Accrued expense	$(10,000)	–0–
Tax deduction	–0–	$(10,000)
Firm CB's realized income	–0–	10,000

Business Bad Debts

It is well established that the tax law does not allow deductions based on reserves or allowances for future or contingent liabilities.[55] Additions to reserves or allowances are based on estimates that fail the crucial all-events test for deductibility. The disallowance of a deduction for such additions causes a temporary difference between book income and taxable income. The most common example of this book/tax difference results from a firm's method of accounting for its bad debts.

When an accrual basis firm sells goods or services and the purchaser doesn't pay cash at the point of sale, the firm records an account receivable for the sales price. Firms anticipate that some portion of their accounts receivable will never be collected because of defaults by customers to whom the firm extended credit. According to GAAP, firms should use the **allowance method** to account for bad debts. Under this method, firms estimate the portion of their accounts receivables that will be uncollectible and establish a bad debt allowance or reserve for this portion. The annual addition to the allowance is recorded as a bad debt expense and matched against sales revenue. For tax purposes, firms must use the **direct write-off method** to account for bad debts. Under this method, firms can deduct accounts receivable (and any other business debts) actually written off as uncollectible during the year.[56]

Accounting for Bad Debts	ABC Inc. began the year with a $298,000 balance in its allowance for bad debts. During the year, it wrote off $155,000 uncollectible accounts receivable against this allowance. On the basis of ABC's year-end accounts receivable, the independent auditors determined that a $173,000 addition to the bad debt allowance was necessary. As a result, the year-end balance in the allowance increased to $316,000.

Beginning allowance for bad debts	$298,000
Actual write-offs during the year	(155,000)
Addition to allowance	173,000
Ending allowance for bad debts	$316,000

---

[55] *Lucas v. American Code Co.*, 280 U.S. 445 (1930).

[56] §166(a).

ABC's income statement shows a bad debt expense of $173,000, while its tax return shows a bad debt deduction of only $155,000. If ABC's book income before tax is $6,700,000 and it has no other book/tax differences, its taxable income is computed as follows.

Book income before tax	$6,700,000
Nondeductible bad debt expense	173,000
Deductible bad debt write-offs	(155,000)
Taxable Income	$6,718,000

Firms occasionally receive payment of an account receivable that was written off as uncollectible in a previous year. For financial statement purposes, this recovery is credited to the allowance for bad debts and has no effect on income. The tax consequences of the recovery are dictated by a long-standing **tax benefit rule.** Under this rule, the recovery of an amount deducted in an earlier year must be included in gross income in the year of recovery.[57] Because the write-off of an account receivable resulted in a bad debt deduction in a previous year, the payment must be included in taxable income.

Recovery of Bad Debt	Two years ago, Sela Company wrote off a $57,000 account receivable as uncollectible. The $57,000 write-off was included in Sela's $589,200 bad debt deduction for that year. This year, the debtor paid $57,000 cash to Sela to settle the old receivable. This recovery has no effect on Sela's book income but increases its taxable income by $57,000.

NET OPERATING LOSSES

In this chapter, we've learned that firms must choose a method of accounting to divide a continuous stream of income into 12-month segments. The choice of accounting method has nothing to do with the measurement of taxable income *over the life* of a firm, but everything to do with the measurement of income for each taxable year. The final section of this chapter focuses on one possible outcome of this annual measurement process: a net operating loss.

The Problem of Excess Deductions

If a taxpayer's annual business operation results in an excess of deductible expenses over gross income, this excess is labeled a **net operating loss (NOL).** Because the taxpayer reports no taxable income, it incurs no tax cost in the year of the NOL. But a more subtle fact is that the excess deductions yield no current tax savings; the taxpayer has the same zero tax cost with or without these deductions. If the excess deductions are wasted because they never yield any tax savings, the taxpayer's average tax rate *over time* could be distorted.

---

[57] Section 111 is a codification of the tax benefit rule. A recovery of a previously deducted amount is taxable only to the extent that the deduction actually reduced the tax base in the year the deduction was allowed.

*Excess
Deductions and
Average Tax Rate*

TUV Inc. conducts a business with a 24-month operating cycle. Its most recent operating cycle generated $300,000 profit.

	Year 1	Year 2	Total
Gross income	$100,000	$625,000	$725,000
Deductible expenses	(300,000)	(125,000)	(425,000)
Profit			$300,000

If TUV had to report its income and pay tax based on strict 12-month intervals, it would report a $200,000 NOL for year 1 and $500,000 taxable income for year 2. At a 34 percent rate, it would owe no tax in year 1 and $170,000 tax in year 2. Thus, TUV's overall tax rate on its profit would be 56.67 percent.

$$\$170,000 \text{ tax} \div \$300,000 \text{ profit} = 56.67\%$$

This inflated rate reflects the fact that $200,000 of TUV's deductible expenses (year 1 NOL) generated no tax savings for the corporation.

Solution: The NOL Deduction

Objective 9
Explain how the NOL deduction smooths taxable income over time.

The tax law prevents the rate distortion that could result from an inflexible one-year reporting period by permitting taxpayers to smooth income over time by deducting excess deductions in one year against income in another. Specifically, a taxpayer may carry an NOL back as a deduction against taxable income reported in the two years immediately before the loss year; the deduction must be used in chronological order beginning with the earlier year in the carryback period.[58] Any NOL in excess of the previous two years' income may be carried forward as a deduction to the next 20 taxable years.

*NOL
Carryback and
Carryforward*

In 2008, Corporation Q generated a $612,000 NOL. The following schedule shows the years in which it used the NOL as a deduction against taxable income.

	2006	2007	2009	2010	2011	2012
Taxable income before NOL deduction	$165,000	$110,000	$138,000	$99,000	$54,000	$125,000
NOL deduction	(165,000)	(110,000)	(138,000)	(99,000)	(54,000)	(46,000)
Taxable income	–0–	–0–	–0–	–0–	–0–	$ 79,000

Corporation Q used $275,000 of the 2008 NOL to reduce 2006 and 2007 taxable income to zero. It used the remaining $337,000 NOL as carryforward deductions in 2009 through 2012.

A taxpayer reports an **NOL carryback** by filing a one-page form with the IRS showing the NOL deducted against prior year income and the recomputed prior year tax.[59] After processing the form, the IRS refunds the tax overpayment. A taxpayer reports an **NOL carryforward** as a deduction on future tax returns until the NOL has been fully utilized or until it expires.

[58] §172.
[59] See Form 1139 Corporation Application for Tentative Refund.

Let's incorporate an NOL deduction into the earlier example involving TUV Inc.

NOL Deduction

Assuming that year 1 was TUV's first taxable year, the NOL in year 1 is carried forward as a deduction into year 2. TUV's tax returns for the two years show the following.

	Year 1	Year 2
Gross income	$ 100,000	$625,000
Deductible expenses	(300,000)	(125,000)
NOL	$(200,000)	
NOL carryforward deduction		(200,000)
Taxable income		$300,000

At a 34 percent rate, TUV owes $102,000 tax in year 2. Because of the NOL carryforward, TUV's taxable income in year 2 equals the $300,000 profit for the 24-month operating cycle, and TUV's tax rate on this profit is 34 percent.

Valuing an NOL Deduction

The value of a deduction equals the tax savings from the deduction. In the case of an NOL deduction, the tax savings (and cash flows) depend on the year (or years) in which the taxpayer takes the deduction against taxable income. If the NOL can be deducted against prior years' income, the taxpayer enjoys the savings immediately in the form of a cash refund.

Cash Flow from an NOL Carryback

Corporation C, which has operated profitably since 1985, experienced a severe business downturn during 2011 and closed the year with a $900,000 loss. The corporation carried this loss back as an NOL deduction to 2009 and 2010.

	2009	2010
Taxable income on original return	$430,000	$1,600,000
NOL carryback from 2011	(430,000)	(470,000)
Recomputed taxable income	–0–	$1,130,000
Tax on original return*	$146,200	$ 544,000
Recomputed tax	–0–	(384,200)
Refund due to Corporation C	$146,200	$ 159,800

*Tax computations are based on the corporate rate schedule.

Corporation C received a $306,000 refund of 2009 and 2010 tax resulting in an *after-tax* loss of $594,000 ($900,000 operating loss minus $306,000 tax savings). In other words, the NOL *deduction* was worth $306,000 to Corporation C.

Now let's modify the example so that 2011 is Corporation C's first taxable year. Consequently, the corporation can use its $900,000 NOL deduction only on a carryforward basis. In this case, the present value of the deduction depends on the corporation's projection of its future income stream.

		2012	2013	2014
NPV of an NOL Carryforward	Corporation C projects that it will generate $350,000 annual income over the next three years. Based on a 9 percent discount rate, the value in 2011 of the NOL carryforward is only $268,958.			

	2012	2013	2014
Projected income	$350,000	$350,000	$350,000
NOL carryforward from 2011	(350,000)	(350,000)	(200,000)
Taxable income	–0–	–0–	$150,000
Tax on projected income*	$119,000	$119,000	$119,000
Actual tax	–0–	–0–	(41,750)
Tax savings from NOL	$119,000	$119,000	$ 77,250
Present value of tax savings	$109,123	$100,198	$ 59,637
NPV of tax savings	$268,958		

*Tax computations are based on the corporate rate schedule.

Because the tax savings from the NOL deduction are deferred into future years, the present value of the deduction decreases. In the carryforward example, Corporation C's after-tax loss is $631,042 ($900,000 − $268,958). Clearly, the longer the period of time over which a taxpayer deducts an NOL carryforward, the less present value of the deduction.

Giving Up an NOL Carryback

An interesting feature of the NOL deduction is that taxpayers can elect to give up the carryback and keep the entire loss as a prospective deduction for future years.[60] In most cases, taxpayers are eager to use an NOL carryback deduction to create immediate cash flow in the form of a tax refund. However, if a taxpayer determines that its marginal tax rate during the two-year carryback period was significantly lower than its projected rate for future years, a decision to forgo the carryback may maximize the value of the NOL deduction.

Giving Up an NOL Carryback	Corporation JM incurs a $20,000 NOL this year, which it could carry back as a deduction against prior year income. However, the marginal tax rate in the carryback year was only 25 percent. JM projects that its marginal tax rate next year will be 39 percent. If JM uses a 7 percent discount rate, the NOL deduction is worth $2,293 more as a carryforward than as a carryback.

Present value of NOL carryforward	
($20,000 × 39% × .935 discount factor)	$7,293
Present value of NOL carryback	
($20,000 × 25%)	(5,000)
	$2,293

[60] §172(b)(3). This election is irrevocable.

Accounting for NOLs

According to GAAP, firms that generate a current net operating loss must report the tax benefit represented by the NOL carryback or carryforward on their current financial statements. If the NOL is carried back, the firm will realize the benefit in the form of a tax refund.

Accounting for NOL Carryback	Herold Inc. generated a $783,000 NOL in 2011, which it carried back as a deduction against prior-year taxable income. This deduction entitled Herold to a $266,220 refund ($783,000 × 34 percent) of prior-year tax. For financial statement purposes, Herold recorded a $266,220 tax refund receivable and a matching $266,220 decrease in 2011 tax expense.

If a firm cannot (or elects not to) carry back an NOL, it will realize the tax benefit in the future year or years in which the NOL carryforward is deducted. In this case, the anticipated benefit is reported as a deferred tax asset.[61]

Accounting for NOL Carryforward	Groh Inc. generated a $492,000 NOL in 2011. Because 2011 was Groh's first taxable year, it carried the NOL forward as a future deduction. Groh accounted for the anticipated tax savings from the carryforward by recording a $167,280 deferred tax asset ($492,000 × 34 percent) and a matching $167,280 decrease in 2011 tax expense.
	In 2012, Groh Inc. generated $1,316,000 taxable income before consideration of its NOL carryforward. Groh could deduct the entire $492,000 carryforward, thereby reducing its 2012 tax payable by $167,280 ($492,000 × 34 percent). Groh accounted for the use of the carryforward by reducing the $167,280 deferred tax asset to zero and recording a matching $167,280 increase in 2012 tax expense.

Conclusion

The computation of taxable income depends on the taxable year and the method of accounting adopted by the firm. Firms often use the same overall method for both financial reporting and tax purposes. Even so, many discrepancies exist between the computations of book and taxable income. In subsequent chapters, we'll encounter many more of these book/tax differences. To make sense of these differences, it may help to keep the following in mind. The goal of generally accepted accounting principles (and financial statements prepared in accordance with GAAP) is to provide useful and pertinent information to management, shareholders, creditors, and other business decision makers. In contrast, the primary (but certainly not the only) goal of the Internal Revenue Code (and the responsibility of the IRS) is to generate and protect federal tax revenues.

---

[61] If the firm's prospect of deducting an NOL carryforward is uncertain, the deferred tax asset may be reduced by a valuation allowance on the balance sheet.

Sources of Book/Tax Differences

Permanent

- Interest on state and local bonds
- Key-person life insurance proceeds and premiums
- Fines and penalties
- Political contributions and lobbying expense
- Meals and entertainment expense
- Domestic production activities deduction

Temporary

- Prepaid income
- Bad debts
- Accrued expenses failing the all-events test
- Compensation accruals
- Related party accruals
- NOL carryforwards

Key Terms

accrual method of accounting *129*
all-events test *134*
allowance method *138*
annualized income *121*
calendar year *119*
cash method of accounting *125*
constructive receipt *126*
deferred tax asset *132*
deferred tax liability *132*
direct write-off method *138*
domestic production activities deduction *125*

economic performance *135*
fiscal year *119*
generally accepted accounting principles (GAAP) *129*
gross income *118*
hybrid method of accounting *128*
key-person life insurance policies *124*
method of accounting *122*
net operating loss (NOL) *139*
NOL carryback *140*

NOL carryforward *140*
payment liabilities *135*
permanent difference *130*
personal service corporations *129*
prepaid income *133*
realization *129*
recognition *122*
recurring item exception *136*
short-period return *120*
tax benefit rule *139*
taxable income *118*
temporary difference *131*

Questions and Problems for Discussion

1. Discuss the choice of a taxable year for the following businesses.
   a. Retail plant and garden center.
   b. French bakery.
   c. Chimney cleaning business.
   d. Moving and transport business.
   e. Software consulting business.

2. Corporation DB operates three different lines of business. Can the corporation elect a different overall method of accounting for each line or must the corporation adopt one overall method?

3. Firm LK bought a warehouse of used furniture to equip several of its clerical offices. An employee discovered a cache of gold coins in a desk drawer. A local court declared Firm LK the rightful owner of the coins, which have a $72,000 FMV. Does Firm LK recognize income because of this lucky event?

4. Lester Inc. owns 55 percent of the outstanding stock of Marvin Corporation. The two corporations engage in numerous intercompany transactions that must be accounted for on both their financial statements and their tax returns. Discuss the circumstances in which the IRS might challenge the method of accounting used to record these intercompany transactions.

5. Discuss the various circumstances in which a firm is required to prepare financial statements in accordance with GAAP.

6. Firm NB, which uses the cash method of accounting, recently received two cases of French wine from a client in settlement of a $1,300 bill. Does Firm NB avoid income recognition because it received a noncash item as payment?

7. For many years, Mr. K, the president of KJ Inc., took the corporation's most important clients to lunch at Al's Steak House several times a week. However, after the tax law was amended to disallow a deduction for 50 percent of the cost of business meals, Mr. K and his clients patronize this restaurant only once or twice a month. What does this scenario suggest about the incidence of the indirect tax increase represented by the meals and entertainment disallowance rule?

8. If a corporation purchases insurance on the life of its chief executive officer and the corporation is named the policy beneficiary, the premium payments are nondeductible. If the officer's spouse and children are named as beneficiaries, the premium payments are deductible. Can you provide a reason for this inconsistent tax treatment?

9. Describe the contrasting treatment of prepaid income under GAAP and under the tax law and explain how each treatment reflects a different principle of conservatism.

10. Describe the book/tax difference resulting from each of the following transactions.

    a. Firm A spent $110 on a business dinner attended by the firm's vice president and a potential client.

    b. Firm B borrowed $50,000 and invested the loan proceeds in tax-exempt City of Los Angeles bonds. This year, Firm B paid $2,800 interest on the loan and earned $3,500 interest on the bonds.

    c. Firm C sent its president and several other key employees to Washington, D.C., to lobby a group of senators to enact legislation that would be extremely beneficial for the firm's business. The cost of this trip was $7,400. While in the capital city, the president attended a "$10,000 a plate" fund-raising dinner sponsored by one senator's reelection committee.

11. The manager of Firm Z, a new business that anticipates a steady growth in profits over the next decade, must decide between the cash method and the accrual method as the overall method for tax purposes. She understands that the difference between the two methods is essentially one of timing and that, over the life of the firm, either method should result in the same taxable income. What she doesn't understand is why the cash method might improve the NPV of the firm's cash flows over the next decade. Can you provide an explanation?

12. Firms generally prefer to engage in transactions that create assets instead of liabilities. However, firms prefer transactions generating deferred tax liabilities to transactions generating deferred tax assets. Can you explain this apparent contradiction?

13. Net operating losses can be carried forward for 20 years, after which time they expire. Why is it unusual for a firm to experience the expiration of an NOL?

14. Why do tax preferences often result in differences between book income and taxable income? Would a book/tax difference from a tax preference be a permanent difference or a temporary difference? Which type of difference is more valuable in NPV terms?

Application Problems

1. Nello Company owed $23,400 overdue rent to its landlord, Bonview Inc. Because Nello is a desirable tenant, Bonview agreed to settle the overdue account for a $15,000 cash payment from Nello. Both Nello and Bonview are accrual basis taxpayers.

    a. What is the tax consequence to Nello of the settlement of its $23,400 account payable to Bonview? Compute Nello's net cash outflow from the settlement assuming its tax rate is 35 percent.

    b. What is the tax consequence to Bonview of the settlement of its $23,400 account receivable from Nello? Compute Bonview's net cash inflow from the settlement assuming its tax rate is 30 percent.

2. PT Inc., which has been in business since 1980, uses a fiscal year ending June 30. The shareholders recently voted to dissolve the corporation under state law. PT ceased operations in September and distributed its remaining assets to its shareholders in October. PT's final tax return for the year beginning on July 1 and ending on October 31 reported $92,000 taxable income.

    a. Compute PT's tax for its last year using the corporate tax rates.

    b. Assume that PT operates an ongoing business and filed the short-period return described above because the IRS granted permission to change from a fiscal year ending June 30 to a fiscal year ending October 31. How does this change in fact affect the tax computation?

3. Assuming a 35 percent marginal tax rate, compute the after-tax cost of the following business expenses.

    a. $5,600 premium on business property and casualty insurance.

    b. $1,200 fine paid to Wisconsin for violation of a state law.

    c. $3,700 premium on key-person life insurance.

    d. $50,000 political contribution.

    e. $7,800 client entertainment.

4. Northwest Company operates manufacturing facilities in Portland, Oregon, and Vancouver, Canada. In 2012, the Portland plant generated $3.1 million net income and the Vancouver plant generated $4.8 million net income. Compute Northwest's 2012 taxable income.

5. Firm B, a calendar year, cash basis taxpayer, leases lawn and garden equipment. During December, it received the following cash payments. To what extent does each payment represent current taxable income to Firm B?

    a. $522 repayment of a loan from an employee. Firm B loaned $500 to the employee six months ago, and the employee repaid the loan with interest.

    b. $600 deposit from a customer who rented mechanical equipment. Firm B must return the entire deposit when the customer returns the undamaged equipment.

    c. $10,000 short-term loan from a local bank. Firm B gave the bank a written note to repay the loan in one year at 9 percent interest.

    d. $888 prepaid rent from the customer described in part *b.* The rent is $12 per day for the 74-day period from December 17 through February 28.

6. Firm F is a cash basis legal firm. In 2012, it performed services for a client, mailed the client a bill for $6,150, and recorded a $6,150 receivable. In 2013, Firm F discovered that the client was under criminal indictment and had fled the country. After learning this news, it wrote off the receivable.

    a. What was the effect of the recording of the account receivable on Firm F's taxable income?

    b. What was the effect of the write-off on Firm F's taxable income?

7. Firm Q operates a cash basis consulting business. In October, Firm Q billed a client for $23,400 of consulting services. In November, the client settled the bill by paying $10,000 cash and transferring marketable securities worth $13,400 to Firm Q. How much taxable income does Firm Q recognize on settlement of the bill?

8. RTY is a calendar year corporation. On December 12, RTY billed a client $17,800 for services rendered during October and November. It had not received payment by December 31. On December 10, RTY received a $4,000 check from a tenant that leases office space from the corporation. The payment was for next year's January and February rent.

   a. If RTY is a cash basis taxpayer, how much income should it recognize from the above transactions this year?

   b. If RTY is an accrual basis taxpayer, how much income should it recognize from the above transactions this year?

9. Brillo Company uses the calendar year and the cash method of accounting. On December 31, 2012, Brillo made the following cash payments. To what extent can Brillo deduct the payment in 2012?

   a. $50,000 for a two-year office lease beginning on February 1, 2013.

   b. $79,000 of inventory items held for sale to customers.

   c. $1,800 to purchase a new refrigerator for the employees' lounge. The refrigerator was delivered on January 8, 2013.

   d. $4,800 retainer to a consultant who spent three weeks in January 2013 analyzing Brillo's internal control system.

   e. $22,300 property tax to the local government for the first six months of 2013.

10. NC Company, a retail hardware store, began business in August and elected a calendar year for tax purposes. From August through December, NC paid $319,000 for inventory to stock the store. According to a physical inventory count on December 31, NC had $64,600 of inventory on hand. Compute NC's cost of goods sold for its first year assuming:

    a. NC adopted the cash method as its overall method of accounting.

    b. NC adopted the accrual method as its overall method of accounting.

11. LSG Company is a calendar year, cash basis taxpayer. On November 1, 2012, LSG paid $9,450 cash to the janitorial service firm that cleans LSG's administrative offices and retail stores. How much of this expenditure can LSG deduct in 2012 assuming that:

    a. The expenditure is a prepayment for six months of cleaning services from November 2012 through April 2013?

    b. The expenditure is a prepayment for 18 months of cleaning services from November 2012 through April 2014?

12. Firm F, a calendar year taxpayer, owes a $200,000 long-term debt to an unrelated creditor. In December, it paid $14,160 to the creditor as interest for the 12-month period from the prior September 1 through August 31 of the following year. Compute the deduction for this payment assuming that:

    a. Firm F uses the cash method of accounting for tax purposes.

    b. Firm F uses the accrual method of accounting for tax purposes.

13. Wahoo Inc., a calendar year taxpayer, leases equipment to a customer for $4,500 monthly rent. On November 27, 2012, Wahoo received a $36,000 rent payment for the eight-month period beginning on December 1. How much of the payment must Wahoo recognize as 2012 taxable income assuming that:

    a. Wahoo uses the cash method of accounting for tax purposes?

    b. Wahoo uses the accrual method of accounting for tax purposes?

14. GreenUp, a calendar year, accrual basis taxpayer, provides landscaping installation and maintenance services to its customers. In August 2012, GreenUp contracted with a university to renovate its lawns and gardens. GreenUp agreed to complete the entire renovation by May 31, 2014, and the university prepaid the entire $100,000 fee. GreenUp completed 20 percent of the work in 2012, 65 percent in 2013, and 15 percent in 2014.

    a. How much revenue should GreenUp report on its financial statements for 2012, 2013, and 2014?

    b. How much taxable income must GreenUp recognize in 2012, 2013, and 2014?

15. Cornish Inc. is an accrual basis, calendar year taxpayer. In December, a flood damaged one of Cornish's warehouses, and Cornish contracted with a construction company to repair the damage. The company estimated that the cost of the repairs could range from $20,000 to $100,000, depending on the severity of the damage. The contract provides that the maximum amount that the company will charge is $100,000. On December 19, the company sent Cornish its first progress bill for $7,200, which Cornish paid on January 8. Cornish's auditors required Cornish to accrue $65,000 of estimated repair expense on its current year financial statements. Compute Cornish's current year deduction for repairs.

16. KLP, a calendar year corporation, sponsored a contest for its customers with a grand prize of $100,000 cash. Contestants could enter the contest from June 1 through November 30. KLP selected the winner and announced her name on December 20. However, it did not present a $100,000 check to the winner until January 13. In which year can KLP deduct the $100,000 payment assuming:

    a. KLP uses the cash method of accounting?

    b. KLP uses the accrual method of accounting?

17. Ernlo is an accrual basis corporation with a June 30 fiscal year-end. On June 2, 2012, Ernlo entered into a binding contract to purchase a six-month supply of heating oil from a local distributor at the current market price of $12,450. This price is guaranteed regardless of the market price on the delivery date. Ernlo did not pay its $12,450 bill from the supplier until July 8, and the distributor delivered the oil on October 15.

    a. In which taxable year can Ernlo deduct its $12,450 cost of heating oil if it does not elect the recurring item exception as its method of accounting for this annual expense?

    b. In which taxable year can Ernlo deduct its $12,450 cost for heating oil if it elects the recurring item exception?

18. HomeSafe, an accrual basis, calendar year corporation, sells and installs home alarm systems. The contract price of a system includes four free service calls. HomeSafe's cost of each call is $75. At the end of 2012, HomeSafe accrued a $48,900 expense and a $48,900 liability for future service calls for systems sold in 2012. By September 15, 2013, HomeSafe had made 362 service calls for 2012 systems; from September 16 through December 31, 2013, HomeSafe made 122 additional service calls for 2012 systems.

    a. If HomeSafe has not adopted the recurring item exception as its method of accounting for service calls, how much of the $48,900 accrued expense can it deduct in 2012 and 2013?

    b. If HomeSafe has adopted the recurring item exception as its method of accounting for service calls, how much of the $48,900 accrued expense can it deduct in 2012 and 2013?

19. BZD, a calendar year corporation, made the following year-end accruals for 2012 financial statement purposes. In each case, determine how much of the accrued expense is deductible on BZD's 2012 federal tax return.

    a. A $55,000 expense and $55,000 liability for unpaid December salaries. BZD paid the entire liability to its employees before the end of January 2013.

    b. A $40,000 expense and $40,000 liability for the CEO's 2012 bonus. BZD paid $20,000 to the CEO on March 1, 2013, and the remaining $20,000 on May 1, 2013. BZD and the CEO are not related parties.

    c. A $219,700 expense and $219,700 liability for accumulated vacation pay. No employees took vacation between January 1 and March 15, 2013.

20. In 2011, AS, an accrual basis corporation, contracted with a nationally prominent artist to paint a mural in the lobby of the new corporate headquarters under construction. The artist's commission was $180,000, payable on completion of the mural. The artist finished her work and received the $180,000 commission in 2013. AS has a 35 percent marginal tax rate and uses a 7 percent discount rate to compute NPV.

    a. Compute AS's after-tax cost of the commission if it can deduct the $180,000 accrued expense in 2011.

    b. Compute AS's after-tax cost of the commission if the economic performance requirement delays the deduction until 2013.

21. Extronic, a calendar year, accrual basis corporation, reported a $41,900 liability for accrued 2011 state income tax on its December 31, 2011, balance sheet. Extronic made the following state income tax payments during 2012.

March 8	Balance due of 2011 tax	$41,900
April 14	1st estimate 2012 state tax	58,000
June 12	2nd estimate 2012 state tax	58,000
September 15	3rd estimate 2012 state tax	58,000
December 13	4th estimate 2012 state tax	58,000

    On December 27, Extronic's tax department calculated that the corporation's actual 2012 state income tax liability was $251,200. Consequently, Extronic accrued a $19,200 liability for state tax payable at year-end. Extronic paid this balance due on March 11, 2013.

    a. If Extronic has not adopted the recurring item exception as its method of accounting for state income tax, compute its 2012 deduction for state income tax.

    b. If Extronic has adopted the recurring item exception as its method of accounting for state income tax, compute its 2012 deduction for state income tax.

22. Company N, an accrual basis taxpayer, owes $90,000 to Creditor K. At the end of 2012, Company N accrued $7,740 interest payable on this debt. It didn't pay this liability until March 3, 2013. Both Company N and Creditor K are calendar year taxpayers. For each of the following cases, determine the year in which Company N can deduct the $7,740 interest expense.

    a. Creditor K is a cash basis taxpayer, and Company N and Creditor K are related parties.

    b. Creditor K is an accrual basis taxpayer, and Company N and Creditor K are related parties.

    c. Creditor K is a cash basis taxpayer, and Company N and Creditor K are unrelated parties.

23. Acme is an accrual basis corporation. Mrs. T, Acme's chief financial officer, is a cash basis individual. In December 2012, Acme's board of directors decided that Mrs. T should receive a $20,000 bonus as additional compensation. Acme paid the $20,000 bonus to Mrs. T on January 12, 2013. In which year can Acme deduct the $20,000 bonus assuming that:

    a. Mrs. T owns no Acme stock?

    b. Mrs. T owns 63 percent of Acme stock?

24. GK Company, a calendar year accrual basis taxpayer, made the following adjustments to its allowance for bad debts this year.

January 1 allowance for bad debts	$86,100
Actual write-offs of accounts receivable	(77,300)
Addition to allowance at year-end	90,000
December 31 allowance for bad debts	$98,800

    a. Compute GK's bad debt expense for financial statement purposes.

    b. Compute GK's tax deduction for bad debts.

25. MG is an accrual basis corporation. In 2012, it wrote off a $65,000 account receivable as uncollectible. In 2013, it received a $65,000 check from the creditor in full payment of this receivable.

    a. What was the effect of the write-off on MG's 2012 financial statement income and taxable income?

    b. What was the effect of the collection of the receivable on MG's 2013 financial statement income and taxable income?

26. EFG, an accrual basis calendar year corporation, reported $500,000 net income before tax on its financial statements prepared in accordance with GAAP. EFG's records reveal the following information.

    • The allowance for bad debts as of January 1 was $58,000. Write-offs for the year totaled $13,800, and the addition to the allowance for the year was $12,500. The allowance as of December 31 was $56,700.

    • EFG paid a $17,500 fine to the state of Delaware for a violation of state pollution control laws.

    • EFG was sued by a consumers group for engaging in false advertising practices. Although EFG's lawyers are convinced that the suit is frivolous, its independent auditors insisted on establishing a $50,000 allowance for contingent legal liability and reporting a $50,000 accrued expense on the income statement.

    • EFG received a $165,000 advanced payment for 10,000 units of inventory on October 20. EFG reported the payment as revenue the following February when the units were shipped.

    Compute EFG's taxable income.

27. Using a 35 percent rate, compute the deferred tax asset or deferred tax liability (if any) resulting from the following:

    a. A transaction resulting in a $31,000 temporary excess of book income over taxable income.

    b. A transaction resulting in an $18,400 permanent excess of book income over taxable income.

    c. A transaction resulting in a $55,000 temporary excess of taxable income over book income.

28. GT Inc.'s net income before tax on its financial statements was $700,000, and its taxable income was $810,000. The $110,000 difference is the aggregate of temporary book/tax differences. GT's tax rate is 34 percent.

    a. Compute GT's tax expense for financial statement purposes.

    b. Compute GT's tax payable.

    c. Compute the net increase in GT's deferred tax assets or deferred tax liabilities (identify which) for the year.

29. Corporation H's auditors prepared the following reconciliation between book and taxable income. H's tax rate is 34 percent.

Net income before tax	$600,000
Permanent book/tax differences	15,000
Temporary book/tax differences	(76,000)
Taxable income	$539,000

    a. Compute Corporation H's tax expense for financial statement purposes.

    b. Compute Corporation H's tax payable.

    c. Compute the net increase in Corporation H's deferred tax assets or deferred tax liabilities (identify which) for the year.

30. Yount Inc.'s auditors prepared the following reconciliation between book and taxable income. Yount's tax rate is 34 percent.

Net income before tax	$378,200
Permanent book/tax differences	(33,500)
Temporary book/tax differences	112,400
Taxable income	$457,100

    a. Compute Yount's tax expense for financial statement purposes.

    b. Compute Yount's tax payable.

    c. Compute the net increase in Yount's deferred tax assets or deferred tax liabilities (identify which) for the year.

31. Micro, an accrual basis corporation, reported $505,100 net income before tax on its financial statements prepared in accordance with GAAP. Micro's records reveal the following information.

    • Micro earned $319,600 net income from its U.S. manufacturing activity and $179,200 from its foreign manufacturing activity.

    • Late in the year, Micro entered into a five-year licensing agreement with an unrelated firm. The agreement entitles the firm to use a Micro trade name in marketing its own product. In return, the firm will pay Micro an annual royalty of 1 percent of gross revenues from sales of the product. The firm paid a $40,000 advanced royalty to Micro on the day the agreement was finalized. For financial statement purposes, this prepayment was credited to an unearned revenue account.

    • At its final meeting for the year, Micro's board of directors authorized a $15,500 salary bonus for the corporation's president to reward him for an outstanding performance. Micro paid the bonus on January 12. The president does not own enough Micro stock to make him a related party for federal tax purposes.

    • Micro was incorporated last year. On its first tax return, it reported a $21,400 net operating loss.

    Compute Micro's taxable income.

32. TRW Inc. began business in 2004 and was profitable for its first three years. In 2007, it generated a $741,000 net operating loss. The following table shows TRW's taxable income *before consideration of this NOL.*

	2004	2005	2006	2007	2008	2009	2010	2011
Taxable income	$20,000	$158,000	$81,000	$(741,000)	$21,000	$398,000	$687,000	$905,000

Recompute TRW's taxable income for this eight-year period assuming that it did not elect to give up the NOL carryback.

33. For its first taxable year, Rony Inc.'s accounting records showed the following:

Operating loss per books	$(800,000)
Temporary book/tax difference	90,000
Net operating loss for tax	$(710,000)

a. Use a 34 percent rate to compute Rony's deferred tax asset with respect to the $90,000 book/tax difference.

b. Use a 34 percent rate to compute Rony's deferred tax asset with respect to its $710,000 NOL carryforward.

c. Compute Rony's tax benefit (negative tax expense) reported on its first income statement.

34. Refer to the facts in the preceding example. For its second taxable year, Rony Inc.'s accounting records showed the following:

Net income before tax	$1,200,000
Reversal of year 1 book/tax difference	(90,000)
Taxable income before NOL deduction	$1,110,000
NOL deduction	(710,000)
Taxable income	$ 400,000

a. Use a 34 percent rate to compute Rony's tax expense for financial statement purposes.

b. Use a 34 percent rate to compute Rony's tax payable.

c. Compute Rony's reduction in its deferred tax assets.

Issue Recognition Problems

Identify the tax issue or issues suggested by the following situations and state each issue in the form of a question.

1. Corporation DS owns assets worth $550,000 and has $750,000 outstanding debts. One of DS's creditors just informed DS that it is writing off a $15,000 account receivable from DS because it believes the receivable is uncollectible. However, even with this debt discharge, DS is insolvent and has no net worth.

2. Two years ago, a professional theater company paid $300 to an antique dealer for an old oil painting that the company used as a prop. This year, the company's prop manager

was cleaning the painting and discovered an older painting hidden beneath the top coat of pigment. To the company's delight, the older painting was signed by Paul Cézanne. Two independent appraisers determined that the painting is worth at least $250,000.

3. BL Inc. has been in business since 1990. This year BL's new CPA discovered that it is using an incorrect accounting method for a certain expense. BL is willing to change to the correct accounting method recommended by the CPA.

4. Company A, a calendar year taxpayer, has always used the cash method of accounting. It completed an engagement for a major client in November 2012 and submitted a bill for its $160,000 fee. Because Company A did not receive payment before year-end, it recognized no income from the engagement on its 2012 tax return. In January 2013, Company A received permission from the IRS to change from the cash method to the accrual method. This change is effective for 2013. On February 2, 2013, Company A received a $160,000 check from the client in payment of the bill.

5. Mr. RJ owns a consulting firm that uses a calendar year and the cash method. In November, Mr. RJ billed a client $3,500 for services performed in September. After waiting several weeks, he called the client to remind her of the bill. The embarrassed client promised to telephone Mr. RJ as soon as she prepared a check for $3,500. Mr. RJ left his business office on December 23 and did not return until January 2. A message on his answering machine said that he could pick up his check from the client's receptionist. The message was dated December 30.

6. Every December, Maxo Inc., an accrual basis, calendar year corporation, purchases 3,500 calendars from a publisher and mails them to its customers as a holiday gift. This year, Maxo received a $14,420 bill from the publisher, which represented a sizable price increase from prior years. Maxo scheduled a January meeting with the publisher to discuss the contested bill.

7. ABC Partnership owns 100 percent of the stock of two corporations, HT (an advertising firm) and LT (a commercial real estate development firm). HT is in a 35 percent marginal tax bracket. LT has an NOL carryforward deduction and will pay no tax this year. HT recently developed a new advertising campaign for LT and charged $75,000 for its services.

8. In 2011, Firm K paid $129,000 real property tax to Jurisdiction J and deducted the payment. In 2012, it successfully contested the property tax assessment. As a result, Jurisdiction J refunded $18,000 of the property tax.

9. In October 2010, Firm G completed a consulting engagement and received a $200,000 cash payment for its services. In December, the client notified Firm G that it was not satisfied with the work and demanded that Firm G refund $50,000 of the payment. Firm G refused and referred the matter to its attorney. In 2012, Firm G settled the dispute by paying the client $30,000. Firm G's 2010 marginal tax rate was 39 percent and its 2012 marginal tax rate was 34 percent.

10. Corporation WJ began business in 2010 and reported taxable income in both 2010 and 2011. In 2012, WJ incurred a $25,000 net operating loss. It wants to carry the NOL back as a deduction against 2011 taxable income because its 2011 marginal tax rate was higher than its 2010 marginal tax rate.

11. BL and TM are both calendar year corporations. On January 1, 2012, BL purchased TM's entire business (all TM's balance sheet assets), and TM's shareholders dissolved the corporation under state law. As of January 1, TM had a $190,000 NOL carryforward. BL's business for 2012 (which includes the business purchased from TM) generated $600,000 taxable income.

Research Problems

1. Bontaine Publications, an accrual basis, calendar year corporation, publishes and sells weekly and monthly magazines to retail bookstores and newsstands. The sales agreement provides that the retailers may return any unsold magazines during the one-month period after purchase. Bontaine will refund one-half of the purchase price of each returned magazine. During December 2012, Bontaine recorded $919,400 of magazine sales. During January 2013, Bontaine refunded $82,717 to retailers that returned magazines purchased during December. Can Bontaine reduce its 2012 income by the refund paid?

2. CheapTrade, an accrual basis, calendar year corporation, operates a discount securities brokerage business. CheapTrade accepts orders to buy or sell marketable securities for its customers and charges them a commission fee for effecting the transaction in a timely, low-cost manner. CheapTrade executes an order on the "trade" date, but title to the securities is not legally transferred and payment to or from the customer is not due until the "settlement date." In the normal five-day interval between the trade and settlement dates, CheapTrade performs administrative and accounting functions to record the transaction. During the last week of 2012, CheapTrade effected over 18,000 transactions with a trading date in 2012 but a settlement date in 2013. CheapTrade's commission from these transactions was $1,712,400. In which year should CheapTrade recognize this income?

3. Moleri, an accrual basis corporation with a fiscal taxable year ending on July 31, owns real estate on which it pays annual property tax to Madison County, Texas. The county assesses the tax for the upcoming calendar year on January 1, and the tax becomes a lien on the property as of the assessment date. Property owners have until March 31 to pay the tax without penalty. Moleri paid its 2012 property tax of $29,820 on March 11, 2012. How much of this tax payment is deductible on Moleri's tax return for the fiscal year ending July 31, 2012?

4. Jetex, an accrual basis, calendar year corporation, engages in the business of long-distance freight hauling. Every year, Jetex is required to purchase several hundred permits and licenses from state and local governments in order to legally operate its fleet of trucks. During 2012, the cost of these permits and licenses totaled $1,119,200. Even though none of the permits and licenses was valid for more than 12 months, a substantial number of them did not expire until sometime in 2013. In fact, Jetex calculated that $612,000 of the total cost incurred in 2012 actually benefited the company in 2013. For financial statement purposes, Jetex capitalized this amount as an asset and expensed only the $507,200 remainder on its 2012 income statement. As an accrual basis taxpayer, is Jetex limited to a $507,200 deduction in 2012?

Tax Planning Cases

1. Company Y began business in February 2012. By the end of the calendar year, it had billed its clients for $3.5 million of services and had incurred $800,000 of operating expenses. As of December 31, it had collected $2.9 million of its billings and had paid $670,000 of its expenses. It expects to collect the remaining outstanding bills and pay the remaining expenses by March 2013. Company Y adopted a calendar year for federal tax purposes. It may use either the cash method or the accrual method of accounting on its first tax return, and has asked you to quantify the value of using the cash method for the first year. In doing so, assume Company Y uses a 7 percent discount rate to compute NPV.

2. Corporation VB's tax returns for 2009, 2010, and 2011 provide the following information.

	2009	*2010*	*2011*
Gross income	$150,000	$1,890,000	$7,810,000
Deductions	(190,000)	(1,830,000)	(7,700,000)
Taxable income or (NOL)	$ (40,000)	$ 60,000	$ 110,000

a. On the basis of the above data, did VB derive any tax benefit from its 2009 NOL? Explain your conclusions.

b. VB generated a $350,000 net operating loss for 2012. It projects that it will continue to operate at a loss through 2013 but should generate at least $1 million taxable income in 2014. On the basis of this projection, compute the net present value of the tax savings from VB's deduction of the 2012 NOL, assuming that VB deducts it as a carryback and carryforward to the extent possible. In making your calculations, refer to the corporate tax rate schedule to compute VB's tax in 2010 and 2011 and use a 7 percent discount rate to compute NPV.

c. Should VB elect to give up the carryback of its 2012 NOL and use the entire NOL as a carryforward deduction? Support your conclusion with calculations.

Chapter **Seven**

Property Acquisitions and Cost Recovery Deductions

Learning Objectives

After studying this chapter, you should be able to:

1. Decide if a business expenditure should be deducted or capitalized.

2. Define the terms *tax basis* and *adjusted basis.*

3. Explain how leverage can reduce the after-tax cost of assets.

4. Compute cost of goods sold for tax purposes.

5. Understand the MACRS framework.

6. Apply the Section 179 expensing election.

7. Incorporate depreciation deductions into the NPV computation.

8. Explain how the cost of intangibles is recovered through amortization.

9. Distinguish between cost depletion and percentage depletion.

In Chapter 6, we learned that taxable income equals the excess of gross income over allowable deductions. We also learned that firms are allowed to deduct their business expenditures over the period of time that the expenditures create value for the firm. If an expenditure benefits the firm only in the current year, the expenditure is generally allowed as a current deduction. If an expenditure will benefit the firm for more than one taxable year, the deduction for the expenditure must be properly matched against future gross income.

In Chapter 7, we address this timing issue: In which taxable year or years can a firm deduct its expenditures? The chapter begins with a discussion of the tax rules that distinguish between deductible expenditures and expenditures that must be capitalized. The discussion then turns to the concept of capitalized costs as the tax basis of business assets. The relationship between basis and cost recovery deductions is explored, and the effect of cost recovery deductions on cash flows is examined. The second part of the chapter focuses on the various methods by which firms recover basis as cost of goods sold or through depreciation, amortization, and depletion deductions.

DEDUCTIBLE EXPENSE OR CAPITALIZED COST?

When a firm expends resources as part of its income-generating activity, the financial cost of the expenditure is reduced by any tax savings from the expenditure. In present value terms, tax savings are usually maximized (and after-tax cost is minimized) if the expenditure is deductible in the current year. The present value of the tax savings decreases if the firm must capitalize the expenditure and postpone its deduction until some future year. For tax accounting purposes, **capitalization** means that an expenditure is recorded as an asset on the balance sheet rather than as a current expense. If the firm is never allowed any tax deduction for the capitalized expenditure, the before-tax cost of the expenditure equals its after-tax cost.

Absent any restrictions, firms would immediately deduct every business expenditure. However, a basic premise of the federal income tax is that *no expenditure is deductible* unless the Internal Revenue Code authorizes the deduction. The Supreme Court has elaborated on this premise by observing that "an income tax deduction is a matter of legislative grace" and "the burden of clearly showing the right to the claimed deduction is on the taxpayer."[1] These observations are consistent with the tax law's conservative attitude toward the measurement of taxable income.

The Internal Revenue Code does allow firms to deduct all "ordinary and necessary expenses paid or incurred during the taxable year in carrying on any trade or business."[2] Because of this generic rule, firms deduct routine operating expenses in the year incurred under the firm's method of accounting. But the Code also prohibits a deduction for payments for "permanent improvements or betterments made to increase the value of any property."[3] As we will learn later in this chapter, the law relaxes this prohibition by allowing firms to recover many capital expenditures in the form of *future* deductions. In these cases, the difference in the tax consequences of current expenses and capitalized costs is the timing of the deduction for each. Even so, in cash flow terms, future deductions are worth less than current deductions, and firms minimize their cost of operations by deducting expenditures as soon as possible.

Objective 1
Decide if a business expenditure should be deducted or capitalized.

What factors determine whether a particular business expenditure is treated as a current deduction or a capital cost? If the expenditure creates or enhances a distinct asset with a useful life substantially beyond the current year, the expenditure must be capitalized.[4] Even if the expenditure does not create or enhance a specific asset, the expenditure must be capitalized if it results in a significant long-term benefit to the firm.[5] Moreover, if the tax treatment of an expenditure is uncertain, capitalization is the norm while deductibility is the exception.[6]

The following example quantifies the difference between deduction and capitalization in cash flow terms.

Current Deduction versus Capitalized Cost	This year, Corporation M raised $1 million of new capital by issuing preferred stock to a group of private investors.[7] The corporation incurred $40,000 of legal and other professional fees related to this transaction. Corporation M's marginal tax rate is 35 percent. Compare the after-tax cash flows under two different assumptions concerning the tax treatment of the $40,000 expenditure.

[1] *Interstate Transit Lines* v. *Commissioner*, 319 U.S. 590, 593 (1943).

[2] §162(a).

[3] §263(a).

[4] *Commissioner* v. *Lincoln Savings & Loan Assn.*, 403 U.S. 345 (1971).

[5] *Indopco Inc. v. Commissioner*, 503 U.S. 79 (1992).

[6] Ibid.

[7] Corporations do not recognize gain on the receipt of cash in exchange for stock. §1032.

	Current Deduction	Capitalized Cost
Proceeds of stock issue	$1,000,000	$1,000,000
Professional fees	(40,000)	(40,000)
Tax savings ($40,000 deduction × 35%)	14,000	–0–
After-tax cash flow	$ 974,000	$ 960,000

In this example, the $40,000 expenditure did not create or enhance a new asset for Corporation M. However, the federal courts have consistently ruled that expenses related to raising capital or reorganizing a firm's capital structure benefit the firm for the duration of its existence and are not deductible.[8] On the basis of this rule of law, Corporation M must charge the $40,000 expenditure against the proceeds of the stock sale, which nets $960,000 for the corporation on an after-tax basis.

Repairs and Cleanup Costs

Every firm that owns tangible operating assets must make incidental repairs and perform routine maintenance to keep the assets in good working order. Repair and maintenance costs that are regular and recurring in nature and do not materially add to either the value or the useful life of an asset are deductible.[9] In contrast, expenditures that substantially increase the value or useful life of an asset are nondeductible capital improvements. Similarly, the expense of adapting an existing asset to a new or different use must be capitalized to the cost of the asset.[10] The distinction between a repair and a capital improvement is not always obvious and is frequently a matter of dispute between taxpayers and the Internal Revenue Service.

Repair or Capital Improvement

Out of concern for earthquake safety, the city of San Francisco required the Fairmont Hotel to either remove or replace the concrete parapets and cornices that had decorated the hotel's exterior since 1907. The hotel spent $3 million to replace the old parapets and cornices with replicas made of lightweight fiberglass. The Fairmont Hotel deducted the expenditure as a repair. The IRS concluded that the expenditure was a capital improvement to the building and disallowed the deduction. In court, the Fairmont's owners argued that the $3 million expenditure was necessary to maintain the classical appearance of the building and to preserve its identity as a "grand hotel of the world." Moreover, the expenditure was not voluntary but was required by city ordinance. In spite of these arguments, the court agreed with the IRS that the expenditure materially prolonged the life and increased the value of the Fairmont Hotel and was not deductible.[11]

The business community and the IRS are constantly debating the proper treatment of environmental cleanup costs. Many firms, either voluntarily or because of government mandate, are spending millions of dollars to clean up pollutants, toxic wastes, and other dangerous substances unleashed on the environment as industrial by-products. The firms argue that cleanup costs should be currently deductible, while the IRS maintains that many such costs must be capitalized.

[8] See *General Bancshares Corp.* v. *Commissioner*, 326 F.2d 712 (CA-8, 1964) and *Mills Estate, Inc.* v. *Commissioner*, 206 F.2d 244 (CA-2, 1953).

[9] Reg. §1.162-4.

[10] Reg. §1.263(a)-1(b).

[11] *Swig Investment Co.* v. *United States,* 98 F.3d 1359 (CA-FC, 1996).

Deductible Cleanup Costs	Lako Transport Inc. purchased farmland in 1980 and constructed a trucking depot on the land. Over the next two decades, the depot generated hazardous wastes that were buried on the land. Three years ago, Lako began the process of remediating the soil and groundwater contaminated by the waste. It excavated and disposed of the contaminated soil, then backfilled the excavation with clean soil. Lako also constructed a groundwater treatment plant to cleanse the contaminated groundwater. The IRS ruled that the costs of remediating the soil did not prolong the land's useful life or increase its value. Instead, the costs merely returned the land to its original condition. The costs are analogous to repairs, and Lako can deduct them as ordinary and necessary expenses. In contrast, the costs of constructing the groundwater treatment plant are capital expenditures that create a new asset for Lako.[12]

Capitalized Cleanup Costs	PNT Company purchased real property from a dry cleaning business. Two months later, PNT discovered that the soil and groundwater were contaminated with dry cleaning fluid that had been improperly stored by the former owners. PNT incurred substantial costs, including legal and consulting fees, laboratory testing fees, supplies, and labor, to decontaminate the land. PNT could not use the real property in its own business until the cleanup process was complete. Unlike Lako in the previous example, PNT acquired the property *in its contaminated state*. Therefore, the IRS ruled that the remediation of the soil and groundwater represented a permanent improvement that increased the value of the land to PNT. Consequently, PNT had to capitalize the cleanup costs as part of the cost of the land.[13]

Asbestos Replacement	Company NM replaced the asbestos insulation in all its manufacturing equipment with nonhazardous insulation and deducted the replacement expense. The company justified the deduction because the replacement was made to protect the health of its employees and did not improve the operating efficiency or increase the value of the equipment. Furthermore, the replacement expense remedied a historic problem and was not related to the generation of future income. Upon audit, the IRS concluded that the asbestos replacement did, in fact, result in a long-term benefit to Company NM by permanently improving the work environment. Therefore, the IRS required the company to capitalize the replacement expense to the cost of the reinsulated equipment.[14]

Deductions of Capital Expenditures as Subsidies

The tax law contains special rules permitting firms to deduct expenditures that clearly are capital in nature. These preferential rules reduce the firm's after-tax cost of the expenditure and thereby represent an indirect federal subsidy. For instance, firms may deduct the first $15,000 of the annual cost of the removal of architectural and transportation barriers from buildings or transportation equipment to make such facilities more accessible to handicapped or elderly people.[15] A more significant preference is the deduction for **research and experimental expenditures.** This deduction is available even if the research leads to the development of an identifiable asset with an extended useful life to the firm.[16] This

---

[12] Rev. Rul. 94-38, 94-1 CB 35.

[13] IRS Letter Ruling 200108029 (February 23, 2001).

[14] IRS Letter Ruling 9240004 (July 29, 1992).

[15] §190.

[16] §174(a).

valuable preference reflects the federal government's belief that basic research is crucial to economic growth and should be encouraged through the tax law.

Self-Created Patent	CPT's research laboratory spent $2 million in the development of a chemical process that eliminates cholesterol from dairy products. CPT applied for and received a patent on the process from the U.S. Patent Office. The patent gave CPT the exclusive right to exploit the process for commercial purposes for 17 years. Even though the patent is an identifiable asset with long-term value, CPT deducted the $2 million cost of this "self-created asset" as a research and experimental expenditure. Consequently, its capitalized cost of the patent is zero.

Many preferential deductions benefit only certain industries. For instance, farmers are allowed to deduct soil and water conservation expenditures, which include the cost of leveling, grading, and terracing land, constructing drainage ditches and earthen dams, and planting windbreaks to inhibit soil erosion.[17] Farmers get a second tax break in the form of a deduction for the cost of fertilizers or other materials used to enrich farmland.[18]

Oil and gas producers can deduct **intangible drilling and development costs (IDC)** associated with locating and preparing wells for production.[19] Expenditures such as wages, fuel, repairs to drilling equipment, hauling, and supplies that contribute to the development of a productive well undeniably result in a long-term benefit to the producer and are usually captialized for financial statement purposes. By allowing a deduction for such IDC, the tax law provides an incentive for producers to undertake new drilling projects.

Advertising costs are deductible, even though a firm's successful advertising campaign can increase its market share and improve its competitive position for years to come.[20] While the IRS acknowledges that the advertising of a particular product or advertising intended to promote name recognition or goodwill may enhance a firm's profitability, it does not require capitalization of advertising costs except in unusual circumstances.[21]

Graphic Design Costs	R.J. Reynolds Tobacco Company deducted $2.2 million of graphic design costs related to its cigarette packs and cartons. Graphic design comprises the verbal information, styles of print, pictures or drawings, shapes, patterns, and colors displayed on the packs and cartons. The IRS disallowed the deduction because the design costs created intangible "brand equity" assets that were distinguishable from the goodwill created by advertising. In court, R.J. Reynolds argued that its graphic designs fit the textbook definition of advertising as any "presentation and promotion of ideas, goods, or services by an identified sponsor, which involves the use of mass media." The judge accepted this argument and held that R.J. Reynolds could deduct the graphic design costs as advertising expenses.[22]

THE CRITICAL ROLE OF TAX BASIS

Objective 2
Define the terms *tax basis* and *adjusted basis*.

When a firm capitalizes an expenditure to a new asset account, the amount of the expenditure becomes the firm's **tax basis** in the asset. Basis can be defined as a taxpayer's investment in any asset or property right—the measure of *unrecovered dollars* represented by the asset. An asset's basis plays a key role in the calculation of cash flows because taxpayers are entitled

[17] §175. This preferential deduction may not exceed 25 percent of the gross income derived from farming during the taxable year.

[18] §180.

[19] §263(c).

[20] Regs. §1.162-1(a) and §1.162-20(a)(2).

[21] Rev. Rul. 92-80, 1992-2 CB 57.

[22] *RJR Nabisco Inc.*, TC Memo 1998-252.

to recover this basis at no tax cost. This recovery occurs either through a series of future deductions or when the taxpayer disposes of the asset. Cost recovery deductions are covered in this chapter, while the tax consequences of asset dispositions are the subject of Chapter 8.

Basis, Cost Recovery, and Cash Flow

When a firm deducts a portion of the capitalized cost of an asset, the deduction has two consequences. The first consequence is that the asset's initial tax basis is reduced by the deduction.[23] The reduced basis is called the asset's **adjusted basis.** The second consequence is that the deduction generates a tax savings that reduces the after-tax cost of the asset.

Basis, Cost Recovery, and After-Tax Cost

Firm J pays $5,000 cash for a business asset. The tax law allows Firm J to deduct the capitalized cost of the asset ratably over five years. In the year of purchase and in each of the four subsequent years, the firm deducts $1,000 and reduces its basis in the asset by this deduction. If the firm has a 35 percent marginal tax rate and uses a 7 percent discount rate to compute net present value (NPV), the after-tax cost of the asset (NPV of cash flows) is $3,464.

Year	Year-End Adjusted Basis	Annual Deduction
0	$4,000	$(1,000)
1	3,000	(1,000)
2	2,000	(1,000)
3	1,000	(1,000)
4	–0–	(1,000)

Cash Flows	Year 0	Year 1	Year 2	Year 3	Year 4
Initial payment	$(5,000)				
Tax savings from deduction	350	$350	$350	$350	$350
Discount factor		.935	.873	.816	.763
NPV	$(4,650)	$327	$306	$286	$267
Total NPV	$ 3,464				

Firm J's adjusted basis in its asset at the end of each year is the $5,000 cost less the accumulated cost recovery deductions. By the end of the fifth year, the firm has recovered its entire investment in the asset, leaving the asset with a zero tax basis. A zero tax basis does not imply anything about the *value* of the asset to the firm; it simply indicates that Firm J has deducted the entire $5,000 expenditure that created the asset.

The difference between Firm J's $5,000 before-tax cost and $3,464 after-tax cost results from the stream of tax savings generated by the cost recovery deductions. If the firm could have recovered its tax basis over a shorter period of time, the present value of this stream would increase and the after-tax cost of the asset would decrease. Conversely, if the

---

[23] §1016(a)(2).

recovery period were longer, the present value of the tax savings would decrease and the after-tax cost of the asset would increase.[24]

Cost Basis

The majority of assets reported on a firm's balance sheet have an initial **cost basis**—the price paid to acquire the asset.[25] Cost basis includes any sales tax paid by the purchaser and any incidental costs related to putting the asset into production. While firms acquire many assets in straightforward cash transactions, they also acquire assets in exchange for property or services. In such case, the cost basis of the asset equals the fair market value (FMV) of the property surrendered or the services performed.[26]

Cost Basis: Exchange for Property	BT Corporation, a manufacturer of heavy equipment, sold inventory to an unrelated land developer. BT agreed to let the developer pay for the inventory by transferring five acres of land to the corporation. The inventory has a FMV of $139,000. BT's cost basis in its new asset (the land) is $139,000, the FMV of the inventory that BT exchanged for the asset.

Cost Basis: Exchange for Note	Modify the previous example by assuming that BT sold the inventory for the developer's written interest-bearing note to pay $139,000 in three years time. BT's cost basis in its new asset (the note receivable) is $139,000, the FMV of the inventory that BT exchanged for the asset.

Cost Basis: Exchange for Services	Firm C, a consulting business, performed professional services for an unrelated corporation and billed the corporation for $17,500. The corporation paid its bill by issuing 1,000 shares of its own common stock to the firm. Firm C recognizes $17,500 gross income and takes a $17,500 cost basis in its new asset (1,000 shares of corporate stock). This basis represents Firm C's investment in these shares—the dollar amount that the firm can recover tax free when it disposes of the stock.

Leveraged Cost Basis

When a firm acquires an asset through debt financing, the cost basis of the asset equals its entire cost, not just the firm's equity in the asset. Refer back to the example on page 162 in which Firm J purchased a business asset for $5,000. Assume that the firm financed the purchase by paying $1,500 from its bank account and borrowing $3,500 from a commercial lender. Firm J gave the lender a lien on the asset to secure the debt. Although the firm's initial investment in the asset is only $1,500, its cost basis is the full $5,000 purchase price.[27] The firm's repayment of the debt will create additional equity in the asset but will have no effect on the tax basis.

---

[24] This calculation of after-tax cost implies that the asset has no residual value after five years. If the firm could sell the asset for cash, the present value of this after-tax cash would reduce the after-tax cost of the asset. The cash flow implications of asset sales are addressed in the next chapter.

[25] §1012.

[26] Fair market value is the price at which property or services would change hands between a willing buyer and a willing seller, neither being under any compulsion to buy or to sell and both having reasonable knowledge of the relevant facts. Reg. §20.2031-1(b). Although this definition is in the estate tax regulations, it is the accepted definition for income tax purposes.

[27] *Crane* v. *Commissioner,* 331 U.S. 1 (1947).

Objective 3
Explain how leverage
can reduce the after-tax
cost of assets.

Tax planners refer to the use of borrowed funds to create tax basis as **leverage.** The use of leverage can reduce the purchaser's after-tax cost of the asset. Let's expand on the Firm J example to demonstrate how the after-tax cost of the $5,000 asset is reduced by the use of borrowed funds.

After-Tax Cost of Leveraged Purchase

Under the terms of its agreement with the commercial lender, Firm J must pay $315 interest (9 percent) at the beginning of each year and repay the $3,500 principal amount at the beginning of the fifth year. The annual interest payments are deductible expenses, while the principal payment is charged against (and retires) the $3,500 debt. The following table reflects each year's net cash flows based on Firm J's 35 percent marginal tax rate and 7 percent discount rate.

	Year 0	Year 1	Year 2	Year 3	Year 4
Initial payment and debt repayment	$(1,500)				$(3,500)
Interest payment		$(315)	$(315)	$(315)	(315)
Tax savings from:					
Cost recovery deduction	350	350	350	350	350
Interest deduction		110	110	110	110
Net cash flow	$(1,150)	$ 145	$ 145	$ 145	$(3,355)
Discount factor		.935	.873	.816	.763
NPV	$(1,150)	$ 136	$ 127	$ 118	$(2,560)
Total NPV	$(3,329)				

By leveraging its purchase of the asset, Firm J reduced the after-tax cost from $3,464 to $3,329. The cash flow data explain this result. Firm J's initial cash outflow to buy the asset was only $1,500. By borrowing the balance of the purchase price, it deferred paying $3,500 cash until the fifth year. This beneficial change in cash flows did not affect the $5,000 tax basis in the asset, the annual cost recovery deductions, or the timing of the stream of tax savings from those deductions. The annual cost of the leverage was $205, which is the after-tax interest on the note ($315 interest payment − $110 tax savings). However, even considering this additional cost, leverage saved the firm $135.[28]

INTRODUCTION TO COST RECOVERY METHODS

The topics covered in the first part of this chapter all relate to a key tax planning concept: The after-tax cost of a capitalized expenditure depends on the time period over which the firm can recover the expenditure as a deduction. Thus, time period variable tax savings are achieved when the cost of a capitalized expenditure is recovered over the shortest possible time period. The remainder of the chapter examines the four basic methods of periodic cost recovery: cost of goods sold, depreciation, amortization, and depletion. If none of these recovery methods is applicable, a cost is recoverable only when the firm disposes of the asset or when that asset ceases to exist.

[28] The leverage was beneficial in this example because Firm J's after-tax interest rate on borrowed funds was 5.85 percent ($205 after-tax interest ÷ $3,500 debt), while its discount rate was 7 percent. If Firm J's after-tax interest rate was higher than its discount rate, the leverage would be detrimental and would increase the after-tax cost of the asset in NPV terms.

INVENTORIES AND COST OF GOODS SOLD

In Chapter 6, we learned that firms maintaining inventories of goods for sale to customers must account for their inventory using the accrual method. In other words, firms can't deduct the cost of manufactured or purchased inventory but must capitalize the cost to an asset account. At the end of each year, the firm ascertains how much inventory is still on hand and how much has been sold during the year. The cost of the inventory on hand is carried on the balance sheet, while the **cost of goods sold** reduces gross income from sales. The following formula summarizes this accounting procedure:

> Cost of inventory on hand at the beginning of the year
> Cost of inventory manufactured or purchased during the year
> _____
> Total cost of inventory available for sale
> (Cost of inventory on hand at the end of the year)
> _____
> Cost of goods sold

Objective 4
Compute cost of goods sold for tax purposes.

This formula is based on two assumptions. The first assumption is that all expenditures that contributed to the value of inventory are capitalized to the inventory account. The second assumption is that the total cost of inventory is properly allocated between the inventory on hand at the end of the year and the inventory sold during the year. Let's examine the tax rules underlying each of these assumptions.

The Unicap Rules

Firms typically prefer to treat expenditures as deductible *period costs* rather than *product costs* that must be capitalized to inventory. Not surprisingly, the tax law contains explicit rules about the expenditures that must be included in inventory. These **uniform capitalization (unicap) rules** are as strict as they are complicated.[29] Under unicap, firms must capitalize all direct costs of manufacturing, purchasing, or storing inventory (direct materials and direct labor) and any indirect costs that "benefit or are incurred by reason of the performance of production or resale activities."[30] Examples of indirect costs that must be capitalized *to the extent they relate to a firm's production or resale function* include:[31]

- Officer's compensation.
- Pension, retirement, and other employee benefits.
- Rents paid on buildings and equipment used in a manufacturing process.
- Premiums paid to carry property insurance on production assets.
- Repair and maintenance of production assets.
- Cost recovery deductions for production assets.

Tax Talk
The Tax Court held that royalties paid for the right to produce trademarked products were indirect manufacturing costs properly capitalized and included in inventory cost for the related products.

The unicap rules may require indirect costs that were expensed for financial statement purposes to be capitalized for tax purposes. For example, the unicap rules require capitalization of indirect payroll department costs, to the extent related to the production function. Such costs would normally be expensed as a period cost under GAAP. The resulting book/tax difference is temporary and will reverse in the year in which the capitalized costs are deducted as cost of goods sold.

---

[29] The unicap rules are found in §263A and the accompanying regulations.
[30] Reg. §1.263A-1(e)(3)(i).
[31] Reg. §1.263A-1(e)(3)(ii).

Book/Tax Difference for Unicap	In 2011, Company MN constructed an inventory item that was on hand at year-end. It incurred $100,000 indirect costs in the construction process. For financial statement purposes, Company MN capitalized $80,000 as inventory product costs and expensed $20,000 as period costs. Under the unicap rules, it had to capitalize $88,000 to inventory and could deduct only $12,000 on its tax return. In 2012, Company MN sold the inventory item. For the two-year period, this temporary book-tax difference resulted in the following:

	Book		Tax		Taxable Income over
2011	*Expense*	*Inventory Cost*	*Deduction*	*Inventory Cost*	*Book Income*
	$20,000	$80,000	$12,000	$88,000	$8,000

2012	*Cost of Goods Sold*	*Cost of Goods Sold*	*Book Income over Taxable Income*
	$80,000	$88,000	$8,000

Computing Cost of Goods Sold

The allocation of costs between ending inventory and cost of goods sold is based on the method of accounting by which a firm tracks the flow of inventory items through its system. If a firm knows the actual cost of each item, it can use the **specific identification method** to value ending inventory and compute cost of goods sold. Real estate developers and antique dealers are good examples of businesses in which specific identification of inventory is possible.

For manufacturing and retail businesses that deal with thousands, if not millions, of inventory items, specific identification of each item is impossible. These firms must use a costing convention that is not based on the physical movement of inventory through the system. The two most commonly used costing conventions are **FIFO** (first-in, first-out) and **LIFO** (last-in, first-out).

The selection of an inventory costing convention may have a substantial effect on annual taxable income. During a period of rising prices, it is generally to a firm's advantage to adopt LIFO because the convention assumes that the last goods manufactured or purchased are the first goods sold. In an inflationary economy, the most recently acquired goods are the most expensive. If a firm assumes these goods are the first to be sold, it maximizes the cost of goods sold and minimizes the cost of ending inventory. While the LIFO convention can offer substantial tax savings, its popularity is diminished by the fact that any firm electing LIFO for tax purposes must also use LIFO to prepare financial statements.[32] Because of this forced conformity, any reduction in taxable income attributable to LIFO is mirrored by a reduction in accounting income and earnings per share reported to the firm's investors.

DEPRECIATION OF TANGIBLE BUSINESS ASSETS

Book and Tax Concepts of Depreciation

Under generally accepted accounting principles (GAAP), firms write off, or *depreciate,* the capitalized cost of tangible assets over their estimated useful lives.[33] As a result, the cost

---

[32] §472(c).

[33] The depreciable cost is reduced by the asset's estimated residual or salvage value.

of an asset is expensed over the years in which the asset contributes to the firm's revenue-generating activity. The concept of **depreciation** applies only to wasting assets that:

- Lose value over time because of wear and tear, physical deterioration, or obsolescence.
- Have a reasonably ascertainable useful life.

Nonwasting tangible assets lacking these characteristics, such as land and works of art acquired for display, are nondepreciable. For financial statement purposes, firms may calculate their annual depreciation expense under a variety of methods and may choose the method resulting in the best matching of the cost of an asset against revenue.

Before 1981, depreciation for tax purposes was also based on the estimated useful life of business property. Because the useful life of any asset is a matter of conjecture, taxpayers and the IRS were constantly wrangling over the question of asset lives. Firms argued for the shortest life over which to recover the tax basis of their assets, while the IRS asserted that a longer recovery period was more realistic. In 1981, Congress enacted a radically new cost recovery system to replace the old depreciation rules. In 1986, Congress refined this system into the **Modified Accelerated Cost Recovery System (MACRS),** which is in effect today.[34] Under MACRS, the estimated useful life of an asset is irrelevant in computing tax depreciation. Because the MACRS computation is independent of the computation of book depreciation, the depreciation deduction on a firm's tax return and depreciation expense on its financial statements are usually different numbers.

Book/Tax Difference for Depreciation

Porter Inc. purchased a depreciable asset for $200,000. First-year depreciation for book purposes was $19,000, while MACRS depreciation was $28,580. The $9,580 excess tax depreciation is a favorable book/tax difference resulting in a $3,353 deferred tax liability ($9,580 × 35 percent tax rate). The temporary difference will reverse in future years when book depreciation exceeds MACRS depreciation. As the difference reverses, the deferred tax liability will be reduced. By the year in which book basis and tax basis of the asset are depreciated to zero, the deferred tax liability will be eliminated.

The MACRS Framework

Objective 5
Understand the MACRS framework.

This section of Chapter 7 presents the MACRS framework: the general rules for computing depreciation for federal tax purposes. Business managers who understand this framework can appreciate the role of MACRS in the tax planning process. They do not need to master the system's fine technical points; consequently, many details of MACRS are omitted from our discussion.

Recovery Periods

MACRS applies to both depreciable realty (buildings, improvements, and other structures permanently attached to the land) and personalty (any tangible asset not part of a building or other permanent structure) used in a trade, business, or income-producing activity. Every depreciable asset is assigned to one of 10 **recovery periods.** Table 7.1 lists these periods and gives examples of assets assigned to each. For the most part, the MACRS recovery period is shorter than the asset's estimated useful life. The shortened time frame over which firms may deduct their investment in operating assets reduces the after-tax cost of the assets and acts as an incentive for firms to make capital acquisitions.

Depreciation Methods

The method by which annual depreciation is calculated is a function of the recovery period. Assets with a 3-year, 5-year, 7-year, or 10-year recovery period are depreciated using a

[34] §168.

MACRS Recovery Period	Assets Included
3 years	Small manufacturing tools, racehorses and breeding hogs, special handling devices used in food manufacturing
5 years	Cars, trucks, buses, helicopters, computers, typewriters, duplicating equipment, breeding and dairy cattle, and cargo containers
7 years	Office furniture and fixtures, railroad cars and locomotives, most machinery and equipment
10 years	Single-purpose agricultural and horticultural structures, assets used in petroleum refining, vessels, barges, and other water transportation equipment, fruit- or nut-bearing trees and vines
15 years	Land improvements such as fencing, roads, sidewalks, bridges, irrigation systems, and landscaping; telephone distribution plants; pipelines; billboards; and service station buildings
20 years	Certain farm buildings, municipal sewers
25 years	Commercial water utility property
27.5 years	Residential rental real property (duplexes and apartments)
39 years	Nonresidential real property (office buildings, factories, and warehouses)
50 years	Railroad grading or tunnel bore

TABLE 7.1
Recovery Periods for Tangible Business Assets

200 percent (i.e., double) declining-balance method. Assets with a 15-year or 20-year recovery period are depreciated using a 150 percent declining-balance method. In each case, the depreciation method switches to straight line when a straight-line computation over the remaining recovery period results in a greater deduction than the declining-balance method. For these six classes of business personalty, MACRS lives up to its name—depreciation deductions are indeed accelerated into the early years of the recovery period. Such front-end loading of depreciation further reduces the after-tax cost of tangible personalty.[35]

Before 1987, buildings and other types of realty could also be depreciated using accelerated declining-balance methods. Since 1987, properties with a 25-year, 27.5-year, 39-year, or 50-year recovery period must be depreciated using the straight-line method. For real property, MACRS is an *accelerated* cost-recovery system in name only.

Depreciation Conventions

The depreciation computation requires some assumption about how much depreciation is allowed in the year of an asset's acquisition or disposition. Under MACRS, all personalty (assets with recovery periods from 3 to 20 years) are assumed to be placed in service or disposed of exactly halfway through the year. This **half-year convention** means that in the first year of the recovery period, six months of depreciation is allowed, regardless of when the asset was actually placed in service. The same convention applies in the year in which an asset is disposed of. Regardless of the actual date of disposition, the firm may claim six months of depreciation.[36]

The half-year convention is subject to an important exception. If more than 40 percent of the depreciable personalty acquired during a taxable year is placed in service during the

[35] Under §168(b)(5), taxpayers may elect the straight-line method (rather than an accelerated method) for any class of property placed in service during the year.

[36] No MACRS depreciation is allowed for property placed in service and disposed of in the same year. Reg. §1.168(d)-1(b)(3)(ii).

last three months of the year, the firm must use a **midquarter convention** with respect to *all* personalty placed in service during the year. Under this convention, assets placed in service during any quarter (three months) of the year are assumed to be placed in service midpoint (one and one-half months) through the quarter. When an asset subject to this convention is disposed of, the disposition is treated as occurring at the midpoint of the quarter in which the disposition occurs. The midquarter requirement constrains a taxpayer that might be tempted to accelerate future-year property acquisitions into the last quarter of the current year to take advantage of cost recovery deductions available under the midyear convention.

Half-Year and Midquarter Conventions	During its calendar taxable year, Company P purchased the following depreciable personalty.

Date Placed in Service	Depreciable Basis
February 27	$ 68,000
July 8	20,000
November 19	55,000
	$143,000

Only 38 percent of the depreciable personalty was placed in service during the last three months of the year. Therefore, Company P uses the half-year convention and calculates six months of depreciation for each asset.

Now assume that Company P purchases a $19,000 depreciable asset on December 4. In this case, 46 percent of the depreciable personalty ($74,000 ÷ $162,000) was placed in service in the last three months of the year. For this reason, Company P must use the midquarter convention with the following result.

Quarter Placed in Service	Depreciable Basis	Months of Depreciation Allowed
First quarter	$ 68,000	10.5 months
Second quarter	–0–	7.5
Third quarter	20,000	4.5
Fourth quarter	74,000	1.5
	$162,000	

A **midmonth convention** applies to the year in which depreciable realty (assets with recovery periods of 25, 27.5, 39, or 50 years) is placed in service or disposed of. Under this convention, realty placed in service (or disposed of) during any month is treated as placed in service (or disposed of) midway through the month.

Midmonth Convention	Company RS placed three buildings into service during its calendar taxable year. It can claim the following months of depreciation for each building.

	Date Placed in Service	Months of Depreciation Allowed
Building 1	April 2	8.5 months
Building 2	July 30	5.5 months
Building 3	December 18	.5 month

Comprehensive Examples

The next two examples illustrate the MACRS calculation.

MACRS Calculation	Firm P, a calendar year taxpayer, buys a computer for $38,000 and places it in service on September 19. The computer has a five-year recovery period, so the firm uses the 200 percent declining-balance method to compute depreciation. Under this method, the straight-line rate of depreciation (20 percent) is doubled, and the resulting rate (40 percent) is applied each year to the unrecovered basis. Firm P will depreciate the computer according to the following schedule.

Year	Unrecovered Basis at Beginning of Year	Recovery Method	Convention	MACRS Depreciation
1	$38,000	200% DB	Half-year	$ 7,600
2	30,400	200% DB		12,160
3	18,240	200% DB		7,296
4	10,944	200% DB		4,378
5	6,566	SL*		4,378
6	2,188	SL		2,188
				$38,000

*$364.78 per month.

- Because only one-half year of depreciation is allowed in year 1, one-half year of depreciation is necessary in year 6 to complete the five-year recovery period.
- The declining-balance method is changed to the straight-line method in year 5 so that the $6,566 unrecovered basis is depreciated ratably over the remaining one and one-half years (18 months) in the recovery period.
- The basis of the computer is reduced to zero. For MACRS purposes, depreciable assets are assumed to have no residual value.

MACRS Calculation in Year of Sale	Refer to the facts in the previous example but assume that Firm P sells the computer on May 3 in year 4. In this case, the half-year convention also applies in the year of disposition.

Year	Unrecovered Basis at Beginning of Year	Recovery Method	Convention	MACRS Depreciation
1	$38,000	200% DB	Half-year	$ 7,600
2	30,400	200% DB		12,160
3	18,240	200% DB		7,296
4	10,944	200% DB	Half-year	2,189

The computer's adjusted basis immediately prior to sale is $8,755 ($10,944 unrecovered basis at beginning of year 4 – $2,189 depreciation in year 4).

IRS Depreciation Tables

To allow taxpayers to avoid the MACRS math process, the IRS publishes a set of convenient tables incorporating the MACRS computational rules. The tables consist of a series of annual percentages that are multiplied against the *initial undepreciated* basis of the asset to result in depreciation for the year. Table 7.2 contains the annual percentages for the six recovery periods for business personalty, based on the half-year convention. The IRS tables that provide the annual percentages for personalty depreciated under a midquarter convention are included in Appendix 7–A.

TABLE 7.2
MACRS for Business Personalty (Half-Year Convention)

Year	3-Year	5-Year	7-Year	10-Year	15-Year	20-Year
			Depreciation Rate			
1	33.33%	20.00%	14.29%	10.00%	5.00%	3.750%
2	44.45	32.00	24.49	18.00	9.50	7.219
3	14.81	19.20	17.49	14.40	8.55	6.677
4	7.41	11.52	12.49	11.52	7.70	6.177
5		11.52	8.93	9.22	6.93	5.713
6		5.76	8.92	7.37	6.23	5.285
7			8.93	6.55	5.90	4.888
8			4.46	6.55	5.90	4.522
9				6.56	5.91	4.462
10				6.55	5.90	4.461
11				3.28	5.91	4.462
12					5.90	4.461
13					5.91	4.462
14					5.90	4.461
15					5.91	4.462
16					2.95	4.461
17						4.462
18						4.461
19						4.462
20						4.461
21						2.231

MACRS Calculation Using IRS Tables

Refer to the facts in the previous two examples. If Firm P holds the equipment until fully depreciated, using Table 7.2 it can compute its annual depreciation deduction for its $38,000 computer as follows:

Year	Initial Basis	Table Percentage	MACRS Depreciation
1	$38,000	20.00%	$ 7,600
2	38,000	32.00	12,160
3	38,000	19.20	7,296
4	38,000	11.52	4,378
5	38,000	11.52	4,378
6	38,000	5.76	2,188
			$38,000

Note that the table percentage in year 1 is one-half the declining balance rate. In other words, the half-year convention for the year of acquisition is built into this table. However, the table percentages for the remaining years reflect a full year of depreciation. If an asset is disposed of before it is fully depreciated, the MACRS deduction for the year is only one-half the amount indicated by the table. If Firm P sells the computer on May 3 of year 4, MACRS depreciation for that year is computed multiplying the otherwise applicable table percentage by 50 percent, as follows:

Year 4 sale $38,000 × 11.52% × 50% = $2,189

TABLE 7.3 MACRS for Residential Real Property (27.5-year property)

Year	Month Placed in Service											
	1	**2**	**3**	**4**	**5**	**6**	**7**	**8**	**9**	**10**	**11**	**12**
	Depreciation Rate											
1	3.485%	3.182%	2.879%	2.576%	2.273%	1.970%	1.667%	1.364%	1.061%	0.758%	0.455%	0.152%
2–27	3.636	3.636	3.636	3.636	3.636	3.636	3.636	3.636	3.636	3.636	3.636	3.636
28	1.970	2.273	2.576	2.879	3.182	3.458	3.636	3.636	3.636	3.636	3.636	3.636
29	0.000	0.000	0.000	0.000	0.000	0.000	0.152	0.455	0.758	1.061	1.364	1.667

TABLE 7.4 MACRS for Nonresidential Real Property (39-year property)

Year	Month Placed in Service											
	1	**2**	**3**	**4**	**5**	**6**	**7**	**8**	**9**	**10**	**11**	**12**
	Depreciation Rate											
1	2.461%	2.247%	2.033%	1.819%	1.605%	1.391%	1.177%	0.963%	0.749%	0.535%	0.321%	0.107%
2–39	2.564	2.564	2.564	2.564	2.564	2.564	2.564	2.564	2.564	2.564	2.564	2.564
40	0.107	0.321	0.535	0.749	0.963	1.177	1.391	1.605	1.819	2.033	2.247	2.461

Tables 7.3 and 7.4 are abridged versions of the IRS tables for computing annual depreciation for 27.5-year and 39-year recovery property. Because these real properties are depreciated by the straight-line method, the tables are really helpful only for the years of acquisition and retirement in which the midmonth convention applies.

MACRS Depreciation for Commercial Building	Bulona Company, a calendar year taxpayer, purchased commercial real property for $3 million and allocated $200,000 cost to the land and $2.8 million to the building. The property was placed in service on June 4 (month 6). According to the IRS table, Bulona can recover the $2.8 cost of the building as follows.

Year 1 ($2.8 million × 1.391 percent) $38,948

Years 2–39 ($2.8 million × 2.564 percent)   71,792

Year 40 ($2.8 million × 1.177 percent)   32,956

Under a straight-line calculation, Bulona's annual depreciation is $71,795 ($2.8 million cost ÷ 39 years), which corresponds to the rounded number generated by the IRS table for years 2 through 39. In year 1, Bulona can deduct only 6.5 months of depreciation, while in year 40, it can deduct the residual 5.5 months of depreciation.

MACRS and FMV

It is important to understand that MACRS deductions do not represent cash outflows, and they do not correlate to any decline in the FMV of the asset. While operating assets typically lose value as they age, the annual MACRS deduction in no way reflects such loss. Moreover, firms may claim depreciation deductions for assets that may actually appreciate in value over time.[37] The adjusted tax basis in a business asset is the capitalized cost that the firm has not yet deducted and conveys no information concerning FMV.

[37] *Noyce*, 97 TC 670 (1991).

Depreciation for an Appreciating Asset?	Richard and Fiona Simon purchased two 100-year-old antique violin bows for $51,500. The couple used the bows in their business as professional violinists and claimed depreciation deductions based on a five-year recovery period. The IRS denied the deductions because the bows were treasured works of art that had actually appreciated in value since they were acquired by the Simons. A federal court concluded that the violin bows met the definition of depreciable property because they suffered "wear and tear" in the taxpayers' business activity. Thus, the Simons could recover their cost and reduce their tax basis in the violin bows to zero even though the bows continued to increase in value.[38]

Limited Depreciation for Passenger Automobiles

The tax law contains a major exception to MACRS for depreciation allowed for passenger automobiles held for business use.[39] **Passenger automobiles** are defined as four-wheeled vehicles manufactured primarily for use on public roads with an unloaded gross vehicle weight of 6,000 pounds or less. Vehicles directly used in the business of transporting people or property for compensation, such as taxicabs, limousines, hearses, ambulances, and delivery vans and trucks, are excluded from the definition of passenger automobiles.

The annual depreciation deduction for passenger automobiles may not exceed the limits provided under a special schedule, which is adjusted annually for inflation. For automobiles placed in service during 2011, annual depreciation was limited to the following:[40]

2011	$3,060
2012	4,900
2013	2,950
2014 and subsequent years	1,775

Passenger Automobile Depreciation	In 2011, WRP Inc. paid $23,000 for a passenger automobile for exclusive business use by its employees. For MACRS purposes, automobiles are five-year recovery property. The following schedule contrasts MACRS depreciation with limited depreciation for a passenger automobile costing $23,000.

Year	*MACRS Depreciation*	*Limited Depreciation*
2011	$ 4,600	$ 3,060
2012	7,360	4,900
2013	4,416	2,950
2014	2,650	1,775
2015	2,650	1,775
2016	1,324	1,775
2017		1,775
2018		1,775
2019		1,775
2020		1,440
	$23,000	$23,000

[38] *Simon*, 103 TC 247 (1994).

[39] §280F(a).

[40] The annual depreciation limits are increased for trucks, vans, and electric automobiles. See Rev. Proc. 2010-18, 2010-9 IRB 427.

Because MACRS depreciation would exceed the annual limits in the initial recovery year, WRP must use limited depreciation for all years. Consequently, WRP will recover its $23,000 cost over 10 years rather than over the normal 6 years in the MACRS recovery period.

Firms that use passenger automobiles in their business cannot avoid the limitation on depreciation by leasing automobiles rather than purchasing them. The tax law provides that deductions for lease payments on passenger automobiles must be limited in a manner that is "substantially equivalent" to the depreciation limitation.[41] IRS Publication 463, *Travel, Entertainment, Gift, and Car Expenses,* includes the complicated procedure by which firms compute their limited deduction for lease payments on passenger automobiles.

Section 179 Expensing Election

Section 179 allows firms to elect to expense (rather than capitalize) a limited dollar amount of the cost of certain property placed in service during the year. The limited dollar amount is $125,000 indexed annually for inflation. However, the Economic Stimulus Act of 2008 and the American Recovery and Reinvestment Tax Act of 2009 temporarily increased the maximum Section 179 deduction to $250,000 for qualifying property placed in service in 2008 and 2009. The Small Business Jobs Act of 2010 provided an even more generous temporary increase for a maximum Section 179 deduction of $500,000 for qualifying property placed in service in 2010 and 2011. Clearly, Congress believes this tax election provides significant economic stimulus. For tax years beginning in 2012, the maximum Section 179 deduction will drop to $139,000 indexed for inflation.

Property that qualifies for the **Section 179 election** includes tangible depreciable personalty and off-the-shelf computer software the cost of which is amortizable over 36 months.[42] The election allows many small firms to simply deduct the cost of their newly acquired assets and avoid the burden of maintaining depreciation or amortization schedules. Firms that purchase qualifying property with an aggregate cost in excess of the limited dollar amount may expense part of the cost of a specific asset or assets. The unexpensed cost is capitalized and recovered through depreciation or amortization.[43]

Objective 6
Apply the Section 179 expensing election.

Section 179 Expensing

In July 2011, Firm B purchased two new items of tangible personalty. Item 1 was seven-year recovery property costing $463,200, and item 2 was five-year recovery property costing $68,000. These were the only items that qualified for the Section 179 election. Firm B elected to expense the entire $463,200 cost of item 1 (because of its longer recovery period) and $36,800 of the cost of item 2. Firm B's cost recovery deduction for item 2 is $43,040.

		Recovery Deductions
Initial cost	$68,000	
Section 179 expense	(36,800)	$ 36,800
Adjusted basis for MACRS	$31,200	
Percentage from Table 7.2	20.00%	
MACRS depreciation	$ 6,240	6,240
		$ 43,040

[41] §280F(c)(3).

[42] §179(d)(1).

[43] In the case of passenger automobiles, any Section 179 deduction is treated as depreciation subject to the limitations of §230F(a).

Firm B's 2011 cost recovery deductions for items 1 and 2 total $506,240 ($463,200 for item 1 + $43,040 for item 2). At the end of 2011, the adjusted tax basis in item 1 is zero, and the adjusted tax basis in item 2 is $24,960 ($68,000 − $43,040).

If the items were purchased in July 2012, the maximum Section 179 expense would be $139,000. Firm B's cost recovery deduction for these items would be $198,928.

		Recovery Deductions
Initial cost of item 1	$463,200	
Section 179 expense	(139,000)	$139,000
Adjusted basis for MACRS	$324,200	
Percentage from Table 7.2	14.29%	
MACRS depreciation on item 1	$ 46,328	46,328
Initial cost of item 2	$ 68,000	
Percentage from Table 7.2	20.00%	
MACRS depreciation on item 2	$ 13,600	13,600
		$198,928

The Section 179 expense election has two limitations. If a firm purchases more than a threshold amount of qualifying property in a year ($2 million in 2010 and 2011, and $560,000 in 2012), the annual dollar amount is reduced by the excess of the total cost of the property over the threshold.[44] Because of this *excess property limitation,* a firm that purchases more than $699,000 of qualifying property in 2012 ($2.5 million in 2011) cannot benefit from a Section 179 election because its limited dollar amount is reduced to zero.

Excess Property Limitation	Firm R purchased $783,000 of equipment in 2012. Consequently, its excess amount of qualifying property was $84,000 ($783,000 − $699,000 threshold). Because of the excess property limitation, Firm R may expense only $55,000 of the cost of its qualifying property ($139,000 limited dollar amount − $84,000). It must capitalize the remaining $728,000 cost and recover it through MACRS depreciation.

Once a firm elects to expense the cost of qualifying property, the expense is generally deductible. However, the *deduction* (not the expense) is limited to taxable business income computed without regard to the deduction. Any nondeductible expense resulting from this *taxable income limitation* carries forward to succeeding taxable years.[45]

Taxable Income Limitation	Firm X purchased $47,800 of tangible personalty in 2011 and elected to expense the entire cost. The firm's taxable income without regard to any Section 179 deduction was $29,600. Because of the taxable income limitation, Firm X could deduct only $29,600, thereby reducing taxable income to zero. The $18,200 nondeductible expense carried forward into 2012. Firm X purchased $41,250 of tangible personalty in 2012 and elected to expense the entire cost. The firm's taxable income without regard to any Section 179 deduction was $394,100. Because the taxable income limitation was inapplicable, the firm's Section 179 deduction was $59,450 ($41,250 + $18,200 carryforward), and its taxable income was $334,650.

[44] §179(b)(2).

[45] §179(b)(3) and Reg. §1.179-3.

Tax Talk

This is the third round of bonus depreciation this decade. For quali-fying property placed in service between September 11, 2001, and May 5, 2003, 30 percent bonus depreciation applied. For property placed in service between May 6, 2003, and December 31, 2004, 50 percent bonus depreciation applied.

The carryforward of a nondeductible expense to a succeeding taxable year does not increase the limited dollar amount for such year. Assume that firm X in the above example purchased $128,000 of qualifying property 2012. In this case, its Section 179 deduction is limited to $139,000 ($128,000 + $11,000 carryforward from 2011), and the firm has a $7,200 remaining carryforward to 2013.

Bonus Depreciation

The 2008 Economic Stimulus Act also provided for 50 percent bonus depreciation in the year of acquisition for qualified property placed in service during 2008.[46] For this provision, quali-fied property includes most new tangible personal property, computer software, and certain leasehold improvements. The adjusted basis of the property is reduced by the amount of bonus depreciation for purposes of computing regular MACRS depreciation over the recovery life of the asset. This provision was also extended by the 2009 Recovery Act and the Small Business Jobs Act of 2010; thus bonus depreciation was available for qualifying acquisitions during 2008, 2009, and 2010. The 2010 Tax Relief Act further enhances this incentive provision, pro-viding for 100 percent bonus depreciation for qualifying property placed in service after Sep-tember 8, 2010, and before January 1, 2012. Thus, qualifying acquisitions during this period are fully deductible in the year acquired. Congress hopes this valuable deduction will provide stimulus for both purchasers and producers of new business assets. As this book goes to press, Congress has not acted to extend 100 percent bonus depreciation beyond 2011. However, 50 percent bonus is available for qualifying property placed in service before January 1, 2013.

If property qualifies both for the Section 179 deduction and 50 percent **bonus deprecia-tion,** Section 179 is applied first.[47] The following example illustrates the joint application of these two stimulus provisions.

Recovery Deductions in 2012 versus 2011

In March 2012, Firm N purchased new tangible personalty costing $250,000. Assume the asset was five-year recovery property and was the firm's only qualifying asset acquisition for the year. If Firm N elects both Section 179 and 50 percent bonus depreciation for this acquisi-tion, its total 2012 recovery deduction for the asset is $710,000.

		Recovery Deductions
Initial cost	$ 250,000	
Section 179 expense	(139,000)	$139,000
Adjusted basis for bonus depreciation	$ 111,000	
50% bonus depreciation	(55,500)	55,500
Adjusted basis for MACRS	$ 55,500	
Percentage from Table 7.2	20.00%	
MACRS depreciation	$ 11,100	11,100
		$205,600

As a result of these incentive provisions, Firm N is able to deduct 82 percent ($205,600 ÷ $250,000) of the cost of the acquisition in 2012. The remaining unrecovered basis of the asset will be depreciated under the normal MACRS rules for the remainder of its recovery life.

Had the asset been placed in service in 2011, bonus depreciation would be $111,000. Through the combination of Section 179 and bonus depreciation, the entire cost of the asset would be deducted in the year of acquisition.

---

[46] §168(k).

[47] Reg. §1.168(k)-1(a)(2)(iii).

Purchase versus Leasing Decision

Objective 7
Incorporate depreciation deductions into the NPV computation.

Business managers routinely make decisions concerning the acquisition of operating assets. One of the more common decisions is whether the firm should purchase an asset or lease it. Both options provide the firm with the use of the asset over time, but the cash flows associated with each option are different. Managers should choose the option that minimizes the after-tax cost of the acquisition in present value terms. The following example illustrates how depreciation deductions are incorporated into a cash flow analysis.

Purchase versus Leasing

SGM must acquire a piece of heavy machinery for use in its construction business. SGM could purchase the machine for $75,000 cash. The machine would be seven-year recovery property. SGM's engineers estimate that the machine would actually last for 10 years, after which time it would have no residual value. Alternatively, SGM could lease the machine for 10 years for $11,300 annual rent. SGM is in a 35 percent marginal tax bracket and uses a 7 percent discount rate to compute NPV. To decide whether to purchase or to lease the machine, SGM must calculate and compare the after-tax cost of each option.

Purchase Option

Purchase price	$(75,000)
Present value of tax savings from depreciation (see following table)	22,193
After-tax cost of purchase option	$(52,807)

Year	MACRS Depreciation	Tax Savings at 35%	Discount Factor	Present Value of Tax Savings
0	$10,717	$3,751	—	$ 3,751
1	18,367	6,428	.935	6,010
2	13,118	4,591	.873	4,008
3	9,367	3,278	.816	2,675
4	6,698	2,344	.763	1,788
5	6,690	2,342	.713	1,670
6	6,698	2,344	.666	1,561
7	3,345	1,171	.623	730
	$75,000			$22,193

Lease Option

Annual lease payment	$(11,300)
Tax savings ($11,300 deduction × 35%)	3,955
After-tax annual payment	$ (7,345)
Present value of year 0 payment	$ (7,345)
Present value of years 1–9 payment ($7,345 × 6.515 discount factor)	(47,853)
After-tax cost of rent option	$(55,198)

A comparison of after-tax cash flows provides SGM with the information necessary to make its decision. SGM should purchase the machine (after-tax cost $52,807) rather than lease it (after-tax cost $55,198) to minimize after-tax cost.

AMORTIZATION OF INTANGIBLE ASSETS

Objective 8
Explain how the cost of intangibles is recovered through amortization.

Firms may own a variety of assets that have no physical substance but that represent a valuable property right or economic attribute. The tax basis in such intangible assets may be recoverable under some type of **amortization** method allowed by the Internal Revenue Code. As a general rule, amortization is allowed only if the intangible asset has a determinable life.[48] For instance, a firm that purchases a patent or copyright can deduct the cost ratably over the number of months during which the patent or copyright confers an exclusive legal right on the owner.[49]

Determinable Life	Refer back to the example beginning on page 161 in which CPT created and patented a chemical process that eliminates cholesterol from dairy products. Hanover, a manufacturer of frozen foods, wanted to use the process to develop a new line of healthy ice cream. Thus, Hanover purchased the patent from CPT for $10 million. At date of purchase, the patent had a remaining legal life of 157 months. Hanover must capitalize the cost of the patent and can amortize the cost at the rate of $63,694 per month ($10 million ÷ 157 months).

The cost basis in an intangible asset with an indeterminable life generally is not amortizable but can be recovered only upon disposition of the asset.

Indeterminable Life	This year, Forman Group purchased 16,000 shares of common stock in ABC Inc. and a 10 percent interest in KLM Partnership. Forman Group must capitalize the cost of both these intangible equity interests. Because the interests represent permanent investments, Forman Group cannot recover the capitalized costs through amortization.

The tax law requires that the capitalized cost basis of a few particular intangible assets be amortized over an arbitrary 15-year period, beginning in the month in which the asset is acquired. This amortization rule applies regardless of how the asset was acquired (self-created or purchased) or the period of time during which the asset confers a legal right or benefit to the owner. The assets subject to this 15-year amortization rule are licenses, permits, and similar rights granted by a government, franchises, trademarks, and trade names.[50]

15-Year Amortization	Perry's Restaurant has been in operation for 12 years. This year, the owners decided to expand their menu to offer wine and beer. They paid $31,500 to the state government for a liquor license that will remain in effect indefinitely. Perry's must capitalize the cost of the license and can amortize the cost over 15 years at the rate of $175 per month ($31,500 ÷ 180 months).

In the following paragraphs, we will analyze three types of intangible assets subject to cost recovery through amortization: organizational and start-up costs, leasehold costs, and business acquisition intangibles.

Organizational and Start-Up Costs

The tax law contains a specific rule for the tax treatment of the **organizational costs** of forming a partnership or corporation. These costs include legal and accounting fees attributable to the formation and any filing or registration fees required under state or local law. A new partnership or corporation can deduct the *lesser* of its actual organizational costs or $5,000. This $5,000 maximum is reduced by the amount by which total costs exceed $50,000. The entity must capitalize any nondeductible organizational cost and may elect to amortize such cost over a 180-month period starting with the month in which business begins.[51]

[48] Reg. §1.167(a)-3.
[49] Reg. §1.197-2(c)(7) and Reg. §1.167(a)-14(c)(4).
[50] §197(a) and (d)(1)(D) and (F).
[51] §709 and §248.

The tax law includes a similar rule for the **start-up expenditures** of any new business, regardless of organizational form. Start-up expenditures include both the up-front costs of investigating the creation or purchase of a business and the routine expenses incurred during the preoperating phase of a business. This preoperating phase ends only when the business has matured to the point that it can generate revenues. A firm may deduct the *lesser* of its actual start-up expenditures or $5,000 (reduced by the amount by which total expenditures exceed $50,000). The firm must capitalize any nondeductible start-up expenditures and may elect to amortize such cost over a 180-month period starting with the month in which business begins.[52]

Organizational and Start-Up Costs	Mr. Dugan and Mrs. Guffman went into partnership to start a new business. Their first step was to engage an attorney to draft a partnership agreement and a CPA to set up an accounting system. The total cost of these professional services was $10,580. DG Partnership spent three months locating and renting suitable office space, hiring and training staff, publicizing the new business on radio and television, and applying for the operating license required under local law. These preoperating expenses totaled $61,200. The partnership received an operating license in late August and opened its doors for business on September 8.

DG Partnership can deduct $5,000 of its organizational costs and must capitalize the $5,580 remainder. Because its start-up expenditures exceeded $55,000, its deduction for these expenditures is reduced to zero, and it must capitalize the entire $61,200. On its first Form 1065 (U.S. Partnership Return of Income), the partnership makes a written election to amortize the $66,780 total of these capitalized costs over 180 months.[53] If the partnership reports on a calendar year basis, its amortization deduction for its first taxable year is $1,284.

$66,780 ÷ 180 months = $371 monthly amortization

$371 × four months (September through December) = $1,484

DG Partnership will amortize the $65,296 remaining capitalized costs over the next 176 months.

The capitalization requirement for start-up expenditures does not apply to the **expansion costs** of an existing business.[54] Once DG Partnership in the above example begins operations, it has established an active business. If DG Partnership expands to a second location, it will repeat the process of renting a facility, hiring and training additional staff, and advertising the new location. Although the expenses with respect to these activities are functionally identical to the $61,200 start-up expenditures, DG Partnership can deduct these expenses because they are incurred in the conduct of an existing business.

Business Start-Up or Expansion?	TresChic Company manufactures and imports perfumes, cosmetics, clothing, and accessories. For many years, TresChic sold its goods only at wholesale. However, three years ago, the company decided to move into the retail market and opened its first "BeBe Boutique." The success of the first boutique prompted the company to open 11 more boutiques nationwide. The boutiques operate in exactly the same manner, have a standardized décor, and carry the same merchandise. TresChic handles the accounting, financing, management, purchasing, and advertising for all the boutiques. The IRS ruled that TresChic's retail operation is a substantially different activity from its wholesale operation. Consequently, the first BeBe Boutique represented a new business, and TresChic had to capitalize its start-up expenditures accordingly. However, the next 11 boutiques represented the expansion of TresChic's existing retail operation. Therefore, TresChic could deduct all the operating expenses associated with each new boutique in the year incurred.[55]

---

[52] §195. According to §195(c)(1), interest expense, taxes, and research and experimentation costs are not start-up expenditures and may be deducted even if incurred during the preoperating phase of a business venture.

[53] The two partners, not the partnership itself, will pay tax on the income generated by the partnership business. Nevertheless, the partnership is required to file an information return on which any elections that affect the computation of taxable income are made. See §703(b).

[54] §195(c)(1)(B).

[55] IRS Letter Ruling 9331001 (April 23, 1993).

Leasehold Costs and Improvements

When a firm rents tangible property for use in its business, it may incur up-front costs to acquire the lease on the property. Such **leasehold costs** must be capitalized and amortized over the term of the lease.[56] In contrast, if a firm pays for physical improvements to leased property, the cost of the **leasehold improvements** must be capitalized to an asset account, assigned to a MACRS recovery period, and depreciated under the MACRS rules. This cost recovery rule applies even when the term of the lease is shorter than the MACRS recovery period.[57]

Leasehold Costs and Improvements	Early in the year, VB Corporation entered into a lease agreement for commercial office space. VB's cost of negotiating the lease was $3,120, and it also spent $28,000 to construct cabinets, bookshelves, and lighting fixtures to conform the leased space to its needs. The term of the lease is 48 months, beginning on May 1. VB Corporation must capitalize the $3,120 lease acquisition cost and amortize it over 48 months ($65 per month for a current year amortization deduction of $520). It must also capitalize the $28,000 cost of the leasehold improvements. These improvements qualify as seven-year recovery property, and VB will recover its cost basis through MACRS depreciation.[58]

Business Acquisition Intangibles

A firm that purchases an entire business is usually acquiring more than just the monetary and operating assets recorded on the business's balance sheet. A substantial portion of the value of the business may consist of intangible assets that may or may not appear on the balance sheet. If the purchaser pays a lump-sum price for the business, it must allocate a portion of the price to each balance sheet asset acquired. The price allocated to each asset equals that asset's FMV and becomes the purchaser's cost basis in the asset.[59]

If the lump-sum price exceeds the value of the balance sheet assets, the excess is allocated to the unrecorded intangible assets of the business. Such assets include **goodwill** (value created by the expectancy that customers will continue to patronize the business) and **going-concern value** (value attributable to the synergism of business assets working in coordination). Other common acquisition intangibles are:

- Information-based intangibles such as accounting records, operating systems or manuals, customer lists, and advertiser lists.
- Customer-based or supplier-based intangibles such as favorable contracts with major customers or established relationships with key suppliers.
- Know-how intangibles such as designs, patterns, formulas, and other intellectual properties.
- Workforce intangibles such as the specialized skills, education, or loyalty of company employees and favorable employment contracts.
- Covenants not to compete and similar arrangements with prior owners of the business.

[56] Reg. §1.162-11(a).

[57] §168(i)(8).

[58] Unless VB Corporation renews its lease on the commercial office space after 48 months, it will not have recovered its entire cost basis in the leasehold improvements when it surrenders the space back to the lessor. The tax consequences of this situation are discussed in the next chapter.

[59] Reg. §1.1060-1.

For tax purposes, firms recover the cost of acquisition intangibles over a 15-year period, regardless of the actual length of time that the intangible asset is expected to yield any commercial benefit.[60] Amortization begins in the month in which the intangible asset is acquired.

Amortization of Acquisition Intangibles	On March 9, BV Company (a calendar year taxpayer) paid $2 million to acquire a business from Mr. Lopez. The sales contract stated that $1.7 million of the lump-sum price was attributable to the appraised value of monetary and tangible operating assets. An additional $50,000 was attributable to the business's customer list, $150,000 was attributable to goodwill, and $100,000 was attributable to a convenant not to compete. Under this covenant, Mr. Lopez cannot engage in a similar business for the next three years. BV Company must capitalize the $300,000 cost of these intangibles and amortize the cost over 15 years at a rate of $1,667 per month ($300,000 ÷ 180 months). Its amortization deduction in the year of purchase is $16,670 ($1,667 for 10 months).

Patents and copyrights are treated as acquisition intangibles *only if* they are acquired as part of the purchase of an *entire business*. In such case, the purchaser must amortize the cost allocated to the patent or copyright over 15 years, regardless of the remaining legal life of the asset.

Patent as Acquisition Intangible	Refer back to the example on page 178 in which Hanover purchased a patent for a chemical process for use in its manufacturing business. This year, Crown Food purchased Hanover's entire business operation. Consequently, Crown Food acquired all Hanover's tangible and intangible assets, including the patent. At date of purchase, the patent had a remaining legal life of only eight years (96 months). But because the patent is included as one of Crown Food's acquisition intangibles, it must recover its cost allocated to the patent over a 15-year amortization period.

Book/Tax Difference for Goodwill

The tax treatment of purchased goodwill is very different from the treatment under GAAP. Firms are not required to amortize the cost of goodwill for financial reporting purposes. Accordingly, the annual deduction for goodwill amortization is a favorable temporary difference between book income and taxable income. For financial reporting purposes, firms must test their purchased goodwill annually for any impairment to its value. If the value of the goodwill is impaired, the firm must record an impairment expense and write down the value of the goodwill reported on its balance sheet.[61] This expense, which is based on an estimate, is not deductible. Consequently, an impairment expense is an unfavorable temporary difference between book income and taxable income.

Book/Tax Difference for Goodwill	In 2002, Grant Inc. purchased a business for a lump-sum price of $12 million. Grant allocated $3.5 million to the goodwill of the acquired business. For tax purposes, Grant is amortizing the capitalized cost of the goodwill at a rate of $19,444 per month ($3.5 million ÷ 180 months). The goodwill is not amortizable for book purposes, so the annual $233,328 amortization deduction is a favorable book/tax difference resulting in an annual $81,665 deferred tax liability ($233,328 × 35 percent tax rate).
	This year, Grant's auditors required the corporation to write the goodwill down to $3 million and record a $500,000 goodwill impairment expense. This nondeductible expense is an unfavorable book/tax difference resulting in a $175,000 reduction ($500,000 × 35 percent tax rate) in Grant's deferred tax liability with respect to its goodwill.

[60] §197(a). The 15-year amortization rule does not apply to equity interests in other businesses, debt instruments, existing leases of tangible property, and computer software available for purchase by the general public. Under §167(f)(1), the cost of such off-the-shelf software is amortizable over 36 months.

[61] SFAS No. 142, *Goodwill and Other Intangible Assets* (2000).

Comprehensive Example of a Lump-Sum Purchase

Firms that pay a lump-sum price to purchase a business must determine the cost basis of each tangible and intangible asset included in the purchase as well as any cost recovery method allowed for each asset. The next example illustrates this important process.

Firm RT's Lump-Sum Purchase

Firm RT purchased the business operated by SW Inc. for a lump-sum price of $1 million. At date of purchase, the appraised values of SW's business assets were:

	Appraised FMV
Accounts receivable	$120,000
Supplies	25,000
Inventory	325,000
Furniture and fixtures	360,000
Lease on real property (8-year remaining term)	40,000
	$870,000

RT was willing to pay $1 million because the business has such an excellent reputation in the local community. The cost basis in each of its newly acquired business assets is:

	Initial Cost Basis
Accounts receivable	$ 120,000
Supplies	25,000
Inventory	325,000
Furniture and fixtures	360,000
Lease on real property	40,000
Purchased goodwill	130,000
	$1,000,000

- RT will recover its basis in the accounts receivable as the receivables are collected.
- RT will recover its basis in the supplies as a deduction when the supplies are consumed.
- RT will recover its basis in the inventory through cost of goods sold.
- RT will recover its basis in the furniture and fixtures through MACRS depreciation.
- RT will recover its basis in the lease through amortization deductions over the eight-year remaining term of the lease.
- RT will recover its basis in the goodwill through amortization deductions over 15 years.

DEPLETION OF NATURAL RESOURCES

Firms engaged in the business of extracting minerals, oil, gas, and other natural deposits from the earth incur a variety of up-front costs to locate, acquire, and develop their operating mines and wells. Some of these costs must be capitalized and recovered over the period of years that the mine or well is productive.[62] The method for recovering a firm's investment in an exhaustible natural resource is called **cost depletion.** The annual cost depletion deduction is based on the following formula.[63]

[62] Oil and gas producers may deduct many intangible drilling and development costs, thereby minimizing the capitalized basis of productive wells.

[63] Reg. §1.611-2(a).

$$\frac{\text{Units of production sold during the year}}{\text{Estimated total units in the ground at the beginning of the year}} \times \text{Unrecovered basis in the mine or well}$$

Cost Depletion	Company M, which operates a mining business, spent $500,000 for geological surveys, mineral rights, and excavation costs, all of which were capitalized as the basis of a new copper mine. At the beginning of the first year of production, the company's engineers estimated that the mine should produce 80,000 tons of copper ore. During the first year, 20,000 tons of ore were extracted and sold. The company's cost depletion deduction was $125,000.

$$\frac{20,000 \text{ tons}}{80,000 \text{ tons}} \times \$500,000 \text{ initial basis} = \$125,000$$

At the beginning of the second year, the engineers revised their estimate of the mine's remaining productivity to 65,000 tons; during the second year, 32,000 tons of copper ore were extracted and sold. The cost depletion deduction was $184,615.

$$\frac{32,000 \text{ tons}}{65,000 \text{ tons}} \times \$375,000 \text{ unrecovered basis} = \$184,615$$

By the year in which the copper deposit is exhausted and the mine is no longer productive, Company M will have recovered its entire $500,000 tax basis through cost depletion deductions. |

Percentage Depletion

Objective 9
Distinguish between cost depletion and percentage depletion.

To encourage the high-risk activity of exploration and extraction, Congress invented **percentage depletion,** an annual deduction based on the gross income generated by a depletable property multiplied by an arbitrary depletion rate. For instance, the statutory depletion rate for sulfur and uranium is 22 percent; the rate for gold, silver, copper, iron ore, and crude oil is 15 percent; and the rate for asbestos, coal, and lignite is 10 percent. In any year, a firm is allowed to deduct the *greater* of the cost depletion or percentage depletion attributable to its properties.[64]

Let's highlight the relationship of cost depletion and percentage depletion by returning to our example of Company M and its copper mine.

Percentage Depletion	Company M can sell its copper ore for $40 per ton, and its percentage depletion equals 15 percent of gross income from sales of the ore. The following table shows the computation of the annual depletion deduction (indicated by bold type).

Year	Estimated Tons/ Beginning of Year	Tons Sold during Year	Gross Income	Unrecovered Basis/ Beginning of Year	Cost Depletion	Percentage Depletion*
1	80,000	20,000	$ 800,000	$500,000	**$125,000**	$120,000
2	65,000	32,000	1,280,000	375,000	184,615	**192,000**
3	30,000	17,000	680,000	183,000	**103,700**	102,000
4	15,000	18,500	740,000	79,300	79,300	**111,000**
5	5,000	4,000	160,000	–0–	–0–	**24,000**
6	2,500	2,000	80,000	–0–	–0–	**12,000**

*15 percent of gross income.

[64] §613(a) and (b).

Note that in years 1 through 4, Company M deducted the *greater* of cost depletion or percentage depletion and reduced the tax basis in the mine accordingly, but in year 4, a curious thing occurred. Company M claimed a $111,000 depletion deduction that exceeded its unrecovered basis in the mine by $31,700! In years 5 and 6, it deducted $36,000 percentage depletion even though it had a zero basis in the copper mine.

Tax Talk

The Obama administration has proposed repeal of both the percentage depletion deduction and immediate deduction of intangible drilling costs. The change would make oil and gas more expensive for the U.S. consumer, reducing the consumption of these fuels.

The magic of the percentage depletion deduction is that it is not limited to the capitalized cost of the mine or well. Percentage depletion is available in every year that the property generates gross income, regardless of the fact that the tax basis has been reduced to zero. In such cases, percentage depletion is not a cost recovery deduction at all but an indirect preferential tax rate on the income earned by the extractive industries.

Not surprisingly, this highly beneficial deduction is subject to restrictions. Annual percentage depletion may not exceed 50 percent of the taxable income from the depletable property (100 percent for oil and gas property).[65] In the oil and gas industry, only independent producers and royalty owners are entitled to percentage depletion. This tax break is denied to the giant integrated companies that extract, refine, and sell oil and gas to retail customers.[66] Even with these restrictions, percentage depletion is a valuable government subsidy.

Conclusion

The after-tax cost of a business expenditure is a function of the time period over which the firm can deduct the expenditure. If an expenditure is not deductible in the current year but must be capitalized to an asset account, its after-tax cost depends on the method (if any) by which the firm can compute cost recovery deductions with respect to the asset. Exhibit 7.1 summarizes the tax treatment of business expenditures and should help you appreciate the key roles that cost of goods sold, depreciation, amortization, and depletion play in the tax planning process.

EXHIBIT 7.1
Tax Treatment of Business Expenditures

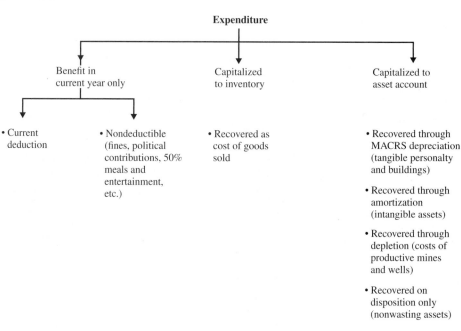

[65] Ibid.
[66] §613A(c).

Sources of Book/Tax Differences	**Permanent**	**Temporary**

Permanent
- Percentage depletion in excess of cost depletion

Temporary
- Intangible drilling costs (IDC)
- Inventory costs capitalized under UNICAP
- MACRS depreciation
- Section 179 deduction
- Bonus depreciation
- Amortization of organizational and start-up costs
- Amortization of purchased intangibles (goodwill)
- Goodwill impairment expense

Key Terms

adjusted basis *162*
amortization *178*
bonus depreciation *176*
capitalization *158*
cost basis *163*
cost depletion *182*
cost of goods sold *165*
depreciation *167*
expansion costs *179*
FIFO *166*
going-concern value *180*
goodwill *180*
half-year convention *168*

intangible drilling and development costs (IDC) *161*
leasehold costs *180*
leasehold improvements *180*
leverage *164*
LIFO *166*
midmonth convention *169*
midquarter convention *169*
Modified Accelerated Cost Recovery System (MACRS) *167*

organizational costs *178*
passenger automobiles *173*
percentage depletion *183*
recovery period *167*
research and experimental expenditures *160*
Section 179 election *174*
specific identification method *166*
start-up expenditures *179*
tax basis *161*
uniform capitalization (unicap) rules *165*

Questions and Problems for Discussion

1. How is the principle of conservatism reflected in the tax law's premise concerning the deductibility of business expenditures?

2. Assume that Congress enacted legislation requiring firms to capitalize advertising costs and amortize them over 20 years. Discuss the potential effects of such legislation on the amount of advertising that firms purchase and the price that advertising companies charge for their product.

3. Discuss the relationship between cost recovery deductions and cash flows.

4. To what extent do cost recovery deductions based on the capitalized cost of a tangible asset reflect a decline in the economic value of that asset?

5. Can a firm have a negative tax basis in an asset?

6. If the tax law did not allow farming businesses to deduct soil and water conservation expenditures but required capitalization of these costs, in what year or years would farmers recover these costs?

7. Corporation J manufactures electrical appliances. Corporation K provides architectural services. During the year, both corporations paid $56,000 annual premiums to carry fire and casualty insurance on their tangible assets. Corporation J was required to capitalize the $56,000 cost for tax purposes while Corporation K was allowed a $56,000 deduction. Can you explain this difference in tax treatment between the two corporations?

8. Identify the tax and nontax issues that firms must consider in adopting the LIFO method of accounting for inventories.

9. Identify four possible differences in the computation of depreciation expense for financial statement purposes and MACRS depreciation.

10. What is the purpose of the MACRS half-year, midquarter, and midmonth conventions?

11. Why do the MACRS tables published by the IRS incorporate a depreciation convention for the first year during an asset's recovery period but not for the year of disposition?

12. Discuss the reasons why the Section 179 election is more valuable to small firms than to large firms.

13. Firm O purchased two items of business personalty this year. The first item cost $135,000 and has a five-year recovery period, and the second item cost $161,500 and has a seven-year recovery period. Firm O wants to make the Section 179 election for one of its new assets. Which asset should the firm choose and why?

14. Discuss the strengths and weaknesses of the tax rule providing for 15-year amortization of the cost of business acquisition intangibles.

15. Describe the difference in tax treatment between start-up costs of a new business and expansion costs of an existing business.

16. On February 1, Mr. B purchased a business from Mr. and Mrs. S for a lump-sum price of $750,000. The business included the following balance sheet assets.

	Appraised FMV
Accounts receivable	$ 27,600
Inventory	195,000
Office supplies (4 months worth)	8,500
Furniture and fixtures	395,000

By buying the business, Mr. B acquired a favorable lease on office space with a remaining term of 31 months; he estimates that the value of this lease is $20,000. The purchase contract stipulates that Mr. and Mrs. S will not engage in a competitive business for the next 36 months. Discuss how Mr. B can recover the cost of each of the business assets acquired in this purchase.

17. Firm W and Firm X both have goodwill and going-concern value worth approximately $1 million. However, only Firm X reports an amortization deduction with respect to its goodwill and going-concern value on its tax return. Can you explain this difference in tax treatment between the two firms?

18. Under what circumstances is percentage depletion not a true cost recovery deduction?

Application Problems

1. Assuming a 25 percent tax rate, compute the after-tax cost of the following business expenditures.

   a. $14,200 cost of a survey capitalized to land.

   b. $44,750 research and experimental expenditure.

   c. $23,000 advertising cost.

   d. $120,000 cost of grading land used in a nonfarming business.

   e. $120,000 cost of grading land used in a farming business.

2. Determine the tax basis of the business asset acquired in each of the following cases.

   a. Firm L paid $5,950 cash plus $416 sales tax plus a $500 installation charge for a satellite dish.

   b. TTP Inc. acquired inventory in exchange for 800 shares of TTP common stock listed on Nasdaq at $212 per share on the date of exchange.

   c. Firm Q acquired machinery in exchange for architectural drawings rendered by Firm's Q's junior partner. The partner spent 20 hours on the drawings, and his hourly billing rate is $350.

   d. Company C purchased equipment by paying $2,000 cash at date of purchase and financing the $18,000 balance of the price under a three-year deferred payment plan.

3. Early this year, ZeZe Inc. paid a $52,000 legal fee in connection with a dispute over ZeZe's title to investment land. ZeZe's auditors required the corporation to expense the payment on this year's financial statements. According to ZeZe's tax adviser, the payment is a nondeductible capital expenditure. ZeZe's tax rate is 35 percent.

   a. Compute the deferred tax asset or a deferred tax liability (identify which) resulting from this difference in accounting treatment.

   b. When will the temporary difference reverse?

4. In 2011, Firm A paid $50,000 cash to purchase a tangible business asset. In 2011 and 2012, it deducted $3,140 and $7,200 depreciation with respect to the asset. Firm A's marginal tax rate in both years was 35 percent.

   a. Compute Firm A's net cash flow attributable to the asset purchase in each year.

   b. Compute Firm A's adjusted basis in the asset at the end of each year.

5. Refer to the facts in problem 4. Now assume that Firm A borrowed $50,000 to purchase the asset. In each year, it paid $3,800 annual interest on the debt. The interest payments were deductible.

   a. How does this change in facts affect Firm A's net cash flow attributable to the asset purchase in each year?

   b. How does this change in facts affect Firm A's adjusted basis in the asset at the end of each year?

6. In year 0, Jarmex paid $55,000 for an overhaul of a tangible operating asset. Jarmex has a 34 percent marginal tax rate and uses a 7 percent discount rate to compute NPV.

   a. Compute the after-tax cost of the overhaul if Jarmex can deduct the $55,000 payment as a repair in year 0.

   b. Compute the after-tax cost of the overhaul if Jarmex must capitalize the $55,000 payment to the asset account and can recover it on a straight-line basis in years 0, 1, 2, and 3.

7. Company XYZ manufactures a tangible product and sells the product at wholesale. In its first year of operations, XYZ manufactured 1,000 units of product and incurred $200,000 direct material cost and $130,000 direct labor costs. For financial statement purposes, XYZ capitalized $85,000 indirect costs to inventory. For tax purposes, it had to capitalize $116,000 indirect costs to inventory under the unicap rules. At the end of its first year, XYZ held 260 units in inventory. Compute XYZ's cost of goods sold for book purposes and for tax purposes.

8. Refer to the facts in problem 7. In its second year of operations, XYZ manufactured 2,000 units of product and incurred $410,000 direct material cost and $275,000 direct labor costs. For financial statement purposes, XYZ capitalized $139,000 indirect costs to inventory. For tax purposes, it had to capitalize $193,000 indirect costs to inventory under the unicap rules. At the end of its second year, XYZ held 300 items in

inventory. Compute XYZ's cost of goods sold for book purposes and for tax purposes assuming that:

a. XYZ uses the FIFO costing convention.

b. XYZ uses the LIFO costing convention.

9. Firm J purchased a depreciable business asset for $62,500. Assuming the firm uses the half-year convention, compute its first-year MACRS depreciation if the asset is:

a. A land irrigation system.

b. Duplicating equipment.

c. An oceangoing barge.

d. Small manufacturing tools.

10. Herelt Inc., a calendar year taxpayer, purchased equipment for $383,600 and placed it in service on April 1, 2012. The equipment was seven-year recovery property, and Herelt used the half-year convention to compute MACRS depreciation.

a. Compute Herelt's MACRS depreciation with respect to the equipment for 2012 and 2013.

b. Compute Herelt's adjusted basis in the equipment on December 31, 2013.

c. Compute Herelt's MACRS depreciation for 2014 if it disposes of the equipment on February 9, 2014.

11. Knute Company purchased only one asset during its calendar taxable year. The asset cost $650,000 and has a three-year recovery period. Compute Knute's MACRS depreciation with respect to this asset over the recovery period assuming that:

a. The asset was placed in service on August 18.

b. The asset was placed in service on November 9.

12. Erwin Company, a calendar year taxpayer, made only two purchases of depreciable personalty this year. The first purchase was five-year recovery property costing $312,800, and the second purchase was seven-year recovery property costing $574,000. Compute Erwin's first-year MACRS depreciation with respect to the personalty assuming that:

a. The first purchase occurred on February 2, and the second purchase occurred on June 18.

b. The first purchase occurred on February 2, and the second purchase occurred on October 13.

13. Suber Inc., a calendar year taxpayer, purchased equipment for $800,000 and placed it in service on March 1. Suber's chief engineer determined that the equipment had an estimated useful life of 120 months and a $50,000 residual value. For financial statement purposes, Suber uses the straight-line method to compute depreciation.

a. Compute book depreciation for the year.

b. Assuming that the equipment has a seven-year recovery period and is subject to the half-year convention, compute MACRS depreciation for the year.

c. Compute Suber's book basis and tax basis in the equipment at the beginning of next year.

14. Ryland Company, a calendar year taxpayer, purchased commercial realty for $2 million and allocated $200,000 cost to the land and $1.8 million cost to the building. Ryland placed the real estate in service on May 21.

a. Compute Ryland's MACRS depreciation with respect to the realty for the year of purchase.

b. How would your answer change if Ryland placed the realty in service on September 2 instead of May 21?

c. How would your answer to part *a* change if the building was a residential apartment complex instead of a commercial office?

15. AP constructed a new manufacturing plant for a total cost of $9,465,000 and placed it in service on March 2. To finance the construction, AP took out a $6 million, 30-year mortgage on the property. Compute AP's MACRS depreciation for the manufacturing plant for the first, second, and third years of operation.

16. On May 12, 2011, Nelson Inc. purchased eight used-passenger automobiles for use in its business. Nelson did not make a Section 179 election to expense any portion of the cost of the automobiles, which are five-year recovery property subject to the half-year convention. Compute Nelson's depreciation deduction with respect to the automobiles for 2011 and 2012 assuming:

    a. The automobiles were Mini Coopers costing $14,300 each.

    b. The automobiles were Buick Lucernes costing $27,000 each.

17. Margo, a calendar year taxpayer, paid $480,000 for machinery (seven-year recovery property) placed in service on August 1, 2012.

    a. Assuming that the machinery was the only tangible property placed in service during the year, compute Margo's maximum cost recovery deduction.

    b. How would your computation change if Margo paid $600,000 for the machinery?

    c. How would your computation change if Margo paid $750,000 for the machinery?

    d. How would your answer to part *a.* change if the machinery was placed in service in 2011?

18. In 2012, Firm L purchased machinery costing $71,300 and elected to expense the entire cost under Section 179. How much of the expense can Firm L deduct in each of the following cases?

    a. Its taxable income before the deduction was $458,000.

    b. Its taxable income before the deduction was $49,200.

    c. Its net operating loss (NOL) before the deduction was $5,016.

19. In 2011, Company W elected under Section 179 to expense $89,300 of the cost of qualifying property. However, it could deduct only $65,000 of the expense because of the taxable income limitation. In 2012, Company W's taxable income before any Section 179 deduction was $812,000. Compute its 2012 Section 179 deduction if:

    a. The total cost of qualifying property purchased in 2012 was $63,600.

    b. The total cost of qualifying property purchased in 2012 was $125,000.

20. Loni Company paid $278,000 for tangible personalty in 2009 and elected to expense $250,000 of the cost (the limited dollar amount for 2009). Loni's taxable income before a Section 179 deduction was $94,100. Loni paid $63,700 for tangible personalty in 2010 and elected to expense the entire cost. Loni's taxable income before a Section 179 deduction was $228,000.

    a. Compute Loni's Section 179 deduction and taxable income for 2009.

    b. Compute Loni's Section 179 deduction and taxable income for 2010.

21. At the beginning of its 2012 tax year, Hiram owned the following business assets.

	Date Placed in Service	Initial Cost	Accumulated Depreciation	Recovery Period	Depreciation Convention
Furniture	6/19/10	$30,750	$11,925	7-year	Half-year
Equipment	5/2/09	70,000	49,840	5-year	Half-year
Machinery	9/30/09	58,000	41,296	5-year	Half-year

On July 8, Hiram sold its equipment. On August 18, it purchased and placed in service new tools costing $189,000; these tools are three-year recovery property. These were Hiram's only capital transactions for the year. Compute Hiram's cost recovery deduction for 2012. In making your computation, assume that taxable income before depreciation exceeds $500,000.

22. In April 2012, Lenape Corporation acquired new business machinery with a total cost of $475,000. Assuming the machinery qualifies for both the Section 179 deduction and bonus depreciation, calculate Lenape's total cost recovery on the machinery for 2012.

23. Ajax Inc. was formed on April 25 and elected a calendar year for tax purposes. Ajax paid $11,200 to the attorney who drew up the articles of incorporation and $5,100 to the CPA who advised the corporation concerning the accounting and tax implications of its organization. Ajax began business operations on July 15. To what extent can Ajax deduct its $16,300 organizational costs on its first tax return?

24. Mr. and Mrs. FB, a retired couple, decided to open a family restaurant. During March and April, they incurred the following expenses.

Prepaid rent on commercial real estate ($2,100 per month from April through December)	$ 18,900
Prepaid rent on restaurant equipment ($990 per month from April through December)	8,910
Advertising of upcoming Grand Opening	900
Staff hiring and training	11,500
	$ 40,210

Mr. and Mrs. FB served their first meal to a customer on May 1. Determine the tax treatment of the above expenses on their tax return.

25. Mr. Z, a calendar year taxpayer, opened a new car wash. Prior to the car wash's grand opening on October 8, Mr. Z incurred various start-up expenditures (rent, utilities, employee salaries, supplies, etc.). In each of the following cases, compute Mr. Z's first-year deduction with respect to these expenditures.

    a. The start-up expenditures totaled $4,750.

    b. The start-up expenditures totaled $27,320.

    c. The start-up expenditures totaled $53,120.

    d. The start-up expenditures totaled $88,380.

26. MNO is a calendar year taxpayer. On March 1, MNO signed a 36-month lease on 2,100 square feet of commercial office space. It paid a $3,240 fee to the real estate agent who located the space and negotiated the lease and $8,800 to install new overhead lighting in the office space. Lighting equipment is seven-year recovery property. Compute MNO's first-year cost recovery deduction with respect to the $12,040 cost relating to the lease space.

27. On April 23, Mrs. Y purchased a taxi business from Mr. M for a $60,000 lump-sum price. The business consisted of a two-year-old taxicab worth $19,000, Mr. M's license to operate a taxi business in Baltimore, his list of regular customers, and his registered business name "On Time Any Time Taxi." Mrs. Y operated the business from April 24 through the end of the year.

    a. Compute Mrs. Y's taxable income from the taxi business if her taxable income *before any cost recovery deductions* was $36,890. Assume Mrs. Y wants to minimize taxable income.

    b. Compute Mrs. Y's taxable income from the taxi business if her taxable income *before any cost recovery deductions* was $17,100. Assume Mrs. Y wants to minimize taxable income.

28. On November 13, Underhill Inc., a calendar year taxpayer, purchased a business for a $750,000 lump-sum price. The business's balance sheet assets had the following appraised FMV.

Accounts receivable	$ 38,000
Inventory	177,000
Tangible personalty	400,000
	$615,000

   a. What is the cost basis of the goodwill acquired by Underhill on the purchase of this business?

   b. Compute Underhill's goodwill amortization deduction for the year of purchase.

   c. Assuming a 35 percent tax rate, compute the deferred tax asset or deferred tax liability (identify which) resulting from Underhill's amortization deduction.

29. SEP, a calendar year corporation, reported $918,000 net income before tax on its financial statements prepared in accordance with GAAP. The corporation's records reveal the following information.

   • SEP incurred $75,000 of research costs that resulted in a new 17-year patent for the corporation. SEP expensed these costs for book purposes.

   • SEP's depreciation expense per books was $98,222, and its MACRS depreciation deduction was $120,000.

   • SEP was organized two years ago. For its first taxable year, it capitalized $27,480 start-up costs and elected to amortize them over 180 months. For book purposes, it expensed the costs in the year incurred.

   Compute SEP's taxable income.

30. TGW, a calendar year corporation, reported $3,908,000 net income before tax on its financial statements prepared in accordance with GAAP. The corporation's records reveal the following information.

   • TGW's depreciation expense per books was $448,000, and its MACRS depreciation deduction was $377,900.

   • TGW capitalized $678,000 indirect expenses to manufactured inventory for book purposes and $802,000 indirect expenses to manufactured inventory for tax purposes.

   • TGW's cost of manufactured goods sold was $2,557,000 for book purposes and $2,638,000 for tax purposes.

   • Four years ago, TGW capitalized $2,250,000 goodwill when it purchased a competitor's business. This year, TGW's auditors required the corporation to write the goodwill down to $1,500,000 and record a $750,000 goodwill impairment expense.

   Compute TGW's taxable income.

31. A&Z incurred $450,000 of capitalized costs to develop a uranium mine. The corporation's geologists estimated that the mine would produce 900,000 tons of ore. During the year, 215,000 tons were extracted and sold. A&Z's gross revenues from the sales totaled $689,000, and its operating expenses for the mine were $200,000. Calculate A&Z's depletion deduction.

32. Jonson Corporation incurred $150,000 in capitalized acquisition costs to develop an oil well. The corporation's geologists estimated that there were 200,000 barrels of oil in the well at the beginning of the year. Jonson produced and sold 20,000 barrels this year, earning $140,000 of gross revenue. Its operating expenses for the well totaled $25,000. Calculate Jonson's allowable depletion deduction.

Issue Recognition Problems

Identify the tax issue or issues suggested by the following situations and state each issue in the form of a question.

1. Corporation J paid $500,000 for six acres of land on which it plans to build a new corporate headquarters. Four months after the purchase, Corporation J paid $20,000 to a demolition company to tear down an old warehouse located on the land and haul away the rubble from the demolition site.

2. Mr. R lived in a two-bedroom, one-bath residence until August when he moved to a new home and converted his old residence into residential rent property. He had no trouble finding tenants who signed a one-year lease and moved in on September 1. As of this date, the market value of the old residence was $120,000. Mr. R purchased the residence six years ago for $180,000.

3. Mrs. K owns her own consulting firm, and her husband, Mr. K, owns a printing business. This year, Mrs. K's consulting business generated $89,000 taxable income. Mr. K's business operated at a loss. In July, Mr. K bought new office furniture for $16,000. This was the only purchase of tangible business personalty by either spouse for the year. Mr. and Mrs. K always file a joint tax return.

4. ROJ Inc. purchased a 20-acre industrial complex consisting of three warehouses and two office buildings surrounded by parking lots. About 12 acres of the land is undeveloped. ROJ paid a lump-sum purchase price of $19.4 million.

5. Firm PY purchased industrial equipment from a Canadian vendor. The firm paid $12,800 to transport the equipment to its manufacturing plant in Florida and a $1,700 premium for insurance against casualty or theft of the equipment while en route.

6. WRT owns a chain of retail bookstores. It recently decided to add coffee bars in each store to sell gourmet coffee drinks and pastries to the bookstore customers. WRT has not yet obtained the necessary licenses required under local law to serve food to the public. However, it has incurred almost $30,000 in up-front expenditures on the coffee bars.

7. In 2009, Firm Z elected to expense the $8,000 cost of a machine, which it reported as the only item of equipment placed in service that year. This year, the IRS audited Firm Z's 2009 return and discovered that it had incorrectly deducted a $10,000 expenditure. According to the IRS, Firm Z should have capitalized this expenditure as the cost of depreciable equipment with a 5-year recovery period.

8. Company JJ, a calendar year corporation, bought an airplane for use in its oil and gas business in December. The manufacturer delivered the plane to the company's hangar on December 19. Because of severe winter weather, JJ's pilot was unable to fly the plane on company business until February 16 of the next year.

9. TCJ bought a 10-acre tract of undeveloped land that it intends to improve and subdivide for sale to real estate customers. This year, TCJ paid $4,300 to a local company to clean up the land by hauling away trash, cutting down dead trees, and spraying for poison ivy.

10. Firm D paid a $500,000 lump-sum price for a commercial office building. A local consulting company approached Firm D with a proposal. For a $15,000 fee, the company would analyze the components of the building (shelving, lighting fixtures, floor coverings, plumbing, etc.) to determine how much of the $500,000 price is attributable to five-year or seven-year recovery property rather than to the building itself.

Research Problems

1. Elsworthy Company operates a number of public golf courses in Florida. This year, Elsworthy constructed six new greens of a type described as "modern" greens. Modern greens contain sophisticated drainage systems that include subsurface drainage tiles and interconnected pipes. These tiles and pipes require replacement about every 20 years. The cost of each modern green was $115,000: $30,000 for earthmoving,

grading, and shaping of the land in preparation for construction and $85,000 for construction of the green itself. What is the correct tax treatment of the total cost of each modern green?

2. On January 1 of every year since 1993, Lanier Corporation has paid a $35,000 retainer fee to the law firm of Myer and Weeble (MW). MW specializes in structuring corporate mergers and acquisitions. In return for the annual payment, MW guarantees that it will represent Lanier for one year. Moreover, MW will not provide legal assistance to any business that Lanier attempts to acquire during the year. MW is entitled to keep the annual retainer regardless of the actual amount of legal work performed for Lanier. On January 1, Lanier paid the annual $35,000 retainer to MW. In August, MW structured Lanier's acquisition of Carstron Manufacturing. MW sent Lanier a bill for $100,000 of additional legal fees in connection with this acquisition.

   The tax law clearly requires Lanier to capitalize the $100,000 additional legal fees as part of the cost of Carstron Manufacturing. But can Lanier deduct (rather than capitalize) the $35,000 retainer paid in January?

3. Last year, Manabee Inc. leased a computer system from ICS Company for five years. After using the system for only 10 months, Manabee realized that it was no longer adequate for its expanding business needs. As a result, Manabee negotiated with ICS to terminate the original lease and enter into a new five-year lease under which ICS would provide Manabee with an expanded, upgraded computer system. ICS would not agree to the arrangement unless Manabee paid a $200,000 lease cancellation fee. Can Manabee deduct this fee as a current expense, or must Manabee capitalize the fee as a leasehold cost and amortize it over the five-year term of the new lease?

4. Peter Nelson is employed full time as an accountant by an insurance company. In his spare time, he operates a secondary business as a self-employed wedding photographer. On January 3, 2012, Peter purchased new video recording equipment for $22,600. During 2012, he used this equipment for personal enjoyment (filming his family members on holidays and during vacations). He also used the equipment for business purposes when a client wanted video coverage of a wedding. Peter did not purchase any other property for business use during the year.

   Peter kept a careful written record of the time that he used the video recording equipment for either personal or business reasons during 2012. This record substantiates that he used the equipment 59 percent of the time for personal reasons and 41 percent of the time for business reasons. Can Peter elect to expense any of the cost of the video recording equipment under Section 179?

Tax Planning Cases

1. MRT, a calendar year corporation, placed the following assets in service this year.

Asset	Initial Cost	Recovery Period	Date Placed in Service
Manufacturing equipment	$259,000	7 years	April 23
Furniture and fixtures	56,000	7 years	May 2
Transportation equipment	225,000	5 years	September 3
Office equipment	120,000	7 years	December 1

   a. Compute MRT's MACRS depreciation with respect to the assets placed in service this year. Assume MRT does not elect to use first-year bonus depreciation or Section 179.

b. In December, MRT decided to purchase $285,000 of additional equipment. The corporation could buy the equipment and place it in service before year-end, or it could postpone the purchase until January. What effect does this decision have on MRT's depreciation with respect to the assets already in service?

2. Company C has a 34 percent marginal tax rate and uses an 8 percent discount rate to compute NPV. The company must decide whether to lease or purchase equipment to use for years 0 through 7. It could lease the equipment for $21,000 annual rent, or it could purchase the equipment for $100,000. The seller would require no money down and would allow Company C to defer payment until year 4 at 11.5 percent simple interest ($11,500 interest payable in years 1, 2, 3, and 4). The equipment would be seven-year MACRS recovery property with no residual value. Should Company C lease or purchase the equipment to minimize the after-tax cost of the use of the property for eight years?

3. MG, a corporation in the 34 percent marginal tax bracket, owns equipment that is fully depreciated. This old equipment is still operating and should continue to do so for four years (years 0, 1, 2, and 3). MG's chief financial officer estimates that repair costs for the old equipment will be $1,400 in year 0, $1,400 in year 1, $1,500 in year 2, and $1,600 in year 3. At the end of year 3, the equipment will have no residual value.

MG could junk the old equipment and buy new equipment for $5,000 cash. The new equipment will have a three-year MACRS recovery period, should not require any repairs during years 0 through 3, and will have no residual value at the end of year 3.

a. Assume MG cannot make a Section 179 election to expense the $5,000 cost of the new equipment. Which option (keep old or buy new) minimizes MG's after-tax cost? In making your calculations, use a 10 percent discount rate.

b. Assume MG can make a Section 179 election to expense the entire $5,000 cost of the new equipment. Under this change in facts, which option (keep old or buy new) minimizes MG's after-tax cost?

4. KP Inc. is negotiating a 10-year lease for three floors of space in a commercial office building. KP can't use the space unless a security system is installed. The cost of the system is $50,000, and it will qualify as seven-year recovery property under MACRS. The building's owner has offered KP a choice. The owner will pay for the installation of the security system and charge $79,000 annual rent. Alternatively, KP can pay for the installation of the security system, and the owner will charge only $72,000 annual rent. Assuming that KP has a 35 percent marginal tax rate, cannot make a Section 179 election to expense the $50,000 cost, and uses a 9 percent discount rate to compute NPV, which alternative should it choose?

5. Mr. S paid $56,600 cash for a tangible asset for use in his new business. The asset is three-year recovery property. Before consideration of any cost recovery deduction, the business generated a net loss this year (year 0). However, Mr. and Mrs. S have other sources of income, so they can deduct the entire business loss on their individual tax return.

Mr. S has two choices with respect to the new asset. He can capitalize the cost and depreciate it under MACRS. Alternatively, he can elect to expense the cost under Section 179. Because his business generates no taxable income, the expense would be nondeductible. However, it would carry forward into future years. Mr. S predicts that the business will operate at a loss for next year (year 1) but should generate at least $60,000 income the following year (year 2). Consequently, he can deduct the Section 179 expense carryforward in that year. If Mr. and Mrs. S's marginal tax rate is 25 percent and they use a 7 percent discount rate to compute NPV, should Mr. S elect to expense the cost of the new business asset?

Midquarter Convention Tables

Midquarter Convention for Business Personalty Placed in Service in First Quarter

Year	Depreciation Rate for Recovery Period					
	3-Year	**5-Year**	**7-Year**	**10-Year**	**15-Year**	**20-Year**
1	58.33%	35.00%	25.00%	17.50%	8.75%	6.563%
2	27.78	26.00	21.43	16.50	9.13	7.000
3	12.35	15.60	15.31	13.20	8.21	6.482
4	1.54	11.01	10.93	10.56	7.39	5.996
5		11.01	8.75	8.45	6.65	5.546
6		1.38	8.74	6.76	5.99	5.130
7			8.75	6.55	5.90	4.746
8			1.09	6.55	5.91	4.459
9				6.56	5.90	4.459
10				6.55	5.91	4.459
11				0.82	5.90	4.459
12					5.91	4.460
13					5.90	4.459
14					5.91	4.460
15					5.90	4.459
16					0.74	4.460
17						4.459
18						4.460
19						4.459
20						4.460
21						0.557

Midquarter Convention for Business Personalty Placed in Service in Second Quarter

Year	Depreciation Rate for Recovery Period					
	3-Year	5-Year	7-Year	10-Year	15-Year	20-Year
1	41.67%	25.00%	17.85%	12.50%	6.25%	4.688%
2	38.89	30.00	23.47	17.50	9.38	7.148
3	14.14	18.00	16.76	14.00	8.44	6.612
4	5.30	11.37	11.97	11.20	7.59	6.116
5		11.37	8.87	8.96	6.83	5.658
6		4.26	8.87	7.17	6.15	5.233
7			8.87	6.55	5.91	4.841
8			3.33	6.55	5.90	4.478
9				6.56	5.91	4.463
10				6.55	5.90	4.463
11				2.46	5.91	4.463
12					5.90	4.463
13					5.91	4.463
14					5.90	4.463
15					5.91	4.462
16					2.21	4.463
17						4.462
18						4.463
19						4.462
20						4.463
21						1.673

Midquarter Convention for Business Personalty Placed in Service in Third Quarter

Year	Depreciation Rate for Recovery Period					
	3-Year	5-Year	7-Year	10-Year	15-Year	20-Year
1	25.00%	15.00%	10.71%	7.50%	3.75%	2.813%
2	50.00	34.00	25.51	18.50	9.63	7.289
3	16.67	20.40	18.22	14.80	8.66	6.742
4	8.33	12.24	13.02	11.84	7.80	6.237
5		11.30	9.30	9.47	7.02	5.769
6		7.06	8.85	7.58	6.31	5.336
7			8.86	6.55	5.90	4.936
8			5.53	6.55	5.90	4.566
9				6.56	5.91	4.460
10				6.55	5.90	4.460
11				4.10	5.91	4.460
12					5.90	4.460
13					5.91	4.461
14					5.90	4.460
15					5.91	4.461
16					3.69	4.460
17						4.461
18						4.460
19						4.461
20						4.460
21						2.788

Midquarter Convention for Business Personalty Placed in Service in Fourth Quarter

Year	Depreciation Rate for Recovery Period					
	3-Year	**5-Year**	**7-Year**	**10-Year**	**15-Year**	**20-Year**
1	8.33%	5.00%	3.57%	2.50%	1.25%	0.938%
2	61.11	38.00	27.55	19.50	9.88	7.430
3	20.37	22.80	19.68	15.60	8.89	6.872
4	10.19	13.68	14.06	12.48	8.00	6.357
5		10.94	10.04	9.98	7.20	5.880
6		9.58	8.73	7.99	6.48	5.439
7			8.73	6.55	5.90	5.031
8			7.64	6.55	5.90	4.654
9				6.56	5.90	4.458
10				6.55	5.91	4.458
11				5.74	5.90	4.458
12					5.91	4.458
13					5.90	4.458
14					5.91	4.458
15					5.90	4.458
16					5.17	4.458
17						4.458
18						4.459
19						4.458
20						4.459
21						3.901

Chapter **Eight**

Property Dispositions

Learning Objectives

After studying this chapter, you should be able to:

1. Distinguish between gain or loss realization and recognition.

2. Apply the installment sale method of accounting.

3. Explain why the tax law disallows losses on related party sales.

4. Identify the two components of the capital gain or loss definition.

5. Apply the limitation on the deduction of capital losses.

6. Apply the Section 1231 netting process.

7. Incorporate the recapture rules into the Section 1231 netting process.

8. Describe the tax consequences of dispositions other than sales or exchanges.

Chapter 8 continues our investigation of the tax consequences of property transactions. In this chapter, we will discuss how taxpayers account for gains or losses from property dispositions. This discussion centers on three basic questions:

- What is the gain or loss recognized on the disposition of property?
- In what taxable year does the recognition occur?
- What is the tax character of the recognized gain or loss?

The answers to these questions determine the tax cost or savings and, in turn, the after-tax cash flows from the property disposition.

For taxpayers disposing of several assets during the tax year, determining the tax consequences of these dispositions is a multistep process. First, the taxpayer computes gain or loss realized on each asset disposition and the amount of such gain or loss recognized in the current year. Second, the character of the recognized gain or loss must be identified. Character is critical to determining the ultimate impact of property transactions on taxable income and tax liability. As we discussed in our exploration of tax planning variables in Chapter 4, the character of income determines whether it is taxed at preferential rates or at the taxpayer's ordinary income rate. In particular, individuals often qualify for preferential tax rates on capital gains from the disposition of capital assets. When property dispositions result in a loss, the character of the loss is important in determining its deductibility. Capital losses can only be deducted against capital gains, whereas ordinary losses are fully deductible against any type of income.

For sales of business assets, the ultimate character of gain or loss is controlled by Section 1231. When Section 1231 assets are sold at a gain, depreciation recapture treats some or all of that gain as ordinary income. Any remaining Section 1231 gain is combined with Section 1231 losses as part of a year-end netting process. The net Section 1231 gain or loss is then characterized as either ordinary or capital. Only after the Section 1231 netting process is complete can the taxpayer determine whether net capital gain exists (with potential preferential rates) or net capital loss results (with limits on deductibility). This chapter explores the details of each of these steps.

COMPUTATION OF GAIN OR LOSS RECOGNIZED

The Internal Revenue Code specifies that gross income includes "gains derived from dealings in property"[1] and allows a deduction for "any loss sustained during the taxable year and not compensated for by insurance or otherwise."[2] These two rules of law mean that firms account for gains and losses from property transactions in the computation of taxable income. The **realized gain or loss** from the disposition of property is computed as follows:[3]

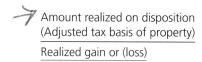

Amount realized on disposition
(Adjusted tax basis of property)

Realized gain or (loss)

This computation reflects the realization principle of accounting. Under this principle, increases or decreases in the value of assets are not accounted for as income. Such increases or decreases are not taken into account until an asset is converted to a different asset through an external transaction with another party. As a simple illustration of this principle, suppose that Firm F bought an asset four years ago for $25,000. Although the market value of the asset has steadily increased, the firm has not reported any of this accrued economic gain on either its financial statements or tax returns. This year, Firm F sells the asset for $60,000 cash, finally realizing a $35,000 gain.

Objective 1
Distinguish between gain or loss realization and recognition.

A third general rule of law is that the gain or loss realized on a property disposition is taken into account for tax purposes.[4] In other words, realized gain or loss becomes **recognized gain or loss** for the year.

Amount realized on disposition
(Adjusted tax basis of property)

Realized gain or (loss)

↓

Recognized gain or (loss)

Most of the property transactions examined in Chapter 8 reflect this linkage between realization and recognition. In Chapter 9, we will explore the exceptions to the general rule: transactions in which realized gain or loss is not recognized in the same year.

[1] §61(a)(3).
[2] §165(a).
[3] §1001(a).
[4] §1001(c).

The realization principle has important planning implications because it gives property owners some control over the timing of gain or loss recognition. Owners of appreciated property can defer gain recognition and the related tax cost for as long as they hold the property. Owners of devalued property can accelerate the deduction of loss and the related tax savings by disposing of the property as soon as possible.

Deferring Gains and Accelerating Losses	Firm K has a $15,000 basis in Asset A and a $141,000 basis in Asset B. Near the end of its taxable year, Firm K has the opportunity to sell each asset for $100,000. It decides to hold Asset A to avoid recognizing its $85,000 economic gain and sell Asset B to recognize its $41,000 economic loss. Firm K can deduct this loss against income that would be taxed at 35 percent. Thus, the loss results in a $14,350 tax savings this year.

The amount of gain or loss that a taxpayer recognizes for tax purposes may not be the same amount reported on the taxpayer's financial statements. If an asset's adjusted tax basis does not equal its book basis, the tax gain or loss realized on disposition will not equal the book gain or loss.

Book/Tax Difference on Asset Disposition

Orlof Inc. purchased a depreciable asset four years ago for $87,400 and sold it this year for $72,000. Orlof's book and tax gain on the sale is computed as follows:

	Book	Tax
Initial cost basis	$87,400	$87,400
Accumulated depreciation	(18,000)	(33,900)
Adjusted basis at date of sale	$69,400	$53,500
Amount realized on sale	$72,000	$72,000
Adjusted basis	(69,400)	(53,500)
Gain realized	$ 2,600	$18,500

Took more depreciation

The $15,900 excess tax gain over book gain is a reversal of the temporary differences between Orlof's book income and taxable income caused by excess tax depreciation over book depreciation during the four years that Orlof held the asset.

Sales and Exchanges

Owners can dispose of property through a sale for cash (including the purchaser's obligation to pay cash in the future) or through an exchange for other property. The owner's **amount realized** on the disposition equals any cash received plus the fair market value (FMV) of any property received.[5] For example, if Company J exchanges equipment for marketable securities and the securities are worth $50,000, Company J's amount realized on the disposition of the equipment is $50,000. While the amount realized equals the value of the cash and/or property received by the seller, the amount realized also equals the value of the property surrendered. In our example, both parties to the transaction must agree that the equipment is also worth $50,000. Why is this so? In an economic setting, no rational

---

[5] §1001(b). The amount realized is reduced by selling costs such as sales commissions and title transfer fees.

person would sell property for less than its value, nor would any purchaser pay more than the property's value. The private market created between seller and purchaser establishes the equal values of the properties changing hands.

Relief of Debt as Amount Realized

In Chapter 7, we learned that the tax basis of property includes any amount that the owner borrowed to acquire the property. In other words, tax basis encompasses both the owner's equity in the property and any debt to which the property is subject. If the owner sells the property and is relieved of debt in the transaction, the owner must include the debt relief in the amount realized on sale.

Relief of Debt

TG Corporation purchased investment land 15 years ago for $450,000. It put $100,000 of its own money into the investment and borrowed the remaining $350,000 from a bank, which took a mortgage on the property. TG's cost basis in the land is $450,000. Each year as TG paid down the principal of the mortgage, the payments increased its equity in the land but had no effect on TG's basis. This year, TG sold the land for $875,000. The purchaser assumed the $200,000 principal balance of the mortgage and paid the $675,000 remaining sales price in cash. TG's realized gain is computed as follows.

Amount realized on sale:	
Cash received	$675,000
Relief of debt	200,000
	$875,000
Basis of land	(450,000)
Realized gain	$425,000

Tax-Free Recovery of Basis and Cash Flow

On a sale or exchange of property, only the excess of amount realized over adjusted basis is taxable income. Accordingly, sellers recover their investment in the property at no tax cost.

Realized Gain and Basis Recovery

Firm R owns an asset with a $5,000 basis. If it sells the asset for $8,000 cash, it realizes a taxable gain of only $3,000. The first $5,000 cash received represents a nontaxable recovery of Firm R's investment in the asset. Assuming that Firm R has a 35 percent marginal tax rate, the sale generates $6,950 cash flow.

	Tax Result	Cash Flow
Amount realized on sale	$8,000	$8,000
Basis	(5,000)	
Gain realized	$3,000	
	.35	
Tax cost of gain	$1,050	(1,050)
After-tax cash flow		$6,950

If a seller realizes a loss on a sale or exchange, the entire amount realized is a tax-free recovery of the seller's investment. Moreover, the seller may be allowed to deduct the *un-recovered* investment (realized loss) in the computation of taxable income.

Realized Loss and Basis Recovery	Refer to the facts in the preceding example. If Firm R sells the asset for only $4,000, it realizes a $1,000 loss. *Assuming that this loss is fully deductible,* the firm recovers its $5,000 investment in the asset in the form of $4,000 cash plus a $1,000 deduction. Because of the tax savings from the deduction, the sale generates $4,350 cash flow.

	Tax Result	Cash Flow
Amount realized on sale	$ 4,000	$4,000
Basis	(5,000)	
Loss realized	$(1,000)	
	.35	
Tax savings from loss	$ (350)	350
After-tax cash flow		$4,350

In these two examples, the realized gain or loss does not enter into the computation of Firm R's net cash flow. Only the tax cost or savings resulting from the gain or loss are cash items.

Taxation of Inflationary Gains

As the preceding examples demonstrate, taxpayers who sell property can recover their basis at no tax cost. In financial terms, a return of investment does not represent income. Only the amount realized in excess of the investment—a return *on* investment—should be recognized as income. This return is overstated if the value of the dollar has changed between the date an asset is purchased and the date that asset is sold. In a period of inflation, the dollars that the taxpayer invested in the asset were worth more in terms of purchasing power than the dollars the taxpayer receives on sale.

Inflationary Gain	Refer to the first example in which Firm R sells an asset with a $5,000 cost basis for an $8,000 amount realized. Because of inflation, a dollar in the year the firm acquired the asset was worth $1.25 of today's dollars. In current dollar terms, Firm R's investment in its asset is $6,250 ($5,000 basis × $1.25), and its economic gain on sale is only $1,750 ($8,000 amount realized − $6,250 inflation-adjusted basis). However, because the tax system fails to account for changes in the dollar's purchasing power over time, Firm R pays tax on a $3,000 gain, $1,250 of which is not economic income but a return of its original investment.[6]

Seller-Financed Sales

In many sale transactions, the seller accepts the purchaser's debt obligation (note) as part of the sale price. Such note represents the purchaser's promise to pay cash to the seller over a specified future period rather than on the date of sale. In an arm's-length **seller-financed sale,**

---

[6] Congress and the Treasury are well aware of this problem. The theoretically sound solution is to allow taxpayers to adjust the basis in their assets for inflation. Lawmakers have been reluctant to enact this solution into law because of the potential revenue loss and the enormous complexity it would add to the computation of basis, cost recovery deductions, and recognized gains and losses.

the seller charges the purchaser a market rate of interest on the note. As a general rule, the seller includes the principal amount of the purchaser's note in the amount realized on sale and computes gain or loss accordingly.

Seller-Financed Sale	Company Q sold property with a $195,000 basis for $300,000. The purchaser paid $30,000 cash on the date of sale and gave Company Q a note for the $270,000 balance of the price. The note obligated the purchaser to pay the $270,000 principal over the next 10 years and carried a 7 percent annual interest rate. Company Q realized a $105,000 gain on this seller-financed sale, even though it received only $30,000 cash in the year of sale.

Installment Sale Method

Objective 2
Apply the installment sale method of accounting.

Taxpayers may use a statutory method of accounting for gains realized on seller-financed sales of certain types of property. Under the **installment sale method,** the seller does not recognize the entire realized gain in the year of sale. Instead, gain recognition is linked to the seller's receipt of cash over the term of the purchaser's note.[7] The seller calculates the gain recognized in the year of sale and each subsequent year by multiplying the cash received during the year by a **gross profit percentage.** This percentage is calculated by dividing the gain realized by the sale price.

Installment Sale Method	In year 1, Firm B sold a five-acre tract of investment land with a $150,000 basis for $214,500. The purchaser paid $14,500 cash on the date of sale and gave Firm B a note for the $200,000 balance of the price. The note provides for annual principal payments of $50,000 in years 2 through 5 plus 6 percent annual interest on the unpaid balance. Firm B's realized gain and gross profit percentage are computed as follows.

Amount realized on sale:	
Cash received	$ 14,500
Purchaser's note	200,000
	$214,500
Basis of land	(150,000)
Realized gain	$ 64,500

$$\frac{\$64,500 \text{ realized gain}}{\$214,500 \text{ sale price}} = 30.07 \text{ gross profit percentage}$$

Firm B will recognize the following taxable gain each year.

Year	Cash Received	Gross Profit Percentage	Taxable Gain Recognized
1	$14,500	30.07%	$ 4,360
2	50,000	30.07	15,035
3	50,000	30.07	15,035
4	50,000	30.07	15,035
5	50,000	30.07	15,035
			$64,500

[7] §453.

Tax Talk
When future payments are contingent on profit, the IRS recently permitted an LLC to recover basis in an installment sale at a rate twice as fast as normal. PLR 200913004.

Note that the annual interest payments that Firm B receives on the installment note do not enter into the computation of recognized gain. The firm must recognize these payments as ordinary income under its overall method of accounting.

Taxpayers can use the installment sale method to defer gain recognition on the sale of many types of business and investment property. (The method has no application to realized losses.) However, the method does not apply to gains realized on the sale of stocks or securities traded on an established market.[8] Nor does the method apply to gains realized on the sale of inventory to customers in the ordinary course of the seller's business.[9] The ordinary income created by any of the depreciation recapture rules discussed later in this chapter is not eligible for deferral under the installment method, and must be recognized in the year of sale.[10]

Installment Sale of Inventory	Refer to the preceding example. If Firm B is a real estate developer that buys and sells land in the ordinary course of business, it cannot use the installment sale method to account for the gain realized on sale of the five-acre tract. Thus, Firm B would recognize the entire $64,500 gain in the year of sale.

Taxpayers generally benefit from the use of the installment sale method to defer gain recognition. In cases in which deferral is not beneficial, taxpayers may make a written election *not* to use the installment sale method.[11] For taxpayers preparing their financial statements according to GAAP, use of the installment sale method generally results in a favorable temporary difference between book income and taxable income. The difference originates in the year of sale and reverses over the years when the taxpayer receives principal payments on the purchaser's note.

Book/Tax Difference from Installment Sale Method	Assume that Firm B in our original example prepares its financial statements in accordance with GAAP. In the year of the land sale, Firm B included its entire $64,500 realized gain in book income but only $4,360 recognized gain in taxable income. This $60,140 excess of book income over taxable income will reverse over the next four years as Firm B recognizes taxable income on receipt of the $50,000 annual principal payments on the purchaser's note.

Seller's Basis in Purchaser's Note

When a seller receives the purchaser's note in a seller-financed sale, the seller generally takes a basis in the note equal to its face value. This basis represents the dollars that the seller will recover as tax-free principal payments.

Note Receivable Basis	Refer back to the example on page 204 in which Company Q sold property for $300,000, accepted the purchaser's note for $270,000, and realized a $105,000 gain. If Company Q recognized the entire gain in the year of sale, its basis in the note receivable is the note's $270,000 face value. The principal payments that Company Q will receive over the next 10 years will reduce both the face value and tax basis of this note to zero.

---

[8] §453(k)(2)(A). Established securities markets include the New York Stock Exchange (NYSE), the American Stock Exchange (AMEX), and Nasdaq.

[9] §453(b)(2).

[10] §453(i).

[11] §453(d).

In the case of an installment sale, the seller is not entitled to a tax-free recovery of the dollars represented by the purchaser's note. Instead, the seller will recognize a percentage of every dollar received as taxable income. Consequently, the seller's tax basis in the installment note is reduced by the deferred gain represented by the note.[12]

Note Receivable Basis— Installment Sale Method	Refer back to the example on page 204 in which Firm B sold a five-acre tract of land for $214,500, accepted the purchaser's note for $200,000, and used the installment sale method to defer gain recognition. Firm B's basis in the note receivable is only $139,860 ($200,000 face value − $60,140 deferred gain). As Firm B receives each $50,000 principal payment, it will recognize a portion of the deferred gain and reduce the face value and tax basis of the note according to the following schedule.

Year	Note Receivable Face Value	Deferred Gain	Note Receivable Basis
1	$200,000	$60,140	$139,860
2	150,000	45,105	104,895
3	100,000	30,070	69,930
4	50,000	15,035	34,965
5	–0–	–0–	–0–

If a taxpayer converts a note receivable to cash, the taxpayer must immediately recognize any deferred gain represented by the note.[13] Assume that Firm B in the preceding example collected only two $50,000 principal payments, then sold the note to a financial institution for its $100,000 face value. Because Firm B accelerated its receipt of cash from the installment sale, it must recognize the remaining $30,070 deferred gain. What if Firm B tried the more subtle technique of pledging the note as collateral for a $100,000 loan from the financial institution? In this case, Firm B still owns the note. Nonetheless, Firm B must recognize the $30,070 deferred gain. The installment sale rules stipulate that a pledge of an installment note is treated as a disposition of the note for cash.[14]

Disallowed Losses on Related Party Sales

Earlier in the chapter, we focused on the general rule that the entire gain or loss realized on a property disposition is recognized for tax purposes. Consequently, firms can usually deduct losses realized on the sale of business assets. One important exception to the general rule is that losses realized on the sale or exchange of property between related parties are nondeductible.[15] For purposes of this exception, the Internal Revenue Code defines related parties as people who are members of the same family, an individual and a corporation if the individual owns more than 50 percent of the value of the corporation's outstanding stock, and two corporations controlled by the same shareholders.[16]

[12] §453B(b).

[13] §453B.

[14] §453A(d).

[15] §267(a)(1).

[16] §267(b)(1), (2), and (3). A person's family includes a spouse, brothers and sisters, ancestors, and lineal descendants. §267(c)(4).

Disallowed Loss	Firm M sold a business asset to Purchaser P for $75,000. Firm M's basis in the asset was $90,000, and it reported a $15,000 realized loss on its financial statements. Firm M and Purchaser P are related parties for federal tax purposes. Consequently, Firm M may not deduct the $15,000 loss in the computation of taxable income. Even though Firm M's loss is disallowed, Purchaser P takes a $75,000 cost basis in the asset.

Objective 3
Explain why the tax law disallows losses on related party sales.

This disallowance rule is based on the theory that a related party loss may not represent an economic loss to the seller. For instance, when a corporation realizes a loss on the sale of an asset to an unrelated purchaser, the loss corresponds to the corporation's unrecovered investment in the asset—a permanent reduction in net worth. If the corporation sells that asset to its controlling shareholder, the underlying ownership of the asset doesn't change. If the value of the asset increases after the sale, the shareholder may eventually recover the corporation's entire investment. In this case, the corporation's loss has no economic substance and should not be deductible in computing taxable income.

A second explanation for the disallowance rule is that related party transactions occur in a fictitious market in which seller and purchaser may not be negotiating at arm's length. Because of this possibility, the government has no assurance that the sale price equals the market value at which the asset would change hands between unrelated parties. If the price is unrealistically low, the seller's loss is inflated and results in an unwarranted tax deduction. Because of this possibility, the loss disallowance rule applies to every related party sale, regardless of the actual bargaining stance between the parties. For instance, if a brother realizes a loss on the sale of a business asset to his sister, the loss is nondeductible, even if the brother can prove that the siblings have been estranged for years, and the transaction between them was strictly at arm's length.

Offset of Gain by Previously Disallowed Loss

From the seller's perspective, the loss disallowance rule causes a permanent difference between loss realized and loss recognized on the sale of property. Thus, the seller never receives the benefit of a tax deduction for the disallowed loss. However, in the right set of circumstances, the *purchaser* may receive some or all of the benefit. If the purchaser subsequently sells the property acquired in the related party transaction and realizes a gain, the purchaser can offset this gain by the previously disallowed loss.[17]

Use of Seller's Disallowed Loss by Purchaser	Refer to the preceding example in which Firm M realized a $15,000 disallowed loss on the sale of an asset to Purchaser P. Assume that the asset was nondepreciable in P's hands. Several years after the related party transaction, Purchaser P sells the asset to an *unrelated* buyer. The tax consequences based on three different assumptions as to the sale price are presented in the following table.

	Assumption 1	Assumption 2	Assumption 3
Amount realized on sale	$93,000	$81,000	$70,000
Basis of asset	(75,000)	(75,000)	(75,000)
Gain (loss) realized	$18,000	$ 6,000	$ (5,000)
Previously disallowed loss	(15,000)	(6,000)	–0–
Gain (loss) recognized	$ 3,000	–0–	$ (5,000)

[17] §267(d).

This example demonstrates that Purchaser P can use Firm M's previously disallowed loss only to *reduce* the gain recognized on a subsequent sale of the asset. The disallowed loss cannot *create* a recognized loss or *increase* the recognized loss on a subsequent sale.

TAX CHARACTER OF GAINS AND LOSSES

Objective 4
Identify the two components of the capital gain or loss definition.

Taxpayers must compute the gain or loss realized on a property disposition and determine the taxable year (or years) in which the gain or loss is recognized. In addition, they must determine the character of the recognized gain or loss. In the tax world, every gain or loss is ultimately characterized as either ordinary or capital. A **capital gain or loss** results from the sale or exchange of a capital asset.[18] Any gain or loss that does not meet this definition is **ordinary** in character.[19]

The capital gain/loss definition has two distinct components. First, the transaction resulting in the gain or loss must be a sale or exchange. Second, the asset surrendered must be a capital asset. If a firm disposes of a capital asset in some way other than a sale or exchange, the realized gain or loss is ordinary in character. Several of these dispositions are discussed later in the chapter. At this point, let's focus our attention on the second component of the capital gain/loss definition: the capital asset requirement.

Capital Asset Defined

The Internal Revenue Code defines the term **capital asset** by exception.[20] For tax purposes, *every* asset is a capital asset unless it falls into one of eight categories:

1. Inventory items or property held by the taxpayer primarily for sale to customers in the ordinary course of business.
2. Accounts or notes receivable acquired in the ordinary course of business (i.e., acquired through the sale of inventory or the performance of services).
3. Supplies used or consumed in the ordinary course of business.
4. Real or depreciable property used in a business (including rental real estate) and intangible business assets subject to amortization.[21]
5. A copyright; literary, musical, or artistic composition; a letter or memorandum; or similar property held by a taxpayer whose personal efforts created the property or a person to whom the property was gifted by the creator.[22]
6. Certain publications of the U.S. government.
7. Commodities derivative financial instruments held by a dealer.
8. Hedging transaction properties.

While the last three categories of capital assets are listed for the sake of completeness, they are not discussed in this text.

Capital asset status is not determined by the intrinsic nature of the asset itself but by the use for which the asset is held by its owner.

---

[18] §1222.

[19] §64 and §65.

[20] §1221.

[21] Reg. §1.167(a)-3 and §197(f)(7).

[22] Taxpayers may elect to treat the sale or exchange of self-created musical compositions or musical copyrights as the sale or exchange of a capital asset.

Capital Asset Defined	Ms. Helm, a professional sculptor, purchased $50 worth of clay and created a work of art that she sold for $5,000 to BVC Corporation. BVC uses the sculpture as decoration in the lobby of its corporate headquarters. The work of art is not a capital asset in the hands of its creator, so Ms. Helm's $4,950 gain recognized on the sale is ordinary income. In contrast, the sculpture is a capital asset to BVC because it is not a *depreciable* business asset. As a result, if the corporation ever sells the sculpture, its recognized gain or loss will be capital in character.

Capital Loss Limitation

Objective 5
Apply the limitation on the deduction of capital losses.

The federal income tax system contains a subset of rules applying to capital gains and losses. One logical way to analyze these rules is to begin with the limitation on capital losses: *Capital losses can be deducted only to the extent of capital gains.*[23] In other words, if the combined result of all sales and exchanges of capital assets during the year is a net loss, the net loss is nondeductible. If the combined result is a net gain, the net gain is included in taxable income. The following diagram depicts the result of this netting process.

The capital loss limitation has a major effect on the tax savings generated by a capital loss. The next three examples demonstrate this effect.

Fully Deductible Capital Loss	Firm SD sold a capital asset with a $100,000 basis for $25,000. If the firm's marginal tax rate is 25 percent, how much tax savings does this $75,000 capital loss generate? If Firm SD recognized at least $75,000 capital gain during the year, the capital loss generates $18,750 current tax savings, and the after-tax loss on the sale is $56,250.

Loss on sale of capital asset	$(75,000)
Current tax savings ($75,000 deductible loss × 25%)	18,750
After-tax loss	$(56,250)

Partially Deductible Capital Loss	Assume that Firm SD recognized only $40,000 capital gain during the year. In this case, the firm can deduct only $40,000 capital loss; its $35,000 **net capital loss** (excess of current year capital loss over capital gain) is nondeductible. The current tax savings generated by the capital loss decreases to $10,000, and the after-tax loss increases to $65,000.

Loss on sale of capital asset	$(75,000)
Current tax savings ($40,000 deductible loss × 25%)	10,000
After-tax loss	$(65,000)

[23] §1211. This strict limitation is relaxed very slightly for individual taxpayers. See the discussion of individual capital losses in Chapter 16.

Nondeductible Capital Loss	In the worst-case scenario, Firm SD recognized no capital gains during the year. Consequently, none of the $75,000 net capital loss is deductible, and the before-tax and after-tax loss are both $75,000.

Loss on sale of capital asset	$(75,000)
Current tax savings	–0–
After-tax loss	$(75,000)

The strict rule that capital losses are deductible only against capital gains is relaxed somewhat for individuals. Individual taxpayers are permitted an annual deduction of up to $3,000 for capital losses in excess of capital gains.

Individual Capital Loss Limitation	Janelle Jones recognized $40,000 of capital gains and $47,000 of capital losses during the current year. Janelle is permitted to deduct $43,000 of her capital losses, resulting in a net capital loss for the year of $3,000.

Loss Carrybacks and Carryforwards

The above examples are incomplete because they show the effect of the capital loss limitation only for an isolated year. If a taxpayer has a nondeductible net capital loss for the year, the law provides a mechanism by which the loss can be deducted in a previous or future year. For no obvious policy reason, the tax law differentiates between capital losses incurred by individuals and those incurred by corporations.

- A nondeductible net capital loss incurred by an *individual* is carried forward indefinitely.[24] In any future year in which the individual recognizes net capital gain (excess of capital gain over capital loss), the loss carryforward is deductible to the extent of such gain.
- A net capital loss incurred by a *corporation* is carried back three years and forward five years, but only as a deduction against net capital gains recognized during this eight-year period.[25] Let's look at an example of the corporate rule.

Capital Loss Carryback	RO, a corporation with a 35 percent marginal tax rate, sold two capital assets in 2011, recognizing a $50,000 gain on the first sale and an $85,000 loss on the second. RO included the $50,000 gain in gross income and deducted $50,000 of the loss on its 2011 tax return; its nondeductible net capital loss is $35,000. RO's taxable income for the three previous years is as follows.

	2008	2009	2010
Ordinary income	$600,000	$400,000	$730,000
Net capital gain	–0–	10,000	12,000
Taxable income	$600,000	$410,000	$742,000

- Because RO had no net capital gain in the earliest year of its carryback period, it can't deduct any of its 2011 net capital loss against 2008 income.

[24] §1212(b)(1).
[25] §1212(a)(1).

- RO may deduct $10,000 and $12,000 of the 2011 loss against the capital gains reported in 2009 and 2010, recompute its tax accordingly, and file for a tax refund.
- RO will carry the $13,000 remaining net capital loss forward for five years to deduct against future capital gains.

Book/Tax Difference for Nondeductible Capital Loss

The characterization of a gain or loss as capital is relevant only for tax purposes. For financial reporting purposes, gains and losses realized during the year generally are included in the computation of book income. Consequently, a nondeductible capital loss results in an excess of tax income over book income. This unfavorable difference is considered temporary because of the loss carryback and carryforward rules.

Book/Tax Difference for Capital Loss	In 2010, Beco Inc. realized a $46,900 loss on sale of an investment asset. The loss was included in 2010 book income but was a nondeductible capital loss for tax purposes. Beco was unable to deduct any of the capital loss as a carryback to earlier years. Because of the unfavorable book/tax difference attributable to the loss, Beco recorded a $16,415 deferred tax asset ($46,900 × 35 percent). In 2011, Beco realized a $31,000 gain on sale of an investment asset. The gain was included in both book and tax income. The gain was a capital gain, so Beco could deduct $31,000 of its capital loss carryforward. Because this favorable book/tax difference was a partial reversal of the 2010 unfavorable difference, Beco reduced the deferred tax asset recorded in 2010 by $10,850 ($31,000 × 35 percent). The balance of the deferred tax asset was $5,565. In 2012, Beco realized a $47,500 gain on sale of an investment asset. The gain was included in both book and tax income. The gain was a capital gain, so Beco could deduct its remaining $15,900 capital loss carryforward ($46,900 − $31,000 deducted in 2011). Because this favorable book/tax difference completely reversed the 2010 unfavorable difference, Beco reduced the deferred tax asset by $5,565 ($15,900 × 35 percent) to zero.

Taxation of Capital Gains

Under the federal income tax system, capital gains have the unique capacity to absorb capital losses. As a result, both corporate and individual taxpayers always prefer capital gains to ordinary income. In a year in which a taxpayer recognizes a net capital gain (excess of capital gain over capital loss), the net gain is included in taxable income. If the taxpayer is a corporation, this net gain is taxed at the same rates as ordinary income. If the taxpayer is an individual, the net capital gain may be taxed at a preferential rate of zero, 15, 25, or 28 percent.[26] Given that the highest marginal rate on ordinary income is 35 percent, the preferential rates on capital gains are extremely valuable to high-income individuals. The details of the preferential rate structure are discussed in Chapter 16.

Capital Asset Definition Revisited

Now that you understand the tax consequences of capital gains and losses, you can appreciate why gain and loss characterization is so important in the tax planning process. As a general rule, taxpayers prefer capital gains to ordinary income, and they prefer ordinary losses to capital losses. As we discussed earlier in this section, the characterization of gain and loss depends on whether the property was a noncapital or a capital asset in the hands of the seller. More specifically, does the property fit into one of the categories of noncapital assets listed in the Internal Revenue Code? If the property does not fit into

---

[26] §1(h). These rates apply only to long-term capital gains, which are derived from the sale of assets held for more than one year. See §1222.

one of these eight categories, the property is a capital asset.[27] This classification scheme is presented in the following diagram.

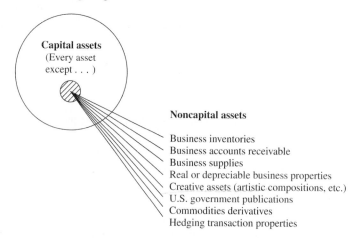

DISPOSITIONS OF NONCAPITAL ASSETS

The expansive definition of a capital asset as every asset except for those specifically excepted may be misleading. In the business context, capital assets are the exception rather than the rule. Most properties listed on a firm's balance sheet fall into one of the first four categories of noncapital assets. In this section of the chapter, we will analyze the tax consequences of the dispositions of these noncapital business assets.

What types of business properties are capital in character? Any asset held by a firm for long-term investment rather than for active business or commercial use is a capital asset. Similarly, equity and creditor interests in other firms, such as stocks, bonds, and partnership interests, are capital in character. Self-created intangible assets such as contracts, technological processes, and patents are capital assets.[28] Finally, the goodwill and going-concern value *created* by a profitable business is a capital asset.[29]

Inventory

The first category of noncapital assets includes any property held as inventory or primarily for sale to customers. When firms sell inventory assets as part of their everyday operations, the recognized gain or loss is the quintessence of ordinary income or loss. For firms engaged in the manufacture, production, wholesaling, distribution, or retailing of tangible goods, the identification of inventory assets is fairly straightforward. Disputes between taxpayers and the IRS concerning the status of property as inventory most frequently arise when the asset in question is land.

Land Sales

If a taxpayer sells a tract of land at a profit, the taxpayer usually prefers to categorize the tract as an investment asset and the profit as capital gain. The IRS might challenge this result if it believes that the taxpayer acquired and held the land primarily for sale to

---

[27] *Arkansas Best Corp.* v. *Commissioner,* 485 U.S. 212 (1988).

[28] §1221(a)(3) and §1235.

[29] See IRS Letter Ruling 200243002 (October 25, 2002). *Purchased* goodwill/going-concern value is not a capital asset to the purchaser. Purchased intangibles fall into the fourth category of noncapital assets, and the tax consequences of their disposition are governed by the specialized rules of §197(f)(1).

customers rather than as a long-term investment. From this perspective, the profit from the sale is ordinary income. The federal courts have been called on many times to resolve this particular difference of opinion. In cases in which the land sale was an unusual or isolated occurrence, the courts have tended to side with the taxpayer. In cases in which the taxpayer sold other tracts of land on a regular and continual basis, subdivided and improved the land prior to sale, or advertised the availability of the land to the general public, the courts have tended to agree with the IRS that the land was an inventory asset.

Land Sales	In 1999, Penro Company paid $175,000 to purchase a seven-acre tract of land. Penro, which operates a service business, held the land as a long-term investment. In 2011, Penro sold the land to Medoc Development Inc. for $340,000. Because Penro held the land as a capital asset, it recognized the $165,000 gain on sale as capital gain. Medoc subdivided the seven-acre tract into one-third acre lots and constructed paved streets and sidewalks, sewers, and utilities. The cost of these improvements totaled $124,800. Medoc advertised the lots in local newspapers and trade journals, and by 2012, it had sold all 21 lots for a total of $647,500. Because Medoc held the land primarily for sale to customers, it recognized its $182,700 gain on sale as ordinary income.

As noted below, land could also qualify as a Section 1231 asset, if used in the taxpayer's trade or business. The taxpayer's motives when acquiring the land and use of the land during the period held must be carefully scrutinized to determine the character of any gain or loss on disposition.

Business Accounts Receivable and Supplies

The second category of noncapital assets includes business accounts receivable from the sale of goods or performance of services. Accrual basis firms realize ordinary income from the transactions that create their receivables. Therefore, the tax basis in their accounts receivable equals face value. Cash basis firms do not realize ordinary income until they collect their receivables. Therefore, the tax basis in their *unrealized* accounts receivable is zero. Firms usually either collect their receivables or write off any uncollectible accounts as bad debts. In an unusual case, a firm that needs immediate cash might sell or *factor* its accounts receivable to a third party (typically a financial institution). The difference between the amount realized and the tax basis of the receivables is ordinary income or loss.

Factoring Accounts Receivable	SP Company has $400,000 accounts receivable that it expects to collect over the next 120 days. To meet a cash emergency, SP factors the receivables with First City Bank for $383,000. If SP uses the accrual method of accounting, it has a $400,000 basis in its accounts receivable and recognizes a $17,000 ordinary loss on their disposition. If SP uses the cash method of accounting, it has a zero basis in its accounts receivable and recognizes $383,000 ordinary income on their disposition.

The third category of noncapital assets includes business supplies. Depending on their method of accounting, firms deduct the cost of supplies either in the year of purchase or in the year in which the supplies are consumed. In an unusual case, a firm with unneeded or excess supplies on hand might sell the supplies to a third party. The difference between the amount realized and the tax basis of the supplies is ordinary income or loss.

Selling Unwanted Supplies	Firm EQP is moving its home office to a new location and does not want to transport its stock of office supplies for which it paid $6,000. EQP sells the supplies to a neighboring business for $5,600. If EQP deducted the $6,000 cost, it has a zero basis in the supplies and recognizes $5,600 ordinary income on their disposition. If EQP capitalized the $6,000 cost, it recognizes a $400 ordinary loss on their disposition.

Section 1231 Assets

The fourth category of noncapital assets includes real or depreciable property used in a business (including rental real estate) and intangible business assets subject to amortization (such as *purchased* goodwill). In other words, the operating assets on a balance sheet are noncapital assets. The tax consequences of a sale of an operating asset depends on the length of time the seller held the asset. If the holding period is a year or less, gain or loss recognized on sale is ordinary in character. If the holding period exceeds one year, the gain or loss is characterized under the complicated rules provided in Section 1231 of the Internal Revenue Code. Consequently, the assets subject to these rules are labeled **Section 1231 assets.**

Objective 6
Apply the Section 1231 netting process.

Section 1231 Assets	Tunley Inc. has the following noncash assets on its tax-basis balance sheet.

Accounts receivable	$ 44,210
Marketable securities	11,400
Merchandise inventory	293,100
Furniture and fixtures	85,800
Machinery and equipment	112,700
Production facility:	
Land	200,000
Building	394,000
Purchased goodwill	150,000

The accounts receivable and inventory are noncapital assets by statutory definition. Tunley's holding periods for all operating assets used in its business exceed one year. Consequently, the furniture and fixtures, machinery and equipment, production facility (both land and building), and amortizable goodwill meet the definition of Section 1231 assets. Tunley's only capital assets are its marketable securities.

The basic rule of Section 1231 is simple. If the *combined result* of all sales and exchanges of Section 1231 assets during the year is a net loss, the loss is treated as an ordinary loss. On the other hand, if the result is a net gain, the gain is treated as a capital gain.[30] The following diagram depicts the Section 1231 netting process and the two possible results.

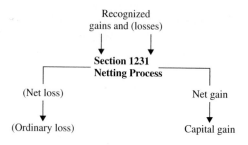

30 §1231(a)(1).

Note that this asymmetric rule offers the best of both worlds to the business community—ordinary loss or capital gain on the sale of operating assets. However, the tax result of any particular Section 1231 asset sale cannot be fully determined until year-end, after application of the netting process. Let's work through two examples of the basic Section 1231 netting process.

Section 1231 Net Loss	During 2012, Company RC sold three Section 1231 assets with the following result.

	Gain or (Loss) Recognized
Asset sale 1	$ 45,000
Asset sale 2	(35,000)
Asset sale 3	(16,000)
Section 1231 net loss	$ (6,000)

Company RC's $6,000 Section 1231 net loss is an ordinary loss, fully deductible in the computation of taxable income.

Section 1231 Net Gain	Assume that asset sale 2 generated only a $5,000 (rather than a $35,000) loss for Company RC. In this case, the company has a net gain on the sale of its Section 1231 assets.

	Gain or (Loss) Recognized
Asset sale 1	$ 45,000
Asset sale 2	(5,000)
Asset sale 3	(16,000)
Section 1231 net gain	$ 24,000

Under Section 1231, Company RC treats the $24,000 net gain as a capital gain. Consequently, the company can deduct up to $24,000 of capital losses or capital loss carryforwards. If the company's capital loss deduction is less than $24,000, the excess Section 1231 gain is treated as net capital gain. If the company's income is taxed at the individual rates (for example, if Company RC is a sole proprietorship), this gain is taxed at the preferential capital gains rates.

Recapture of Prior Year Ordinary Losses

Objective 7
Incorporate the recapture rules into the Section 1231 netting process.

Before Company RC can treat its Section 1231 net gain as a capital gain, it must consider an exception to the basic characterization rule. This exception applies if a taxpayer has a Section 1231 net gain in the current year but had a Section 1231 net loss in any of the five preceding taxable years. In such case, the taxpayer must **recapture** the prior year loss (which was deductible as ordinary loss) by characterizing an equivalent amount of current year gain as ordinary income.[31] The next diagram incorporates this recapture rule.

---

[31] §1231(c).

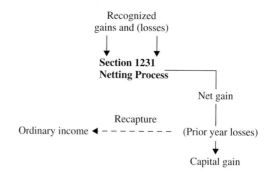

<table>
<tr><td rowspan="2">Recapture of Prior Year Losses</td></tr>
</table>

Recapture of Prior Year Losses

In our previous example, Company RC recognized a $24,000 net Section 1231 gain in 2012. Before Company RC can characterize this gain, it must look back for five years to identify any **nonrecaptured Section 1231 loss.** Here is a schedule of prior year information.

	2007	2008	2009	2010	2011
Section 1231 gains	–0–	1,350	5,200	–0–	–0–
Section 1231 losses	–0–	–0–	(11,400)	(900)	–0–
Net gain or (loss)	–0–	1,350	(6,200)	(900)	–0–

In 2009 and 2010, Company RC deducted a total of $7,100 of net Section 1231 losses against ordinary income. So in 2012, the company must recapture these losses by characterizing $7,100 of its $24,000 net Section 1231 gain as ordinary income. The $16,900 remaining gain is treated as capital gain.

Tax Talk
RIA Federal Taxes Weekly Alert offers this advice to taxpayers: "Avoid being snared by unexpected depreciation recapture. The sheer volume and complexity of these rules make planning and communication essential if unexpected bombshells are to be avoided."

Once a taxpayer has recaptured a prior year Section 1231 loss, the loss is not recaptured again. If Company RC has a Section 1231 net gain in 2012, the entire gain is treated as capital gain because the company has no *nonrecaptured* losses for the preceding five-year period.

Depreciation Recapture

The pro-business rule of Section 1231 is modified when applied to gains recognized on the sale of depreciable or amortizable property. The modification requires that gain attributable to prior year depreciation or amortization deductions be characterized as ordinary income rather than Section 1231 gain. Thus, depreciation recapture merely changes the character of gain on the sale of Section 1231 property. It does not create additional gain. This **depreciation recapture** rule has three components: full recapture, partial recapture, and 20 percent recapture. Before analyzing each component, let's add the basic recapture rule to our diagram.

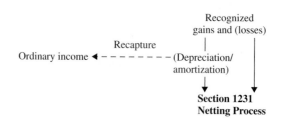

Full Recapture Rule

The full recapture rule applies to gains recognized on sales of depreciable personalty and amortizable intangibles. Under this rule, an amount of gain equal to accumulated depreciation or amortization (including any Section 179 expense deduction) through date of sale is recharacterized as ordinary income.[32] Put another way, depreciation recapture equals the lesser of the gain recognized or the accumulated depreciation or amortization. The Code section requiring full recapture is Section 1245. Consequently, tax professionals commonly refer to the requirement as **Section 1245 recapture.**

The rationale for Section 1245 recapture can best be explained through a numeric example.

Rationale for Recapture	Firm D purchased a tangible asset several years ago for $100,000 and has accumulated $40,000 MACRS depreciation through date of sale. As a result, its adjusted basis in the asset is $60,000. If the firm sells the asset for $100,000, it recognizes a $40,000 gain. *Absent a recapture requirement*, this gain is a Section 1231 gain with the potential for capital gain treatment. However, the entire gain is attributable to previous years' cost recovery deductions, which reduced *ordinary income* in those years by $40,000.

Section 1245 recapture prevents this conversion of ordinary income into capital gain. In our example, Firm D must characterize its $40,000 gain as ordinary income. If we modify the example by changing the amount realized on sale, the amount of recaptured ordinary income also changes. The following table illustrates the recapture computation based on four different amounts realized.

	Assumption 1	Assumption 2	Assumption 3	Assumption 4
Amount realized	$100,000	$ 90,000	$105,000	$ 48,000
Cost of asset $100,000				
Depreciation (40,000)				
Adjusted basis	(60,000)	(60,000)	(60,000)	(60,000)
Gain (loss) recognized	$ 40,000	$ 30,000	$ 45,000	$(12,000)
Section 1245 recapture	$ 40,000	$ 30,000	$ 40,000	–0–
Section 1231 gain (loss)	–0–	–0–	5,000	$(12,000)
	$ 40,000	$ 30,000	$ 45,000	$(12,000)

- Assumption 1 reflects the original facts in the Firm D example. The $40,000 gain recognized equals the $40,000 accumulated depreciation, and the entire gain is recaptured as ordinary income.

---

[32] §1245 and §197(f)(7).

- Under Assumption 2, the $30,000 gain recognized *is less than* accumulated depreciation. In this case, the entire gain is recaptured as ordinary income.
- Under Assumption 3, the $45,000 gain *is more than* accumulated depreciation. In this case, only $40,000 of the gain (an amount equal to accumulated depreciation) is recaptured, and the remaining $5,000 gain (appreciation in the value of the asset) is Section 1231 gain.
- Under Assumption 4, Firm D recognizes a $12,000 loss on the sale. This is a Section 1231 loss; the recapture rules don't apply to losses.

Partial Recapture Rule for Realty

The recapture rule applying to gains recognized on sales of depreciable realty (buildings, improvements, and other permanent attachments to land) is less stringent than the full recapture rule.[33] Although Congress has changed the details of this rule many times over the past decades, the essential concept is that only *accelerated depreciation in excess of straight-line depreciation* is recaptured. Tax professionals commonly refer to the partial recapture requirement as **Section 1250 recapture.**

Section 1250 Recapture

Company NB sold a residential apartment complex for $1 million: $200,000 for the underlying land and $800,000 for the building. NB purchased the property in 1986 for $1,120,000 and allocated $170,000 and $950,000 of this cost basis to the land and building, respectively. NB deducted $700,000 accelerated depreciation with respect to the building through date of sale. Straight-line depreciation over the same period would have been $628,000; consequently, NB deducted $72,000 *excess* accelerated depreciation. The computation of NB's recognized gain on sale and characterization of that gain is as follows.

		Land		Building
Amount realized		$ 200,000		$800,000
Cost of asset	$170,000		$ 950,000	
Depreciation	–0–		(700,000)	
Adjusted basis		(170,000)		(250,000)
Gain recognized		$ 30,000		$550,000
Section 1250 recapture		–0–		$ 72,000
Section 1231 gain		$ 30,000		478,000
		$ 30,000		$550,000

In Chapter 7, we learned that buildings placed in service after 1986 *must* be depreciated under the straight-line method. Consequently, Section 1250 recapture applies only to buildings placed in service before 1987. By 2012, any such building has been depreciated for more than 20 years. During the later years of a cost recovery period, the excess of accelerated over straight-line depreciation diminishes and eventually disappears when the building is fully depreciated (adjusted tax basis is zero). So with each passing year, the significance of Section 1250 recapture diminishes and eventually will disappear.

---

[33] Nonresidential realty (commercial buildings, warehouses, and so on) placed in service after 1980 and before 1987 and depreciated under an accelerated method is subject to the full recapture rule. See §1245(a)(5) before its amendment by the Tax Reform Act of 1986.

Twenty Percent Recapture by Corporations

Corporate taxpayers must contend with a special recapture rule for gain recognized on sales of depreciable realty.[34] Corporations must compute the excess of the gain that would be characterized as ordinary income under the Section 1245 full recapture rule over any gain characterized as ordinary income under the Section 1250 partial recapture rule. The corporation must then recapture 20 percent of this excess as additional ordinary income. Tax professionals commonly refer to the 20 percent recapture requirement as Section 291 recapture.

Section 1250 and 20 Percent Recapture	If Company NB in the preceding example is a corporation, it must apply the 20 percent recapture rule to the $550,000 gain recognized on sale of the building. This gain is less than the $700,000 accumulated depreciation through date of sale. Consequently, the entire gain would be recaptured as ordinary income under the Section 1245 full recapture rule. However, only $72,000 of the gain was actually recaptured under the Section 1250 partial recapture rule. So Corporation NB must recapture an additional $95,600 ordinary income computed as follows:

Section 1245 recapture	$550,000
Section 1250 recapture	(72,000)
Excess	$478,000
	.20
20 percent recapture	$ 95,600

In summary, Corporation NB recognized a $550,000 gain on sale of the building, $167,600 of which was ordinary income ($72,000 + $95,600) and $382,400 of which was Section 1231 gain.

Twenty percent recapture is particularly significant for sales of buildings placed in service after 1986. Because such buildings are depreciated under the straight-line method, Section 1250 recapture does not apply. Even so, corporate sellers must recapture 20 percent of the gain that would be ordinary income under a full recapture rule.

Twenty Percent Recapture	Enwerd Inc. purchased a building for use in its business and placed it in service in 1994. This year, it sold the building for $1,975,000. Enwerd's adjusted basis at date of sale was $790,750 ($1,400,000 cost − $609,250 accumulated straight-line depreciation), so the corporation recognized a $1,184,250 gain on sale.

Amount realized	$1,975,000
(Adjusted basis)	(790,750)
Gain recognized	$1,184,250

The gain is not subject to Section 1250 recapture because the building was depreciated under the straight-line method. However, the gain is subject to 20 percent recapture.

---

[34] §291(a)(1).

Section 1245 recapture	$609,250
Section 1250 recapture	–0–
Excess	$609,250
	.20
Twenty percent recapture	$121,850

In summary, Enwerd recognized a $121,850 ordinary gain and a $1,062,400 Section 1231 gain on sale of the building.

Summary

Exhibit 8.1 provides a summary of the depreciation recapture rules. Remember that recapture only applies to recognized gain on sale of a Section 1231 asset. If a Section 1231 asset is sold at a loss, the recognized loss is characterized as a Section 1231 loss subject to the Section 1231 netting process.

EXHIBIT 8.1
Summary of Recapture Rules

Recognized GAIN on Sale or Exchange of Section 1231 Asset	Recapture Rule
• Tangible personalty	Section 1245 recapture of depreciation
• Amortizable intangibles	Section 1245 recapture of amortization
• Nondepreciable realty [land]	No recapture
• Depreciable realty [buildings] placed in service before 1987	Section 1250 recapture of excess accelerated depreciation and 20 percent recapture by corporations
• Depreciable realty [buildings] placed in service after 1986	20 percent recapture by corporations

Comprehensive Example

The tax rules governing the character of gains and losses recognized on the sale or exchange of business operating assets are quite difficult. Before leaving this subject, let's review the rules by working through a comprehensive example.

Characterizing Gains and Losses

In 2012, BC, a calendar year corporation, recognized a $145,000 capital loss on the sale of marketable securities. The corporation did not sell any other capital assets during the year. Therefore, BC cannot deduct any of the capital loss *unless* it recognized a Section 1231 net gain for the year.

BC recognized the following gains and losses on 2012 sales of operating assets. The column headed *Accumulated Depreciation* reflects the correct MACRS depreciation through date of sale.

	Date Placed in Service	Date Sold	Initial Basis	Accumulated Depreciation	Sale Price	Gain (Loss)
Office equipment	11/3/11	2/14	$ 8,200	$ 2,300	$ 5,100	$ (800)
Copying equipment	8/16/08	5/14	4,000	3,650	2,350	2,000
Furniture	12/19/10	5/31	18,000	4,900	20,400	7,300
Hauling equipment	2/12/11	8/28	32,000	12,000	19,250	(750)
Real property:						
Land	4/12/07	11/3	100,000	–0–	125,000	25,000
Building	4/12/07	11/3	500,000	62,000	550,000	112,000

[handwritten margin notes: 2350, −356]

These gains and losses are characterized as follows.

	Gain (Loss)	Ordinary Income or (Loss)	Section 1231 Gain or (Loss)
Office equipment	$ (800)	$ (800)	
Copying equipment	2,000	2,000	
Furniture	7,300	4,900	$ 2,400
Hauling equipment	(750)		(750)
Real property:			
Land	25,000		25,000
Building	112,000	12,400	99,600
Current year totals		$18,500	$126,250

- BC owned the office equipment for less than a year. Therefore, this asset is neither a capital asset nor a Section 1231 asset, and the loss recognized on sale is ordinary.
- Gain recognized on sale of the copying equipment is less than accumulated depreciation. Therefore, the entire gain is recaptured as ordinary income.
- Gain recaptured as ordinary income on sale of the furniture is limited to accumulated depreciation. The rest of the gain is Section 1231 gain.
- Loss recognized on sale of the hauling equipment is Section 1231 loss.
- Gain recognized on sale of the land is Section 1231 gain.
- Gain recognized on sale of the building is subject to 20 percent recapture. Therefore, $12,400 (20 percent of $62,000 accumulated depreciation) is recaptured as ordinary income. The rest of the gain is Section 1231 gain.

BC's tax returns for the previous five years show $8,400 nonrecaptured Section 1231 net losses. Thus, the final step in characterizing the corporation's gains and losses is to recapture this loss.

	Ordinary Income or (Loss)	Section 1231 Gain or (Loss)
Current year totals	$18,500	$126,250
Prior year loss recapture	8,400	(8,400)
	$26,900	$117,850

   In summary, BC's sales of operating assets generated $26,900 ordinary income and $117,850 Section 1231 gain. BC treats the Section 1231 gain as capital gain. As a result, the corporation can deduct $117,850 of its $145,000 capital loss from the security sale. The $27,150 nondeductible capital loss can be deducted only on a carryback or carryforward basis.

The diagram below summarizes the steps discussed in this chapter for determining the tax consequences of property dispositions.

OTHER PROPERTY DISPOSITIONS

Objective 8
Describe the tax consequences of dispositions other than sales or exchanges.

To this point in the chapter, our consideration of the tax consequences of property dispositions has been limited to the consequences of sales and exchanges. While sales and exchanges are the most common ways to dispose of assets, they are not the only ways. In this section, we consider three other property dispositions and their effect on taxable income.

Abandonment and Worthlessness

If a firm formally relinquishes its ownership interest in an asset, any unrecovered basis in the asset represents an **abandonment loss**.[35] An abandonment loss is an ordinary deduction even if the abandoned asset is a Section 1231 or capital asset because the loss is not realized on a sale or exchange. To claim a loss, a firm must take overt action to indicate that it has no intention of reviving its interest or reclaiming the asset in the future.[36]

[35] Regs. §1.165-1(b), §.165-2, and §1.167(a)-8.
[36] *Echols v. Commissioner,* 950 F.2d 209 (CA-5, 1991).

Abandonment Loss	Firm WB occupied leased office space for eight years. During this time, it capitalized the cost of several leasehold improvements to an asset account. This year, WB had a serious dispute with its landlord, broke its lease, and relocated to a new office. Unfortunately, the leasehold improvements were not portable so WB had to leave them behind. WB's adjusted basis in these improvements was $28,200, so it can claim a $28,200 abandonment loss as an ordinary deduction.

Firms typically don't abandon property unless the property no longer has any value and is worthless to the firm. The Internal Revenue Code contains a special rule for securities that become worthless during the taxable year.[37] The owner must treat the securities as if they were sold on the last day of the year for a price of zero. This fictitious sale triggers a realized loss equal to the owner's basis in the securities. If the securities were capital assets in the owner's hands, the loss is characterized as a capital loss because it resulted from a deemed sale. For purposes of this rule, securities include corporate stocks and bonds, debentures, or other corporate or government debt instruments that bear interest coupons or are in registered form.

Worthless Securities	Colbert Company owns 1,400 shares of stock in NewHigh Inc., a publicly held corporation. Colbert purchased the stock as an investment 10 years ago for $5,500. This year, NewHigh declared bankruptcy and made a public announcement that its stock is worthless. Colbert must treat the NewHigh shares as if they were sold on the last day of Colbert's taxable year for a price of zero. Colbert recognizes a $5,500 capital loss from the deemed sale of worthless securities.

An important modification to the worthless securities rule applies if a corporation owns worthless securities in an affiliated corporation.[38] An **affiliated corporation** is any 80 percent or more controlled domestic subsidiary that has always derived more than 90 percent of its annual gross receipts from the conduct of an active business. In this case, the corporation can treat the securities as a noncapital asset. Accordingly, the corporation's loss is not subject to the capital loss limitation but is fully deductible.

Securities in an Affiliated Corporation	BGH, a calendar year corporation, owns XYZ bonds with a $290,000 tax basis. BGH also owns 90 percent of the outstanding stock of Subsidiary S, a domestic corporation deriving all its gross receipts from a manufacturing business. BGH's basis in this stock is $500,000. Both the bonds and the stock are capital assets. This year, BGH's chief financial officer determined that the XYZ bonds and the Subsidiary S stock are worthless. For tax purposes, BGH recognizes a loss as if it sold both securities on December 31 for an amount realized of zero. The $290,000 loss from the deemed bond sale is a capital loss. However, the $500,000 loss from the deemed stock sale qualifies as an ordinary loss because Subsidiary S qualifies as an affiliated corporation.

[37] §165(g)(1).
[38] §165(g)(3).

Foreclosures

If a firm owns property that is collateral for a debt, the firm will lose the property if it fails to service the debt and the creditor forecloses. The tax consequences of a foreclosure depend on whether the debt is recourse or nonrecourse in nature. A **recourse debt** is one for which the debtor is personally liable; the debtor is obligated to repay the debt out of any and all of its assets. A **nonrecourse debt** is secured by only the specific property pledged as collateral; the debtor is not personally liable for repayment of the debt.

Recourse Debt Foreclosure	Company T owned a tract of land for which it paid $400,000 and which was subject to a $275,000 recourse mortgage. Because of financial difficulties, Company T failed to make the required payments on the mortgage. As a result, the creditor foreclosed and took possession of the land. As part of the foreclosure proceedings, Company T and the creditor agreed that the FMV of the land was $240,000.[39] Therefore, Company T was obligated to pay $35,000 cash to the creditor in full satisfaction of the $275,000 recourse mortgage.
	For tax purposes, Company T treats the foreclosure as if it sold the land for its $240,000 FMV, thereby realizing a $160,000 loss.[40] The character of the loss depends on Company T's use of the land. If Company T operates a real estate business and held the land as inventory, the loss is ordinary. If it used the land in the operation of its business, the loss is a Section 1231 loss. If it held the land as an investment, the loss is a capital loss.

Now change the facts in the preceding example by assuming that Company T is in such poor financial condition that it could not pay the $35,000 cash to fully satisfy the mortgage. If the creditor decides not to pursue its legal claim to such payment, Company T must recognize $35,000 ordinary cancellation-of-debt income.[41] This subsequent development does not affect the tax consequences of the land foreclosure itself.

Nonrecourse Debt Foreclosure	Refer to the facts in the preceding example but assume that the $275,000 mortgage on the land was a nonrecourse debt. The creditor's only right when Company T defaulted on the debt was to foreclose on the land. From the creditor's perspective, it received an asset worth only $240,000 in full settlement of a $275,000 debt and, as a result, incurred a $35,000 bad debt loss. Company T treats the foreclosure as a deemed sale for an amount realized of $275,000—the full amount of the nonrecourse debt—and recognizes a $125,000 loss.[42]

Casualties and Thefts

In this uncertain world, firms may dispose of assets involuntarily because of a sudden, destructive event such as a fire, flood, earthquake, or other act of nature, or through some human agency such as theft, vandalism, or riot. If a firm is adequately insured, the reimbursement from the insurance company should compensate for the economic loss from such casualties. If the insurance reimbursement is less than the adjusted basis of the destroyed property, the firm can claim the unrecovered basis as an ordinary deduction.[43]

---

[39] FMV is frequently established by the creditor's subsequent sale of the property at public auction.

[40] Reg. §1.1001-2(c), Example 8.

[41] §61(a)(12). If Company T is insolvent, only the cancellation-of-debt income in excess of the insolvency is taxable. If Company T is involved in bankruptcy proceedings, none of the cancellation-of-debt income is taxable. §108(a). See *Frazier,* 111 T.C. No. 11 (1998).

[42] Reg. §1.1001-2(c), Example 7, and *Commissioner* v. *Tufts,* 461 U.S. 300 (1983).

[43] Reg. §1.165-7(b). This general statement disregards the complex casualty gain/loss netting rule of §1231(a)(4)(C).

If the reimbursement exceeds the adjusted basis, the firm must recognize the excess as taxable income unless it takes advantage of a deferral opportunity discussed in the next chapter.

Casualty Loss	Firm JBJ recently suffered a casualty loss when a flood destroyed four automobiles used in its business. The firm carried property insurance and received a $42,000 reimbursement after filing a claim with its insurance company. The adjusted basis of the four automobiles was $53,800. JBJ can deduct its $11,800 unrecovered basis as an ordinary loss in the computation of taxable income.

Theft Loss	Firm W operates a construction company. Over a recent weekend when one of the firm's jobsites was unoccupied, thieves stole construction materials with a total cost of $5,000 and construction tools with an original cost of $4,000 and accumulated tax depreciation of $1,550. The loss was not reimbursed by insurance. Firm W is entitled to an ordinary loss deduction for the cost of the stolen materials and the adjusted tax basis of the tools. The total deductible loss is $7,450 ($5,000 + $4,000 − $1,550).

Conclusion

The rules governing the tax consequences of property transactions are among the most complicated in the tax law. Nevertheless, business managers must understand how these rules operate to determine the taxable gain or deductible loss triggered by sales, exchanges, and other dispositions of assets. The rules relate both to the timing of gain or loss recognition and the character of the gain or loss. The critical distinction between ordinary and capital gain or loss can result in significant differences in tax cost or tax savings. Managers who do not understand this distinction may miss tax planning opportunities that can dramatically improve after-tax cash flows from asset dispositions. In the next chapter, we continue our discussion of property transactions by examining still another type of asset disposition—a nontaxable exchange.

Sources of Book/Tax Differences

Permanent

- Loss on related party sale

Temporary

- Disposition of asset with different book/tax basis
- Seller-financed sale eligible for installment sale method
- Net capital loss

Key Terms

abandonment loss   *222*
affiliated corporation   *223*
amount realized   *201*
capital asset   *208*
capital gain or loss   *208*
depreciation recapture   *216*
gross profit percentage   *204*
installment sale
    method   *204*

net capital loss   *209*
nonrecaptured Section
    1231 loss   *216*
nonrecourse debt   *224*
ordinary gain or loss   *208*
realized gain or loss   *200*
recapture   *215*
recognized gain or
    loss   *200*

recourse debt   *224*
Section 1231 asset   *214*
Section 1245
    recapture   *217*
Section 1250
    recapture   *218*
seller-financed sale   *203*
20 percent
    recapture   *219*

Questions and Problems for Discussion

1. BBB Company, which manufactures industrial plastics, owns the following assets. Characterize each asset as either a capital, ordinary, or Section 1231 asset.

   a. A computer system used in BBB's main office.

   b. A 50 percent interest in a business partnership organized to conduct a mining operation in Utah.

   c. Heavy equipment used to mold BBB's best-selling plastic item.

   d. BBB's customer list developed over 12 years of business.

   e. BBB's inventory of raw materials used in the manufacturing process.

   f. An oil painting of BBB's founder and first president that hangs in the boardroom.

   g. A patent developed by BBB's research and development department.

   h. BBB's company airplane.

2. For tax purposes, what is the difference between a sale of property and an exchange of property?

3. Under what circumstances could a taxpayer have an amount realized on the disposition of an asset without any inflow of cash or property?

4. Under what circumstances would a taxpayer elect not to use the installment sale method of reporting gain?

5. Does the characterization of gain or loss as either ordinary or capital have any effect on the computation of net income per books?

6. Distinguish between a firm's tax basis in an asset and its equity in that asset.

7. Corporation A and Corporation Z both have business goodwill worth approximately $1 million. The goodwill is a capital asset to Corporation A and a Section 1231 asset to Corporation Z. Can you explain this apparently inconsistent tax characterization?

8. Mrs. Carly called her accountant with a question. She is planning to sell nine acres of land for $380,000 cash. She purchased the land eight years ago for $195,000. She asks her accountant if her gain on sale will be a capital gain, and his answer is "It depends." Can you explain why the accountant could not answer Mrs. Carly's simple question?

9. Two years ago, Firm OP bought a tract of land for $600,000, paying $50,000 down and borrowing the balance of the purchase price from a commercial lender. The land is the collateral for OP's debt. To date, OP has not repaid any of the loan.

   a. If the debt is recourse, to what extent do OP and the commercial lender bear the risk of loss if the FMV of the land decreases to $475,000?

   b. How does your answer change if the debt is nonrecourse?

10. Mr. K realized a loss on the sale of an asset to Mr. P, his best friend for 20 years. Does this sale represent an arm's-length transaction? Are Mr. K and Mr. P related parties for tax purposes?

11. Why do both corporate and noncorporate taxpayers prefer capital gains to ordinary income? Why is the preference stronger for noncorporate taxpayers?

12. Why is Section 1250 recapture inapplicable to sales of realty subject to MACRS depreciation?

13. Does a taxpayer always realize a loss on the involuntary disposition of property because of a casualty or a theft?

14. Firm F's adjusted basis in operating asset A is $75,000. If the firm carries $75,000 of property insurance on this asset, is it adequately protected against risk of loss?

Application Problems

1. Lento Inc. owned machinery with a $30,000 initial cost basis. Accumulated book depreciation with respect to the machinery was $12,000, and accumulated tax depreciation was $19,100. Lento sold the machinery for $13,000 cash. Lento's marginal tax rate is 30 percent.

   a. Compute Lento's book gain or loss on sale.

   b. Compute Lento's tax gain or loss on sale.

   c. Compute Lento's after-tax cash flow from the sale.

2. Several years ago, PTR purchased business equipment for $50,000. PTR's accumulated book depreciation with respect to the equipment is $37,200, and its accumulated tax depreciation is $41,000.

   a. Compute PTR's book and tax basis in the equipment.

   b. Using a 35 percent tax rate, compute PTR's deferred tax asset or liability (identify which) resulting from the difference between accumulated book and tax depreciation.

   c. Compute PTR's book and tax gain if it sells the equipment for $14,750.

   d. Explain the effect of the sale on the deferred tax asset or liability computed in *b*.

3. Firm CS performed consulting services for Company P. The two parties agreed that Company P would pay for the services by transferring investment securities to Firm CS. At date of transfer, the securities had a 38,500 FMV. Company P's tax basis in the securities was $25,000.

   a. How much income must Firm CS recognize on receipt of the securities? What is the character of this income? What is Firm CS's tax basis in the securities?

   b. How much income must Company P recognize on disposition of the securities? What is the character of the income?

   c. Does disposition of the securities result in a deduction for Company P? If so, what is the amount of the deduction?

4. Company L sold an inventory item to Firm M for $40,000. Company L's marginal tax rate is 35 percent. In each of the following cases, compute Company L's after-tax cash flow from the sale.

   a. Firm M's payment consisted of $10,000 cash and its note for $30,000. The note is payable two years from the date of sale. Company L's basis in the inventory item was $15,700.

   b. Firm M's payment consisted of $5,000 cash and its note for $35,000. The note is payable two years from the date of sale. Company L's basis in the inventory item was $47,000.

   c. Firm M's payment consisted of $40,000 cash. Company L's basis in the inventory item was $18,000.

   d. Firm M's payment consisted of $40,000 cash. Company L's basis in the inventory item was $44,000.

5. KNB sold real property to Firm P for $15,000 cash and Firm P's assumption of the $85,000 mortgage on the property.

   a. What is KNB's amount realized on sale?

   b. Compute KNB's after-tax cash flow from the sale if its adjusted basis in the real property is $40,000, and its marginal tax rate is 34 percent.

6. Firm UT sold realty to an unrelated buyer for $40,000 cash plus the buyer's assumption of a $166,700 mortgage on the property. UT's initial cost basis in the realty was $235,000, and accumulated tax depreciation through date of sale was $184,200.

   a. Compute UT's gain recognized on sale.

   b. Assuming a 35 percent marginal tax rate, compute UT's after-tax cash flow from the sale.

7. TPW, a calendar year taxpayer, sold land with a $535,000 tax basis for $750,000 in February. The purchaser paid $75,000 cash at closing and gave TPW an interest-bearing note for the $675,000 remaining price. In August, TPW received a $55,950 payment from the purchaser consisting of a $33,750 principal payment and a $22,200 interest payment.

   a. Compute gain realized on the sale.

   b. Compute gain recognized in the year of sale if TPW elects not to use the installment sale method of accounting. Compute TPW's tax basis in the note at the end of the year.

   c. Compute gain recognized in the year of sale if TPW uses the installment sale method of accounting. Compute TPW's tax basis in the note at the end of the year.

8. Refer to the facts in the preceding problem and assume that TPW uses the installment sale method of accounting.

   a. Compute the difference between TPW's book and tax income resulting from the installment sale method.

   b. Is this difference favorable or unfavorable?

   c. Using a 35 percent tax rate, compute PTR's deferred tax asset or liability (identify which) resulting from the book/tax difference.

9. Refer to the facts in problem 7. In the first year after the year of sale, TPW received payments totaling $106,900 from the purchaser. The total consisted of $67,500 principal payments and $39,400 interest payments.

   a. Compute TPW's gain recognized under the installment sale method.

   b. Compute TPW's tax basis in the note at the end of the year.

10. Refer to the facts in the preceding problem.

   a. Compute the difference between TPW's book and tax income resulting from the installment sale method.

   b. Is this difference favorable or unfavorable?

   c. Using a 35 percent tax rate, determine the effect of the difference on the deferred tax asset or liability generated in the year of sale.

11. In 2009, Aldo sold investment land with a $61,000 tax basis for $95,000. Payment consisted of $15,000 cash down and the purchaser's note for $80,000. The note is being paid in 10 annual installments of $8,000, beginning in 2010.

   a. Compute Aldo's recognized gain under the installment sale method in 2009 and 2010.

   b. In 2012, Aldo pledged the note as partial collateral for a $75,000 bank loan. The unpaid principal at date of pledge was $56,000. Determine the tax consequences of this pledge to Aldo.

12. Refer to the facts in the preceding problem but assume that Aldo's basis in the investment land was $100,000 rather than $61,000.

   a. Compute Aldo's recognized loss in 2009.

b. In 2012, Aldo pledged the note received from the purchaser as partial collateral for a $75,000 bank loan. The unpaid principal at date of pledge was $56,000. Determine the tax consequences of this pledge to Aldo.

13. Firm J sold marketable securities to Company B. Firm J's tax basis in the securities was $45,250. Compute Firm J's recognized gain or loss if:

    a. The selling price was $60,000, and Firm J and Company B are unrelated parties.

    b. The selling price was $60,000, and Firm J and Company B are related parties.

    c. The selling price was $38,000, and Firm J and Company B are unrelated parties.

    d. The selling price was $38,000, and Firm J and Company B are related parties.

14. Silo Inc. sold investment land to PPR Inc. for $110,000 cash. Silo's basis in the land was $145,000. Mr. and Mrs. J own 100 percent of the stock of both corporations.

    a. What is PPR's tax basis in the land purchased from Silo?

    b. PPR holds the land as an investment for seven years before selling it to an unrelated buyer. Compute the gain or loss recognized if the amount realized on sale is (1) $100,000, (2) $116,000, or (3) $150,000.

15. Firm J, an accrual basis taxpayer, recorded a $40,000 account receivable on the sale of an asset on credit. Its basis in the asset was $33,000. Two months after the asset sale, Firm J sold the receivable to a local bank for $38,000.

    a. Assuming that the asset was an inventory item, determine the amount and character of Firm J's gain or loss recognized on sale of (1) the asset and (2) the receivable.

    b. Assuming that the asset was a capital asset, determine the amount and character of Firm J's gain or loss recognized on sale of (1) the asset and (2) the receivable.

16. Four years ago, Firm RD paid $468,000 for 12 acres of undeveloped land. This year, the firm sold the land for $1 million. What is the character of RD's $532,000 recognized gain under each of the following assumptions?

    a. RD improved the land by adding roads and utilities, then subdivided the land into 36 one-third-acre tracts that RD held for sale to local builders.

    b. RD made no improvements to the land and sold the entire 12 acres to a Japanese purchaser.

17. On July 8, Divo Company sold office supplies for $13,000. Determine the amount and character of Divo's gain or loss on sale under each of the following assumptions.

    a. Divo is a retail store that sells office supplies to customers. Under the LIFO method of accounting, Divo's cost basis in the supplies was $11,900.

    b. Divo is a law firm. Divo sold the supplies because it was overstocked and needed the storage space for a different purpose. Under its method of accounting, Divo expenses the cost of office supplies when purchased.

    c. Divo is an accounting firm. Divo sold the supplies because it is liquidating its business. Divo's capitalized cost of the supplies was $14,250.

18. *Shenandoah Skies* is the name of an oil painting by artist Kara Lee. In each of the following cases, determine the amount and character of the taxpayer's gain or loss on sale of the painting.

    a. The taxpayer is Kara Lee, who sold her painting to the Reller Gallery for $6,000.

    b. The taxpayer is the Reller Gallery, who sold the painting purchased from Kara to a regular customer for $10,000.

    c. The taxpayer is Lollard Inc., the regular customer that purchased the painting from the Reller Gallery. Lollard displayed the painting in the lobby of its corporate headquarters until it sold *Shenandoah Skies* to a collector from Dallas. The collector paid $45,000 for the painting.

19. Koil Corporation generated $718,400 ordinary income from the sale of inventory to its customers. It also sold three noninventory assets during the year. Compute Koil's taxable income assuming that:

    a. The first sale resulted in a $45,000 capital gain; the second sale resulted in a $12,000 capital loss, and the third sale resulted in a $19,000 capital loss.

    b. The first sale resulted in a $17,000 ordinary gain; the second sale resulted in a $22,300 capital gain, and the third sale resulted in a $58,000 capital loss.

    c. The first sale resulted in a $9,000 capital gain; the second sale resulted in a $16,100 capital loss, and the third sale resulted in an $8,800 ordinary loss.

20. This year, PRS Corporation generated $300,000 income from the performance of consulting services for its clients. It sold two assets during the year, recognizing a $36,000 gain on the first sale and a $49,000 loss on the second sale. Compute PRS's taxable income assuming that:

    a. Both the gain and the loss were capital.

    b. Both the gain and the loss were ordinary.

    c. The gain was ordinary, and the loss was capital.

    d. The gain was capital, and the loss was ordinary.

21. Zeno Inc. sold two capital assets in 2012. The first sale resulted in a $53,000 capital loss, and the second sale resulted in a $25,600 capital gain. Zeno was incorporated in 2008, and its tax records provide the following information.

	2008	2009	2010	2011
Ordinary income	$443,000	$509,700	$810,300	$921,000
Net capital gain	22,000	0	4,120	13,600
Taxable income	$465,000	$509,700	$814,420	$934,600

(handwritten: 2008, 2009, 2010 above table years)

    a. Using a 34 percent tax rate, compute Zeno's tax refund from the carryback of its 2012 nondeductible capital loss.

    b. Compute Zeno's capital loss carryforward into 2013.

22. In its first year, Firm KZ recognized $427,300 ordinary business income and a $13,590 loss on the sale of an investment asset. In its second year, Firm KZ recognized $500,800 ordinary business income and a $19,300 Section 1231 gain and a $7,400 Section 1231 loss on two sales of operating assets.

    a. Compute KZ's book and tax income for its first year.

    b. Using a 34 percent tax rate, compute KZ's deferred tax asset or liability (identify which) on its balance sheet on the last day of the year.

    c. Compute KZ's book and tax income for its second year.

    d. Compute KZ's deferred tax asset or liability (identify which) on its balance sheet on the last day of the year.

23. Firm OCS sold business equipment with a $20,000 initial cost basis and $7,315 accumulated tax depreciation. In each of the following cases, compute OCS's recaptured ordinary income and Section 1231 gain or loss on sale.

    a. Amount realized was $10,000.

    b. Amount realized was $13,000.

    c. Amount realized was $17,500.

    d. Amount realized was $22,500.

24. This year, Zeron Company generated $87,200 income from the performance of services for its clients. It also sold several assets during the year. Compute Zeron's taxable income under each of the following assumptions about the tax consequences of the asset sales.

    a. Zeron recognized $1,000 recaptured ordinary income, a $2,400 net Section 1231 gain, and a $7,000 capital loss.

    b. Zeron recognized a $6,600 net Section 1231 loss and a $1,700 capital loss.

    c. Zeron recognized $3,900 recaptured ordinary income, a $1,510 net Section 1231 gain, and a $1,200 capital gain.

    d. Zeron recognized a $10,300 net Section 1231 loss and a $4,000 capital gain.

    e. Zeron recognized a $2,800 net Section 1231 gain, a $5,200 capital gain, and a $6,300 capital loss.

25. This year, QIO Company generated $192,400 income from its routine business operations. In addition, it sold the following assets, all of which were held for more than 12 months. Compute QIO's taxable income.

	Initial Basis	Acc. Depr.*	Sale Price
Computer equipment	$ 22,400	$ 18,600	$ 4,500
Construction equipment	175,000	121,700	50,000
Furniture	6,000	1,500	4,750
Transportation equipment	83,200	26,000	55,000

*Through date of sale.

26. This year, Sigma Inc. generated $612,000 income from its routine business operations. In addition, the corporation sold the following assets, all of which were held for more than 12 months.

	Initial Basis	Acc. Depr.*	Sale Price
Marketable securities	$144,000	–0–	$ 64,000
Production equipment	93,000	$76,000	30,000
Business realty:			
Land	165,000	–0–	180,000
Building	200,000	58,300	210,000

*Through date of sale.

    a. Compute Sigma's taxable income assuming that it used the straight-line method to calculate depreciation on the building and has no nonrecaptured Section 1231 losses.

    b. Recompute taxable income assuming that Sigma sold the securities for $150,000 rather than $64,000.

27. EzTech, a calendar year accrual basis corporation, generated $994,300 ordinary income from its business this year. It also sold the following assets, all of which were held for more than 12 months.

	Initial Basis	Acc. Depr.*	Sale Price
Machinery	$ 97,500	$39,660	$ 70,000
Office equipment	50,000	12,470	57,500
Warehouse	163,500	21,620	125,000
Investment securities	72,700	n/a	83,100
Investment land	350,000	n/a	328,000

*Through date of sale.

EzTech used the straight-line method to calculate depreciation on the warehouse and has no nonrecaptured Section 1231 losses.

a. Compute EzTech's taxable income.

b. Recompute taxable income assuming that EzTech used the land in its business instead of holding it for investment.

28. Corporation Q, a calendar year taxpayer, has incurred the following Section 1231 net gains and losses since its formation in 2009.

	2009	2010	2011
Section 1231 gains	$ 14,800	$ 5,700	–0–
Section 1231 losses	(13,000)	(9,000)	$(3,100)
Net gain or (loss)	$ 1,800	$(3,300)	$(3,100)

a. In 2012, Corporation Q sold only one asset and recognized a $4,000 Section 1231 gain. How much of this gain is treated as capital gain and how much is ordinary?

b. In 2013, Corporation Q recognized a $16,700 Section 1231 gain on the sale of one asset and a $2,000 Section 1231 loss on the sale of a second asset. How much of the $14,700 net gain is treated as capital gain and how much is ordinary?

29. In 2001, Lynn Inc. purchased a warehouse for $315,000. This year, the corporation sold the warehouse to Firm D for $80,000 cash and D's assumption of a $225,000 mortgage. Through date of sale, Lynn deducted $92,300 straight-line depreciation on the warehouse.

a. Compute Lynn's gain recognized on sale of the warehouse.

b. What is the character of this gain?

c. How would your answers change if Lynn is a noncorporate business?

30. Firm P, a noncorporate taxpayer, purchased residential realty in 1985 for $1 million. This year it sold the realty for $450,000. Through date of sale, Firm P deducted $814,000 accelerated depreciation on the realty. Straight-line depreciation would have been $625,000.

a. Determine the amount and character of Firm P's recognized gain on sale.

b. How would your answer change if Firm P was a corporation?

31. Six years ago, Corporation CN purchased a business and capitalized $200,000 of the purchase price as goodwill. Through this year, CN has deducted $74,000 amortization with respect to this goodwill. At the end of the year, CN sold the business for $2 million, $250,000 of which was allocable to goodwill. Determine the amount and character of CN's gain from its sale of goodwill.

32. Company B disposed of obsolete computer equipment with a $32,000 initial cost basis and $27,000 accumulated depreciation. Determine the amount and character of Company B's recognized gain or loss if:

    a. It sold the equipment for $7,000.

    b. It sold the equipment for $1,000.

    c. It dumped the equipment in a local landfill.

33. Firm L owns a commercial building that is divided into 23 offices. Several years ago, it leased an office to Company K. As part of the lease agreement, Firm L spent $29,000 to construct new interior walls to conform the office to Company K's specifications. It capitalized this expenditure to an asset account and has deducted $6,200 depreciation with respect to the asset. Early this year, Company K broke its lease and vacated the office. Firm L has found a prospective tenant that wants Firm L to demolish the interior walls before it will sign a lease. What are the tax consequences to Firm L if it agrees to the demolition?

34. A taxpayer owned 1,000 shares of common stock in Barlo Corporation, which manufactures automobile parts. The taxpayer's cost basis in the stock was $82,700. Last week, Barlo declared bankruptcy and its board of directors issued a news release that Barlo common stock should be considered worthless. Determine the character of the $82,700 loss if the taxpayer is

    a. An individual who purchased the stock as an investment.

    b. A corporation that purchased the stock as an investment.

    c. Barlo's parent corporation that owned 96 percent of Barlo's outstanding common stock.

35. Lyle Company owns commercial real estate with a $360,000 initial cost basis and $285,000 accumulated straight-line depreciation. The real estate is subject to a $120,000 recourse mortgage and has an appraised FMV of only $100,000. The mortgage holder is threatening to foreclose on the real estate because Lyle failed to make the last four mortgage payments. Determine the tax consequences of foreclosure assuming that:

    a. Lyle must pay $20,000 cash to the mortgage holder in full satisfaction of its recourse debt.

    b. The mortgage holder agrees to accept the real estate in full satisfaction of the recourse debt.

36. Change the facts in the preceding problem by assuming that the $120,000 mortgage on Lyle's real estate is nonrecourse. Determine the tax consequence to Lyle if the mortgage holder forecloses on the real estate.

37. Five years ago, Firm SJ purchased land for $100,000 with $10,000 of its own funds and $90,000 borrowed from a commercial bank. The bank holds a recourse mortgage on the land. For each of the following independent transactions, compute SJ's positive or negative cash flow. Assume that SJ is solvent, any recognized loss is fully deductible, and SJ's marginal tax rate is 35 percent.

    a. SJ sells the land for $33,000 cash and the buyer's assumption of the $80,000 principal balance of the mortgage.

    b. SJ sells the land for $113,000 cash and pays off the $80,000 principal balance of the mortgage.

    c. SJ sells the land for $82,000 cash and pays off the $80,000 principal balance of the mortgage.

     d. SJ defaults on the $80,000 mortgage. The bank forecloses and sells the land at public auction for $64,000. The bank notifies SJ that it will not pursue collection of the $16,000 remaining debt.

     e. SJ defaults on the $80,000 mortgage. The bank forecloses and sells the land at public auction for $64,000. The bank requires SJ to pay off the $16,000 remaining debt.

38. Firm R owned depreciable real property subject to a $300,000 nonrecourse mortgage. The property's FMV is only $250,000. Consequently, the firm surrendered the property to the creditor rather than continue to service the mortgage. At date of surrender, Firm R's adjusted basis in the property was $195,000. Determine Firm R's cash flow consequences of the disposition, assuming that the gain recognized is taxed at 25 percent.

39. A fire recently destroyed a warehouse owned by Company J. Its adjusted basis in the warehouse was $489,000. However, the warehouse's replacement value (cost to rebuild) was $610,000. Determine the tax consequences of this property disposition assuming that:

     a. The building was insured, and Company J received a $450,000 reimbursement from the insurance company.

     b. The building was uninsured.

40. Calvin Corporation's office was burglarized. The thieves stole 10 laptop computers and other electronic equipment. The lost assets had an original cost of $35,000 and accumulated tax depreciation of $19,400. Calvin received an insurance reimbursement of $10,000 related to the theft loss. Determine the amount and character of gain or loss recognized as a result of this theft.

41. Bali Inc. reported $605,800 net income before tax on this year's financial statements prepared in accordance with GAAP. The corporation's records reveal the following information.

    • Depreciation expense per books was $53,000, and MACRS depreciation was $27,400.

    • Bali sold business equipment for $100,000 cash. The original cost of the equipment was $125,000. Book accumulated depreciation through date of sale was $48,000, and MACRS accumulated depreciation through date of sale was $63,000.

    • Bali sold investment land to Coroda, a corporation owned by the same person that owns Bali. The amount realized on sale was $115,000, and Bali's basis in the land was $40,000.

    • Bali sold marketable securities to its sole shareholder. The amount realized on sale was $51,450, and Bali's basis in the securities was $75,000.

    Compute ZEJ's taxable income.

42. St. George Inc. reported $711,800 net income before tax on this year's financial statement prepared in accordance with GAAP. The corporation's records reveal the following information.

    • Four years ago, St. George realized a $283,400 gain on sale of investment property and elected the installment sale method to report the sale for tax purposes. Its gross profit percentage is 50.12, and it collected $62,000 principal and $14,680 interest on the installment note this year.

    • Five years ago, St. George purchased investment property for $465,000 cash from an LLC. Because St. George and the LLC were related parties, the LLC's $12,700 realized loss on sale was disallowed for tax purposes. This year, St. George sold the property to an unrelated purchaser for $500,000.

- A flood destroyed several antique carpets that decorated the floors of corporate headquarters. Unfortunately, St. George's property insurance does not cover damage caused by rising water, so the loss was uninsured. The carpets' adjusted book basis was $36,000, and their adjusted tax basis was $28,400.

Compute St. George's taxable income.

43. Ms. D sold a business that she had operated as a sole proprietorship for 18 years. On date of sale, the business balance sheet showed the following assets.

	Tax Basis
Accounts receivable	$ 32,000
Inventory	125,000
Furniture and equipment:	
Cost	45,800
Accumulated depreciation	(38,000)
Leasehold improvements:	
Cost	29,000
Accumulated depreciation	(5,100)

The purchaser paid a lump-sum price of $300,000 cash for the business. The sales contract stipulates that the FMV of the business inventory is $145,000, and the FMV of the remaining balance sheet assets equals adjusted tax basis. Assuming that Ms. D's marginal tax rate on ordinary income is 35 percent and her rate on capital gain is 15 percent, compute the net cash flow from the sale of her business.

44. Twelve years ago, Mr. and Mrs. Chang purchased a business. This year, they sold the business for $750,000. On date of sale, the business balance sheet showed the following assets.

		Tax Basis
Accounts receivable		$ 41,200
Inventory		515,000
Furniture and fixtures:		
Cost	$395,500	
Accumulated depreciation	(321,800)	
		73,700
Purchased goodwill:		
Cost	$250,000	
Accumulated amortization	(203,600)	
		46,400
Total tax basis		$676,300

The sales contract allocated $40,000 of the purchase price to accounts receivable, $515,000 to inventory, and $70,000 to furniture and fixtures. Assuming that the Changs' marginal tax rate on ordinary income is 33 percent and their rate on capital gain is 15 percent, compute the net cash flow from the sale of their business.

Issue Recognition Problems

Identify the tax issue or issues suggested by the following situations, and state each issue in the form of a question.

1. On March 1, DS Company, a calendar year taxpayer, recognized a $15,000 loss on sale of marketable securities. On May 12, it recognized an $85,000 Section 1231 gain on sale of an office building. In forecasting current taxable income, DS's chief financial officer plans to deduct the $15,000 loss against the $85,000 gain.

2. Firm LD, a calendar year taxpayer, owns 20,000 shares of MXP stock with a $160,000 basis. In November, LD's chief financial officer learned that MXP had just declared bankruptcy. The CFO was unable to determine if MXP's board of directors intend to try to save the corporation or dissolve it under state law.

3. A fire damaged industrial equipment used by Firm L in its manufacturing process. Immediately before the fire, the equipment was worth $40,000. After the fire, the equipment was worth only $15,000. Firm L's adjusted basis in the equipment was $14,000, and it received only $10,000 insurance reimbursement for its loss.

4. Company LR owns a commercial office building. Four years ago, LR entered into a long-term lease with Lessee M for 2,400 square feet of office space. LR spent $13,600 to finish out the space to meet Lessee M's requirements. The leasehold improvements included several interior walls and special purpose electrical wiring. This year, Lessee M terminated the lease and moved out of the office space. To make the space more marketable, LR tore down the interior walls and removed the special purpose wiring.

5. Two years ago, Corporation M loaned $80,000 to its employee Mr. E. The corporation received Mr. E's properly executed note in which he promised to repay the loan at the end of seven years and to pay annual interest of 9 percent (the market interest rate on the date of the loan). This year, when interest rates were 6 percent, Corporation M sold the $80,000 note to an unrelated party for $92,700.

6. In its second taxable year, Corporation NM generated a $25,000 net operating loss and recognized an $8,000 net capital loss. The corporation's tax return for its first year reported $15,000 taxable income, $10,000 of which was capital gain.

7. Firm WD sold depreciable realty for $225,000. The firm purchased the realty 12 years earlier for $350,000 and deducted $155,000 MACRS depreciation through date of sale. During an audit of the tax return on which the sale was reported, the IRS determined that WD had incorrectly computed its depreciation with respect to the realty. The correct depreciation through date of sale should have been $200,000.

8. Corporation AD operates four antique dealerships. Last year, it sold a 200-year-old desk to its sole shareholder, Mr. C, for $35,000. AD reported its $2,700 gain as ordinary income from the sale of inventory. This year, Mr. C sold the desk to an unrelated collector for $60,000 and reported a $25,000 capital gain on his tax return.

9. Mr. V sold his sole proprietorship to an unrelated party for a lump-sum price of $900,000. The contract of sale specifies that $100,000 is for a covenant not to compete—Mr. V's promise not to operate a similar business anywhere in the state for the next four years.

10. Corporation TJ ceased business operations and was dissolved under state law. On the last day of its existence, TJ's balance sheet showed $2,200 unamortized organizational costs and $12,000 unamortized goodwill.

11. At the beginning of the year, Firm GH owned 8,200 shares of common stock in LSR, a publicly held corporation. GH's basis in these shares was $290,000. On a day when

LSR stock was trading at $1.14 per share, GH delivered the 8,200 shares to its broker with a letter stating that it was formally abandoning ownership of its LSR equity interest.

Research Problems

1. For the last 12 years, George Link has operated his appliance repair business out of a 1,000-square-foot, ground floor office in a four-story commercial building called 129 Main. Last year, George signed a five-year lease with Kramer Management, the owner of 129 Main. This year, Kramer decided to convert the building into condominiums and is negotiating with all its tenants to surrender their leasehold rights and vacate their space in 129 Main. Kramer has offered George a $50,000 cash payment and the use of a 1,200-square-foot office in a new shopping center recently constructed by Kramer. If George accepts Kramer's offer, he can use the new office rent free for 36 months. The fair rental value of this office is $1,300 per month. What are the tax consequences to George if he accepts Kramer's offer and moves his business location?

2. Six years ago, Graham Inc., an accrual basis corporation, sold investment land (basis $562,250) to Jervil LLC and accepted Jervil's note for the entire $865,000 sale price. The land was the collateral for the note, and Graham used the installment sale method of reporting its taxable gain on sale. This year, Jervil defaulted on the note, and Graham repossessed the land. At the date of repossession, the principal of the note was $644,000. Graham also had $40,800 accrued interest receivable on the note. How much gain must Graham recognize on repossession, and what is its new tax basis in the repossessed land?

3. In 1988, Big Skye Partnership paid $695,500 for a Christmas tree farm in northern Arizona. In 1991, over 300 farms and ranches in the area were granted allocations of water from a newly completed irrigation project funded by the U.S. Department of the Interior. This year, Big Skye Partnership discontinued its tree farming operation and converted the property to a sheep ranch. Because the property no longer needed irrigation, Big Skye sold its federal water rights to a neighboring farm for $175,000. What is the amount and character of Big Skye's gain or loss on disposition of its water rights?

4. The BPL Corporation is considering selling investment land to Kaier Partnership for the land's independently appraised FMV of $1.2 million. BPL purchased the land in 1993 for $1.32 million cash. Mr. Larry Bass is the largest shareholder in BPL; he owns 892 of 2,000 BPL shares outstanding. Larry's sister, Mrs. Ann Olsen, owns 165 BPL shares, and various investors who are unrelated to Larry and Ann own the remaining shares outstanding. Ann is a limited partner in Kaier Partnership; she owns a 35 percent interest in Kaier's profits and capital. Ann's daughter, Suzanne Olsen, owns a 22 percent limited interest in Kaier's profits and capital. Ann and Suzanne are unrelated to any other Kaier partner and are not involved in any aspect of the management of the partnership. If BPL sells its land to Kaier Partnership, can it recognize the $120,000 loss that it will realize on the sale?

Tax Planning Cases

1. Firm Z, a corporation with a 35 percent tax rate, has $100,000 to invest in year 0 and two investment choices. Investment 1 will generate $12,000 taxable cash flow annually for years 1 through 5. In year 5, the firm can sell the investment for $100,000. Investment 2 will not generate any taxable income or cash flow in years 1 through 5, but in year 5, the firm can sell Investment 2 for $165,000.

   a. Assuming a 6 percent discount rate, which investment has the greater NPV?

b. Would your answer change if Firm Z is a noncorporate taxpayer with a 35 percent tax rate and the gain on sale of Investment 2 is eligible for the 15 percent capital gains rate?

2. Mr. RH purchased 30 acres of undeveloped ranch land 10 years ago for $935,000. He is considering subdividing the land into one-third-acre lots and improving the land by adding streets, sidewalks, and utilities. He plans to advertise the 90 lots for sale in a local real estate magazine. Mr. RH projects that the improvements will cost $275,000 and that he can sell the lots for $20,000 each. He is also considering an offer from a local corporation to purchase the 30-acre tract in its undeveloped state for $1.35 million. Assuming that Mr. RH makes no other property dispositions during the year and has a 35 percent tax rate on ordinary income and a 15 percent tax rate on capital gain, which alternative (develop or sell as is) maximizes his cash flow?

3. For its first four years of operation, Corporation Y reported the following taxable income.

	2008	2009	2010	2011
Ordinary income	$12,000	$ 6,000	$150,000	$600,000
Net capital gain	–0–	19,000	4,000	–0–
Taxable income	$12,000	$25,000	$154,000	$600,000

(handwritten annotations above the year headers: "2009" above 2008, "2009" above 2009, "2010" above 2011)

In 2012, Corporation Y generated $900,000 ordinary income and recognized a $20,000 loss on the sale of a capital asset. It is considering selling a second capital asset *before the close of 2012.* This sale would generate a $21,000 capital gain that would allow the corporation to deduct its entire capital loss. Alternatively, it could carry its $20,000 net capital loss back to 2009 and 2010 and receive a tax refund. Which course of action do you recommend and why?

4. Olno Inc. has a $52,100 capital loss carryforward into its current taxable year that will expire at the end of the year. During the year, Olno realized a $141,900 capital gain on sale of land. The purchaser paid 10 percent down and gave Olno an interest-bearing note for the 90 percent remainder of the sale price. Under the installment sale method, Olno will recognize $14,190 gain this year and $14,190 in each of the following nine years. If Olno's marginal tax rate is 35 percent and it uses a 6 percent discount rate to compute NPV, should Olno elect out of the installment sale method?

5. Rocky Corporation is experiencing cash flow problems. It needs to generate an additional $60,000 of working capital and is considering selling off assets to meet this need. Rocky's marginal tax rate is 34 percent and it has no prior year capital gains. It is considering three alternatives, as follows.

Alternative 1: Sell land for $60,000. The land was acquired three years ago as an investment at a cost of $90,000. Ground contamination caused by industrial dumping has caused the property value to decline.

Alternative 2: Sell land and a building used in Rocky's business. The two assets together could be sold for $60,000, of which $50,000 is attributable to the building and $10,000 is attributable to the land. The building has an adjusted tax basis of $23,000; the land has an adjusted tax basis of $17,000.

Alternative 3: Sell obsolete business machinery and equipment. The machinery has an adjusted basis of $100,000 and can be sold for $60,000.

Determine the impact of each of these alternatives on *current year* cash flow. Which alternative or alternatives provide the needed cash flow?

CPA REVIEW

CPA Exam Simulation

Please visit the text website for the online CPA simulations: mhhe.com/sjones2013.

Earlier this year, Investment, Inc. sold one of its stock investments and realized a loss. What code section and subsection provide the authority regarding the treatment by corporate taxpayers of this realized loss?

Topics covered in the simulation:

- Tax research
- Capital loss limitations

Option #1

900,000
1,000
―――――
901,000

900,000

Option 1   Sell now (2ᴺᴰ Asset

Option 2   Carry back loss

Nontaxable Exchanges

Learning Objectives

After studying this chapter, you should be able to:

1. Compute the substituted basis of property received in a nontaxable exchange.

2. Compute gain recognized when boot is received in a nontaxable exchange.

3. Identify properties that qualify for like-kind exchange treatment.

4. Describe the effect of the relief and assumption of debt in a like-kind exchange.

5. Compute gain recognized and the basis of replacement property in an involuntary conversion.

6. Explain the tax consequences of the exchange of property for equity in a corporation or partnership.

7. Describe the tax consequences of a wash sale.

In our analysis of property dispositions thus far, we've been working under the premise that any realized gain or loss is recognized (taken into account for tax purposes) in the year of disposition. In Chapter 9, we will examine a number of transactions that trigger gain or loss realization but do not result in current recognition of some or all of that gain or loss. These transactions are called **nontaxable exchanges,** and each one is authorized by a provision of the Internal Revenue Code. Congress enacted these provisions for particular tax policy reasons, which we will discuss as we look at the details of selected provisions.

TAX NEUTRALITY FOR ASSET EXCHANGES

The nontaxable exchange provisions are extremely useful because they allow taxpayers to convert property from one form to another without a tax cost. In other words, a nontaxable exchange provision makes the tax law *neutral* with respect to certain business and investment decisions.

Neutrality of Nontaxable Exchange	Firm T, which has a 35 percent marginal tax rate, owns an investment asset with a $50,000 basis and a $110,000 fair market value (FMV). The asset generates $6,600 annual income, which represents a 6 percent return on FMV. Firm T is considering selling this asset and reinvesting the proceeds in a new venture that promises a 7 percent return on capital. If the sale of the investment asset is taxable, Firm T will have only $89,000 after-tax proceeds to reinvest.

Amount realized on sale	$110,000
Basis in investment asset	(50,000)
Gain realized and recognized	$ 60,000
	.35
Tax cost	$ 21,000
After-tax cash ($110,000 − $21,000)	$ 89,000

The annual income from an $89,000 investment at a 7 percent rate of return is only $6,230. Therefore, Firm T should not undertake the sale/reinvestment because of the front-end tax cost.

On the other hand, if the conversion of the investment to an equity interest in the new venture can be accomplished with no front-end tax cost, the new investment is superior to the old, and Firm T should undertake the sale/reinvestment.

Unfortunately for taxpayers in the same strategic position as Firm T, tax neutrality for asset exchanges is the exception rather than the rule. An asset exchange is taxable unless it meets the requirements of one of the nontaxable exchange provisions scattered throughout the Internal Revenue Code. These requirements vary substantially across provisions. Some nontaxable exchange provisions are mandatory, while others are elective on the part of the taxpayer. Some apply only to realized gains, while others apply to both realized gains and losses. Certain provisions require a direct exchange of noncash assets, while others allow the taxpayer to be in a temporary cash position. Nevertheless, all the nontaxable exchanges share several characteristics. We begin the chapter by analyzing these common characteristics in the context of a generic exchange. By doing so, we can focus on the structure of nontaxable exchanges before considering the details of any particular exchange.

A GENERIC NONTAXABLE EXCHANGE

Exchanges of Qualifying Property

Every nontaxable exchange transforms one property interest into another. The type of property that can be swapped tax free depends on the unique qualification requirements of the relevant IRC section. But only the disposition and receipt of **qualifying property** can be a nontaxable exchange. Consider the diagram of a nontaxable exchange between Firm A and Firm B in Exhibit 9.1 on page 243. Given that the exchange involves only qualifying property, it is nontaxable to both firms. What else do we know about this exchange? Assuming that Firms A and B are unrelated parties dealing at arm's length, they must have agreed that the properties are of equal value.

To quantify the respective tax consequences of the exchange to each firm, we must know the FMV of the property received and the tax basis in the property surrendered.

EXHIBIT 9.1

EXHIBIT 9.2

This information is presented in Exhibit 9.2 above. Because Firm A disposed of property with a $140,000 basis in return for property worth $200,000, it realized a $60,000 gain. Because the exchange involved qualifying property, Firm A does not recognize any gain in the current year. Similarly, Firm B's disposition of qualifying property with a $185,000 basis in return for qualifying property worth $200,000 resulted in a $15,000 realized but unrecognized gain.

The Substituted Basis Rule

Objective 1
Compute the substituted basis of property received in a nontaxable exchange.

The nontaxable exchange label is a misnomer. The tax law does not intend that gains and losses realized on nontaxable exchanges should escape recognition permanently. Instead, the exchange provisions are designed so that unrecognized gains and losses are merely deferred until some future year in which the qualifying property is disposed of in a taxable transaction. This deferral is accomplished through the rule for calculating the tax basis of qualifying property acquired in the exchange: The basis of this property equals the basis of the qualifying property surrendered. In the Firm A/Firm B exchange, each firm expended $200,000 (FMV of the property surrendered) to acquire their new properties. Because the exchange was nontaxable, the firms did not take a cost basis. Instead, Firm A's basis in its new property is $140,000, while Firm B's basis in its new property is $185,000.

This **substituted basis** rule causes the unrecognized gain or loss on a nontaxable exchange to be embedded in the basis of the qualifying property acquired. The gain or loss remains dormant as long as the taxpayer holds the property.[1] If and when the taxpayer makes a taxable disposition of the property, the deferral ends, and the unrecognized gain or loss on the nontaxable exchange is finally recognized.

To demonstrate this important concept, return to the facts in the Firm A/Firm B exchange. If Firm A eventually sells its new property for $200,000 cash, it will recognize a $60,000 gain, even though the property has not appreciated in value since Firm A acquired it. Similarly, if Firm B sells its new property for $200,000, it will recognize the $15,000 gain deferred on the exchange. This observation suggests an alternate method for computing the basis of qualifying property acquired in a nontaxable exchange: Basis equals the property's

---

[1] If the qualifying property is depreciable or amortizable, the embedded gain or loss is recognized over the recovery period for the substituted basis.

EXHIBIT 9.3

FMV *minus* deferred gain or *plus* deferred loss on the exchange. The substituted basis rule for nontaxable exchanges is summarized as follows.

$$\text{Basis of property surrendered} = \underline{\text{Basis of qualifying property acquired}}$$

Alternate method: FMV of qualifying property acquired
− Deferred gain or
+ Deferred loss
──────────────────────────
Basis of qualifying property acquired

The Effect of Boot

The facts of our generic exchange between Firm A and Firm B are contrived because the FMVs of the properties are equal. A more realistic scenario is that the FMVs of the properties qualifying for nontaxable exchange treatment are unequal. In this case, the party owning the property of lesser value must transfer additional value in the form of cash or nonqualifying property to make the exchange work.

Objective 2
Compute gain recognized when boot is received in a nontaxable exchange.

In tax terminology, any cash or nonqualifying property included in a nontaxable exchange is called **boot.** The presence of boot does not disqualify the entire exchange. Instead, the party receiving the boot must recognize a portion of realized gain equal to the FMV of the boot. Refer to Exhibit 9.3 above in which the FMV of the property surrendered by Firm B was only $192,000. For Firm A to agree to the exchange, Firm B had to pay $8,000 cash so that Firm A received $200,000 total value in exchange for its asset worth $200,000. In this case, Firm A received $8,000 boot and must recognize $8,000 of its $60,000 realized gain.

Because Firm A must recognize an $8,000 gain, it can increase its basis in its new assets by this amount. In other words, Firm A's investment in the new assets has increased to $148,000 ($140,000 basis in the surrendered property plus $8,000 gain recognized). Firm A must allocate this $148,000 basis between the two assets acquired: $8,000 cash and the qualifying property. Cash always takes a basis equal to monetary value. Consequently, only $140,000 of basis is allocated to the qualifying property. This $140,000 basis can also be derived by subtracting Firm A's $52,000 deferred gain from the $192,000 FMV of the qualifying property. The modification to the substituted basis rule when boot is *received* in a nontaxable exchange is summarized as follows.

Basis of qualifying property surrendered
+ Gain recognized
− FMV of boot received
──────────────────────────
Basis of qualifying property acquired

The fact that Firm B *paid* boot in the exchange did not cause it to recognize gain. Firm B surrendered property with an aggregate basis of $193,000 ($8,000 cash + $185,000 basis of surrendered property) to acquire property worth $200,000. As a result, Firm B realized a

$7,000 gain, none of which is recognized. Firm B's basis in the new property is $193,000, the aggregate basis of the cash and property surrendered. This $193,000 basis equals the $200,000 FMV of the new property less $7,000 deferred gain. The substituted basis rule when boot is *paid* in a nontaxable exchange is summarized as follows.

$$\begin{array}{l} \text{Basis of qualifying property surrendered} \\ \underline{+ \text{ FMV of boot paid}} \\ \text{Basis of qualifying property acquired} \end{array}$$

Tax Talk

A company that exchanged gold mines for coal mines subject to long-term supply contracts treated the exchange as nontaxable. The IRS argued that the contracts were boot, so the company must recognize gain equal to the contracts' FMV. The Tax Court ruled in favor of the company because the contracts and the coal mines were "inseparable" and represented a single qualifying property.

Two more facts concerning boot should be mentioned. First, the receipt of boot can never trigger recognition of more gain than the recipient realized on the exchange. For example, if Firm A received $70,000 cash and qualifying property worth $130,000, the receipt of $70,000 boot would trigger recognition of the entire $60,000 gain realized. (After all, Firm A would recognize only $60,000 gain if it sold the property for $200,000 cash!) In this case, Firm A's basis in the qualifying property would be $130,000 ($140,000 basis of qualifying property surrendered + $60,000 gain recognized − $70,000 boot received).

Second, the receipt of boot does not trigger loss recognition. Consider the new set of facts in Exhibit 9.4 in which Firm A surrendered qualifying property with a $230,000 basis in exchange for $8,000 cash and qualifying property worth $192,000. As a result, it realized a $30,000 loss, none of which is recognized. Firm A's $230,000 basis in the surrendered property must be allocated between the $8,000 cash received and the new property. Because the cash absorbed $8,000 of the substituted basis, Firm A's basis in the qualifying property is $222,000 ($230,000 basis of qualifying property surrendered − $8,000 boot received). This basis can also be derived by *adding* Firm A's $30,000 deferred loss to the $192,000 FMV of the property.

EXHIBIT 9.4

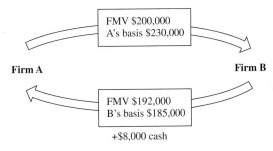

+$8,000 cash

Book/Tax Difference from Nontaxable Exchange

For financial reporting purposes, gains and losses realized on property exchanges often are included in book income.[2] In such cases, nontaxable exchanges cause a difference between book income and taxable income. The book basis of the property received in the exchange (the property's FMV) is different from the property's tax basis. Consequently, the book/tax difference caused by the exchange is temporary and will reverse as the newly acquired property is depreciated or when it is disposed of in a taxable transaction.

Book/Tax Difference from Nontaxable Exchange	Hogan Inc. exchanged old property ($138,200 book and tax basis) for new property ($210,000 FMV). Hogan's $71,800 realized gain was included in book income but was not recognized as taxable income because the old and new properties qualified for nontaxable exchange treatment. Hogan's depreciable book basis in the new property is $210,000, and its depreciable tax basis is only $138,200. Therefore, the $71,800 excess of book income over taxable income resulting from the exchange will reverse as future excesses of book depreciation over MACRS depreciation.

---

[2] See ASC 845, *Nonmonetary Transactions.*

Summary

The Internal Revenue Code contains an assortment of nontaxable exchange provisions with different definitional and operational rules. Nonetheless, these provisions share the following generic characteristics.

- The exchange must involve qualifying property, as defined in the provision.
- The gain or loss realized on the exchange is deferred.
- The basis of the qualifying property received equals the basis of the qualifying property surrendered (substituted basis rule).
- The receipt of boot triggers gains recognition to the extent of the boot's FMV.

The remainder of the chapter focuses on four nontaxable exchanges with particular relevance in the business world: like-kind exchanges, involuntary conversions, formations of business entities, and wash sales. Before proceeding, refer back to the diagram on page 200 that links gain or loss realization and gain or loss recognition. Let's expand the diagram to include the possibility of gain or loss deferral on a nontaxable exchange.

LIKE-KIND EXCHANGES

Objective 3
Identify properties that qualify for like-kind exchange treatment.

No gain or loss is recognized on the exchange of business or investment property for property of a like kind.[3] Nonrecognition is mandatory for qualifying exchanges. This rule allows firms to convert one asset to another asset with the same function or purpose at no tax cost. The rule's scope, however, is limited: It does not apply to exchanges of inventory property, equity or creditor interests (stocks, bonds, notes, etc.), or partnership interests.

Like-Kind Personalty

The definition of **like-kind property** for depreciable tangible personalty is determined under a detailed IRS classification system.[4] Under this system, automobiles and taxis constitute one class of like-kind property, while buses constitute another. Accordingly, the exchange of a business automobile for another automobile is nontaxable, while the exchange of an automobile for a bus is taxable. Airplanes and helicopters are like-kind properties, while airplanes and tugboats are not. The logic of the classification system is not always apparent. Office furniture and copying equipment are like-kind properties, while copying equipment and computers are not. Livestock of the same sex are like-kind properties, while

---

[3] §1031.

[4] Reg. §1.1031(a)-2(b)(1) and Rev. Proc. 87-56, 1987-2 CB 674.

livestock of different sexes are not.[5] If a rancher swaps a bull held for breeding purposes for another bull, the exchange is nontaxable, but if he swaps the bull for a breeding heifer, the exchange is taxable. Clearly, firms that want to dispose of tangible business personalty through a nontaxable exchange should consult their tax advisers to determine exactly which assets qualify as like-kind.

Tangible Personalty	Petra Inc., which operates a motor vehicle leasing service, exchanged 20 passenger automobiles with a $106,200 aggregate adjusted tax basis for 10 sports utility vehicles (SUVs). The SUVs had an aggregate FMV of $290,000. The IRS has ruled that passenger automobiles and SUVs are like-kind property. Consequently, Petra's exchange is nontaxable, and it has a $106,200 substituted basis in the 10 SUVs.[6]

Like-Kind Personalty with Boot Given	Quantum Corporation wishes to upgrade its laser printer. It has identified a new printer with an FMV of $5,000. The seller has agreed to accept the old printer as a trade-in, along with $3,800 cash. Quantum's adjusted tax basis in the old printer is $500. Because the two printers are considered like-kind property, the exchange is nontaxable to Quantum. For the seller, however, the new printer is inventory and it will recognize ordinary income on the sale. The tax consequences of the exchange to Quantum are as follows.

Amount realized	$5,000
Basis of property surrendered:	
Old printer	(500)
Cash	(3,800)
Gain realized	$ 700
Gain recognized	$ 0
Gain deferred	700
	$ 700

Quantum's basis in the newly acquired laser printer is determined as follows:

Basis of printer surrendered	$ 500
Boot paid	3,800
Gain recognized	0
Basis of printer acquired	$4,300

Tax Talk

Exchanges of emission allowances under EPA's emission allowance program can be treated as a like-kind exchange that qualifies for nonrecognition treatment.

The IRS does not provide a classification system for identifying like-kind intangible personalty. According to Treasury regulations, whether one intangible asset is of a like-kind to another intangible asset depends on the nature or character of the legal rights involved and the nature or character of the underlying property to which the intangible relates.[7] The regulations do include one bright-line rule: The goodwill of one business is not of a like kind to the goodwill of any other business.

[5] §1031(e).

[6] Reg. §1.168(i)-6 provides complicated rules for computing MACRS depreciation for recovery property acquired in a like-kind exchange or involuntary conversion.

[7] Reg. §1.1031(a)-2(c).

Intangible Personalty	Lorna Publishing House exchanged the copyright on one novel for a copyright on a different novel. The two copyrights confer identical legal rights on the owner, and the underlying properties are both literary compositions. Consequently, the copyrights are like-kind, and the exchange is nontaxable. If Lorna had exchanged the copyright on a novel for a copyright on a song, the underlying properties would not have the same character, the copyrights would not be like-kind, and the exchange would be taxable.

Like-Kind Realty

In contrast to the narrow rules defining like-kind personalty, virtually all types of business and investment real estate are considered like-kind. As a result, any swap of realty for realty can be structured as a nontaxable exchange.[8]

Like-Kind Realty	An Arizona firm that owned undeveloped investment land in Tucson negotiated with a New York firm that owned an apartment in Manhattan to trade their properties. This exchange is diagrammed in Exhibit 9.5. The investment land has an $800,000 FMV, while the apartment has a $925,000 FMV. As a result, the Arizona firm paid $125,000 cash to the New York firm to equalize the values exchanged. The tax consequences of this exchange are summarzied as follows:

	Arizona Firm	New York Firm
Amount realized:		
FMV of realty acquired	$925,000	$800,000
Boot received	–0–	125,000
	$925,000	$925,000
Basis of property surrendered:		
Realty	(500,000)	(485,000)
Boot paid	(125,000)	–0–
Gain realized	$300,000	$440,000
Gain recognized*	–0–	$125,000
Gain deferred	$300,000	315,000
	$300,000	$440,000

*Lesser of FMV of boot received or gain realized.

The final step in the analysis of this like-kind exchange is to determine each party's basis in its newly acquired realty.

	Arizona Firm	New York Firm
Basis of realty surrendered	$500,000	$485,000
Boot paid	125,000	–0–
Gain recognized	–0–	125,000
Boot received	–0–	(125,000)
Basis of realty acquired	$625,000	$485,000

Note that the Arizona firm's basis in its Manhattan property equals the $925,000 FMV less the $300,000 gain deferred in the exchange. The New York firm's basis in its Tucson property equals the $800,000 FMV less the $315,000 gain deferred in the exchange.

[8] Reg. §1.1031(a)-1(b).

EXHIBIT 9.5

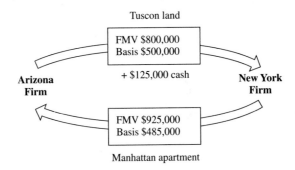

Tuscon land

| FMV $800,000 |
| Basis $500,000 |

Arizona Firm   + $125,000 cash   **New York Firm**

| FMV $925,000 |
| Basis $485,000 |

Manhattan apartment

The above example suggests a practical question. How did the Arizona firm and the New York firm find each other? Most like-kind exchanges of realty are arranged by *qualified intermediaries:* real estate professionals who specialize in *three-party* exchanges. In a prototype three-party exchange, a taxpayer that wants to sell property without recognizing gain and a prospective buyer use a qualified intermediary to locate replacement property that is suitable to the seller. The seller relinquishes its property to the intermediary who transfers it to the buyer, the buyer transfers cash to the intermediary, and the intermediary uses the cash to purchase the replacement property for the seller. The tax law governing like-kind exchanges is flexible enough so that the seller is treated as exchanging the relinquished property directly for the replacement property.[9]

Three-Party Exchange	Talmadge Partnership wants to dispose of rental property with a $900,000 FMV, and Vernon Inc. is willing to buy the property for cash. However, Talmadge's tax basis in the property is only $100,000, and it does not want to recognize gain on the disposition. Talmadge and Vernon work through a qualified intermediary to facilitate a three-party exchange. Talmadge relinquishes its property to the intermediary who transfers it to Vernon for $900,000 cash. The intermediary then uses the cash to purchase replacement property on Talmadge's behalf. For tax purposes, Talmadge has made a nontaxable exchange of the relinquished property for the replacement property.

Exchanges of Mortgaged Properties

Objective 4
Describe the effect of the relief and assumption of debt in a like-kind exchange.

Many real property interests involved in like-kind exchanges are subject to mortgages that are transferred along with the property and become the legal liability of the new owner. As we learned in Chapter 8, a taxpayer that is relieved of debt on a property disposition must treat the relief as an amount realized from the disposition. In the like-kind exchange context, a party that surrenders mortgaged property receives boot equal to the debt relief. In other words, the relief of debt is treated exactly like cash received in the exchange, while the assumption of debt is treated as cash paid.

Exchange of Mortgaged Property	ABC Inc. and XYZ Partnership exchanged a Chicago shopping mall and a commercial office building located in St. Louis. This exchange is diagrammed in Exhibit 9.6. The net value of the shopping mall is $500,000 ($730,000 FMV − $230,000 mortgage), and the FMV of

[9] Reg. §1.1031(b)-2 and Reg. §1.1031(k)-1(g)(4). The various steps in a three-party exchange must be completed within a 180-day time period.

the office building is $500,000. The tax consequences of this exchange are summarized as follows:

	ABC Inc.	XYZ Partnership
Amount realized:		
FMV of realty acquired	$500,000	$730,000
Boot received (debt relief)	230,000	–0–
	$730,000	$730,000
Basis of property surrendered:		
Realty	(295,000)	(413,000)
Boot paid (debt assumed)	–0–	(230,000)
Gain realized	$435,000	$ 87,000
Gain recognized*	$230,000	–0–
Gain deferred	205,000	$ 87,000
	$435,000	$ 87,000
Basis of realty surrendered	$295,000	$413,000
Boot paid	–0–	230,000
Gain recognized	230,000	–0–
Boot received	(230,000)	–0–
Basis of realty acquired	$295,000	$643,000

*Lesser of FMV of boot received or gain realized.

EXHIBIT 9.6

In a like-kind exchange in which both properties are subject to a mortgage so that both parties are relieved of debt, only the *net* amount of debt is treated as boot given and boot received.[10]

Net Debt Relief as Boot	Firm O and Firm R entered into a like-kind exchange of realty. The property surrendered by Firm O was subject to a $120,000 mortgage, and the property surrendered by Firm R was subject to a $100,000 mortgage. Firm O was relieved of a $20,000 net amount of debt and therefore received $20,000 boot in the exchange. Firm R assumed a $20,000 net amount of debt and therefore paid $20,000 boot in the exchange. Consequently, Firm O must recognize $20,000 of realized gain, while Firm R has a totally nontaxable exchange.

[10] Reg. §1.1031(b)-1(c).

INVOLUNTARY CONVERSIONS

Objective 5
Compute gain recognized and the basis of replacement property in an involuntary conversion.

Firms generally control the circumstances in which they dispose of property. Occasionally, a disposition is involuntary; property may be stolen or destroyed by a natural disaster such as a flood or a fire. If the property is not insured or if the insurance proceeds are less than the property's adjusted basis, the owner can deduct the unrecovered basis as an ordinary casualty loss. However, if the property is insured and the insurance proceeds are more than the adjusted basis, the disposition actually results in a realized gain. Another example of an **involuntary conversion** is a condemnation of private property by a government agency that takes the property for public use. If a government has the right of eminent domain, it can compel an owner to sell property to the agency for its FMV. If the condemnation proceeds exceed the basis of the condemned property, the owner realizes a gain.

A taxpayer that realizes a gain on the involuntary conversion of property can elect to defer the gain if two conditions are met.[11] First, the taxpayer must reinvest the amount realized on the conversion (the insurance or condemnation proceeds) in **property similar or related in service or use.** This condition requires taxpayers to replace their original property to avoid paying tax on the realized gain.[12] Both the IRS and the courts have been strict in their interpretation of the concept of similar or related property. For instance, the IRS ruled that a taxpayer who owned a land-based seafood processing plant that was destroyed by fire and who used the insurance proceeds to purchase a floating seafood processing vessel was ineligible for nonrecognition treatment because the properties were not similar in function.[13]

The second condition is that replacement of the involuntarily converted property must occur within the two taxable years following the year in which the conversion took place. Thus, taxpayers making the deferral election usually have ample time to locate and acquire replacement property.

If the cost of replacement property equals or exceeds the amount realized on an involuntary conversion, none of the taxpayer's realized gain is recognized. If the taxpayer does not reinvest the entire amount realized in replacement property (i.e., the taxpayer uses some of the insurance or condemnation proceeds for other purposes), the amount not reinvested is treated as boot, and the taxpayer must recognize gain accordingly. In either case, the basis of the replacement property is its cost less unrecognized gain. As a result, unrecognized gain is deferred until the taxpayer disposes of the replacement property in a future taxable transaction.

Tax Talk
A beekeeper whose beehives were destroyed when pesticides were sprayed on an adjacent property suffered an involuntary conversion. Gain from the receipt of compensation for his loss was eligible for deferral.

Gain Recognized on Involuntary Conversion

Company UL owned equipment that was completely destroyed in the most recent California earthquake. The equipment's adjusted basis was $80,000. The company collected $100,000 of insurance proceeds, thereby realizing a $20,000 gain on the involuntary conversion. Company UL purchased identical equipment in the year after the disaster. The following table shows the tax consequences under four different assumptions about the cost of the replacement property.

---

[11] §1033.

[12] If real property held for business or as an investment is condemned by a government agency, the owner may replace it with like-kind property (any realty held for business or as an investment) rather than realty similar or related in service or use to the property so condemned. §1033(g).

[13] Rev. Rul. 77-192, 1977-1 CB 249.

	Cost of				Basis of
Insurance Proceeds	Replacement Property	Unreinvested Proceeds	Gain Recognized	Gain Deferred	Replacement Property*
$100,000	$135,000	–0–	–0–	$20,000	$115,000
100,000	100,000	–0–	–0–	20,000	80,000
100,000	92,000	$ 8,000	$ 8,000	12,000	80,000
100,000	77,000	23,000	20,000	–0–	77,000

*Cost less gain deferred.

The involuntary conversion rule provides relief to taxpayers deprived of property through circumstances beyond their control and who want nothing more than to return to the status quo by replacing that property. The rule applies to the involuntary conversion of any type of asset.[14] Moreover, the rule is elective; taxpayers that would benefit by recognizing the entire gain realized on an involuntary conversion may do so.

FORMATIONS OF BUSINESS ENTITIES

Objective 6
Explain the tax consequences of the exchange of property for equity in a corporation or partnership.

In the early days of the federal income tax, Congress decided that the tax law should be neutral with respect to the formation of business entities. If entrepreneurs wanted to organize a new business as a corporation or partnership for legal or financial reasons, they should not be discouraged from doing so because of a front-end tax cost. Congress achieved this neutrality with a pair of nontaxable exchange provisions that the business community has relied on for decades. These provisions allow organizers to transfer assets to a corporation or a partnership in exchange for an equity interest without the recognition of gain. In this section of the chapter, we will examine the basic operation of these two extremely useful nontaxable exchanges.

Corporate Formations

No gain or loss is recognized when property is transferred to a corporation solely in exchange for that corporation's stock if the transferors of property are in control of the corporation immediately after the exchange.[15] In this context, the term *property* is defined broadly to include cash, tangible, and intangible assets. Personal services are not property; individuals who perform services in exchange for corporate stock must recognize the FMV of the stock as compensation income. To satisfy the control requirement for this nontaxable exchange, the transferors of property *in the aggregate* must own at least 80 percent of the corporation's outstanding stock immediately after the exchange.[16]

Corporate Formation	Mr. Jiang and Ms. Kirt each owned a business. The two individuals combined forces by transferring their respective operating assets to newly incorporated J&K Inc. Based on recent appraisals, Mr. Jiang's assets have a $375,000 FMV, and Ms. Kirt's assets have a $250,000

---

[14] The involuntary conversion rules apply to business and investment assets, as well as assets owned by individuals and used for personal enjoyment and consumption.

[15] §351.

[16] More precisely, the transferors must own stock possessing at least 80 percent of the voting power represented by all outstanding voting shares and at least 80 percent of the total number of shares of all nonvoting classes of stock. §368(c) and Rev. Rul. 59-259, 1959-2 CB 115.

FMV. Therefore, the corporation's beginning balance sheet reflected operating assets with a $625,000 total FMV. The articles of incorporation authorize J&K to issue 100 shares of voting common stock. These shares were issued in proportion to the FMV of the contributed assets: 60 shares to Mr. Jiang and 40 shares to Ms. Kirt. This corporate formation is diagrammed in Exhibit 9.7.

EXHIBIT 9.7

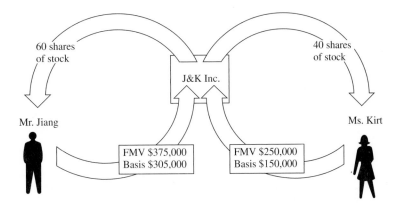

Tax Consequences of Formation

Mr. Jiang's adjusted basis in the assets transferred to J&K was $305,000. Ms. Kirt's adjusted basis in the assets transferred to J&K was $150,000. Consequently, the two transferors realized the following gains on the exchange of property for stock.

	Mr. Jiang	Ms. Kirt
Amount realized (FMV of stock)	$ 375,000	$ 250,000
Basis of property transferred	(305,000)	(150,000)
Gain realized	$ 70,000	$ 100,000

Because Mr. Jiang and Ms. Kirt *in the aggregate* own 100 percent of J&K's stock immediately after the exchange, neither recognizes any gain. Each takes a substituted basis in the shares of stock ($305,000 stock basis for Mr. Jiang and $150,000 stock basis for Ms. Kirt).[17] Thus, their unrecognized gains on the corporate formation are deferred until they dispose of the stock in a taxable transaction.

The nontaxable exchange provision governing corporate formations also applies to transfers of property to an existing corporation. However, if the transferor fails to satisfy the 80 percent control requirement, the exchange of property for stock is taxable.

Taxable Exchange of Property for Stock

Two years after J&K is formed, a third individual, Mr. Larkin, contributes real property with a $285,000 FMV and a $240,000 adjusted basis in exchange for 50 shares of newly issued stock. Immediately after the exchange, Mr. Larkin (the only transferor in the transaction) owns only 33 percent of J&K's stock. Because he does not satisfy the control requirement, Mr. Larkin must recognize the $45,000 gain realized on the exchange. Because the exchange is taxable, Mr. Larkin takes a $285,000 cost basis in his J&K shares.

---

[17] §358(a)(1).

Tax Consequences to the Corporation

Corporations that issue stock in exchange for property never recognize gain or loss on the exchange, regardless of whether the exchange is nontaxable or taxable to the transferor of the property.[18] However, a corporation's tax basis in the property received does depend on whether the exchange is nontaxable or taxable to the transferor. If the exchange is nontaxable (because the transferor satisfies the 80 percent control requirement), the corporation's basis in the property received equals the transferor's basis.[19] In other words, the corporation takes a **carryover basis** in the property.

Carryover Basis of Property	Refer back to Exhibit 9.7 in which Mr. Jiang and Ms. Kirt transferred operating assets to J&K Inc. in exchange for stock. This exchange was nontaxable to the two transferors because they satisfied the control requirement immediately after the exchange. The exchange also was a nontaxable event to J&K. The corporation's carryover tax basis in the assets received from Mr. Jiang is $305,000, and its carryover tax basis in the assets received from Ms. Kirt is $150,000. For financial reporting purposes, J&K Inc. recorded the assets received in the exchange at FMV. Consequently, the corporation has a $375,000 book basis in the assets received from Mr. Jiang, and a $250,000 book basis in the assets received from Ms. Kirt. The difference in J&K's book and tax basis will be eliminated over time as the corporation depreciates or amortizes the assets or when it disposes of the assets.

If a corporation issues stock in exchange for property and the exchange is taxable to the transferor (because the transferor does not satisfy the 80 percent control requirement), the corporation takes a cost basis in the property.[20]

Cost Basis of Property	Again, refer back to the example on page 253 in which Mr. Larkin transfers real property to J&K Inc. in exchange for stock. The exchange is taxable to Mr. Larkin because he does not satisfy the control requirement immediately after the exchange. However, J&K does not recognize any gain on the issuance of its stock in exchange for Mr. Larkin's real property. The corporation's tax basis in the real property is its $285,000 cost (FMV of the shares issued to Mr. Larkin), which equals the book basis of the property for financial reporting purposes.

Partnership Formations

The tax law treats partnership formations in the same way that it treats corporate formations. Specifically, neither the partners nor the partnership recognizes gain or loss when property is exchanged for an equity interest in the partnership.[21] If Mr. Jiang and Ms. Kirt in our earlier example had decided to become partners, they could have transferred their appreciated assets to J&K Partnership in exchange for a 60 percent and 40 percent interest without recognizing gain. Mr. Jiang's basis in his partnership interest would be a $305,000 substituted basis, and Ms. Kirt's basis in her partnership interest would be a $150,000 substituted basis.[22] The partnership would take a carryover basis in their contributed assets of $305,000 and $150,000, respectively.[23]

---

[18] §1032.

[19] §362(a).

[20] Reg. §1.1032-1(d).

[21] §721.

[22] §722.

[23] §723.

While this nontaxable exchange provision is clearly a first cousin to the corporate provision, it lacks any control requirement and is more flexible. For example, if our third individual, Mr. Larkin, wants to become a partner in some future year, he can do so without recognizing gain. If he contributes appreciated real property ($285,000 FMV and $240,000 adjusted basis) for a one-third equity interest in J&K Partnership, the transaction qualifies as a nontaxable exchange, and his $45,000 realized gain escapes current taxation. Of course, Mr. Larkin's substituted basis in his new interest and the partnership's carryover basis in its new property would be only $240,000.

WASH SALES

Objective 7
Describe the tax consequences of a wash sale.

The **wash sale** rule is a nontypical nontaxable exchange provision because it defers only the recognition of *losses* realized on certain sales of marketable securities.[24] A wash sale occurs when an investor sells securities at a loss and reacquires substantially the same securities within 30 days before or 30 days after the sale. This rule prohibits investors from selling securities to generate a tax loss, while simultaneously buying the stock back to keep their investment portfolio intact. If the wash sale rule applies, the cost of the reacquired securities is increased by the unrecognized loss realized on the sale.

Wash Sale	BNJ Company owns 10,000 shares of Acme stock with an $85,000 basis. The stock is trading at $6 per share so that the BNJ's holding is worth only $60,000. BNJ believes that the stock is an excellent long-term investment and that the depression in the market price is temporary. Nonetheless, it sells the stock on July 13 to trigger a $25,000 tax loss. If BNJ purchases 10,000 shares of Acme stock during the period beginning on June 13 and ending on August 12, it cannot recognize the $25,000 loss. If BNJ paid $61,000 for the replacement shares, its basis in these shares is $86,000 ($61,000 cost + $25,000 unrecognized loss).

Taxpayers who sell stock at a loss can easily avoid the wash sale rule by waiting for more than 30 days to reestablish their investment position. The risk, of course, is that in the time between sale and repurchase, the market value of the securities rebounds and the taxpayer must pay a higher price for the same securities. This additional cost could easily exceed the tax benefit of the recognized loss.

Conclusion

Business managers may defer the recognition of gain realized on the conversion of property from one form to another by structuring the conversion as a nontaxable exchange. The deferral reduces the tax cost of the conversion and increases the value of the transaction. While the advantages offered by the various nontaxable exchange provisions are considerable, these transactions require careful planning and a respect for the technical nuances differentiating one from the other.

Chapter 9 is the final chapter in Part Three in which we focused on the measurement of taxable income from business operations. You've learned how firms account for their routine activities and how that accounting can differ under generally accepted accounting principles (GAAP) and the tax law. You've been introduced to the tax consequences of asset acquisitions and dispositions and determined how property transactions affect taxable income. In Part Four of the text, we turn to the next issue: how the tax on that income is calculated and paid to the federal government.

[24] §1091.

Sources of Book/Tax Differences	**Permanent**	**Temporary**
	None	• Like-kind exchange • Involuntary conversion • Nontaxable exchange of property for equity • Wash sale of securities

Key Terms

boot *244*

carryover basis *254*

involuntary
  conversion *251*

like-kind property *246*

nontaxable exchange *241*

property similar or related
  in service or use *251*

qualifying property *242*

substituted basis *243*

wash sale *255*

Questions and Problems for Discussion

1. Four years ago, Company PJ acquired 1,000 acres of undeveloped land. On the date of the exchange, the land's FMV was $700,000. During the past four years, the land appreciated in value by $600,000; a recent appraisal indicated that it is worth $1.3 million today. However, if Company PJ sells the land for $1.3 million, the taxable gain will be $825,000. Can you explain this result?

2. In a nontaxable exchange between unrelated parties, are the amounts realized by the parties always equal?

3. In a nontaxable exchange, do the tax consequences to one party in any way depend on the tax consequences to the other party?

4. Is the substituted basis of the qualifying property received in a nontaxable exchange more or less than the cost of that property?

5. Determine if each of the following transactions qualifies as a nontaxable exchange.

   a. Firm A exchanges a 2 percent interest in MG Partnership for a 10 percent interest in KLS Partnership.

   b. Mr. B exchanges investment land for common stock in RV Inc. Immediately after the exchange, Mr. B owns 42 percent of RV's outstanding stock.

   c. Corporation C exchanges business equipment for a 25 percent interest in a residential apartment complex.

   d. Company D exchanges 15,000 units of inventory for a new computer system.

6. Firm Q, a real estate broker, exchanged 16 acres of land for a commercial warehouse owned by Company M. Company M, a light industrial business, plans to hold the land as a long-term investment. Is this exchange nontaxable to Firm Q and Company M?

7. Company W exchanged the following assets for Blackacre, investment land worth $2 million.

	Company W's Basis	*FMV*
Real property used in Company W's business	$800,000	$1,750,000
Marketable securities	30,000	250,000

   Does Company W recognize any gain on this exchange?

8. Under what conditions can the destruction of property by casualty or theft result in an economic loss but a realized gain?

9. In what way is the nontaxable exchange rule for partnership formations more flexible than the nontaxable exchange rule for corporate formations?

10. Explain the difference between a substituted basis in an asset and a carryover basis in an asset.

11. If a corporation engages in a nontaxable exchange of assets, could the transaction result in a book/tax difference? Is this difference a permanent or a temporary difference?

12. When a taxpayer transfers appreciated property to a corporation in exchange for newly issued stock and the exchange is nontaxable, the gain deferred on the exchange actually doubles. Can you explain this?

13. Why doesn't Congress extend the wash sale rule to apply to realized gains?

14. This year, Firm B recognized a $100,000 capital gain on the sale of investment land. Toward the end of the year, the firm plans to sell stock from its investment portfolio to generate a $100,000 capital loss. It has two blocks of stock that are candidates for sale (basis exceeds FMV by $100,000). However, Firm B plans to reacquire whichever block it sells on the 31st day after the sale. How should it decide which block of stock to sell and reacquire?

15. Why is the label "nontaxable exchange" a misnomer?

Application Problems

1. Company Z exchanged old equipment (FMV $16,000) for new equipment (FMV $16,000). Company Z's tax basis in the old equipment was $9,300.

   a. Compute Company Z's realized gain, recognized gain, and tax basis in the new equipment assuming the exchange was a taxable transaction.

   b. Compute Company Z's realized gain, recognized gain, and tax basis in the new equipment assuming the exchange was a nontaxable transaction.

   c. Six months after the exchange, Company Z sold the new equipment for $16,850 cash. How much gain does Company Z recognize if the exchange was taxable? How much gain if the exchange was nontaxable?

2. Business K exchanged old machinery (FMV $95,000) for new machinery (FMV $95,000). Business K's tax basis in the old machinery was $107,000.

   a. Compute Business K's realized loss, recognized loss, and tax basis in the new machinery assuming the exchange was a taxable transaction.

   b. Compute Business K's realized loss, recognized loss, and tax basis in the new machinery assuming the exchange was a nontaxable transaction.

   c. Six months after the exchange, Business K sold the new machinery for $100,000 cash. How much gain or loss does Business K recognize if the exchange was taxable? How much gain or loss if the exchange was nontaxable?

3. Rufus Inc. and Hardy Company are negotiating a nontaxable exchange of business properties. Rufus's property has a $50,000 tax basis and a $77,500 FMV. Hardy's property has a $60,000 tax basis and a $90,000 FMV.

   a. Which party to the exchange must pay boot to make the exchange work? How much boot must be paid?

   b. Assuming the boot payment is made, how much gain or loss will Rufus realize and recognize on the exchange and what tax basis will Rufus take in the property acquired?

c. Assuming the boot payment is made, how much gain or loss will Hardy realize and recognize on the exchange and what tax basis will Hardy take in the property acquired?

4. Firm A exchanged an old asset with a $20,000 tax basis for a new asset with a $32,000 FMV. Under each of the following assumptions, apply the generic rules to compute A's realized gain, recognized gain, and tax basis in the new asset.

a. Old asset and new asset are not qualified property for nontaxable exchange purposes.

b. Old asset and new asset are qualified property for nontaxable exchange purposes.

c. Old asset and new asset are not qualified property for nontaxable exchange purposes. To equalize the values exchanged, Firm A paid $1,700 cash to the other party.

d. Old asset and new asset are qualified property for nontaxable exchange purposes. To equalize the values exchanged, Firm A paid $1,700 cash to the other party.

e. Old asset and new asset are not qualified property for nontaxable exchange purposes. To equalize the values exchanged, Firm A received $4,500 cash from the other party.

f. Old asset and new asset are qualified property for nontaxable exchange purposes. To equalize the values exchanged, Firm A received $4,500 cash from the other party.

5. Firm Q exchanged old property with an $80,000 tax basis for new property with a $65,000 FMV. Under each of the following assumptions, apply the generic rules to compute Q's realized loss, recognized loss, and tax basis in the new property.

a. Old property and new property are not qualified property for nontaxable exchange purposes.

b. Old property and new property are qualified property for nontaxable exchange purposes.

c. Old property and new property are not qualified property for nontaxable exchange purposes. To equalize the values exchanged, Firm Q paid $2,000 cash to the other party.

d. Old property and new property are qualified property for nontaxable exchange purposes. To equalize the values exchanged, Firm Q paid $2,000 cash to the other party.

e. Old property and new property are not qualified property for nontaxable exchange purposes. To equalize the values exchanged, Firm Q received $8,000 cash from the other party.

f. Old property and new property are qualified property for nontaxable exchange purposes. To equalize the values exchanged, Firm Q received $8,000 cash from the other party.

6. Firm M exchanged an old asset with a $9,100 tax basis and a $21,000 FMV for a new asset worth $18,500 and $2,500 cash.

a. If the exchange is nontaxable, compute Firm M's realized and recognized gain and tax basis in the new asset.

b. How would your answers change if the new asset were worth only $7,000, and Firm M received $14,000 cash in the exchange?

7. This year, Neil Inc. exchanged a business asset for an investment asset. Both assets had a $932,000 appraised FMV. Neil's book basis in the business asset was $604,600, and its tax basis was $573,000.

a. Compute Neil's book gain and tax gain assuming the exchange was a taxable transaction.

b. Determine Neil's book and tax basis of the investment asset acquired in the taxable exchange.

    c. Compute Neil's book gain and tax gain assuming the exchange was a nontaxable transaction.

    d. Determine Neil's book and tax basis of the investment asset acquired in the nontaxable exchange.

8. Refer to the facts in the preceding problem. Three years after the exchange, Neil sold the investment asset for $1 million cash.

    a. Compute Neil's book gain and tax gain on sale assuming Neil acquired the investment asset in a taxable exchange.

    b. Compute Neil's book gain and tax gain on sale assuming Neil acquired the investment asset in a nontaxable exchange.

9. CC Company exchanged a depreciable asset with a $17,000 initial cost and a $10,000 adjusted basis for a new asset priced at $16,000.

    a. Assuming that the assets do not qualify as like-kind property, compute the amount and character of CC's recognized gain and its basis in the new asset.

    b. Assuming that the assets qualify as like-kind property, compute the amount and character of CC's recognized gain and its basis in the new asset.

10. XYZ exchanged old equipment for new like-kind equipment. XYZ's adjusted basis in the old equipment was $13,000 ($30,000 initial cost − $17,000 accumulated depreciation), and its FMV was $20,000. Because the new equipment was worth $28,500, XYZ paid $8,500 cash in addition to the old equipment.

    a. Compute XYZ's realized gain and determine the amount and character of any recognized gain.

    b. Compute XYZ's basis in its new equipment.

11. OCD exchanged old furniture for new like-kind furniture. OCD's adjusted basis in the old furniture was $31,700 ($60,000 initial cost − $28,300 accumulated depreciation), and its FMV was $48,000. Because the new furniture was worth only $45,000, OCD received $3,000 cash in addition to the new furniture.

    a. Compute OCD's realized gain and determine the amount and character of any recognized gain.

    b. Compute OCD's basis in its new furniture.

12. Firm ML, a noncorporate taxpayer, exchanged residential rental property plus $15,000 cash for 20 acres of investment land with a $200,000 FMV. ML used the straight-line method to compute depreciation on the rental property.

    a. Assuming that ML's exchange was negotiated at arm's length, what is the FMV of the rental property?

    b. If the adjusted basis of the rental property is $158,000, compute ML's realized and recognized gain. What is the character of the recognized gain?

    c. Compute ML's basis in the 20 acres of investment land.

13. Refer to the facts in the preceding problem, but assume that ML exchanged the residential rental property for the 20 acres of investment land plus $22,000 (i.e., ML *received* cash in the exchange).

    a. Assuming that ML's exchange was negotiated at arm's length, what is the FMV of the rental property?

    b. If the adjusted basis of the rental property is $158,000, compute ML's realized and recognized gain. What is the character of the recognized gain?

    c. Compute ML's basis in the 20 acres of investment land.

14. Firm PO and Corporation QR exchanged the following business real estate.

	Marvin Gardens (exchanged by PO)	Boardwalk (exchanged by QR)
FMV	$1,040,000	$325,000
Mortgage	(715,000)	–0–
Equity	$325,000	$325,000

a. If PO's adjusted basis in Marvin Gardens was $403,000, compute PO's realized gain, recognized gain, and basis in Boardwalk.

b. If QR's adjusted basis in Boardwalk was $78,000, compute QR's realized gain, recognized gain, and basis in Marvin Gardens.

15. Company B and Firm W exchanged the following business real estate.

	Blackacre (exchanged by B)	Whiteacre (exchanged by W)
FMV	$400,000	$525,000
Mortgage	(100,000)	(225,000)
Equity	$300,000	$300,000

a. If B's adjusted basis in Blackacre was $240,000, compute B's realized gain, recognized gain, and basis in Whiteacre.

b. If W's adjusted basis in Whiteacre was $100,000, compute W's realized gain, recognized gain, and basis in Blackacre.

16. On June 2, 2011, a tornado destroyed the building in which FF operated a fast-food franchise. FF's adjusted basis in the building was $214,700. In each of the following cases, determine FF's recognized gain or loss on this property disposition and FF's basis in the replacement building. Assume that FF would elect to defer gain recognition when possible.

a. On September 8, 2011, FF received a $250,000 reimbursement from its insurance company. On August 10, 2012, it completed construction of a replacement building for a total cost of $300,000.

b. On September 8, 2011, FF received a $250,000 reimbursement from its insurance company. On August 10, 2012, it completed construction of a replacement building for a total cost of $235,000.

c. On September 8, 2011, FF received a $200,000 reimbursement from its insurance company. On August 10, 2012, it completed construction of a replacement building for a total cost of $300,000.

17. On January 10, 2010, a fire destroyed a warehouse owned by NP Company. NP's adjusted basis in the warehouse was $530,000. On March 12, 2010, NP received a $650,000 reimbursement from its insurance company. In each of the following cases, determine NP's recognized gain on this property disposition. Assume that NP would elect to defer gain recognition when possible.

a. NP's board of directors decided not to replace the warehouse.

b. On January 2, 2012, NP paid $700,000 to acquire a warehouse to store its inventory.

c. On February 8, 2013, NP paid $700,000 to acquire a warehouse to store its inventory.

18. RP owned residential real estate with a $680,000 adjusted basis that was condemned by City Q because it needed the land for a new convention center. RP received $975,000 condemnation proceeds for the real estate. Assume that RP would elect to defer gain recognition when possible.

    a. What are the tax consequences if RP spent $200,000 of the proceeds to expand its inventory and the remaining $775,000 to purchase new residential real estate? What is RP's basis in the inventory and the new real estate?

    b. How would your answer change if RP's basis in the condemned real estate was $850,000 rather than $680,000?

    c. How would your answer change if RP invested the entire condemnation proceeds plus an additional $100,000 cash in new residential real estate?

19. On October 18, 2012, a flood washed away heavy construction equipment owned by Company K. The adjusted tax basis in the equipment was $416,000. On December 8, 2012, Company K received a $480,000 reimbursement from its insurance company. On April 8, 2013, Company K purchased new construction equipment for $450,000.

    a. How much 2012 gain must Company K recognize because of the involuntary disposition of the equipment?

    b. What is Company K's tax basis in the new equipment?

    c. How would your answers change if Company K paid $492,000 for the new equipment?

20. Calvin Corporation's office was burglarized. The thieves stole 10 laptop computers and other electronic equipment. The lost assets had an original cost of $35,000 and accumulated tax depreciation of $19,400. Calvin received an insurance reimbursement of $20,000 related to the theft loss, and immediately purchased new replacement computer equipment. In each of the following cases, determine Calvin's recognized gain, if any, and the tax basis of the replacement property. Assume that Calvin would elect to defer gain recognition when possible.

    a. The replacement property cost $27,000.

    b. The replacement property cost $18,000.

21. Mr. Boyd and Ms. Tuck decide to form a new corporation named BT Inc. Mr. Boyd transfers $10,000 cash and business inventory ($20,000 FMV; adjusted tax basis $3,200), and Ms. Tuck transfers business equipment (FMV $60,000; adjusted tax basis $41,500) to BT. In exchange for their cash and property, BT issues 1,200 shares of common stock to its two shareholders.

    a. How many shares should Mr. Boyd and Ms. Tuck each receive?

    b. Compute Mr. Boyd's realized and recognized gain on his exchange of property for stock, and determine his tax basis in his BT common shares.

    c. Compute Ms. Tuck's realized and recognized gain on her exchange of property for stock, and determine her tax basis in her BT common shares.

    d. Determine BT Inc.'s book and tax basis in the inventory transferred by Mr. Boyd and the equipment transferred by Ms. Tuck.

22. PV Inc. transferred the operating assets of one of its business divisions into newly incorporated SV Inc. in exchange for 100 percent of SV's stock. PV's adjusted basis in the operating assets was $4 million, and their FMV was $10 million.

    a. Discuss the business reasons why a parent corporation like PV operates a business through a subsidiary like SV.

    b. Compute PV's realized gain, recognized gain, and basis in its SV stock.

23. Mr. ZJ owns a sole proprietorship. The business assets have a $246,000 aggregate adjusted basis. According to an independent appraisal, the business is worth $400,000. Mr. ZJ transfers his business to ZJL Corporation in exchange for 1,000 shares of ZJL stock. In each of the following cases, compute Mr. ZJ's recognized gain on the exchange of assets for stock.

    a. Immediately after the exchange, ZJL has 20,000 shares of outstanding stock of which Mr. ZJ owns 1,000 shares.

    b. Immediately after the exchange, ZJL has 1,500 shares of outstanding stock of which Mr. ZJ owns 1,000 shares.

    c. Immediately after the exchange, ZJL has 1,200 shares of outstanding stock of which Mr. ZJ owns 1,000 shares.

24. Refer to the facts in the preceding problem. Assume that Mrs. L, who is Mr. ZJ's business colleague, transfers $200,000 cash to ZJL Corporation in exchange for 500 shares of ZJL stock. Mr. ZJ and Mrs. L's transfers occur on the same day, and after the exchange ZJL has 1,500 shares of outstanding stock (1,000 owned by Mr. ZJ and 500 owned by Mrs. L).

    a. Compute Mr. ZJ's recognized gain on the exchange of assets for stock.

    b. Compute Mr. ZJ and Mrs. L's tax basis in their ZJL stock.

    c. Compute ZJL's tax basis in the assets transferred from Mr. ZJ.

25. Corporation A and Corporation Z go into partnership to develop, produce, and market a new product. The two corporations contribute the following properties in exchange for equal interests in AZ Partnership.

	Corporation A	Corporation Z
Cash	$100,000	$50,000
Business equipment (FMV)	30,000	80,000

    Corporation A's tax basis in the contributed equipment is $34,000, and Corporation Z's tax basis in the contributed equipment is $12,000.

    a. Compute each corporation's realized and recognized gain or loss on the formation of AZ Partnership.

    b. Compute each corporation's tax basis in its half interest in AZ Partnership.

    c. Compute the partnership's tax basis in the equipment contributed by each corporate partner.

26. In 2004, Ms. Dee purchased 1,000 shares of Fox common stock for $124 per share. On June 2, 2012, she sold 500 shares for $92 per share. Compute Ms. Dee's recognized loss on sale assuming that:

    a. She purchased 600 shares of Fox common stock on June 28, 2012, for $94 per share.

    b. She purchased 600 shares of Fox common stock on August 10, 2012, for $99 per share.

    c. Compute Ms. Dee's tax basis in the 600 shares purchased in *a.*

    d. Compute Ms. Dee's tax basis in the 600 share purchased in *b.*

27. In 2005, SW purchased 1,000 shares of Delta stock. On May 20, 2012, it sold these shares for $90 per share. In each of the following cases, compute SW's recognized gain or loss on this sale.

    a. SW's cost basis in the 1,000 shares was $104 per share. It did not purchase any other Delta shares during 2012.

    b. SW's cost basis in the 1,000 shares was $104 per share. It purchased 1,200 shares of Delta on May 1, 2012, for $92 per share.

    c. SW's cost basis in the 1,000 shares was $104 per share. It purchased 1,200 shares of Delta on June 8, 2012, for $92 per share.

   d. SW's cost basis in the 1,000 shares was $79 per share. It purchased 1,200 shares of Delta on June 8, 2012, for $92 per share.

28. Refer to the facts in the preceding problem. In each case in which SW purchased 1,200 Delta shares in 2012, compute its tax basis in the shares.

29. KAI, a calendar year corporation, reported $500,000 net income before tax on its financial statements prepared in accordance with GAAP. The corporation's records reveal the following information.

   • KAI received an $80,000 insurance reimbursement for the theft of equipment with a $62,000 book basis and a $58,000 tax basis. KAI used $75,000 to replace the equipment and the remaining $5,000 to pay Christmas bonuses.

   • KAI exchanged investment real estate with a $250,000 book and tax basis for commercial real estate with a $600,000 FMV.

   Compute KAI's taxable income. In making your computation, assume that the corporation defers the recognition of gain when possible.

30. Alfix, a calendar year corporation, reported $789,300 net income before tax on its financial statements prepared in accordance with GAAP. The corporation's records reveal the following information.

   • Depreciation expense per books was $15,890, and MACRS depreciation was $40,120.

   • Two years ago, Alfix exchanged one tract of investment land (Whiteacre) for a different tract of investment land (Greenacre). Alfix's tax basis in Whiteacre was $500,000, and Greenacre's FMV was $835,000. This year, Alfix sold Greenacre for $820,000 cash.

   • Alfix transferred business property worth $112,000 to Dundee Inc. in exchange for 400 shares of Dundee stock. After the exchange, Dundee had 800 shares of stock outstanding. Alfix had a $91,000 book basis and a $68,200 tax basis in the business property.

   Compute Alfix's taxable income.

Issue Recognition Problems

Identify the tax issue or issues suggested by the following situations, and state each issue in the form of a question.

1. ST Inc. and Firm WX are negotiating an exchange of the following business properties.

	Office Building (owned by ST)	Warehouse (owned by WX)
FMV	$2,000,000	$1,700,000
Mortgage	(450,000)	–0–

   ST agrees to pay $150,000 cash to WX to equalize the value of the exchange. ST's adjusted basis in the office building is $700,000, and WX's adjusted basis in the warehouse is $500,000.

2. Company JK disposed of the following items of business equipment in a like-kind exchange.

	Initial Cost	Acc. Depr.	FMV
Item 1	$75,000	$38,000	$45,000
Item 2	30,000	16,000	10,000

   In exchange for the two items, JK received like-kind equipment worth $50,000 and $5,000 cash.

3. NBV, a California corporation, exchanged commercial real estate located in San Francisco for commercial real estate located in Tokyo, Japan. NBV's gain realized was $16.3 million.

4. FM Inc. operates a dairy farm. The local government required the corporation to destroy 150 head of cattle because the herd had been exposed to mad cow disease. None of the cattle displayed any symptoms of the disease before they were destroyed. The local government paid $150,000 to FM as compensation for the loss. FM's adjusted basis in the herd was $105,000.

5. Company T operated a drive-in movie theater from 1980 through 2007. The company ceased operations because so few people were attending the outdoor facility. This year, the entire facility (movie screen, projection building, snack bar, 15 picnic tables, and playground equipment) was destroyed by a tornado. Company T received a $360,000 insurance reimbursement. The aggregate adjusted basis in the destroyed properties was $200,000. Four months after the twister, Company T purchased a new four-screen movie theater complex located in an urban shopping mall.

6. In 2009, an office building owned by Firm F was completely destroyed by fire. F's adjusted basis in the building was $485,000, and its insurance reimbursement was $550,000. On its 2009 tax return, F elected to defer the $65,000 gain realized on the involuntary conversion. In 2010, F invested $560,000 in another office building. In 2012, F settled a dispute with its insurance company concerning the 2009 claim. Pursuant to the settlement, it received a $25,000 additional reimbursement.

7. In 2010, an industrial plant owned by Company C, a calendar year taxpayer, was destroyed in a flood. C's adjusted basis in the plant was $1.65 million, and the company received a $2 million insurance reimbursement. On its 2010 tax return, C elected to defer the gain realized on the involuntary conversion. C promptly began construction of a new plant on the site of the old. However, because of unexpected delays, construction was not completed until January 2013, and C did not place the new industrial plant into service until March 2013. The total construction price was $3 million.

8. In 2011, transportation equipment owned by Corporation ABC was stolen. The adjusted basis in the equipment was $105,000, and ABC received a $400,000 insurance reimbursement. It immediately paid $440,000 for replacement transportation equipment. On its 2011 tax return, ABC elected to defer the $295,000 gain realized on the involuntary conversion. In 2012, ABC generated a $7 million net operating loss—the first in its history. ABC's aggregate taxable income on its 2010 and 2011 returns was $3.2 million.

9. Mr. P, a professional architect, entered into an agreement with Partnership M under which he designed three buildings for the partnership and transferred a copyright for design software to the partnership. Mr. P had no tax basis in this software. In exchange for the services and computer software, Mr. P received a 35 percent interest in Partnership M.

10. On May 19, WJ realized a $48,000 loss on the sale of 10,000 shares of voting common stock in XZY Corporation. On May 30, WJ purchased 3,200 shares of XZY nonvoting preferred stock.

Research Problems

1. Kiley Communication Inc. owns and operates radio and television stations that broadcast throughout the northwestern United States. This year, Kiley entered into an agreement with another broadcasting company under which Kiley surrendered one AM and two FM radio station licenses in Oregon for one television station license in California. Kiley realized a $3.9 million gain on the exchange. Must it recognize this gain for tax purposes?

2. Mr. Bryan Olgivie owned an indoor roller-skating rink as a sole proprietorship. On April 9, a flood completely destroyed the rink. Mr. Olgivie's adjusted basis in the rink was $833,400. On May 15, he received a check for $1.1 million from his insurance company in complete settlement of his damage claim. Mr. Olgivie is planning to use the entire insurance settlement to purchase 100 percent of the outstanding stock of IceMagic Inc., a corporation that owns an indoor ice-skating rink. Can he defer the recognition of gain on the involuntary conversion of his roller-skating rink by purchasing the IceMagic stock?

3. On February 2, Mr. Eugene Pomeroy transferred all the assets of his sole proprietorship (Pomeroy's Ski Shop) to a newly created corporation, Pomeroy Ski Inc. In exchange for the business assets, Mr. Pomeroy received all 1,000 shares of the corporation's newly issued voting common stock. On February 3, Mr. Pomeroy gave 100 shares of this stock to each of his five children and three grandchildren, leaving him with 200 shares. Does Mr. Pomeroy's exchange of business assets for corporate stock qualify as a nontaxable exchange even though he reduced his ownership interest from 100 percent to only 20 percent on the day after Pomeroy Ski Inc. was incorporated?

4. On April 1, 2012, Bullen Company transferred machinery used in its business to Eaton Inc. in exchange for Eaton common stock. Both Bullen and Eaton use the calendar year for tax purposes. Bullen's exchange of property for stock qualified as a nontaxable exchange under Section 351. Consequently, Bullen's adjusted tax basis in the machinery carried over to become Eaton's tax basis. Bullen purchased the machinery in 2010 for $413,000 cash. The machinery was seven-year recovery property, and Bullen deducted a total of $160,161 MACRS depreciation in 2010 and 2011. Compute the 2012 MACRS depreciation deduction with respect to the machinery allowed to Bullen Company and to Eaton Inc.

Tax Planning Cases

1. Firm NS owns 90 percent of Corporation T's outstanding stock. NS also owns business realty that T needs for use in its business. The FMV of the realty is $4 million, and NS's adjusted basis is $5.6 million. Both NS and T are in the 35 percent marginal tax bracket. Discuss the tax implications of each of the following courses of action, and decide which course you would recommend to NS.

   a. NS could exchange the realty for newly issued shares of T stock worth $4 million.

   b. NS could sell the realty to T for $4 million cash.

   c. NS could lease the realty to T for its annual fair rental value of $600,000.

2. Firm K, a noncorporate taxpayer, has owned investment land with a $600,000 basis for four years. Two unrelated parties want to acquire the land from K. Party A has offered $770,000 cash, and Party B has offered another tract of land with a $725,000 FMV. If K accepts Party B's offer, it would hold the new land for no more than two years before selling it. The FMV of this land should appreciate 10 percent annually. K's tax rate on capital gain is 15 percent, and it uses a 7 percent discount rate to compute NPV. Which offer should K accept to maximize the NPV of the transaction?

3. This year, Corporation EF decides to replace old, outmoded business equipment (adjusted basis $50,000) with new, improved equipment. The corporation has two options.

   - Sell the old equipment for $120,000 cash and use the cash to purchase the new equipment. This option has no transaction cost.

   - Exchange the old equipment for the new like-kind equipment. This exchange has a $6,000 transaction cost that EF could deduct in the current year.

   The new equipment has a MACRS recovery period of five years, and EF will use the half-year convention. EF cannot make a Section 179 election for the cost of the new equipment. Which option should EF choose? In making your computations, assume a 35 percent tax rate and a 6 percent discount rate.

4. DM Inc. incurred a $25,000 net capital loss in 2010 that has carried forward into 2011. During 2011, a hurricane destroyed business assets with a $120,000 basis. DM received a $150,000 insurance reimbursement which it immediately used to purchase replacement assets. The new assets have a three-year MACRS recovery period. Should DM elect to defer the gain recognized on the involuntary conversion?

Comprehensive Problems for Part Three

1. Croyden is a calendar year, accrual basis corporation. Mr. and Mrs. Croyden (cash basis taxpayers) are the sole corporate shareholders. Mr. Croyden is president and Mrs. Croyden is vice president of the corporation. Croyden's financial records, prepared in accordance with GAAP, show the following information for the year.

Revenues from sales of goods	$12,900,000
Cost of goods sold (LIFO)	(9,260,000)
Gross profit	$ 3,640,000
Bad debt expense	$ 24,000
Administrative salaries and wages	612,000
State and local business taxes	135,000
Interest expense	33,900
Advertising	67,000
Annual property insurance premiums	19,800
Annual life insurance premiums	7,300
Depreciation expense	148,800
Repairs, maintenance, utilities	81,000

Croyden's records reveal the following facts.

- Under the UNICAP rules, Croyden had to capitalize $142,800 of administrative wages to inventory. These wages were expensed for financial statement purposes.
- Because of the UNICAP rules, Croyden's cost of goods sold for tax purposes exceeds cost of goods sold for financial statement purposes by $219,000.
- Bad debt expense equals the addition to the corporation's allowance for bad debts. Actual write-offs of uncollectible accounts during the year totaled $31,200.
- Administrative salaries include an accrued $50,000 year-end bonus to Mr. Croyden and an accrued $20,000 year-end bonus to Mrs. Croyden. These bonuses were paid on January 17 of the following year.
- The life insurance premiums were on key-person policies for Mr. and Mrs. Croyden. The corporation is the policy beneficiary.
- Croyden disposed of two assets during the year. (These dispositions are *not* reflected in the financial statement information shown above.) It sold office furnishings for $45,000. The original cost of the furnishings was $40,000, and accumulated MACRS depreciation through date of sale was $12,700. It also exchanged transportation equipment for a 15 percent interest in a partnership. The original cost of the transportation equipment was $110,000, and accumulated MACRS depreciation through date of exchange was $38,900.
- MACRS depreciation for assets placed in service in prior years (including the office furnishings and transportation equipment disposed of this year) is $187,600.

The only asset acquired this year was new equipment costing $275,000. The equipment has a seven-year recovery period and was placed in service on February 11.

- Croyden's prior year tax returns show no nonrecaptured Section 1231 losses and a $7,400 capital loss carryforward.

Solely on the basis of the above facts, compute Croyden's taxable income.

2. LN Consulting is a calendar year, cash basis unincorporated business. The business is not required to provide audited financial statements to any external user. LN's accounting records show the following.

Cash receipts:	
Revenues from service contracts	$292,000
Proceeds from sale of mutual fund shares	18,000
Insurance reimbursement for fire loss	7,000
Cash disbursements:	
Administrative salaries	$ 32,000
Professional fees	800
Business meals and entertainment	1,090
State and local business taxes	5,000
Interest expense	7,600
Advertising	970
Office expense	1,200
Office rent	14,400
New office equipment	8,300

LN's records reveal the following facts.

- In December, the bookkeeper prepaid $1,500 interest on a business debt. This interest is related to the next taxable year.
- LN disposed of two assets during the year. It exchanged computer equipment for office furniture. (These assets are not like-kind for federal tax purposes.) The original cost of the computer equipment was $13,000, and accumulated MACRS depreciation through date of exchange was $9,700. The office furniture has a $6,000 FMV. It sold 1,200 shares in a mutual fund for $18,000. LN purchased the shares as a short-term investment of excess working capital. The cost of the shares was $16,600.
- An electrical fire completely destroyed a company car. The adjusted basis of the car was $9,100, and LN's property insurance company paid $7,000 in complete settlement of its damage claim. LN used the insurance money to pay various operating expenses.
- MACRS depreciation for assets placed in service in prior years (including the computer equipment and company car) is $4,600. The only asset acquired this year (in addition to the office furniture) was office equipment costing $8,300. The equipment was placed in service on August 19.

On the basis of the above facts, compute the taxable income generated by LN Consulting's activities.

Part **Four**

The Taxation of Business Income

10 Sole Proprietorships, Partnerships, LLCs, and S Corporations

11 The Corporate Taxpayer

12 The Choice of Business Entity

13 Jurisdictional Issues in Business Taxation

Chapter **Ten**

Sole Proprietorships, Partnerships, LLCs, and S Corporations

Learning Objectives

After studying this chapter, you should be able to:

1. Compute net profit or loss from a sole proprietorship.

2. Compute the FICA payroll taxes and the federal SE tax.

3. Differentiate between a distributive share of partnership income and cash flow.

4. Adjust the tax basis in a partnership interest.

5. Apply the basis limitation on the deduction of partnership losses.

6. Explain how limited liability companies (LLCs) are treated for federal tax purposes.

7. Determine if a corporation is eligible to be an S corporation.

8. Apply the basis limitation on the deduction of S corporation losses.

In Part Three of *Principles of Taxation for Business and Investment Planning,* we learned that taxable income from business transactions and activities equals gross income minus allowable deductions.[1] In Part Four of the text, we will learn how to compute the tax on business income. Throughout Part Three, we used the labels *firm* and *company* to refer to business organizations. We could get by with these generic labels because we were concentrating on the *measurement of taxable income.* The measurement process does not depend on the type of legal entity operating the business. As stated in Chapter 4, the tax law is essentially neutral across business entities with respect to the tax base. But to make the actual *tax computation,* we must focus on the specific organizational form of the business.

For tax purposes, business organizations fall into one of two categories. The first category consists of organizations that are not taxable entities. The income generated by the organization is taxed directly to the owners. This category includes sole proprietorships, partnerships, limited liability companies (LLCs), and S corporations, all of which are discussed in Chapter 10. The second category consists of corporations (often referred to as

[1] §63(a).

EXHIBIT 10.1
Categories of Business Organization

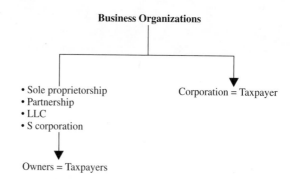

regular or C corporations), which are both persons under the law and taxpayers in their own right. Corporations pay tax on their income at the entity level. If a corporation distributes after-tax earnings to its owners, the distributed income is taxed a second time at the owner level. This potential for double taxation, as well as other characteristics of corporate taxpayers, is examined in detail in Chapter 11. Exhibit 10.1 contrasts the two categories of business organizations in terms of the identity of the taxpayer.

Part Four includes two more chapters that complete our discussion of the taxation of business income. Chapter 12 compares the tax advantages and disadvantages of the various business entities and identifies tax planning strategies unique to each. Finally, Chapter 13 introduces the complexities that develop when business entities operate in more than one taxing jurisdiction.

SOLE PROPRIETORSHIPS

The simplest form of business organization is a **sole proprietorship,** defined as an unincorporated business activity owned by one individual.[2] A sole proprietor owns the business assets in his or her own name and is personally liable for the business debts. In other words, the business has no legal identity separate from that of its owner. Sole proprietorships are the most common form of business entity in the United States. According to recent Internal Revenue Service data, over 22.7 million nonfarm sole proprietorships operate in this country, and nearly three of every four businesses that report to the IRS are operated by sole proprietors.[3]

Overview of Schedule C

Objective 1
Compute net profit or loss from a sole proprietorship.

The taxable income from a sole proprietorship is reported on Schedule C (Profit or Loss From Business) of the proprietor's Form 1040 (U.S. Individual Income Tax Return).[4] This schedule is the proprietorship's income statement for the year. Gross income from the sale of goods to customers or performance of services for clients is accounted for in Part I. The proprietorship's deductible operating expenses and cost recovery deductions are listed in Part II. An excess of gross income over deductions is reported as net profit, while an excess of deductions over gross income is reported as net loss.

---

[2] This definition includes businesses in which the owner's spouse has an equity interest in the business under state property law. As discussed later in this chapter, a single member LLC whose owner is an individual is treated as a sole proprietorship.

[3] IRS Statistics of Income Bulletin, Summer 2011.

[4] Agricultural business operations are reported on Schedule F (Profit or Loss From Farming).

Faux Antique— *Sole* *Proprietorship*	Mr. Tom Owen owns and operates a firm that manufactures reproductions of antique furniture. The business name for this sole proprietorship is Faux Antique. For 2011, the business records reflect the following items of revenue and expense.

Revenue from furniture sales	$1,117,300
Sales returns	(21,000)
Expenses: Advertising	6,200
Accounts written off as uncollectible	8,900
Attorney and CPA fees	2,150
Business license tax	2,500
Cost of goods sold	599,700
Interest to Credit Union	7,300
MACRS depreciation	3,600
Payroll taxes	9,250
Property and liability insurance	5,600
Rent on workroom	23,200
Repairs to tools and equipment	17,900
Supplies	18,000
Utilities	14,000
Wages	73,200

Mr. Owen used the above information to prepare the Schedule C included in his Form 1040. Page 1 of this Schedule C is shown as Exhibit 10.2. The $304,900 net profit reported on Schedule C was included in Mr. Owen's 2011 taxable income.

Note that the tax on net profit is not computed on Schedule C. Instead, the net profit carries to the first page of Form 1040 as ordinary income and is combined with all other income items recognized during the year. Consequently, the individual's business income is just one component of total income on which tax is computed. Similarly, if the sole proprietorship operated at a loss, the loss carries to the first page of Form 1040 to be deducted against other income for the year. If the business loss exceeds other income, the individual can carry the excess loss back two years and forward 20 years as a net operating loss (NOL) deduction.

Individual Net *Operating Loss*	Mr. Zeller reported the following items on his Form 1040 for 2011.

Salary from employer	$21,600
Interest and dividend income from investments	1,200
Business loss from sole proprietorship	(26,810)
Net operating loss	$ (4,010)

Mr. Zeller can use his $4,010 net operating loss as a carryback deduction (to 2009 and 2010) or as a carryforward deduction for the next 20 years.[5]

Cash Flow Implications

The after-tax cash generated by a sole proprietorship belongs to the individual owner. The individual can retain the cash for use in the business, spend it for personal consumption, or

---

[5] This example ignores the computational details of the individual NOL deduction. In general, the following items are not allowed when computing the individual NOL: personal exemptions, net capital losses, nonbusiness deductions in excess of nonbusiness income, and the domestic production activities deduction.

invest it in other income-producing property. In the latter case, earnings from the owner's investments (interest, dividends, rents, etc.) are not considered business income and are not reported on Schedule C.[6]

Faux Antique Cash to Mr. Owen	Refer back to the example on page 273 in which Mr. Tom Owen owns and operates Faux Antique. During 2009, Mr. Owen transferred $261,300 cash from his business bank account to his personal bank account. Mr. Owen and his wife, Claire, pay all their household expenses out of the personal account. The transfer of cash has absolutely no effect on the computation of Faux Antique's net profit reported on Schedule C.

EXHIBIT 10.2

SCHEDULE C (Form 1040)

Department of the Treasury
Internal Revenue Service (99)

Profit or Loss From Business
(Sole Proprietorship)

▶ For information on Schedule C and its instructions, go to *www.irs.gov/schedulec*
▶ Attach to Form 1040, 1040NR, or 1041; partnerships generally must file Form 1065.

OMB No. 1545-0074

2011

Attachment Sequence No. **09**

Name of proprietor: Tom G. Owens

Social security number (SSN): 497-45-9058

A Principal business or profession, including product or service (see instructions): manufacturing - furniture

B Enter code from instructions ▶ 3 3 7 0 0 0

C Business name. If no separate business name, leave blank.: Faux Antiques

D Employer ID number (EIN), (see instr.): 2 6 1 1 4 7 1 3 1

E Business address (including suite or room no.) ▶ 1012 East Main
City, town or post office, state, and ZIP code: Widener, NY 42714

F Accounting method: **(1)** ☐ Cash **(2)** ☑ Accrual **(3)** ☐ Other (specify) ▶

G Did you "materially participate" in the operation of this business during 2011? If "No," see instructions for limit on losses ☑ Yes ☐ No

H If you started or acquired this business during 2011, check here ▶ ☐

I Did you make any payments in 2011 that would require you to file Form(s) 1099? (see instructions) ☐ Yes ☑ No

J If "Yes," did you or will you file all required Forms 1099? ☐ Yes ☐ No

Part I Income

1a	Merchant card and third party payments. For 2011, enter -0-	1a	
b	Gross receipts or sales not entered on line 1a (see instructions)	1b	
c	Income reported to you on Form W-2 if the "Statutory Employee" box on that form was checked. **Caution.** See instr. before completing this line	1c	
d	**Total gross receipts.** Add lines 1a through 1c	1d	1,117,300
2	Returns and allowances plus any other adjustments (see instructions)	2	21,000
3	Subtract line 2 from line 1d	3	1,096,300
4	Cost of goods sold (from line 42)	4	599,700
5	**Gross profit.** Subtract line 4 from line 3	5	496,600
6	Other income, including federal and state gasoline or fuel tax credit or refund (see instructions)	6	
7	**Gross income.** Add lines 5 and 6 ▶	7	496,600

Part II Expenses   Enter expenses for business use of your home only on line 30.

8	Advertising	8	6,200	**18**	Office expense (see instructions)	18	
9	Car and truck expenses (see instructions)	9		**19**	Pension and profit-sharing plans	19	
10	Commissions and fees	10		**20**	Rent or lease (see instructions):		
11	Contract labor (see instructions)	11		**a**	Vehicles, machinery, and equipment	20a	23,200
12	Depletion	12		**b**	Other business property	20b	
13	Depreciation and section 179 expense deduction (not included in Part III) (see instructions)	13	3,600	**21**	Repairs and maintenance	21	17,900
				22	Supplies (not included in Part III)	22	
				23	Taxes and licenses	23	11,750
14	Employee benefit programs (other than on line 19)	14		**24**	Travel, meals, and entertainment:		
15	Insurance (other than health)	15	5,000	**a**	Travel	24a	
16	Interest:			**b**	Deductible meals and entertainment (see instructions)	24b	18,000
a	Mortgage (paid to banks, etc.)	16a		**25**	Utilities	25	14,000
b	Other	16b	7,300	**26**	Wages (less employment credits)	26	73,200
17	Legal and professional services	17	2,150	**27a**	Other expenses (from line 48)	27a	bad debts 8,900
				b	Reserved for future use	27b	
28	**Total expenses** before expenses for business use of home. Add lines 8 through 27a ▶					28	191,700
29	Tentative profit or (loss). Subtract line 28 from line 7					29	304,900
30	Expenses for business use of your home. Attach Form 8829. Do **not** report such expenses elsewhere					30	
31	Net profit or (loss). Subtract line 30 from line 29.						

• If a profit, enter on both **Form 1040, line 12** (or **Form 1040NR, line 13**) and on **Schedule SE, line 2.** If you entered an amount on line 1c, see instr. Estates and trusts, enter on **Form 1041, line 3.**
• If a loss, you **must** go to line 32.

31	304,900

32 If you have a loss, check the box that describes your investment in this activity (see instructions).

• If you checked 32a, enter the loss on both **Form 1040, line 12, (or Form 1040NR, line 13)** and on **Schedule SE, line 2.** If you entered an amount on line 1c, see the instructions for line 31. Estates and trusts, enter on **Form 1041, line 3.**
• If you checked 32b, you **must** attach Form 6198. Your loss may be limited.

32a ☐ All investment is at risk.
32b ☐ Some investment is not at risk.

For Paperwork Reduction Act Notice, see your tax return instructions.   Cat. No. 11334P   Schedule C (Form 1040) 2011

---

[6] Chapter 16 discusses the taxation of investment income earned by an individual taxpayer.

Tax Talk

The IRS estimates that the annual "tax gap" (taxes that people legally owe but don't pay) equals $345 billion. About $109 billion of the gap is attributable to sole proprietors who understate revenue (often received in cash) or overstate deductions.

Dispositions of Business Assets

Only the results of the sole proprietorship's routine operations are reported on Schedule C. If the owner disposes of assets used in the business, recognized gains and losses are reported on Form 4797 (Sales of Business Property). The tax consequences of the disposition are based on the rules discussed in Chapters 8 and 9. For instance, if the owner sells business equipment at a gain, he must report Section 1245 depreciation recapture as ordinary income and any additional gain as Section 1231 gain. If he sells the equipment at a loss, the loss is a Section 1231 loss.

Interest Expense

If an individual borrows money for a business purpose relating to her sole proprietorship, the interest paid on the debt is deductible on Schedule C. The deductibility of business interest is in sharp contrast to the tax treatment of other types of interest expense. For example, individuals can't deduct the interest paid on debt incurred to purchase consumer goods such as a family car or a new wardrobe. If the sole proprietorship fails to generate enough cash to service the business debt, the individual owner is personally liable for repayment, and the business creditors can look to the owner's nonbusiness assets for satisfaction.

Home Office Deduction

If an individual uses a portion of his personal residence as an office for his sole proprietorship, the expenses allocable to the home office may qualify as a business deduction.

Home Office Deduction	Mrs. Greer, a self-employed consultant, uses one room of her home as a business office. This room represents 15 percent of the home's square footage. This year, Mrs. Greer incurred the following expenses in connection with her home.

Home mortgage interest	$18,000
Property tax on residence	4,300
Homeowner's insurance	2,950
Utilities	3,600
House cleaning service	2,400
Repairs	1,900
	$33,150

If Mrs. Greer's office meets the tax law requirements, she can deduct $4,973 (15 percent of the total expenses) as a business deduction on her Schedule C.[7] She can also claim a MACRS depreciation deduction based on 15 percent of the cost of the residence.

The possibility of deducting some percentage of monthly household expenses might prompt the conversion of many a spare bedroom into a home office—even if the use of such office is extraneous to the conduct of the homeowner's business. The tax law limits the potential for abuse through a set of tough requirements for qualifying a portion of a residence as a home office. Essentially, the office must be *exclusively* used on a regular basis as the principal place of any business operated by the homeowner or as a place to meet with patients, clients, or customers.[8] A home office used exclusively for administrative or management activities qualifies as a principal place of business if the taxpayer has no other fixed location where such activities are conducted.

[7] Mrs. Greer can deduct the remainders of her home mortgage interest and property tax as itemized deductions. See Chapters 14 and 17.

[8] §280A(c)(1).

Principal Place of Business	Dr. Milby is a self-employed obstetrician who treats patients at three different urban hospitals. Although Dr. Milby spends more than 12 hours during an average week at each hospital, he does not maintain an office in any of the hospitals. He does all his medical reading, patient billing and record keeping, and other administrative tasks in his home office where he spends two to three hours each day. Patient treatment is the most significant aspect of Dr. Milby's business, and he spends more hours working at the hospitals than in his home office. Nevertheless, his home office qualifies as Dr. Milby's principal place of business, and he can deduct the expenses allocable to the office.

Even when an individual meets the requirements for a home office, the home office deduction is limited to the taxable income of the business before consideration of the deduction.[9] In other words, the home office deduction can't create or increase a net loss. A sole proprietor who claims a home office deduction must isolate the deduction on line 30, Schedule C, and attach a separate Form 8829 to show the detailed computation of the deduction. Clearly, the IRS is very sensitive about home office deductions. Sole proprietors who are entitled to the deduction should carefully document the underlying expenses and be prepared to justify the necessity of a home office if their tax return is audited.

Employment Taxes

A sole proprietor may be the only person working in the business or the proprietor may have any number of employees. In the latter case, the sole proprietor must obtain an **employer identification number** from the IRS and comply with the state and federal employment tax requirements imposed on every business organization.

Unemployment and FICA Tax

Objective 2
Compute the FICA payroll taxes and the federal SE tax.

Employers must pay both a state and federal unemployment tax based on the compensation paid to their employees during the year.[10] As we discussed in Chapter 1, these taxes fund the national unemployment benefits program. Employers must also pay the tax authorized by the Federal Insurance Contribution Act (FICA) that funds our national Social Security and Medicare systems. This **employer payroll tax** has two components: a Social Security tax of 6.2 percent of a base amount of compensation paid to each employee and a Medicare tax of 1.45 percent of the employee's total compensation.[11] Congress increases the Social Security base periodically: In 2011, the base is $106,800. For 2012, the base is increased to $110,100.

Employer Payroll Tax	Mr. Carr has a full-time employee, Mrs. Stroh, who manages Mr. Carr's sole proprietorship. Mrs. Stroh's 2012 salary was $112,000, and Mr. Carr's employer payroll tax on this salary was $8,450.

Social Security tax (6.2% × $110,100)	$6,826
Medicare tax (1.45% × $112,000)	1,624
Employer payroll tax	$8,450

In addition to paying unemployment and payroll taxes, employers must collect the FICA tax levied on their employees.[12] For tax years prior to and after 2011, this **employee payroll tax** is computed in exactly the same manner as the employer payroll tax. However,

---

[9] §280A(c)(5). *Michael H. Visin,* T.C. Memo 2003-246.
[10] §3301.
[11] §3111.
[12] §3102.

for wages received during 2011, the 2010 Tax Relief Act provides a temporary reduction of the employee Social Security tax from 6.2 percent to 4.2 percent. Congress has extended the 4.2 percent rate through 2012.[13] Absent an additional extension by Congress, in 2013 the employee Social Security tax will revert back to 6.2 percent.

Employee Payroll Tax Withholding	Based on the facts in the preceding example, Mrs. Stroh's 2012 employee payroll tax was $6,248.[14]

Social Security tax (4.2% × $110,100)	$4,624
Medicare tax (1.45% × $112,000)	1,624
Employee payroll tax	$6,248

Mr. Carr withheld this tax from Mrs. Stroh's salary and remitted it along with his employer payroll tax to the U.S. Treasury for a total payment of $14,698 ($8,450 employer payroll tax + $6,248 employee payroll tax). Thus, Mr. Carr is the collection agent for the federal government with respect to the employee payroll tax.

The temporary reduction in employee payroll taxes for 2011 and 2012 is intended as an economic stimulus. In effect, it gives employees a 2 percent raise in take-home pay, which Congress hopes they will spend in support of the U.S. economy!

Employers should take seriously their responsibility to withhold and remit employee payroll tax. If an employer fails to remit the proper FICA tax for an employee, the federal government may collect both halves of the tax (the employer and the employee portions) from the employer.[15]

Income Tax Withholding on Employee Compensation

Employers are required to withhold federal income tax (and possibly state income tax) from the compensation paid to their employees.[16] Employers must remit the withholding to the U.S. Treasury periodically throughout the year. The withholding for each employee is based on the information on the employee's Form W-4 (Employee's Withholding Allowance Certificate) and computed by reference to withholding tables provided by the IRS.

Gross and Net Compensation	During 2012, Mr. Carr also withheld $22,900 federal income tax from Mrs. Stroh's $112,000 gross salary. Therefore, Mrs. Stroh received only $82,852 after-tax (net) compensation.

Gross salary	$112,000
FICA tax withheld	(6,248)
Federal income tax withheld	(22,900)
Net salary received	$ 82,852

---

[13] As this book goes to press, Congress is still debating a full 12 month extension of the payroll tax reduction. While all indications are that the extension will pass, a legislative stalemate is always possible. If Congress ultimately settles for a less than 12 month extension, please go to our website for a technical update on this issue.

[14] §3101. The employee payroll tax is nondeductible for federal income tax purposes.

[15] The employer is not technically liable for an employee's payroll tax. However, an employer that fails to "collect, truthfully account for, and pay over" this tax is subject to a penalty equal to 100 percent of such tax. In other words, the penalty on the employer equals the uncollected employee tax. §6672. This penalty has been described as the "iron fist" of the FICA tax system.

[16] §3402.

At the end of each year, employers are required to provide information concerning the gross wages or salary paid to each employee during the year and the payroll and income tax withheld from that gross income. This information is summarized on the familiar Form W-2 (Wage and Tax Statement).

Income Tax Consequences to the Employer

Business organizations can deduct the gross compensation paid to their employees.[17] They can also deduct state and federal unemployment taxes and the employer payroll tax because these taxes are ordinary and necessary expenses incurred in the conduct of an active business.[18] Let's summarize the relationship between these deductible expenses, the employer's withholding requirements, and the net compensation paid to employees by referring back to Mr. Carr's sole proprietorship.

Compensation and Cash Disbursements	For 2012, Mr. Carr deducted $112,000 compensation expense and $8,450 employer payroll tax on that compensation. He withheld $6,248 employee payroll tax and $22,900 income tax from Mrs. Stroh's compensation ($29,148 total) and remitted $37,598 tax to the U.S. Treasury.		

	Deductible Business Expense	Cash Disbursed to:	
		Mrs. Stroh	*U.S. Treasury*
Salary	$112,000	$82,852	$29,148
Employer FICA tax	8,450		8,450
	$120,450	$82,852	$37,598

Self-Employment Tax

While sole proprietors are responsible for collecting and remitting payroll and income taxes from their employees, sole proprietors themselves are not employees and do not receive a salary from the business. Sole proprietors are self-employed and must pay the federal **self-employment (SE) tax** on their business income.[19] Refer to Schedule C in Exhibit 10.2 and note how line 31 instructs the sole proprietor to carry net profit to Schedule SE. The self-employment tax is computed on this schedule and paid along with the individual's income tax for the year.

The SE tax has two components: a Social Security tax of 10.4 percent (for 2011 and 2012) of a base amount of net earnings from self-employment and a Medicare tax of 2.9 percent of total net earnings. For 2011 and 2012, the Social Security base is $106,800 and $110,100, respectively. For years after 2012, the Social Security tax component of the SE tax is scheduled to increase to 12.4 percent of the base amount.

Note that the SE tax rates equal the *combined* employer/employee payroll tax rates and the Social Security base is the same for both taxes. The SE tax was enacted to complement the FICA tax; the federal government collects the same tax on a sole proprietor's self-employment income as it would collect on an identical amount of compensation. To complete the parallel, sole proprietors can claim as an income tax deduction that portion

---

[17] Unless some or all the compensation must be capitalized to inventory under the uniform capitalization (unicap) rules discussed in Chapter 7.

[18] See Rev. Rul. 80-164, 1980-1 CB 109.

[19] §1401. Self-employed individuals are not eligible to receive unemployment benefits and, therefore, are not subject to state and federal unemployment taxes.

of the SE tax equivalent to the employer payroll tax. For tax years other than 2011 or 2012, the tax deduction is simply one-half of the SE tax. For 2011 and 2012, the tax deduction equals 59.6 percent of the Social security tax and 50 percent of the Medicare tax.[20]

In calculating after-tax business income, sole proprietors must factor in both the income tax and the SE tax levied on that income.

Self-Employment Tax 2012	Mr. Carr's sole proprietorship generated $200,000 net profit in 2012. If his marginal income tax rate was 33 percent, the after-tax income from the business was $120,330.	

Schedule C net profit		$200,000
Self-employment tax:		
Net earnings from self-employment[21]	$184,700	
Social Security tax (10.4% × $110,100)	11,450	
Medicare tax (2.9% × $184,700)	5,356	
Total SE tax		(16,806)
Income tax:		
Schedule C net profit	$200,000	
59.6% of Social Security tax	(6,824)	
One-half of Medicare tax	(2,678)	
	$190,498	
	.33	
		(62,864)
After-tax business income		$120,330

Note that the SE tax is not a progressive tax because the combined 13.3 percent rate applies to the first dollar of self-employment income. For sole proprietors who earn modest incomes, the SE tax can be a heavier burden than the income tax.

PARTNERSHIPS

Entrepreneurs who pool their resources by becoming co-owners of a business can organize the business as a partnership. **Partnerships** are unincorporated entities created by contractual agreement among two or more business associates.[22] Such associates can be individuals, corporations, and even other partnerships. All 50 states and the District of Columbia have enacted statutes (generally patterned after the Revised Uniform Partnership Act and the Revised Uniform Limited Partnership Act) to define the characteristics and requirements for partnerships operating within their jurisdiction.

Tax Talk
Recent IRS statistics indicate nearly 3 million partnership returns are filed each year.

Forming a Partnership

The first step in the formation of a partnership is the drafting of an agreement by the prospective partners.[23] A partnership agreement is a legal contract stipulating both the rights and obligations of the partners and the percentage of profits and losses allocable to each. The agreement gives the partners flexibility to customize their business arrangement to suit

---

[20] §164(f).

[21] The statutory base for the SE tax is "net earnings from self-employment." Net earnings equals net profit minus a deduction equal to 7.65 percent of such profit. §1402(a)(12). Schedule SE builds this deduction into its computation of net earnings by defining that number as 92.35 percent of Schedule C net profit.

[22] The term *partnership* encompasses syndicates, groups, pools, joint ventures, or any other unincorporated business organization. §761(a).

[23] See the discussion of organizational and start-up costs in Chapter 7.

their unique situation. The partners can agree to share all profits and losses equally, or they can decide on different sharing ratios for special items of income, gain, deduction, or loss. Ideally, a partnership agreement should be drafted by an attorney, should be in writing, and should be signed by all the partners. However, even oral partnership agreements have been respected as binding contracts by the courts.[24]

A partnership can be a **general partnership** in which all partners have unlimited personal liability for debts incurred by the partnership. Alternatively, a partnership can be a **limited partnership** in which one or more limited partners are liable for partnership debt only to the extent of their capital contributions to the partnership. Limited partnerships must have at least one general partner. A limited partner's role is restricted to that of a passive investor; state law typically prohibits limited partners from active involvement in the partnership business. Limited partners who violate this prohibition may forfeit their limited liability for the partnership's debts.

Individuals who perform professional services for patients or clients, such as doctors, attorneys, and CPAs, often form **limited liability partnerships (LLPs).** General partners in an LLP are not personally liable for malpractice-related claims arising from the professional negligence of any other partner. However, they are personally liable for other debts of the LLP.[25]

Limited Liability Partnership	Doctors Jeff Batson, Susan Lloyd, and Cary Carew formed an LLP to conduct their medical practice. The three doctors are general partners. This year, the LLP is the defendant in two lawsuits.
	The first lawsuit was initiated by a former LLP employee who claims that she was fired from her job because of age discrimination. Consequently, the ex-employee is suing the LLP for $600,000 damages. The second lawsuit was initiated by the family of a patient who died shortly after Dr. Carew performed a routine surgical procedure. Because the family believes that Dr. Carew was grossly negligent, it is suing the LLP for $1.2 million damages.
	If the LLP loses the first lawsuit, the three general partners are personally liable for any portion of the $600,000 settlement not covered by the LLP's insurance. If the LLP loses the second lawsuit, only Dr. Carew is personally liable for any portion of the $1.2 million settlement not covered by the LLP's or his own malpractice insurance.

Tax Basis in Partnership Interests

Partnerships are both legal entities (title to property can be held and conveyed in the partnership name) and accounting entities (financial books and records are maintained by the partnership). An equity interest in a partnership is an intangible asset, the value of which depends on the underlying value of the partnership business. Partnership interests are considered illiquid assets because partnership agreements usually prevent partners from disposing of their interests without the consent of the other partners. A partner's initial tax basis in a partnership interest equals the cash plus the adjusted basis of any property transferred to the partnership in exchange for the equity interest.[26]

As legal entities, partnerships can borrow money in their own name. Nonetheless, general partners have unlimited liability for repayment of debt to the partnership's creditors. If the partnership business does not generate enough cash to service its debts, the general partners must contribute funds to satisfy any unpaid liabilities.[27] As a result, a

---

[24] See, for example, *Elrod*, 87 T.C. 1046 (1986) and *Kuhl* v. *Garner*, 894 P.2d 525 (Oregon, 1995).

[25] The Big Four public accounting firms are LLPs.

[26] The exchange of property for a partnership interest is nontaxable to both the partner and the partnership. §721. See the discussion of partnership formations in Chapter 9.

[27] In this respect, a general partner's risk with respect to the partnership business is equivalent to a sole proprietor's business risk.

partner's economic investment consists of the initial investment of cash or property *plus* the share of partnership debt for which the partner may ultimately be responsible. The tax law acknowledges this responsibility by providing that a partner's share of partnership debt is included in the basis in her partnership interest.[28]

Basis in Partnership Interest	Three individuals each contributed $10,000 cash to a new partnership in which they are equal general partners. The partnership immediately borrowed $24,000 from a local bank and used the money to purchase equipment and supplies. Each partner's basis in his partnership interest is $18,000: the initial cash contribution plus an equal share of partnership debt.[29]

Partnership Reporting Requirements

The Internal Revenue Code states that "a partnership as such shall not be subject to the income tax. . . . Persons carrying on a business as partners shall be liable for income tax only in their separate or individual capacities."[30] Although partnerships are not taxable entities, they are required to file an annual Form 1065 (U.S. Partnership Return of Income) with the IRS.[31]

The taxable income generated by partnership activities is measured and characterized at the entity level. All items of gross income and deduction relating strictly to business operations are reported on page 1 of Form 1065. The net of these items is reported on line 22 as ordinary income or loss. This income or loss is allocated among the partners according to the sharing ratio specified in the partnership agreement. The partners report their share of income or loss on their respective returns and include it in the calculation of taxable income. Accordingly, net profit from a partnership business is taxed directly to the partners; the tax rate depends on whether the partner is an individual or a corporation.[32] Because partnerships serve only as conduits of income, they are described as **passthrough entities.**

Faux Antique— Partnership	Refer back to our earlier example in which Mr. Tom Owen operates a furniture business (Faux Antique) as a sole proprietorship. Let's change the facts by assuming that Mr. Owen and two co-owners organized Faux Antique as a partnership. Mr. Owen owns a 60 percent equity interest as a general partner. Faux Antique generated $304,900 ordinary business income for 2011. Page 1 of the partnership's Form 1065 is shown as Exhibit 10.3.

Partnerships frequently recognize items of income, gain, expense, or loss that don't relate to business operations. For example, a partnership might invest excess cash in marketable securities that pay dividends and interest. The partnership might recognize gain or loss on

---

[28] §752(a).

[29] The regulatory rules for calculating a partner's share of partnership debt are extremely complex. The simplest summary of these rules is that recourse debt is shared only by general partners on the basis of their relative loss-sharing ratios and nonrecourse debt is shared by all partners on the basis of their profit-sharing ratios. Reg. §1.752-2 and Reg. §1.752-3.

[30] §701.

[31] As a general rule, partnerships are required to use the same taxable year as that used by their partners. Under this rule, a partnership consisting of individual partners who are calendar year taxpayers files its Form 1065 on a calendar year basis. §706(b).

[32] If partnership income is allocated to a partner that is a passthrough entity (another partnership, LLC, or S corporation), the income is passed through again until it is finally allocated to a taxable entity (an individual or corporation).

EXHIBIT 10.3

Form **1065**	**U.S. Return of Partnership Income**	OMB No. 1545-0099
Department of the Treasury Internal Revenue Service	For calendar year 2011, or tax year beginning _____, 2011, ending _____, 20 ___. ▶ See separate instructions.	**2011**

A Principal business activity manufacturing		Name of partnership Faux Antiques	D Employer identification number 81-1138419
B Principal product or service furniture	Print or type.	Number, street, and room or suite no. If a P.O. box, see the instructions. 1012 East Main	E Date business started February 1, 1990
C Business code number 337000		City or town, state, and ZIP code Widener, NY 42714	F Total assets (see the instructions) $ 1,136,640

G Check applicable boxes: **(1)** ☐ Initial return **(2)** ☐ Final return **(3)** ☐ Name change **(4)** ☐ Address change **(5)** ☐ Amended return
(6) ☐ Technical termination - also check (1) or (2)
H Check accounting method: **(1)** ☐ Cash **(2)** ☑ Accrual **(3)** ☐ Other (specify) ▶ _____
I Number of Schedules K-1. Attach one for each person who was a partner at any time during the tax year ▶ 3
J Check if Schedules C and M-3 are attached . . . . ☐

Caution. Include **only** trade or business income and expenses on lines 1a through 22 below. See the instructions for more information.

Income	**1a**	Merchant card and third-party payments (including amounts reported on Form(s) 1099-K). For 2011, enter -0-	**1a**		
	b	Gross receipts or sales not reported on line 1a (see instructions)	**1b**	1,117,300	
	c	Total. Add lines 1a and 1b	**1c**	1,117,300	
	d	Returns and allowances plus any other adjustments to line 1a (see instructions)	**1d**	21,000	
	e	Subtract line 1d from line 1c	**1e**	1,096,300	
	2	Cost of goods sold (attach Form 1125-A)	**2**	599,700	
	3	Gross profit. Subtract line 2 from line 1e	**3**		496,600
	4	Ordinary income (loss) from other partnerships, estates, and trusts (attach statement) . .	**4**		
	5	Net farm profit (loss) (attach Schedule F (Form 1040))	**5**		
	6	Net gain (loss) from Form 4797, Part II, line 17 (attach Form 4797)	**6**		
	7	Other income (loss) (attach statement)	**7**		
	8	**Total income (loss).** Combine lines 3 through 7	**8**		496,600
Deductions (see the instructions for limitations)	**9**	Salaries and wages (other than to partners) (less employment credits)	**9**		73,200
	10	Guaranteed payments to partners	**10**		
	11	Repairs and maintenance	**11**		17,900
	12	Bad debts	**12**		8,800
	13	Rent	**13**		23,200
	14	Taxes and licenses	**14**		11,750
	15	Interest	**15**		7,300
	16a	Depreciation (if required, attach Form 4562)	**16a**	3,600	
	b	Less depreciation reported on Form 1125-A and elsewhere on return	**16b**		
			16c		3,600
	17	Depletion **(Do not deduct oil and gas depletion.)**	**17**		
	18	Retirement plans, etc.	**18**		
	19	Employee benefit programs	**19**		
	20	Other deductions (attach statement)	**20**		45,950
	21	**Total deductions.** Add the amounts shown in the far right column for lines 9 through 20 .	**21**		191,700
	22	**Ordinary business income (loss).** Subtract line 21 from line 8	**22**		304,900

Sign Here	Under penalties of perjury, I declare that I have examined this return, including accompanying schedules and statements, and to the best of my knowledge and belief, it is true, correct, and complete. Declaration of preparer (other than general partner or limited liability company member manager) is based on all information of which preparer has any knowledge.		May the IRS discuss this return with the preparer shown below (see instructions)? ☐ **Yes** ☐ **No**
	▶ Signature of general partner or limited liability company member manager	▶ _____ Date	

Paid Preparer Use Only	Print/Type preparer's name	Preparer's signature	Date	Check ☐ if self- employed	PTIN
	Firm's name ▶			Firm's EIN ▶	
	Firm's address ▶			Phone no.	

For Paperwork Reduction Act Notice, see separate instructions.   Cat. No. 11390Z   Form **1065** (2011)

the sale of one of these securities. Or the partnership could make a contribution to a local charity. These items are not included in the calculation of ordinary business income or loss. Instead, they are reported on Schedule K of Form 1065 and allocated to the partners for inclusion on the partners' returns.[33] These **separately stated items** retain their tax character as they pass through to the partners.[34]

---

[33] More specifically, Reg. §1.702-1(a)(8)(ii) explains that each partner must be able to take into account separately his or her distributive share of any partnership item that results in an income tax liability different from that which would result if the item were not accounted for separately.

[34] §702(b).

EXHIBIT 10.4

Form 1065 (2011)   Page **4**

Schedule K		Partners' Distributive Share Items			Total amount	
Income (Loss)	1	Ordinary business income (loss) (page 1, line 22)		1	304,900	
	2	Net rental real estate income (loss) (attach Form 8825)		2		
	3a	Other gross rental income (loss)	3a			
	b	Expenses from other rental activities (attach statement)	3b			
	c	Other net rental income (loss). Subtract line 3b from line 3a		3c		
	4	Guaranteed payments		4		
	5	Interest income		5		
	6	Dividends: **a** Ordinary dividends		6a	1,680	
		b Qualified dividends	6b	1,680		
	7	Royalties		7		
	8	Net short-term capital gain (loss) (attach Schedule D (Form 1065))		8		
	9a	Net long-term capital gain (loss) (attach Schedule D (Form 1065))		9a		
	b	Collectibles (28%) gain (loss)	9b			
	c	Unrecaptured section 1250 gain (attach statement) . .	9c			
	10	Net section 1231 gain (loss) (attach Form 4797)		10		
	11	Other income (loss) (see instructions) Type ▶		11		
Deductions	12	Section 179 deduction (attach Form 4562)		12		
	13a	Contributions		13a	3,000	
	b	Investment interest expense		13b		
	c	Section 59(e)(2) expenditures: **(1)** Type ▶ _____ **(2)** Amount ▶		13c(2)		
	d	Other deductions (see instructions) Type ▶		13d		
Self-Employ-ment	14a	Net earnings (loss) from self-employment		14a	304,900	
	b	Gross farming or fishing income		14b		
	c	Gross nonfarm income		14c		
Credits	15a	Low-income housing credit (section 42(j)(5))		15a		
	b	Low-income housing credit (other)		15b		
	c	Qualified rehabilitation expenditures (rental real estate) (attach Form 3468)		15c		
	d	Other rental real estate credits (see instructions) Type ▶		15d		
	e	Other rental credits (see instructions) Type ▶		15e		
	f	Other credits (see instructions) Type ▶		15f		
Foreign Transactions	16a	Name of country or U.S. possession ▶				
	b	Gross income from all sources		16b		
	c	Gross income sourced at partner level		16c		
		Foreign gross income sourced at partnership level				
	d	Passive category ▶ _____ **e** General category ▶ _____ **f** Other ▶		16f		
		Deductions allocated and apportioned at partner level				
	g	Interest expense ▶ _____ **h** Other . . . . ▶		16h		
		Deductions allocated and apportioned at partnership level to foreign source income				
	i	Passive category ▶ _____ **j** General category ▶ _____ **k** Other ▶		16k		
	l	Total foreign taxes (check one): ▶ Paid ☐ Accrued ☐		16l		
	m	Reduction in taxes available for credit (attach statement)		16m		
	n	Other foreign tax information (attach statement)		16n		
Alternative Minimum Tax (AMT) Items	17a	Post-1986 depreciation adjustment		17a		
	b	Adjusted gain or loss		17b		
	c	Depletion (other than oil and gas)		17c		
	d	Oil, gas, and geothermal properties—gross income		17d		
	e	Oil, gas, and geothermal properties—deductions		17e		
	f	Other AMT items (attach statement)		17f		
Other Information	18a	Tax-exempt interest income		18a		
	b	Other tax-exempt income		18b		
	c	Nondeductible expenses		18c		
	19a	Distributions of cash and marketable securities		19a	250,000	
	b	Distributions of other property		19b		
	20a	Investment income		20a	1,680	
	b	Investment expenses		20b		
	c	Other items and amounts (attach statement)				

Form **1065** (2011)

Separately Stated Items	For several years, Faux Antique partnership invested its excess cash in a mutual fund. In 2011, the partnership received a $1,680 ordinary dividend from the fund and recognized a $3,710 capital gain on sale of fund shares. During 2011, Faux Antique made a $3,000 donation to the United Way and distributed $250,000 cash to its partners. The dividend, capital gain, donation, and distribution were not included in the computation of ordinary business income. Instead, these items were separately stated on Schedule K of Form 1065, which is shown as Exhibit 10.4.

Tax Consequences to Partners

Objective 3
Differentiate between
a distributive share of
partnership income and
cash flow.

Distributive Shares and Cash Flows

After the close of its taxable year, a partnership issues a Schedule K-1 (Partner's Share of Income, Credits, Deductions, etc.) to each partner. Schedule K-1 provides detailed information concerning the partner's **distributive share** of the partnership's ordinary business income or loss and any separately stated items. The instructions to the schedule tell individual partners how and where to include each item on their tax return. For instance, a partner's distributive share of ordinary income or loss is reported on Schedule E of Form 1040.

Partners must pay tax on their distributive share of partnership taxable income, regardless of the cash flow from the partnership during the year. In an extreme case, partners may decide to retain all available cash in the partnership. As a result, each partner must find another source of funds to pay the tax on his share of partnership income. Alternatively, partners may decide to withdraw enough cash to pay their taxes. Another possibility is that the partners withdraw all available cash for personal consumption. The important point is that the cash flow is irrelevant in determining the partners' taxable income.

Schedule K-1 for Partner	Each partner in Faux Antique received a 2011 Schedule K-1 showing a distributive share of ordinary business income, dividend income, capital gain, donation, and cash distribution. Tom Owen's Schedule K-1, which reflects his 60 percent share of each partnership item, is shown as Exhibit 10.5. Mr. Owen reported his $182,940 share of Faux Antique's business income as ordinary income on his Form 1040. He reported his $1,008 share of dividend income as investment income and his $2,226 share of capital gain as capital gain on his Form 1040. He included his $1,800 share of Faux Antique's donation in his total personal charitable contributions for 2011.[35] His $150,000 share of the cash distribution had no effect on his 2011 taxable income.

Guaranteed Payments

The personal involvement of individual partners in the partnership business can vary greatly across partners. Limited partners, by definition, do not actively participate in the day-to-day operation of the business and, at most, may take part in major management decisions. General partners may have different levels of participation; some may be sporadically involved, while others may devote 100 percent of their workweek to the business.

Partners who work for the partnership on a continual basis expect to be compensated. These partners typically receive **guaranteed payments** from the partnership based on the value of their work. Guaranteed payments to partners are analogous to the salaries paid to partnership employees. The partnership deducts guaranteed payments in computing ordinary income, and partners report guaranteed payments as ordinary income.[36] However, partners can't be employees of their partnerships any more than individuals can be employees of their sole proprietorships. Because a guaranteed payment is not a salary, neither the partnership nor the partner pays FICA payroll tax. Nor does the partnership withhold any federal income tax from the guaranteed payment. If a partner earns a $10,000 monthly guaranteed payment, that partner receives $10,000 cash each month. At the end of the year, the partnership does not issue a Form W-2 to the partner. Instead, the total guaranteed payments are reported as an ordinary income item on the partner's Schedule K-1.

---

[35] The tax consequences of personal charitable contributions are discussed in Chapter 17.
[36] §707(c).

EXHIBIT 10.5

651111

☐ Final K-1	☐ Amended K-1	OMB No. 1545-0099

Schedule K-1
(Form 1065)

20**11**

Department of the Treasury
Internal Revenue Service

For calendar year 2011, or tax
year beginning _____, 2011
ending _____, 20 ___

**Partner's Share of Income, Deductions,
Credits, etc.** ▶ See back of form and separate instructions.

Part I	Information About the Partnership

A Partnership's employer identification number
81-1138419

B Partnership's name, address, city, state, and ZIP code

Faux Antiques
1012 East Main
Widener, NY 42714

C IRS Center where partnership filed return
Cincinnati

D ☐ Check if this is a publicly traded partnership (PTP)

Part II	Information About the Partner

E Partner's identifying number
498-45-9058

F Partner's name, address, city, state, and ZIP code

Tom G. Owen
330 Aspen Lane
Widener, NY 42714

G ☒ General partner or LLC member-manager   ☐ Limited partner or other LLC member

H ☐ Domestic partner   ☐ Foreign partner

I What type of entity is this partner? Individual

J Partner's share of profit, loss, and capital (see instructions):

	Beginning	Ending
Profit	60 %	60 %
Loss	60 %	60 %
Capital	60 %	60 %

K Partner's share of liabilities at year end:

Nonrecourse	$	
Qualified nonrecourse financing	$	13,612
Recourse	$	21,050

L Partner's capital account analysis:

Beginning capital account	$	25,000
Capital contributed during the year	$	
Current year increase (decrease)	$	184,374
Withdrawals & distributions	$ (	150,000)
Ending capital account	$	59,374

☐ Tax basis   ☐ GAAP   ☒ Section 704(b) book
☐ Other (explain)

M Did the partner contribute property with a built-in gain or loss?
☐ Yes   ☒ No
If "Yes," attach statement (see instructions)

Part III	Partner's Share of Current Year Income, Deductions, Credits, and Other Items		
1	Ordinary business income (loss) 182,940	15	Credits
2	Net rental real estate income (loss)		
3	Other net rental income (loss)	16	Foreign transactions
4	Guaranteed payments		
5	Interest income		
6a	Ordinary dividends 1,008		
6b	Qualified dividends 1,008		
7	Royalties		
8	Net short-term capital gain (loss)		
9a	Net long-term capital gain (loss) 2,226	17	Alternative minimum tax (AMT) items
9b	Collectibles (28%) gain (loss)		
9c	Unrecaptured section 1250 gain		
10	Net section 1231 gain (loss)	18	Tax-exempt income and nondeductible expenses
11	Other income (loss)		
		19	Distributions
12	Section 179 deduction	A	150.000
13	Other deductions A 1,800	20	Other information
		A	Investment_inc_1,800
14	Self-employment earnings (loss) 182,940		

*See attached statement for additional information.

For IRS Use Only

For Paperwork Reduction Act Notice, see Instructions for Form 1065.   Cat. No. 11394R   **Schedule K-1 (Form 1065) 2011**

Self-Employment Income

Individual general partners are considered to be self-employed. Consequently, any guaranteed payments plus their distributive share of ordinary business income are net earnings from self-employment subject to SE tax.[37] Limited partners are not considered self-employed and are not required to pay self-employment tax on their distributive share of ordinary income.[38]

[37] §1402(a).
[38] §1402(a)(13).

<table>
<tr><td>*Self-Employment Income*</td><td>Refer to Mr. Owen's Schedule K-1 from the Faux Antique partnership (Exhibit 10.5). Line 14 shows that Mr. Owen's $182,940 distributive share of business income represents net earnings from self-employment. Mr. Owen must report these earnings on a Schedule SE and compute his SE tax accordingly.</td></tr>
</table>

Comprehensive Example

To summarize our discussion of the tax consequences of partnerships, consider the case of ABC Partnership. This business is owned by three individual partners. Ms. Alton and Mr. Bach are general partners who work in the business, and Ms. Cole is a limited partner. The partnership agreement provides that Ms. Alton and Mr. Bach are each allocated 40 percent of income or loss, while Ms. Cole is allocated the remaining 20 percent. ABC pays a $3,000 monthly guaranteed payment to Ms. Alton and a $1,100 monthly guaranteed payment to Mr. Bach. For 2009, ABC's ordinary business income (after deducting the guaranteed payments) was $90,800. ABC also earned $3,300 interest income from a mutual bond fund investment. On December 24, ABC distributed $20,000 cash to its partners ($8,000 to Ms. Alton and Mr. Bach and $4,000 to Ms. Cole). ABC reported the following information on each partner's 2009 Schedule K-1.

ABC Partnership 2009 Schedule K-1s			
	Ms. Alton	**Mr. Bach**	**Ms. Cole**
Guaranteed payments	$36,000	$13,200	–0–
Distributive shares:			
Ordinary business income	36,320	36,320	$18,160
Interest income	1,320	1,320	660
Net earnings from self-employment	72,320	49,520	–0–
Cash distribution	8,000	8,000	4,000

The partners included their guaranteed payments and their share of business and interest income in taxable income, and Ms. Alton and Mr. Bach paid SE tax on their net earnings from self-employment. Assuming that Ms. Alton was in a 28 percent marginal tax bracket and both Mr. Bach and Ms. Cole were in a 31 percent marginal tax bracket, each partner's after-tax cash flow from ABC is computed as follows.

ABC Partner Cash Flows			
	Ms. Alton	**Mr. Bach**	**Ms. Cole**
Guaranteed payments	$36,000	$13,200	–0–
Cash distribution	8,000	8,000	$ 4,000
SE tax*	(10,218)	(6,997)	–0–
Income tax	(19,189)	(14,676)	(5,834)
After-tax cash flow	$14,593	$ (473)	$ (1,834)
Income tax calculation:			
Guaranteed payments	$36,000	$13,200	–0–
Ordinary business income	36,320	36,320	$18,160
Interest income	1,320	1,320	660
One-half SE tax	(5,109)	(3,499)	–0–
Taxable income	$68,531	$47,341	$18,820
	.28	.31	.31
Income tax	$19,189	$14,676	$ 5,834

*Self-employment tax based on 92.35 percent of net earnings from self-employment. See footnote 20.

Ms. Alton had positive cash flow from the partnership, but both Mr. Bach and Ms. Cole had negative cash flows. This cash flow information reflects the fact that the three partners paid tax on partnership profits that they did not withdraw as cash from the business.

Adjusting the Basis of a Partnership Interest

Objective 4
Adjust the tax basis in a partnership interest.

When a partner is allocated a share of partnership income but does not receive a cash distribution of that income, the partner is making an additional investment in the partnership. The partner should be entitled to recover this investment tax-free at some future date. When a partner receives a cash distribution, the distribution is treated as a nontaxable return of investment.[39] These investment increases and decreases are captured as positive and negative year-end adjustments to the tax basis in the partner's interest in the partnership.[40] Let's continue the comprehensive example by computing the ABC partners' basis adjustments for 2009. The partner's initial basis on January 1, 2009 carries forward from 2008 and is assumed as shown below.

ABC Partner Basis Adjustments for 2009*			
	Ms. Alton	**Mr. Bach**	**Ms. Cole**
Adjusted basis on January 1	$35,000	$60,000	$100,000
Increased by:			
Ordinary business income	36,320	36,320	18,160
Interest income	1,320	1,320	660
Decreased by:			
Cash distribution	(8,000)	(8,000)	(4,000)
Adjusted basis on December 31	$64,640	$89,640	$114,820

*This comprehensive example ignores any changes in partnership liabilities that would affect the partners' basis.

When a partnership generates an ordinary business loss or a separately stated loss, each partner's share of the loss represents a decrease in the partner's investment that is captured as a negative basis adjustment. Year-end basis adjustments for losses are made after any adjustments for income items or cash distributions.[41]

To illustrate the negative basis adjustment for losses, assume that ABC Partnership generated a $99,200 operating loss (after deducting Ms. Alton's and Mr. Bach's guaranteed payments) in 2010. ABC earned $2,400 interest income and recognized a $19,600 capital loss on the sale of mutual fund shares. The partnership made no cash distributions to its partners. ABC reported the following information on each partner's 2010 Schedule K-1.

ABC Partnership 2010 Schedule K-1s			
	Ms. Alton	**Mr. Bach**	**Ms. Cole**
Guaranteed payments	$36,000	$13,200	–0–
Distributive shares:			
Ordinary business loss	(39,680)	(39,680)	$(19,840)
Interest income	960	960	480
Capital loss	(7,840)	(7,840)	(3,920)
Net earnings from self-employment	(3,680)	(26,480)	–0–
Cash distribution	–0–	–0–	–0–

[39] §731(a) and §733. If a partner receives a cash distribution that exceeds the partner's basis, the excess distribution is recognized as capital gain.

[40] §705(a). Basis is also increased for a partner's distributive share of tax-exempt income.

[41] Reg. §1.705-1(a). Basis is also decreased by a partner's distributive share of nondeductible expenses.

The partners included their guaranteed payments and their share of interest income in taxable income. They also deducted their share of ordinary business loss and included their share of ABC's capital loss in their net capital gain or loss for 2010.[42] Because Ms. Alton and Mr. Bach had negative earnings from self-employment, they paid no SE tax for the year.

ABC Partner Basis Adjustments for 2010			
	Ms. Alton	**Mr. Bach**	**Ms. Cole**
Adjusted basis on January 1	$ 64,640	$ 89,640	$114,820
Increased by:			
Interest income	960	960	480
Decreased by:			
Ordinary business loss	(39,680)	(39,680)	(19,840)
Capital loss	(7,840)	(7,840)	(3,920)
Adjusted basis on December 31	$ 18,080	$ 43,080	$ 91,540

Basis Limitation on Loss Deductions

Objective 5
Apply the basis limitation on the deduction of partnership losses.

As a general rule, partners may deduct their distributive share of partnership losses for the year. However, they must reduce the basis in their partnership interest by their share of losses, and the basis cannot be reduced below zero. If a partner's share of losses exceeds basis, the excess is not deductible in the current year.[43] The partner can carry the nondeductible loss forward indefinitely and can deduct it in a future year in which basis in the partnership interest is restored.

Suppose that ABC Partnership had another bad year in 2011. The partnership did not make any guaranteed payments to Ms. Alton or Mr. Bach. Even with this frugality, ABC's business generated a $160,000 operating loss. ABC did earn $3,000 interest income from its mutual fund and reported the following information on each partner's 2011 Schedule K-1.

ABC Partnership 2011 Schedule K-1s			
	Ms. Alton	**Mr. Bach**	**Ms. Cole**
Guaranteed payments	–0–	–0–	–0–
Distributive shares:			
Ordinary business loss	$(64,000)	$(64,000)	$(32,000)
Interest income	1,200	1,200	600
Net earnings from self-employment	(64,000)	(64,000)	–0–
Cash distribution	–0–	–0–	–0–

Ms. Alton's and Mr. Bach's deduction for their share of loss is limited to the adjusted basis in their partnership interest immediately before the negative basis adjustment for the loss.

---

[42] This example assumes that the §465 at-risk limitation and the §469 passive activity loss limitation are inapplicable for all three partners. These limitations are discussed in Chapter 16.
[43] §704(d).

ABC Partner Basis Adjustments for 2011			
	Ms. Alton	**Mr. Bach**	**Ms. Cole**
Adjusted basis on January 1	$18,080	$ 43,080	$ 91,540
Increased by:			
Interest income	1,200	1,200	600
Decreased by:			
Deductible loss	(19,280)	(44,280)	(32,000)
Adjusted basis on December 31	–0–	–0–	$ 60,140
Nondeductible loss carryforward	$(44,720)	$(19,720)	–0–

In 2011, all three partners must include their share of ABC's interest income in taxable income. Ms. Cole can deduct her entire $32,000 share of ABC's ordinary business loss. Ms. Alton can deduct only $19,280 and Mr. Bach can deduct only $44,280 of their share of loss. Ms. Alton and Mr. Bach can carry their nondeductible loss into future taxable years, but they must restore basis in their partnership interests to deduct the carryforward. These partners could easily create basis by investing more money in ABC Partnership. But if the partnership's business is failing (as the 2010 and 2011 losses suggest), Ms. Alton and Mr. Bach could lose their additional investment. In such case, they would have made the mistake of throwing good money after bad to secure a tax deduction. Of course, if ABC's business becomes profitable again, the partners' shares of future income will create basis against which Ms. Alton and Mr. Bach can deduct their loss carryforwards.

Let's complete our comprehensive example with one more year of ABC Partnership's operations. In 2012, the partnership generated $64,400 ordinary business income after deducting an $18,000 guaranteed payment to Ms. Alton and a $6,600 guaranteed payment to Mr. Bach. ABC earned $3,400 interest income and recognized an $11,000 capital gain on the sale of mutual fund shares. ABC reported the following information on each partner's 2012 Schedule K-1.

ABC Partnership 2012 Schedule K-1s			
	Ms. Alton	**Mr. Bach**	**Ms. Cole**
Guaranteed payments	$18,000	$ 6,600	–0–
Distributive shares:			
Ordinary business income	25,760	25,760	$12,880
Interest income	1,360	1,360	680
Capital gain	4,400	4,400	2,200
Net earnings from self-employment	43,760	32,360	–0–
Cash distribution	–0–	–0–	–0–

The partners included their guaranteed payments and their share of business, interest, and capital gain in taxable income, and Ms. Alton and Mr. Bach paid SE tax on their net earnings from self-employment. The partners increased the basis in their partnership interests by their share of income, and, as a result, Ms. Alton could deduct $31,520 and Mr. Bach could deduct $19,720 of their 2011 loss carryforwards in the computation of 2012 taxable income. Ms. Alton has a $13,200 remaining loss carryforward that she can deduct to the extent of future increases in the basis in her ABC interest.

ABC Partner Basis Adjustments for 2012			
	Ms. Alton	**Mr. Bach**	**Ms. Cole**
Adjusted basis on January 1	–0–	–0–	$60,140
Increased by:			
Ordinary business income	$ 25,760	$25,760	12,880
Interest income	1,360	1,360	680
Capital gain	4,400	4,400	2,200
	$ 31,520	$31,520	$75,900
Decreased by:			
Deductible loss carryforward	(31,520)	(19,720)	–0–
Adjusted basis on December 31	–0–	$11,800	$75,900
Remaining loss carryforward	$(13,200)	–0–	–0–

Limited Liability Companies

Objective 6
Explain how limited liability companies (LLCs) are treated for federal tax purposes.

Business owners often prefer the partnership form to the corporate form because partnership income is not taxed at the entity level but only at the owner level. The partnership form also provides the greatest flexibility in the manner in which business income can be divided among the co-owners. The major disadvantage of the partnership form is the unlimited personal liability of the general partners for business debt.

Every state (and the District of Columbia) permits business owners to organize as a **limited liability company (LLC)** as an alternative to a general or limited partnership. An LLC is an unincorporated legal entity owned by one or more *members.* In contrast to a partnership, every member has limited liability for the LLC's debts. This limited liability protects even those members who are actively involved in the LLC's business. State laws do not limit the number of members nor the type of entity that can be a member in an LLC. Thus, an LLC's membership can include individuals, partnerships, corporations, and even other LLCs.

Under Treasury regulations that classify business entities for federal tax purposes (the check-the-box regulations), an LLC with two or more members is classified as a partnership.[44] Consequently, income earned by an LLC is not taxed at the entity level but passes through to the various members. An LLC with only one member (i.e., one owner) is a *disregarded entity* for federal tax purposes. If the single member is an individual, the LLC is treated as a sole proprietorship. If the single member is an entity, the LLC is treated as a division or branch of the entity.

LLCs offer business owners a terrific combination: one owner-level tax on income and limited liability for business debt. Moreover, LLCs are not subject to many of the bothersome restrictions that apply to S corporations (our next topic). As a result, LLCs are an attractive option for business ventures. However, because LLCs are a relatively new organizational form, many tax questions concerning their operation have yet to be resolved. Business owners and their advisers must consider this element of uncertainty in making the decision to organize an LLC.

One major unresolved issue is the extent to which members are subject to self-employment tax on their LLC income. The self-employment tax statute was written before the advent of LLCs and is silent as to whether distributive shares of LLC business income are net earnings from self-employment. In 1997, the Treasury attempted to resolve this

Tax Talk

The Second Circuit Court of Appeals recently held the owner of a single-member LLC personally liable for the LLC's unpaid payroll tax. The court held that under the check-the-box regulations, the LLC was treated as a "sole proprietorship" for federal tax purposes and "disregarded as an entity separate from its owner." The court rejected the taxpayer's argument that the regulations wrongfully ignored the limited liability provided to LLC owners under state law. McNamee v. Treasury, (CA 2) 99 AFTR 2d 2007-2871.

---

[44] Reg. §301.7701-3(b)(1). Under this regulation, an LLC can elect to be classified as a corporation for federal tax purposes. There is no obvious reason why a domestic LLC would make such an election.

issue through proposed regulations.[45] The regulations contain elaborate rules for determining whether an LLC member may be regarded as a limited partner. If so, the member's share of LLC income is not self-employment income. If a member may not be regarded as a limited partner, both guaranteed payments and any share of LLC income are self-employment income. The tax professional community's reaction to these proposed regulations was extremely critical. Congress responded to the criticism by issuing a moratorium that prevented the Treasury from finalizing the 1997 regulations. To date, the Treasury has declined to make a second attempt to resolve this issue.

Self-Employment Income or Not?	Mrs. Miller is a member in Wooster LLC. She does not work for Wooster on a daily basis and does not receive any guaranteed payments. However, last year she worked about 175 hours during October and November on a special marketing campaign for Wooster. Mrs. Miller's share of Wooster's ordinary business income last year was $38,170. Since she is not involved in Wooster's business on a regular basis, Mrs. Miller could argue that she should be regarded as a limited partner and should not pay SE tax on her share of LLC income. However, the IRS could argue that Mrs. Miller did perform substantial personal services for the LLC and therefore should treat her LLC income as earned income subject to SE tax.

SUBCHAPTER S CORPORATIONS

Tax Talk
Recent IRS statistics indicate over 4 million S corporation returns are filed each year.

Before the advent of LLCs, business owners who wanted to avoid both the corporate income tax and the risk of unlimited personal liability had only one choice: the **subchapter S corporation.** This form of business organization is a corporate entity, organized as such under state law.[46] A predominant characteristic of corporations is the limited liability of their shareholders. If a corporation gets into financial trouble and can't pay its debts, the corporate creditors have no claim against the personal assets of the shareholders. Thus, the shareholders' risk is limited to their investment in the corporation.

For federal tax purposes, a subchapter S corporation is a passthrough entity; its business income is allocated and taxed directly to the corporation's shareholders.[47] The statutory rules providing for this passthrough are almost identical to the partnership rules. The ordinary income or loss generated by an S corporation's business is reported on page 1 of Form 1120S (U.S. Income Tax Return for an S Corporation). This income or loss is allocated among the shareholders based on their percentage ownership of the corporation's outstanding stock.[48] Recall from our discussion of partnerships that considerable flexibility is allowed in the allocation of income and loss items to partners. This flexibility is not permitted to S corporations and their shareholders. All S corporation allocations are strictly based on percentage ownership of stock.

Faux Antique—S Corporation	Refer back to our earlier example involving Mr. Tom Owen and his antique furniture restoration business. Let's change the facts again by assuming that Mr. Owen and his two co-owners incorporated the business as Faux Antique Inc., which is an S corporation for federal tax purposes. Tom Owen owns 60 percent of the outstanding stock. Faux Antique Inc. generated $304,900 ordinary business income in 2011. Page 1 of the S corporation's Form 1120S is shown as Exhibit 10.6.

[45] Prop. Reg. §1.1402(a)-2(h).

[46] While a partnership must have at least two co-owners as partners, a corporation may be owned by one shareholder.

[47] §1363(a) and §1366.

[48] §1377(a).

EXHIBIT 10.6

Form **1120S**	**U.S. Income Tax Return for an S Corporation**	OMB No. 1545-0130
Department of the Treasury Internal Revenue Service	▶ Do not file this form unless the corporation has filed or is attaching Form 2553 to elect to be an S corporation. ▶ See separate instructions.	20**11**

For calendar year 2011 or tax year beginning		, 2011, ending	, 20	

A S election effective date		**Name**	**D** Employer identification number
February 1, 1990	**TYPE**	Faux Antiques	81-1138419
B Business activity code number *(see instructions)*	**OR**	Number, street, and room or suite no. If a P.O. box, see instructions.	**E** Date incorporated
337000	**PRINT**	1012 East Main	February 1, 1990
		City or town, state, and ZIP code	**F** Total assets *(see instructions)*
C Check if Sch. M-3 attached ☐		Widener, NY 42714	$ 1,136,640

G Is the corporation electing to be an S corporation beginning with this tax year? ☐ Yes ☐ No   If "Yes," attach Form 2553 if not already filed
H Check if: **(1)** ☐ Final return **(2)** ☐ Name change **(3)** ☐ Address change **(4)** ☐ Amended return **(5)** ☐ S election termination or revocation
I Enter the number of shareholders who were shareholders during any part of the tax year . . . . ▶   3
Caution. *Include **only** trade or business income and expenses on lines 1a through 21. See the instructions for more information.*

Income	**1a**	Merchant card and third-party payments. For 2011, enter -0- . . .	**1a**		
	b	Gross receipts or sales not reported on line 1a (see instructions) . .	**1b**	1,117,300	
	c	Total. Add lines 1a and 1b	**1c**	1,117,300	
	d	Returns and allowances plus any other adjustments (see instructions)	**1d**	21,000	
	e	Subtract line 1d from line 1c		**1e**	1,096,300
	2	Cost of goods sold (attach Form 1125-A)		**2**	599,700
	3	Gross profit. Subtract line 2 from line 1e		**3**	496,600
	4	Net gain (loss) from Form 4797, Part II, line 17 *(attach Form 4797)* . . .		**4**	
	5	Other income (loss) *(see instructions—attach statement)*		**5**	
	6	**Total income (loss).** Add lines 3 through 5 . . . . ▶		**6**	496,600
Deductions (see instructions for limitations)	**7**	Compensation of officers		**7**	
	8	Salaries and wages (less employment credits)		**8**	73,200
	9	Repairs and maintenance		**9**	17,900
	10	Bad debts		**10**	8,800
	11	Rents		**11**	23,200
	12	Taxes and licenses		**12**	11,750
	13	Interest		**13**	7,300
	14	Depreciation not claimed on Form 1125-A or elsewhere on return *(attach Form 4562)* . . .		**14**	3,600
	15	Depletion **(Do not deduct oil and gas depletion.)**		**15**	
	16	Advertising		**16**	6,200
	17	Pension, profit-sharing, etc., plans		**17**	
	18	Employee benefit programs		**18**	
	19	Other deductions *(attach statement)*		**19**	39,750
	20	**Total deductions.** Add lines 7 through 19 . . . . ▶		**20**	191,700
	21	**Ordinary business income (loss).** Subtract line 20 from line 6		**21**	304,900
Tax and Payments	**22a**	Excess net passive income or LIFO recapture tax *(see instructions)* . .	**22a**		
	b	Tax from Schedule D (Form 1120S)	**22b**		
	c	Add lines 22a and 22b (see *instructions for additional taxes*)		**22c**	
	23a	2011 estimated tax payments and 2010 overpayment credited to 2011	**23a**		
	b	Tax deposited with Form 7004	**23b**		
	c	Credit for federal tax paid on fuels *(attach Form 4136)*	**23c**		
	d	Add lines 23a through 23c		**23d**	
	24	Estimated tax penalty *(see instructions)*. Check if Form 2220 is attached . . . . ▶ ☐		**24**	
	25	**Amount owed.** If line 23d is smaller than the total of lines 22c and 24, enter amount owed . .		**25**	
	26	**Overpayment.** If line 23d is larger than the total of lines 22c and 24, enter amount overpaid . .		**26**	
	27	Enter amount from line 26 **Credited to 2012 estimated tax** ▶	Refunded ▶	**27**	

Sign Here	Under penalties of perjury, I declare that I have examined this return, including accompanying schedules and statements, and to the best of my knowledge and belief, it is true, correct, and complete. Declaration of preparer (other than taxpayer) is based on all information of which preparer has any knowledge.	May the IRS discuss this return with the preparer shown below (see instructions)? ☐ Yes ☐ No
	▶ Signature of officer Date ▶ Title	

Paid Preparer Use Only	Print/Type preparer's name	Preparer's signature	Date	Check ☐ if self-employed	PTIN
	Firm's name ▶			Firm's EIN ▶	
	Firm's address ▶			Phone no.	

For Paperwork Reduction Act Notice, see separate instructions.   Cat. No. 11510H   Form **1120S** (2011)

If an S corporation recognizes items of income, gain, deduction, or loss that don't relate to ordinary business operations, these items are separately stated on Schedule K of Form 1120S and retain their tax character as they flow through to the shareholders.

Separately Stated Items	In 2011, Faux Antique Inc. received a $1,680 ordinary dividend from a mutual fund and recognized a $3,710 capital gain on sale of fund shares. During 2011, the corporation made a $3,000 donation to the United Way and distributed $250,000 cash to its shareholders. The dividend, capital gain, donation, and distribution were not included in the computation of ordinary business income. Instead, these items were separately stated on Schedule K of Form 1120S, which is shown as Exhibit 10.7.

EXHIBIT 10.7

Schedule K	Shareholders' Pro Rata Share Items				Total amount
Income (Loss)	1 Ordinary business income (loss) (page 1, line 21)			1	304,900
	2 Net rental real estate income (loss) (attach Form 8825)			2	
	3a Other gross rental income (loss)	3a			
	b Expenses from other rental activities (attach statement)	3b			
	c Other net rental income (loss). Subtract line 3b from line 3a			3c	
	4 Interest income			4	
	5 Dividends: a Ordinary dividends			5a	1,680
	b Qualified dividends	5b	1,680		
	6 Royalties			6	
	7 Net short-term capital gain (loss) (attach Schedule D (Form 1120S))			7	
	8a Net long-term capital gain (loss) (attach Schedule D (Form 1120S))			8a	3,710
	b Collectibles (28%) gain (loss)	8b			
	c Unrecaptured section 1250 gain (attach statement)	8c			
	9 Net section 1231 gain (loss) (attach Form 4797)			9	
	10 Other income (loss) (see instructions) . . . . Type ▶			10	
Deductions	11 Section 179 deduction (attach Form 4562)			11	
	12a Contributions			12a	3,000
	b Investment interest expense			12b	
	c Section 59(e)(2) expenditures (1) Type ▶_____ (2) Amount ▶			12c(2)	
	d Other deductions (see instructions) . . . . Type ▶			12d	
Credits	13a Low-income housing credit (section 42(j)(5))			13a	
	b Low-income housing credit (other)			13b	
	c Qualified rehabilitation expenditures (rental real estate) (attach Form 3468)			13c	
	d Other rental real estate credits (see instructions) Type ▶_____			13d	
	e Other rental credits (see instructions) . . . . Type ▶			13e	
	f Alcohol and cellulosic biofuel fuels credit (attach Form 6478)			13f	
	g Other credits (see instructions) . . . . Type ▶			13g	
Foreign Transactions	14a Name of country or U.S. possession ▶_____				
	b Gross income from all sources			14b	
	c Gross income sourced at shareholder level			14c	
	Foreign gross income sourced at corporate level				
	d Passive category			14d	
	e General category			14e	
	f Other (attach statement)			14f	
	Deductions allocated and apportioned at shareholder level				
	g Interest expense			14g	
	h Other			14h	
	Deductions allocated and apportioned at corporate level to foreign source income				
	i Passive category			14i	
	j General category			14j	
	k Other (attach statement)			14k	
	Other information				
	l Total foreign taxes (check one): ▶ ☐ Paid ☐ Accrued			14l	
	m Reduction in taxes available for credit (attach statement)			14m	
	n Other foreign tax information (attach statement)				
Alternative Minimum Tax (AMT) Items	15a Post-1986 depreciation adjustment			15a	
	b Adjusted gain or loss			15b	
	c Depletion (other than oil and gas)			15c	
	d Oil, gas, and geothermal properties—gross income			15d	
	e Oil, gas, and geothermal properties—deductions			15e	
	f Other AMT items (attach statement)			15f	
Items Affecting Shareholder Basis	16a Tax-exempt interest income			16a	
	b Other tax-exempt income			16b	
	c Nondeductible expenses			16c	
	d Property distributions			16d	250,000
	e Repayment of loans from shareholders			16e	
Other Information	17a Investment income			17a	1,680
	b Investment expenses			17b	
	c Dividend distributions paid from accumulated earnings and profits			17c	
	d Other items and amounts (attach statement)				
Reconciliation	18 **Income/loss reconciliation.** Combine the amounts on lines 1 through 10 in the far right column. From the result, subtract the sum of the amounts on lines 11 through 12d and 14l			18	

Objective 7
Determine if a corporation is eligible to be an S corporation.

Eligible Corporations

Only domestic corporations formed under the law of one of the 50 states or the District of Columbia are eligible to be S corporations for federal tax purposes. Eligibility is based on three statutory requirements.[49]

[49] §1361. Corporations that have been operating as regular corporations and that meet the eligibility requirements can be converted to S corporations. Converted S corporations are subject to several troublesome corporate level taxes that don't apply to original S corporations. See §1374 and §1375. In addition, an LLC which has "checked the box" to be treated as a corporation could also elect S status.

1. Only individuals, estates, certain trusts, and tax-exempt organizations may be shareholders, and nonresident aliens (persons who are neither citizens nor permanent residents of the United States) cannot be shareholders. This requirement ensures that the S corporation's income is taxed at the individual rates.

2. The number of shareholders is limited to 100. A family may elect for all family members to be treated as one shareholder.

3. The corporation can have only a single class of outstanding common stock; an S corporation cannot include preferred stock in its capital structure. Because of this requirement, shares of stock in an S corporation carry identical rights to corporate profits and assets. This requirement is not violated if the outstanding shares have different voting rights.

There are no statutory limits on an S corporation's invested capital, volume of sales, or number of employees. Consequently, S corporations can be very large corporate enterprises.

Subchapter S Election

An eligible corporation becomes an S corporation by the unanimous election of its shareholders.[50] The election is permanent for the life of the corporation unless shareholders owning a majority of the stock revoke the election.[51] The election is immediately terminated if the corporation loses its eligibility. For example, if a shareholder sells shares to a partnership (an ineligible shareholder), the election terminates as of the date of sale.[52] The corporation is no longer a passthrough entity and is subject to the corporate income tax.

The inadvertent termination of an S election can be a tax planning disaster for the shareholders. Moreover, they generally cannot make a new election for five years.[53] Because of the potential severity of the problem, the tax law provides a relief measure. If shareholders discover that an inadvertent termination has occurred and take immediate steps to correct the situation (repurchase the corporate stock from the partnership in our example), the IRS may allow the original S election to remain in effect.[54]

Shareholders of closely held corporations, including S corporations, often enter into shareholder agreements to prevent negative consequences associated with undesirable transfers of stock. Shareholder agreements may provide that the corporation, or other shareholders, has a right of first refusal if one shareholder wishes to dispose of his or her stock. Such an agreement could prevent a transfer to an ineligible shareholder, avoiding an inadvertent termination of the S corporation election.

Tax Basis in S Corporation Stock

A shareholder's initial tax basis in stock issued by an S corporation equals the cash plus the adjusted basis of any property transferred to the corporation in exchange for the stock.[55] When an S corporation incurs a debt, no shareholder has any personal liability. Accordingly, no S corporation debt is included in a shareholder's stock basis, even if the shareholder has guaranteed the debt.

---

[50] §1362(a). To document consent to the election, each shareholder must file a signed Form 2553 with the IRS.

[51] §1362(d)(1).

[52] §1362(e)(1).

[53] §1362(g).

[54] §1362(f).

[55] The transfer of property to a corporation in exchange for stock is nontaxable to the transferors if they have at least 80 percent control of the corporation immediately after the transfer. §351. See the discussion of corporate formations in Chapter 9.

Basis in S Corporation Stock	Three individuals each contributed $10,000 cash to form a new S corporation. Each individual received 100 shares of the 300 shares of outstanding stock. The S corporation immediately borrowed $24,000 from a local bank and used the money to purchase equipment and supplies. The bank required the shareholders to personally guarantee repayment of the loan. Each shareholder's basis in her S corporation stock is $10,000: the initial cash contribution to the corporation.

Tax Consequences to Shareholders

After the close of its taxable year, an S corporation issues a Schedule K-1 (Shareholder's Share of Income, Credits, Deductions, etc.) to each shareholder. The Schedule K-1 has the same function as a partnership Schedule K-1; it informs the owners of their **pro rata share** of business income or loss and any separately stated items.[56]

The S corporation shareholders must incorporate the information on Schedule K-1 into their individual tax returns. Thus, the corporate income is taxed at the individual rates, and the shareholders pay the tax. The cash (if any) that the shareholders received from the corporation is irrelevant in determining their taxable income.

Schedule K-1 for Shareholder	Each shareholder in Faux Antique received a 2011 Schedule K-1 showing a pro rata share of ordinary business income, dividend income, capital gain, donation, and cash distribution. Tom Owen's Schedule K-1, which reflects his 60 percent share of each corporate item, is shown as Exhibit 10.8. Mr. Owen reported his $182,940 share of Faux Antique's business income as ordinary income on his Form 1040. He reported his $1,008 share of dividend income as investment income and his $2,226 share of capital gain as capital gain on his Form 1040. He included his $1,800 share of Faux Antique's donation in his total personal charitable contributions for 2011. His $150,000 share of the cash distribution had no effect on his 2011 taxable income.

Salary Payments

A significant difference between partnerships and S corporations is that an owner (shareholder) can be an employee of the corporation. Shareholders who work in the corporate business receive salaries as compensation for their services. Both the corporation and the employee pay the FICA payroll tax on the salary, and the corporation withholds federal income tax. At the end of the year, the corporation issues a Schedule K-1 and a Form W-2 to any shareholder/employee. S corporation shareholders are not considered to be self-employed. Therefore, their share of corporate business income is not subject to self-employment tax.[57]

Payments to Shareholder/ Employees	Milo Todd owns 20 percent of the stock in Sussex Inc., a calendar year S corporation, and is employed as the corporation's CEO. This year, Milo's salary from Sussex was $75,000, from which Sussex withheld both employee FICA tax and state and local income tax. Sussex's ordinary business income (after deduction of all employee compensation) was $984,000, and Milo's share of this income was $196,800. Milo received a $160,000 cash distribution from Sussex with respect to his stock. Milo must include $271,800 ($75,000 salary + $196,800 share of corporate income) in taxable income. The $160,000 cash distribution has no effect on Milo's taxable income.

[56] As previously discussed, partners are taxed on their distributive share of partnership income. In contrast, S corporation shareholders are taxed on their pro rata share of S corporation income. This difference in terminology is not simply semantics. The partnership allocation rules provide for considerably more flexibility in determining income allocations than the S corporation rules.

[57] Rev. Rul. 59-221, 1959-1 CB 225.

EXHIBIT 10.8

671111

☐ Final K-1 ☐ Amended K-1	OMB No. 1545-0130

Schedule K-1 (Form 1120S)
Department of the Treasury
Internal Revenue Service

For calendar year 2011, or tax
year beginning _____, 2011
ending _____, 20 ____

2011

Shareholder's Share of Income, Deductions, Credits, etc. ► See back of form and separate instructions.

Part I — Information About the Corporation

A Corporation's employer identification number
81-1138419

B Corporation's name, address, city, state, and ZIP code

Faux Antiques
1012 East Main
Widener, NY 42714

C IRS Center where corporation filed return
Cincinnati

Part II — Information About the Shareholder

D Shareholder's identifying number
487-45-9058

E Shareholder's name, address, city, state, and ZIP code

Tom G. Owen
330 Aspen Lane
Widener, NY 42714

F Shareholder's percentage of stock
ownership for tax year . . . . _____ 60 %

For IRS Use Only

Part III — Shareholder's Share of Current Year Income, Deductions, Credits, and Other Items

1	Ordinary business income (loss) 182,940	13	Credits
2	Net rental real estate income (loss)		
3	Other net rental income (loss)		
4	Interest income		
5a	Ordinary dividends 1,008	14	Foreign transactions
5b	Qualified dividends 1,008		
6	Royalties		
7	Net short-term capital gain (loss)		
8a	Net long-term capital gain (loss) 2,226		
8b	Collectibles (28%) gain (loss)		
8c	Unrecaptured section 1250 gain		
9	Net section 1231 gain (loss)		
10	Other income (loss)	15	Alternative minimum tax (AMT) items
11	Section 179 deduction	16	Items affecting shareholder basis
12	Other deductions A donation_1,800		
		17	Other information D distribution_150,000

* See attached statement for additional information.

For Paperwork Reduction Act Notice, see Instructions for Form 1120S.   Cat. No. 11520D   Schedule K-1 (Form 1120S) 2011

Note that salary payments to S corporation shareholders are generally deductible in computing ordinary income from the business. Thus, a shareholder receiving a salary payment will report greater salary income and less ordinary income. While the net impact on the shareholder's taxable income may be zero, the payroll tax cost of the salary payment creates an incentive for S corporations to understate salary payable to shareholders. As a result, the IRS tends to carefully scrutinize salary payments to S corporation shareholders to ensure that adequate compensation (and adequate payroll tax) is paid given the shareholder's efforts.

Adequate Salary Payments to Shareholder/ Employees	Maxwell owns 100 percent of the stock of Golden Inc., a calendar year S corporation. Maxwell spends 60 hours a week working for the corporation. During 2012, Golden earned $200,000 of ordinary income, before any salary payments to Maxwell. If Maxwell is paid $100,000 of salary, the corporation will owe $7,650 employer payroll taxes on this income. Remaining corporate ordinary income, allocated and taxable to Maxwell, will be $92,350. Maxwell will pay $5,650 employee payroll tax on his salary income, and personal income tax on $192,350, his salary and income allocated from the S corporation. If Maxwell's marginal tax rate is 35 percent, his income tax on his salary and S corporation earnings is $67,323, and his total tax burden (payroll and income tax) related to his S corporation is $72,973. If Maxwell does not take a salary from Golden, he will report and pay tax on $200,000 total S corporation earnings, resulting in additional tax liability of only $70,000. However, if the IRS audits either Maxwell or Golden, it will likely assert that Maxwell should be reasonably compensated for his work on behalf of the corporation, and assess additional payroll tax liability on both the corporation and the shareholder.

Adjusting the Basis of S Corporation Stock

Shareholders make positive and negative adjustments to the basis in their S corporation stock in much the same way as partners adjust the basis in their partnership interests.[58] Specifically, shareholders increase the basis in their stock by their share of the corporation's income and gain for the year. Conversely, shareholders reduce the basis by their share of any corporate losses. Cash distributed by an S corporation to a shareholder is a nontaxable return of investment that reduces stock basis.[59] Recall, however, that the basis of S corporation stock does not reflect changes in entity debt.

Basis Limitation on Loss Deductions

Objective 8
Apply the basis limitation on the deduction of S corporation losses.

The tax law imposes the same limitation on S corporation losses as it does on partnership losses: Such losses are currently deductible only to the extent of the owner's investment. Under the limitation rule for S corporations, a shareholder can deduct an amount of loss that reduces his stock basis to zero.[60] If a shareholder also has basis in any debt obligation from the S corporation, the shareholder may deduct additional loss to reduce the debt basis to zero.[61] In other words, a shareholder's investment that can be recovered through tax deductions includes both his equity investment *and* his investment as a corporate creditor.

Nondeductible S Corporation Loss	Ms. Jentz owns 25 percent of the outstanding stock of SGM, a calendar year S corporation. At the beginning of 2010, Ms. Jentz's basis in her stock was $81,000. Several years ago, Ms. Jentz loaned $30,000 to SGM in return for its interest-bearing note. For 2011, SGM incurred a $500,000 operating loss. Although Ms. Jentz's Schedule K-1 reflects a $125,000 loss, Ms. Jentz can deduct only $111,000 of the loss on her Form 1040.

	Stock Basis	*Note Basis*
Beginning of year	$ 81,000	$30,000
Deductible loss	(81,000)	(30,000)
End of year	–0–	–0–
Nondeductible loss	$(14,000)	

---

[58] §1367(a).

[59] Salary payments to shareholder/employees have no effect on stock basis. If a shareholder receives a cash distribution that exceeds stock basis, the excess distribution is recognized as a capital gain. §1368.

[60] §1366(d)(1)(A).

[61] §1366(d)(1)(B).

Ms. Jentz's $14,000 nondeductible loss is carried forward into future years. If she creates basis by making an additional investment in SGM as either a shareholder or a creditor, she can deduct the loss to the extent of the additional basis. Alternatively, if SGM generates future income, Ms. Jentz's share of *undistributed* income will first increase the basis in her note to its $30,000 face amount and will then increase her stock basis.[62] Ms. Jentz can deduct her loss carryforward to the extent of her restored basis.

Basis Restoration	Ms. Jentz's 25 percent share of SGM's 2012 income is $50,000. The corporation made no cash distributions during the year. The undistributed income increases Ms. Jentz's investment basis and allows her to deduct the $14,000 loss carryforward from 2011 on her 2012 return.

	Stock Basis	Note Basis
Beginning of year	–0–	–0–
Share of income:		
Increase to note basis		$30,000
Increase to stock basis	$20,000	
	$20,000	$30,000
Loss carryforward	(14,000)	
End of year	$ 6,000	$30,000

Because of the deduction for her loss carryforward, Ms. Jentz's 2011 taxable income includes only $36,000 SGM income.

If SGM were to repay the $30,000 loan from Ms. Jentz before her basis in the note was restored to its face amount, the repayment is treated as an amount realized on sale of the note. Because the note is a capital asset to Ms. Jentz, she would recognize a capital gain equal to the excess of the repayment over her basis.[63]

Gain on Repayment of Debt	Change the facts in the previous example by assuming that SGM retired its debt to Ms. Jentz by paying her $30,000 (plus accrued interest) on June 30, 2012. Assume also that SGM distributed $50,000 cash to Ms. Jentz to match her $50,000 share of 2012 income. In this case, Ms. Jentz had no 2012 *undistributed* income to restore basis in either her SGM note or her SGM stock. Consequently, she must recognize a $30,000 long-term capital gain on repayment of the note and cannot deduct any of her 2011 loss carryforward.

Conclusion

In this chapter, we've examined the tax consequences of operating a business as a sole proprietorship or as a passthrough entity. In the case of a sole proprietorship, the business income is included in the owner's taxable income and taxed at the individual rates. In the case of a general or limited partnership, LLC, or S corporation, the business income is allocated to the owners of the entity. The income is taxed directly to the partners, members, or shareholders at their marginal rate. Many owners deliberately use these organizational forms to avoid paying an entity level tax on business income. This tax strategy is one of the topics covered in Chapter 11. Before we can evaluate this strategy, we must examine the tax consequences of operating a business as a regular corporation.

[62] §1367(b)(2).
[63] §1271(a)(1) and Rev. Rul. 64-162, 1964-1 CB 304.

Key Terms

distributive share   *284*

employee payroll tax   *276*

employer identification number   *276*

employer payroll tax   *276*

general partnership   *280*

guaranteed payment   *284*

limited liability company (LLC)   *290*

limited liability partnership (LLP)   *280*

limited partnership   *280*

partnership   *279*

passthrough entity   *281*

pro rata share   *295*

self-employment (SE) tax   *278*

separately stated item   *282*

sole proprietorship   *272*

subchapter S corporation   *291*

Questions and Problems for Discussion

1. Can a sole proprietorship be described as a passthrough entity?

2. Mrs. Liu owns a business as a sole proprietor. Near the end of her taxable year, she is evaluating a new opportunity that would generate $25,000 additional income for her business. What marginal tax rate should Mrs. Liu use to compute the tax cost of this opportunity?

3. This year, Mr. Pitt's sole proprietorship generated a $17,000 net loss. Can Mr. Pitt use this loss as an net operating loss carryback deduction?

4. This year, Firm Q, a cash basis taxpayer, remitted $26,800 FICA payroll tax to the federal government. However, the firm deducted only $13,400 FICA tax on its income tax return. Can you explain this apparent inconsistency?

5. Critique the employee payroll tax on the normative standards of convenience to the taxpayer and vertical equity.

6. Define the tax base for the self-employment tax. When do sole proprietors pay the self-employment tax to the federal government?

7. Why is only half of a sole proprietor's self-employment tax deductible in the computation of taxable income?

8. Tom, Angela, and Peter want to become co-owners of a business enterprise. Compare their personal liability for the debts incurred by the enterprise if they organize as:

   a. A general partnership.

   b. A limited partnership.

   c. An LLC.

   d. An S corporation.

9. Why are certain items of income, gain, deduction, or loss separately stated on a partnership or an S corporation tax return?

10. This year, Soya Partnership disposed of only one operating asset and recognized a $22,000 loss on the disposition. Why must Soya report this net Section 1231 loss as a separately stated item rather than deducting the loss in the computation of ordinary business income?

11. Mr. A and Mr. Z are both sole proprietors. This year, each proprietorship generated $85,000 net cash flow from business operations. Mr. A used the cash to expand his business, while Mr. Z used the cash to make the down payment on a new home for his family. Discuss how the different uses of cash affect each man's federal income tax for the year.

12. Four years ago, Mr. Bates purchased 1,000 shares of UPF Inc. for $10,000. These shares represent a 30 percent equity interest in UPF, which is an S corporation. This year, UPF defaulted on a $120,000 unsecured debt to a major creditor.

    a. To what extent can the creditor demand repayment of the debt from Mr. Bates?

    b. Would your answer change if UPF is a partnership in which Mr. Bates is a 30 percent general partner?

    c. Would your answer change if UPF is a partnership in which Mr. Bates is a 30 percent limited partner?

    d. Would your answer change if UPF is an LLC in which Mr. Bates is a 30 percent member?

13. Mr. Yang sold his interest in a business to an unrelated purchaser for $500,000 cash. How does Mr. Yang determine his adjusted basis for purposes of computing gain or loss realized on the sale if the business is:

    a. A sole proprietorship?

    b. A partnership?

    c. An S corporation?

14. Corporation ABC sold its interest in KK Partnership on October 9 for $150,000. KK Partnership uses a calendar year for tax purposes. Explain the reason why Corporation ABC cannot compute gain or loss realized on the date that the sale occurs.

Application Problems

1. James Jones is the owner of a small retail business operated as a sole proprietorship. During 2011, his business recorded the following items of income and expense:

Revenue from inventory sales	$147,000
Cost of goods sold	33,500
Business license tax	2,400
Rent on retail space	42,000
Supplies	15,000
Wages paid to employees	22,000
Payroll taxes	1,700
Utilities	3,600

    a. Compute taxable income attributable to the sole proprietorship by completing Schedule C to be included in James's 2011 Form 1040.

    b. Compute self-employment tax payable on the earnings of James's sole proprietorship by completing a 2011 Schedule SE, Form 1040.

2. Rhea is a self-employed professional singer. She resides in a rented apartment and uses one room exclusively as a business office. This room includes 225 of the 1,500 square feet of living space in the apartment. Rhea performs in recording studios and concert halls, but she conducts all of the administrative duties with respect to the business in her home office. This year, Rhea's apartment rent was $48,000. She paid $5,200 to a housekeeping service that cleaned the entire apartment once a week and $2,000 for renter's insurance on the apartment furnishings. Compute Rhea's home office deduction assuming that:

    a. Her net profit before the deduction was $300,000.

    b. Her net profit before the deduction was $4,000.

3. Colin, a self-employed consultant, uses a room of his home as a business office. This room represents 10 percent of the home's square footage. This year, Colin incurred the following expenses in connection with his home.

Home mortgage interest	$12,980
Property tax on residence	2,200
Homeowner's insurance	1,475
Utilities	2,100
Furnace repairs	300

Colin purchased the home in 2000 for $225,000. For MACRS depreciation purposes, he allocated $185,000 to the building and $40,000 to the land.

   a. If Colin's gross business income exceeded his operating expenses by $75,000, compute his net profit for the year.

   b. If Colin's gross business income exceeded his operating expenses by $1,800, compute his net profit for the year.

4. Mr. Williams is employed by BDF Inc. Compute BDF's 2012 employer payroll tax with respect to Mr. Williams assuming that:

   a. His annual compensation is $60,000.

   b. His annual compensation is $200,000.

5. Refer to the facts in the preceding problem. Assume that in the year 2013, the Social Security base amount increases to $112,000. Compute BDF's 2013 employer payroll tax with respect to Mr. Williams assuming that:

   a. His annual compensation is $60,000.

   b. His annual compensation is $200,000.

6. Mrs. Singer owns a profitable sole proprietorship. For each of the following cases, use a Schedule SE, Form 1040, to compute her 2011 self-employment tax and her income tax deduction for such tax.

   a. Mrs. Singer's net profit from Schedule C was $51,458. She had no other earned income.

   b. Mrs. Singer's net profit from Schedule C was $51,458, and she received a $70,000 salary from an employer.

   c. Mrs. Singer's net profit from Schedule C was $12,685, and she received a $110,000 salary from an employer.

7. In 2012, Wilma Way's sole proprietorship, WW Bookstore, generated $120,000 net profit. In addition, Wilma recognized a $17,000 gain on the sale of business furniture and shelving, all of which was recaptured as ordinary income. The business checking account earned $960 interest income.

   a. Which of these income items are subject to self-employment tax?

   b. Compute Wilma's 2012 self-employment tax.

   c. Compute Wilma's 2012 taxable income from her bookstore activity.

8. JC recently graduated from veterinary school and opened her own professional practice. This year, her net profit was $32,000. Compute JC's after-tax income from her practice assuming:

   a. Her self-employment tax is $4,522, and her marginal income tax rate is 25 percent.

   b. What percentage of the federal tax burden on JC's business income is represented by the self-employment tax?

9. Jane is a self-employed attorney. This year, her net profit exceeded $250,000, which put her in the 35 percent tax bracket. Early in the year, Jane hired Ben as a paralegal and paid him a $33,000 salary.

   a. Compute the employer payroll tax on Ben's salary.

   b. In addition to the employer payroll tax, Jane paid $400 unemployment tax on Ben's salary. The salary and tax expense reduced Jane's net earnings from self-employment, thereby saving $962 in self-employment tax. Compute Jane's after-tax cost of hiring Ben.

10. AB Corporation and YZ Corporation formed a partnership to construct a shopping mall. AB contributed $500,000 cash and YZ contributed land ($500,000 FMV and $430,000 basis) in exchange for a 50 percent interest in ABYZ Partnership. Immediately after its formation, ABYZ borrowed $250,000 from a local bank. The debt is recourse (unsecured by any specific partnership asset). Compute each partner's initial basis in its partnership interest, assuming that:

   a. AB and YX are both general partners.

   b. AB is a general partner, and YZ is a limited partner.

11. This year, FGH Partnership generated $600,000 ordinary business income. FGH has two equal partners: Triad LLC and Beta, an S corporation. Triad LLC has three members: Mr. T, who owns a 40 percent interest; Mrs. U, who owns a 35 percent interest; and V Inc., which owns a 25 percent interest. Beta has 100 shares of outstanding stock, all of which are owned by Ms. B. Identify the taxpayers who must pay tax on the partnership income and determine how much income must be reported by each.

12. Rochelle is a partner in Megawatt Partnership. For 2011, her schedule K-1 from the partnership reported the following share of partnership items.

Ordinary income	$25,000
Section 1231 loss	(3,000)
Nondeductible expense	1,000
Cash distribution	5,000

   a. Describe the impact of each of the above items on Rochelle's 2011 taxable income.

   b. Assume that Rochelle's marginal tax rate is 35 percent. Calculate her 2011 after-tax cash flow as a result of her interest in Megawatt.

13. KLMN Partnership's financial records show the following.

Gross receipts from sales	$670,000
Cost of goods sold	(460,000)
Operating expenses	(96,800)
Business meals and entertainment	(6,240)
Section 1231 loss on equipment sale	(13,500)
Charitable contribution	(1,500)
Distributions to partners	(10,000)

   Compute KLMN's ordinary business income for the year.

14. Refer to the facts in the preceding problem. Mr. T is a 10 percent general partner in KLMN. During the year, he received a $1,000 cash distribution from KLMN.

   a. Compute Mr. T's share of partnership ordinary income and separately stated items.

   b. If Mr. T's adjusted basis in his KLMN interest was $45,000 at the beginning of the year, compute his adjusted basis at the end of the year. Assume that KLMN's debt did not change during the year.

   c. How would your basis computation change if KLMN's debt at the end of the year was $28,000 more than its debt at the beginning of the year?

15. Jayanthi and Krish each own a 50 percent general partner interest in the JK Partnership. The following information is available regarding the partnership's 2011 activities.

Sales revenue	$500,000
Selling expenses	200,000
Depreciation expense	30,000
Long-term capital gain	9,000
Nondeductible expenses	2,000
Partnership debts, beginning of the year	100,000
Partnership debts, end of the year	120,000
Partnership distributions	
Jayanthi	50,000
Krish	50,000

a. Calculate the partnership's ordinary (nonseparately stated) income and indicate which items must be separately stated.

b. Calculate Jayanthi's allocable share of partnership items.

c. If Jayanthi has no other sources of taxable income, what is her total gross income for 2011?

d. At the beginning of the year, Jayanthi's adjusted tax basis in her partnership interest was $25,000. Calculate her ending adjusted tax basis in her partnership interest.

16. Refer to the facts in the preceding problem.

a. Complete Schedule K, Form 1065, for the partnership.

b. Complete Schedule K-1, Form 1065, for Jayanthi.

17. This year, individual X and individual Y formed XY Partnership. X contributed $50,000 cash, and Y contributed business assets with a $50,000 FMV. Y's adjusted basis in these assets was only $10,000. The partnership agreement provides that income and loss will be divided equally between the two partners. Partnership operations for the year generated a $42,000 loss. How much loss may each partner deduct currently, and what basis will each partner have in her interest at the beginning of next year?

18. AV Inc. is a member of an LLC. This year, AV received a Schedule K-1 reporting a $1,200 share of capital loss and a $4,000 share of Section 1231 gain. During the year, AV recognized a $5,000 capital loss on the sale of marketable securities and a $17,000 Section 1231 loss on the sale of business equipment. What effect do the LLC losses have on AV's taxable income?

19. Bonnie and George are equal general partners in BG Partnership. Bonnie receives a $4,000 monthly guaranteed payment for services. This year, BG generated $95,000 profit (before consideration of Bonnie's guaranteed payments).

a. Compute each partner's distributive share of ordinary business income.

b. Compute each partner's self-employment income.

c. How would your answers change if BG's profit was only $32,000 instead of $95,000?

20. Zelda owns a 60 percent general interest in YZ Partnership. At the beginning of 2011, the adjusted basis in her YZ interest was $95,000. For 2011, YZ generated a $210,000 business loss, earned $14,600 dividend and interest income on its investments, and recognized a $6,200 capital gain. YZ made no distributions to its partners and had no debt.

a. How much of her share of YZ's loss can Zelda deduct on her 2011 return?

b. Compute Zelda's adjusted basis in her YZ interest at the end of 2011.

c. Would your answers change if Zelda received a $5,000 cash distribution from YZ during 2011?

21. Refer to the facts in the preceding problem. In 2012, YZ generated $7,000 ordinary business income and $18,000 dividend and interest income. The partnership made no distributions. At the end of the year, YZ had $21,000 debt.

    a. How much partnership income will Zelda report on her 2012 return?

    b. Compute Zelda's adjusted basis in her YZ interest at the end of 2012.

22. At the beginning of 2012, Ms. P purchased a 20 percent interest in PPY Partnership for $20,000. Ms. P's Schedule K-1 reported that her share of PPY's debt at year-end was $12,000 and her share of ordinary loss was $28,000. On January 1, 2013, Ms. P sold her interest to another partner for $2,000 cash.

    a. How much of her share of PPY's loss can Ms. P deduct on her 2012 return?

    b. Compute Ms. P's recognized gain on sale of her PPY interest.

23. On January 1, 2010, Leo paid $15,000 for 5 percent of the stock in BLS, an S corporation. In November, he loaned $8,000 to BLS in return for a promissory note. BLS generated a $600,000 operating loss in 2010.

    a. How much of his share of the loss can Leo deduct on his 2010 return?

    b. Compute Leo's basis in his BLS stock and his BLS note at the end of 2010.

24. Refer to the facts in the preceding example. BLS generated $408,000 ordinary business income in 2011.

    a. How much of Leo's share of this income is included in his 2011 taxable income?

    b. Compute Leo's basis in his BLS stock and his BLS note at the end of 2011.

    c. How would your answers change if BLS's ordinary business income was only $220,000?

25. Refer to the facts in part *c* of the preceding problem. In 2012, BLS repaid its $8,000 debt to Leo before he restored any basis in the debt. What are the consequences of the loan repayment to Leo?

26. Evan is the sole shareholder of Magic Roofing Company, a calendar year S corporation. Although Evan spends at least 30 hours per week supervising Magic's employees, he has never drawn a salary from Magic. Magic has been in existence for five years and has earned a profit every year. Evan withdraws $50,000 of cash from the S corporation each year.

    a. Explain the tax consequences of Evan's cash withdrawals from the S corporation and their impact on Evan's taxable income and Magic's ordinary income.

    b. An IRS agent has just begun examining the last three years (2008, 2009, and 2010) of tax returns filed by Evan and Magic. He has questioned whether the $50,000 withdrawals should be characterized as salary payments to Evan instead of shareholder distributions. What are the income tax consequences to Evan and Magic if these distributions are characterized as salary payments?

    c. What are the payroll tax consequences to Evan and Magic if the distributions are characterized as salary payments? Calculate the total potential underpayment of both employee and employer payroll tax that could result from this audit.

Issue Recognition Problems

Identify the tax issue or issues suggested by the following situations and state each issue in the form of a question.

1. Ellie has operated a sole proprietorship for six years during which net profit has been stable and Ellie's marginal tax rate has been a constant 25 percent. Ellie projects that her profit next year will be the same as this year. Consequently, she estimates her tax cost

for next year based on a 25 percent rate. Late in the year, Ellie's husband graduated from law school and accepted an excellent offer of employment from a local firm.

2. Javier is a full-time employee of B Inc. and also operates a sole proprietorship. This year, his salary was $70,000, and his net earnings from self-employment were $60,000.

3. Mr. and Mrs. Chou file a joint income tax return. Mr. Chou reports the income from his full-time landscaping business on a Schedule C, which lists him as the sole proprietor. He also reports 100 percent of the net profit as his self-employment income and pays SE tax accordingly. During the last several years, Mrs. Chou has worked at least 20 hours per week in her husband's business. However, Mr. Chou does not pay her any salary or wage for her services.

4. Travis is a professional writer who maintains his business office in one room of his personal residence. The office contains Travis's desk, filing cabinets, personal computer and printer, copying machine, phone system, and fax machine. It also contains his family's library of videotapes, music CDs, popular novels, and the set of encyclopedias used by his three children for their schoolwork.

5. Lola owns a 15 percent limited interest in AF Partnership, which uses a calendar year for tax purposes. On April 12, Lola sold her entire interest to the R Corporation; consequently, she was a partner for only 102 days during the year. AF generated $845,000 ordinary business income this year and recognized a $70,000 capital gain on the November 13 sale of marketable securities.

6. Nine years ago, Fred paid $20,000 cash for a 2 percent limited interest in a very profitable partnership. Every year Fred has properly included his distributive share of partnership income in taxable income. This year, Fred sold his interest to an unrelated party for $80,000 and computed a $60,000 gain recognized on sale.

7. The 18 partners in KT Limited Partnership unanimously voted to convert their partnership to an LLC. To make the conversion, each partner will exchange his interest in KT for a membership interest in the newly formed LLC.

8. Four individuals are evaluating the tax cost of operating their business as an S corporation. They assume that the corporation will pay no tax on its annual business income. They plan to incorporate the business in a state with a 7 percent corporate income tax.

9. Mr. Yang just sold his entire 20 percent interest in DK Partnership to an unrelated purchaser for $7,500. Mr. Yang's adjusted basis in the interest was zero, and he had a $12,000 carryforward of DK loss.

10. Paula's Schedule K-1 from an LLC reported a $12,000 share of ordinary loss and a $1,900 share of capital loss. Paula's adjusted basis in her LLC interest before consideration of these losses was $6,200.

11. Marcus, a cash basis individual, is a general partner in MNOP Partnership. Both Marcus and MNOP use a calendar year for tax purposes. According to the partnership agreement, MNOP pays a $10,000 guaranteed payment to Marcus on the last day of every calendar month. However, because of a bookkeeping error, the partnership did not pay (and Marcus did not receive) his final guaranteed payment for 2009 until January 10, 2010.

12. David's Schedule K-1 from DES, an S corporation, reported $8,900 tax-exempt interest and $4,700 ordinary loss. David's adjusted basis in his stock before consideration of these items was $2,000.

13. Mr. and Mrs. West are the only shareholders in WW, an S corporation. This year, WW paid $21,000 to the caterers who provided food for the couple's silver wedding anniversary celebration.

14. The 100 shares of NS's outstanding stock are owned by seven unrelated individuals. NS has an S corporation election in effect. Late in the year, one individual announces to his fellow shareholders that he intends to give his NS shares to his son-in-law, who is a citizen and resident of Canada.

15. BR Inc. owns a 20 percent interest in a limited partnership. All the other partners are individual shareholders in BR. This year, BR sold land to the partnership for use in the partnership's business activity. BR's basis in the land was $400,000, and the selling price was $275,000. This price was determined by an independent appraiser.

16. JKL Partnership uses the calendar year for tax purposes. For 2009, the partnership generated $1 million ordinary business income. Corporation L, a 10 percent limited partner in JKL, uses a fiscal year ending June 30 as its tax year.

17. FG Inc. owned a 3 percent limited interest in a partnership that has been unprofitable for several years. The partnership recently informed its partners that they must contribute additional capital if the partnership is to survive. FG decided not to contribute any more money and sent written notification to the general partner relinquishing its equity interest. On the date of notification, FG's adjusted basis in the interest was $15,500.

Research Problems

1. Don Ferris and Lou Lindberg are the two partners in F&L Partnership. The partnership agreement provides that all income is allocated equally between Don and Lou but in no case shall the allocation to Don be less than $75,000 per year. (In other words, Don has a minimum guarantee of $75,000.) This year, F&L generated $107,200 net profit. Compute F&L's taxable income for the year and each partner's distributive share of that income.

2. Max Coen is employed as a full-time police officer by the Memphis Police Department. He is required to abide by the Department's rules of conduct, which apply whether he is on-duty or off-duty. With the Department's permission, Max "moonlights" as a security guard for several public school districts. While serving as a security guard, he is required to wear his police uniform and to carry police equipment (gun, handcuffs, etc.). The school districts pay security guards on an hourly basis and do not withhold income tax or payroll tax. This year, Max earned a $32,000 salary from the city of Memphis and $8,100 wages from the school districts. Do Max's wages constitute net earnings from self-employment on which he must pay SE tax?

3. Herold had been a calendar year S corporation since 1990. On October 10, 2011, Mrs. Hughes sold 18 shares of Herold stock to a foreign partnership, thereby terminating Herold's S election. Herold's taxable income for the entire 2011 calendar year was $592,030. Describe the federal tax returns that Herold must file for 2011, determine how much income must be reported on each, and compute any corporate income tax that Herold must pay.

4. At the beginning of 2011, Sandy Brewer had a zero basis in her 38 shares of stock in Lindlee, an S corporation, a zero basis in a $5,000 note from Lindlee, and a $7,400 carryforward of a 2010 ordinary loss from Lindlee that she was unable to deduct because of the basis limitation. Early in February 2011, Sandy was notified by Lindlee's attorney that the corporation was bankrupt. Consequently, Lindlee was defaulting on its $5,000 debt to Sandy, and Sandy's 38 shares of stock were worthless. Describe the consequences to Sandy of the worthlessness of her Lindlee investments.

Tax Planning Cases

1. Mr. and Mrs. Janus operate a restaurant business as a sole proprietorship. The couple has decided to purchase $85,000 of new kitchen equipment for the restaurant. They also want to buy two new automobiles—one for their personal use and one for

their 19-year-old son's personal use. The two automobiles will cost $65,000. Mr. and Mrs. Janus have $70,000 in a savings account that they can use to partially fund these purchases. They intend to borrow the additional $80,000 from a local bank at 7 percent annual interest. What steps should the couple take to minimize the after-tax cost of the borrowed funds?

2. On March 1, 2011, Eve and Frank each contributed $30,000 cash to the newly formed EF Partnership in exchange for a 50 percent general interest. The partnership immediately borrowed $50,000 from an unrelated creditor, a debt that it does not have to repay for two years. In November, the partners estimate with reasonable certainty that EF's 2011 operating loss will be $100,000. However, EF's business has started to generate positive cash flow, and the partners also estimate that EF will be profitable in 2012, perhaps generating as much as $125,000 ordinary income. In anticipation of these future profits, Eve and Frank are considering withdrawing their initial cash contributions from EF before Christmas. Eve and Frank are both in the 35 percent tax bracket. What tax planning advice can you offer the partners?

3. In the current year (year 0), Amisha became a shareholder in Sultan Inc., a calendar year S corporation, by contributing $15,000 cash in exchange for stock. Shortly before the end of the year, Sultan's CFO notified Amisha that her pro rata share of ordinary loss for the year would be $55,000. Amisha immediately loaned $40,000 to Sultan in exchange for a two-year, interest-bearing corporate note. Consequently, she had enough stock and debt basis to allow her to deduct the $55,000 loss on her current year return.

   Compute the NPV of Amisha's cash flow *associated with her loan* in the following three cases. In each case, assume she has a 35 percent marginal tax rate on ordinary income, a 15 percent rate on capital gains, and uses a 6 percent discount rate.

   a. For the next two years (years 1 and 2), Amisha's share of Sultan's ordinary income totaled $49,000, and Sultan did not distribute any cash to its shareholders. However, it did repay the $40,000 loan plus $3,800 interest in year 2.

   b. For the next two years (years 1 and 2), Amisha's share of Sultan's ordinary income totaled $19,100, and Sultan did not distribute any cash to its shareholders. However, it did repay the $40,000 loan plus $3,800 interest in year 2.

   c. For the next two years (years 1 and 2), Amisha's share of Sultan's ordinary loss totaled $11,400. In year 2, the corporation declared bankruptcy and defaulted on all its debts, including the loan from Amisha.

4. Marla recently inherited $50,000 and is considering two alternatives for investing these funds. Investment A is stock of a C corporation, expected to pay annual dividends of 8 percent. Investment B is stock of an S corporation. Based on income projections, Marla's share of the S corporation's ordinary income would be approximately $10,000 per year. However, the S corporation does not expect to make any cash distributions for the foreseeable future. Marla would hold either investment for three years, at which time she believes the C corporation stock could be sold for $60,000 and the S corporation stock could be sold for $90,000.

   Assume that the initial investment would be made in year 0, dividends on the C corporation stock would be received in years 1, 2, and 3, S corporation earnings would be allocated in years 1, 2, and 3, and either investment would be sold in year 3. Also assume that Marla's marginal tax rate on ordinary income is 35 percent. Using a 4 percent discount rate, calculate the net present value of after-tax cash flows attributable to either investment and make a recommendation to Marla regarding which investment she should choose.

CPA REVIEW

CPA Exam Simulation

Please visit the text website for the online CPA simulation: mhhe.com/sjones2013.

Miller, Smith and Tucker decided to form a partnership to perform engineering services. The new entity, MST Consulting Services, LLP, began operations on January 1, year 1, and uses the calendar year for reporting purposes. The partners expect to work full time for MST, and each contributed cash and other property to the partnership sufficient to commence operations.

Topics covered in the simulation:

- Basis of contributed property
- Depreciation of contributed property

Chapter **Eleven**

The Corporate Taxpayer

Learning Objectives

After studying this chapter, you should be able to:

1. Identify the four primary legal characteristics of corporations.

2. Compute the corporate dividends-received deduction.

3. Prepare a reconciliation of book and taxable income.

4. Compute the regular tax on corporate taxable income.

5. Discuss the purpose of the corporate alternative minimum tax.

6. Describe the corporate tax payment and return filing requirements.

7. Explain why corporate profits distributed as dividends are double-taxed.

8. Discuss the incidence of the corporate income tax.

In the previous chapter, we studied business organizations that are not taxable entities: sole proprietorships, partnerships, limited liability companies (LLCs), and S corporations. These organizations are conduits of business income to the owners who are taxed directly on such income. In Chapter 11, we turn to the rules governing the taxation of business income earned by corporations.[1] In contrast to sole proprietorships and passthrough entities, corporations are taxpayers in their own right. The tax on corporate profits is determined without reference to the tax situations of the shareholders who own the corporation.

Chapter 11 begins with a discussion of the legal characteristics of corporations. The discussion then shifts to the computation of corporate taxable income and the reconciliation of that income with financial statement income. The corporate tax rate structure is examined, the function of tax credits is explained, and the corporate alternative minimum tax is introduced. The chapter concludes by analyzing the tax consequences of distributions of earnings to corporate investors.

---

[1] Corporations for which a subchapter S election is not in effect are referred to as regular corporations or C corporations. In this text, any reference to a corporation means the taxable, rather than the passthrough, variety.

LEGAL CHARACTERISTICS OF CORPORATIONS

Objective 1
Identify the four primary legal characteristics of corporations.

A corporation is an entity formed under state law to conduct a business enterprise. Ownership of the entity is represented by the outstanding shares of corporate stock. **Closely held corporations** are privately owned by a relatively small number of shareholders. These shareholders are often personally involved in the operation of the corporate business, and their ownership is stable over time. In contrast, the stock in **publicly held corporations** is traded on established securities markets such as the New York Stock Exchange or Nasdaq. The ownership of these corporations may be diffused over thousands of shareholders and may change on a daily basis.

Many entrepreneurs operate in the corporate form because of the advantageous legal and financial characteristics. One important legal characteristic is the **limited liability** of shareholders. The rights of corporate creditors and other claimants extend only to corporate assets and not to the personal assets of the corporation's owners. While this characteristic protects shareholders against many types of business risk, the scope of the protection is narrowed by two facts. First, financial institutions may refuse to lend money to closely held corporate businesses unless the shareholders personally guarantee repayment of the debt. Second, licensed professionals, such as physicians, attorneys, and CPAs, cannot avoid personal liability for their negligence or misconduct by operating in the corporate form. Even if they offer their services to the public as employees of a personal service corporation, professionals typically must protect themselves by carrying personal malpractice insurance.

Tax Talk
For 2010, the corporate income tax accounted for nearly 12 percent of gross federal tax collections and only 1 percent of returns filed with the IRS.

A second attractive characteristic is the **unlimited life** of a corporation. Under state and federal law, corporations are persons separate and distinct from their owners. Consequently, their legal existence is not affected by changes in the identity of their shareholders. This characteristic gives corporations the vitality and stability so conducive to a successful enterprise. A related characteristic is the **free transferability** of equity interests in corporations. Stock in publicly held corporations is a highly liquid asset; investors can buy and sell this stock with maximum convenience and minimal transaction cost in a regulated market. As a result, publicly held corporations have access to millions of potential investors and can raise large amounts of venture capital.

In the context of closely held corporations, the characteristic of free transferability may be conspicuously absent. Shareholders are often family members or colleagues who want to protect the ownership of the business from outsiders. To this end, the stock in closely held corporations is usually subject to some type of **buy-sell agreement.** The agreement may prohibit the owner from disposing of the stock without approval of the other shareholders, or it may restrict the owner from transferring the stock to anyone but the existing shareholders or the corporation itself.

A fourth corporate characteristic is **centralized management.** Unlike a sole proprietorship or a general partnership, a corporation is not directly managed by its owners. Instead, managerial decisions are made by a board of directors appointed by and acting on behalf of the shareholders and by the officers who are hired by the board of directors. This characteristic is crucial to the efficient management of publicly held corporations with thousands of shareholders. In contrast, the shareholders of closely held corporations usually serve on the board of directors and are employed as corporate officers. In such case, the characteristic of centralized management has little significance.

Affiliated Groups

For various legal, financial, and managerial reasons, a single corporate entity may not be the best organizational form for a multifaceted enterprise. The enterprise may operate more efficiently if it is compartmentalized into several corporate entities that form an **affiliated group.** Affiliated groups consist of a parent corporation that directly owns 80 percent or more of at least one subsidiary corporation plus all other subsidiaries that are 80 percent owned within the group.[2] Only taxable, domestic corporations are included in an affiliated group. The following diagram illustrates an affiliated group consisting of four corporations.

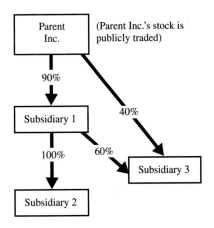

Parent Inc. is the parent corporation of the affiliated group because of its direct 90 percent ownership of Subsidiary 1. Subsidiaries 2 and 3 are also included in the group because 100 percent of each corporation's outstanding stock is owned within the group.

An affiliated group may consist of just two corporations or a conglomerate with hundreds of subsidiaries. Regardless of an affiliated group's size, the tax law treats it as one entity. For instance, an affiliated group may elect to file a **consolidated tax return**—one return reporting the combined results of the operations of all corporations in the group.[3] The major advantage of consolidated filing is that a net loss generated by one corporate member can offset the taxable income generated by other members.

Consolidated Return Filing

Refer to the affiliated group illustrated in the above diagram. This year, the separate operations of the group members resulted in the following.

	Net Income (Loss)
Parent Inc.	$960,000
Subsidiary 1	(750,000)
Subsidiary 2	225,000
Subsidiary 3	114,000

If the corporations file on a separate basis, Parent Inc., Subsidiary 2, and Subsidiary 3 report their incomes on their respective tax returns and Subsidiary 1 reports a $750,000 net operating loss on its tax return. This loss would generate an immediate tax benefit only to the extent that Subsidiary 1 could deduct it as an NOL carryback. If the group files a consolidated return, the taxable income on the return is $549,000 (combined net income and loss for the four members). Consequently, Subsidiary 1's loss generates an immediate tax benefit by reducing the affiliated group's taxable income by $750,000.

---

[2] §1504(a)(1).

[3] §1501.

Nonprofit Corporations

Many corporations are formed to conduct philanthropic, rather than profit-motivated, activities. As a general rule, these **nonprofit corporations** are nontaxable entities. Specifically, any corporation formed exclusively for "religious, charitable, scientific, testing for public safety, literary, or educational purposes, or to foster national or international amateur sports competition" is exempt from federal income taxation.[4] The IRS is generous in granting tax-exempt status to thousands of organizations devoted to some aspect of the public good. Nonetheless, a tax-exempt corporation that conducts a profitable sideline activity unrelated to its philanthropic purpose may find itself liable for the corporate tax on unrelated business taxable income.[5]

Unrelated Business Taxable Income	Phi Delta Theta is a national fraternity organized as a tax-exempt corporation. The fraternity published a quarterly magazine, *The Scroll,* that featured articles concerning the achievements of fraternity members and alumni. The publication costs were paid from the earnings from an endowment fund which generated over $100,000 annual investment income. The IRS determined that publication of *The Scroll* was incidental to the educational purpose that justified Phi Delta Theta's tax-exempt status. Consequently, the annual income from the endowment fund was unrelated business income on which the fraternity must pay tax.[6]

COMPUTING CORPORATE TAXABLE INCOME

Corporations report their taxable income and calculate the federal tax on that income on Form 1120 (U.S. Corporation Income Tax Return). The information on page 1, Form 1120, is essentially the corporation's income statement for tax accounting purposes.

Form 1120	Movement Plus Inc., a calendar year, accrual basis corporation, operates aerobics and dance studios. The first page of Movement Plus's Form 1120 is reproduced as Exhibit 11.1. The corporation recognized $834,390 gross profit from fees and memberships (lines 1c and 3) and $1,410 interest income from short-term investments of excess working capital (line 5). These two items represent Movement Plus's total income of $835,800 on line 11. The corporation's deductible operating expenses are listed on lines 12 through 26 and totaled to $510,860 on line 27. Movement Plus had a $6,700 NOL carryforward reported as a deduction on line 29c. The corporation's $318,240 taxable income is reported on line 30.

As discussed in Chapter 6, taxable income equals gross income minus allowable deductions. The rules discussed in Chapters 6 through 9, for determining gross income, ordinary and necessary business deductions, cost recovery deductions, and the tax treatment of property transactions, apply in determining corporate taxable income. In addition, a number of

[4] §501(a) and (c)(3).

[5] §511 and §512.

[6] *Phi Delta Theta Fraternity* v. *Commissioner,* 887 F.2d 1302 (CA-6, 1989).

EXHIBIT 11.1

Form **1120**

Department of the Treasury
Internal Revenue Service

U.S. Corporation Income Tax Return

For calendar year 2011 or tax year beginning _____, 2011, ending _____, 20 ____

▶ See separate instructions.

2011

A Check if:			
1a Consolidated return (attach Form 851)	☐		
b Life/nonlife consolidated return	☐	TYPE OR PRINT	
2 Personal holding co. (attach Sch. PH)	☐		
3 Personal service corp. (see instructions)	☐		
4 Schedule M-3 attached	☐		

Name: Movement Plus Inc.

Number, street, and room or suite no. If a P.O. box, see instructions.
4800 Sun Valley Road

City or town, state, and ZIP code
Albuquerque, NM 87121

B Employer identification number
28-4288317

C Date incorporated
August, 15, 1998

D Total assets (see instructions)
$ 642,212

E Check if: (1) ☐ Initial return   (2) ☐ Final return   (3) ☐ Name change   (4) ☐ Address change

Income	1a	Merchant card and third-party payments. For 2011, enter -0-	1a	
	b	Gross receipts or sales not reported on line 1a (see instructions)	1b	834,390
	c	Total. Add lines 1a and 1b	1c	834,390
	d	Returns and allowances plus any other adjustments (see instructions)	1d	
	e	Subtract line 1d from line 1c	1e	834,390
	2	Cost of goods sold from Form 1125-A, line 8 (attach Form 1125-A)	2	
	3	Gross profit. Subtract line 2 from line 1e	3	834,390
	4	Dividends (Schedule C, line 19)	4	
	5	Interest	5	1,410
	6	Gross rents	6	
	7	Gross royalties	7	
	8	Capital gain net income (attach Schedule D (Form 1120))	8	
	9	Net gain or (loss) from Form 4797, Part II, line 17 (attach Form 4797)	9	
	10	Other income (see instructions—attach schedule)	10	
	11	**Total income. Add lines 3 through 10**	11	835,800
Deductions (See instructions for limitations on deductions.)	12	Compensation of officers from Form 1125-E, line 4 (attach Form 1125-E)	12	40,000
	13	Salaries and wages (less employment credits)	13	255,100
	14	Repairs and maintenance	14	16,900
	15	Bad debts	15	
	16	Rents	16	43,300
	17	Taxes and licenses	17	24,750
	18	Interest	18	
	19	Charitable contributions	19	35,350
	20	Depreciation from Form 4562 not claimed on Form 1125-A or elsewhere on return (attach Form 4562)	20	42,600
	21	Depletion	21	
	22	Advertising	22	12,200
	23	Pension, profit-sharing, etc., plans	23	
	24	Employee benefit programs	24	
	25	Domestic production activities deduction (attach Form 8903)	25	
	26	Other deductions (attach schedule)	26	40,650
	27	**Total deductions. Add lines 12 through 26**	27	510,860
	28	Taxable income before net operating loss deduction and special deductions. Subtract line 27 from line 11	28	324,940
	29a	Net operating loss deduction (see instructions)	29a	6,700
	b	Special deductions (Schedule C, line 20)	29b	
	c	Add lines 29a and 29b	29c	6,700
Tax, Refundable Credits, and Payments	30	**Taxable income.** Subtract line 29c from line 28 (see instructions)	30	318,240
	31	Total tax (Schedule J, Part I, line 11)	31	107,364
	32	Total payments and refundable credits (Schedule J, Part II, line 21)	32	
	33	Estimated tax penalty (see instructions). Check if Form 2220 is attached ▶ ☐	33	110,000
	34	**Amount owed.** If line 32 is smaller than the total of lines 31 and 33, enter amount owed	34	
	35	**Overpayment.** If line 32 is larger than the total of lines 31 and 33, enter amount overpaid	35	2,636
	36	Enter amount from line 35 you want: **Credited to 2012 estimated tax** ▶ _____ Refunded ▶	36	2,636

Sign Here

Under penalties of perjury, I declare that I have examined this return, including accompanying schedules and statements, and to the best of my knowledge and belief, it is true, correct, and complete. Declaration of preparer (other than taxpayer) is based on all information of which preparer has any knowledge.

▶ Signature of officer _____ Date _____   ▶ Title _____

May the IRS discuss this return with the preparer shown below (see instructions)? ☐ Yes ☐ No

Paid Preparer Use Only

Print/Type preparer's name	Preparer's signature	Date	Check ☐ if self-employed	PTIN

Firm's name ▶ _____   Firm's EIN ▶ _____

Firm's address ▶ _____   Phone no. _____

For Paperwork Reduction Act Notice, see separate instructions.   Cat. No. 11450Q   Form **1120** (2011)

Tax Talk

Recent IRS statistics indicate approximately 2.5 million Form 1120 corporate income tax returns are filed each year.

special rules apply only to corporate taxpayers. Two such special rules are the limitation on deductibility of corporate charitable contributions and the dividends-received deduction.

Corporations are allowed a deduction for charitable contributions. The annual deduction is limited to 10 percent of taxable income *before* the deduction. Contributions in excess of this limit are carried forward for five years as a deduction against future income.[7]

---

[7] §170(b)(2) and (d)(2). For purposes of this limitation, taxable income is computed without any dividend-received deduction or loss carrybacks into the year.

Limit on Contribution Deduction	Movement Plus Inc. contributed $40,000 to local charities. However, its deduction for the contribution is limited to $35,360, as shown on line 19, Form 1120. This limitation is computed as follows:

Total income (line 11)	$835,800
Deductions *excluding* line 19 and *including* NOL deduction	(482,200)
Taxable income *before* charitable contribution deduction	$353,600
	.10
Charitable contribution deduction	$ 35,360

Movement Plus has a $4,640 contribution carryforward ($40,000 contribution − $35,360 contribution deduction) into next year.

The Dividends-Received Deduction

Objective 2
Compute the corporate dividends-received deduction.

The last deduction listed on the first page of Form 1120 (and described on line 29b as a special deduction) is the **dividends-received deduction.**[8] Corporations that receive dividends from other taxable, domestic corporations are entitled to this deduction. Note that dividends received from foreign corporations are generally not eligible for the deduction. In addition, noncorporate shareholders are not eligible for the dividends-received deduction. The dividends-received deduction equals a percentage of the total dividends included in gross income. The percentage depends on the recipient corporation's investment in the corporation paying the dividend, as shown in the following schedule.

• If the recipient corporation owns *less than 20 percent* of the stock of the paying corporation, the deduction equals 70 percent of the dividends received.
• If the recipient corporation owns *at least 20 percent but less than 80 percent* of the stock of the paying corporation, the deduction equals 80 percent of the dividends received.
• If the recipient corporation owns *80 percent or more* of the stock of the paying corporation, the deduction equals 100 percent of the dividend received.

Dividends-Received Deduction	ABC Inc. owns 5 percent of the stock of Corporation X, 50 percent of the stock of Corporation Y, and 83 percent of the stock of Corporation Z. The three corporations in which ABC invested are taxable, domestic entities. ABC's gross income includes the following dividends.

Corporation X dividend	$ 24,000
Corporation Y dividend	8,000
Corporation Z dividend	90,000
	$122,000

ABC's dividends-received deduction is $113,200.

Deduction for Corporation X dividend ($24,000 × 70%)	$ 16,800
Deduction for Corporation Y dividend ($ 8,000 × 80%)	6,400
Deduction for Corporation Z dividend ($90,000 × 100%)	90,000
	$113,200

[8] §243. If corporate taxable income *before* the dividends-received deduction is less than the corporation's dividend income, the 70 percent and 80 percent deductions are limited to the respective percentages of such taxable income by §246(b)(1).

Because of the dividends-received deduction, only $8,800 of ABC's gross dividend income is included in taxable income. If ABC's marginal tax rate is 35 percent, the tax on this income is $3,080, and ABC's tax rate on its dividend income is only 2.5 percent ($3,080 ÷ $122,000). This low rate is not as generous as it first may seem. The dividends that ABC included in gross income represent after-tax dollars because Corporations X, Y, and Z already paid federal income tax on the earnings distributed as dividends to their investors (including ABC). As we will discuss in a later section of this chapter, ABC's dividends-received deduction simply prevents most of these earnings from being taxed again at the corporate level.

Reconciling Book Income and Taxable Income

Objective 3
Prepare a reconciliation of book and taxable income.

Because of differences between the measurement of income for federal tax purposes and the measurement of income under generally accepted accounting principles (GAAP), the taxable income reported on page 1, Form 1120, is usually not the same as the net income reported on the corporation's financial statements. The corporation must reconcile the two numbers so that the IRS can identify the differences between financial statement income and taxable income. Until 2004, all corporations provided this reconciliation on Schedule M-1, page 4, Form 1120. In 2004, the IRS developed a new reconciliation Schedule M-3 for use by corporations with total assets of $10 million or more. Schedule M-3 requires much more detailed information than Schedule M-1 and should make the book/tax reconciliation more transparent to revenue agents. According to the IRS, "the new schedule will enable us to focus our compliance resources on returns and issues that need to be examined and avoid those that do not." Schedule M-3 is included as Appendix 11–A to this chapter.

Corporations with total assets of less than $10 million may continue to provide their book/tax reconciliation on Schedule M-1. Here is an example of such reconciliation.

Book/Tax Reconciliation

Diamont Inc., which has total assets of $6.81 million, reported $343,093 net income after tax on its audited financial statements and $453,364 taxable income on its Form 1120. Here is Schedule M-1 reconciling these numbers:

Schedule M-1	Reconciliation of Income (Loss) per Books With Income per Return				
	Note: Schedule M-3 required instead of Schedule M-1 if total assets are $10 million or more—see instructions				
1	Net income (loss) per books	343,093	7	Income recorded on books this year not included on this return (itemize):	
2	Federal income tax per books	181,474		Tax-exempt interest $	
3	Excess of capital losses over capital gains .	20,500			
4	Income subject to tax not recorded on books this year (itemize): .... Prepaid rent	8,100		Deferred gain like-kind exchange	71,200
5	Expenses recorded on books this year not deducted on this return (itemize):		8	Deductions on this return not charged against book income this year (itemize):	
a	Depreciation . . . . $		a	Depreciation . . . . $ 43,812	
b	Charitable contributions $		b	Charitable contributions $	
c	Travel and entertainment $ ...... 13,909 Bad debts 1,300	15,209			43,812
6	Add lines 1 through 5	568,376	9	Add lines 7 and 8	115,012
			10	Income (page 1, line 28)—line 6 less line 9	453,364

(handwritten margin note: "Unfavorable increases (Taxable Inc)")

- Diamont's net income per books is entered on line 1, and the federal income tax expense per books is entered on line 2.[9] This expense is not deductible in the computation of taxable income.
- Diamont realized a $20,500 net capital loss on the sale of investment securities and included the loss in financial statement income. This nondeductible loss is entered on line 3.
- Diamont received $8,100 prepaid rent that was recorded as a liability for unearned revenues for financial statement purposes. This taxable income is entered on line 4.

---

[9] See the discussion of tax expense versus tax payable in Chapter 6.

- Diamont incurred $27,818 meal and entertainment expense. The nondeductible half of this expense is entered on line 5(c).
- Diamont's addition to its allowance for bad debts exceeded its actual write-off of uncollectible accounts receivable by $1,300. This nondeductible excess is entered on line 5.

The total on line 6 is financial statement income increased by (1) taxable income items not included in book income and (2) expense items not deducted on the tax return.

- Diamont realized a $71,200 gain on an exchange of commercial real estate. The exchange involved like-kind properties so the realized gain was not recognized for tax purposes. The deferred gain is entered on line 7.
- Diamont's MACRS depreciation deduction exceeded its depreciation expense per books by $43,812. This excess is entered on line 8(a).

The total on line 9 equals (1) book income items not included in taxable income and (2) allowable deductions not reported as expenses for book purposes.

Line 10 is the final number in the reconciliation: taxable income reported on page 1, Form 1120, *before* any NOL deduction and dividends-received deduction. Diamont had neither of these special deductions this year. Consequently, it paid federal tax on $453,364 income.

Schedule M-1 is organized so that unfavorable book/tax differences (those increasing taxable income) are reported on the left-hand side of the form, while favorable book/tax differences (those decreasing taxable income) are reported on the right-hand side of the form. As noted in the example, line 10 of Schedule M-1 is not bottom-line taxable income. Instead, line 10 equals taxable income before any NOL deduction and the dividends-received deduction. For corporations with such special deductions, Schedule M-1 does not provide a full reconciliation to taxable income.

COMPUTING THE REGULAR CORPORATE TAX

Objective 4
Compute the regular tax on corporate taxable income.

The final section on the first page of Form 1120 (Exhibit 11.1) is labeled "Tax and Payments." After the corporation has computed taxable income, it must calculate the federal tax on that income. The first step in the calculation is to determine the corporation's regular tax, which is based on the following rate schedule.[10]

If taxable income is:	The tax is:
Not over $50,000	15% of taxable income
Over $50,000 but not over $75,000	$7,500 + 25% of the excess over $50,000
Over $75,000 but not over $100,000	$13,750 + 34% of the excess over $75,000
Over $100,000 but not over $335,000	$22,250 + 39% of the excess over $100,000
Over $335,000 but not over $10,000,000	$113,900 + 34% of the excess over $335,000
Over $10,000,000 but not over $15,000,000	$3,400,000 + 35% of the excess over $10,000,000
Over $15,000,000 but not over $18,333,333	$5,150,000 + 38% of the excess over $15,000,000
Over $18,333,333	$6,416,667 + 35% of the excess over $18,333,333

Technically, this rate structure is progressive: Observe the 15 percent, 25 percent, and 34 percent rates on the first $100,000 of taxable income. The marginal rate increases to 39 percent on taxable income in excess of $100,000 but drops back to 34 percent for taxable income from $335,000 to $10 million. The additional 5 percent on income between

[10] §11(b)(1).

$100,000 and $335,000 is actually a **surtax,** or extra tax, that recoups the benefit of the 15 percent and 25 percent rates on the first $75,000 of taxable income. This benefit equals $11,750, computed as follows.

Tax on $75,000 at 34%		$25,500
Tax on $50,000 at 15%	$7,500	
Tax on $25,000 at 25%	6,250	
		(13,750)
Benefit of 15% and 25% rates		$11,750

The maximum 5 percent surtax is $11,750 ($235,000 × 5 percent). Accordingly, corporations with taxable income between $335,000 and $10 million actually pay tax at a flat 34 percent rate.

Regular Tax Calculation	Corporation M's taxable income is $4 million. Based on the corporate rate schedule, the regular tax on this income is $1,360,000.

Taxable income	$4,000,000
	(335,000)
Taxable income in excess of $335,000	$3,665,000
Marginal rate on excess	.34
	$1,246,100
Tax on $335,000 (from rate schedule)	113,900
	$1,360,000

Because Corporation M's taxable income is between $335,000 and $10 million, its regular tax can be calculated by simply multiplying $4 million by 34 percent.

Corporate taxable income in excess of $10 million is taxed at 35 percent. A second surtax of 3 percent is levied on taxable income from $15 million to $18.33 million. The maximum 3 percent surtax is $100,000 ($3.33 million × 3 percent), which equals the difference between a 34 percent and a 35 percent rate on the first $10 million of taxable income. Because of this second surtax, corporations with taxable income in excess of $18.33 million pay tax at a flat 35 percent rate.

Regular Tax Calculation	Corporation R's taxable income is $40 million. Based on the corporate rate schedule, the regular tax on this income is $14 million.

Taxable income	$ 40,000,000
	(18,333,333)
Taxable income in excess of $18,333,333	$ 21,666,667
Marginal rate on excess	.35
	$ 7,583,333
Tax on $18,333,333 (from rate schedule)	6,416,667
	$ 14,000,000

Because Corporation R's taxable income exceeds $18.33 million, its regular tax can be calculated by simply multiplying $40 million by 35 percent.

Personal Service Corporations

Closely held corporations owned by individuals who perform services in the fields of health, law, engineering, architecture, accounting, actuarial science, performing arts, or consulting for the corporation's clientele are denied even the minimal progressivity of the corporate rate schedule. The income earned by these **personal service corporations** is taxed at a flat 35 percent rate.[11]

Defining the Field of Accounting	A recent Tax Court ruling found that a corporation providing bookkeeping and tax return preparation services was a personal service corporation taxable at a flat 35 percent rate. The corporation had argued that it qualified to use the graduated rates because it employed no CPAs and did not meet Nevada state law requirements for providing "accounting services."[12]

Reduced Tax Burden on Domestic Manufacturers

The current tax rate structure applies to corporate taxable income, regardless of the type of activity generating the income or the geographic location of the activity. Consequently, income from sales of tangible goods is taxed at the same statutory rate as income from the performance of services, and income from domestic activities is taxed at the same rate as income from foreign activities. In recent years, Congress has struggled to find a way to reduce the tax burden on domestic production activities because it believes that a lower tax on domestic manufacturers will improve their cash flow, stimulate investment in domestic facilities, and ultimately increase the number of manufacturing jobs in the United States.

Tax Talk
For 2008, corporations claimed over $18 billion of domestic production activities deductions.

Acting on this belief, Congress enacted a radical new tax deduction as part of the American Jobs Creation Act of 2004. This deduction is available to any U.S. taxpayer deriving income from a qualified activity: the "lease, rental, license, sale, exchange, or other disposition" of tangible property, computer software, and sound recordings that are "manufactured, produced, grown, or extracted by the taxpayer in whole or in significant part within the United States."[13] This **domestic production activities deduction** equals the following percentage of the *lesser* of the corporation's net income from the qualified activity or its taxable income computed before the deduction.

For taxable years beginning in:	
2005 and 2006	3 percent
2007, 2008, 2009	6 percent
2010 and later	9 percent

The amount of the deduction allowed for any taxable year cannot exceed 50 percent of the total compensation that the corporation pays to its U.S. workforce.

---

[11] §11(b)(2) and §448(d)(2).

[12] *Rainbow Tax Service, Inc. v. Commissioner,* 128 T.C. 5.

[13] §199, effective for taxable years beginning after December 31, 2004. While this deduction is available to noncorporate taxpayers, it clearly was enacted as a corporate tax relief measure.

Domestic Production Activities Deduction	PeriProducts is a New York corporation engaged exclusively in the domestic manufacture and sale of electrical components. Assume that in 2012, it earns $800,000 net income from this qualified activity. Before the domestic production activities deduction, its taxable income is also $800,000, and the compensation paid to its workforce is $219,675. PeriProducts' domestic production activities deduction for 2012 is $72,000 (9 percent × $800,000), which is less than 50 percent of total compensation paid. Therefore, the corporation's 2012 federal income tax is $247,520.

Taxable income before the deduction	$800,000
Domestic production activities deduction	(72,000)
Taxable income	$728,000
Tax rate	.34
Tax	$247,520

The domestic production activities deduction is artificial in that it does not correspond to any expense, loss, or cash outflow incurred by the corporate taxpayer. *Consequently, it is equivalent to a reduced tax rate on the income from any qualified activity.* In our example, the $247,520 federal tax that PeriProducts pays on $800,000 net income equates to a 30.94 percent effective tax rate, even though its explicit tax rate is 34 percent. The domestic production activities deduction results in a permanent difference between book and taxable income.

TAX CREDITS

A corporate (or noncorporate) taxpayer's regular tax is offset by any tax credits for which the taxpayer is eligible. A **tax credit** is a direct dollar-for-dollar reduction in tax liability. As a result, the value of a credit is greater than the value of a deduction of the same amount.

Deduction versus Credit	Jodi Inc.'s taxable income is $600,000, and its regular tax (at 34 percent) is $204,000. If Jodi is allowed an additional $50,000 deduction, the tax decreases to $187,000, and the tax savings from the deduction is $17,000 (34 percent of $50,000). In comparison, if Jodi is entitled to a $50,000 tax credit, the tax decreases to $154,000, and the tax savings from the credit is $50,000.

	Deduction	Credit
Taxable income	$600,000	$600,000
Additional deduction	(50,000)	
Recomputed taxable income	$550,000	$600,000
	.34	.34
Precredit tax	$187,000	$204,000
Tax credit		(50,000)
Recomputed tax	$187,000	$154,000

Tax credits are generally nonrefundable, which means they can reduce current year tax to zero, but any credit in excess of precredit tax does not generate a refund from the Treasury. However, the tax law may provide that an excess credit can be carried back or forward to reduce tax in a different year.

Because tax credits reduce the regular tax on business income, they are equivalent to a preferential tax rate. Thus, tax credits utilize the character variable, discussed in Chapter 4, to reduce tax liability. To be eligible for a particular credit, taxpayers must engage in very specific activities or transactions that Congress believes are worthy of government support. From this perspective, tax credits are instruments of fiscal policy and are enacted by Congress to increase the efficiency of the tax system as an agent of economic change. Currently, the tax law provides a **general business credit,** which is the sum of 26 different credits for the tax year.[14]

Most of these 26 credits are narrow in scope and are available to relatively few businesses. Moreover, the list of credits changes as Congress experiments with new credits and discards those that fail to produce the intended behavioral result. To learn how a tax credit can induce a certain behavior, we will look at the mechanics of just one credit.

Rehabilitation Credit

Taxpayers who renovate or reconstruct commercial buildings originally placed in service before 1936 or buildings certified as historic structures by the U.S. Department of the Interior are entitled to a **rehabilitation credit.**[15] The credit equals 10 percent of the rehabilitation costs of a qualifying commercial building and 20 percent of the rehabilitation costs of a certified historic structure. Congress designed this credit to encourage businesses to undertake urban renewal projects that might be financially unfeasible without the tax savings from the credit.

Rehabilitation Credit	
	Quick Corporation must locate a suitable facility to house one of its regional offices and has narrowed its search to two buildings. One building is newly constructed and ready for occupancy. The second building was constructed in 1925 and is in need of extensive renovation. The purchase price of the first building is $10 million, while the purchase price of the second building is only $3 million. Quick estimates that the rehabilitation costs for the second building would be $7.5 million. For tax purposes, Quick's cost basis in either building ($10 million for the new building or $10.5 million for the old building) can be depreciated over the same 39-year recovery period.

Without the rehabilitation credit, the cost of the new building is less than that of the old building, and Quick has no reason to invest in the older structure. However, the credit reduces the cost of the old building to $9,750,000.

Purchase price	$ 3,000,000
Rehabilitation cost	7,500,000
	$10,500,000
Tax savings from credit ($7,500,000 × 10%)	(750,000)
After-tax cost	$ 9,750,000

Because of the rehabilitation credit, Quick minimizes its cost by purchasing the old building. Note that the tax savings from the credit is not a function of Quick's marginal tax rate. But the savings calculation is based on the assumption that precredit tax is sufficient to allow full use of the credit in the current year. If this is not the case and Quick must carry forward some of the credit for use in a future year, the present value of the carryforward might be insufficient to tip the scale in favor of the rehabilitation project.

---

[14] §38. The general business credit that a taxpayer can use each year is limited to $25,000 plus 75 percent of precredit tax in excess of $25,000. §38(c). Any unused credit can be carried back one year and forward 20 years. §39(a).

[15] §47.

Save a Building, Save Tax	The National Park Service released a report summarizing the positive effects of the rehabilitation credit on historic preservation. According to the report, 2,967 historic buildings were preserved in the five-year period of the report, including Chicago office towers, Baltimore row houses, St. Louis warehouses, and Miami art deco hotels. The Park Service concluded that the tax credit "leverages private investment in depressed neighborhoods, creates jobs, promotes community preservation, fosters heritage education, enhances state and local tax revenues, and increases property values." Not bad for a tax credit![16]

Other popular corporate tax credits, included in the general business credit, include the following: the research activities credit, promoting basic scientific research activities; the empowerment zone employment credit, for the hiring of employees in designated economically distressed areas; the low-income housing credit, for construction or renovation of multi-unit low-income housing; and the tax credit for alternative-fuel vehicles. The details of these credits are beyond the scope of this text. The foreign tax credit, intended to mitigate double taxation of foreign earnings of U.S. taxpayers, is discussed in more detail in Chapter 13.

ALTERNATIVE MINIMUM TAX

Objective 5
Discuss the purpose of the corporate alternative minimum tax.

The **alternative minimum tax (AMT)** is a second federal tax system parallel to the regular income tax system described throughout the text. Congress enacted the corporate AMT primarily for political reasons. Under the regular tax system, corporations with substantial economic income can occasionally take advantage of tax exclusions, deductions, or credits to dramatically reduce, or even eliminate, their tax. In past years, these occasions received a great deal of publicity and caused people to lose respect for a tax system so riddled with "loopholes" that huge companies can escape taxation altogether. In response to this embarrassing public perception, Congress created a backup system to ensure that every corporation pays a "fair share" of the federal tax burden.

Every newly formed corporation is exempt from AMT for its first taxable year. After the first year, a corporation is exempt from AMT for each year in which it passes a gross receipts test. The test is based on the corporation's average annual gross receipts for the three-year period (or portion thereof) *preceding* the test year. A corporation is exempt for its *first* test year if its average annual gross receipts for the testing period do not exceed $5,000,000. For all subsequent test years, the corporation is exempt if its average annual gross receipts for the testing period do not exceed $7,500,000. If a corporation fails the gross receipts test, it is subject to AMT for the test year and all subsequent years.[17]

AMT Exemption	Hermann Inc. was incorporated on January 1, 2008, and adopted a calendar year. It had the following gross receipts for its first five taxable years.

2008	$ 4,890,000
2009	6,520,000
2010	9,891,000
2011	10,037,000
2012	11,440,000

---

[16] "Tax Matters," *Journal of Accountancy*, September 2001, p. 107.
[17] §55(e).

Hermann was exempt from AMT for 2008 (its first taxable year). Thus, Hermann's first test year was 2009, and the testing period for that year was 2008. Because average annual gross receipts for the testing period ($4,890,000) did not exceed $5,000,000, it was exempt from AMT for 2009.

Hermann's second test year was 2010, and the testing period for that year was the two-year period 2008–2009. Average annual gross receipts for this period were $5,705,000 [($4,890,000 + $6,520,000) ÷ 2]. Because this average did not exceed $7,500,000, Hermann was exempt from AMT for 2010.

Hermann's third test year was 2011, and the testing period was the three-year period 2008–2010. Average annual gross receipts for this period were $7,100,333 [($4,890,000 + $6,520,000 + $9,891,000) ÷ 3]. Because this average did not exceed $7,500,000, Hermann was exempt from AMT for 2011.

Hermann's fourth test year was 2012, and the testing period was the three-year period 2009–2011. Average annual gross receipts for this period were $8,816,000 [($6,520,000 + $9,891,000 + $10,037,000) ÷ 3]. Because this average exceeded $7,500,000, Hermann was subject to AMT for 2012 and all subsequent taxable years.

Alternative Minimum Taxable Income

The base for the corporate AMT is **alternative minimum taxable income (AMTI).**[18] The computation of AMTI begins with taxable income for regular tax purposes. This income number is increased or decreased by a series of complicated **AMT adjustments** and increased by specific **tax preferences.** The computation of AMTI is presented in the following formula.

Taxable income for regular tax purposes
+ or − AMT adjustments
+ AMT tax preferences

Alternative minimum taxable income

Tax Talk
For property placed in service in 2008–2012 on which bonus depreciation is claimed, AMT depreciation equals regular depreciation. Thus, no AMT depreciation adjustment is required for these qualifying acquisitions.

To get a sense of the nature of AMT adjustments and preferences, let's examine four of the more common: the depreciation adjustment, excess percentage depletion, the ACE adjustment, and the NOL adjustment.

Depreciation Adjustment

Under MACRS, business assets with a 3-year, 5-year, 7-year, or 10-year recovery period are depreciated under the 200 percent declining balance method. For AMT purposes, depreciation on these assets is computed under a 150 percent declining-balance method.[19] Consequently, the MACRS deduction with respect to these assets is greater than its AMT counterpart in the early years of an asset's life, and the excess MACRS becomes a positive adjustment in the AMTI computation. At some point in the asset's life, the situation reverses and AMT depreciation exceeds MACRS depreciation. At this point, the annual AMT adjustment becomes negative. Over the life of the asset, MACRS and AMT depreciation are equal, and the positive and negative AMT adjustments zero out.

---

[18] §55(b)(2).

[19] §56(a)(1). For property placed in service before January 1, 1999, AMT depreciation is based on the extended recovery periods under the alternative depreciation system (ADS) described in §168(g).

	MACRS	AMT Depreciation	AMT Adjustment
Asset 1	$17,800	$12,000	$5,800
Asset 2	2,100	4,300	(2,200)
	$19,900	$16,300	$3,600

AMT Depreciation

JS Inc. owns two depreciable assets. This year, the MACRS depreciation, AMT depreciation, and AMT adjustment for each asset is:

JS has a $5,800 positive AMT adjustment for Asset 1 (excess MACRS over AMT depreciation) and a $2,200 negative AMT adjustment for Asset 2 (excess AMT depreciation over MACRS). JS must add its $3,600 aggregate positive adjustment to regular taxable income in the computation of AMTI.

Excess Percentage Depletion

As we discussed in Chapter 7, the percentage depletion that corporations deduct over the productive life of a mine or well is not limited to the tax basis in the mineral property. If a corporation has recovered its entire basis and continues to deduct percentage depletion, the depletion deduction in excess of the zero basis is an AMT tax preference.[20]

Depletion Preference

JS Inc. had $240,000 unrecovered basis in a mining property at the beginning of the year. The percentage depletion deduction with respect to this property for the year was $310,000. JS has $70,000 excess depletion and must add this preference to regular taxable income in the AMTI computation.

ACE Adjustment

The **ACE adjustment** is targeted at publicly held corporations that report robust earnings to their shareholders but only modest income on their federal tax returns. To determine this adjustment, corporations first must compute their adjusted current earnings (ACE), a number that broadly approximates book income for financial reporting purposes.[21] Consequently, ACE ropes in items of nontaxable income that are not tax preference items per se, such as tax-exempt interest, gain deferred under the installment sale method of accounting, and dividend income sheltered by the 70 percent dividends-received deduction.

The ACE adjustment equals 75 percent of the excess of ACE over AMTI (computed before the ACE adjustment or NOL deduction for the year).[22] If ACE is less than AMTI, a negative ACE adjustment is allowed but is limited to the cumulative amount of positive ACE adjustments for prior years.

[20] §57(a)(1).
[21] Joint Committee on Taxation, *General Explanation of the Tax Reform Act of 1986*, p. 449.
[22] §56(g).

Positive ACE Adjustment	This year, JS Inc. has $2.504 million adjusted current earnings and $2.088 million AMTI before the ACE adjustment. ACE exceeds this AMTI number by $416,000, so JS's ACE adjustment is $312,000 (75% × $416,000), and its AMTI is $2.4 million ($2.088 million + $312,000).

Negative ACE Adjustment	This year is JS's second taxable year. Its ACE adjustment for its first year was $81,000; its ACE adjustment this year is $312,000; and its cumulative positive adjustment is $393,000. Assume that next year, JS's ACE is $2.020 million and its AMTI before the ACE adjustment is $2.76 million. Because AMTI exceeds ACE by $740,000, JS is allowed a negative ACE adjustment. The adjustment equals $555,000 (75% × $740,000) *limited to* $393,000 (cumulative positive adjustments for prior years). Consequently, JS's AMTI next year is $2.367 million ($2.76 million − $393,000).

NOL Deduction

Even if a corporation generates a profit, it may have no taxable income because it has an NOL carryforward or carryback into the year. For AMT purposes, the NOL deduction is limited to 90 percent of AMTI.[23]

AMT NOL Deduction	JS Inc.'s taxable income before any NOL deduction is $2 million, and it has a $3 million NOL carryforward into the year. For regular tax purposes, JS can deduct $2 million of the carryforward, thereby reducing taxable income to zero. JS's AMTI before the NOL deduction is $2.4 million. Under the AMT rules, JS can deduct only $2.16 million of its NOL carryforward (90 percent of $2.4 million), resulting in $240,000 AMTI.

Calculating AMT

Calculation of the corporate AMT is a three-step process.[24] First, AMTI is decreased by any exemption to which the corporation is entitled. The basic exemption is $40,000. This exemption is reduced by 25 percent of AMTI in excess of $150,000. Consequently, the exemption is reduced to zero for corporations with AMTI in excess of $310,000.

AMTI Exemption	IQP Corporation's AMTI is $293,000, and its exemption is $4,250.

AMTI	$ 293,000
	(150,000)
Excess AMTI	$ 143,000
	.25
Reduction in exemption	$ 35,750
Basic exemption	$ 40,000
	(35,750)
IQP's exemption	$ 4,250

---

[23] §56(a)(4) and §56(d). Because the AMT NOL is calculated under the AMT system, the AMT NOL deduction can be different from the NOL deduction for regular tax purposes.

[24] §55 provides the rules for the AMT computation.

In the second step of the AMT calculation, AMTI in excess of the exemption is multiplied by a flat 20 percent rate to compute **tentative minimum tax.** In the third step, the tentative minimum tax is compared to the corporation's regular tax. Any excess of tentative minimum tax over regular tax becomes AMT, which the corporation pays *in addition to* its regular tax.[25] The AMT calculation is demonstrated in the next example.

AMT Calculation	In 2011, Bantam Inc. has $5,000,000 taxable income and $9,750,000 AMTI. Bantam's tax is computed as follows.	
	AMTI	$ 9,750,000
	Exemption	–0–
		$ 9,750,000
		.20
	Tentative minimum tax	$ 1,950,000
	Regular tax ($5,000,000 × 34%)	(1,700,000)
	AMT	$ 250,000
	Total tax (regular tax + AMT)	$ 1,950,000

Although Bantam's AMTI is almost twice its taxable income, its AMT is relatively small. Because the 20 percent AMT rate is so much less than the 34 percent or 35 percent regular tax rate, tentative minimum tax won't exceed regular tax unless AMTI is significantly greater than taxable income. Therefore, corporations with modest AMT adjustments and preferences escape the AMT. Nonetheless, the additional record keeping necessary to compute annual AMTI increases the tax compliance costs of these corporations.

Minimum Tax Credit

Tax Talk
For 2008, corporations claimed nearly $2 billion of minimum tax credits.

In the preceding example, the fact that Bantam's $1,950,000 tax bill consists of both regular tax and AMT may seem of little practical importance. Even so, corporations must keep careful track of their AMT because this tax payment is transformed into a **minimum tax credit.** This credit carries forward indefinitely and reduces the corporation's regular tax in subsequent years. However, the credit cannot reduce regular tax to less than the corporation's tentative minimum tax for the year.[26] The logic behind this credit is that the corporate AMT is not designed as a permanent tax increase. Instead, AMT merely accelerates the payment of tax into years when corporate taxable income is dramatically less than AMTI. To demonstrate the important function of the minimum tax credit, refer back to Bantam's situation.

[25] In the AMT context, regular tax generally equals a corporation's precredit tax liability.
[26] §53.

Minimum Tax Credit

In 2012, Bantam has $7,500,000 taxable income and $8,000,000 AMTI. Bantam's tax is computed as follows.

AMTI	$8,000,000
Exemption	–0–
	$8,000,000
	.20
Tentative minimum tax	$1,600,000
Regular tax ($7,500,000 × 34%)	$2,550,000
AMT (regular tax *exceeds* tentative minimum tax)	–0–
Minimum tax credit from 2010	(250,000)
Total tax	$2,300,000

In this two-year example, the AMT affected only the timing and not the amount of Bantam's income tax. With or without AMT, Bantam pays $4,250,000 total tax for the two years.

	Two-Year Summary for Bantam	
	Total Tax with AMT	*Total Tax without AMT*
2011	$1,950,000	$1,700,000
2012	2,300,000	2,550,000
	$4,250,000	$4,250,000

The effect of the AMT over the two-year period was to accelerate $250,000 tax into the earlier year, not to permanently increase that tax. Realistically, AMT may take any number of years to reverse as minimum tax credits against regular tax. For growing businesses, each successive year's tentative minimum tax may exceed regular tax. In such case, use of the minimum tax credit is postponed indefinitely. Of course, regardless of the fact that a corporation may recoup AMT in a future year, that AMT always increases the corporation's tax cost in present value terms.

PAYMENT AND FILING REQUIREMENTS

Objective 6
Describe the corporate tax payment and return filing requirements.

Corporations are required to pay their federal income tax for the year in four install-ments.[27] Each installment is 25 percent of the annual tax, and the installments are due by the 15th day of the 4th, 6th, 9th, and 12th months of the taxable year. Corporations that fail to make their required installment payments on a timely basis incur an **underpayment penalty.** If the total of the installment payments is less than the actual tax reported on Form 1120, the corporation must pay the balance due by the 15th day of the third month

---

[27] §6655.

following the close of the taxable year.[28] If the total is more than the actual tax, the corporation is entitled to a refund of the overpayment.

The required installment payments must total to 100 percent of the tax reported on Form 1120. Because corporations can't know their exact tax liability until after year-end, they must base their installment payments on their best estimate. Corporations that underestimate their tax incur the underpayment penalty. The law provides some leeway for small corporations (defined as corporations with less than $1 million taxable income). These corporations escape the underpayment penalty if their total installment payments equal 100 percent of the tax reported on the *previous* year's tax return.[29] This *safe harbor* provision is useful to newly formed corporations with rapidly growing businesses.

Safe Harbor Estimate	In 2011, Corporation DF's taxable income was $400,000, and its tax was $136,000. During 2012, DF made four $35,000 installment payments. Its 2012 taxable income was $930,000, and its tax was $316,200. Although DF paid only $140,000 tax during 2012, it did not incur an underpayment penalty because the payment exceeded 100 percent of its 2011 tax.

Corporations must file their annual income tax returns with the IRS by the 15th day of the third month following the close of the taxable year.[30] Corporations that are unable to meet this filing deadline may request an automatic six-month extension of time to file their returns, and corporations routinely take advantage of this grace period.[31] It should come as no surprise that corporations that file delinquent returns may incur late-filing penalties.[32] An extension of the filing deadline does *not* extend the payment deadline for any balance of tax due for the year. Corporations must pay any estimated balance due by the 15th day of the third month after the close of the year even if they file an extended tax return. Beginning in 2006, corporations with assets of $50 million or more are required to file their federal tax returns electronically. Beginning in 2007, the asset threshold drops to $10 million.

Payment and Filing Requirements	Keno, a calendar year corporation, filed a Form 7004 (Application for Automatic Extension of Time to File Corporation Income Tax Return) on March 3, 2012, on which it requested a six-month extension for its 2011 return. On the application, Keno reported that its estimated 2011 tax was $258,500 and its quarterly installment payments of that tax totaled $244,000. Therefore, Keno paid its $14,500 estimated balance due with the Form 7004. Keno filed its 2011 return on August 29, 2012. The actual tax reported on the return was $255,039, which entitled Keno to a $3,461 refund of 2011 tax ($258,500 total payments − $255,039 actual tax).

DISTRIBUTIONS OF PROFITS TO INVESTORS

The corporate form of business organization allows an unlimited number of investors to contribute capital to the business. Investors can become creditors, either by lending money directly to the corporation in exchange for a promissory note or by purchasing the

---

[28] Corporations do not send tax payments directly to the IRS. Instead, they use the Electronic Federal Tax Payment System (EFTPS) or a Federal Tax Deposit Coupon to deposit their payments in a government account maintained by a qualified depositary, such as a commercial bank.

[29] Large corporations with highly fluctuating patterns of annual income may look to other statutory exceptions to the strict 100 percent requirement for relief from the underpayment penalty.

[30] §6072(b).

[31] Reg. §1.6081-3.

[32] §6651 describes the penalties for late filing. These penalties are discussed in more detail in Chapter 18.

corporation's debt instruments traded on a public bond market. Alternatively, investors can become owners by contributing money or property directly to the corporation in exchange for shares of equity stock, purchasing shares from other shareholders, or purchasing shares traded on a public stock market.

Of course, both creditors and shareholders expect a return on their investment. Creditors receive interest income on their corporate notes or bonds. On the other side of the transaction, corporations can deduct the interest paid on their debt obligations. As a result, the business profit flowing through to investors as interest is not taxed at the corporate level but only to the investors. Corporate stockholders may receive a return on their investment in the form of dividends. Corporations *cannot* deduct dividend payments in the computation of taxable income. The business profit flowing through to investors as dividends is taxed both at the corporate level and again to the shareholders receiving the dividends.

Objective 7

Explain why corporate profits distributed as dividends are double-taxed.

This double taxation of corporate earnings is one of the dominant characteristics of the federal income tax system. The fact that dividends are paid with after-tax dollars is a major consideration affecting the choice of organizational form—a consideration we will analyze in the next chapter. This fact also justifies the corporate dividends-received deduction. Without this deduction, business profit would be taxed over and over again as it is distributed through a chain of corporate investors before final distribution to individual shareholders for personal consumption.

From the corporate perspective, the nondeductibility of dividend payments creates a bias in favor of debt financing.[33] A corporation that raises capital by borrowing can deduct the interest paid on the debt. At a 35 percent tax rate, the after-tax cost of the capital is only 65 percent of the before-tax cost. In effect, the federal government pays 35 percent of the return on the creditors' investment. If the corporation raises capital by selling stock, the after-tax cost of the dividends paid on that stock equals the before-tax cost. Of course, the choice of debt financing has serious nontax implications, one of the more important of which is that interest and principal payments (unlike dividends paid on common stock) are not discretionary on the part of management. Corporations with high debt-to-equity ratios have more burdensome cash flow commitments and a greater risk of insolvency than corporations with less debt in their capital structures. Companies that break faith with their creditors suffer financial distress that may even lead to bankruptcy. In many situations, the nontax costs associated with debt financing outweigh the tax savings from the corporate interest deduction.[34]

Alternatives to Double Taxation

How could the present income tax system be reformed to eliminate the double taxation of corporate income? One alternative would be to treat corporations as passthrough entities by requiring them to allocate income to their shareholders on an annual basis. Shareholders would include share of corporate earnings in gross income and pay tax accordingly. This alternative would be administratively cumbersome, if not impossible, for publicly held corporations in which stock ownership changes daily. In addition, this alternative could cause cash flow problems for investors who find themselves owing tax on their share of corporate income but who did not receive a commensurate cash distribution from the corporation.

Another alternative is to make dividends nontaxable to individual investors so that the only tax on corporate income is at the entity level. Congress recently took an unprecedented step in this direction by enacting a 15 percent preferential tax rate for dividend income

[33] Richard A. Brealey and Stewart C. Myers, *Principles of Corporate Finance,* 5th ed. (New York: McGraw-Hill, 1996), p. 418.
[34] Ibid., p. 421.

received by individuals. However, any preferential treatment of dividends is vulnerable to political attack as a tax break for the wealthy who receive much more dividend income than middle- and lower-income individuals. A variation on this alternative would be to allow corporations to deduct dividend payments (in the same way that they deduct interest payments) so that distributed corporate income would be taxed only at the shareholder level.

Still another alternative is a system in which individuals are allowed a tax credit for the corporate tax attributable to the dividends included in their gross income. For example, if a shareholder received a $6,500 dividend, representing $10,000 income on which the corporation already paid $3,500 tax, the shareholder would include the full $10,000 ($6,500 cash received grossed up by $3,500 tax) in income and compute his tax accordingly. The shareholder would then reduce that tax by a $3,500 credit. The end result is that $10,000 income is taxed only once at the individual's rate. Variations of this credit system are currently used in Canada and several western European nations.

Over the past decades, Congress and the Treasury have considered all these alternatives as solutions to the structural problem of double taxation. While the alternatives have theoretical merit, their implementation would result in significant revenue loss. Thus, it is unlikely that any of the alternatives will be enacted into law in the near future.

INCIDENCE OF THE CORPORATE TAX

Objective 8
Discuss the incidence of the corporate income tax.

Because corporations are taxpayers in their own right and yet have no human persona, they become easy political targets in any debate on tax reform. People don't enjoy paying taxes and often believe that their tax burden is too heavy because some other taxpayer's burden is too light. Impersonal corporate taxpayers are scapegoats as the hue and cry becomes "raise taxes on the corporate giants, not middle-class Americans." This sentiment ignores the fact that corporations are nothing more than a form in which people organize their business, and that an increase in the corporate tax represents an additional cost of conducting that business.

Just who does pay the corporate income tax? The answer to this question varies across corporations, depending on the nature of the markets in which they compete. In some markets, corporations may shift their tax costs directly to their customers as part of the price of goods and services. In markets in which price competition is fierce, management may offset tax costs by trimming production costs. In such case, the tax is passed on to the corporation's suppliers (smaller orders for materials), employees (lower compensation or workforce reductions), and even to consumers (lower quality). Still another possibility is that tax costs simply reduce the corporation's net income. In this case, the tax is paid by shareholders in the form of shrinking dividends or reduced market price for their stock. The question of the economic incidence of the corporate tax and whether that tax falls hardest on consumers, suppliers, labor, or capital has been researched and argued for decades without a definitive answer. Nonetheless, one conclusion is inescapable: Corporations do not pay taxes—people do.

Have You Paid Your Corporate Tax Today?	According to a recent study, in 2011 the average American will work 102 days just to pay their taxes. Included in these estimates are 36 days worked to pay individual income taxes, 22 days worked to cover payroll taxes, and 12 days to pay corporate income taxes! The study explained: "The reason these taxes are rightly counted as part of the nation's tax burden is that taxes on businesses are ultimately passed on to individuals: consumers, employees, and shareholders in the form of higher prices, lower wages or employment levels, and lower share value."[35]

---

[35] "Tax Freedom Day Arrives on April 12," *The Tax Foundation,* Special Report No. 1490, March 2011, p. 6.

Conclusion

Corporations have many legal and financial characteristics that make them the entity of choice for many enterprises and the only option for publicly held companies. Corporations are taxable entities in their own right, paying tax at progressive rates ranging from 15 percent to 35 percent on annual income. When corporations distribute after-tax income as dividends to their shareholders, the income is taxed a second time. In the next chapter, we will consider the impact of this double taxation on the choice of business entity and the entire tax planning process.

Sources of Book/Tax Differences

Permanent

• Dividends-received deduction
• U.S. production activities deduction

Temporary

• Corporate charitable contributions

Key Terms

ACE adjustment   *323*
affiliated group   *311*
alternative minimum tax (AMT)   *321*
alternative minimum taxable income (AMTI)   *322*
AMT adjustments   *322*
buy-sell agreement   *310*
centralized management   *310*
closely held corporation   *310*

consolidated tax return   *311*
dividends-received deduction   *314*
domestic production activities deduction   *318*
free transferability   *310*
general business credit   *320*
limited liability   *310*
minimum tax credit   *325*
nonprofit corporation   *312*

personal service corporation   *318*
publicly held corporation   *310*
rehabilitation credit   *320*
surtax   *317*
tax credit   *319*
tax preferences   *322*
tentative minimum tax   *325*
underpayment penalty   *326*
unlimited life   *310*

Questions and Problems for Discussion

1. To what extent does the corporate characteristic of limited liability protect shareholder/employees who perform professional services for corporate clients?

2. The corporate form of business is characterized by centralized management. Describe this characteristic as it applies to publicly held corporations and closely held corporations.

3. The corporate form of business is characterized by free transferability of equity interests. Describe this characteristic as it applies to publicly held corporations and closely held corporations.

4. Mr. and Mrs. Dane and their six children own 100 percent of the stock in three family corporations. Do these corporations qualify as an affiliated group eligible to file a consolidated corporate tax return?

5. RP Inc. owns 59 percent of QV's voting stock. RP's board of directors elects the majority of the members of QV's board of directors and thereby controls QV's management. Are RP and QV an affiliated group eligible to file a consolidated corporate tax return?

6. Libretto Corporation owns a national chain of retail music stores. The corporation wants to expand into a new, extremely competitive, and highly specialized business—the composition and production of rock music videos. Can you identify any nontax

reasons why Libretto may want to operate its new business through a controlled subsidiary corporation?

7. Corporations are allowed a dividends-received deduction for dividends from other domestic, taxable corporations. Why is this deduction not available for dividends from foreign corporations?

8. Corporations subject to the AMT are penalized because they took advantage of tax preferences during the year. If Congress doesn't want corporations to take advantage of a certain tax preference, why doesn't Congress simply repeal the preference?

9. For the last six years, Corporation V's AMTI has exceeded its regular taxable income, but it has never paid AMT. Can you explain this result?

10. In your own words, explain the conclusion that corporations do not pay tax—people do.

Application Problems

1. The stock of AB and YZ is publicly traded, and no shareholder owns more than a 1 percent interest in either corporation. AB owns 40 percent and YZ owns 60 percent of the stock of Alpha, which owns 90 percent of the stock of Beta. YZ and Beta each own 50 percent of the stock of Kappa. Which of the corporations identified in this problem form an affiliated group eligible to file a consolidated tax return?

2. The stock of Grommet Corporation, a U.S. company, is publicly traded, with no single shareholder owning more than 5 percent of its outstanding stock. Grommet owns 95 percent of the outstanding stock of Staple Inc., also a U.S. company. Staple owns 100 percent of the outstanding stock of Clip Corporation, a Canadian company. Grommet and Clip each own 50 percent of the outstanding stock of Fastener Inc., a U.S. company. Grommet and Staple each own 50 percent of the outstanding stock of Binder Corporation, a U.S. company. Which of these corporations form an affiliated group eligible to file a consolidated tax return?

3. Corporation P owns 93 percent of the outstanding stock of Corporation T. This year, the corporations' records provide the following information.

	Corporation P	Corporation T
Ordinary operating income (loss)	$500,000	$(200,000)
Capital gain (loss)	(8,300)	6,000
Section 1231 gain (loss)	(1,000)	5,000

  a. Compute each corporation's taxable income if they file separate tax returns.

  b. Compute consolidated taxable income if Corporation P and Corporation T file a consolidated tax return.

4. This year, Napa Corporation received the following dividends.

KLP Inc. (a taxable Delaware corporation in which Napa holds an 8% stock interest)	$ 55,000
Gamma Inc. (a taxable Florida corporation in which Napa holds a 90% stock interest)	120,000

Napa and Gamma do not file a consolidated tax return. Compute Napa's dividends-received deduction.

5. This year, GHJ Inc. received the following dividends.

BP Inc. (a taxable California corporation in which GHJ holds a 2% stock interest)	$17,300
MN Inc. (a taxable Florida corporation in which GHJ holds a 52% stock interest)	80,800
AB Inc. (a taxable Canadian corporation in which GHJ holds a 21% stock interest)	17,300

Compute GHJ's dividends-received deduction.

6. In its first year, Camco Inc. generated a $92,000 net operating loss, and it also made a $5,000 cash donation to a local charity. In its second year, Camco generated a $210,600 profit, and it also made a $10,000 donation to the same charity. Compute Camco's taxable income for its second year.

7. This year, Fig Corporation made a $100,000 contribution to charity. In each of the following situations, compute the after-tax cost of this contribution assuming that Fig uses a 6 percent discount rate to compute NPV.

   a. Fig had $8 million taxable income before consideration of the contribution.

   b. Fig had $490,000 taxable income before consideration of the contribution. Next year, Fig's taxable income is $6 million, and it makes no charitable contributions.

   c. Fig had $190,000 taxable income before consideration of the contribution. For the next five years, Fig's annual taxable income is $130,000, and it makes no charitable contributions.

8. Cranberry Corporation, a North Dakota company, is a producer of low-budget independent films. It engages in this activity both within the United States and in Canada. For 2012, it earned $200,000 of net income within the United States and $300,000 within Canada. Compensation paid to its U.S. workforce was $150,000, and total compensation paid to its Canadian workforce was $100,000. Total taxable income, before any domestic production activities deduction, was $450,000.

   a. Cranberry is unsure whether film production is a qualifying activity for purposes of the domestic production activities deduction. If it is, calculate Cranberry's allowable deduction, its 2012 taxable income, and its 2012 regular income tax liability.

   b. If film production does not qualify, calculate Cranberry's 2012 regular income tax liability.

   c. Compare your answers to *a* and *b* above to compute the potential tax savings for Cranberry attributable to the domestic production activities deduction. Comment on whether you feel this tax savings will influence the company to shift future production activities from Canada to the United States.

9. Hallick, a Michigan corporation, operates two facilities for the manufacture of tangible goods; one facility is located in Michigan and the other is located in Canada. In 2012, Hallick earned the following net income from these facilities.

	Michigan	*Canada*
Gross receipts from sales	$ 1,978,000	$ 1,642,000
Cost of goods sold	(1,233,000)	(1,001,000)
Gross manufacturing profit	$ 745,000	$ 641,000
Other deductible expenses	(316,000)	(298,000)
Net income	$ 429,000	$ 343,000

Hallick's total compensation paid to its U.S. workforce was $635,000, and total compensation paid to its Canadian workforce was $409,000. In addition to its manufacturing income, Hallick earned $39,400 taxable investment income in 2012.

    a. Compute Hallick's 2012 taxable income.

    b. How would your computation change if Hallick's Canadian facility generated a $112,700 loss instead of $343,000 net income?

10. Landover Corporation is looking for a larger office building to house its expanding operations. It is considering two alternatives. The first is a newly constructed building at a cost of $6 million. It would require only minor modifications to meet Landover's needs, at an estimated cost of $500,000. The second building was constructed in 1910, and is a certified historic structure. It could be purchased for $3 million, but would require an additional $4 million in renovations to be suitable for Landover.

    a. Calculate Landover's allowable rehabilitation credit if it chooses to purchase and renovate the certified historic structure, and the after-tax purchase price of the building.

    b. Based on your analysis, which building should Landover acquire?

    c. How might your analysis and conclusion change if Landover is currently experiencing net operating losses and does not expect to pay regular tax for several years?

11. Western Corporation, a calendar year, accrual basis corporation, reported $500,000 of net income after tax on its financial statements prepared in accordance with GAAP. The corporation's books and records reveal the following information:

- Western's book income included $15,000 of dividends, received from a domestic corporation in which Western owns less than 1 percent of the outstanding stock.

- Western's depreciation expense per books was $55,000, and its MACRS depreciation was $70,000.

- Western earned $5,000 of interest from municipal bonds and $6,000 of interest from corporate bonds.

- Western's capital losses exceeded its capital gains by $2,000.

- Western's federal income tax expense per books was $249,000.

    a. Compute Western's federal taxable income and regular tax liability.

    b. Prepare a Schedule M-1, page 5, Form 1120, reconciling Western's book and taxable income.

12. EFG, a calendar year, accrual basis corporation, reported $479,900 net income after tax on its 2011 financial statements prepared in accordance with GAAP. The corporation's financial records reveal the following information.

- EFG earned $314,800 from a qualified domestic production activity.

- EFG earned $10,700 on an investment in tax-exempt municipal bonds.

- EFG's allowance for bad debts as of January 1 was $21,000. Write-offs for the year totaled $4,400, while the addition to the allowance was $3,700. The allowance as of December 31 was $20,300.

- On August 7, EFG paid a $6,000 fine to a municipal government for a violation of a local zoning ordinance.

- EFG's depreciation expense per books was $44,200, and its MACRS depreciation deduction was $31,000.

- This is EFG's second taxable year. In its first taxable year, it recognized an $8,800 net capital loss. This year, it recognized a $31,000 Section 1231 gain on the sale of equipment. This was EFG's only disposition of noninventory assets.

- In its first taxable year, EFG capitalized $6,900 organizational costs for tax purposes and elected to amortize the costs over 180 months. For book purposes, it expensed the costs.
- EFG's federal income tax expense per books was $241,589.

a. Compute EFG's taxable income and regular tax.

b. Prepare a Schedule M-1, page 5, Form 1120, reconciling EFG's book and taxable income.

13. Grim Corporation has income and expenses for its fiscal year ended April 30, 2012, recorded under generally accepted accounting principles, as shown in the schedule below. In addition, a review of Grim's books and records reveals the following information:

- Grim expensed, for book purposes, meals and entertainment costs totaling $100,000. These costs were incurred by Grim sales personnel, are reasonable in amount, and are documented in company records.

- During January 2012, Grim was sued by one of its employees as a result of a work-related accident. The suit has not yet gone to court. However, Grim's auditors required the company to record a contingent liability (and related book expense) for $50,000, reflecting the company's likely liability from the suit.

- Grim recorded federal income tax expense for book purposes of $130,000.

- Grim uses the reserve method for calculating bad debt expenses for book purposes. Its 2012 book income statement reflects bad debt expense of $30,000, calculated as 1.5 percent of sales revenue. Actual write-offs of accounts receivable during 2012 totaled $22,000.

- MACRS depreciation for the year totals $95,000.

a. Complete the table shown below, reflecting Grim's book/tax differences for the current year, whether such differences are positive (increase taxable income) or negative (decrease taxable income), and the final numbers to be included in the calculation of taxable income on Grim's tax return.

	GAAP Book Income	Book/Tax Differences	Taxable Income
Sales revenue	$ 2,000,000		
Cost of goods sold	(1,200,000)		
Net profit	$ 800,000		
Meals and entertainment expense	(100,000)		
Bad debt expense	(30,000)		
Depreciation expense	(80,000)		
Other operating expenses	(220,000)		
Contingent loss	(50,000)		
Income before taxes	$ 320,000		
Federal income tax expense	(130,000)		
Net income	$ 190,000		

b. Prepare a Schedule M-1, page 5, Form 1120, reconciling Grim's book and taxable income.

14. Corporation AB's marginal tax rate is 15 percent, and Corporation YZ's marginal tax rate is 35 percent.

a. If both corporations are entitled to an additional $5,000 deduction, how much tax savings will the deduction generate for each corporation?

    b. If both corporations are entitled to a $5,000 tax credit, how much tax savings will the credit generate for each corporation? (Assume that each corporation's precredit tax exceeds $5,000.)

15. In each of the following cases, compute the corporation's regular tax.

    a. Allen Corporation, which produces motion pictures, has $160,000 taxable income.

    b. Benson Corporation, a personal service corporation providing medical care, has $160,000 taxable income.

    c. Carver Corporation, which develops and operates golf resorts, has $3.91 million taxable income.

    d. Damon Corporation, which drills oil wells, has $16.8 million taxable income.

    e. Edmonds Corporation, which manufactures farm equipment, has $57 million taxable income.

16. Refer to the cases in the preceding problem. In each case, identify the corporation's marginal tax rate, and compute its average tax rate.

17. Myamo was incorporated on January 1, 2010, and adopted a calendar year for tax purposes. It had the following gross receipts for its first three taxable years.

2010	$5,118,300
2011	3,520,000
2012	5,291,000

    For which of these three years is Myamo exempt from AMT?

18. Northup was incorporated on January 1, 2007, and adopted a calendar year for tax purposes. It had the following gross receipts for its first six taxable years.

2007	$4,282,000
2008	8,418,000
2009	7,002,000
2010	9,668,000
2011	5,219,000
2012	3,843,000

    For which of these years is Northup exempt from AMT?

19. Perkin Corporation's regular taxable income is $100,000, and it has positive AMT adjustments totaling $45,000 and a $22,000 AMT tax preference. Compute Perkin's AMT (if any).

20. Raise Corporation's regular taxable income is $3,590,000, and it has positive AMT adjustments totaling $980,000 and AMT tax preferences totaling $315,000. Compute Raise's AMT (if any).

21. Grand Inc. has taxable income of $1.25 million before any NOL deduction. It has $2.8 million of NOL carryforwards but no other AMT adjustments or preferences. Compute Grand's tax.

22. Camden Corporation, a calendar year accrual basis corporation, reported $5 million of net income after tax on its financial statements prepared in accordance with GAAP. In addition, the following information is available from Camden's books and records:

- Federal income tax expense per books was $2 million.
- Camden incurred $30,000 of meals and entertainment expenses.

- Camden sold two pieces of equipment used in its business for total sales proceeds of $400,000. The equipment's original cost was $2 million. Book depreciation prior to sale totaled $1.2 million; tax depreciation totaled $1.5 million.
- Camden uses the reserve method of accounting for bad debts. Additions to the reserve during the year totaled $400,000. Accounts receivable actually written off during the year totaled $450,000.
- Camden's depreciation expense for book purposes totaled $900,000. Tax depreciation computed under MACRS is $1.2 million.

    a. Determine Camden's taxable income and complete Schedule M-1, page 5, Form 1120.

    b. For the current year, Camden has AMT preferences and positive AMT adjustments totaling $2 million. Calculate Camden's alternative minimum taxable income, tentative minimum tax, regular tax before credits, and final tax due.

23. Assume the following tentative minimum tax and regular tax amounts have been calculated for Krolick Corporation:

	Year 1	Year 2	Year 3
Tentative minimum tax	$150,000	$130,000	$110,000
Regular tax	110,000	150,000	150,000

    Complete the following table by calculating any minimum tax credit generated, any such credit usable, and the final tax liability for Krolick Corporation for each year.

	Year 1	Year 2	Year 3
Minimum tax credit generated			
Minimum tax credit used			
Final tax liability			
Minimum tax credit carryforward			

24. Hall Corporation was formed in 2008 and was exempt from AMT for that year. For 2009 through 2011, its regular tax and tentative minimum tax were as follows.

Year	Regular Tax	Tentative Minimum Tax
2009	$ 200,000	$ 160,000
2010	870,000	900,000
2011	1,500,000	1,820,000

    a. Compute Hall's tax for 2009, 2010, and 2011.

    b. Compute Hall's tax for 2012 if its regular taxable income is $9 million, and its AMTI is $11 million.

    c. Compute Hall's tax for 2012 if its regular taxable income is $9 million, and its AMTI is $14.8 million.

25. In 2012, NB Inc.'s federal income tax was $242,000. Compute the required installment payments of 2013 tax in each of the following cases.

    a. NB's 2013 taxable income is $593,000.

    b. NB's 2013 taxable income is $950,000.

    c. NB's 2013 taxable income is $1,400,000.

26. James, who is in the 35 percent marginal tax bracket, owns 100 percent of the stock of JJ Inc. This year, JJ generates $500,000 taxable income and pays a $100,000 dividend to James. Compute his tax on the dividend under each of the following assumptions.

    a. The federal tax rules currently in effect apply to the dividend payment.

    b. The federal tax system has been amended to allow shareholders to gross up dividend income by the corporate tax paid with respect to the dividend and credit this tax against their individual tax.

27. Shine Inc. manufactures laundry detergent and other cleaning products. This year, the government increased the corporate tax rate by 2 percent. The marketing department determined that Shine could not raise its prices and retain its market share. The production department concluded that manufacturing costs cannot be reduced by another penny. Consequently, Shine's before-tax profits remain constant, while after-tax profits decline by the full tax increase. The stock market reaction to the decline in earnings is a fall in Shine's stock price.

    a. Who bears the incidence of the increase in Shine's corporate tax?

    b. How would your answer change if Shine held its after-tax profit constant by shutting down the on-site day care center for its employees' preschool children and eliminating this operating cost from its budget?

28. Griffin Corporation received $50,000 of dividend income from Eagle, Inc. Griffin owns 5 percent of the outstanding stock of Eagle. Griffin's marginal tax rate is 35 percent.

    a. Calculate Griffin's allowable dividends-received deduction and its after-tax cash flow as a result of the dividend from Eagle.

    b. How would your answers to *a* change if Griffin owned 55 percent of the stock of Eagle?

    c. How would your answers to *b* change if Griffin owned 85 percent of the stock of Eagle?

Issue Recognition Problems

Identify the tax issue or issues suggested by the following situations, and state each issue in the form of a question.

1. Greentown Foundation is a nonprofit corporation exempt from federal income tax. Its purpose is to solicit volunteers to plant and tend public gardens and greenbelts located in inner cities. The board of directors is considering publishing a gardener's newsletter that Greentown could sell in retail bookstores to raise money for its various projects.

2. TK Enterprises, an accrual basis corporation, needs to raise capital. One idea is for TK to sell bonds to the public for $625 each. These bonds would have no stated rate of interest but would be redeemable from TK in five years for a redemption price of $1,000.

3. Bandera Corporation has not paid a dividend for six years. This year, the board of directors decides to declare a dividend. It hires a consultant to update the shareholder records so that the dividend can be distributed to the proper people. The consultant's fee for her services is $16,800.

4. M&M is a publicly held corporation, and its stock trades on Nasdaq. This year, M&M contributed 15,000 shares of its newly issued common stock to a local charity. At date of contribution, the stock was selling at $7.12 per share.

5. Twenty years ago, Chemco Corporation developed, manufactured, and marketed Kepone, a chemical pesticide. As a result of manufacturing practices that violated state environmental standards, harmful levels of Kepone were discharged into the soil and groundwater.

A state agency sued Chemco for damages, and the corporation was indicted for criminal negligence for the unlawful discharge of toxic substances. The judge imposed a $1 million fine on Chemco. After extensive meetings with the judge and prosecutors, Chemco created the Midwest Environment Foundation, the purpose of which is to alleviate the effects of Kepone waste. Chemco contributed $950,000 to this nonprofit organization, and the judge promptly reduced the fine to $50,000.

6. Several years ago, Ferris Corporation purchased heavy machinery for $618,000. It sold the machinery this year for $500,000. Through date of sale, MACRS depreciation on the machinery was $320,000, while AMT depreciation was $198,000. Ferris has paid AMT in three of its last five taxable years and expects to do so again this year.

7. In its first year of operations, Talon Corporation incurred a $120,000 NOL. The director of tax projects that Talon will generate $40,000 taxable income in each of the next three years. Consequently, the director estimates that Talon will pay no tax in these years because of the NOL carryforward deduction.

8. Wiggins Corporation is a calendar year taxpayer. For the past nine years, its taxable income has been stable, averaging $2 million per year. Through November of this year, its taxable income was $1.81 million. In April, June, and September, Wiggins made a $175,000 installment payment of tax. In December, it recognized a $5 million gain on the sale of investment land.

Research Problems

1. In 2011, Connor Inc. announced its intention to construct a manufacturing facility in the Shenandoah Valley. In order to persuade Connor to locate the facility in Augusta County, the county government contributed a six-acre tract of undeveloped county land to the corporation. The appraised FMV of the land at date of contribution was $280,000. Soon after accepting the contribution, Connor paid $3,300 to an attorney to do a title search to make sure that it had uncontested ownership of the land. Connor also paid $12,900 for a survey and site map of the six acres and $1,360 for two water wells drilled on the land. Did Connor recognize income because of the receipt of the land? What is the proper tax treatment of Connor's $17,560 expenditure with respect to the land?

   In 2012, Connor's attorney discovered that the Estate of Elsa Reynolds claimed title to the six acres and was preparing to file suit in Virginia state court to regain ownership and possession. The attorney advised Connor that the estate's claim appeared valid and would be upheld. Consequently, Connor informed Augusta County that it was renouncing all claim to the land and would build its new manufacturing facility 200 miles away in Rockingham County. Did Connor recognize a loss when it renounced its claim to the land?

2. On December 10, 2010, the representative of a national charitable organization contacted the CEO of Wilkie Inc., a calendar year accrual basis corporation, to solicit a $100,000 donation. The CEO presented the solicitation to Wilkie's board of directors on December 19, and the board unanimously authorized the donation. Pursuant to this authorization, Wilkie transferred ownership of 3,973 shares of Gydo Inc. common stock to the charity on March 20, 2011. Wilkie purchased the Gydo stock in 1998 for $71,800 and held it as an investment. On March 20, Gydo common was selling on the NYSE for $25.17 per share. Before consideration of this donation, Wilkie's taxable income for both 2010 and 2011 exceeded $8 million. In which year is Wilkie allowed a charitable deduction for this donation, and what is the amount of the deduction?

3. Barry and Lynette Majors own 36 percent of the outstanding stock of Echo Valley, which has approximately $5 million earnings and profits. Echo Valley owns 38 tracts of undeveloped land in central Colorado. Barry and Lynette want to acquire one of the tracts (tract D6) to develop as a campground and recreational park. The appraised FMV of tract D6 is $420,000 although the corporation's tax basis is only $211,000. At the most recent shareholder meeting, Barry and Lynette convinced the other shareholders to distribute tract D6 to them as a dividend. (The other shareholders would receive equivalent cash dividends proportionate to their stock ownership.) Would the distribution of tract D6 as a dividend be a taxable event to Echo Valley? How much dividend income would the Majors recognize, and what would be their tax basis in tract D6?

4. This year, Prewer Inc. received a $160,000 dividend on its investment consisting of 16 percent of the outstanding stock of TKS Inc., a taxable domestic corporation. Before considering this dividend, Prewer had a $43,500 operating loss for the year. It also had a $31,300 NOL carryover deduction from 2007. What is Prewer's taxable income this year?

Tax Planning Cases

1. Congress recently enacted a nonrefundable credit based on the cost of qualifying alcohol and drug abuse counseling programs provided by any corporate employer to its employees. The credit is limited to 50 percent of the total cost of the program. If a corporation elects the credit, none of the program costs are allowed as a deduction. Any credit in excess of current year tax may not be carried back or forward to another year.

   a. TMM Corporation spent $80,000 for a qualifying counseling program this year. If TMM has $500,000 taxable income before consideration of this expense, should it elect the credit or deduct the program's cost as an ordinary business expense?

   b. Would your answer change if TMM had only $70,000 taxable income before consideration of the expense?

2. A&Z Inc. averages $4 million taxable income a year. Because it needs an infusion of cash, the board of directors is considering two options: selling a new issue of preferred stock to the public for a total offering price of $500,000 or borrowing $500,000 from a local bank. The market dividend rate on preferred stock is only 5.6 percent, while the bank's interest rate is 9 percent. Which option minimizes the after-tax cost of the new capital?

3. In 2011, Elspeth Corporation paid both regular tax ($2,714,000) and AMT ($129,300). The director of tax forecasts that Elspeth will be in an AMT position for 2012 and 2013. However, its tentative minimum tax in 2014 will be significantly less than its regular tax. Assuming a 6 percent discount rate, calculate the cost of the 2011 AMT in present value terms.

4. Wingo Inc, which has a 34 percent income tax rate, is considering making a substantial investment in marketable securities that should generate $400,000 income/cash flow this year. Compute Wingo's after-tax cash flow under each of the following assumptions.

   a. The investment is in tax-exempt bonds, and Wingo is not in an AMT position (Wingo will pay regular income tax but no AMT this year).

   b. The investment is in publicly traded stock, the $400,000 cash dividend is eligible for a 70 percent dividends-received deduction, and Wingo is not in an AMT position.

   c. The investment is in tax-exempt bonds. Wingo is in an AMT position and has a positive ACE adjustment before consideration of the interest income.

   d. The investment is in publicly traded stock, and the $400,000 cash dividend is eligible for a 70 percent dividends-received deduction. Wingo is in an AMT position and has a positive ACE adjustment before consideration of the dividend income.

CPA REVIEW

**CPA Exam
Simulation**

Please visit the text website for the online CPA simulation: mhhe.com/sjones2013.

A client operates a small business organized as a sole proprietorship and is considering changing the business to operate as a C corporation. The client wants to know how certain deductible items are treated for tax purposes by a business conducted as a C corporation filing Form 1120, *U.S. Corporation Income Tax Return,* as compared to the way they are treated as a sole proprietorship filing Form 1040, *U.S. Individual Income Tax Return.*

Topics covered in the simulation:

- Charitable contribution limitations
- Payments to owners for services rendered
- Payments for health insurance for owners
- Business meals and entertainment expenses

Appendix **11–A**

Schedule M-3 for Reconciling Book and Taxable Income

During 2004, the IRS developed Schedule M-3 with the goal of increasing transparency between reported net income for financial accounting purposes and reported net income for tax purposes. The new schedule replaces Schedule M-1 for tax years ending on or after December 31, 2004, for corporations with total assets of $10 million or more. Schedule M-3 reports significantly more detailed information than Schedule M-1, including the temporary versus permanent characterization of book-tax differences and the detail of book income and expense amounts for each line item on Schedule M-3.

Schedule M-3 is divided into three parts. Part I reports the source of the financial information used in the tax return, whether it be from SEC Form 10-K, a certified audited income statement, or simply the corporations books and records. In addition, for a consolidated group of corporations, Part I reconciles worldwide financial statement net income to the financial statement net income of those corporations permitted to be included in the U.S. consolidated tax return group.

Parts II and III of Schedule M-3 reconcile the elements of financial statement net income to taxable income, using four columns and more than 60 specific categories, many of which require attachment of detailed supporting schedules. Part II focuses on income (loss) items, while Part III details expense/deduction items. The end result of the reconciliation process, line 30 of Part II, must equal line 28, page 1, Form 1120.

SCHEDULE M-3 (Form 1120) Department of the Treasury Internal Revenue Service	**Net Income (Loss) Reconciliation for Corporations With Total Assets of $10 Million or More** ▶ Attach to Form 1120 or 1120-C. ▶ See separate instructions.	OMB No. 1545-0123 20**11**

Name of corporation (common parent, if consolidated return)	Employer identification number

Check applicable box(es): (1) ☐ Non-consolidated return (2) ☐ Consolidated return (Form 1120 only)

(3) ☐ Mixed 1120/L/PC group (4) ☐ Dormant subsidiaries schedule attached

Part I **Financial Information and Net Income (Loss) Reconciliation** (see instructions)

1a Did the corporation file SEC Form 10-K for its income statement period ending with or within this tax year?
  ☐ **Yes.** Skip lines 1b and 1c and complete lines 2a through 11 with respect to that SEC Form 10-K.
  ☐ **No.** Go to line 1b. See instructions if multiple non-tax-basis income statements are prepared.
 b Did the corporation prepare a certified audited non-tax-basis income statement for that period?
  ☐ **Yes.** Skip line 1c and complete lines 2a through 11 with respect to that income statement.
  ☐ **No.** Go to line 1c.
 c Did the corporation prepare a non-tax-basis income statement for that period?
  ☐ **Yes.** Complete lines 2a through 11 with respect to that income statement.
  ☐ **No.** Skip lines 2a through 3c and enter the corporation's net income (loss) per its books and records on line 4a.
2a Enter the income statement period: Beginning   MM/DD/YYYY   Ending   MM/DD/YYYY
 b Has the corporation's income statement been restated for the income statement period on line 2a?
  ☐ **Yes.** (If "Yes," attach an explanation and the amount of each item restated.)
  ☐ **No.**
 c Has the corporation's income statement been restated for any of the five income statement periods preceding the period on line 2a?
  ☐ **Yes.** (If "Yes," attach an explanation and the amount of each item restated.)
  ☐ **No.**
3a Is any of the corporation's voting common stock publicly traded?
  ☐ **Yes.**
  ☐ **No.** If "No," go to line 4a.
 b Enter the symbol of the corporation's primary U.S. publicly traded voting common stock . . . .
 c Enter the nine-digit CUSIP number of the corporation's primary publicly traded voting common stock . . . .

4a Worldwide consolidated net income (loss) from income statement source identified in Part I, line 1 .	**4a**	
b Indicate accounting standard used for line 4a (see instructions):		
(1) ☐ GAAP (2) ☐ IFRS (3) ☐ Statutory (4) ☐ Tax-basis (5) ☐ Other (specify) _____		
5a Net income from nonincludible foreign entities (attach schedule)	**5a**	( )
b Net loss from nonincludible foreign entities (attach schedule and enter as a positive amount) . . .	**5b**	
6a Net income from nonincludible U.S. entities (attach schedule)	**6a**	( )
b Net loss from nonincludible U.S. entities (attach schedule and enter as a positive amount)	**6b**	
7a Net income (loss) of other includible foreign disregarded entities (attach schedule)	**7a**	
b Net income (loss) of other includible U.S. disregarded entities (attach schedule)	**7b**	
c Net income (loss) of other includible entities (attach schedule)	**7c**	
8 Adjustment to eliminations of transactions between includible entities and nonincludible entities (attach schedule)	**8**	
9 Adjustment to reconcile income statement period to tax year (attach schedule)	**9**	
10a Intercompany dividend adjustments to reconcile to line 11 (attach schedule)	**10a**	
b Other statutory accounting adjustments to reconcile to line 11 (attach schedule)	**10b**	
c Other adjustments to reconcile to amount on line 11 (attach schedule)	**10c**	
11 **Net income (loss) per income statement of includible corporations.** Combine lines 4 through 10 . .	**11**	
Note. Part I, line 11, must equal the amount on Part II, line 30, column (a), and Schedule M-2, line 2.		

12 Enter the total amount (not just the corporation's share) of the assets and liabilities of all entities included or removed on the following lines.

	Total Assets	Total Liabilities
a Included on Part I, line 4 . . . . . . ▶		
b Removed on Part I, line 5 . . . . . . ▶		
c Removed on Part I, line 6 . . . . . . ▶		
d Included on Part I, line 7 . . . . . . ▶		

For Paperwork Reduction Act Notice, see the Instructions for Form 1120. Cat. No. 37961C Schedule M-3 (Form 1120) 2011

Schedule M-3 (Form 1120) 2011 | Page **2**

Name of corporation (common parent, if consolidated return)	Employer identification number

Check applicable box(es): **(1)** ☐ Consolidated group   **(2)** ☐ Parent corp   **(3)** ☐ Consolidated eliminations   **(4)** ☐ Subsidiary corp   **(5)** ☐ Mixed 1120/L/PC group

Check if a sub-consolidated: **(6)** ☐ 1120 group   **(7)** ☐ 1120 eliminations

Name of subsidiary (if consolidated return)	Employer identification number

Part II   **Reconciliation of Net Income (Loss) per Income Statement of Includible Corporations With Taxable Income per Return** (see instructions)

Income (Loss) Items (Attach schedules for lines 1 through 11)	(a) Income (Loss) per Income Statement	(b) Temporary Difference	(c) Permanent Difference	(d) Income (Loss) per Tax Return
1 Income (loss) from equity method foreign corporations				
2 Gross foreign dividends not previously taxed . . .				
3 Subpart F, QEF, and similar income inclusions . .				
4 Section 78 gross-up				
5 Gross foreign distributions previously taxed . . .				
6 Income (loss) from equity method U.S. corporations				
7 U.S. dividends not eliminated in tax consolidation				
8 Minority interest for includible corporations . . .				
9 Income (loss) from U.S. partnerships				
10 Income (loss) from foreign partnerships				
11 Income (loss) from other pass-through entities . .				
12 Items relating to reportable transactions (attach details)				
13 Interest income (attach Form 8916-A)				
14 Total accrual to cash adjustment				
15 Hedging transactions				
16 Mark-to-market income (loss)				
17 Cost of goods sold (attach Form 8916-A)	( )			( )
18 Sale versus lease (for sellers and/or lessors) . . .				
19 Section 481(a) adjustments				
20 Unearned/deferred revenue				
21 Income recognition from long-term contracts . .				
22 Original issue discount and other imputed interest .				
23a Income statement gain/loss on sale, exchange, abandonment, worthlessness, or other disposition of assets other than inventory and pass-through entities				
b Gross capital gains from Schedule D, excluding amounts from pass-through entities				
c Gross capital losses from Schedule D, excluding amounts from pass-through entities, abandonment losses, and worthless stock losses				
d Net gain/loss reported on Form 4797, line 17, excluding amounts from pass-through entities, abandonment losses, and worthless stock losses				
e Abandonment losses				
f Worthless stock losses (attach details)				
g Other gain/loss on disposition of assets other than inventory				
24 Capital loss limitation and carryforward used . . .				
25 Other income (loss) items with differences (attach schedule)				
26 **Total income (loss) items.** Combine lines 1 through 25				
27 **Total expense/deduction items** (from Part III, line 38)				
28 Other items with no differences				
29a Mixed groups, see instructions. All others, combine lines 26 through 28				
b PC insurance subgroup reconciliation totals . . .				
c Life insurance subgroup reconciliation totals . . .				
30 **Reconciliation totals.** Combine lines 29a through 29c				

Note. Line 30, column (a), must equal the amount on Part I, line 11, and column (d) must equal Form 1120, page 1, line 28.

Schedule M-3 (Form 1120) 2011

Schedule M-3 (Form 1120) 2011   Page **3**

Name of corporation (common parent, if consolidated return)	Employer identification number

Check applicable box(es): **(1)** ☐ Consolidated group   **(2)** ☐ Parent corp   **(3)** ☐ Consolidated eliminations   **(4)** ☐ Subsidiary corp   **(5)** ☐ Mixed 1120/L/PC group
Check if a sub-consolidated: **(6)** ☐ 1120 group   **(7)** ☐ 1120 eliminations

Name of subsidiary (if consolidated return)	Employer identification number

Part III   Reconciliation of Net Income (Loss) per Income Statement of Includible Corporations With Taxable Income per Return—Expense/Deduction Items (see instructions)

Expense/Deduction Items	(a) Expense per Income Statement	(b) Temporary Difference	(c) Permanent Difference	(d) Deduction per Tax Return
1 U.S. current income tax expense				
2 U.S. deferred income tax expense				
3 State and local current income tax expense				
4 State and local deferred income tax expense				
5 Foreign current income tax expense (other than foreign withholding taxes)				
6 Foreign deferred income tax expense				
7 Foreign withholding taxes				
8 Interest expense (attach Form 8916-A)				
9 Stock option expense				
10 Other equity-based compensation				
11 Meals and entertainment				
12 Fines and penalties				
13 Judgments, damages, awards, and similar costs				
14 Parachute payments				
15 Compensation with section 162(m) limitation				
16 Pension and profit-sharing				
17 Other post-retirement benefits				
18 Deferred compensation				
19 Charitable contribution of cash and tangible property				
20 Charitable contribution of intangible property				
21 Charitable contribution limitation/carryforward				
22 Domestic production activities deduction				
23 Current year acquisition or reorganization investment banking fees				
24 Current year acquisition or reorganization legal and accounting fees				
25 Current year acquisition/reorganization other costs				
26 Amortization/impairment of goodwill				
27 Amortization of acquisition, reorganization, and start-up costs				
28 Other amortization or impairment write-offs				
29 Section 198 environmental remediation costs				
30 Depletion				
31 Depreciation				
32 Bad debt expense				
33 Corporate owned life insurance premiums				
34 Purchase versus lease (for purchasers and/or lessees)				
35 Research and development costs				
36 Section 118 exclusion (attach schedule)				
37 Other expense/deduction items with differences (attach schedule)				
38 **Total expense/deduction items.** Combine lines 1 through 37. Enter here and on Part II, line 27, reporting positive amounts as negative and negative amounts as positive				

Schedule M-3 (Form 1120) 2011

Chapter Twelve

The Choice of Business Entity

Learning Objectives

After studying this chapter, you should be able to:

1. Explain the advantage of start-up losses in a passthrough entity.

2. Calculate after-tax cash flow from passthrough entities and taxable corporations.

3. Describe how families can use partnerships or S corporations to shift income.

4. Define the term *constructive dividend*.

5. Explain why individuals no longer can use corporations as tax shelters.

6. Explain the purpose of the accumulated earnings tax and the personal holding company tax.

7. Apply the tax rates to income earned by a controlled corporate group.

In the two preceding chapters, we identified the basic forms of business organization and learned how the choice of form determines whether business income is taxed at the individual or corporate rates. These chapters concentrated on the tax rules and regulations applying to different business entities. In Chapter 12, we will build on this technical knowledge as we consider the tax planning implications of the choice of business entity. The first half of the chapter focuses on the advantages of conducting a business as a passthrough entity. The second half explains how business owners can control the tax cost of operating in the corporate form. Throughout the chapter, we will analyze how planning strategies affect after-tax cash flow available to the business owners.

No one organizational form is ideal for every business. The tax characteristics of one form may be advantageous in one case and disadvantageous in another. In some cases, a passthrough entity accomplishes the owners' tax objectives, while in other cases, a taxable corporation is the better option. Oftentimes, owners have compelling nontax reasons for operating their business in a particular form. As the business matures and the owners' financial situations evolve, the optimal form may change. Finally, business owners must reevaluate the form in which they conduct their business every time Congress amends the Internal Revenue Code. Even minor alterations in the law can affect the tax pros and cons of passthrough entities and taxable corporations.

TAX PLANNING WITH PASSTHROUGH ENTITIES

From Chapter 10, we know that businesses organized as partnerships, LLCs, and S corporations are not subject to federal income tax at the entity level. Instead, income passes through the entity to be reported by and taxed to the owners. If the business operates at a loss, the loss passes through and is reported as a deduction by the owners. Cash distributions from passthrough entities are generally nontaxable. These cash flows represent a return of the owners' investment in the business and do not affect the income or loss reported by the owners. For many individuals, this combination of rules helps them control tax costs and maximize the cash flow from their business.

Tax Benefit of Start-Up Losses

Objective 1
Explain the advantage of start-up losses in a passthrough entity.

Organizers of a new business may expect to lose money during the start-up phase. If the business is organized as a passthrough entity, these initial losses can generate an immediate tax savings to the owners. If the business is organized as a corporation, the losses do not flow through but are trapped at the entity level as NOL carryforwards. As a result, the tax savings from the start-up losses are deferred until the corporation can deduct them against future income. The following example focuses on this important difference in timing.

Start-Up Losses

A group of individuals owns a business with the following income and deductions for its first three years.

Year	Gross Income	Allowable Deductions	Net Income or Loss
0	$ 420,000	$ (720,000)	$(300,000)
1	800,000	(920,000)	(120,000)
2	1,530,000	(1,000,000)	530,000

If the owners organized the business as a passthrough entity, they could deduct the operating losses in years 0 and 1.[1] In year 2, they paid tax on $530,000 business income. If the owners organized the business as a corporation with no S election, the losses in years 0 and 1 carried forward and resulted in $110,000 corporate taxable income in year 2. To isolate the tax effect of the timing difference, let's use a hypothetical 35 percent tax rate for both the individual owners and the corporation and a 5 percent discount rate.

Tax Savings and Costs

	Passthrough Entity			
Year	(Deduction) or Taxable Income	Tax Savings or (Cost)	Discount Factor	Present Value of Tax Savings or (Cost)
0	$(300,000)	$ 105,000		$ 105,000
1	(120,000)	42,000	.952	39,984
2	530,000	(185,500)	.907	(168,249)
		$ (38,500)		$ (23,265)

[1] If a passthrough loss exceeds the owner's other income for the year, the excess loss is a net operating loss. The owner can carry the NOL back as a deduction to the two preceding years or forward as a deduction for 20 years.

	Corporation			
Year	(NOL Carryforward) or Taxable Income	Tax Savings or (Cost)	Discount Factor	Present Value of Tax Savings or (Cost)
0	$(300,000)	–0–		–0–
1	(120,000)	–0–		–0–
2	110,000	$(38,500)	.907	$(34,920)
		$(38,500)		$(34,920)

In this simple case, the present value of the tax cost is minimized if the business was organized as a passthrough entity rather than as a corporation. The dramatic difference in tax cost is *entirely attributable* to the timing of the deduction for the first two years of losses. With a passthrough entity, these losses were deductible in the year incurred. Consequently, the owners received the tax savings from the deduction in years 0 and 1. With a corporate entity, the tax savings from the loss deduction were postponed until year 2, so the savings decreased in present value terms.

Avoiding a Double Tax on Business Income

Objective 2
Calculate after-tax cash flow from passthrough entities and taxable corporations.

People who own their own business often depend on the cash flow from the business to meet their family's consumption needs. Their basic financial strategy is to maximize the cash transferred from the business bank account to their personal checking account. This strategy usually dictates that they operate their business as a passthrough entity, rather than as a corporation, so that income is taxed only once.

Single versus Double Tax

Mr. and Mrs. Gilbert are the sole shareholders in an S corporation that conducts a restaurant business.[2] The restaurant generates $100,000 taxable income annually and an equal cash flow. The corporation distributes all available cash to the Gilberts each year. Assuming a 28 percent individual tax rate, the after-tax cash flow from their business is $72,000.

Annual cash from operations	$100,000
Individual tax	
($100,000 taxable income × 28%)	(28,000)
After-tax cash flow	$ 72,000

If Mr. and Mrs. Gilbert had not elected subchapter S status for their corporation, the $100,000 income would be taxed at the entity level and the corporation itself would pay $22,250 tax. The cash available for distribution would be only $77,750. Moreover, the distribution would be a dividend to Mr. and Mrs. Gilbert, and the after-tax cash available for their personal consumption would be only $66,087.

Annual cash from operations	$100,000
Corporate tax	(22,250)
Cash distributed to shareholders	$ 77,750
Individual tax	
($77,750 dividend × 15%)	(11,663)
After-tax cash flow	$ 66,087

[2] To keep the example simple, assume that neither shareholder is an employee of the corporation.

In Mr. and Mrs. Gilbert's case, the double tax resulting from the corporate form would result in a 33.9 percent tax rate on their business income ($33,913 total tax ÷ $100,000 income). Clearly, Mr. and Mrs. Gilbert are minimizing their income tax and maximizing the money they can spend by operating their restaurant as a passthrough entity.

Income Shifting among Family Members

Objective 3
Describe how families can use partnerships or S corporations to shift income.

The creation of a family partnership or S corporation can be an effective way to divide business income among a number of taxpayers. To the extent that this division causes income to be taxed at a lower marginal rate, the total tax burden on the business shrinks. This strategy is an application of the entity variable, discussed in Chapter 4. Let's illustrate this concept with a simple example.

Shift of Business Income	Mrs. Alm owns a sole proprietorship generating $150,000 annual taxable income. Mrs. Alm is in the 35 percent tax bracket but has two children in the 25 percent tax bracket. If Mrs. Alm could convert her business into a passthrough entity in which she and her children are equal owners, the annual income would be allocated among three individual taxpayers. If the shift of $50,000 business income from Mrs. Alm to each child decreased the tax rate on the income from 35 percent to 25 percent, the tax savings would be $10,000.

Tax on $100,000 at 35%	$ 35,000
Tax on $100,000 at 25%	(25,000)
	$ 10,000

While Mrs. Alm should be impressed with this tax strategy, she must understand that the strategy will not just shift *income* to her children—it will shift *dollars* to them as well. As owners, the children are entitled to an equal share of any cash distributions from the business. When the business eventually terminates or is sold, each child will receive one-third of any remaining property or any amount realized on sale. In other words, if Mrs. Alm wants to shift two-thirds of the business income, she must part with two-thirds of the wealth represented by the business.

Statutory Restrictions

The tax savings achieved through income shifts to family members with low tax rates can be substantial. Not surprisingly, the Internal Revenue Code restricts the use of both partnerships and S corporations as income-shifting devices. Let's first consider the statutory rules pertaining to family partnerships.

If partnership income is primarily attributable to the work performed by individual partners rather than to the property owned by the partnership, any allocation of that income to nonworking partners is an unjustified assignment of earned income. Accordingly, a family member cannot be a partner in a personal service business unless he or she is qualified to perform services for the business.[3] In contrast, a family member can be a partner in a business in which property is a material income-producing factor.[4] Unlike a service partnership,

---

[3] *Commissioner* v. *Culbertson,* 337 U.S. 733 (1949).

[4] §704(e)(1). Property is a material income-producing factor if the business requires substantial inventories or a substantial investment in plant, machinery, or equipment. Reg. §1.704-1(e)(1)(iv).

the mere ownership of an equity interest in a capital-intensive partnership entitles a partner to a share of profits.

Does a Family Partnership Exist?	Elizabeth and Emerson Winkler, who lived on a farm in Illinois, had five children. Emerson was in poor health and was frequently hospitalized. Elizabeth and one or more of her children always drove Emerson to the hospital. During these trips, the family usually purchased three $1 lottery tickets at the gas station where they stopped for fuel. The money was contributed by any family member who happened to have a dollar bill, and Elizabeth kept all the tickets in her china cabinet. The family often joked about how they would spend their winnings from these "family" tickets. On one trip, Elizabeth used her own money to purchase the three tickets. That night, one of these tickets won $6.5 million. The family agreed that Elizabeth and Emerson should each receive 25 percent of the jackpot, while each child should receive 10 percent. Consequently, when Elizabeth received the $6.5 million, she paid $650,000 to each of her five children. The IRS contended that no family partnership existed among the Winklers, and that Elizabeth and Emerson made gifts (the lottery winnings) to the children on which they owed gift tax of over $116,000. But the federal court disagreed with the IRS. The court concluded that the Winklers formed a family partnership to purchase lottery tickets. Each family member contributed capital to the partnership when he or she spent a dollar to buy a ticket and each contributed services by going into the gas station to make the purchase. Consequently, the division of the jackpot was a distribution of profits to partners rather than a taxable gift from Elizabeth and Emerson to their children.[5]

Family partnerships are often created when a business owner makes a gift of an equity interest to a relative, thereby creating a partnership between donor and donee. Alternatively, the owner could sell the equity interest to the relative to create the partnership. In either case, the business income must be allocated among the partners based on their proportionate interests in partnership capital.[6]

Family Partnership	Refer to the example on page 348 involving Mrs. Alm and her two children. Mrs. Alm can convert her sole proprietorship to a family partnership only if capital is a material income-producing factor. In other words, if Mrs. Alm is a self-employed physician earning $150,000 from her medical practice, she can't make her children partners unless they are qualified to provide some type of service to the practice. On the other hand, if Mrs. Alm's business is a retail clothing store, she can transfer the business assets to a partnership and give her children a capital interest in the new entity. If each child receives a one-third interest, the partnership income can be allocated in equal shares to the partners. If Mrs. Alm gives each child only a 10 percent capital interest, only 10 percent of the income can be shifted to each child.

If the partner who gave away or sold an equity interest to a family member provides services to the partnership, the partner must receive a guaranteed payment as compensation.[7] The partnership is allowed to deduct the payment, and the remaining income is allocated in proportion to the capital interests.

---

[5] *Estate of Emerson Winkler,* T.C. Memo 1997-4.

[6] In nonfamily partnerships, the allocation of income does not have to be in proportion to each partner's ownership of capital. For example, the partnership agreement could provide that a partner who owns 50 percent of the capital is allocated 80 percent of the business income or loss.

[7] §704(e).

<table>
<tr><td>

Compensation for Services to a Family Partnership

</td><td>

Refer to the preceding example and assume that Mrs. Alm formed a family partnership by giving a one-third equity interest in her retail clothing business to each of her two children. Mrs. Alm works 40 hours a week managing the business. If her services are reasonably worth $60,000 a year, the partnership must pay her a $60,000 guaranteed payment. If partnership income after deduction of this guaranteed payment is $90,000, the maximum allocation to each child is $30,000. Because of this allocation rule, Mrs. Alm can't increase the income shifted to her children by working for free on their behalf.

</td></tr>
</table>

When a business is operated as an S corporation, annual income is allocated pro rata to the outstanding shares of corporate stock. Therefore, the percentage of income allocable to any one individual is based strictly on the number of shares owned. If Mrs. Alm converted her sole proprietorship to an S corporation and gave each child one-third of the stock, each child would be allocated one-third of the business income. If she gave each child only 10 percent of the stock, their pro rata share of the income drops to 10 percent. Before any corporate income is allocated to the shareholders, Mrs. Alm must receive a reasonable salary for any services performed for the corporation.[8]

Transaction Costs

Even with these statutory restrictions, partnerships and S corporations are a viable way to reduce the aggregate income tax burden on a family business. The potential tax savings must be compared to the transaction costs of forming the entity. If an individual creates a family partnership or S corporation by giving an equity interest in an established business to a family member, the donative transfer may be subject to the federal gift tax. This tax is based on the FMV of the transferred interest and must be paid by the *donor* (the individual making the gift). If the business has considerable value, the gift tax may represent a substantial transaction cost.[9] The various nontax transaction costs associated with the formation and operation of a separate legal entity should also be factored into the decision to create a family partnership or S corporation.

<table>
<tr><td>

Transaction Costs of Partnership Formation

</td><td>

Refer back to the preceding example in which Mrs. Alm formed a family partnership by giving a one-third equity interest in her retail clothing business to each of her two children. Immediately before the formation, the business had an appraised FMV of $950,000. Consequently, the FMV of Mrs. Alm's gift to each child was $316,667. If Mrs. Alm has not made prior taxable gifts, she would owe no current gift tax due to the lifetime gift tax exemption. However, if she has fully utilized her lifetime gift tax exemption, the gift tax due on these transfers could be as high as $212,567! The partnership paid $2,750 to the attorney who drafted the partnership agreement and an $800 fee to transfer title in the business real estate to the partnership. Thus, the transaction costs of forming the family partnership could total as much as $216,117. The gift tax is a nondeductible personal expense. The attorney's fee is a deductible organizational cost. The title transfer fee is capitalized to the partnership's basis in the real estate.[10]

</td></tr>
</table>

Nontax Considerations

Entrepreneurs should carefully determine the extent to which the formation of a family-owned entity will dilute their control of the business. Many business owners who are willing to shift income and dollars to their relatives may be reluctant to give those relatives a

---

[8] §1366(e).

[9] The federal gift tax is discussed in more detail in Chapter 16.

[10] Reg. §1.709-2.

voice in management. A limited partnership in which the entrepreneur is the sole general partner can eliminate this concern. Another option is for the entrepreneur to create an S corporation capitalized with both voting and nonvoting stock. The entrepreneur can keep the voting stock and give the nonvoting stock to his family, thereby retaining complete control of the business.

Individuals who transfer equity interests to a family member should understand that the transfer must be complete and legally binding. The recipient becomes the owner of an intangible property right. Absent any restrictions, the recipient is free to dispose of this right, with or without the blessing of the other owners. *Buy-sell agreements* among the partners or shareholders are commonly used to restrict family members from selling or assigning their equity interest to an unrelated third party.

Still another important consideration is that the transfer of an equity interest must be irrevocable; the transferor can't simply change his mind and take the interest back. If the transferor becomes estranged from his family, an income-shifting arrangement could turn into a bitterly resented trap. A parent who has an ill-favored child can always disinherit the child. It is another matter entirely if the child owns stock in the family S corporation. A change in the relative economic circumstances of family members can also undermine an income-shifting strategy. Consider a situation in which a high-income taxpayer suffers a severe economic setback. An irreversible arrangement that shifts income away from this taxpayer could cause a personal financial crisis. These unhappy possibilities emphasize a point made earlier in the text: Tax strategies must be evaluated on the basis of flexibility. If a business owner is uneasy about her family's ability to cooperate, a family partnership or S corporation may be a bad idea.

A Family Partnership Gone Wrong	Refer one last time to the family partnership created by Mrs. Alm and her two children. Six years after the partnership was formed, one of the children died in an accident and his widow inherited his one-third interest in the partnership. The widow cannot get along with Mrs. Alm and the surviving child and contests every decision they make concerning the management of the retail clothing business. Because of the continual discord, the three partners finally discontinue the business and terminate the partnership.

PARTNERSHIP OR S CORPORATION?

Tax Talk
Although LLCs are increasingly popular, S corporations still dominate the small business landscape. In 2010, the IRS received 4.5 million returns from S corporations and only 3.5 million returns from partnerships and LLCs.

Entrepreneurs who organize their business as a passthrough entity must choose between some type of partnership and an S corporation. The choice depends on the tax and nontax characteristics that differentiate these two organizational forms. In the next few paragraphs, we will compare and contrast several important characteristics that enter into the decision-making process. Then we will analyze two planning cases.

Contrasting Characteristics

Costs of Entity Formation and Operation

The transfer of cash or property to a new partnership or corporation in exchange for a controlling equity interest is a nontaxable exchange.[11] Consequently, forming a new business entity has no up-front income tax cost. The owners will incur legal, accounting, and professional fees incidental to the formation. If the owners form a corporation, they must file a timely subchapter S election with the IRS. In addition, they must incur the incremental

---

[11] See the discussion of §721 and §351 in Chapter 9.

cost of monitoring the ownership structure to ensure that their S corporation continues to meet the eligibility requirements. If an S corporation loses its eligibility and the election terminates, the corporation automatically reverts to a taxable entity. An S corporation may be more expensive to operate than a partnership because of state tax costs. Several states, including New York, Tennessee, and Texas, impose entity-level income or franchise taxes on S corporations. In contrast, partnerships are typically exempt from state tax at the entity level.

Flexibility of Income and Loss-Sharing Arrangement

Partnerships offer owners the maximum flexibility to tailor their business arrangement to fit their needs. The partnership agreement specifies the amount and type of capital each partner contributes to the business and can create special sharing ratios for different items of income, gain, deduction, and loss. Moreover, the partners can amend their agreement every year. S corporations offer less flexibility because of the statutory restrictions on capital structure. S corporations can have only a single class of stock, and each share must represent an identical claim on the income and assets of the business.

Subchapter K versus Subchapter S

Although both partnerships and S corporations are passthrough entities, they are governed by different sections in the Internal Revenue Code. The sections governing partnerships are located in Subchapter K, while the sections governing S corporations are located in Subchapter S. Many provisions of Subchapter K, which originated with the Internal Revenue Code of 1954, are archaic and exceedingly difficult to apply. Subchapter K is particularly outmoded with respect to LLCs, which became widely available as an organizational form 30 years *after* Subchapter K was enacted. In comparison, Subchapter S was completely revised in 1982 to accommodate the modern S corporation and presents few difficulties in its application.

Self-Employment Tax

As we discussed in Chapter 10, general partners and LLC members who work for the LLC must treat their share of the entity's business income as net earnings from self-employment on which they pay self-employment tax. Shareholders in S corporations are not considered to be self-employed and therefore do not pay self-employment tax on their share of corporate income.

SE Tax Comparison	Mr. Biglow is a general partner in a partnership, and Ms. Tippee is a shareholder in an S corporation. Both individuals work full-time for the entity; Mr. Biglow receives a guaranteed payment, while Ms. Tippee receives a salary. This year, both individuals were allocated a $100,000 share of the entity's business income. Mr. Biglow must pay self-employment tax on both his guaranteed payment and his $100,000 share of partnership income. Ms. Tippee must pay employee payroll tax on her salary, but she does not pay self-employment tax on her $100,000 share of S corporation income.

Owner Liability

Historically, an S corporation was the only choice for owners who wanted to pay a single tax on business income at the owner level and avoid unlimited personal liability for claims against the business. In contrast, the traditional partnership involved significant financial risk for general partners, who have unlimited liability for business debt. In recent years, traditional partnerships have been supplanted by LLPs and LLCs, both of which offer greater protection against financial risk. In an LLP, a partner is not personally liable for malpractice-related claims arising from the professional misconduct of another partner. In many states, professionals such as CPAs and attorneys organize their practices as LLPs to safeguard themselves against the negligent actions of any one individual partner. In an LLC, every member has limited liability for all debts of or claims against the business. Consequently, an LLC combines the tax advantages of a passthrough entity *and* the legal protection of the corporate form, without the costs or complications of the latter. The number of these organizations is growing at a phenomenal rate, and the LLC is now the entity of choice for many new businesses.

Two Planning Cases

To complete our discussion of the relative advantages and disadvantages of partnerships and S corporations, let's develop two cases in which differences between them are key variables in the planning process.

Leveraged Real Property Venture	Six individuals decide to form a company to purchase, rehabilitate, and manage a hotel. The hotel property is subject to a $3 million nonrecourse mortgage, and the owner is willing to sell his equity in the property for only $50,000. The commercial lender holding the mortgage has agreed to the conveyance of the hotel to the new company. The individuals will each contribute $20,000 cash in exchange for equal ownership interests, and the company will use the cash to buy the hotel and begin the necessary renovations. The individuals forecast that the company will generate a $264,000 tax loss for its first year. Most of this loss is from cost recovery deductions with respect to the hotel building and its furnishings.
	The individuals intend to organize the company as a passthrough entity; consequently, each individual will be allocated $44,000 of the first-year loss. The individuals can deduct the loss only to the extent of the tax basis in their equity interest. If the company is organized as an S corporation, each individual's stock basis is $20,000—the cash contributed to the corporation. Therefore, each can deduct only $20,000 of the first-year loss.
	If the company is organized as an LLC, the tax basis in each member's interest includes both the contributed cash *and* a portion of the LLC's debts. Because of the $3 million non-recourse mortgage on the hotel, each individual has an initial basis of $520,000 ($20,000 cash + one-sixth of the mortgage). Because the LLC debt is included in basis, the individuals can deduct their entire shares of the first-year business losses.[12]
	With respect to risk of financial loss, the individuals are indifferent between an LLC and an S corporation. In either case, the commercial lender can look only to the hotel property for satisfaction of the mortgage. The choice of entity should not affect the *total* business loss that each individual will eventually deduct. In the S corporation case, each shareholder can carry his $24,000 disallowed loss forward as a deduction against future income from the hotel business. The disadvantage of the S corporation is that the loss deduction is deferred. By operating their company as an LLC, the individuals can deduct the loss in the year incurred, thereby maximizing the value of the tax savings from the loss.
Transferring Equity to Successive Generations	Mr. and Mrs. Traub are approaching retirement age and want to begin transferring their business to their three children and, ultimately, to their seven grandchildren. The grandchildren range from 1 year to 18 years of age, and the adults agree that it would be premature to make any grandchild an owner. Mr. and Mrs. Traub could create a family partnership to give their children an ownership interest in the business. In this case, a legally drafted partnership

[12] This statement assumes that the mortgage is qualified nonrecourse financing for at-risk purposes and the passive activity loss limitation is inapplicable. The passive activity loss limitation is discussed in Chapter 16.

agreement would create and define the equity interests of each family member. But what happens in four years when one partner wants to transfer a portion of her equity to the eldest grandchild, or in six years when Mr. Traub wants to withdraw from the business and divide his equity among his three children? Every time the family modifies the ownership structure, the partnership agreement must be amended and the partnership interests redefined—a procedure that may be both inconvenient and costly.

As an alternative, Mr. and Mrs. Traub could incorporate their business as an S corporation with a specified number of shares of stock. Each share would represent a pro rata interest in the business. Mr. and Mrs. Traub, and eventually their children, can modify the ownership structure of the corporation by simply giving shares to another relative. By choosing an S corporation rather than a partnership, Mr. and Mrs. Traub can minimize the transaction costs associated with a systematic transfer of ownership to their offspring.

TAX PLANNING WITH CLOSELY HELD CORPORATIONS

At some point in the life of a small business, the owners may decide to change from a passthrough entity to a corporation. Perhaps the organization has become so complex that the partnership form is unwieldy. Or perhaps the business has grown to the extent that the owners want to sell stock to the public, and the corporate form becomes a legal necessity. Regardless of the size or nature of the enterprise or the number of shareholders, the double taxation of income is the predominant tax problem associated with the corporate form. In this section of the chapter, we will discuss how the owners of closely held corporations cope with the problem.

Getting Cash out of the Corporation

Owners of closely held corporations are aware that dividends have a high tax cost. Consequently, they can become very creative in devising ways to bail cash out of their corporations. The standard tactic is for an individual shareholder to assume an additional role with respect to the corporation. For instance, shareholders commonly serve as corporate officers or executives. In their role as employees, they are entitled to salaries that create cash flow to them and are deductible by the corporation. As a result, the business dollars paid as compensation are taxed only once at the individual level. Similarly, shareholders can become creditors by lending money to their corporations; the interest paid by the corporation on the debt is a deductible expense. Shareholders may lease property to their corporations for rent payments that the corporation can deduct. In all these cases, the cash received by the shareholder, whether as salary, interest, or rent, is taxable as ordinary income. The critical difference is at the corporate level where dividends are paid with after-tax dollars but salaries, interest, and rent are paid with before-tax dollars.

Prior to the enactment of the Jobs and Growth Tax Relief Reconciliation Act of 2003, individual shareholders paid tax on their dividends at the regular progressive rates. Beginning in 2003, dividends are taxed at a maximum 15 percent rate.[13] Because this new preferential rate decreases the double-tax burden on dividends, owners of closely held corporations now have less incentive to pay themselves salaries, interest, and rent instead of dividends.

Objective 4
Define the term
constructive dividend.

Constructive Dividends

The IRS has no quarrel with shareholders who transact with their corporations if the transaction is based on reasonable terms comparable to those that would be negotiated between

---

[13] §1(h)(3)(B). The 15 percent rate drops to 0 percent for dividend income that would be taxed at 15 percent or less under the regular rate structure.

unrelated parties. Even so, the IRS understands that shareholders have an incentive to violate this arm's-length standard. When revenue agents audit closely held corporations, they pay special attention to any deductions for payments to shareholders. If an agent concludes that the payment is unreasonable in light of the facts and circumstances, the IRS may conclude that the unreasonable portion is a **constructive dividend.**

Unreasonable Compensation	Mr. Maupin, sole shareholder and chief executive officer of MP Inc., receives a $450,000 annual salary. If other companies comparable in size and function to MP pay salaries to their CEOs ranging from $400,000 to $500,000 and if Mr. Maupin has the talent and experience to merit such compensation, his salary appears reasonable, and MP can deduct it. Conversely, if the CEO salaries paid by comparable firms average only $300,000 and Mr. Maupin spends more time on the golf course than at corporate headquarters, the IRS may conclude that some portion of his salary is unreasonable.[14]

Let's build on the preceding example by assuming that the IRS decides that $150,000 of Mr. Maupin's annual salary is unreasonable and should be treated as a dividend. What are the tax consequences of this decision?

Constructive Dividend	The following table compares the net tax cost of a $450,000 payment from MP Inc. to Mr. Maupin when the entire payment is treated as salary with the net tax cost when only $300,000 is treated as salary and $150,000 is treated as a dividend. The table assumes that Mr. Maupin's marginal rate on ordinary income is 35 percent and MP's marginal rate is 34 percent. (The comparison ignores the difference in payroll taxes under the two assumptions.)

	Salary	Salary/ Dividend
Mr. Maupin's salary	$450,000 .35	$300,000 .35
Mr. Maupin's *tax cost* of salary	$157,500	$105,000
Mr. Maupin's dividend	–0–	$150,000 .15
Mr. Maupin's *tax cost* of dividend		$22,500
MP's deduction for the payment	$450,000 .34	$300,000 .34
MP's *tax savings* from the deduction	$153,000	$102,000
Net tax cost of payment *(tax costs less tax savings)*	$ 4,500	$ 25,500

Note that the reduction in Mr. Maupin's tax cost attributable to his 15 percent preferential rate on dividends is not enough to offset the reduction in MP Inc.'s tax savings attributable to payment of a nondeductible dividend. The $21,000 increase in the net tax cost when $150,000 of the $450,000 payment must be treated as a dividend falls squarely on Mr. Maupin as the sole owner of the corporation.

---

[14] The topic of reasonable compensation is discussed in more detail in Chapter 15.

These next two examples illustrate constructive dividends in two other contexts.

Unreasonable Rent Payments	Mr. Serednesky rented office space from an unrelated third party for $8,000 annual rent, then subleased the office space to his wholly owned corporation for $16,604. The corporation deducted the $16,604 payment as rent expense on its tax return. The IRS determined that only $8,000 of the payment represented a reasonable, arm's-length rent, and that $8,604 of the payment was a nondeductible dividend.[15]

Shareholder Expenses	Mr. Leonard was the sole shareholder and employee of a personal service corporation. The corporation paid $1,663 of Mr. Leonard's personal travel and entertainment expenses and deducted the payment as a business expense. The IRS treated the payment as a nondeductible constructive dividend that Mr. Leonard had to include in his taxable income. The federal court agreed with the IRS's evaluation of the transaction. When Mr. Leonard protested that the tax consequences unfairly penalized him for operating a business in corporate form, the court replied, "The corporate bed may have lumps; once chosen, however, a taxpayer must endure a sleepless night every now and then."[16]

Thin Capitalization

The organizers of closely held corporations usually understand that if they invest funds in exchange for a corporate debt obligation, the corporation can deduct the interest paid on the debt. Moreover, a loan is temporary, and the organizers will receive a return of their investment according to a fixed repayment schedule or even on demand. On the other hand, if they invest funds in exchange for equity stock, their investment is permanent, and any dividends paid on the investment are nondeductible. As a result, organizers are motivated to include as much debt as possible in their corporation's capital structure.

If the debt held by shareholders is excessive, the IRS may contend that some or all of the debt is disguised equity. As a result, interest payments are actually nondeductible dividends. Even worse, principal repayments may be reclassified as constructive dividends.[17] Because these repayments were nondeductible to the corporation, their reclassification doesn't affect the corporation's taxable income. However, the shareholders who believed they were receiving a nontaxable return of investment must recognize the repayments as income.

Disguised Equity	Mr. and Mrs. Vance formed V&V Inc. in 2004 by contributing $1,000 for 100 shares of common stock (the minimum capitalization under state law). The couple also loaned $25,000 to V&V in exchange for the corporation's note. The note had no fixed repayment schedule but did provide for annual interest. The corporation has never paid a dividend and paid no interest on the note from 2004 through 2009. Late in 2010, V&V distributed $36,250 to Mr. and Mrs. Vance. According to the corporate financial records, the distribution was a repayment of the 2004 loan plus $11,250 accrued interest. The corporation deducted the $11,250 interest on its tax return, and Mr. and Mrs. Vance reported $11,250 interest income on their tax return. The revenue agent who audited V&V's 2010 return concluded that Mr. and Mrs. Vance's loan was, in substance, an equity investment. Thus, the entire $36,250 distribution was a dividend—nondeductible to V&V and taxable to Mr. and Mrs. Vance.

[15] *Social Psychological Services, Inc.*, T.C. Memo 1993-565.

[16] *Leonard*, T.C. Memo 1989-432.

[17] This is typically the case when the debt held by the shareholders is in proportion to their stock interests. As a result, principal repayments are treated as distributions under §302(d) and are taxable as dividends to the extent of the corporation's earnings and profits.

The IRS is most likely to challenge the validity of shareholder debt when a closely held corporation is **thinly capitalized,** with an unusually high ratio of debt to equity. From the government's perspective, the debt-equity ratio is a measure of the business risk borne by the corporation's creditors. A capital structure can become so top heavy with debt that repayment depends on the corporation's continuing profitability rather than on the security of the underlying equity base. In such case, the purported debt has the economic character-istics of common stock. Although the tax law does not contain a safe harbor, a debt-equity ratio of 3 to 1 or less is generally considered immune from IRS attack.[18] Regardless of the corporate debt-equity ratio, shareholders should take care that any loan to their corporation has all the attributes of arm's-length debt. The loan should be evidenced by the corpora-tion's written unconditional promise to repay the principal by a specified date plus a fixed market rate of interest. Ideally, the debt should not be subordinated to other corporate li-abilities, and the shareholders should not hold debt in the same proportion as they own the corporate stock. By respecting these formalities, shareholders can minimize the possibility that the IRS will question the capital structure of their corporation.

Under the current tax regime, individual shareholders may prefer dividend treatment to interest treatment (ignoring, of course, recharacterization of principal payments), because divi-dends are taxed at preferential rates while interest is taxable at ordinary income rates. Corpo-rate shareholders almost always prefer dividend treatment because of the dividends-received deduction. The loss of the corporate-level deduction for interest payments, and the related tax savings, must be balanced against the lower tax cost of dividends to the recipient shareholder.

Decline of the Corporate Tax Shelter

A Historical Perspective

For most of the history of the federal income tax, the tax rates for individuals were signifi-cantly higher than the tax rates for corporations. For example, from 1965 through 1980, the top marginal rate for individuals was 70 percent, while the top marginal rate for cor-porations hovered around 48 percent. Business owners could take advantage of the rate differential by operating their businesses in the corporate form. Of course, this arbitrage strategy was effective only to the extent that the owners could do without annual dividends from their closely held corporations.

Individual shareholders who had their corporations *accumulate* (i.e., retain) after-tax earnings instead of distributing dividends did not permanently avoid the double tax on such earnings. The accumulated earnings increased the shareholders' equity and thus the value of the corporate stock. As long as shareholders held on to their stock, the unrealized appreciation in value was not taxed. But if and when a shareholder disposed of stock in a taxable transaction, the shareholder recognized the appreciation as capital gain and paid an indirect second tax on the corporation's accumulated earnings. Because this second tax was postponed until the year of the stock disposition, its cost was reduced in present value terms. Furthermore, the second tax was computed at the preferential capital gain rate in-stead of the regular rate on ordinary income. This combination of *deferral* and *conversion* (of ordinary income into capital gain) enhanced the attraction of the corporate tax shelter.

The Classic Corporate Tax Shelter	Many years ago, when the top individual tax rate was 70 percent and the top corporate tax rate was only 48 percent, Mr. and Mrs. Van Sant organized a new business as V&S Inc. For its first year (year 0), V&S generated $200,000 taxable income, paid $96,000 income tax, and

[18] Boris I. Bittker and James S. Eustice, *Federal Income Taxation of Corporations and Shareholders,* 6th ed. (Boston: Warren Gorham Lamont, 1994), pp. 4–35.

accumulated $104,000. If the Van Sants had organized their business as a passthrough entity, their year 0 individual tax on $200,000 income would have been $140,000.

The Van Sants held their V&S stock until year 15 when they sold it to a competitor. Their capital gain on sale, which was taxed at a 20 percent preferential rate, reflected 15 years of appreciation in value attributable to V&S's accumulated earnings. Therefore, the indirect second tax on the $104,000 earnings accumulated in year 0 was $20,800. The NPV of this tax at an 8 percent discount rate was $6,552, and the double tax on the corporate income in present value terms totaled $102,552. By organizing their business as a corporation instead of a passthrough entity, the Van Sants saved $37,448 tax ($140,000 individual tax − $102,552 double tax) on their year 0 income.

The Current Environment

Objective 5
Explain why individuals no longer can use corporations as tax shelters.

In 1981, Congress began gradually to decrease the top marginal rates for both individual and corporate taxpayers and to diminish the spread between the rates. The Jobs and Growth Tax Relief Reconciliation Act of 2003 finally equalized the top marginal rates at 35 percent. As you learned in Chapter 11, only a minuscule amount of corporate income is taxed at the progressive rates below 34 percent. Consequently, in today's tax environment, the opportunity for individuals to exploit the differences between the individual and the corporate rate structures is exceedingly narrow.

No More Shelter

What if the Van Sants were to begin their new business today? Could they save any tax by organizing as a corporation rather than a passthrough entity? Let's compare the tax outcomes under two different assumptions about the amount of 2012 income generated by the business.

If the business generates $200,000 income and is organized as a corporation, the 2012 corporate tax would be $61,250, and accumulated earnings would be $138,750. If the Van Sants sell their stock in 2027 (after 15 years), their indirect second tax on the $138,750 accumulated earnings at a 15 percent capital gains rate will be $20,813. The NPV of this tax at an 8 percent discount rate is $6,556, and the double tax on the corporate income in present value terms totals $67,806. But if the Van Sants organize their business as a passthrough entity, their 2012 tax on $200,000 *computed at the highest marginal rate* would be $70,000, which is a mere $2,194 more than the corporate alternative.

If the business generates $400,000 income and is organized as a corporation, the 2012 corporate tax would be $136,000, and accumulated earnings would be $264,000. If the Van Sants sell their stock in 2027, their indirect second tax on the $264,000 accumulated earnings at a 15 percent capital gains rate will be $39,600. The NPV of this tax at an 8 percent discount rate is $12,474, and the double tax on the corporate income in present value terms totals $148,474. But if the Van Sants organize their business as a passthrough entity, their 2012 tax on $400,000 *computed at the highest marginal rate* would be $140,000, which is $8,474 *less* than the corporate alternative!

This example demonstrates that entrepreneurs like the Van Sants can save tax by organizing their business as a corporation only if the business income is very small *and* if the entrepreneurs are willing to forgo cash flow (dividends) from the business for a long period of time. For most individuals, the corporate form offers no tax shelter whatsoever and a passthrough entity is the logical choice.

Objective 6
Explain the purpose of the accumulated earnings tax and the personal holding company tax.

Penalty Taxes on Corporate Accumulations

Prior to the equalization of the top individual and corporate rates, individuals could reduce their tax costs significantly by operating their businesses as corporations. Decades ago, Congress resolved to discourage the use of closely held corporations as tax shelters by enacting two penalty taxes on corporations that fail to distribute dividends to their individual shareholders. These two taxes, the accumulated earnings tax and the personal holding company tax, are still part of the tax law even though the glory days of corporate tax shelters are over. A corporation that finds itself liable for either tax must pay it *in addition to* its income tax for the year.

Accumulated Earnings Tax

The IRS can impose an **accumulated earnings tax** on any corporation "formed or availed of for the purpose of avoiding the income tax with respect to its shareholders by permitting earnings and profits to accumulate instead of being divided or distributed."[19] This tax avoidance purpose is presumed to exist when a corporation accumulates earnings beyond the reasonable needs of its business. The penalty tax equals 15 percent of the corporation's *accumulated taxable income* (roughly defined as taxable income less income tax and dividends paid). For example, a corporation with $660,000 after-tax income that pays no dividends and has no business justification to accumulate earnings could owe a $99,000 accumulated earnings tax ($660,000 × 15 percent).

Tax Talk

Recent changes in IRS audit procedure suggest that the Service is targeting for audit corporate tax returns that show accumulated earnings that may have been accumulated beyond the reasonable needs of the business.

The accumulated earnings tax is clearly intended to coerce corporations to pay dividends. It is not a self-imposed tax, but is instead imposed by the IRS on audit. The IRS's application of the tax is uncertain and subjective. Many corporations have accumulated millions of dollars, and their shareholders have never worried about the penalty tax because they have documented reasons justifying the accumulation.[20] The corporate balance sheet may show that retained earnings financed the development of a new product line, the geographic expansion of the business, the retirement of long-term debt, or the construction of a new manufacturing facility. On the other hand, corporations vulnerable to the tax display two common traits. They have a history of minimal or no dividend payments, and their balance sheets reveal an overabundance of nonbusiness assets such as long-term certificates of deposit, marketable securities, investment real estate, and, most damning of all, substantial loans to shareholders.

The tax law gives newly incorporated businesses some leeway to retain after-tax income on a "no-questions-asked" basis. Specifically, every corporation can accumulate $250,000 without establishing business need and without exposure to the penalty tax.[21]

"No-Questions-Asked" Accumulation	Selby Inc., a calendar year corporate taxpayer, was formed in 2010. On December 31, 2010, Selby's accumulated earnings were $82,700. Consequently, Selby was immune to the accumulated earnings tax for 2010. By December 31, 2011, Selby's accumulated earnings had increased to $204,900. Because this accumulation was still less than $250,000, Selby's immunity continued for 2011. In 2012, Selby's after-tax earnings were $400,000, and the corporation did not pay any dividends. Shelby can accumulate only $45,100 ($250,000 − $204,900 prior years' accumulated earnings) in 2012 on a "no-questions-asked" basis. It must be able to demonstrate a reasonable business need for the additional $354,900 accumulation to avoid exposure to a 2012 accumulated earnings tax on these earnings.

Personal Holding Company Tax

Corporations qualifying as personal holding companies may be liable for a **personal holding company tax**.[22] The statutory definition of a **personal holding company** is technically complex—suffice it to say that personal holding companies are owned by a small number

---

[19] §532(a). Sections 531 through 537 describe the accumulated earnings tax.

[20] Publicly held corporations are normally immune to the accumulated earnings tax because their dividend policies are not controlled by their shareholders.

[21] Personal service corporations may accumulate only $150,000 without establishing reasonable business need.

[22] §541. Sections 541 through 547 describe the personal holding company tax.

of individuals and earn primarily nonbusiness income such as dividends, interest, rents, and royalties. The penalty tax equals 15 percent of undistributed after-tax corporate income for the year. For example, a personal holding company with $2,450,000 undistributed after-tax income owes a $367,500 personal holding company tax ($2,450,000 × 15 percent). Personal holding companies that distribute 100 percent of after-tax earnings are not liable for any penalty tax.[23]

Congress enacted the personal holding company tax more than 60 years ago. Its purpose was to discourage individuals from incorporating their investment portfolios to take advantage of corporate tax rates that were 45 percentage points less than individual rates. Today, there is no difference between the highest corporate and individual rates, and individuals have no tax incentive to incorporate their portfolios. Nevertheless, a corporation qualifying as a personal holding company must attach a Schedule PH showing the computation of any additional penalty tax to its annual Form 1120.

Controlled Corporate Groups

Objective 7
Apply the tax rates to income earned by a controlled corporate group.

The corporate tax rates are mildly progressive on taxable income up to $335,000, at which point the rate becomes a flat 34 percent. This rate applies until taxable income reaches $10 million, at which point the marginal rate increases to 35 percent. The rates again become slightly progressive until taxable income reaches $18,333,333, at which point the rate becomes a flat 35 percent. The owners of a corporate business might be tempted to take advantage of the progressivity in the tax rates by fragmenting their business into multiple corporate entities. For instance, if a business that generates $1 million annual income is organized as *one* corporation, its annual tax is $340,000. However, if that business could be splintered into *five* corporations, each reporting $200,000 taxable income, the annual tax would be reduced to $306,250 ($61,250 tax on $200,000 income × 5).

The law prevents this tax avoidance strategy through the rules applying to controlled groups of corporations. Specifically, a **controlled group** has only "one run" up the progressive rates because the rates apply to the group's aggregate taxable income instead of the taxable incomes of each group member.[24] Additionally, the controlled group as a whole can retain only $250,000 after-tax earnings without establishing a reasonable business need for the accumulation.[25]

The tax law identifies two types of controlled corporate groups. The first type is a brother-sister group consisting of two or more corporations controlled by the same set of individual shareholders. The second type is a parent-subsidiary group consisting of a parent corporation that owns one or more controlled subsidiaries. Both types of controlled groups are pictured in Exhibit 12.1.

Parent-subsidiary controlled groups often qualify as affiliated groups eligible to file a consolidated tax return.[26] Parent-subsidiary groups that elect to file on a consolidated basis compute the group's income tax based on consolidated taxable income. Similarly, the accumulated earnings tax rules apply with reference to consolidated after-tax earnings. Thus, the controlled group rules concern only those parent-subsidiary groups that file separate returns rather than a consolidated return. Brother-sister controlled groups, however, are not eligible to file consolidated tax returns. Consequently, the controlled group rules concern all brother-sister groups. While individual shareholders may create brother-sister corporate groups for good nontax reasons, they do not derive any tax advantage by doing so.

---

[23] Personal holding companies are not subject to the accumulated earnings tax. §532(b)(1).

[24] §1561(a)(1).

[25] §1561(a)(2).

[26] See the discussion of consolidated tax returns in Chapter 11.

EXHIBIT 12.1
Controlled Corporate Groups

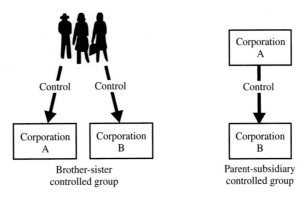

Brother-sister
controlled group

Parent-subsidiary
controlled group

Conclusion

This chapter concludes our study of the five basic forms of business organization. Four of these forms—sole proprietorships, partnerships, LLCs, and S corporations—are not taxable entities for federal purposes. Individuals who use these forms pay a single tax on their business income. Only the fifth form—corporations—is taxed at the entity level, and shareholders pay a second tax when they receive dividends from the corporation. Business owners who want to engage in successful tax planning must understand the basic tax rules that differentiate passthrough entities and corporations. By taking advantage of these rules, the owners can control tax costs, maximize after-tax income available for personal consumption, and enhance the value of their investment in the business.

Key Terms

accumulated earnings tax   *359*
constructive dividend   *355*
controlled group   *360*
personal holding company   *359*
personal holding company tax   *359*
thinly capitalized   *357*

Questions and Problems for Discussion

1. Mr. and Mrs. Velotta are self-employed professional musicians. Their average annual income from performance fees and music lessons is $130,000. The couple wants to shift income to their two children, ages 19 and 22. Can Mr. and Mrs. Velotta organize their music business as a family partnership and give each child a 25 percent interest?

2. Mr. and Mrs. Barnes own a fast-food restaurant that generates $160,000 average annual income. The couple wants to shift some of this income to their two children, ages 19 and 22. Can Mr. and Mrs. Barnes organize their restaurant as a family partnership and give each child a 25 percent interest?

3. Ms. Johnson is eager to create a family partnership to generate income and cash flow for her three college-age children. She owns two businesses, either of which could be organized as a partnership. Ms. Johnson established the first business 15 years ago. This business consists of operating assets with a $15 million FMV. Ms. Johnson established the second business only 10 months ago. This business is growing rapidly and already is generating taxable income. However, its operating assets have only a $300,000 FMV. Which business is the better candidate for a family partnership? Explain your reasoning.

4. Discuss the tax and nontax reasons why the stock in an S corporation is typically subject to a buy-sell agreement.

5. Mr. Eros operates an antique store located on the first floor of a four-story office building owned by Mr. Eros. The top three stories are leased to business tenants. Mr. Eros

is considering giving a one-third interest in both the antique store and the building to each of his two grandchildren and operating the businesses in one passthrough entity. Mr. Eros wants to receive 100 percent of the rent from his tenants for several years but is willing to distribute one-third of the net profit from the antique store to his grandchildren each year. On the basis of this objective, which form of organization should he choose?

6. Dr. Quinn, Dr. Rose, and Dr. Tanner are dentists who practice as equal owners of QRT Dental Services. A patient of Dr. Rose's recently sued him for medical malpractice and was awarded a $500,000 judgment. Discuss each owner's personal liability for this judgment assuming that:

   a. QRT is a general partnership.

   b. QRT is an LLP.

   c. QRT is an LLC.

7. Refer to the facts in the previous problem. QRT purchased $30,000 of dental equipment on credit. When QRT failed to pay its bill, the seller took it to court and won a judgment for $30,000. Discuss each owner's personal liability for this judgment assuming that:

   a. QRT is a general partnership.

   b. QRT is an LLP.

   c. QRT is an LLC.

8. Mrs. Tran and Mrs. Nutter each owns a small business that averages $80,000 annual income. Each woman is in the 35 percent marginal tax bracket. Mrs. Tran has decided to incorporate her business as a taxable corporation, while Mrs. Nutter has decided to continue to operate as a sole proprietorship. Both decisions maximize the after-tax value of the business to its owner. How can you explain this apparent contradiction?

9. BNC, a closely held corporation, was organized in 1987. To date, it has accumulated over $10 million after-tax income. This year, BNC's taxable income is $750,000, and its federal tax is $255,000. Describe two different ways that BNC can avoid exposure to the accumulated earnings tax for the year.

10. Describe the FICA payroll tax implications when the IRS classifies a portion of a salary payment to a shareholder/employee as a constructive dividend.

11. When the IRS classifies a portion of a salary payment to a shareholder/employee as a constructive dividend, which party (corporation or shareholder) bears the economic burden of the tax consequences?

12. Ms. Knox recently loaned $20,000 to her closely held corporation, which needed the money for working capital. She sees no reason to document the loan other than as a "loan payable—shareholder" on the corporate balance sheet. She also sees no reason for her corporation to pay interest on the loan. What advice can you offer Ms. Knox concerning this related-party transaction?

13. Explain the logic of the tax rate for both the accumulated earnings tax and the personal holding company tax.

14. In what way does a corporate balance sheet provide information concerning the corporation's exposure to the accumulated earnings tax?

15. Why are publicly held corporations such as General Motors generally immune from the accumulated earnings tax?

16. How would the tax shelter potential of closely held corporations be affected by:

   a. An increase in the highest individual tax rate to 43 percent?

b. A decrease in the preferential tax rate on individual capital gains to 5 percent?

c. Repeal of the accumulated earnings tax?

17. Both brother-sister groups and parent-subsidiary groups are controlled groups for federal tax purposes. However, the qualification as a controlled group is more of an issue for brother-sister groups than for parent-subsidiary groups. Can you explain why?

Application Problems

1. Mr. Tuck and Ms. Under organized a new business as an LLC in which they own equal interests. The new business generated a $4,800 operating loss for the year.

   a. If Mr. Tuck's marginal tax rate before consideration of the LLC loss is 35 percent, compute his tax savings from the first-year LLC loss.

   b. Assume that Ms. Under has no taxable income for the year. However, her taxable income last year was enough to put her into the 28 percent tax bracket. Compute her tax savings from the LLC loss.

   c. Assume that Ms. Under has no taxable income for the year or for the two preceding years. Does she have any tax savings from the LLC loss? Explain briefly.

2. Mr. and Mrs. Lund and their two children (Ben and June) are the four equal partners in LBJ Partnership. This year, LBJ generated $36,000 ordinary income. Compute the tax cost for the business if Mr. and Ms. Lund's marginal rate is 33 percent, Ben's marginal rate is 28 percent, and June's marginal rate is 15 percent. (Ignore SE tax consequences.)

3. Ms. Kona owns a 10 percent interest in Carlton LLC. This year, the LLC generated $72,400 ordinary income. Ms. Kona's marginal tax rate is 33 percent, and she does not pay SE tax on her LLC income.

   a. Compute the tax cost on Ms. Kona's share of Carlton's income assuming that she received a $35,000 cash distribution this year.

   b. Compute the tax cost on Ms. Kona's share of Carlton's income assuming that she received no cash distribution this year.

4. Mrs. Franklin, who is in the 35 percent tax bracket, owns a residential apartment building that generates $80,000 annual taxable income. She plans to create a family partnership by giving each of her two children a 20 percent equity interest in the building. (She will retain a 60 percent interest.) Mrs. Franklin will manage the building, and value of her services is $15,000 per year. If Mrs. Franklin's children are in the 15 percent tax bracket, compute the tax savings from this income-shifting arrangement. (Ignore any payroll tax consequences.)

5. WRT, a calendar year S corporation, has 100 shares of outstanding stock. At the beginning of the year, Mr. Wallace owned all 100 shares. On September 30, he gave 25 shares to his brother and 40 shares to his daughter. WRT's ordinary income for the year was $216,000. What portion of this income must each shareholder include in income?

6. Angela and Thomas are planning to start a new business. Thomas will invest cash in the business but not be involved in day-to-day operations. Angela plans to work full-time overseeing business operations.

   The two currently project that the business will generate $200,000 of annual taxable income before consideration of any payments to Angela for her services. Both agree that Angela's services are worth $100,000.

   Angela and Thomas plan to form a passthrough entity but are unsure whether to choose a partnership or an S corporation. In either case, they will be equal owners of the entity. Given their other sources of income, both Thomas and Angela have a 35 percent marginal tax rate on ordinary income. (Ignore any payroll or self-employment tax consequences.)

  a. If the business is operated as a partnership, calculate ordinary income allocated to each owner and explain the treatment by the partnership and by Angela of her $100,000 payment for services.

  b. If the business is operated as an S corporation, calculate ordinary income allocated to each owner and explain the treatment by the corporation and by Angela of her $100,000 payment for services.

  c. Given your analysis above, explain to Angela and Thomas whether and to what extent income tax consequences should control their choice of entity.

7. Refer to the facts in the preceding problem.

  a. If the business is operated as a partnership, explain the payroll tax/self-employment tax implications for the entity, Thomas, and Angela. (No calculations required.)

  b. If the business is operated as an S corporation, explain the payroll tax/self-employment tax implications for the entity, Thomas, and Angela. (No calculations required.)

  c. Given your discussion above, how might payroll tax/self-employment taxes influence Thomas and Angela's choice of entity through which to operate their business?

8. Mr. Lion, who is in the 35 percent tax bracket, is the sole shareholder of Toto, which manufactures greeting cards. Toto's average annual net profit (before deduction of Mr. Lion's salary) is $200,000. For each of the following cases, compute the income tax burden on this profit. (Ignore any payroll tax consequences.)

  a. Mr. Lion's salary is $100,000, and Toto pays no dividends.

  b. Mr. Lion's salary is $100,000, and Toto distributes its after-tax income as a dividend.

  c. Toto is an S corporation. Mr. Lion's salary is $100,000, and Toto makes no cash distributions.

  d. Toto is an S corporation. Mr. Lion draws no salary, and Toto makes no cash distributions.

  e. Toto is an S corporation. Mr. Lion draws no salary, and Toto makes cash distributions of all its income to Mr. Lion.

9. Mr. Pauper and Mrs. Queen are the equal shareholders in Corporation PQ. Both shareholders have a 35 percent marginal tax rate. PQ's financial records show the following.

Gross income from sales of goods	$880,000
Operating expenses	(410,000)
Interest paid on debt to Mr. P and Mrs. Q	(62,000)
Dividend distributions:	
Mr. Pauper	(50,000)
Mrs. Queen	(50,000)

  a. Compute the combined tax cost for PQ, Mr. Pauper, and Mrs. Queen.

  b. How would your computation change if the interest on the shareholder debt was $162,000 and PQ paid no dividends?

10. American Corporation has two equal shareholders, Mr. Freedom and Brave Inc. In addition to their investments in American stock, both shareholders have made

substantial loans to American. During the current year, American paid $100,000 interest each to Mr. Freedom and Brave Inc. Assume that American and Brave have 34 percent marginal tax rates and Mr. Freedom's marginal tax rate on ordinary income is 35 percent.

    a. Calculate American's tax savings from deduction of these interest payments and their after-tax cost.

    b. Calculate Brave's tax cost and after-tax earnings from its receipt of interest income from American.

    c. Calculate Mr. Freedom's tax cost and after-tax earnings from his receipt of interest income from American.

    d. If an IRS agent concludes that American is thinly capitalized and the shareholder loans should be treated as equity, explain the impact on American, Brave, and Mr. Freedom.

    e. Recalculate Brave's tax cost and after-tax earnings assuming its receipt of interest from American is treated as a constructive dividend.

    f. Recalculate Mr. Freedom's tax cost and after-tax earnings assuming his receipt of interest from American is treated as a constructive dividend.

11. Ms. Xie, who is in the 35 percent tax bracket, is the sole shareholder and president of Xenon. The corporation's financial records show the following.

Gross income from sales of goods	$1,590,000
Operating expenses	(930,000)
Salary paid to Ms. Xie	(300,000)
Dividend distributions	(200,000)

    a. Compute the combined tax cost for Xenon and Ms. Xie. (Ignore payroll tax.)

    b. How would your computation change if Ms. Xie's salary was $500,000 and Xenon paid no dividends?

12. Mr. Vernon is the sole shareholder of Teva. He also owns the office building that serves as corporate headquarters. Last year, Teva paid $180,000 annual rent to Mr. Vernon for use of the building. Teva's marginal tax rate was 34 percent, and Mr. Vernon's marginal tax rate was 35 percent. The revenue agent who audited Teva's return concluded that the fair rental value of the office building was $125,000.

    a. What effect does this conclusion have on Mr. Vernon's tax?

    b. What effect does this conclusion have on Teva's tax?

13. In 1994, Mr. and Mrs. Adams formed ADC by transferring $50,000 cash in exchange for 100 shares of common stock and a note from the corporation for $49,000. The note obligated ADC to pay 10 percent annual interest and to repay the $49,000 principal on demand. ADC has never declared a dividend nor made any interest payments on the note. Last year, it distributed $25,000 cash to Mr. and Mrs. Adams as a principal repayment. When the IRS audited ADC's tax return, the revenue agent determined that this payment was a constructive dividend.

    a. What is the effect of the constructive dividend on ADC's tax if its marginal tax rate was 34 percent?

    b. What is the effect of the constructive dividend on Mr. and Mrs. Adams's tax if their marginal tax rate was 35 percent?

14. During a recent IRS audit, the revenue agent decided that the Parker family used their closely held corporation, Falco, to avoid shareholder tax by accumulating earnings beyond the reasonable needs of the business. Falco's taxable income was $900,000, it paid no dividends, and it had no business need to retain any income. Compute Falco's accumulated earnings tax assuming that:

    a. It had accumulated $4 million after-tax income in prior years.

    b. It had accumulated $129,000 after-tax income in prior years.

15. Graham is the sole shareholder of Logan Corporation. For the past five years, Logan has reported little or no taxable income, as a result of paying Graham a salary of $500,000 per year. During a recent IRS audit, the revenue agent determined that Graham's educational and business experience, and his time devoted to managing Logan, justified a salary of only $200,000. Thus, the agent recharacterized $300,000 of the payments from the corporation as a dividend.

    a. Calculate the additional income tax liability for Logan as a result of this constructive dividend treatment. (Ignore any payroll tax consequences.)

    b. What are the tax consequences to Graham as a result of the constructive dividend treatment? Calculate the change in Graham's income tax liability as a result of this change. (Ignore any payroll tax consequences.)

    c. Given your calculations above, determine the total impact on Treasury tax collections as a result of this audit finding.

16. Refer to the facts in the preceding problem. Briefly explain the payroll tax consequences of the revenue agent's conclusions.

17. Megan operates a house-cleaning business as a sole proprietorship. She oversees a team of 10 cleaning personnel, markets the business, and provides supplies and equipment. The business has been generating net taxable profits of $50,000 per year.

    a. Assume that Megan's marginal tax rate on ordinary income is 35 percent and that she has no pressing need for cash flow from this business. Would you recommend that Megan consider incorporating and operating the business through a C corporation? Provide calculations to support your conclusion. (Ignore any payroll or self-employment tax considerations.)

    b. How would your conclusion in part change if Megan's marginal tax rate is only 28 percent?

18. Alpha Corporation generates taxable income of $100,000 per year. Beta Corporation generates taxable income of $75,000 per year.

    a. Calculate regular income tax liability for Alpha and Beta.

    b. How would your answers to part change if John Smith is the sole shareholder of both Alpha and Beta?

    c. Would the ownership of the two corporations impact their tax liability if Alpha and Beta each generated taxable income of $500,000? Provide calculations to support your conclusion.

Issue Recognition Problems

Identify the tax issue or issues suggested by the following situations, and state each issue in the form of a question.

1. Mr. and Mrs. Keck are in the highest marginal tax bracket. Their son, a freshman in college, earns minimal income from his summer job, and his marginal tax rate is

10 percent. Mr. and Mrs. Keck are considering making their son an equal owner in a family business that generates over $200,000 taxable income each year. They believe that every dollar of income shifted to their son will save more than 25 cents of tax for the family.

2. Mr. Jackson owns a 40 percent interest in newly formed JKL Partnership. The partners organized their business as a passthrough entity so that the start-up loss would generate an immediate tax savings. Mr. Jackson, however, had a substantial loss from another business and has no taxable income against which to deduct his share of the JKL loss.

3. Mr. and Mrs. Braun own 100 percent of the stock of BB Inc., which operates a temporary employment business. Late last year, Mr. Braun was short of cash in his personal checking account. Consequently, he paid several personal bills by writing checks on the corporate account and recorded the payments as miscellaneous expenses. Three months later he repaid the corporation in full.

4. REW Inc. is closely held by six members of the REW family. The corporation owns two vans that employees use for various business transportation purposes. However, for at least eight weeks during each year, the shareholders use the vans to take their families on extended vacation trips.

5. Eight years ago, Mr. and Mrs. Lauffer created a family partnership with their son, the son's wife, their daughter, and the daughter's husband. Each of these six individuals owns an equal interest in the partnership. This year, the son and his wife decide to divorce.

6. LSN, a calendar year S corporation, has 13 shareholders. Since its incorporation, LSN has retained over $800,000 income to reinvest in its business. Because LSN is a passthrough entity, the shareholders have paid tax on this undistributed income and increased their stock basis accordingly. The shareholders want to revoke the S election and operate LSN as a regular corporation. LSN has only $69,000 in its corporate bank account.

7. Last year, Mrs. Kahn and Mrs. Toms each contributed the assets of their respective sole proprietorships to a new corporation. The shareholders believed that by combining their businesses, they could increase profitability. They were encouraged to do so because they could transfer their assets in exchange for stock without recognizing gain. Unfortunately, Mrs. Kahn and Mrs. Toms discovered that they couldn't work together effectively. They agreed to part company by dissolving the corporation and taking back ownership of their respective assets (essentially just reversing the incorporation process).

8. Taha is closely held by eight family members. Taha purchased investment land 12 years ago for $100,000. The land was recently appraised at a FMV of $3 million. A buyer has offered to pay cash for the land. Because the shareholders need the cash, they plan to have Taha distribute the land to them as a dividend. They will then sell the land and recognize a capital gain taxable at the 15 percent preferential individual rate.

9. Mr. and Mrs. Crandall own 100 percent of the stock in CR Inc., which recently hired the couple's nephew at a $30,000 annual salary. The nephew, age 20, has been in several scrapes with the law and needs financial help, and the Crandall family agreed that a low-stress job with the family business is just what he needs for a year or two.

10. WQ Corporation, a closely held family business, has not paid a dividend for the last seven years. Each year, the minutes of the board of directors' December meeting state

that WQ must accumulate after-tax income to pay for a new manufacturing facility. Until plans for construction are finalized, WQ has been investing its excess cash in marketable securities. This year, WQ curtails its manufacturing business and abandons its plan for the new facility.

Research Problems

1. Fifteen years ago, Mr. and Mrs. Boyer created Brovo, a regular corporation, through which to operate a service business. The Boyers own all of Brovo's 1,000 shares of stock with a $1.6 million aggregate tax basis. The corporate business has been extremely successful; at the beginning of the year, Brovo's balance sheet reflected over $2 million retained earnings. According to a recent appraisal, its stock is worth $2.5 million. The Boyers want to withdraw $500,000 cash from Brovo for their personal use, but they do not want Brovo to pay them a dividend. Instead, they plan to have Brovo distribute $500,000 in exchange for 200 shares of their stock. The Boyers believe that they will recognize a $180,000 gain on this redemption, which will qualify as capital gain. Are the Boyers correct in their analysis of the tax consequences of the redemption?

2. On March 1, Mr. and Mrs. Trent formed Trent Properties Inc. through which to operate a real estate management business. Both Mr. and Mrs. Trent worked full-time for modest, but reasonable, salaries. In early December, the Trents estimated that the corporation would incur a $325,000 net loss for its first 10 months of operation. They decided to adopt a calendar year for Trent Properties Inc. and make an S election so that they could deduct the loss on their individual tax return. Can the Trents make an S election for Trent Property Inc.'s first taxable year?

3. Fair View Inc. owns and operates a golf club, which includes two 18-hole courses, a driving range, a restaurant, and a pro shop. The club's facilities can be used only by its membership, which includes all the individual shareholders as well as nonshareholders. All the members are charged a greens fee for each round of play plus an additional fee for use of a golf cart. However, the fees for shareholders are 30 percent less than the fees for nonshareholders. Shareholders also enjoy a 30 percent discount on the price of food and drink purchased in the club restaurant and merchandise purchased in the pro shop. Do these discounts have any income tax consequences to Fair View's shareholders?

4. Four years ago, Amy Huang contributed four acres of undeveloped land to Richter Company in exchange for a 12 percent equity interest in Richter. Amy's tax basis in the land was $275,000, and the land's appraised FMV on date of contribution was $430,000. The exchange of land for equity was nontaxable to both Amy and Richter. Since the exchange, Richter has held the land as a long-term investment. This year, Richter sold the land to an unrelated purchaser for $550,000. How much capital gain does Richter recognize on the sale? How much of this gain is allocated to Amy if Richter is an LLC? How much gain is allocated to Amy if Richter is an S corporation?

5. Leonard Grant is the sole shareholder of Great Yards Corporation, a landscaping business. During the current year, Leonard's wife, Lisa, and his sister, Lena, formed a catering business, Take for Granted Inc. Both businesses are operated as regular corporations. Lisa and Lena are equal shareholders in Take for Granted. Are Great Yards and Take for Granted considered a controlled group for purposes of calculating the corporate income tax?

Tax Planning Cases

1. Mr. and Mrs. Tinker own a sizeable investment portfolio of stock in publicly held corporations. The couple has four children, ages 20, 22, 25, and 27, with whom they want to share their wealth. Unfortunately, none of the children has demonstrated any ability to manage money. As a result, Mr. and Mrs. Tinker plan to transfer their portfolio to a new corporation in exchange for 20 shares of voting stock and 400 shares of nonvoting stock. They will give 100 nonvoting shares to each child. The couple will serve as the directors of the corporation, manage the investment portfolio, and distribute cash dividends when their children need money. They estimate that the portfolio will generate $72,000 annual dividend income.

   a. If the Tinker Family Corporation is operated as an S corporation, compute the annual income tax burden on the dividend income generated by the investment portfolio. Assume that Mr. and Mrs. Tinker are in the 35 percent tax bracket and each child is in the 15 percent tax bracket. To simplify the case, ignore any value of the couple's management service to the corporation.

   b. Compute the tax burden for the first year if Tinker Family Corporation does not have an S election in effect and distributes a $100 annual dividend per share.

2. Agatha is planning to start a new business venture and must decide whether to operate as a sole proprietorship or incorporate. She projects that the business will generate annual cash flow and taxable income of $100,000. Agatha's personal marginal tax rate, given her other sources of income, is 35 percent.

   a. If Agatha operates the business as a sole proprietorship, calculate the annual after-tax cash flow available for reinvestment in the business venture.

   b. If Agatha operates the business as a regular (C) corporation that makes no dividend distributions, calculate the annual after-tax cash flow available for reinvestment in the business.

   c. Now suppose that Agatha wishes to withdraw $20,000 per year from the business, and will reinvest any remaining after-tax earnings. What are the tax consequences to Agatha and the business of such a withdrawal if the business is operated as a sole proprietorship? How much after-tax cash flow will remain for reinvestment in the business? How much after-tax cash flow will Agatha have from the withdrawal?

   d. What are the tax consequences to Agatha and the business of a $20,000 withdrawal in the form of a dividend if the business is operated as a C corporation? How much after-tax cash flow will remain for reinvestment in the business? How much after-tax cash flow will Agatha retain from the dividend?

   e. If Agatha wishes to operate the business as a corporation but also wishes to receive cash flow from the business each year, what would you recommend to get a better tax result?

3. Mr. Young operates a photography studio as a sole proprietorship. His average annual income from the business is $100,000. Because Mr. Young does not need the entire cash flow for personal consumption, he is considering incorporating the business. He will work as a corporate employee for a $40,000 annual salary, and the corporation will accumulate its after-tax income to fund future business expansion. For purposes of this case, assume that Mr. Young's marginal income tax rate is 33 percent and ignore any employment tax consequences.

   a. Assuming that the new corporation would not be a personal service corporation, would Mr. Young decrease the annual tax burden on the business by incorporating?

   b. How would your answer change if the new corporation would be a personal service corporation?

Chapter **Thirteen**

Jurisdictional Issues in Business Taxation

Learning Objectives

After studying this chapter, you should be able to:

1. Define the term *nexus.*

2. Apportion corporate taxable income among states according to UDITPA.

3. Explain the significance of a permanent establishment.

4. Compute a foreign tax credit.

5. Compare the tax consequences of a foreign branch and a foreign subsidiary.

6. Compute a deemed paid foreign tax credit.

7. Explain the tax consequences of subpart F income earned by a CFC.

8. Describe the role of Section 482 in the international transfer pricing area.

Chapter 13 introduces the issues that arise when firms operate in more than one taxing jurisdiction. Firms that span territorial boundaries must understand that an overlap in jurisdictions can cause the same income to be taxed more than once. In this chapter, we will learn how firms can minimize the burden of such duplicative taxation. We will also discover how the differences in tax costs across jurisdictions create planning opportunities. Firms can implement many effective strategies to shift income away from jurisdictions with high tax costs. These strategies relate back to our maxim that tax costs decrease and cash flows increase when income is generated in a jurisdiction with a low tax rate.

Chapter 13 begins with an overview of state and local taxes as a cost of doing business, then focuses on the key issues involving state income taxation. The first issue concerns the states' right to tax interstate commerce and the federal restrictions on such right. The concept of income apportionment is introduced, and strategies for reducing the aggregate tax burden on multistate businesses are discussed. The remainder of the chapter deals with the taxation of international business. We will learn that the United States has a global tax system that can result in the double taxation of foreign source income. The major role of the foreign tax credit in mitigating double taxation and the limitations on the credit are covered in some detail. We will consider how U.S. firms can organize overseas operations to control the tax consequences of those operations. Finally, we will discuss how U.S. corporations use foreign subsidiaries to defer income recognition and reduce the tax cost of international business.

STATE AND LOCAL TAXATION

In the United States, even the smallest firm is subject to three taxing jurisdictions: local government, state government, and the federal government. Historically, firms concentrated their tax planning efforts at the federal level and devoted less attention to state and local tax costs. Recently, firms have become more aware of their state and local tax burden. In response to demand by the business community, public accounting firms have developed specialized state and local tax (SALT) practices to provide expert professional help. More than ever before, firms and their tax advisers are formulating strategies to minimize real and personal property taxes, unemployment taxes, and sales and use taxes.

In the first section of this chapter, we focus on planning opportunities in the area of state income taxation. As we learned in Chapter 1, most states impose both a personal (individual) and a corporate income tax. Consequently, business income is subject to state tax whether the business is organized as a passthrough entity or a corporation. For federal purposes, corporations are allowed to deduct state income tax in the computation of taxable income.[1] The tax savings from this deduction reduce the cost of the state tax.

Federal Deduction for State Income Tax	Zeta Inc. paid $45,000 state income tax this year. If Zeta's federal tax rate is 34 percent, the after-tax cost of the payment is only $29,700.

State tax paid	$(45,000)
Federal tax savings ($45,000 deduction × 34%)	15,300
After-tax cost	$(29,700)

Nonetheless, Zeta's aggregate tax burden is increased because it must pay income tax at both the state and federal level. If Zeta's before-tax income is $900,000 and the state tax rate is 5 percent, Zeta's tax rate for the year is 37.3 percent.

State tax[2] ($900,000 taxable income × 5%)	$ 45,000
Federal tax ($855,000 taxable income × 34%)	290,700
Total income tax	$335,700

$$\$335,700 \div \$900,000 \text{ before-tax income} = 37.3\%$$

Constitutional Restrictions on State Jurisdiction

Objective 1
Define the term *nexus*.

A state has jurisdiction to tax all individuals who reside in the state and all corporations formed under the laws of the state. This jurisdiction extends to nonresident individuals and corporations conducting business within the state. Thus, firms engaged in interstate

---

[1] For individual taxpayers, the state tax on both business and nonbusiness income is allowed as an itemized deduction. See Chapter 17.

[2] State income tax payments are not deductible in the computation of taxable income for state purposes. Three states (Alabama, Iowa, and Missouri) allow corporations to deduct a limited amount of federal tax in the computation of taxable income for state purposes.

EXHIBIT 13.1
Show-Me Inc.

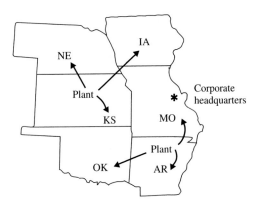

commerce may be subject to tax in any number of states. Given that thousands of U.S. companies conduct business in more than one state, if not all 50 states, some degree of national coordination is necessary to avert fiscal anarchy.

Article 1 of the U.S. Constitution grants the federal government the power to "regulate commerce with foreign nations, and among the several states, and with the Indian tribes." This **Commerce Clause** empowers Congress and the federal courts to establish ground rules for state tax laws. For a state tax to be constitutional, it must not discriminate against interstate commerce. For instance, an income tax with a 3 percent rate for resident corporations and a 6 percent rate for nonresident corporations would be blatantly unconstitutional. In addition, state taxes can be levied only on businesses having nexus with the state. **Nexus** means the degree of contact between a business and a state necessary to establish jurisdiction.

The Issue of Nexus

Let's examine the concept of nexus by considering the regional business conducted by Show-Me Inc., which is incorporated in Missouri. Show-Me's corporate headquarters are in St. Louis, and its two manufacturing plants are in Kansas and Arkansas. The corporation uses a common carrier to ship its products to customers in Missouri, Kansas, Arkansas, Iowa, Nebraska, and Oklahoma. Show-Me's business is illustrated in Exhibit 13.1.

Because Show-Me is formed and protected under Missouri law and is commercially domiciled in the state, the corporation has nexus with Missouri. Show-Me has employees and owns real and personal property located in Kansas and Arkansas, and these states provide public benefits (fire and police protection, roads and highways, etc.) that add value to the corporation's business. Thus, Show-Me's physical presence in these two states creates nexus allowing both Kansas and Arkansas to tax the corporation.

But what about the other three states in Show-Me's region? According to the facts, Show-Me has no physical presence in Iowa, Nebraska, or Oklahoma. Under a long-standing federal statute, Public Law 86-272, firms do not establish nexus by simply selling tangible goods to customers residing in a state. Firms can even send traveling salespeople into a state to solicit orders for such goods without creating nexus.[3] Because of this federally mandated immunity, Show-Me is not subject to income tax in Iowa, Nebraska, and Oklahoma.

P.L. 86-272 does not pertain to business activities other than the sale of tangible goods. As a result, nonresident firms providing services (including the leasing of tangible property) or marketing intangible property to in-state residents are not immune to the state's taxing jurisdiction. Currently, the issue of nexus with respect to these in-state activities is unsettled. Several states have taken the aggressive position that any firm conducting a regular

Tax Talk
A new statute in New York requires online retailers to collect sales tax on sales to NY residents if the retailer pays commissions or other compensation to NY residents for customer referrals. Amazon.com's challenge of the law as violating the Commerce Clause was denied by a NY appellate court.

[3] 15 U.S.C. 381-384 (1959).

commercial activity within the state has established *economic* nexus. Accordingly, the state has jurisdiction to tax the firm regardless of the lack of physical presence in the state.[4]

The issue of economic nexus is being hotly debated by lawmakers, tax policy groups, and taxpayers alike. Several bills have been introduced in Congress attempting to provide a common standard across the states, but to date no legislation has passed.[5] In June 2007, the U.S. Supreme Court declined to hear two taxpayer appeals in cases in which states (West Virginia and New Jersey) assessed income and franchise taxes on companies with no physical presence in the state. Absent federal legislation restricting the economic nexus approach, some commentators predict a surge in state assessment of tax on businesses without a physical presence but with economic presence and earnings in the state.

Economic Nexus	Show-Me's research division recently developed a manufacturing process that the corporation patented with the federal government. Show-Me licensed this patent to a number of companies, three of which operate in South Carolina. The companies pay an annual royalty for use of the patent. Although Show-Me has no physical presence (tangible property or employees) in South Carolina, it does earn revenue from marketing an intangible asset to South Carolina customers. On the basis of this economic nexus, South Carolina claims jurisdiction to tax Show-Me's royalty income.

The nexus issue is particularly uncertain for firms that sell goods and services over the Internet. Traditional nexus concepts make little sense when applied to business conducted in cyberspace. Consequently, firms may be hesitant about expanding their Internet operations for fear of inadvertently creating nexus with states in which they have no physical presence. In turn, state governments are concerned that the anticipated growth in electronic commerce will result in a loss of sales tax and income tax revenues from traditional commercial activities. The business community, the Internet industry, and state governments all acknowledge the need for a workable tax policy with respect to electronic commerce. Such policy should "facilitate, not impede, the growth of new technologies, while ensuring that no unfair tax advantage accrues to companies that develop or utilize such technologies."[6]

No Taxes in Cyberspace	On October 1, 1998, the Internet Tax Freedom Act went into effect. The act included a moratorium on new state and local taxes imposed on Internet access and a Congressional declaration that the Internet should be free of all international tariffs, trade barriers, and other restrictions. Supporters of the act maintain that the Internet is still in its infancy and must be protected against unbridled taxation. Critics claim that the act establishes the Internet as a giant tax shelter and that "for a bunch of nerds, computer types have proven to be very effective lobbyists."[7] The act has been extended several times, most recently until November 1, 2014.

Apportionment of Business Income

The federal courts established the principle that states may tax only the income attributable to a firm's in-state business activity; the state may not tax income attributable to

---

[4] The landmark case in this area is *Geoffrey, Inc. v. South Carolina Tax Commission,* 437 S.E.2d 13 (1993), *cert. denied,* 510 U.S. 992 (1993).

[5] See, for example, H.R. 1083, the Business Activity Tax Simplification Act of 2009.

[6] Houghton and Friedman, "Lost in [Cyber] Space?" 97 *State Tax Notes* 174-25.

[7] Lee Sheppard, "What Does 'No New Internet Taxes' Mean?" 97 *State Tax Notes* 141-51.

the firm's *extraterritorial value*. To comply with this principle, state law must provide a rational and fair method for determining the portion of a firm's total income subject to that state's tax.

In 1957, a National Conference of Uniform State Laws drafted the **Uniform Division of Income for Tax Purposes Act (UDITPA)** as a recommended method for apportioning income among multiple state jurisdictions. Today, most states use an apportionment formula modeled after UDITPA. Firms apply these formulas to derive an **apportionment percentage**, which determines the income taxable by each state. The UDIPTA formula is based on three equally weighted factors: the sales factor, the payroll factor, and the property factor.

$$\frac{\text{Sales factor} + \text{Payroll factor} + \text{Property factor}}{3} = \text{State apportionment percentage}$$

Objective 2
Apportion corporate taxable income among states according to UDITPA.

Each factor itself is a percentage computed as follows.

- The sales factor is the ratio of gross receipts from sales to in-state customers divided by total gross receipts from sales.
- The payroll factor is the ratio of compensation paid to employees working in-state divided by total compensation.
- The property factor is the ratio of the cost of real or tangible personal property located in-state divided by the total cost of such property.

To demonstrate the mechanics of income apportionment, let's examine the following data for Duo, a corporation conducting business in just two states, North Dakota and Montana.

| *Apportionment Formulas* | Duo's financial records provide the following information. (All numbers are in thousands of dollars.) |

	North Dakota	Montana	Total
Gross receipts from sales	$ 8,200	$ 6,800	$15,000
Payroll expense	1,252	697	1,949
Property costs	18,790	10,004	28,794

Because both states use a three-factor UDITPA formula, each state's apportionment percentage is computed as follows.

	North Dakota	Montana
Sales factor	54.67% ($8,200 ÷ $15,000)	45.33% ($6,800 ÷ $15,000)
Payroll factor	64.24% ($1,252 ÷ $1,949)	35.76% ($697 ÷ $1,949)
Property factor	65.26% ($18,790 ÷ $28,794)	34.74% ($10,004 ÷ $28,794)

$$\text{North Dakota} \quad \frac{54.67\% + 64.24\% + 65.26\%}{3} = \underline{\underline{61.39\%}}$$

$$\text{Montana} \quad \frac{45.33\% + 35.76\% + 34.74\%}{3} = \underline{\underline{38.61\%}}$$

If Duo's annual income is $40 million, the portion taxable by North Dakota is $24.556 million (61.39 percent × $40 million) and the portion taxable by Montana is $15.444 million (38.61 percent × $40 million). Under these simple assumptions, exactly 100 percent of Duo's income is taxed. No income is taxed twice or escapes state taxation altogether.

Realistically, state apportionment methods never achieve this mathematical precision. One major reason is that a majority of states now use a modified three-factor formula in which sales are *double-weighted* (the sales factor is counted twice and the factor total is divided by four) or otherwise given greater weight than the payroll and property factors. At least a dozen states either require or permit the use of single-factor apportionment, in which only the sales factor is considered in apportioning income. For example, Missouri permits seven different apportionment methods, including a traditional three-factor formula and a single-factor formula based only on sales. Another reason is that the definitions of the factors vary from state to state. For instance, the payroll factor under Virginia law includes compensation paid to corporate executive officers, while this compensation is excluded from North Carolina's payroll factor. Similarly, the definition of apportionable income is inconsistent across states. For instance, New Jersey law excludes interest and dividend income from the apportionment base, while New York law includes both as apportionable income. Clearly, states do not conform to a strictly uniform method of apportionment, and the federal courts have not required them to do so.[8] As a result, the division of taxable income among states inevitably results in some overlap or omission.

Tax Talk
South Dakota has the most "business friendly" tax system, and New York has the least, according to the Tax Foundation's 2011 State Business Climate Index.

Tax Planning Implications

Multistate businesses can reduce their overall tax cost to the extent that they can shift income from a high-tax state to a low-tax state. This strategy often involves the manipulation of the state apportionment formulas. Let's refer back to our Duo example. Currently, North Dakota's tax rate on corporate income is 6.5 percent, while Montana's tax rate is 6.75 percent. Because of this rate differential, every $100 of income that Duo can shift from Montana's jurisdiction to North Dakota's jurisdiction saves $0.25 of tax.

Manipulating the Property Factor

Duo plans to build a new manufacturing plant at an estimated cost of $25 million. If the plant is built in North Dakota, the corporation's property factors will be revised as follows. (All numbers are in thousands of dollars.)

	North Dakota	Montana	Total
Property costs	$18,790	$10,004	$28,794
New manufacturing plant	25,000	–0–	25,000
Revised property costs	$43,790	$10,004	$53,794
Revised property factors	81.4%	18.6%	

Consequently, North Dakota's apportionment percentage will increase, while Montana's apportionment percentage will decrease.

$$\text{North Dakota} \quad \frac{54.67\% + 64.24\% + 81.4\%}{3} = \underline{66.77\%}$$

$$\text{Montana} \quad \frac{45.33\% + 35.76\% + 18.6\%}{3} = \underline{33.23\%}$$

---

[8] *Moorman Manufacturing Co. v. Bair, Director of Revenue of Iowa,* 437 U.S. 267 (1978).

Because Duo's decision to build a new plant in North Dakota increases that state's apportionment percentage, the decision shifts income from Montana to North Dakota and saves $5,380 state tax.[9]

Revised Apportionment

	Original Apportionment	
	North Dakota	Montana
Total taxable income	$40,000,000	$40,000,000
Apportionment percentage	.6139	.3861
State taxable income	$24,556,000	$15,444,000
	.065	.0675
State tax	$ 1,596,140	$ 1,042,470
	Revised Apportionment	
	North Dakota	Montana
Total taxable income	$40,000,000	$40,000,000
Apportionment percentage	.6677	.3323
State taxable income	$26,708,000	$13,292,000
	.065	.0675
State tax	$ 1,736,020	$ 897,210
Total state tax:		
Original apportionment	$ 2,638,610	
Revised apportionment	(2,633,230)	
Tax savings	$ 5,380	

Of course, the tax savings from the income shift is only one factor in the selection of the optimal site for the plant. Duo should certainly consider how its real and personal property tax costs will be affected by the geographic location of the plant. Nontax factors, such as the local cost of construction and the availability of a skilled workforce, are key elements in the selection process. While Duo may minimize its state income tax cost by locating its new manufacturing facility in North Dakota, this location is not necessarily the best choice for maximizing the value of the facility to the corporation.

Gross Receipts Taxes

Although most states apply a net income tax to business earnings, several states have adopted tax systems that tax gross revenues instead of net earnings. For example, Ohio assesses a commercial activity tax (CAT) for the privilege of doing business in Ohio. The CAT tax rate is generally 0.26 percent of gross receipts from business operations, without reduction for cost of goods sold or other business expenses. Texas assesses the Texas margin tax (TMT) on gross receipts reduced by the greater of cost of goods sold or compensation paid to employees. The TMT tax rate is generally 1 percent. Washington's gross receipts tax is called the business and occupation tax (B&O). B&O rates vary by industry, taxing gross receipts without reduction for expenses.

---

[9] The North Dakota apportionment percentage will also reflect any increase in the North Dakota payroll factor attributable to the new manufacturing facility.

Michigan State Taxation—What Next?	Michigan's state tax system has changed dramatically in the past five years, and continues to evolve. Prior to 2008, Michigan assessed a single business tax (SBT) that was a type of value-added tax. That system was replaced in 2008 with a combined business income tax (BIT) and gross receipts tax (GRT). In addition, a surcharge of 21.99 percent was assessed on the combined liability under the BIT and GRT. The BIT, GRT, and surcharge taxes applied to businesses operated by individuals, corporations, and passthrough entities.
	Effective in 2012, Michigan has repealed the BIT, GRT, and surcharge taxes, replacing them with a 6 percent corporate income tax (CIT) levied only on C corporations. Individuals and passthrough entities are exempt from the new system.

TAX CONSEQUENCES OF INTERNATIONAL BUSINESS OPERATIONS

In the current business environment, firms operating on a multinational level are becoming the rule rather than the exception. Globalization is creating exciting opportunities for U.S. businesses to expand into the emerging markets of eastern Europe, Africa, Asia, and South America. These opportunities are coupled with formidable obstacles. Firms with international aspirations must cope with differences across currencies, languages, technological sophistication, and cultural and political traditions.

Firms must be aware of the foreign tax implications of international operations. When a U.S. firm plans to expand its activities into another country, it should identify the taxes included in the country's fiscal structure. The firm's liability for these taxes will depend on the nature and extent of its activity within the country and whether such activity triggers the country's taxing jurisdiction. If the foreign country imposes a net income tax, its jurisdiction may depend on whether a tax treaty is in effect between the country and the United States.

Income Tax Treaties

Objective 3
Explain the significance of a permanent establishment.

An **income tax treaty** is a bilateral agreement between the governments of two countries defining and limiting each country's respective tax jurisdiction. The treaty provisions pertain only to individuals and corporations that are residents of either country and override the countries' general jurisdictional rules.[10] Under a typical treaty, a firm's income is taxable only by the country of residence (the home country) *unless* the firm maintains a **permanent establishment** in the other country (the host country). In this case, income attributable to the permanent establishment can be taxed by the host country. A permanent establishment is a fixed location, such as an office or factory, at which the firm carries on its regular commercial operations.[11] Because of this rule, a U.S. firm conducting business in a treaty country avoids that country's income tax if it does not maintain a fixed place of business in the host country.

Permanent Establishment	Adam Inc., a U.S. manufacturer, sells its products to many major customers in Italy. The United States and Italy have an income tax treaty under which Italy does not have jurisdiction to tax Adam unless the corporation maintains a permanent establishment within Italy. If Adam maintains a permanent establishment (such as a sales office in Rome), Italy has jurisdiction to tax the portion of Adam's income attributable to such establishment.

[10] The term *resident* includes individuals who are citizens or permanent residents of a country and corporations formed under the laws of the country or a political subdivision thereof.

[11] U.S. Treasury Department, Model Income Tax Treaty, article 5.

Tax Talk

At last count, the United States has entered into or is in the process of negotiating tax treaties with over 60 foreign countries.

If a U.S. firm conducts any business in a country that does not have an income tax treaty with the United States, the host country's jurisdiction depends on its unique tax laws. Consequently, the U.S. firm must research these laws to determine the level of activity that triggers jurisdiction. This determination is often subjective and results in considerable uncertainty for the firm. Moreover, the requisite level of business activity in nontreaty countries is often much less than the maintenance of a permanent establishment in the country.

U.S. Jurisdiction to Tax Global Income

The United States has a global tax system under which its citizens, permanent residents, and domestic corporations are taxed on *worldwide* income. In other words, when the United States is the home country, it claims jurisdiction to tax income regardless of where the income is earned. The United States does not surrender this primary jurisdiction when a U.S. firm engages in **outbound transactions** with residents of other nations, even if the income from the transaction is taxed by a foreign government.[12] Thus, a fundamental issue confronting U.S. firms operating abroad is the potential double taxation of their income.

As we learned in Chapter 6, firms can deduct foreign income taxes paid or accrued during the taxable year. However, a deduction is an imperfect remedy for double taxation.

Deduction of Foreign Income Tax

Corporation Q, which pays a 35 percent U.S. income tax, generates $1 million income subject to another nation's 22 percent income tax. Even with a deduction for the foreign income tax (and disregarding state tax), Corporation Q's global tax rate on this foreign income is 49.3 percent.

Foreign tax ($1 million taxable income × 22%)	$220,000
U.S. tax ($780,000 taxable income × 35%)	273,000
Global income tax	$493,000

$493,000 ÷ $1 million before-tax income = 49.3%

The federal government understands that U.S. firms facing this tax burden could be at a competitive disadvantage in the global marketplace. Therefore, the tax law contains the powerful mechanism of a foreign tax credit to alleviate double taxation at the international level.

FOREIGN TAX CREDIT

U.S. citizens, residents, and domestic corporations may elect to credit foreign income tax paid or accrued during the year against their U.S. tax.[13] Taxpayers electing the credit are not allowed a deduction for foreign income taxes.[14] The **foreign tax credit** is available only for

---

[12] The United States also taxes business income earned in this country by nonresident aliens and foreign corporations. §871(b) and §882. Any discussion of the tax rules applying to these *inbound transactions* is beyond the scope of this text.

[13] §901(a). The election to claim a foreign tax credit is made annually so that taxpayers can choose either the credit or the deduction on a year-to-year basis.

[14] §275(a)(4)(A).

income taxes; foreign excise, value-added, sales, property, and transfer taxes are not creditable.[15] Let's refer back to the example involving Corporation Q to demonstrate the power of the foreign tax credit.

Credit for Foreign Income Tax	If Corporation Q does not deduct its $220,000 foreign tax payment and elects the tax credit, its U.S. tax decreases to $130,000, and its global tax rate decreases to 35 percent.

Precredit U.S. tax ($1 million taxable income × 35%)	$ 350,000
Foreign tax credit	(220,000)
U.S. tax	$ 130,000
Foreign tax ($1 million taxable income × 22%)	$ 220,000
U.S. tax	130,000
Global income tax	$ 350,000

$350,000 ÷ $1 million before-tax income = 35%

By permitting Corporation Q to claim the foreign tax credit, the United States relinquished its taxing jurisdiction to the extent that another nation exercised its jurisdiction. In other words, the United States reduced its 35 percent rate by the 22 percent foreign rate so that Corporation Q paid only 13 percent U.S. tax on its foreign income.

Limitation on the Annual Credit

Objective 4
Compute a foreign tax credit.

The foreign tax credit is subject to a major limitation: The annual credit cannot exceed a specific percentage of the precredit U.S. tax for the year. This percentage is computed by dividing the taxpayer's **foreign source income** by taxable income.[16]

Foreign Tax Credit Limitation	In 2012, Corporation RH had $800,000 taxable income, $300,000 of which was generated by business activities in Country M. RH paid $123,900 foreign tax (at more than a 40 percent rate) to Country M.[17] Its U.S. income tax is computed as follows.

U.S. source income	$500,000	
Foreign source income	300,000	
Taxable income		$ 800,000
U.S. tax rate		.34
Precredit U.S. tax		$ 272,000
Foreign tax credit (limited)		(102,000)
U.S. tax		$ 170,000

[15] Firms either deduct or capitalize their noncreditable taxes relating to their foreign business activities.

[16] §904(a). The Internal Revenue Code contains elaborate and lengthy rules for distinguishing between foreign source and U.S. source income. See §861 through §865.

[17] The statement assumes that Country M and the United States use the same definition of taxable income. Actually, the definition of taxable income varies considerably from country to country.

RH's foreign tax credit is *limited* to the precredit U.S. tax of $272,000 multiplied by the ratio of foreign source income to taxable income.

$$\$272,000 \times \frac{\$300,000 \text{ foreign source income}}{\$800,000 \text{ taxable income}} = \$102,000$$

Even though RH paid $123,900 foreign income tax, only $102,000 is creditable against U.S. tax. Note that the limited credit equals the *entire precredit U.S. tax* on RH's foreign source income ($300,000 × 34 percent = $102,000). Note also that the U.S. tax equals 34 percent of $500,000 U.S. source income. Because of the foreign tax credit, RH pays no U.S. tax on its foreign source income. Because of the limitation on that credit, it pays the full U.S. tax on its *domestic* income.

Excess Credit Carrybacks and Carryforwards

When a firm is subject to the foreign tax credit limitation, the **excess foreign tax credit** (foreign tax paid but not credited) can be carried back one year and forward 10 years.[18] The firm can use its excess credits in a carryback or carryforward year, subject to the annual limitation.

Excess Credit Carryback

In the preceding example, RH had a $21,900 excess credit ($123,900 foreign tax paid − $102,000 limited credit) in 2012. Its 2011 U.S. tax return showed the following.

U.S. source income	$350,000	
Foreign source income	250,000	
Taxable income		$ 600,000
U.S. tax rate		.34
Precredit U.S. tax		$ 204,000
Foreign tax credit (actual tax paid)		(77,500)
U.S. tax		$ 126,500

The credit limitation did not apply because the $77,500 foreign tax paid was less than the $85,000 limitation.

$$\$204,000 \times \frac{\$250,000 \text{ foreign source income}}{\$600,000 \text{ taxable income}} = \$85,000$$

Consequently, RH had a $7,500 excess limitation in 2011 ($85,000 limitation − $77,500 credited foreign tax). Because of the excess limitation, RH can carry back $7,500 of its 2012 excess credit and obtain a $7,500 refund of 2011 tax. The remaining $14,400 excess credit is available as a carryforward to 2013.

Cross-Crediting

If a firm's foreign source income is taxed by a foreign jurisdiction at a rate *lower* than the U.S. rate, the firm's global rate on such income is the higher U.S. rate. In such case, the

[18] §904(c) as amended by the American Jobs Creation Act of 2004.

firm has an excess limitation equal to the U.S. tax paid on its foreign source income. If the foreign source income is taxed by a foreign jurisdiction at a rate *higher* than the U.S. rate, the global rate is the higher foreign rate. In this case, the firm pays no U.S. tax on its foreign source income. It will, however, have an excess foreign tax credit.

If a firm earns income in both low-tax and high-tax foreign jurisdictions, the excess credit from the high-tax income can be used to the extent of the excess limitation from the low-tax income. This **cross-crediting** reduces the firm's global tax rate on its foreign source income. Let's develop a case to illustrate this important result.

Cross-Crediting

CVB Inc. has the following taxable income.

U.S. source income	$350,000
Foreign source income:	
Country L	100,000
Country H	100,000
Taxable income	$550,000

Country L has a 15 percent income tax, and Country H has a 42 percent income tax. Thus, CVB paid $15,000 income tax to Country L and $42,000 income tax to Country H. Its U.S. tax is $130,000.

Taxable income	$550,000
U.S. tax rate	.34
Precredit U.S. tax	$187,000
Foreign tax credit (actual tax paid)	(57,000)
U.S. tax	$130,000

The credit limitation does not apply because the $57,000 foreign tax paid is *less* than the $68,000 limitation.

$$\$187,000 \times \frac{\$200,000 \text{ foreign source income}}{\$550,000 \text{ taxable income}} = \$68,000$$

In this example, CVB pays only $11,000 U.S. tax on its $200,000 foreign source income.

Foreign source income	$200,000
U.S. tax rate	.34
	$ 68,000
Foreign tax credit	(57,000)
U.S. tax on foreign source income	$ 11,000

Therefore, CVB's global rate on this income is 34 percent, even though the $100,000 earned in Country H was taxed at 42 percent. Because CVB blended low-tax and high-tax income in computing its foreign tax credit limitation, it reduced its U.S. tax bill by every dollar of foreign tax paid for the year.

ORGANIZATIONAL FORMS FOR OVERSEAS OPERATIONS

U.S. firms expanding internationally must decide on the form in which to operate their overseas activities. This section of the chapter surveys the basic organizational choices for foreign business ventures.

Branch Offices and Foreign Partnerships

Objective 5
Compare the tax consequences of a foreign branch and a foreign subsidiary.

U.S. firms wanting to establish a presence in a foreign country can open a branch office. A *branch office* is not a separate legal entity but is merely an extension of the U.S. firm. Any income or loss generated by the foreign branch is commingled with income and losses from the firm's other business activities. If the branch is profitable, its income is subject to U.S. tax. Any foreign tax paid on branch income is included in the computation of the foreign tax credit. The same tax consequences result if a U.S. firm becomes a partner in a foreign partnership. The firm reports its share of the partnership's foreign source income or loss and is entitled to a tax credit for its share of foreign income taxes paid by the partnership.

Foreign Partnership

SC, an Oklahoma corporation engaged in oil and gas drilling, owns a 60 percent interest in a partnership formed under South African law. This year, the foreign partnership generated $3 million income from its drilling activities in Africa and paid $420,000 income tax to various African jurisdictions. SC must include $1.8 million (60 percent × $3 million) foreign source income in its taxable income and may include $252,000 (60 percent × $420,000) of the African taxes paid by the partnership in computing its foreign tax credit.

Domestic Subsidiaries

U.S. corporations often create wholly owned subsidiaries to operate foreign businesses. Because of the parent's limited liability as a shareholder, this strategy confines the risks of the foreign operation to the subsidiary corporation. If the subsidiary is a domestic corporation, the tax consequences are virtually identical to those of a foreign branch. The parent and subsidiary can file a consolidated U.S. tax return so that profits and losses generated by the overseas business are combined with those of the parent and any other domestic subsidiaries.[19] The group can elect a consolidated foreign tax credit for income taxes paid by the subsidiary and any other corporation in the group.

Domestic Subsidiary

SC, the Oklahoma corporation described in the preceding example, owns 100 percent of the outstanding stock of Pacifica, a California corporation. Pacifica conducts oil drilling activities in several countries in Southeast Asia. This year, Pacifica generated $14 million income and paid $3.1 million income tax to its host countries. SC files a consolidated federal tax return that includes Pacifica. Consequently, Pacifica's $14 million foreign source income is included in consolidated taxable income, and the $3.1 million foreign income tax paid by Pacifica is included in the computation of the SC consolidated group's foreign tax credit.

---

[19] See the discussion of consolidated corporate returns in Chapter 11.

Foreign Subsidiaries

Another alternative is for a U.S. corporation to create a subsidiary under the laws of a foreign jurisdiction. In such case, the subsidiary is a foreign corporation, although it is completely controlled by a U.S. parent. The foreign jurisdiction is *both* home and host country to the subsidiary even though a U.S. shareholder owns the corporation. Multinational corporations typically have strong political and legal reasons for using foreign subsidiaries, such as the public image of the business in the host country or prohibitions against foreign ownership of real property located in the host country. When a U.S. corporation conducts business through a foreign subsidiary, the subsidiary's activities cannot be combined with those of the parent because foreign subsidiaries cannot be included in a U.S. consolidated tax return.[20] Thus, income generated by the subsidiary is not included in consolidated taxable income. Losses incurred by the subsidiary are isolated; the parent can't use these losses to shelter its own income from U.S. taxation. Depending on the tax laws of the foreign jurisdiction, the corporation may be allowed to carry the loss back or forward as a net operating loss deduction.

Foreign Subsidiary	SC, our Oklahoma oil and gas corporation, owns 100 percent of the outstanding stock of Latina, a Brazilian corporation. Latina conducts its business activities only in Brazil. This year, Latina generated $9 million income and paid $2.25 million Brazilian income tax. Although SC files a consolidated federal tax return with all its domestic subsidiaries, the return does not include Latina. Because Latina is a foreign corporation operating exclusively in a foreign jurisdiction, it does not pay U.S. income tax.

Dividends from Foreign Subsidiaries

When a U.S. corporation receives a dividend from another corporation (the payer), the dividend is included in the recipient's gross income. If the payer is a U.S. corporation, the recipient is allowed a dividends-received deduction. Consequently, little if any of the dividend is included in the recipient's taxable income.[21] If the payer is a foreign corporation, the recipient is not entitled to a dividends-received deduction.[22] The dividend is included in the recipient's taxable income, and the issue of double taxation again takes center stage.

Many countries (including the United States) impose a tax on dividends paid by resident corporations to foreign shareholders. The payer must withhold the tax from the dividend payment and remit it to the government. Consequently, the amount received by the shareholder is net of this **withholding tax.** The withholding tax rates vary across countries and are often specified in a country's income tax treaties. For example, Spain imposes a withholding tax on dividends paid by Spanish corporations to foreign shareholders, and the tax treaty between the United States and Spain specifies that the withholding tax rate is 15 percent. A U.S. corporation that receives a dividend net of a foreign withholding tax is entitled to a foreign tax credit.

---

[20] §1504(b)(3).

[21] See the discussion of the dividend-received deduction in Chapter 11. Intercompany dividends between members of an affiliated group filing a consolidated return are eliminated from consolidated taxable income. Reg. §1.1502-13(f)(2).

[22] §245 contains several exceptions to this general rule.

Credit for Foreign Withholding Tax	Domino, a U.S. corporation, owns 2 percent of the stock of Carmela, a Spanish corporation. This year, Domino received a $265,000 dividend from Carmela net of the 15 percent Spanish withholding tax. Thus, Domino received only $225,250 *cash* ($265,000 dividend − $39,750 withheld foreign tax). The $265,000 dividend is included in Domino's foreign source taxable income, and the $39,750 withholding tax is a creditable foreign income tax.

Deemed Paid Foreign Tax Credit

Objective 6
Compute a deemed paid foreign tax credit.

A U.S. corporation's dividends received from a foreign corporation are included in taxable income and subject to U.S. tax. Regardless of whether the dividends are subject to a foreign withholding tax, they represent after-tax earnings if the foreign corporation had to pay income tax to its home country. If a U.S. corporation owns 10 percent or more of the voting stock of the foreign corporation, it is entitled to a **deemed paid foreign tax credit.**[23] This credit is based on the income tax paid by the foreign corporation and not on any tax paid directly by the U.S. corporation. The best way to explain the computation of the deemed paid foreign tax credit is through an example.

Deemed Paid Credit	YNK, a U.S. corporation, formed FC Inc. under the laws of Country F. In its first year of operation, FC generated $100,000 income and paid $25,000 tax to Country F. The foreign subsidiary distributed its $75,000 after-tax income to YNK as a dividend, which was not subject to any withholding tax by Country F. The preliminary step in the computation of YNK's deemed paid credit is to increase (gross up) this dividend by the foreign tax that FC paid. Because FC distributed its entire after-tax income, the $75,000 dividend is grossed up by the entire $25,000 Country F tax. Therefore, YNK reports a $100,000 grossed-up dividend as foreign source income.[24] YNK is now entitled to a credit for the $25,000 foreign tax deemed paid on YNK's behalf by FC. Because of this credit, YNK's U.S. tax on the dividend is only $10,000.

Foreign source income (grossed-up dividend)	$100,000
U.S. tax rate	.35
Precredit U.S. tax	$ 35,000
Deemed paid foreign tax credit	(25,000)
U.S. tax	$ 10,000

YNK's $25,000 credit is not limited because the 25 percent foreign tax rate is *less* than the U.S. tax rate. Because of the deemed paid credit, the global tax on the $100,000 foreign source income earned by YNK through FC is $35,000: $25,000 foreign tax paid by FC and $10,000 U.S. tax paid by YNK.

Now change the facts by assuming that FC distributed only $10,000 of its $75,000 after-tax income as a dividend. In this case, FC's tax attributable to the dividend is $3,333 ([$10,000 ÷ $75,000] × $25,000 Country F tax). The grossed-up dividend is $13,333, and YNK's U.S. tax on the dividend is $1,333.

[23] §902(a).
[24] §78.

Grossed-up dividend	$13,333
U.S. tax rate	.35
Precredit U.S. tax	$ 4,666
Deemed paid foreign tax credit	(3,333)
U.S. tax	$ 1,333

The global tax on the $13,333 foreign source income earned by YNK through FC is $4,666: $3,333 foreign tax paid by FC and $1,333 U.S. tax paid by YNK.

DEFERRAL OF U.S. TAX ON FOREIGN SOURCE INCOME

Foreign source income earned by a foreign corporation is not subject to U.S. tax unless and until the corporation pays a dividend to a U.S. shareholder. Accordingly, U.S. corporations that don't *repatriate* (bring home) the earnings of their foreign subsidiaries are deferring U.S. tax on such earnings. If a U.S. parent has no pressing need for cash from its overseas operations, this deferral can go on indefinitely. Let's develop a case that quantifies the value of such deferral.

Deferral of U.S. Tax

RWB, a California corporation with a 35 percent U.S. tax rate, has two foreign operations, one organized as a branch office and the other organized as a foreign subsidiary. In year 0, both the branch and the subsidiary earned $500,000 income subject to a 20 percent foreign tax. Both operations reinvested their after-tax earnings in their respective businesses.

In year 0, RWB's U.S. tax on the $500,000 foreign source income earned by the branch is $75,000.

Foreign source income	$ 500,000
U.S. tax rate	.35
Precredit U.S. tax	$ 175,000
Foreign tax credit	(100,000)
U.S. tax	$ 75,000

RWB's global tax on the branch income is $175,000 ($100,000 foreign tax + $75,000 U.S. tax). In contrast, RWB's global tax on the $500,000 income earned by its foreign subsidiary is only $100,000, which is the tax paid by the subsidiary to its home country.

Note that RWB pays U.S. tax on the branch's income even though it did not withdraw any cash from the branch. If and when RWB does withdraw cash from the branch, the withdrawal will have no tax consequences. In contrast, RWB pays no U.S. tax on the income earned by the subsidiary *until* it withdraws cash (i.e., receives a dividend) from the subsidiary.

Tax Savings from Deferral

RWB's foreign subsidiary pays no dividends until year 6, when it distributes $400,000 to its parent. This distribution represents the after-tax income earned by the subsidiary in year 0. RWB's U.S. tax on this dividend is $75,000.

Dividend received	$400,000
Gross-up for tax paid by subsidiary	100,000
Foreign source income	$500,000
U.S. tax rate	.35
Precredit U.S. tax	$175,000
Deemed paid foreign tax credit	(100,000)
U.S. tax	$ 75,000

At a 9 percent discount rate, the present value of this tax in year 0 is $44,700, and the present value of RWB's global tax on the $500,000 income earned by its subsidiary in year 0 and repatriated in year 6 is $144,700.

Foreign tax paid by subsidiary in year 0	$100,000
Present value of U.S. tax paid in year 6	
($75,000 × .596 discount factor)	44,700
NPV of global tax	$144,700

This cost is $30,300 less than the $175,000 global tax on the year 0 income of the branch operation: a tax savings resulting entirely from the deferral of U.S. tax on foreign source income.

Tax deferral through foreign subsidiaries is possible only if the subsidiary's income is taxed at a foreign rate *less* than the U.S. rate. If a subsidiary operating in a high-tax country repatriates after-tax income as a dividend, the deemed paid foreign tax credit reduces the parent's U.S. tax on the dividend to zero. Thus, the parent's only tax on the foreign source income is the foreign income tax paid by the subsidiary in the year the income was earned.

Dividend from High-Tax Subsidiary

Vernon, a Georgia corporation with a 35 percent U.S. tax rate, has a foreign subsidiary subject to a 40 percent corporate income tax. The subsidiary distributed a $315,000 dividend that represents $525,000 before-tax income reduced by $210,000 foreign income tax. Vernon's U.S. tax on the dividend is zero.

Dividend received	$315,000
Gross-up for tax paid by subsidiary	210,000
Foreign source income	$525,000
U.S. tax rate	.35
Precredit U.S. tax	$183,750
Deemed paid foreign tax credit (limited)	(183,750)
U.S. tax	–0–

Although the subsidiary paid $210,000 foreign tax with respect to the earnings repatriated to Vernon, Vernon's credit for this tax is limited to the precredit U.S. tax on the dividend. Because of the limitation, Vernon has a $26,250 excess credit to use as a carryback or carryforward.

EXHIBIT 13.2
Tax Haven Subsidiary

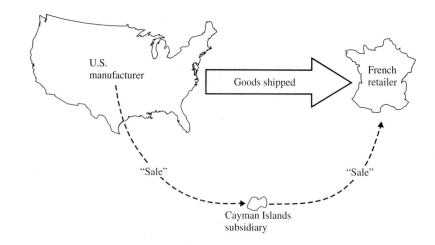

Controlled Foreign Corporations

Tax Talk
Recent federal legislative proposals would label the Cayman Islands and 33 other locations as "offshore secrecy jurisdictions" where U.S. citizens' financial activity would be automatically suspect.

U.S. corporations with foreign subsidiaries in low-tax countries (countries with tax rates less than the U.S. rate) can minimize tax by shifting as much income as possible to those subsidiaries. Before 1962, U.S. corporations routinely created subsidiaries in **tax haven** jurisdictions—countries with minimal or no corporate income tax. In many cases, the tax haven subsidiary existed only on paper, performing no function other than providing tax shelter. Consider the case of a U.S. manufacturer exporting its goods through a French subsidiary for retail sale in the European market. If the U.S. parent sold its goods directly to this marketing subsidiary at an arm's-length price, it would pay U.S. tax on the income from the outbound transaction. Furthermore, the subsidiary would pay French tax on the income from its retail sales of the goods. If, however, the U.S. parent also owned a subsidiary incorporated in the Cayman Islands, a Caribbean nation with no corporate income tax, the parent could sell its goods to this subsidiary for a very low price. The Cayman subsidiary could then sell the goods to the French subsidiary for a very high price. This three-party transaction is diagrammed in Exhibit 13.2.

Even though the U.S. parent sold its goods to the Cayman subsidiary, it shipped the goods directly to the French subsidiary's warehouse outside of Paris. The Cayman subsidiary was not involved in the actual production or distribution process. Nevertheless, the subsidiary's intermediate legal title to the goods shifted most of the income from the outbound transaction to the Cayman corporation. Until such time as this corporation paid a dividend to its U.S. parent, no income taxes at all were levied on the income.

Objective 7
Explain the tax consequences of subpart F income earned by a CFC.

This classic tax avoidance scheme is just one example of the creative strategies used by international firms to divert income to tax haven jurisdictions. In 1962, Congress ended the most abusive strategies by enacting a set of "antideferral" rules applying to controlled foreign corporations. A **controlled foreign corporation (CFC)** is a foreign corporation in which U.S. shareholders own more than 50 percent of the voting power or stock value.[25] If a CFC earns certain types of income, the law treats such income as if it were immediately distributed to the CFC's shareholders.[26] Any U.S. shareholder with a 10 percent or more interest must pay tax on its pro rata share of this constructive dividend. These shareholders are entitled to increase the tax basis in their CFC stock by their constructive dividend.[27] If

---

[25] §957(a).

[26] §951(a)(1)(A).

[27] §961.

the CFC subsequently makes cash distributions to its shareholders, the distributions are nontaxable to the extent of any prior year constructive dividends and reduce the tax basis in the shareholder's CFC stock.[28]

Deferral versus Constructive Dividends	In 2010, ABC created a wholly owned CFC, Flortez, in Country B. In 2010, 2011, and 2012, Flortez earned $20,000 income and paid $3,000 tax to Country B. Flortez paid no dividends in 2010 and 2011 and a $51,000 cash dividend in 2012.

The following chart reflects the tax consequences to ABC under two different assumptions. Under the "Deferral" assumption, ABC is not required to pay U.S. tax on Flortez's income until Flortez repatriates the income by paying a dividend. Under the "Constructive Dividend" assumption, ABC must recognize Flortez's $17,000 annual after-tax income as a constructive dividend in the year the CFC earns the income.

	Deferral	Constructive Dividend
2010:		
Cash received by ABC from Flortez	–0–	–0–
Dividend recognized by ABC	–0–	$17,000
Gross-up for Country B tax paid	–0–	3,000
ABC's foreign source income from Flortez	–0–	20,000
Increase in ABC's basis in Flortez stock	–0–	17,000
2011:		
Cash received by ABC from Flortez	–0–	–0–
Dividend recognized by ABC	–0–	$17,000
Gross-up for Country B tax paid	–0–	3,000
ABC's foreign source income from Flortez	–0–	20,000
Increase in ABC's basis in Flortez stock	–0–	17,000
2012:		
Cash received by ABC from Flortez	$51,000	$51,000
Dividend recognized by ABC	51,000	17,000
Gross-up for Country B tax paid	9,000	3,000
ABC's foreign source income from Flortez	60,000	20,000
Decrease in ABC's basis in Flortez stock	–0–	34,000

The only difference in the tax consequences under the two assumptions is the *timing* of ABC's recognition of its foreign source income from Flortez. Under both assumptions, ABC is entitled to a deemed paid foreign tax credit in the year it recognizes an actual or a constructive dividend from Flortez.

Subpart F Income

Not all foreign source income earned by a CFC must be constructively repatriated to its U.S. shareholders. Only narrowly defined categories of income (labeled **subpart F income** in the Internal Revenue Code) are treated as constructive dividends. Conceptually, subpart F income is artificial income because it has no commercial or economic connection to the CFC's home country. Subpart F income has many complex components, one of the more important of which is income derived from the sale of goods if (1) the CFC either buys the goods from or sells the goods to a related party and (2) the goods are neither manufactured nor sold for use within the CFC's home country.[29] In our Cayman Islands example, the Cayman CFC is related to both the U.S. manufacturer and the French distributor because all three corporations are members of

---

[28] §959.

[29] Such income constitutes foreign base company sales income per §954(d)(1). Subpart F income is defined in §952 through §954.

one controlled group. Moreover, the goods described in the example never touched Cayman soil and have no connection to the country. Quite clearly, the Cayman subsidiary's entire taxable income is subpart F income on which the U.S. parent must pay current tax.

Subpart F Income	Petroni owns 100 percent of the stock of RYM, a CFC operating in Country M. This year, RYM earned $1 million taxable income, $700,000 of which related to RYM's commercial activities within Country M and $300,000 (30 percent) of which was subpart F income. RYM paid $100,000 income tax to Country M and made no cash distributions to Petroni. Nonetheless, Petroni must recognize a constructive dividend equal to RYM's after-tax earnings attributable to its subpart F income.

Petroni's constructive dividend from RYM (30% × RYM's $900,000 after-tax earnings)	$270,000
Gross-up for foreign tax paid by RYM	30,000
Petroni's foreign source income from RYM	$300,000
Petroni's deemed paid foreign tax	$ 30,000

Petroni can increase the basis in its RYM stock by the $270,000 constructive dividend.

Investment of CFC Earnings in U.S. Parent

Corporations can use CFCs to defer U.S. tax if three conditions are satisfied.

1. The CFC generates foreign source income in a jurisdiction with a tax rate *less* than the U.S. rate.
2. The foreign source income is not subpart F income.
3. The CFC accumulates after-tax earnings instead of paying dividends.

If the U.S. parent is content to reinvest the CFC's earnings in foreign activities, the third condition may not be an obstacle. But if the parent needs cash from its overseas operations, it may try to maneuver around this condition. An obvious strategy is for the parent to borrow money from or sell shares of its own stock to the CFC. Neither transaction results in taxable gain to the parent but both result in positive cash flow. Unfortunately for the parent, this strategy doesn't work. The tax law treats a CFC's debt or equity investment in its U.S. parent as a repatriation of earnings: a constructive dividend on which the parent must pay U.S. income tax.[30]

U.S. Investment of CFC Earnings	Dykeman owns 100 percent of the stock of FV, a CFC operating in a country with a 20 percent income tax. This year, FV earned $100,000 taxable income (none of which was subpart F income) and paid no dividends. However, FV paid $40,000 cash to Dykeman for 1,600 shares of newly issued Dykeman stock. Because of this "back door" repatriation of FV's earnings, Dykeman must recognize $50,000 foreign source income.

Dykeman's constructive dividend from FV (cash received in payment for stock)	$40,000
Gross-up for foreign tax paid by FV	10,000
Dykeman's foreign source income from FV	$50,000
Dykeman's deemed paid foreign tax	$10,000

Dykeman can increase the basis in its FY stock by the $40,000 constructive dividend.

---

[30] §951(a)(1)(B) and §956.

Transfer Pricing and Section 482

Objective 8
Describe the role of Section 482 in the international transfer pricing area.

While the subpart F rules are potent, they do not extend to many types of foreign source income earned by CFCs. Consequently, U.S. parents benefit when they shift income to their foreign subsidiaries in low-tax jurisdictions. If a U.S. parent has subsidiaries in high-tax jurisdictions (such as Japan, France, Germany, and the United Kingdom), the tax strategy can be reversed. In such case, the parent wants to use its domestic subsidiaries as tax shelters.

Controlled groups of corporations can shift income among the members through their pricing structure for intercompany transactions. Consider the possibilities for income shifting if a U.S. parent owns an Irish subsidiary that manufactures consumer goods for worldwide export. Although the Irish subsidiary is a CFC, its profit from sales of goods manufactured in Ireland and sold to unrelated purchasers is not subpart F income. As a result, the income is subject only to the much lower Irish corporate tax until the CFC pays dividends to its parent. If the parent (or any domestic subsidiary) sells raw materials to the Irish subsidiary, the lower the price charged for the materials, the greater the income shifted to Ireland. If the U.S. parent provides administrative, marketing, or financial services to the Irish subsidiary, the parent could further inflate the subsidiary's profits (and deflate its own) by charging a nominal fee for the services rendered. Similarly, if the parent owns patents, copyrights, licenses, or other intangible assets that add value to the Irish manufacturing process, it could forgo royalty payments for the subsidiary's use of the intangible.

All the above pricing strategies shift income to the Irish subsidiary. Not surprisingly, the United States and most foreign countries, mindful of the income distortion resulting from artificial **transfer prices,** demand that related entities deal with each other in the same arm's-length manner as they deal with unrelated parties. Under federal tax law, Section 482 gives the IRS the authority to apportion or allocate gross income, deductions, or credits between related parties to correct any perceived distortion resulting from unrealistic transfer prices.[31]

Section 482 Adjustment

BSX, a California corporation, owns a CFC that manufactures and sells goods in the Asian market. The CFC is incorporated in a country with no corporate income tax. Several years ago, BSX sent a team of system engineers to advise the CFC on improving inventory management. BSX did not charge the CFC a fee for this service. In the same year, BSX sold industrial equipment to the CFC for a price of $385,000. During its audit of BSX's tax return, the IRS determined that a reasonable transfer price for the advisory services was $150,000, and a reasonable transfer price for the equipment was $500,000. Consequently, the IRS allocated $265,000 gross income to BSX from its CFC and assessed U.S. tax on this Section 482 adjustment.

Over the past decades, the IRS has not hesitated to use its Section 482 power to ensure that domestic corporations pay U.S. tax on an appropriate amount of their international income. While corporations certainly can challenge the IRS in court, the prevailing judicial attitude is that the IRS's determination of an arm's-length transfer price should be upheld unless the corporation can demonstrate that the determination is "arbitrary, capricious, or unreasonable."[32] Clearly, multinational corporations are in a defensive posture concerning their transfer pricing practices and must be constantly aware of any Section 482 exposure created by their intercompany transactions.

---

[31] §482 was introduced in Chapter 6.
[32] *Liberty Loan Corp.* v. *U.S.,* 498 F.2d 225 (CA-8, 1974), *cert. denied,* 419 U.S. 1089.

Transfer Pricing—An Issue of Global Proportion	Ernst & Young conducted a survey of the tax directors of over 450 multinational companies concerning transfer pricing issues. The survey results led to the following observations. • Companies throughout the world regard transfer pricing as the most important international tax issue they will face in the future. • Fiscal authorities in both developed and emerging markets are paying increased attention to transfer pricing compliance. • Intercompany services are the transactions most susceptible to transfer pricing disputes. • Nearly two-thirds of the companies surveyed report that their intercompany transactions have already been the target of a transfer pricing examination. • Eight in 10 multinationals expect to face a transfer pricing examination in the future.

Book/Tax Differences Related to Foreign Operations

Under GAAP, financial statements typically include the worldwide operations of a corporate group, including its foreign subsidiaries. However, the U.S. consolidated corporate income tax return will include only U.S. affiliated corporations. To the extent the income of foreign subsidiaries is not currently taxable in the United States, book/tax differences will result. Such differences could be either temporary or permanent, depending on their nature.

Tax versus Financial Statement Reporting of Foreign Subsidiaries	Westbrook Inc. is a U.S. multinational conducting business in several foreign jurisdictions through foreign subsidiaries. For 2011, its consolidated GAAP financial statements included $2 million of book income from foreign subsidiaries. It received cash dividend payments from its foreign subsidiaries of $750,000 (out of non-subpart F earnings), with associated "deemed paid" foreign taxes of $250,000. In addition, it must report $200,000 of subpart F income related to the activities of its foreign subsidiaries. Westbrook's federal income tax return will report $1.2 million of foreign taxable income ($750,000 cash dividend + $250,000 gross-up for deemed paid taxes + $200,000 subpart F income), resulting in a favorable book-tax difference of $800,000 ($2 million book income from foreign sources −$1.2 million taxable income from foreign sources). This book-tax difference is generally temporary, under the expectation that the foreign earnings will eventually be repatriated to the U.S. parent corporation and taxed at that future date. However, if Westbrook can demonstrate that it intends to permanently reinvest its unrepatriated foreign earnings outside the United States, it can treat the book-tax difference as permanent.

Conclusion

In the preceding chapter, we discussed the tax implications when owners select a particular entity through which to conduct business. In this chapter, we added a new tax planning variable—the jurisdiction in which the entity is taxed. To the extent that owners can manipulate this variable by operating in low-tax jurisdictions, tax costs can be controlled. When a business stretches across jurisdictions, the owners run the risk that double taxation will erode their after-tax profits. If the competing jurisdictions are state governments, income is divided according to each state's apportionment rule. Businesses can often take advantage of anomalies in these rules and differences in state tax rates to reduce their tax burden. If the competing jurisdictions are the United States and a foreign government, the foreign tax credit is an invaluable mechanism for preventing double taxation.

Multinational U.S. corporations can achieve substantial tax savings by incorporating foreign subsidiaries in low-tax jurisdictions. As a general rule, the income earned by these subsidiaries is not subject to U.S. tax until it is repatriated. To take advantage of this deferral, U.S. parent corporations must carefully avoid the subpart F rules and be content with reinvesting their foreign earnings in overseas ventures. They must steer clear of transfer pricing disputes with the IRS and the tax enforcement agencies of other nations. Certainly, international tax planning is a complex and challenging specialty that will become more valuable as the global economy continues to develop.

Sources of Book/Tax Differences	**Permanent**	**Temporary**
	• Permanently reinvested earnings of foreign subsidiaries	• Most unrepatriated earnings of foreign subsidiaries

Key Terms

apportionment 375
Commerce Clause 373
controlled foreign
  corporation (CFC) 388
cross-crediting 382
deemed paid foreign tax
  credit 385
excess foreign tax
  credit 381

foreign source
  income 380
foreign tax credit 379
income tax treaty 378
nexus 373
outbound transaction 379
permanent
  establishment 378
subpart F income 389

tax haven 388
transfer price 391
Uniform Division of
  Income for Tax Purposes
  Act (UDITPA) 375
withholding tax 384

Questions and Problems for Discussion

In the questions, problems, and cases for Chapter 13, corporations are U.S. corporations unless otherwise stated.

1. Why does a corporation's state income tax cost depend on its marginal income tax rate for federal purposes?

2. NY is a New York corporation that manufactures office equipment in a factory located in New York. In which of the following cases does NY have nexus with Pennsylvania?

   a. NY owns two retail outlets for its products in Pennsylvania.

   b. NY owns no tangible property in Pennsylvania. It employs two salespeople who travel throughout Pennsylvania soliciting orders for office equipment from regular customers. NY fills the orders out of its New York factory and ships the equipment to the customers by common carrier.

   c. NY owns no tangible property in Pennsylvania and does not have any employees who work in the state. It does have Pennsylvania customers who order equipment directly from the New York factory by telephone or fax.

   d. Refer to the facts in part c above. NY employs two technicians who travel throughout Pennsylvania providing repair and maintenance services to NY's customers.

3. Distinguish between the concepts of physical presence nexus and economic nexus.

4. Does the federal government require states to use a three-factor formula to apportion the income of an interstate business for state income tax purposes?

5. Borden Inc. conducts a business that spans four states. Its total income for the year was $32 million. However, the total of the taxable incomes reported on Borden's four state income tax returns was $34.8 million. Discuss the possible reasons for such discrepancy.

6. In what situation would a multistate business deliberately create nexus with a state so that the state has jurisdiction to tax a portion of the business income?

7. Distinguish between a home country and a host country in the international tax context.

8. What is the purpose of a bilateral income tax treaty between two countries?

9. Lefty Inc. sells its products to customers residing in Country X and Country Y. Both foreign jurisdictions have a 20 percent corporate income tax. This year, Lefty made more than $30 million of sales in both Country X and Country Y. However, it paid income tax only to Country X. What factors could account for this result?

10. Posse Corporation plans to form a foreign subsidiary through which to conduct a new business in Country J. Posse projects that this business will operate at a loss for several years.
    a. To what extent will the subsidiary's losses generate U.S. tax savings?
    b. To what extent will the subsidiary's losses generate a savings of Country J income tax?

11. Halifax Inc. operates its business in Country U through a subsidiary incorporated under Country U law. The subsidiary has never paid a dividend and has accumulated over $10 million after-tax earnings.
    a. Country U has a 45 percent corporate income tax. Describe the tax consequences to Halifax if it receives a $5 million dividend from the subsidiary.
    b. How would the tax consequences change if Country U's corporate income tax rate is only 20 percent?

12. Togo Inc. has a subsidiary incorporated in Country H, which does not have a corporate income tax. Which of the following activities generates subpart F income?
    a. The subsidiary buys woolen clothing products manufactured by a Swedish company and sells the products to unrelated wholesalers in the United States. Togo owns the Swedish company.
    b. The subsidiary buys coffee beans grown on plantations located in Country H and sells the beans to Togo, which makes coffee products.
    c. The subsidiary buys building materials from a Mexican company and sells the materials to construction companies operating in Country H. Togo owns the Mexican company.

13. Column Corporation has a subsidiary operating exclusively in Country A and a subsidiary operating exclusively in Country Z.
    a. Both subsidiaries were incorporated under Delaware law and are therefore U.S. corporations. Can Column use the losses from the Country A subsidiary to reduce the income from the Country Z subsidiary?
    b. Would your answer change if both subsidiaries are foreign corporations?

14. Delta Partnership carries on business in the United States and four other countries. Explain why the ordinary income generated by the foreign business is a separately stated item on Delta's Schedule K, Form 1065.

15. Kantor Inc. owns 100 percent of Sub 1 (a CFC in a country with a 50 percent corporate tax) and 90 percent of Sub 2 (a CFC in a country with a 10 percent corporate tax). Kantor sells goods and services to both CFCs. Is the IRS more interested in Kantor's transfer pricing for sales to Sub 1 or sales to Sub 2?

16. In what situation is the United States a tax haven for an international business operation?

Application Problems

1. This year, Mesa Inc.'s before-tax income was $9,877,000. It paid $419,000 income tax to Minnesota and $385,000 income tax to Illinois.
    a. Compute Mesa's federal income tax.
    b. What is Mesa's tax rate on its income?

2. Oldham Inc. conducts business in State M and State N, which both use the UDITPA three-factor formula to apportion income. State M's corporate tax rate is 4.5 percent, and State N's corporate tax rate is 7 percent. This year, Oldham had the following sales, payroll, and property (in thousands of dollars) in each state.

	State M	State N	Total
Gross receipts from sales	$3,000	$7,500	$10,500
Payroll expense	800	1,200	2,000
Property costs	900	1,000	1,900

   If Oldham's before-tax income was $3 million, compute its State M and State N tax.

3. Refer to the facts in the preceding problem. Compute Oldham's State M and State N tax if State N uses an apportionment formula in which the sales factor is double-weighted.

4. Refer to the facts in problem 2. Compute the state income tax savings if Oldham could relocate its personnel so that payroll expense in State M increased to $1,900 (thousand) and payroll expense in State N decreased to $100 (thousand).

5. Cromwell Corporation does business in two states, A and B. State A uses an equal-weighted three-factor apportionment formula and has a 5 percent state tax rate. State B uses an apportionment formula that double-weights the sales factor and has a 6 percent state tax rate. Cromwell's state-level taxable income, before apportionment, is $2 million. It has identified the following components of its sales, payroll, and property factors:

	State A	State B	Total
Sales	$6,000,000	$4,000,000	$10,000,000
Payroll	2,000,000	1,200,000	3,200,000
Average Property	1,000,000	800,000	1,800,000

   a. Calculate Cromwell's apportionment factors, income apportioned to each state, and state tax liability.

   b. State B is considering changing its apportionment formula to place 100 percent of the weight on the sales factor, ignoring payroll and property for apportionment purposes. Given its current levels of activity, would such a change increase or decrease Cromwell's state income tax burden? Provide calculations to support your conclusion.

6. Akita is a U.S. corporation. This year, it earned $8 million before-tax income and paid $450,000 income tax to jurisdictions other than the United States. Compute Akita's U.S. income tax assuming that:

   a. The other jurisdictions were the states of Montana, Colorado, California, and Arizona.

   b. The other jurisdictions were Italy and Spain, and Akita's foreign tax credit was not limited.

7. Zenon Inc. has the following taxable income.

U.S. source income	$1,900,000
Foreign source income	240,000
Taxable income	$2,140,000

   Zenon paid $33,000 foreign income tax. Compute its U.S. income tax.

8. Refer to the facts in the preceding problem. How would your answer change if Zenon conducted its foreign operations through a foreign subsidiary that made no shareholder distributions during the current year?

9. Jackson Inc. has the following taxable income.

U.S. source income	$18,800,000
Foreign source income	2,690,000
Taxable income	$21,490,000

Jackson paid $1,040,000 foreign income tax. Compute its U.S. income tax.

10. Refer to the facts in the preceding problem. How would your answer change if Jackson conducted its foreign operations through a foreign subsidiary that made no shareholder distributions during the current year?

11. Elmo Inc. is a U.S. corporation with a branch office in foreign country Z. During the current year, Elmo had $340,000 of U.S. source income and $60,000 of foreign source income from Z, on which Elmo paid $28,000 of country Z income tax.

   a. Calculate Elmo's U.S. tax liability before foreign tax credit, maximum foreign tax credit allowable, and net U.S. tax liability after foreign tax credit.

   b. If Elmo had paid only $10,000 of country Z income tax, calculate Elmo's foreign tax credit allowable and net U.S. tax liability after foreign tax credit.

   c. For which fact situation (foreign tax of $28,000 or $10,000) could Elmo have reduced its worldwide tax burden by operating in country Z using a foreign subsidiary rather than a branch operation? Explain briefly.

12. Axtell Corporation has the following taxable income.

U.S. source income	$1,620,000
Foreign source income:	
Country A	550,000
Country B	2,000,000
Country C	2,900,000
Taxable income	$7,070,000

Axtell paid $600,000 income tax to Country B and $1.3 million income tax to Country C. Country A does not have a corporate income tax. Compute Axtell's U.S. income tax.

13. Transcom, an Ohio corporation, earned $700,000 U.S. source income from sales of goods to U.S. customers and $330,000 foreign source income from sales of goods to customers in Canada. Canada's corporate income tax rate is 40 percent, and the United States and Canada have a bilateral tax treaty.

   a. Compute Transcom's U.S. tax if it does not maintain a permanent establishment in Canada.

   b. Compute Transcom's U.S. tax if it does maintain a permanent establishment in Canada.

14. Aqua, a South Carolina corporation, is a 20 percent partner in a Swiss partnership. This year, Aqua earned $2 million U.S. source income and $190,000 foreign source income. It paid no foreign income tax. The Swiss partnership earned $1.73 million

foreign source income and paid $660,000 income tax to Switzerland, France, and Austria. Compute Aqua's U.S. tax.

15. The Trio affiliated group consists of Trio, a New Jersey corporation, and its three wholly owned subsidiaries. This year, the four corporations report the following.

	Net Income (Loss)
Trio	$ 412,000
Subsidiary 1	(180,000)
Subsidiary 2	389,000
Subsidiary 3	600,000

If Trio elects to file a consolidated return, compute consolidated taxable income assuming that:

a. Subsidiary 1 is a domestic corporation, and Subsidiaries 2 and 3 are foreign corporations.

b. Subsidiaries 2 and 3 are domestic corporations, and Subsidiary 1 is a foreign corporation.

16. Comet operates solely within the United States. It owns two subsidiaries conducting business in the United States and several foreign countries. Both subsidiaries are U.S. corporations. This year, the three corporations report the following.

	Foreign Source Income	U.S. Source Income	Foreign Income Tax Paid
Comet	–0–	$600,000	–0–
Sub 1	$3,500,000	150,000	$ 380,000
Sub 2	4,700,000	410,000	2,350,000

a. If Comet and its two subsidiaries file a consolidated U.S. tax return, compute consolidated income tax.

b. How would the aggregate tax of the group change if the three corporations file separate U.S. tax returns?

c. Identify the reason for the difference in the tax liability in parts *a* and *b* above.

17. Velox Inc. began operations in 2010. For its first two taxable years, Velox's records show the following.

	2010	2011
U.S. source income	$300,000	$270,000
Foreign source income	200,000	630,000
Taxable income	$500,000	$900,000
Foreign income tax paid	$ 82,000	$151,000

Compute Velox's U.S. tax for both years.

18. Minden Corporation's records show the following results for its first three years of operations.

	2009	*2010*	*2011*
U.S. source income	$180,000	$350,000	$ 800,000
Foreign source income	92,000	500,000	680,000
Taxable income	$272,000	$850,000	$1,480,000
Foreign tax paid	$ 21,000	$152,000	$ 224,400

In 2012, Minden generated $2 million taxable income ($900,000 of which was foreign source) and paid $370,000 foreign income tax.

a. Compute Minden's U.S. tax for 2009, 2010, and 2011.

b. Compute Minden's U.S. tax for 2012.

c. Compute the refund generated by the carryback of the 2012 excess credit.

19. Omaha Inc. owns 100 percent of the stock in Franco, a foreign corporation. All Franco's income is foreign source, and its foreign income tax rate is 20 percent. This year, Franco distributed a $50,000 dividend to Omaha.

a. Assuming that Omaha is in the 35 percent tax bracket, compute its U.S. tax on the dividend.

b. How would your computation change if the foreign income tax rate was 45 percent?

20. Dixie Inc., a Tennessee corporation, conducts business through branch offices in the United States, Mexico, and Canada. Dixie owns 100 percent of the stock of two foreign subsidiaries, Dix-Col Inc. and Dix-Per Inc., through which it conducts its South American business. This year, Dixie recognized the following items of taxable income.

U.S. source income from domestic branch	$4,922,000
Foreign source income from foreign branches	1,031,000
Cash dividends received from Dix-Col	249,000
Cash dividends received from Dix-Per	186,000

During the year, Dixie paid $116,200 income tax to Mexico and $286,700 income tax to Canada. It paid no direct income taxes to any other foreign country. However, Dix-Col paid a 20 percent income tax to the country of Colombia, and Dix-Per paid a 37 percent income tax to the country of Peru.

a. Compute Dixie's taxable income.

b. Compute Dixie's U.S. tax.

21. Jumper Inc., which has a 34 percent marginal tax rate, owns 40 percent of the stock of a CFC. At the beginning of 2011, Jumper's basis in its stock was $660,000. The CFC's 2011 income was $1 million, $800,000 of which was subpart F income. The CFC paid no foreign income tax and distributed no dividends.

a. Does Jumper have any 2011 tax consequences with respect to its investment in the CFC?

b. Compute Jumper's basis in its CFC stock at the beginning of 2012.

22. Refer to the facts in the preceding problem. In 2012, the CFC's income was $600,000, none of which was subpart F income, and it distributed a $300,000 dividend to its shareholders ($120,000 to Jumper). What is the tax consequence to Jumper of this dividend?

23. Yasmin Corporation, which has a 35 percent marginal tax rate, owns 100 percent of Luna Corporation, a foreign corporation in a country with a 15 percent corporate income tax. Luna has never paid a dividend and has accumulated $18 million

after-tax income (none of which is subpart F income). This year, Luna lends $1 million to Yasmin. What is the tax consequence to Yasmin of this loan?

24. Alamo, a Texas corporation, manufactures plastic components that it sells to Vegas, a Mexican corporation, for assembly into a variety of finished goods. Alamo owns 60 percent of Vegas' stock. Alamo's cost per component is $85, its selling price per component is $100, and it sold 70,000 components to Vegas this year. Alamo's taxable income as reported on its Form 1120 was $900,000, and Vegas's taxable income as reported on its Mexican corporate income tax return was $1.2 million. Determine the effect on the taxable incomes of both corporations if the IRS determines that an arm's-length transfer price per plastic component is $108.

25. Cotton Comfort Corporation is a U.S. shirt manufacturer with a foreign subsidiary in Country X. Cloth to make shirts is woven in the United States, at a cost of $14 per shirt and shipped to Country X where it is cut and sewn at a cost of $15 per shirt. These shirts are sold in Europe for $90 per shirt. The profit on each shirt is $61, a portion of which is U.S. source income and a portion of which is foreign source income, depending on the price at which the cloth is transferred from the United States to Country X.

    a. If the tax rate in Country X is lower than the U.S. tax rate, would Cotton Comfort prefer a high transfer price or a low transfer price? At what transfer price would all of the profit on these shirts be tax in Country X? Explain briefly.

    b. If the tax rate in Country X is higher than the U.S. tax rate, would Cotton Comfort prefer a high transfer price or a low transfer price? At what transfer price would all of the profit on these shirts be tax in the United States? Explain briefly.

26. Refer to the facts in the preceding problem. Assume that the tax rate in Country X is 15 percent and Cotton Comfort's U.S. marginal tax rate is 35 percent. The corporation and its subsidiary have agreed to a transfer price for the cloth of $30 per shirt.

    a. At this price, how much profit per shirt will be taxed in the United States?

    b. At this price, how much profit per shirt will be taxed in Country X?

    c. If the IRS chooses to challenge Cotton's Comfort's transfer price for the cloth, would you expect it to argue for a higher or lower transfer price? Explain briefly.

Issue Recognition Problems

Identify the tax issue or issues suggested by the following situations and state each issue in the form of a question.

1. State E wants to encourage the development of a local wine industry. Consequently, it decreased its excise tax rate on retail sales of locally produced wines to 3 percent. The state's excise tax on wines produced out-of-state but sold in-state is 10 percent.

2. ABC operates a meat and poultry business. The corporation distributes its products in six states and pays income tax to each based on the meat and poultry income apportionable to each. Last year, ABC invested in a motion picture. The picture was a commercial success, and ABC received a royalty check for $1,800,000 from the movie's producer.

3. Durbin Corporation is incorporated and has its commercial domicile in State N. This year, Durbin sold its manufactured products to customers in State N (61 percent of sales), State O (28 percent of sales), and State P (11 percent of sales). Durbin has nexus with State N and State O. However, it has no physical presence in State P and therefore is not taxed by that state. Both State N and State O use the three-factor UDITPA formula to apportion income.

4. The United States has a tax treaty with the United Kingdom that provides certain tax benefits to U.K. corporations conducting business in the United States. The United States does not have an income tax treaty with Chile. Silas Company, a Chilean firm that exports goods to the United States, decides to operate its export business through a shell corporation formed under U.K. law.

5. Benton is a consulting firm with its headquarters in New York City. This year, it entered into a consulting contract with a multinational corporation. Mrs. Kalle, an employee, spent 33 days working at Benton headquarters, 28 days in London, 50 days in Paris, and 14 days in Hong Kong performing the professional services specified in the contract. Benton received a $1 million fee upon completion of Mrs. Kalle's work.

6. Homely Corporation operates a fleet of oceangoing cargo vessels. During the year, one Homely vessel was docked at its home port in New Orleans for 55 days, was on the high seas for 120 days, and was docked at various foreign ports of call for the remaining 190 days. Homely's net income from operation of this vessel was $620,000.

7. Funk Corporation conducts business in a foreign jurisdiction that imposes a 1 percent tax on gross receipts from sales within the jurisdiction. This year, Funk paid $750,000 gross receipts tax to the jurisdiction.

8. Lincoln manufactures paper products in the United States and sells the products internationally. Because most of its foreign sales are in high-tax jurisdictions, Lincoln has excess foreign credits from its paper business. This year, Lincoln earned $8 million interest income on long-term bonds issued by Country NT, which has no income tax.

9. Hastings Corporation has a foreign subsidiary conducting a manufacturing business in Country Z, which has a 25 percent corporate income tax. The IRS recently challenged the transfer price at which Hastings performs managerial services for the subsidiary and used its Section 482 authority to reallocate $10 million income from the subsidiary to Hastings. The taxing authorities in Country Z maintain the transfer price was perfectly accurate.

10. Williams Inc. is a U.S. corporation that manufacturers toys in a factory located near Milwaukee, Wisconsin. Williams sells the toys to its foreign subsidiary, which is incorporated in Carnema, a Caribbean country with no corporate income tax. Williams actually ships the toys to a warehouse in Carnema, where the toys are sealed in protective plastic wrappings and labeled. The foreign subsidiary resells the sealed and labeled toys in the European market. This year, the foreign subsidiary's profit from toy sales will exceed $25 million.

11. Bertrand owns a foreign subsidiary with over $8 million accumulated foreign source income (on which Bertrand has never paid U.S. tax). The subsidiary recently purchased $500,000 worth of stock in a publicly held U.S. corporation with over 30,000 shareholders.

Research Problems

1. Visit the website for Federation of Tax Administrators (**www.taxadmin.org**) and use the Links button to go to the Illinois Department of Revenue website. Locate a copy of the Corporate Income and Replacement Tax Return (Form IL-1120), scrutinize Step 4 and describe how Illinois's apportionment percentage is computed. Return to the FTA website and link to the Ohio Department of Taxation website. Locate a copy of the Ohio Corporation Franchise Tax Report (Form FT-1120), scrutinize Schedule D, and describe how Ohio's apportionment percentage is computed.

2. Endless Summer is a Florida corporation that operates a fleet of cruise ships. It offers two categories of cruises. The first category includes round-trip cruises on ships that depart from Miami, visit various Caribbean and South American ports, then return to Miami at the end of the cruise. The second category includes one-way cruises on ships that depart from Miami and travel to various South American ports. The passengers disembark and are responsible for arranging their return travel from the destination port. The ship then takes on a new group of passengers at the South American port for a one-way journey to Miami. This year, Endless Summer earned $4,912,000 from its round-trip cruises and $5,018,000 from its one-way cruises. How much of Endless Summer's $9,930,000 total transportation income is U.S. source income, and how much is foreign source income?

3. In 1995, Jenson Investments, a Delaware corporation with a 35 percent federal tax rate, formed Bestmark, a wholly owned German subsidiary. Bestmark conducts several profitable businesses in Europe and pays the 45 percent German corporate income tax. Bestmark has never paid a dividend to its U.S. parent and has accumulated $8.2 million after-tax earnings. Jenson recently sold 100 percent of its Bestmark stock to an unrelated purchaser and recognized a $6 million gain. Compute Jenson's U.S. tax on this gain.

Tax Planning Cases

1. Lydell Corporation currently operates in two states, P and Q. State P has a 5 percent tax rate and uses an equally weighted three-factor apportionment formula. State Q has a 9 percent tax rate and uses an apportionment formula that double-weights the sales factor. For the current year, Lydell's state taxable income before apportionment was $1,500,000. Below is information regarding Lydell's current activity within each state.

	State P	State Q	Total
Sales	$3,000,000	$2,000,000	$5,000,000
Payroll	1,000,000	500,000	1,500,000
Average property	1,200,000	800,000	2,000,000

Lydell is considering expanding its operations by constructing a new production facility. The facility would increase Lydell's total property and payroll by $1 million and $400,000, respectively. The company projects that, as a result of the new facility, total sales would increase by $800,000, of which half of these new sales would be to customers in State P and half would be to customers in State Q. Total net income would increase by $300,000. Solely on the basis of state income tax considerations, in which state would you recommend Lydell locate the new facility?

2. Minden Corporation wants to open a branch operation in eastern Europe and must decide between locating the branch in either Country R or Country S. Labor costs are substantially lower in Country R than in Country S. For this reason, the Country R branch would generate $700,000 annual income, while the Country S branch would generate only $550,000 annual income. However, Country R has a 20 percent corporate income tax, while Country S has a 10 percent corporate income tax. On the basis of these facts, in which country should Minden locate its eastern European branch?

3. Echo Inc., which has a 35 percent U.S. tax rate, plans to expand its business into Country J. It could open a branch office, or it could create a foreign subsidiary in Country J. The branch office would generate $5,000,000 income in year 0. The foreign subsidiary would incur incremental legal costs and, as a result, would generate only $4,750,000 income in year 0. This income would be taxed at Country J's 18 percent corporate rate. Echo plans to defer repatriation of the subsidiary's year 0 after-tax earnings until year 4. Assuming a 6 percent discount rate, should Echo open

the branch office or form the subsidiary to maximize the NPV of the year 0 foreign source income?

4. Rand Corporation owns 100 percent of the stock of Flo, a foreign corporation conducting business in Portugal. Flo generates $100,000 before-tax annual income on which it pays a 30 percent Portuguese tax. Flo can reinvest its after-tax earnings for an indefinite time period in Europe at a 7 percent before-tax rate of return. Alternatively, Flo could distribute its after-tax earnings to Rand, which could invest the funds in the United States at a 9 percent before-tax rate of return. Assuming that Rand's U.S. tax rate is 35 percent, should it repatriate Flo's earnings to maximize its rate of return?

5. Chloe Inc. is an Oklahoma corporation that generates $2 million U.S. source income annually. Chloe recently opened a branch office in Country A, which has a 38 percent income tax. Chloe forecasts that this branch will earn $1 million foreign source income this year. Chloe is planning to open a second branch office in either Country D or Country G. Chloe forecasts that a Country D branch would earn $425,000 foreign source income subject to Country D's 13 percent tax. A Country G branch would earn $530,000 foreign source income subject to Country G's 32.5 percent tax. Given that Chloe's U.S. tax rate is 34 percent, where should Chloe open its second branch office to maximize its global after-tax income?

Comprehensive Problems for Part Four

1. Univex is a calendar year, accrual basis retail business. Its financial statements provide the following information for the year.

Revenues from sales of goods	$ 783,200
Cost of goods sold (FIFO)	(417,500)
Gross profit	$ 365,700
Interest income from certificates of deposit	1,300
Dividend income from IBM stock	6,720
Gain from sale of IBM stock purchased in 2000	8,615
Bad debt expense	3,900
Administrative salaries and wages	153,400
Business and employment taxes	31,000
Interest expense on debt incurred to buy inventory	5,100
Advertising	7,000
Meals and entertainment	3,780
Property insurance premiums	4,300
Depreciation	10,800
Repairs and maintenance	18,700
Supplies	4,120
Utilities	21,000
Contributions to charity	5,000

Univex's records reveal the following facts.

- Bad debt expense equals the addition to an allowance for bad debts. Actual write-offs of uncollectible accounts totaled $2,000.
- MACRS depreciation for the year was $21,240.
- Univex made no dispositions of operating assets.
- The owners did not receive any compensation or withdraw any funds from Univex.
- Univex is entitled to an $1,800 general business credit.

a. Assume Univex is a sole proprietorship. Compute net profit on Schedule C, Form 1040, and identify the items from Univex's records that do not appear on Schedule C. Complete Schedule C, Form 1040.

b. Assume Univex is an LLC. Compute ordinary income on page 1, Form 1065, and complete Schedule K, Form 1065.

c. Assume Univex is a corporation operating in a state without a corporate income tax. Univex made estimated federal tax payments totaling $23,500. Compute taxable income on page 1, Form 1120, calculate Univex's federal income tax, and complete page 1, Form 1120, and Schedule M-1, page 5, Form 1120.

2. Dollin Inc. is incorporated under Virginia law and has its corporate headquarters in Richmond. Dollin is a distributor; it purchases tangible goods from manufactureres and sells the goods to retailers. It has a branch office through which it sells goods in the United Kingdom and owns 100 percent of a French corporation (French Dollin) through which it sells goods in France. Dollin's financial records provide the following information for the year.

Before-tax net income from sales:	
Domestic sales	$ 967,900
U.K. sales (foreign source income)	415,000
	$1,382,900
Dividend income:	
Brio Inc.	$ 8,400
French Dollin (foreign source income)	33,800

- Dollin pays state income tax in Virginia, North Carolina, and South Carolina. All three states tax their apportioned share of Dollin's net income from worldwide sales. Because Virginia is Dollin's commercial domicile, it also taxes Dollin's U.S. source (but not foreign source) dividend income net of any federal dividends-received deduction. The states have the following apportionment factors and tax rates.

	Apportionment Factor	Tax Rate
Virginia	43.19%	6.00%
North Carolina	11.02%	7.75%
South Carolina	39.52%	5.00%

- Dollin paid $149,200 income tax to the United Kingdom.
- Brio Inc. is a taxable U.S. corporation. Dollin owns 2.8 percent of Brio's stock.
- The $33,800 dividend from French Dollin is a distribution of after-tax earnings with respect to which French Dollin paid $17,000 French income tax.
- Dollin elects to claim the foreign tax credit rather than to deduct foreign income taxes.

Solely on the basis of the above facts, compute the following.

a. Dollin's state income tax for Virginia, North Carolina, and South Carolina.

b. Dollin's federal income tax. Assume that Dollin paid the state taxes during the year, and no state income tax is allocable to foreign source income.

Part Five

The Individual Taxpayer

14 The Individual Tax Formula

15 Compensation and Retirement Planning

16 Investment and Personal Financial Planning

17 Tax Consequences of Personal Activities

Chapter **Fourteen**

The Individual Tax Formula

Learning Objectives

After studying this chapter, you should be able to:

1. Determine an individual's filing status.

2. List the four steps for computing individual taxable income.

3. Explain the relationship between the standard deduction and itemized deductions.

4. Compute an exemption amount.

5. Compute the regular tax on ordinary income.

6. Explain why a marriage penalty exists in the federal income tax system.

7. Describe the child credit and dependent care credit.

8. Recognize circumstances that may trigger the individual AMT.

9. Describe the individual tax payment and return filing requirements.

Parts Three and Four of *Principles of Taxation for Business and Investment Planning* are concerned with the taxation of business income. In Part Three, we learned how to measure income for federal tax purposes, and we identified the important differences between taxable income and financial statement income determined under generally accepted accounting principles (GAAP). In Part Four, we discovered that the computation of taxable income does not vary significantly across business entities, but the rate at which the income is taxed does depend on the type of entity. Income earned by a sole proprietorship or an S corporation is taxed at the individual rates. Income earned by a regular corporation is taxed at the corporate rates. Income earned by a partnership is allocated to either individual or corporate partners and taxed accordingly.

In Part Four, we observed that a corporation's business income is essentially equivalent to its taxable income. In contrast, an individual's business income is just one component of the total tax base reported on Form 1040 (U.S. Individual Income Tax Return). Unlike corporate taxpayers, people engage in many nonbusiness activities. If a person engages in a nonbusiness activity that results in an economic benefit, he or she may have to recognize the value of the benefit as income. If the activity involves an expense or loss, the person may be allowed to deduct it. Therefore, before we can compute individual taxable income and the federal tax on that income, we must turn our attention to the nonbusiness transactions in which people commonly engage.

Part Five of the text is devoted to the individual taxpayer. Chapter 14 lays the groundwork with an overview of the individual tax base and the individual tax computation. The chapter also describes the tax payment and return filing requirements for individuals. Chapter 15 concentrates on the tax implications of compensation arrangements from the perspective of both employer and employee. Chapter 16 turns to the tax consequences of investment activities, while Chapter 17 focuses on personal activities. Throughout Part Five, we will emphasize the planning opportunities and the cash flow consequences for individual taxpayers.

FILING STATUS FOR INDIVIDUALS

Tax Talk
Same-sex couples are prohibited from filing joint federal income tax returns even if legally married under state law. For federal tax purposes, marriage is restricted to a "legal union between a man and woman as husband and wife."

Every individual who is either a citizen or a permanent resident of the United States is a taxable entity who may be required to file a federal income tax return.[1] One of the first items of information that must be provided on this return is **filing status.** Filing status, which reflects an individual's marital and family situation, affects the calculation of taxable income and determines the rates at which that income is taxed.

Married Individuals and Surviving Spouses

An individual who is married on the last day of the taxable year can elect to file a **joint return** with his or her spouse.[2] A joint return reflects the combined activities of both spouses for the entire year. A husband and wife who file a joint return have **joint and several liability** for their tax bill. In other words, each spouse is responsible for paying the entire tax (not just one-half).[3] With respect to a joint return, any reference to the taxpayer is actually a reference to two people.

Married Filing Jointly	Mr. and Mrs. Lane were legally married under Hawaiian law on December 12, 1994. For federal tax purposes, their marital status was determined on December 31. The newlyweds filed a joint return for 1994 that reported their combined incomes for the entire calendar year.

Objective 1
Determine an individual's filing status.

For the taxable year in which a married person dies, the widow or widower can file a joint return with the deceased.[4] If the widow or widower maintains a home for a dependent child, he or she qualifies as a **surviving spouse** for the two taxable years following the year of death.[5] A surviving spouse can use the married filing jointly tax rates for these two years.

Surviving Spouse	Refer to the facts in the preceding example. Mrs. Lane died on September 14, 2009, and Mr. Lane has not remarried. Mr. Lane filed a 2009 joint return reflecting his deceased wife's activities from January 1 through September 14 and his activities for the entire year. The couple had two children, ages 6 and 10, who live with their father. Because Mr. Lane met the definition of surviving spouse, he was entitled to compute his tax for 2010 and 2011 using the married filing jointly rates.

---

[1] §7701(b) distinguishes between resident aliens and nonresident aliens. The former are subject to the same tax rules as U.S. citizens. Nonresident aliens are subject to federal income tax only if they earn U.S. source income.

[2] §6013(a).

[3] §6013(d)(3).

[4] §6013(a)(2).

[5] §2(a). A person does not qualify as a surviving spouse if he or she remarries within these two years.

As an alternative to joint filing, married individuals can file **separate returns** that reflect each spouse's independent activity and separate taxable income. In a few situations, individuals can derive some negligible tax benefit by filing separately, but most couples who file separate returns do so for nontax reasons.

Married Filing Separately	Mr. and Mrs. Conrad have been legally separated for six years but have not divorced because of their religious faith. They live in different cities and have no joint financial dealings or obligations. Because the Conrads lead independent lives, they choose to file separate tax returns.

Unmarried Individuals

An individual who is unmarried on the last day of the year, who is not a surviving spouse, and who maintains a home that is the principal place of abode for a child or other dependent family member qualifies as a **head of household** for filing purposes.[6]

Head of Household	Refer back to our example involving Mr. Lane, a widower with two dependent children living at home. In 2010 and 2011, Mr. Lane filed his tax return as a surviving spouse. In 2012, his filing status changed to head of household. Mr. Lane will continue to qualify as a head of household until his children grow up and move out of his home or until he remarries.

An unmarried individual who is neither a surviving spouse nor a head of household files as a **single taxpayer.** Note that the tax law does not provide any special filing status for minor or dependent children. Regardless of age, children who earn income in their own name must file as single taxpayers, even if the income is collected and controlled by their parents.[7]

OVERVIEW OF THE TAXABLE INCOME COMPUTATION

Tax Talk
Senator John McCain and his wife Cindy have always filed separate returns. Senator McCain's 2007 Form 1040 reported about $500,000 taxable income. Mrs. McCain's Form 1040 reported more than $4.1 million taxable income.

Objective 2
List the four steps for computing individual taxable income.

A pragmatic way to approach the computation of individual taxable income is to observe how the computation is presented on Form 1040. In this section of the chapter we will do just that, concentrating on the basic structure of the computation without devoting much attention to its separate elements. In subsequent chapters, we will examine the more important of these elements in detail. This overview of the taxable income computation from a compliance perspective offers a practical benefit: It will help you to read and interpret your own Form 1040. The federal tax return is, after all, a legal document that individuals must sign. By doing so, they are attesting that they have examined the return and that the information on the return is "true, correct, and complete." Therefore, every person, even if he or she uses a professional tax return preparer, should understand the flow of information on a Form 1040.

The Four-Step Procedure

The computation of taxable income on an individual return follows four procedural steps contained on pages 1 and 2 of Form 1040.

[6] §2(b).
[7] §73.

Step 1: Calculate Total Income

As the first step, an individual must list all items of income recognized in the year on page 1, Form 1040. On the basis of the material in earlier chapters, we know that this list includes taxable income from any business in which the individual engaged. If the individual operated a sole proprietorship, the net profit (as computed on Schedule C) is carried to page 1. Similarly, if the individual conducted business through a partnership or owned stock in an S corporation, a share of the passthrough entity's income is carried from Schedule E to page 1. The list of income items also includes any salary or wage payments that the individual earned as an employee and any income from the individual's investments. The listed items are added together to result in the individual's **total income.**

Mr. and Mrs. Volpe: Step 1	James and Nancy Volpe are a married couple who file a joint income tax return. In 2011, the couple recognized three items of income.	

Mr. Volpe's salary from his employer	$ 46,600
Interest income on certificates of deposit	1,400
Business income from Mrs. Volpe's sole proprietorship	56,730
Total income	$104,730

The first page of Mr. and Mrs. Volpe's Form 1040 on which these income items are listed is shown as Exhibit 14.1.

Step 2: Calculate Adjusted Gross Income

The second step is the calculation of the individual's adjusted gross income. **Adjusted gross income (AGI)** equals total income less the specific deductions listed on page 1, Form 1040.[8] One example is the deductible portion of any self-employment tax owed by the individual.[9] We will identify other so-called **above-the-line deductions** throughout the rest of the text.

While AGI represents an intermediate step in the computation of individual taxable income, it is an extremely important number in its own right. As we will soon discuss, many individual deductions and credits are limited by reference to the taxpayer's AGI. As a result, the amount of deduction or credit is a function of the AGI reported on the last line of page 1, Form 1040.

Mr. and Mrs. Volpe: Step 2	Mrs. Volpe's 2011 self-employment tax (computed on Schedule SE, Form 1040) is $6,968, and $4,008 of this tax is deductible in the computation of AGI. In June, Mr. Volpe cashed in a one-year certificate of deposit after holding it for only 10 months. Because of the early withdrawal, the bank charged a $435 penalty. The Volpes are allowed to deduct this penalty in computing their AGI. Both these above-the-line deductions are reported on page 1, Form 1040 (Exhibit 14.1). Line 37 (the last line on page 1) reports that the couple's AGI is $100,287.

Step 3: Subtract Standard Deduction or Itemized Deductions

Objective 3
Explain the relationship between the standard deduction and itemized deductions.

In the third step of the taxable income computation, AGI is reduced by the *greater of* a standard deduction or allowable itemized deductions.

---

[8] §62 provides the list of above-the-line deductions that are subtracted in the AGI calculation.

[9] §164(f). In 2011, this deduction equaled 59.6 percent of the Social Security portion and 50 percent of the Medicare portion of the SE tax. See Chapter 10 for a complete discussion of SE tax.

EXHIBIT 14.1

Form **1040**	Department of the Treasury—Internal Revenue Service (99) **U.S. Individual Income Tax Return**	2011	OMB No. 1545-0074	IRS Use Only—Do not write or staple in this space.

For the year Jan. 1–Dec. 31, 2011, or other tax year beginning _____ , 2011, ending _____ , 20___   **See separate instructions.**

Your first name and initial	Last name	Your social security number
James L.	Volpe	7 8 4 4 5 9 0 4 2
If a joint return, spouse's first name and initial	Last name	Spouse's social security number
Nancy J.	Volpe	5 1 7 3 8 0 0 8 1

Home address (number and street). If you have a P.O. box, see instructions.   Apt. no.

10 St. Martin Circle

▲ Make sure the SSN(s) above and on line 6c are correct.

City, town or post office, state, and ZIP code. If you have a foreign address, also complete spaces below (see instructions).

Exeter, CN 04012

Presidential Election Campaign
Check here if you, or your spouse if filing jointly, want $3 to go to this fund. Checking a box below will not change your tax or refund. ☑ You ☑ Spouse

Foreign country name	Foreign province/county	Foreign postal code

Filing Status

Check only one box.

1 ☐ Single
2 ☑ Married filing jointly (even if only one had income)
3 ☐ Married filing separately. Enter spouse's SSN above and full name here. ▶
4 ☐ Head of household (with qualifying person). (See instructions.) If the qualifying person is a child but not your dependent, enter this child's name here. ▶
5 ☐ Qualifying widow(er) with dependent child

Exemptions

6a ☑ **Yourself.** If someone can claim you as a dependent, **do not** check box 6a . . . . .
b ☑ **Spouse** . . . .

c **Dependents:**		(2) Dependent's social security number	(3) Dependent's relationship to you	(4) ✓ if child under age 17 qualifying for child tax credit (see instructions)
(1) First name	Last name			
Sara M.	Volpe	2 4 9 9 8 1 3 2 2	daughter	☑
Shana E.	Volpe	3 1 2 0 5 7 8 8 6	daughter	☑
				☐
				☐

If more than four dependents, see instructions and check here ▶ ☐

Boxes checked on 6a and 6b **2**
No. of children on 6c who:
• lived with you **2**
• did not live with you due to divorce or separation (see instructions) ___
Dependents on 6c not entered above ___
Add numbers on lines above ▶ **4**

d   Total number of exemptions claimed . . . .

Income

Attach Form(s) W-2 here. Also attach Forms W-2G and 1099-R if tax was withheld.

If you did not get a W-2, see instructions.

Enclose, but do not attach, any payment. Also, please use Form 1040-V.

7	Wages, salaries, tips, etc. Attach Form(s) W-2	7	46,600
8a	**Taxable** interest. Attach Schedule B if required	8a	1,400
b	Tax-exempt interest. **Do not** include on line 8a . . .	8b		
9a	Ordinary dividends. Attach Schedule B if required	9a	
b	Qualified dividends	9b		
10	Taxable refunds, credits, or offsets of state and local income taxes	10	
11	Alimony received	11	
12	Business income or (loss). Attach Schedule C or C-EZ	12	56,730
13	Capital gain or (loss). Attach Schedule D if required. If not required, check here ▶ ☐	13	
14	Other gains or (losses). Attach Form 4797	14	
15a	IRA distributions . [15a]	b Taxable amount . . .	15b	
16a	Pensions and annuities [16a]	b Taxable amount . . .	16b	
17	Rental real estate, royalties, partnerships, S corporations, trusts, etc. Attach Schedule E	17	
18	Farm income or (loss). Attach Schedule F	18	
19	Unemployment compensation	19	
20a	Social security benefits [20a]	b Taxable amount . . .	20b	
21	Other income. List type and amount	21	
22	Combine the amounts in the far right column for lines 7 through 21. This is your **total income** ▶	22	104,730

Adjusted Gross Income

23	Educator expenses	23		
24	Certain business expenses of reservists, performing artists, and fee-basis government officials. Attach Form 2106 or 2106-EZ	24		
25	Health savings account deduction. Attach Form 8889	25		
26	Moving expenses. Attach Form 3903	26		
27	Deductible part of self-employment tax. Attach Schedule SE .	27	4,008	
28	Self-employed SEP, SIMPLE, and qualified plans . . .	28		
29	Self-employed health insurance deduction	29		
30	Penalty on early withdrawal of savings	30	435	
31a	Alimony paid b Recipient's SSN ▶	31a		
32	IRA deduction	32		
33	Student loan interest deduction	33		
34	Tuition and fees. Attach Form 8917	34		
35	Domestic production activities deduction. Attach Form 8903	35		
36	Add lines 23 through 35 . . . . ▶	36		4,443
37	Subtract line 36 from line 22. This is your **adjusted gross income** . . . . . . ▶	37		100,287

For Disclosure, Privacy Act, and Paperwork Reduction Act Notice, see separate instructions.   Cat. No. 11320B   Form **1040** (2011)

Standard Deduction

The **standard deduction** is a function of filing status. The basic deductions for 2012 are:

Married filing jointly and surviving spouses	$11,900
Married filing separately	5,950
Head of household	8,700
Single	5,950

EXHIBIT 14.1
(continued)

Tax and Credits	38	Amount from line 37 (adjusted gross income)	38	100,287
	39a	Check { You were born before January 2, 1947, ☐ Blind. } Total boxes if: { Spouse was born before January 2, 1947, ☐ Blind. } checked ▶ 39a		
Standard Deduction for—	b	If your spouse itemizes on a separate return or you were a dual-status alien, check here ▶ 39b ☐		
• People who check any box on line 39a or 39b **or** who can be claimed as a dependent, see instructions.	40	**Itemized deductions** (from Schedule A) **or** your **standard deduction** (see left margin)	40	17,070
	41	Subtract line 40 from line 38	41	83,217
	42	**Exemptions.** Multiply $3,700 by the number on line 6d.	42	14,800
	43	**Taxable income.** Subtract line 42 from line 41. If line 42 is more than line 41, enter -0-	43	68,417
	44	**Tax** (see instructions). Check if any from: **a** ☐ Form(s) 8814 **b** ☐ Form 4972 **c** ☐ 962 election	44	9,413
• All others: Single or Married filing separately, $5,800	45	**Alternative minimum tax** (see instructions). Attach Form 6251	45	
	46	Add lines 44 and 45 ▶	46	9,413
Married filing jointly or Qualifying widow(er), $11,600	47	Foreign tax credit. Attach Form 1116 if required	47		
	48	Credit for child and dependent care expenses. Attach Form 2441	48	870	
Head of household, $8,500	49	Education credits from Form 8863, line 23	49		
	50	Retirement savings contributions credit. Attach Form 8880	50		
	51	Child tax credit (see instructions)	51	2,000	
	52	Residential energy credits. Attach Form 5695	52		
	53	Other credits from Form: **a** ☐ 3800 **b** ☐ 8801 **c** ☐	53		
	54	Add lines 47 through 53. These are your **total credits**	54	2,870
	55	Subtract line 54 from line 46. If line 54 is more than line 46, enter -0- ▶	55	6,543
Other Taxes	56	Self-employment tax. Attach Schedule SE	56	6,968
	57	Unreported social security and Medicare tax from Form: **a** ☐ 4137 **b** ☐ 8919	57	
	58	Additional tax on IRAs, other qualified retirement plans, etc. Attach Form 5329 if required	58	
	59a	Household employment taxes from Schedule H	59a	
	b	First-time homebuyer credit repayment. Attach Form 5405 if required	59b	
	60	Other taxes. Enter code(s) from instructions _____	60	
	61	Add lines 55 through 60. This is your **total tax** ▶	61	13,511
Payments	62	Federal income tax withheld from Forms W-2 and 1099	62	2,496	
	63	2011 estimated tax payments and amount applied from 2010 return	63	12,000	
If you have a qualifying child, attach Schedule EIC.	64a	**Earned income credit (EIC)**	64a		
	b	Nontaxable combat pay election 64b			
	65	Additional child tax credit. Attach Form 8812	65		
	66	American opportunity credit from Form 8863, line 14	66		
	67	First-time homebuyer credit from Form 5405, line 10	67		
	68	Amount paid with request for extension to file	68		
	69	Excess social security and tier 1 RRTA tax withheld	69		
	70	Credit for federal tax on fuels. Attach Form 4136	70		
	71	Credits from Form: **a** ☐ 2439 **b** ☐ 8839 **c** ☐ 8801 **d** ☐ 8885	71		
	72	Add lines 62, 63, 64a, and 65 through 71. These are your **total payments** ▶	72	14,496
Refund	73	If line 72 is more than line 61, subtract line 61 from line 72. This is the amount you **overpaid**	73	985
	74a	Amount of line 73 you want **refunded to you.** If Form 8888 is attached, check here ▶ ☐	74a	
Direct deposit? ▶ See instructions.	b	Routing number ▶ c Type: ☐ Checking ☐ Savings		
	d	Account number		
	75	Amount of line 73 you want **applied to your 2012 estimated tax** ▶ 75	985	
Amount You Owe	76	**Amount you owe.** Subtract line 72 from line 61. For details on how to pay, see instructions ▶	76	
	77	Estimated tax penalty (see instructions) 77		

Third Party Designee Do you want to allow another person to discuss this return with the IRS (see instructions)? ☐ **Yes.** Complete below. ☐ **No**

Designee's name ▶ _____ Phone no. ▶ _____ Personal identification number (PIN) ▶ ☐☐☐☐☐

Sign Here Under penalties of perjury, I declare that I have examined this return and accompanying schedules and statements, and to the best of my knowledge and belief, they are true, correct, and complete. Declaration of preparer (other than taxpayer) is based on all information of which preparer has any knowledge.

Joint return? See instructions.
Keep a copy for your records.

Your signature	Date	Your occupation	Daytime phone number
Spouse's signature. If a joint return, **both** must sign.	Date	Spouse's occupation	If the IRS sent you an Identity Protection PIN, enter it here (see inst.) ☐☐☐☐☐☐

Paid Preparer Use Only

Print/Type preparer's name	Preparer's signature		Date	Check ☐ if self-employed	PTIN
Firm's name ▶				Firm's EIN ▶	
Firm's address ▶				Phone no.	

Form **1040** (2011)

An individual who has reached age 65 by the last day of the year is entitled to an additional deduction. An individual who is legally blind is also entitled to an additional deduction. For 2012, the additional deductions are:

Married filing jointly or separately and surviving spouse	$1,150
Head of household or single	1,450

Both the basic and the additional standard deductions are indexed for inflation and may change every year.[10]

Standard Deduction	Mr. and Mrs. O'Neil file a joint return and are 79 and 75 years of age, respectively. Mr. O'Neil is legally blind. Their standard deduction for 2012 is $15,350.

Basic standard deduction	$11,900
Additional deductions for Mr. O'Neil:	
Age 65 or older	1,150
Legally blind	1,150
Additional deduction for Mrs. O'Neil:	
Age 65 or older	1,150
	$15,350

Limited Standard Deduction for Dependent

In the case of an individual who is claimed as a dependent on another person's tax return (see the discussion of dependents on page 413), the basic standard deduction on the dependent's own return may be limited. In 2012, the basic standard deduction may not exceed the *greater* of (1) $950 or (2) the dependent's earned income (wages, salary, or self-employment income) plus $300. (Both numbers in this limitation are indexed for inflation.)

Limited Standard Deduction	Jerry, age 17, and Janice, age 15, are claimed as dependents on their parents' 2012 return. In 2012, Jerry earned $3,940 wages from his summer job, and Janice earned $486 from babysitting. Jerry and Janice each own a savings account funded with a small inheritance from their grandmother. The 2012 interest income on each account was $712. Jerry's AGI is $4,652 (wages + interest income), and his standard deduction as a single taxpayer ($5,950) is limited to $4,240 ($3,940 earned income + $300). Janice's AGI is $1,198 ($486 babysitting income + $712 interest income), and her standard deduction is limited to $950.

Itemized Deductions

As a category, **itemized deductions** include any deduction allowed to an individual that cannot be subtracted in the calculation of AGI.[11] Individuals elect to itemize (i.e., subtract itemized deductions from AGI) only if their total deduction amount exceeds the standard deduction for the year. This situation is the exception rather than the rule; only about 35 percent of individual return filers elect to itemize.[12] Itemized deductions are reported on Schedule A, Form 1040.

Itemized deductions create a tax savings only if the individual elects to itemize. In a year in which the individual claims the standard deduction, any itemized deductions yield no tax benefit.

[10] §63(c) and (f).

[11] §63(d).

[12] "Individual Income Tax Returns Publication 1304 (Complete Report)," *Statistics of Income Division,* Internal Revenue Service.

Election to Itemize	Assume that Mr. and Mrs. O'Neil in the example on page 413 accumulated $14,000 of itemized deductions in 2012. Because this total is less than their $15,350 standard deduction, they use the standard deduction to compute taxable income, and their itemized deductions yield no tax benefit.
	Now assume that their itemized deductions totaled $16,000. In this case, they would elect to itemize by subtracting this amount from AGI. If their marginal tax rate is 28 percent, their itemized deductions save $4,480 in tax ($16,000 × 28 percent). However, the standard deduction would have saved $4,298 ($15,350 × 28 percent). Consequently, the incremental tax savings from the itemized deductions is only $182 ($650 excess itemized deductions × 28 percent).

This example leads to a key observation about individual tax deductions. A deduction listed as an above-the-line deduction *always* reduces taxable income. A deduction that must be itemized may have limited or even no effect on taxable income. Congress decides which deductions are above-the-line and which deductions are itemized. The classification often reflects tax policy concerns and can change from year to year. For example, individuals are allowed to deduct attorney fees and other costs of lawsuits based on unlawful discrimination by the individual's employer. Before the enactment of the American Jobs Creation Act of 2004, this deduction was an itemized deduction. The act reclassified it as an above-the-line deduction in order to improve the equity of the tax law for individuals involved in such lawsuits.

Bunching Itemized Deductions

People can often maximize the value of their itemized deductions through a tax planning technique called **bunching.** By controlling the timing of their deductible expenses, they can concentrate the deductions into one year. By doing so, they create a critical mass of itemized deductions, the total of which exceeds their standard deduction. The following example illustrates this technique.

Bunching of Itemized Deductions	Mr. Norris, a single taxpayer with a 25 percent marginal tax rate, routinely incurs $5,500 annual expenses qualifying as itemized deductions. This amount is less than his annual standard deduction. If his pattern of expenses is level from year to year, he will derive no benefit from the expenses. In contrast, if Mr. Norris can shift $2,000 of the expenses from 2012 to 2013, he can take his standard deduction in 2012 and elect to itemize in 2013.

	Level Pattern of Itemized Deductions	*Bunched Deductions*
2012:		
Itemized deductions	$5,500	$ 3,500
Standard deduction (single)	5,950	5,950
2013:		
Itemized deductions	$5,500	$ 7,500
Standard deduction (single)	5,950	(5,950)
Itemized deductions in excess of standard deduction		$ 1,550
		.25
Tax savings from bunching		$ 388

How can Mr. Norris shift deductible expenses from 2012 to 2013? As a cash basis taxpayer, he recognizes deductions in the year of payment. By *postponing* payment of an expense from December until January, he shifts the deduction to the next year. At the end of 2013, Mr. Norris may want to *accelerate* payment of deductible expenses that he normally would pay in 2014, when he will take the standard deduction under his cyclical bunching strategy.

Mr. and Mrs. Volpe: Step 3	During 2011, Mr. and Mrs. Volpe incurred the following expenses that qualify as itemized deductions.

Connecticut individual income tax	$5,140
Real estate tax on the Volpes' personal residence	1,920
Home mortgage interest	8,080
Charitable donations	1,930

These deductions are listed on Schedule A (shown as Exhibit 14.2) and totaled on line 29. Because the Volpes' $17,070 total itemized deductions exceeded their standard deduction, they elected to itemize by carrying the $17,070 total to line 40, page 2, Form 1040 (see Exhibit 14.1).

Step 4: Subtract Exemption Amount

Objective 4
Compute an exemption amount.

As the fourth and last step in the computation of taxable income, AGI is reduced by the individual's exemption amount.[13] This amount equals the annual inflation-adjusted **exemption amount** ($3,800 for 2012) multiplied by the number of people in the individual's family. The family consists of the taxpayer (two taxpayers on a joint return) plus the taxpayer's dependents. A **dependent** must be either a qualifying child or a qualifying relative of the taxpayer. In addition, a dependent cannot file a joint tax return with a spouse and must be a U.S. citizen or a resident of the United States, Mexico, or Canada.

The definition of **qualifying child** is much broader than the term suggests. The definition includes not only the taxpayer's children and their descendants (grandchildren and so on) but also the taxpayer's sisters and brothers (including stepsisters and stepbrothers) and their descendants (nieces and nephews and so on). However, for any of these relatives to be a qualifying child, the relative:

- Must have the same principal place of abode as the taxpayer for more than one-half of the year.
- Must be younger than the taxpayer and less than 19 years old or a student less than 24 years old.[14]
- Must not have provided more than one-half of his or her own financial support for the year.
- Must not have filed a joint tax return with a spouse unless such return was filed only as a refund claim.

[13] §151 and §152 contain the exemption rules and definitions.
[14] This age requirement is waived for a relative who is permanently and totally disabled.

EXHIBIT 14.2

SCHEDULE A		Itemized Deductions	OMB No. 1545-0074

SCHEDULE A
(Form 1040)

Department of the Treasury
Internal Revenue Service (99)

► **Attach to Form 1040.**   ► **See Instructions for Schedule A (Form 1040).**

Itemized Deductions

OMB No. 1545-0074

20**11**

Attachment
Sequence No. **07**

Name(s) shown on Form 1040

James L. and Nancy J. Volpe

Your social security number

784-45-9042

Medical and Dental Expenses		**Caution.** Do not include expenses reimbursed or paid by others.			
	1	Medical and dental expenses (see instructions)	1		
	2	Enter amount from Form 1040, line 38 ☐ 2			
	3	Multiply line 2 by 7.5% (.075)	3		
	4	Subtract line 3 from line 1. If line 3 is more than line 1, enter -0-		4	
Taxes You Paid	5	State and local **(check only one box):**			
		a ☑ Income taxes, **or** ⎫	5	5,140	
		b ☐ General sales taxes ⎭			
	6	Real estate taxes (see instructions)	6	1,920	
	7	Personal property taxes	7		
	8	Other taxes. List type and amount ► _____	8		
	9	Add lines 5 through 8		9	7,060
Interest You Paid	10	Home mortgage interest and points reported to you on Form 1098	10	8,080	
	11	Home mortgage interest not reported to you on Form 1098. If paid to the person from whom you bought the home, see instructions and show that person's name, identifying no., and address ► _____	11		
Note. Your mortgage interest deduction may be limited (see instructions).	12	Points not reported to you on Form 1098. See instructions for special rules	12		
	13	Mortgage insurance premiums (see instructions)	13		
	14	Investment interest. Attach Form 4952 if required. (See instructions.)	14		
	15	Add lines 10 through 14		15	8,080
Gifts to Charity	16	Gifts by cash or check. If you made any gift of $250 or more, see instructions	16	1,930	
If you made a gift and got a benefit for it, see instructions.	17	Other than by cash or check. If any gift of $250 or more, see instructions. You **must** attach Form 8283 if over $500 . . .	17		
	18	Carryover from prior year	18		
	19	Add lines 16 through 18		19	1,930
Casualty and Theft Losses	20	Casualty or theft loss(es). Attach Form 4684. (See instructions.)		20	
Job Expenses and Certain Miscellaneous Deductions	21	Unreimbursed employee expenses—job travel, union dues, job education, etc. Attach Form 2106 or 2106-EZ if required. (See instructions.) ► _____	21		
	22	Tax preparation fees	22		
	23	Other expenses—investment, safe deposit box, etc. List type and amount ► _____	23		
	24	Add lines 21 through 23	24		
	25	Enter amount from Form 1040, line 38 ☐ 25			
	26	Multiply line 25 by 2% (.02)	26		
	27	Subtract line 26 from line 24. If line 26 is more than line 24, enter -0-		27	
Other Miscellaneous Deductions	28	Other—from list in instructions. List type and amount ► _____		28	
Total Itemized Deductions	29	Add the amounts in the far right column for lines 4 through 28. Also, enter this amount on Form 1040, line 40		29	17,070
	30	If you elect to itemize deductions even though they are less than your standard deduction, check here . . . . ► ☐			

For Paperwork Reduction Act Notice, see Form 1040 instructions.   Cat. No. 17145C   Schedule A (Form 1040) 2011

Qualifying Child

Mr. and Mrs. White provide a home not only for their 15-year-old son Jake but also for their 17-year-old niece Karen, who has lived with her aunt and uncle for four years. This year, both Jake and Karen had summer jobs, but their earnings represented far less than 50 percent of their financial support for the year. Both Jake and Karen meet the definition of qualifying child. Consequently, the Whites can claim both of them as dependents on their Form 1040.

Qualifying Married Child	Mr. Wiggen provides a home for his 23-year-old son Richard and Richard's 19-year-old wife Colleen. Richard is a full-time student at a local university. Colleen earns the minimum wage at her job, so Mr. Wiggen provides about 80 percent of the couple's financial support. Richard and Colleen filed a joint income tax return this year only to receive a refund of the $962 tax withheld by Colleen's employer. Richard meets the definition of qualifying child even though he is married, and Mr. Wiggen can claim Richard as a dependent on his Form 1040.

The definition of **qualifying relative** includes specific members of the taxpayer's family or stepfamily (ancestors and descendants, siblings, aunts and uncles, nieces and nephews, and various in-laws) who do not meet the definition of qualifying child. The definition also includes any person who is not related to the taxpayer but who has the same principal place of abode and is a member of the taxpayer's household for the year. For a relative or household member to be a qualifying relative, the person:

- Must receive more than one-half of his or her financial support for the year from the taxpayer.
- Must not have gross income for the year in excess of the exemption amount.

Qualifying Relative	Ms. Blake, a single individual, has provided a home and complete financial support for Nan and Bobby Anderson since 2005. Nan and Bobby are the daughter and son of Ms. Blake's college roommate, who was killed in a plane crash. This year, Nan had a summer job and earned $4,790 gross salary. Bobby had no gross income for the year. Nan and Bobby are members of Ms. Blake's household and receive more than one-half of their support from Ms. Blake. However, because Nan's gross income exceeds the $3,800 exemption amount, she does not meet the definition of qualifying relative. Because Bobby has no gross income, he does meet the definition, and Ms. Blake can claim him as a dependent on her Form 1040.

Nonqualifying Relative	Refer to the earlier example in which Mr. Wiggen provides a home for son Richard and daughter-in-law Colleen. Colleen earned $10,965 wages that were reported on the joint return that she filed with her husband. Even though Colleen is Mr. Wiggen's relative and he provides more than one-half of her financial support, she is not a qualifying relative because her gross income exceeds the $3,800 exemption amount.

No Exemption on Dependent's Return

An individual who is claimed as a dependent on another person's tax return may be required to file his or her own return. In such case, the dependent may not claim an exemption on the return.

No Exemption Allowed	John Lenox is a 23-year-old college student who meets the definition of a qualifying child of his parents, Max and Lynn Lenox. As a result, Mr. and Mrs. Lenox claimed John as a dependent on their 2012 Form 1040. However, John earned $7,900 from a part-time job and was required to report this income on his own Form 1040. He deducted a $5,950 standard deduction but was not allowed to deduct an exemption amount. Consequently, John's 2012 taxable income was $1,950.

Mr. and Mrs. Volpe: Step 4	Mr. and Mrs. Volpe have two daughters (ages 7 and 10) who live with their parents and depend on them for financial support. Mr. and Mrs. Volpe also provide about 80 percent of the annual financial support for Annie Jarvis, Mrs. Volpe's widowed mother (age 82). Mrs. Jarvis received $4,216 taxable interest from several savings accounts in 2011. The Volpes claimed exemptions for themselves and their two children on line 6, page 1, Form 1040 (Exhibit 14.1). They could not claim Annie Jarvis as a dependent because her gross income exceeded the 2011 exemption amount. The Volpes' total exemption amount of $14,800 ($3,700 × 4) is reported on line 42, page 2, Form 1040 (Exhibit 14.1).

The Taxable Income Formula

The four-step procedure for computing individual taxable income can be summarized as follows.

> Total income
> (Above-the-line deductions)
> Adjusted gross income
> (Standard or itemized deductions)
> (Exemption amount)
> Taxable income

Tax Talk
The IRS estimates that 43 million Americans file tax returns but pay no tax because of the standard deduction and exemption amount.

The AGI reported on Form 1040 is the closest gauge of a taxpayer's disposable income. The standard deduction and exemption amount are not based on monetary expenses or economic losses and are unrelated to specific cash flows. The purpose of these two subtractions from AGI is to shelter a base amount of disposable income from tax. If a person's AGI is less than the tax-free threshold represented by the combined standard deduction and exemption amount, his taxable income is zero. Theoretically, such person must spend every dollar of AGI to buy the necessities of life and has no financial ability to pay income tax.

Mr. and Mrs. Volpe: Taxable Income	Pages 1 and 2 of Mr. and Mrs. Volpe's Form 1040 (Exhibit 14.1) reflect the following computation of taxable income.

Total income (line 22)	$104,730
Above-the-line deductions (line 36)	(4,443)
AGI (line 37)	$100,287
Itemized deductions (line 40)	(17,070)
Exemption amount (line 42)	(14,800)
Taxable income (line 43)	$ 68,417

COMPUTING INDIVIDUAL TAX

The tax on individual taxable income is computed under the rate schedule determined by the taxpayer's filing status.[15] These rate schedules are adjusted annually for inflation. Here are the 2012 rate schedules.

Individual Tax Rate Schedules

Married Filing Jointly and Surviving Spouse

If taxable income is:	The tax is:
Not over $17,400	10% of taxable income
Over $17,400 but not over $70,700	$1,740.00 + 15% of the excess over $17,400
Over $70,700 but not over $142,700	$9,735.00 + 25% of the excess over $70,700
Over $142,700 but not over $217,450	$27,735.00 + 28% of the excess over $142,700
Over $217,450 but not over $388,350	$48,665.00 + 33% of the excess over $217,450
Over $388,350	$105,062.00 + 35% of the excess over $388,350

Married Filing Separately

If taxable income is:	The tax is:
Not over $8,700	10% of taxable income
Over $8,700 but not over $35,350	$870.00 + 15% of the excess over $8,700
Over $35,350 but not over $71,350	$4,867.50 + 25% of the excess over $35,350
Over $71,350 but not over $108,725	$13,867.50 + 28% of the excess over $71,350
Over $108,725 but not over $194,175	$24,332.50 + 33% of the excess over $108,725
Over $194,175	$52,531.00 + 35% of the excess over $194,175

Heads of Household

If taxable income is:	The tax is:
Not over $12,400	10% of taxable income
Over $12,400 but not over $47,350	$1,240.00 + 15% of the excess over $12,400
Over $47,350 but not over $122,300	$6,482.50 + 25% of the excess over $47,350
Over $122,300 but not over $198,050	$25,220.00 + 28% of the excess over $122,300
Over $198,050 but not over $388,350	$46,430.00 + 33% of the excess over $198,050
Over $388,350	$109,229.00 + 35% of the excess over $388,350

Single

If taxable income is:	The tax is:
Not over $8,700	10% of taxable income
Over $8,700 but not over $35,350	$870.00 + 15% of the excess over $8,700
Over $35,350 but not over $85,650	$4,867.50 + 25% of the excess over $35,350
Over $85,650 but not over $178,650	$17,442.50 + 28% of the excess over $85,650
Over $178,650 but not over $388,350	$43,482.50 + 33% of the excess over $178,650
Over $388,350	$112,683.50 + 35% of the excess over $388,350

Objective 5
Compute the regular tax on ordinary income.

Each tax rate schedule consists of six income brackets with progressively higher rates. These brackets are listed in the left column. The right column gives the *cumulative* tax on the income in all lower brackets and the marginal rate for the bracket. To compute the tax on a given amount of income, refer to the left column to determine the income bracket and

[15] Form 1040 instructions require individuals with taxable incomes less than $100,000 to use a Tax Table to compute tax. These tables are derived from the rate schedules and eliminate the arithmetic required to use the schedules.

the *excess* taxable income over the bracket floor. Refer to the right column and multiply the *excess* by the marginal rate for the bracket. Add the result to the cumulative tax to equal the total tax on the income.

Tax on Ordinary Income

Mr. and Mrs. Ames (married filing jointly), Mr. Boyd (head of household), and Ms. Croll (single) each report $180,000 taxable income for 2012. Their tax (rounding up to whole dollars) is computed as follows.

	Mr. and Mrs. Ames (Married Filing Jointly)	Mr. Boyd (Head of Household)	Ms. Croll (Single)
Taxable income	$ 180,000	$ 180,000	$ 180,000
Bracket floor	(142,700)	(122,300)	(178,650)
Excess over floor	$ 37,300	$ 57,700	$ 1,350
Bracket rate	.28	.28	.33
	$ 10,444	$ 16,156	$ 445
Cumulative tax	27,735	25,220	43,483
Tax	$ 38,179	$ 41,376	$ 43,928

Preferential Rates

The tax computation must take into account any preferential rate applying to dividends or capital gains included in taxable income. The complicated preferential rate structure is discussed in detail in Chapter 16. This next example illustrates the basic effect of a preferential rate on the tax computation.

Tax on Ordinary Income and Capital Gain

Assume that Ms. Croll recognized a $25,000 capital gain as part of her taxable income. This gain is eligible for a 15 percent preferential tax rate. Consequently, Ms. Croll's 2012 tax is computed as follows.

Taxable income	$180,000
Capital gain	(25,000)
Ordinary income portion of taxable income	$155,000
Bracket floor	(85,650)
Excess over floor	$ 69,350
Bracket rate	.28
	$ 19,418
Cumulative tax	17,443
Tax on ordinary income	$ 36,861
Tax on capital gain ($25,000 × 15%)	3,750
Tax	$ 40,611

The 15 percent capital gains rate reduced Ms. Croll's tax from $43,928 to $40,611 for a $3,317 tax savings.

The Marriage Penalty Dilemma

Objective 6
Explain why a marriage penalty exists in the federal income tax system.

In our example in which a married couple (Mr. and Mrs. Ames) and a single individual (Ms. Croll) both had $180,000 ordinary taxable income, the couple's tax was $38,179, while the single's tax was $43,928. The rationale for this difference is straightforward: Two people can't live as well as one on the same income. Mr. and Mrs. Ames presumably have less financial ability to pay than Ms. Croll and should pay less tax.

But now suppose that Mr. and Mrs. Ames are both employed and earn identical salaries. Assume that their separate returns would each reflect $90,000 taxable income (half their combined income). If they could use the rate schedule for single taxpayers, each would owe $18,661 tax, and their combined tax burden would be only $37,322. On the basis of a comparison of this number with their $38,179 joint tax, the couple could complain that they are paying an $857 penalty for being married.[16]

These comparisons show that the federal income tax system is not marriage neutral. However, in the Jobs and Growth Tax Relief Reconciliation Act of 2003, Congress provided relief from the marriage penalty for lower-income individuals. Currently, the amount of income in the 10 percent and 15 percent brackets for married couples is exactly twice the amount of income in these brackets for single taxpayers. Furthermore, the standard deduction for married couples is exactly twice the standard deduction for single taxpayers.

Marriage Penalty Relief

In 2012, Kelli Burns earned a $26,000 salary and her fiancé, Bob Tully, earned $19,300 wages. Here is a comparison of their combined tax burden if they marry before the end of the year or if they remain single.

	Married Filing Jointly	Single (Kelli)	Single (Bob)
AGI	$ 45,300	$26,000	$19,300
Standard deduction	(11,900)	(5,950)	(5,950)
Exemption	(7,600)	(3,800)	(3,800)
Taxable income	$ 25,800	$16,250	$ 9,550
Tax	$ 3,000 =	$ 2,003 +	$ 997

The couples' tax if they marry and file a joint return would equal their combined tax if they do not marry and file as single taxpayers. Thus, the income tax is a neutral factor in their wedding plans.

Why can't Congress design an income tax system that is *completely* marriage neutral? The answer to this tax policy conundrum can be demonstrated by a simple set of facts. Assume that four people, A, B, C, and D, are taxed under a hypothetical system consisting of a 20 percent rate on income up to $30,000 and a 30 percent rate on income in excess of

---

[16] The couple can't avoid the marriage penalty by filing separately. Because of the married filing separately rate structure, the combined tax of the spouses equals their tax on a joint return.

$30,000. The following table presents the relevant information if A, B, C, and D each file their own tax return.

Taxpayer	Taxable Income	Tax
A	$30,000	$ 6,000
B	30,000	6,000
C	10,000	2,000
D	50,000	12,000

Now assume that A marries B and C marries D. If the system requires the couples to file joint returns, the result is as follows.

Taxpayer	Taxable Income	Tax
AB	$60,000	$15,000
CD	60,000	15,000

As married couples, AB and CD have equal taxable incomes and equal tax. For couple AB, this tax is $3,000 more than their combined tax as single people. Because A and B aggregated their incomes on the joint return, $30,000 of that income was boosted out of the 20 percent bracket into the 30 percent bracket. As a result, the tax increased by $3,000. For couple CD, the tax on their joint return is $1,000 more than their combined single tax. In CD's case, the aggregation of their incomes boosted only $10,000 into the higher tax bracket.

The marriage penalties on AB and CD disappear if each spouse could file as a single taxpayer. Couple AB would file two returns, each reporting $6,000 tax, for a $12,000 combined tax burden. Couple CD would also file two returns, with C's return reporting $2,000 tax, and D's return reporting $12,000 tax. Couple CD's tax burden would be $14,000, *$2,000 more than Couple AB's tax burden.* Couple CD could certainly protest that this result is unfair because it violates the standard of horizontal equity. In our society, married couples are regarded as an economic unit, and their financial ability to pay tax should be a function of their aggregate income. Therefore, couples with the same aggregate income (such as AB and CD) should pay the same tax, regardless of which spouse earned the income. As this set of facts illustrates, a progressive income tax system that allows married couples to file joint returns can be marriage neutral or horizontally equitable—but not both.

The Elusive Marginal Tax Rate

The marginal tax rate is the percentage applying to the *next* dollar of taxable income. Obviously taxpayers must know their marginal rate to compute tax costs and after-tax cash flows from any income-generating transaction. Individuals can determine their apparent marginal rate by comparing their projected taxable income for the year to the applicable rate schedule. For instance, if a single taxpayer estimates that his 2012 income will be $200,000, he can refer to the rate schedule and observe that his statutory marginal rate is 33 percent. However, this apparent rate is not necessarily the actual marginal rate.

When an individual recognizes an additional dollar of income, AGI generally increases by one dollar. This increase changes the calculation of any deduction or credit limited by

Tax Talk
Edwin S. Cohen, former Assistant Secretary for Tax Policy, noted the mathematical impossibility of a progressive tax being both marriage neutral and horizontally equitable: "No algebraic equation, no matter how sophisticated, can solve this dilemma. Both ends of a seesaw cannot be up at the same time."

reference to AGI. Later in this chapter, we will learn about several important tax credits that are reduced or even eliminated as AGI climbs above a threshold level. In subsequent chapters, we will encounter more of these AGI-sensitive items. If an additional dollar of AGI triggers a decrease in one or more deductions or credits, the tax cost of such dollar will be greater than the apparent marginal rate would suggest.

Increased AGI and Marginal Tax Rate	Ms. Grant, a single individual with an apparent 35 percent marginal rate, needs to calculate her after-tax cash flow from a transaction expected to generate $10,000 taxable cash flow. The $10,000 increase in her AGI will cause a certain itemized deduction to decrease by $700. Consequently, the $10,000 incremental income will result in $10,700 more taxable income and $3,745 more tax ($10,700 × 35 percent). Ms. Grant's actual marginal rate on the incremental income will be 37.45 percent, and her after-tax cash flow from the transaction will be $6,255 ($10,000 cash − $3,745 tax cost).

The lesson of this example is that the individual marginal tax rate can be an elusive number. The inverse relationship between AGI and certain deductions and credits can cause a hidden surtax not reflected by the apparent statutory rate. The only sure way to calculate the incremental tax from a proposed transaction is to "run the numbers" by incorporating the tax consequences of the transaction into a complete tax calculation.

Some Perspective on Marginal Rate	Currently, the top statutory rate for the U.S. individual income tax is 35 percent. This rate compares favorably with the top rates in other industrialized countries. For instance, the top rate is 40 percent in France and Japan, 45 percent in Germany, and 50 percent in the United Kingdom. From a historical perspective, the 35 percent rate seems like a bargain compared to the top federal rate in 1951 (92 percent), 1964 (77 percent), and even 1981 (50 percent).

Marginal Rate on Child's Unearned Income

Before leaving the topic of marginal tax rate, let's introduce the special rule for computing tax on the unearned income of certain children. Recall from earlier in the chapter that the law is quite restrictive with respect to individuals who file a tax return in their own right but who are claimed as a dependent on another taxpayer's return. Such individuals (typically children) are allowed only a limited standard deduction and no personal exemption. For any child under the age of 18, the tax law contains an additional restriction.[17] The child's unearned (investment) income in excess of an inflation-adjusted base amount ($1,900 in 2012) is taxed at the *parents'* marginal rate. This peculiar computation is popularly described as the **kiddie tax.**

---

[17] §1(g). The kiddie tax also applies to certain children between the ages of 18 and 24 whose annual earned income does not exceed 50 percent of their annual support. It does not apply to a child if both parents are deceased at the close of the year or if the child files a joint return with a spouse.

Kiddie Tax	Ben Lee, 17 years old, is claimed as a dependent on his parents' tax return. Ben's only item of gross income on his Form 1040 was $18,390 interest from a trust fund established by Ben's grandfather. Ben's tax is computed as follows.

Ben's unearned income	$18,390
Base amount	(1,900)
Excess unearned income	16,490
Parents' marginal tax rate	.35
Tax on excess earned income	$ 5,772
Ben's remaining unearned income	$ 1,900
Standard deduction	(950)
Personal exemption	-0-
Remaining taxable income	$ 950
Tax rate for single individual	.10
Tax on remaining income	$ 95

Ben's tax on his Form 1040 is $5,867 ($5,772 + $95).

INDIVIDUAL TAX CREDITS

Individuals can reduce their tax by any tax credits for which they are eligible. People who conduct business as a sole proprietorship or in a passthrough entity are entitled to the general business credit discussed in Chapter 11. People who pay foreign income tax are entitled to the foreign tax credit discussed in Chapter 13. In addition to these credits, individuals may qualify for many other credits, four of which are described in the following paragraphs.

Child Credit

Objective 7
Describe the child credit and dependent care credit.

Under current law, individuals can claim a $1,000 **child credit** for a dependent who is a qualifying child under age 17 at the close of the year.[18] This credit phases out for high-income taxpayers. On a joint return, the total credit is reduced by $50 for every $1,000 increment (or portion thereof) of AGI in excess of $110,000. For single individuals and heads of households, the credit phaseout begins when AGI exceeds $75,000. For married individuals filing separate returns, the phaseout begins when AGI exceeds $55,000.

Child Credit	Mr. and Mrs. Dale reported $117,890 AGI on their Form 1040. They have four qualifying children who were ages 18, 14, 12, and 10 on December 31. Mr. and Mrs. Dale's child credit is $2,600.

Adjusted gross income	$117,890
AGI threshold	(110,000)
Excess AGI	$ 7,890
Excess AGI divided by $1,000 and rounded up to nearest whole number	8
Maximum total credit ($1,000 × three children under age 17)	$ 3,000
Phaseout ($50 × 8)	(400)
Child credit	$ 2,600

[18] §24. The child credit may be refundable for low-income families.

Dependent Care Credit

Individuals with one or more dependents who are either under age 13 or physically or mentally incapable of caring for themselves may be eligible for a **dependent care credit.**[19] The credit is based on the cost of caring for these dependents. Such costs include compensation paid to caregivers who work in the home (nannies, housekeepers, and babysitters) and fees paid to child care or day care centers. The purpose of the credit is to provide tax relief to people who must incur these costs to be gainfully employed. Consequently, the annual cost on which the credit is based is limited to the taxpayer's earned income for the year. On a joint return, the limit is based on the *lesser* of the husband's or wife's earned income. The cost is further limited to $3,000 if the taxpayer has only one dependent and $6,000 if the taxpayer has two or more dependents.

The credit equals a percentage of dependent care costs (subject to the limitation described in the preceding paragraph). The percentage is determined by reference to AGI and equals 35 percent reduced by 1 point for each $2,000 (or fraction thereof) by which AGI exceeds $15,000. The percentage is reduced to a minimum of 20 percent (for all taxpayers with AGI over $43,000).

Dependent Care Credit	Mr. and Mrs. Axel spent $1,300 this year on child care for their six-year-old daughter. Their AGI is $25,400, and their dependent care credit percentage is 29 percent computed as follows.

AGI	$25,400
AGI floor	(15,000)
Excess AGI	$10,400
Reduction (excess AGI divided by $2,000)	5.2
Maximum credit percentage	35%
Reduction (rounded up to whole point)	(6)
Mr. and Mrs. Axel's percentage	29%

The Axels' dependent care credit is $377 ($1,300 cost × 29%).

Earned Income Credit

Tax Talk

According to former Treasury Secretary Henry Paulson, the earned income credit helps "people who are often on the first step of the economic ladder, gaining the experience and skills to land a better job and earn a higher income in the future."

Many individuals pay no federal income tax because of the shelter provided by the standard deduction and the exemption amount. However, low-income families are not sheltered from the employee payroll tax, which is levied on the first dollar of wages or salary earned. Congress enacted the **earned income credit** to offset the burden of the payroll tax on low-income workers and to encourage individuals to seek employment rather than to depend on welfare.

The credit is based on a percentage of the individual's earned income.[20] The percentage depends on whether the individual has no children, one child, or more than one child. For 2012, the maximum credit available to a family with three or more children is $5,891. If earned income exceeds a dollar threshold, the credit is phased out. For a married couple with three or more children, the 2012 phaseout threshold is $22,300, and the credit is reduced to zero when earned income reaches $50,270. The earned income credit differs from most other credits because it is *refundable:* Taxpayers may receive a refund of the credit that exceeds precredit income tax.

[19] §21.

[20] §32.

Refund of Earned Income Credit

Mr. and Mrs. Wong's precredit income tax liability for 2012 was $2,215, and the income tax withheld by Mr. Wong's employer was $2,000. Based on their earned income and the number of their children, the Wongs were entitled to a $3,480 earned income credit. The credit reduced their income tax liability to zero and resulted in a $3,265 refund ($1,265 credit in excess of tax + $2,000 withholding).

The IRS estimates that 23 million families, the poorest fifth of this country's workforce, qualify for the earned income credit. The IRS computes the credit for those taxpayers who request such assistance when filing their income tax returns.

Excess Social Security Tax Withholding Credit

The federal employee Social Security tax equals 6.2 percent (4.2 percent in 2011 and 2012) of an annual base amount of an employee's compensation. Employers are required to withhold this tax from their employees' paychecks and remit the withholding to the Treasury. When an employee changes jobs, the new employer must withhold Social Security tax without regard to the amount withheld by any former employer. As a result, the employee may indirectly overpay his Social Security tax for the year.

Excess Social Security Tax Withholding

Mrs. Vaughn worked for FM Inc. for the first nine months of 2012, then resigned to take a job with CN Company. Her 2012 salary from FM was $100,000 from which FM withheld $4,200 Social Security tax (4.2% × $100,000). Her 2012 salary from CN was $56,000 from which CN withheld $2,352 Social Security tax (4.2% × $56,000). Consequently, Mrs. Vaughn had $1,928 excess Social Security tax withheld in 2012.

Mrs. Vaughn's withholding:	
FM Inc.	$4,200
CN Company	2,352
	$6,552
Maximum 2012 tax:	
(4.2% × $110,100 annual base)	(4,624)
Excess tax withheld	$1,928

Mrs. Vaughn is allowed to claim this **excess Social Security tax withholding credit** against her 2012 income tax.[21] Her tax credit has no effect on the two firms that employed her during the year. Neither FM Inc. nor CN Company is entitled to any refund of the employer Social Security tax on Mrs. Vaughn's compensation.

Mr. and Mrs. Volpe: Credits

Refer back to page 2 of Mr. and Mrs. Volpe's Form 1040 (Exhibit 14.1). Line 43 reports $68,417 taxable income, and line 44 reports $9,413 tax computed on that income.

During the year, the Volpes paid $4,350 to an after-school activities program for their two young daughters. This dependent care cost was less than Mr. Volpe's $46,600 salary (lesser of either spouse's earned income) and less than the $6,000 limit for two dependents. Consequently, the Volpes were entitled to an $870 dependent care credit ($4,350 cost × 20%) reported on line 48.

The Volpes were also entitled to a $2,000 child credit reported on line 51. These two credits totaled to $2,870 on line 54 and reduced their tax to $6,543 on line 55.

---

[21] §31. The excess Social Security tax withholding credit is refundable.

ALTERNATIVE MINIMUM TAX

Individuals are subject to the alternative minimum tax (AMT) system and may owe AMT in addition to their regular income tax.[22] The individual AMT is based on alternative minimum taxable income (AMTI), which is computed under the formula introduced in Chapter 11.

> Taxable income for regular tax purposes
> + or − AMT adjustments
> + AMT tax preferences
>
> Alternative minimum taxable income

Objective 8
Recognize circumstances that may trigger the individual AMT.

Many AMT adjustment and preference items are common to both corporate and individual taxpayers. However, several items are unique to individuals. For instance, the standard deduction and exemption amount are AMT adjustments that must be added back to taxable income in the AMTI computation.[23] We will identify other individual AMT items in subsequent chapters.

Individual AMT is based on AMTI in excess of an exemption amount, which is determined by the individual's filing status. The AMT exemption is phased out for high-income taxpayers. Specifically, the exemption amount is reduced by 25 percent of AMTI in excess of a threshold. The following table presents the 2011 exemption amounts, the AMTI threshold, and the AMTI at which the exemption is reduced to zero (AMTI maximum). Congress has not yet determined the exemption amounts for 2012.

	Exemption	AMTI Threshold	AMTI Maximum
Married filing jointly and surviving spouses	$ 74,450	$150,000	$447,800
Married filing separately	37,225	75,000	223,900
Head of household or single	48,450	112,500	306,300

AMT Exemption   Ms. Epps, a head of household, has $91,000 AMTI. Because her AMTI is below the threshold, her exemption is $48,450.

Mr. and Mrs. Floyd, who file a joint return, have $513,000 AMTI. Because their AMTI is greater than the AMTI maximum, their exemption is reduced to zero.

Mr. and Mrs. Giles, who file a joint return, have $215,000 AMTI, which falls in the phase-out range. Consequently, their exemption is $58,200, computed as follows.

AMTI	$ 215,000
AMTI threshold	(150,000)
AMTI in excess of threshold	$ 65,000
	.25
Reduction in exemption	$ 16,250
Exemption for married filing jointly	$ 74,450
Reduction	(16,250)
Exemption for Mr. and Mrs. Giles	$ 58,200

[22] §55.
[23] §56(b)(1)(E).

Computing AMT

The individual AMT equals any *excess* of tentative minimum tax over the individual's precredit regular income tax. Tentative minimum tax is based on a rate structure consisting of two brackets:

- 26 percent on the first $175,000 AMTI in excess of the exemption ($87,500 for married filing separately).
- 28 percent of any additional excess AMTI.

If an individual's taxable income includes dividend income and capital gain taxed at a preferential rate (generally 15 percent), the same preferential rate applies in computing the tentative minimum tax on the dividend income/capital gain component of AMTI.[24]

Tentative Minimum Tax	Refer to the three taxpayers in the preceding example. Assuming their AMTI does not include any dividend income or capital gain, their tentative minimum tax is calculated as follows.

	Ms. Epps	Mr. and Mrs. Floyd	Mr. and Mrs. Giles
AMTI	$ 91,000	$ 513,000	$ 215,000
Exemption	(48,450)	–0–	(58,200)
AMTI in excess of exemption	$ 42,550	$ 513,000	$ 156,800
26% of first $175,000 excess AMTI	$ 11,063	$ 45,500	$ 40,768
28% of additional excess AMTI	–0–	94,640	–0–
Tentative minimum tax	$ 11,063	$ 140,140	$ 40,768

After computing AMTI and tentative minimum tax, individuals compare their tentative minimum tax to their regular income tax to determine if they owe any AMT. If they do, they must pay the AMT *in addition to* their regular tax.

AMT	The three taxpayers in the preceding example must compare their tentative minimum tax with their regular income tax. Here is the comparison.

	Ms. Epps	Mr. and Mrs. Floyd	Mr. and Mrs. Giles
Tentative minimum tax	$ 11,063	$ 140,140	$ 40,768
Regular income tax	(14,216)	(148,900)	(38,200)
AMT	–0–	–0–	$ 2,568

While Ms. Epps and Mr. and Mrs. Floyd pay only regular income tax, Mr. and Mrs. Giles pay both regular tax *and* AMT, for a total tax bill of $40,768.

Individuals who pay AMT may be allowed to carry some portion of the payment forward as a credit against future regular tax.[25] The amount of the minimum tax credit used in any future year generally is limited to the excess of regular tax over tentative minimum tax for that year.

---

[24] §55(b)(3).

[25] See §53 for the complicated calculation of the precise amount of the minimum tax credit.

Minimum Tax Credit	Assume that Mr. and Mrs. Giles can carry $1,400 of their current-year $2,568 AMT into next year as a minimum tax credit. Next year, their regular tax is $45,718, while their tentative minimum tax is only $44,888. The Giles owe no AMT (because regular tax exceeds tentative minimum tax), and they can use $830 of the credit to reduce their *regular tax* to $44,888. The couple has a $570 remaining minimum tax credit carryforward ($1,400 − $830) into future years.

The AMT Trap

The original purpose of the individual AMT was to guarantee that high-income taxpayers who dramatically reduced their regular tax by overindulging in tax preferences would still pay a fair share of income tax. But in recent years, more and more middle-income taxpayers with modest amounts of AMT adjustments or preferences are finding themselves paying AMT. This trend is attributable to the fact that the regular income tax rates are adjusted annually for inflation but the AMT rates are not. As the regular rates on a given amount of income decrease and the AMT rates remain the same, the probability that the regular tax on that income will fall below the tentative minimum tax increases. In fact, this narrowing of the spread between the regular and AMT rates can trigger an AMT even for an individual with no AMT adjustments or preferences for the year.

Blindsided by the AMT	In 2012, Mr. and Mrs. Booth's $472,000 taxable income consisted of $330,000 ordinary income and $142,000 dividends and capital gain. The couple had no AMT adjustments or preferences, so their AMTI also was $472,000, and their AMTI exemption was zero. To their complete surprise, the Booths owed a $3,093 AMT.

Tentative minimum tax:	
26% × $175,000 ordinary AMTI	$ 45,500
28% × $155,000 ($330,000 ordinary AMTI − $175,000)	43,400
15% × $142,000 dividends and capital gain	21,300
	$110,200
Regular tax:	
Regular tax (MFJ) on $330,000 ordinary income	$ 85,807
15% × $142,000 dividends and capital gain	21,300
Regular tax on taxable income	$107,107
AMT ($110,200 − $107,107)	$ 3,093

The AMT, which was intended to apply to a handful of high-income taxpayers, has evolved into a broad-based tax. To date, Congress has been unwilling to confront the AMT problem head on. Until it does so, the AMT will remain a chronic irritant and, in some cases, a costly burden for millions of individuals.

PAYMENT AND FILING REQUIREMENTS

Objective 9
Describe the individual tax payment and return filing requirements.

Individuals are required to pay their income and self-employment tax to the federal government periodically over the course of the year. The income tax on compensation is paid automatically; employers are required to withhold income tax from each wage or salary payment and remit this withholding to the Treasury on their employees' behalf.[26]

[26] §3402. The withholding is based on the information concerning marital and family status provided by the employee to the employer on Form W-4. Employees can also specify a dollar amount of income tax to be withheld during the year.

The tax on other income items, such as net profit from a sole proprietorship, distributive shares of partnership income, or investment income must be paid in four equal installments.[27] The first three of these **estimated tax payments** are due on April 15, June 15, and September 15 of the current year, while the fourth installment is due on January 15 of the following year.

Individuals who fail to make timely payments of at least 90 percent of their current tax in the form of withholding and quarterly payments may incur an underpayment penalty.[28] Because of the uncertainty inherent in estimating the tax owed for the year in progress, the law provides a **safe-harbor estimate.** Individuals with AGI of $150,000 or less in the preceding year may pay current tax equal to 100 percent of the preceding year's tax.[29] By doing so, they avoid any underpayment penalty, regardless of their actual current tax. The safe-harbor estimate for individuals with AGI *in excess* of $150,000 is 110 percent of the preceding year's tax.[30]

Safe-Harbor Estimate	Mrs. Ruiz works for a local corporation and knows that her income tax withholding for this year will be $14,000. Mr. Ruiz recently started a new business venture and doesn't know how much income it might generate. The couple knows that their AGI for the preceding year was $92,000, and they paid $25,116 income and self-employment tax. Therefore, they can make a safe-harbor estimate for this year by paying in $25,116. If they make four estimated tax payments of $2,779 each, their total payments plus Mrs. Ruiz's withholding will equal $25,116, and they are immune to penalty regardless of their actual tax for the year.

Form 1040 must be filed by the 15th day of the 4th month following the close of the taxable year; for calendar year taxpayers, this is the familiar April 15 due date.[31] If the tax paid throughout the year (withholding and estimated payments) is *less* than the tax computed on the return, the taxpayer must pay the balance due with the return.[32] If the prepayment is *more* than the tax, the return serves as a claim for refund of the overpayment.

Paying Taxes with Plastic	The IRS has arranged with private credit card companies to allow individuals to charge their federal tax. Individuals can now use American Express, Visa, Discover, or MasterCard to pay any balance of tax due for the year as well as to make their estimated payments. While the IRS does not impose a fee for credit card payments, the credit card companies may impose convenience fees based on the tax amounts charged.

Undeliverable Refunds	The IRS is searching for 99,123 individuals whose 2010 refund checks were returned to the IRS by the U.S. Post Office because of an incorrect mailing address. These checks represent a total of about $153 million owed to people who should have left a forwarding address! Individuals expecting to receive a tax refund can visit the "Where's My Refund?" feature on the IRS website to determine the status of their refund.

[27] §6654(c).
[28] §6654(a) and (d)(1)(B)(i).
[29] §6654(d)(1)(B)(ii).
[30] §6654(d)(1)(C).
[31] §6072(a).
[32] §6151(a).

Individuals who are not ready to file a completed return by the due date may request an automatic six-month extension of the filing deadline (October 15 for a calendar year taxpayer).[33] This extension applies only to the return filing requirement; individuals who estimate that they still owe tax should pay the estimated balance due with the extension request to avoid interest and penalties.

Automatic Extension	Mr. Sanchez simply couldn't find the time to complete his 2011 Form 1040 before April 15, 2012. He estimated that his 2011 tax liability would be no more than $14,500. Because his 2011 withholding was $13,850, Mr. Sanchez concluded that he owed $650 additional tax. So Mr. Sanchez filed Form 4686 (Application of Time to File U.S. Individual Income Tax Return) on April 12 and attached his check for $650 with the application. Consequently, the filing date for his 2011 Form 1040 was extended until October 15, 2012. Mr. Sanchez filed his return on July 29. The return showed an actual tax liability of $14,210, so Mr. Sanchez was due a $290 refund ($14,500 tax paid − $14,210 tax owed) from the government.

Let's conclude the discussion of payment and filing requirements by returning one last time to our comprehensive Form 1040 example.

Mr. and Mrs. Volpe: Tax Refund	Refer back to page 2 of Mr. and Mrs. Volpe's Form 1040 (Exhibit 14.1). Mrs. Volpe's $6,968 self-employment tax is reported on line 56. The couple's $13,511 total tax (income and self-employment) is reported on line 61. During the year, Mr. Volpe's employer withheld $2,496 income tax (line 62) from Mr. Volpe's salary, and the couple made $12,000 estimated tax payments (line 63). These two payments total $14,496 on line 72. Because the Volpes overpaid their tax by $985, the Treasury owed the Volpes a refund (line 73). The entry on line 75 shows that the couple applied the $985 refund to their 2012 estimated tax.

Conclusion

Chapter 14 provides the "big picture" with respect to individual taxpayers. In this chapter, we developed the formula for the computation of taxable income and discussed the significance of AGI in this formula. We learned how to compute the regular tax on individual income, identified the most common individual tax credits, and considered the threat of the alternative minimum tax. The chapter closed with a synopsis of the payment and filing requirements for individual taxpayers.

In the next three chapters, we will explore the incredible variety of transactions that affect the computation of individual taxable income. Our discussions of the tax consequences of many specific transactions will reinforce your understanding of the individual tax formula and will lead to new tax planning ideas. Hopefully, the material in these chapters will also give you a real appreciation of the complexities and nuances that make the study of individual taxation so challenging and yet so fascinating.

---

[33] Reg. §1.6081-4T.

Key Terms

above-the-line deduction *410*	estimated tax payments *430*	joint return *408*
		kiddie tax *423*
adjusted gross income (AGI) *410*	excess Social Security tax withholding credit *426*	qualifying child *415*
		qualifying relative *417*
bunching *414*	exemption amount *415*	safe-harbor estimate *430*
child credit *424*	filing status *408*	separate returns *409*
dependent *415*	head of household *409*	single taxpayer *409*
dependent care credit *425*	itemized deduction *413*	standard deduction *411*
	joint and several liability *408*	surviving spouse *408*
earned income credit *425*		total income *410*

Questions and Problems for Discussion

1. Discuss the extent to which adjusted gross income (AGI) is actually a net income number.

2. Explain why AGI is considered a better measure of individual disposable income than taxable income.

3. Discuss possible tax policy reasons why individuals who are age 65 or older receive an additional standard deduction.

4. Individuals who are legally blind receive an additional standard deduction, while individuals with other disabilities, such as deafness or paralysis, are not entitled to an additional deduction. Is there a tax policy justification for the different treatment?

5. Identify the reasons why individual taxpayers benefit more from above-the-line deductions than from itemized deductions.

6. While checking the computations on his Form 1040, Mr. G realized he had misclassified a $10,800 expense as a business deduction on Schedule C. The expense should have been an itemized deduction on Schedule A. Mr. G did not correct the error because he assumed the correction would not affect taxable income. Is this assumption correct?

7. Individuals who plan to bunch itemized deductions into one year can either postpone the payment of expenses from an earlier year or accelerate the payment of expenses from a later year. Which technique is preferable from a cash flow standpoint?

8. Describe the restrictions on tax benefits available to an individual taxpayer who is claimed as a dependent on another taxpayer's Form 1040.

9. Under the current rate structure, a single person could pay more tax than a married couple on the same income. What economic circumstances might a single person cite to argue that his ability to pay tax is not necessarily greater than a married couple's ability to pay tax on the same income?

10. Single individuals S and Z were married this year and filed their first joint return. To what extent did this change in filing status affect the following?

    a. S and Z's aggregate standard deduction.

    b. S and Z's aggregate exemption amount.

    c. S and Z's aggregate child credit.

    d. S and Z's aggregate AMT exemption.

11. Explain why an individual's combined standard deduction and exemption amount can be considered a bracket of income taxed at a zero rate.

12. Why is the formula for computing individual taxable income so much more complicated than the formula for computing corporate taxable income?

13. The tax law provides for both refundable and nonrefundable credits. What is the difference between the two types of credit?

14. Congress enacted the earned income credit to relieve the burden of the payroll tax on low-income workers. Why did Congress not accomplish this goal by providing a payroll tax exemption for a base amount of annual compensation paid by an employer to an employee?

15. When he accepted his job, Mr. MG instructed his employer to withhold substantially more federal income tax from his monthly paycheck than was indicated by his marital and family situation. As a result, he routinely overpays his tax and receives a refund each spring, which he invests in a mutual fund. Mr. MG views this strategy as an efficient means of enforced savings. Do you agree?

16. Ms. JR has been very ill since the beginning of the year and unable to attend to any financial matters. Her CPA advised that she request an automatic extension of time to file her prior year Form 1040. Ms. JR likes this idea because she believes the balance of tax due with the return will be at least $20,000, and she wants to avoid paying this tax for as long as possible. By requesting the extension, how long can Ms. JR delay paying the $20,000 to the Treasury?

Application Problems

For the following problems, assume the taxable year is 2012.

1. Determine Ms. A's filing status in each of the following independent cases.
   a. Ms. A and Mr. Z have been living together since 2010. They were married on December 13, 2012.
   b. Ms. A married Mr. P in 2005. They were divorced on November 8, 2012.
   c. Ms. A married Mr. P in 2005. They separated in 2011 and have not lived together since, but have not divorced.
   d. Ms. A divorced Mr. P in 2012. She maintains a home for herself and her dependent grandmother.

2. Determine Mr. J's filing status in each of the following independent cases.
   a. Mr. J and Mrs. J were divorced on November 18. Mr. J has not remarried and has no dependent children.
   b. Mr. J and the first Mrs. J were divorced on April 2. Mr. J remarried the second Mrs. J on December 15. He has no dependent children.
   c. Mrs. J died on July 23. Mr. J has not remarried and has no dependent children.
   d. Mrs. J died on October 1, 2010. Mr. J has not remarried and maintains a home for one dependent child.
   e. Mrs. J died on May 30, 2011. Mr. J has not remarried and has no dependent children.
   f. Mr. J and Mrs. J were divorced on May 30, 2009. Mr. J has not remarried and maintains a home for his two dependent children.

3. Mr. and Mrs. K file a joint income tax return. Compute their standard deduction assuming that:
   a. Mr. K is age 68, and Mrs. K is age 60.
   b. Mr. K is age 70, and Mrs. K is age 68.
   c. Mr. K is age 70, and Mrs. K is age 68. Mrs. K is legally blind.

4. Ms. W is an unmarried individual. Determine if each of the following unmarried individuals is either a qualifying child or a qualifying relative for whom Ms. W can claim an exemption.

   a. Daughter Dee, age 20, who is a student at State University but lists Ms. W's home as her permanent residence. Ms. W provides 80 percent of Dee's financial support. Dee earned $6,320 from her summer internship with a bank.

   b. Sister Lulu, who is 39 years old and mentally handicapped. Lulu lives in a privately operated group home, and Ms. W provides 100 percent of her financial support. Lulu has no gross income.

   c. Son Bryan, age 13, who lives in Ms. W's home but receives 65 percent of his financial support from his father.

   d. Niece Betsy, age 25, who lives in Ms. W's home. Ms. W provides 60 percent of Betsy's financial support. Betsy is a part-time student and holds a part-time job at which she earned $10,450 this year.

5. Mr. and Mrs. O file a joint income tax return. Determine if each of the following unmarried individuals is either a qualifying child or a qualifying relative for whom the couple can claim an exemption.

   a. Son Jack, age 20, who lives in his parents' home and works full-time as an auto mechanic. Jack is self-supporting except for the fact that he does not pay rent to his parents.

   b. Daughter Brenda, age 22, who is a full-time college student. Brenda lives in a dormitory during the school year, but her parents' home is her permanent residence, and her parents provide 100 percent of her financial support.

   c. Nephew Eddie, age 16, who has lived in Mr. and Mrs. O's home since 2008. Eddie is a high school student who earned $6,690 this summer working for a plumber. Since his aunt and uncle provide 100 percent of his financial support, Eddie is saving his earnings for college.

   d. Mr. O's mother, Mildred, age 64, who lives in a retirement community. Mr. and Mrs. O provide about 65 percent of her financial support. Mildred earned $4,650 this year as a part-time librarian.

   e. Mrs. O's father, Richard, age 76, who has lived in Mr. and Mrs. O's home since 2007. Mr. and Mrs. O provide about 30 percent of his financial support. The rest of his support comes from Social Security.

6. Ms. G earned a $91,250 salary, and Mr. H earned a $171,000 salary. Neither individual had any other income and neither can itemize deductions.

   a. Compute Ms. G and Mr. H's combined tax if they file as single individuals.

   b. Compute Ms. G and Mr. H's tax if they are married and file a joint return.

7. Mr. O earned an $89,000 salary, and Mrs. O earned a $40,330 salary. The couple had no other income and cannot itemize deductions.

   a. Compute their combined tax if they file separate returns.

   b. Compute their tax if they file a joint return.

8. Mr. and Mrs. D had the following income items.

Mr. D's salary	$52,500
Mrs. D's Schedule C net profit	41,800
Interest income	1,300

Mrs. D's self-employment tax was $5,134, and her above-the-line deduction for this tax was $2,953. The couple had $8,070 itemized deductions and no children or other dependents. Compute their income tax on a joint return.

9. Mr. and Mrs. S have the following income items.

Mr. S's Schedule C net profit	$91,320
Mrs. S's Schedule C net loss	(7,480)
Mrs. S's taxable pension	12,300

Mr. S's self-employment tax was $11,217, and his above-the-line deduction for this tax was $6,451. The couple had $13,050 itemized deductions. They provide 100 percent of the financial support of Mr. S's 82-year-old mother, who resides in their home. Compute the couple's income tax on a joint return.

10. Ms. T. an unmarried individual, has the following income items.

Schedule C net profit	$31,900
NOL carryforward deduction	(9,190)
Interest income	725

Ms. T's self-employment tax was $3,918, and her above-the-line deduction for this tax was $2,253. She had $6,270 itemized deduction and one dependent child (age 9) who lives in her home. Compute Ms. T's income tax.

11. Mr. and Mrs. K had the following income items.

Mr. K's salary	$145,000
Mrs. K's salary	110,000
Ordinary partnership income	51,750

The couple had $28,200 itemized deductions and two dependent children over age 17. Compute Mr. and Mrs. K's income tax on a joint return.

12. Mr. C, an unmarried individual, had the following income items.

Interest income	$ 14,200
Ordinary loss from an S corporation	(8,400)
Ordinary income from an LLC	179,000

He had $17,300 itemized deductions and no dependents. Compute Mr. C's income tax.

13. Mr. and Mrs. L had the following income items.

Dividend eligible for 0% preferential rate	$ 3,400
Capital gain eligible for 0% preferential rate	2,900
Mrs. L's salary	24,325

Mr. L is age 66, and Mrs. L is age 68. Their itemized deductions totaled $6,390, and they have no dependents. Compute their income tax on a joint return.

14. Mr. RG, an unmarried individual, had the following income items.

Salary	$412,100
Interest income	19,700
Dividend eligible for 15% rate	31,000

He had $34,000 itemized deductions and four dependent children (ages 5 through 15) plus two dependent parents who live in his home. Compute Mr. RG's income tax.

15. Ms. E, a single individual, had $115,000 taxable income. Compute her income tax assuming that:

    a. Taxable income includes no capital gain.

    b. Taxable income includes $22,000 capital gain eligible for the 15 percent preferential rate.

16. Ms. B, an unmarried individual, has $186,300 taxable income. Compute her income tax in each of the following cases.

    a. Ms. B is a single taxpayer.

    b. Ms. B is a head of household.

    c. Ms. B is a surviving spouse.

17. Refer to your computations for Ms. B in the previous problem. For each case, identify Ms. B's statutory marginal rate and compute her average tax rate.

18. Mr. G, a single taxpayer, has $15,700 AGI. Compute his taxable income in each of the following cases.

    a. Mr. G's AGI consists entirely of interest income. He is 19 years old and claimed as a dependent on his parents' tax return.

    b. Mr. G's AGI consists entirely of wage income. He is 19 years old and claimed as a dependent on his parents' tax return.

    c. Mr. G's AGI consists entirely of interest income. He is 70 years old.

19. Danny Liu is 20 years old and claimed as a dependent on his parents' tax return. Compute Danny's taxable income in each of the following cases.

    a. Danny's only income item was $2,712 interest earned on a certificate of deposit.

    b. Danny had two income items: $2,712 interest earned on a certificate of deposit and $3,276 wages from a part-time job.

    c. How would your answers change if Danny is not claimed as a dependent on his parents' return?

20. Mr. and Mrs. PJ celebrated the birth of their third child on November 18. Compute the effect of this event on their tax liability, assuming that:

    a. Their AGI was $99,000, and their taxable income before considering the new dependent was $84,200.

    b. Their AGI was $260,000, and their taxable income before considering the new dependent was $228,800.

21. Mr. M's salary was $208,000, and Mrs. M's salary was $114,000. They had no other income items, no deductions, and no dependents.

    a. Compute their tax on a joint return.

    b. Compute their combined tax if they file separate returns.

    c. Compute their marriage penalty (excess of tax on a joint return over combined tax on two returns filed as single taxpayers).

22. Ms. NM, a single taxpayer, projects that she will incur $6,000 of expenses qualifying as itemized deductions in both 2012 and 2013. Assuming that her standard deduction is $5,950 in both years, compute the effect on taxable income for each year if she can shift $2,500 of expenses from 2012 to 2013.

23. Mrs. A is an unmarried taxpayer with one dependent child living in her home. Her AGI is $40,000, and she does not itemize deductions. The 18-year-old child earned $6,980 from a part-time job and incurred no deductible expenses.
    a. Compute Mrs. A's income tax.
    b. Compute her child's income tax.

24. Callie is the 11-year-old daughter and dependent of Mr. and Mrs. Santo. This year, Callie filed a Form 1040 on which the only item of gross income was $10,557 interest from an investment bond portfolio that Callie inherited from a great aunt. Compute Callie's income tax if her parents' marginal tax rate is 33 percent.

25. Ms. GW, an unmarried taxpayer, had the following income items.

Salary	$33,400
Net income from a rental house	3,200

    Ms. GW has a four-year-old son, who attends a day care center while she is at work. Ms. GW paid $4,380 to this center and has no itemized deductions. Compute her income tax.

26. Mr. and Mrs. C have three dependent children, ages 3, 6, and 9. Compute their child credit if AGI on their joint return is:
    a. $88,300.
    b. $131,600.
    c. $167,000

27. Mr. and Mrs. OP have two dependent children. They paid $7,200 wages to a housekeeper to care for the children and $549 employer payroll tax on her wages. Mr. and Mrs. OP file a joint return. In each of the following cases, compute their dependent care credit.
    a. One child is age 10, and the other is age 15. Mr. OP's earned income is $75,000, and Mrs. OP has no earned income. Their AGI is $81,300.
    b. One child is age 2, and the other is age 6. Mr. OP's earned income is $45,000, and Mrs. OP's earned income is $28,000. Their AGI is $81,300.

28. Mr. and Mrs. Coulter have four dependent children, ages 1, 4, 7, and 11. Mr. Coulter's salary was $21,400, Mrs. Coulter's wages totaled $16,200, and the couple had no other income or above-the-line deductions this year. The Coulters paid $3,600 for day care and after-school child care.
    a. Compute the Coulters' child credit.
    b. Compute the Coulters' dependent care credit.
    c. Recompute the Coulters' child and dependent care credits if Mr. Coulter's salary was $100,000, Mrs. Coulter's wages totaled $32,000, and the couple earned $5,700 taxable interest income.

29. On March 31, Mr. R quit his job with MT Inc. and began a new job with PK Company. His salary from MT was $82,600, and his salary from PK was $93,000. Compute his excess Social Security tax withholding credit.

30. Mr. and Mrs. K's AGI (earned income) was $14,610. Their federal income tax withholding was $850. They had no itemized deductions and two dependent children, ages 18 and 19. If Mr. and Mrs. K are entitled to a $4,716 earned income credit, compute their income tax refund.

31. In each of the following cases, compute AMT (if any). For all cases, assume that taxable income does not include any dividend income or capital gain, and use the 2011 exemption amounts.

    a. Mr. and Mrs. BH's taxable income on their joint return was $200,000, and their AMTI before exemption was $203,000.

    b. Mr. CK's taxable income on his single return was $77,300, and his AMTI before exemption was $98,000.

    c. Ms. W's taxable income on her head of household return was $181,000, and her AMTI before exemption was $229,500.

32. Jaclyn Biggs, who files as a head of household, never paid an AMT before 2012. In 2012, her $197,900 taxable income included $178,000 ordinary income and a $19,900 capital gain taxed at 15 percent. Her 2012 AMTI in excess of her exemption amount was $218,175.

    a. Compute Jaclyn's total income tax for 2012.

    b. Assume that Jaclyn has a $5,200 minimum tax credit carryforward from 2012. Her 2013 taxable income is $178,100, all of which is ordinary income. Her 2013 AMTI in excess of her exemption amount is $146,900. Compute Jaclyn's total tax for 2013. (Use the 2012 tax rates.)

33. In January, Ms. NW projects that her employer will withhold $25,000 from her 2013 salary. However, she has income from several other sources and must make quarterly estimated tax payments. Compute the quarterly payments that result in a 2013 safe-harbor estimate assuming that:

    a. Her 2012 AGI was $176,000, and her tax was $47,200.

    b. Her 2012 AGI was $139,000, and her tax was $36,800.

Issue Recognition Problems

Identify the tax issue or issues suggested by the following situations and state each issue in the form of a question.

1. Mr. LR died on April 16. Mr. and Mrs. LR had been married for 11 years and had always filed a joint return. Mrs. LR remarried on December 21.

2. Mr. and Mrs. JC were married in 1995. This year they traveled to Reno, Nevada, immediately after Christmas and obtained a divorce on December 29. They spent two weeks vacationing in California, returned to their home in Texas on January 13, and remarried the next day.

3. Until March of this year, Mr. GS took care of his invalid mother in his own home and provided 100 percent of her financial support. In March, she became eligible for Medicaid, and Mr. GS moved her into a state-provided room in a nursing home.

4. Mr. T is a 20-year-old college student. This year he lived on campus for nine months and in his parents' home during the summer. His parents paid for all Mr. T's living expenses, but a scholarship paid for his $22,000 college tuition.

5. Mr. and Mrs. TB have an 11-year old child. The couple is divorced, and Mrs. TB has sole custody of the child. However, Mr. TB pays his former wife $1,200 child support each month.

6. Mr. G, age 90, lives in a nursing home. He has no gross income and is financially dependent on his four adult children, each of whom pays 25 percent of the cost of the home.

7. Mr. and Mrs. WQ both have full-time jobs. They employ Mrs. WQ's 18-year-old sister as an after-school babysitter for their 10-year-old son.

8. Mr. TJ, a self-employed attorney, has sole custody of his nine-year-old daughter. This year she spent eight weeks during the summer at a recreational camp. The total cost was $3,800.

9. During the first eight months of the year, Ms. V was self-employed and earned $63,200 net income. In September, she accepted a job with MW Company and earned $51,000 salary through the end of the year.

10. Mr. and Mrs. P own a sole proprietorship that generates approximately $60,000 annual net profit. This business is the couple's only source of income. In April, June, and September, they paid their estimated tax payments. In December, they won $250,000 in a state lottery.

11. In November, Mr. K discovered that his combined income tax withholding and estimated tax payments would be less than his prior year tax and, therefore, would not be a safe-harbor estimate. He immediately requested that his employer withhold enough tax from his December paycheck to result in a safe-harbor estimate.

12. Mr. P's AGI includes an $8,700 dividend paid by a German corporation and $11,600 interest paid by a Canadian bank. He paid $3,000 foreign income tax this year.

13. Mr. and Mrs. CD engage a CPA to prepare their Form 1040. For the last two years, their itemized deductions totaled $11,014 and $12,300. The CPA estimates that $750 of his fee relates to the preparation of the Schedule A on which the itemized deductions are detailed.

Research Problems

1. Sam Maceo, a single individual, is a third-grade teacher at Lewis Elementary School. This year, Sam spent $440 of his own money to buy Halloween classroom decorations, various art supplies, and reference books for his students because the school district had no funds for such items. Sam's unreimbursed expenditure qualifies as a deductible business expense under Section 162. Before consideration of the expenditure, Sam's AGI was $40,200, and he had only $1,300 of itemized deductions. Compute the after-tax cost of Sam's classroom expenditures.

2. Bert Baker and Ernestine Moffet were never formally married but have lived together as husband and wife for the last 14 years. Bert and Ernestine reside in Washington, D.C., a jurisdiction that recognizes common law marriages as valid. Consequently, they filed both a joint district income tax return and a joint federal income tax return for the last eight years. Bert and Ernestine are planning to move their household to Frederick, Maryland, and become permanent residents of that state. Maryland does not recognize common law marriages. Will Bert and Ernestine's change in residence allow them to avoid the marriage penalty by filing as single individuals?

3. Tim Loker is the five-year-old godson of Mr. and Mrs. Bryant. Tim's parents died in an accident on December 18 of last year. Tim was seriously injured in the accident and remained hospitalized until August 12 of this year. After his discharge from the hospital, Tim moved into the Bryants' home. The Bryants have provided 100 percent of Tim's financial support since the accident and intend to raise him as their own child. Can the Bryants claim Tim as a dependent on this year's tax return?

4. Bill Young, a single taxpayer, reported the following information on his 2012 Form 1040.

Salary from part-time job	$ 16,600
Interest on savings account	400
Net loss from sole proprietorship	(22,100)
Alimony received	3,600
AGI	$ (1,500)
Standard deduction	(5,950)
Exemption	(3,800)
Taxable income	$ (11,250)

Does Bill have a net operating loss (NOL) that he can carry back or forward as a deduction in another taxable year?

Tax Planning Cases

1. Mr. and Mrs. WG's AGI averages $425,000, and they are in the 35 percent tax bracket. They support their 22-year-old son who is a full-time college student. Mr. and Mrs. WG are considering giving him a bond portfolio that generates $20,000 annual interest income. He could support himself with this income stream (he would be financially independent) and would file his own tax return. Compute the annual tax savings to the family resulting from this plan.

2. Assume that the tax law allows individuals to claim an itemized deduction for the cost of music lessons for the taxpayer or any member of his family. Instead of this deduction, individuals may claim the first $1,000 of the cost as a nonrefundable tax credit (no carryforward or carryback of any excess credit). In each of the following situations, advise the taxpayer as to whether she should take the deduction or credit. In each situation the taxpayer is single.

   a. Ms. M has $95,000 AGI. Before consideration of the $5,000 cost of her music lessons, she has no itemized deductions.

   b. Ms. N has $27,000 AGI. Before consideration of the $5,000 cost of her music lessons, she has $6,075 itemized deductions.

   c. Ms. O has $95,000 AGI. Before consideration of the $5,000 cost of her music lessons, she has $7,200 itemized deductions.

3. In November 2012, Mr. and Mrs. Fenton have the opportunity to sell a 192-acre tract of investment land. Their gain on sale would be $360,000, which would qualify as capital gain eligible for the 15 percent preferential rate. Before consideration of this gain, the Fentons' 2012 taxable income is $146,100, all of which is taxable at the regular rates, and their alternative minimum taxable income (AMTI) reduced by a $75,000 exemption is $83,000. If the Fentons close the sale before year-end, the inclusion of the $360,000 gain in their AMTI would eliminate their entire exemption, resulting in $518,000 taxable AMTI ($83,000 + $75,000 + $360,000). Based on these facts, compute the Fentons' marginal tax rate on the $360,000 prospective capital gain.

Chapter Fifteen

Compensation and Retirement Planning

Learning Objectives

After studying this chapter, you should be able to:

1. Distinguish between employees and independent contractors.

2. List the factors determining reasonable compensation for a shareholder/employee.

3. Identify the most common nontaxable employee fringe benefits.

4. Describe the tax consequences of stock options.

5. Compare the after-tax wealth accumulated in a qualified and a nonqualified retirement plan.

6. Distinguish between defined-benefit and defined-contribution plans.

7. Explain why employers use nonqualified deferred-compensation plans.

8. Describe the tax benefit of a Keogh plan to a self-employed individual.

9. Describe the tax benefits of IRAs and Roth IRAs.

The first item of income listed on page 1, Form 1040, and the most important (if not the only) item of income recognized by millions of individuals is the compensation they earn as employees.[1] Such compensation can consist of an hourly wage, an annual salary, sales commissions, tips, fees, fringe benefits, bonuses, severance pay, or any other economic benefit received for services rendered in the course of employment.[2] In the first part of Chapter 15, we will concentrate on this broad category of income by describing some popular compensation techniques and analyzing the tax and cash flow implications of each. In the second part of the chapter, we will consider the arrangements through which people convert current compensation into retirement income. Through long-range tax planning, individuals can maximize the cash flow available for consumption and enjoyment during their postemployment years.

---

[1] According to IRS data, wages and salaries constitute about 70 percent of the total income reported by individual taxpayers.

[2] Reg. §1.61-2.

THE COMPENSATION TRANSACTION

Tax Talk
The difference in transactional markets may help explain the fact that between 1970 and 2005, the median salary for top corporate executives increased by 430 percent, while the average wage for all workers increased by only 26 percent.

The payment of compensation is a transaction with tax consequences to two parties: the employer making the payment and the employee receiving the payment. The nature and amount of the compensation are determined by contractual agreement between these parties. The employer's objective in negotiating the contract is to minimize the after-tax cost of the compensation paid; the employee's objective is to maximize the after-tax value of the compensation received. High-ranking employees can usually negotiate with their employers on a personal basis. Because they are transacting in a private market, employer and employee can work together to achieve their objectives. Specifically, they can compare different compensation arrangements and evaluate the tax consequences to both parties. By doing so, employer and employee can design a package offering the greatest overall tax savings divided between them on a mutually satisfactory basis. In contrast, rank-and-file employees typically transact with their employers in an impersonal public market. These employees can only accept or reject the compensation arrangement offered by the employer. In such case, both employee and employer must pursue their tax planning objectives independently.

EMPLOYEE OR INDEPENDENT CONTRACTOR?

Objective 1
Distinguish between employees and independent contractors.

The employer/employee relationship is characterized by the employer's right to direct and control how, when, and where the employee's duties are performed.[3] The relationship is continual because an **employee** works according to a regular schedule in return for periodic payments from the employer. The relationship is also exclusive because an employee provides services for one employer rather than the general public.

As an alternative to hiring an employee, a firm can engage an independent contractor to do the job. An **independent contractor** is a self-employed individual who performs services for monetary consideration and who controls the way the services are performed. The independent contractor's clients don't oversee his work but can only accept or reject the final product. The relationship between client and independent contractor is impermanent, and the contractor can have any number of clients at the same time.

Tax Consequences of Worker Classification

The distinction between employee and independent contractor is critical for tax purposes. As you learned in Chapter 10, employers must pay federal and state payroll taxes on the compensation paid to their employees. In addition, employers are required to withhold both employee payroll tax and federal, state, and local income tax from their employees' wages and salaries. At the end of the calendar year, employers must issue a Form W-2 (Wage and Tax Statement) to each employee.[4] This form provides detailed information about the various taxes withheld by the employer on the employee's behalf.

Form W-2	Robin Simms is employed by Crockett Products. During 2011, Robin earned a $117,500 salary. Her monthly *net* paycheck was $6,791, which equaled her $9,792 *gross* salary less federal income tax, federal Social Security and Medicare tax, and state income tax withheld by Crockett Products. Robin's Form W-2 is shown as Exhibit 15.1.

[3] Reg. §31.3401(c)-1(b).

[4] §6051(a). Employers must issue Form W-2s by January 31. If an employee who terminates employment during the year submits a written request for a Form W-2, the employer must issue the form within 30 days of receipt of the request.

EXHIBIT 15.1

a Employee's social security number 496-45-3150	OMB No. 1545-0008	Safe, accurate, FAST! Use	IRS e-file	Visit the IRS website at www.irs.gov/efile

b Employer identification number (EIN) 87-4009325	1 Wages, tips, other compensation 117,500	2 Federal income tax withheld 22,655

c Employer's name, address, and ZIP code	3 Social security wages 106,800	4 Social security tax withheld 4,486

Crockett Products

P.O. Box 92252

Wilmington, DE 12899

| 5 Medicare wages and tips 117,500 | 6 Medicare tax withheld 1,704 |

| 7 Social security tips | 8 Allocated tips |

| d Control number | 9 | 10 Dependent care benefits |

| e Employee's first name and initial   Last name   Suff. | 11 Nonqualified plans | 12a See instructions for box 12 |
| Robin L.   Simms | | |

| 13 Statutory employee / Retirement plan / Third-party sick pay | 12b |

108 Brunswick Court

Wilmington, DE 12890

| 14 Other | 12c |
| | 12d |

| f Employee's address and ZIP code |

| 15 State DE | Employer's state ID number 400648 | 16 State wages, tips, etc. 117,500 | 17 State income tax 7,163 | 18 Local wages, tips, etc. | 19 Local income tax | 20 Locality name |

Form **W-2** Wage and Tax Statement   **2011**   Department of the Treasury—Internal Revenue Service

Copy B—To Be Filed With Employee's FEDERAL Tax Return.
This information is being furnished to the Internal Revenue Service.

When clients engage independent contractors, the fees paid are not subject to FICA payroll taxes, and clients are not required to withhold income tax. At the end of the year, clients must issue a Form 1099-MISC (Miscellaneous Income) to each independent contractor stating the annual compensation paid. Independent contractors who are sole proprietors (rather than in partnership with other individuals) report this compensation as business income on Schedule C, Form 1040. Independent contractors pay self-employment tax on the net profit from their business and make quarterly estimated payments of both self-employment and federal income tax.

Form 1099-MISC	Sam Lincoln is an independent contractor who performs occasional professional services for Crockett Products. During 2011, Sam earned total fees of $34,700 from Crockett. His Form 1099-MISC on which these fees are reported is shown as Exhibit 15.2.

Worker Classification Controversy

The classification of a worker as either employee or independent contractor depends on the facts and circumstances of each case.[5] The classification is usually straightforward. But occasionally, the nature of the working relationship does not clearly indicate whether the worker is an employee or an independent contractor.

The Firm's Viewpoint

When a firm hires a worker whose classification is ambiguous, it has a financial incentive to treat the worker as an independent contractor. By doing so, the firm avoids both the employer payroll tax and the administrative cost of the various withholding requirements. Moreover, it doesn't have to provide independent contractors with the fringe benefits available to its permanent workforce. The payroll cost for an employee includes both base compensation (wage or salary) and any benefits (medical and life insurance, paid vacation, sick leave, retirement

---

[5] In Rev. Rul. 87-41, 1987-1 CB 296, the IRS lists 20 factors for determining whether an individual is an employee or an independent contractor.

EXHIBIT 15.2

☐ CORRECTED (if checked)

PAYER'S name, street address, city, state, ZIP code, and telephone no.		1 Rents	OMB No. 1545-0115	
Crockett Products P.O. Box 92252 Wilmington, DE 12899		$	**2011**	**Miscellaneous Income**
		2 Royalties $	Form **1099-MISC**	
		3 Other income $	4 Federal income tax withheld $	**Copy B For Recipient**
PAYER'S federal identification number 87-4009325	RECIPIENT'S identification number 165-39-2238	5 Fishing boat proceeds $	6 Medical and health care payments $	
RECIPIENT'S name **Sam Lincoln**		7 Nonemployee compensation $ 34,700	8 Substitute payments in lieu of dividends or interest $	This is important tax information and is being furnished to the Internal Revenue Service. If you are required to file a return, a negligence penalty or other sanction may be imposed on you if this income is taxable and the IRS determines that it has not been reported.
Street address (including apt. no.) **88 Fernglade #316**		9 Payer made direct sales of $5,000 or more of consumer products to a buyer (recipient) for resale ► ☐	10 Crop insurance proceeds $	
City, state, and ZIP code **Stafford, DE 12891**		11	12	
Account number (see instructions)		13 Excess golden parachute payments $	14 Gross proceeds paid to an attorney $	
15a Section 409A deferrals $	15b Section 409A income $	16 State tax withheld $ $	17 State/Payer's state no.	18 State income $ $

Form **1099-MISC**   (keep for your records)   Department of the Treasury - Internal Revenue Service

pensions, etc.) for which the employee is eligible. If the firm can engage an independent contractor for the same base compensation, it eliminates the incremental cost of the benefits.

The IRS's Viewpoint

In theory, the federal government should be indifferent as to whether workers are employees or independent contractors. The IRS should collect the same employment tax on the worker's compensation, either as payroll tax or self-employment tax. Similarly, the compensation is subject to income tax in either case. Realistically, the IRS has a higher probability of collecting these taxes if the worker is an employee. In this case, the employer is legally responsible for remitting both the employment tax and the income tax on the compensation to the government.

If a firm classifies a worker as an independent contractor, the responsibility for paying tax shifts to the contractor. The IRS has determined that self-employed individuals as a group have a relatively low level of compliance, either because they fail to file a tax return or because they understate their business income. For this reason, the IRS takes an aggressive stance with respect to worker classification. Firms that classify workers as independent contractors must be aware of the risk that a revenue agent may challenge this classification on audit. If the agent concludes that facts and circumstances tip the scales in favor of employee status, the firm may find itself liable for unpaid taxes, interest, and penalties because it failed to carry out its responsibilities as an employer.

Talking the Talk

Companies that use independent contractors may head off a dispute with the IRS by making sure that all written references to such contractors contain the proper terminology. For example, independent contractors are not "hired" or "fired" or paid "wages" or "salaries." Instead, they are "retained" or "discontinued" and paid "remuneration" or "fees." The company should never refer to itself as the "employer" but as the "principal" or "client." Finally, the department that deals with independent contractors should not be labeled "human resources" but "contractor relations."[6]

[6] Daniel P. O'Meara and Jeffrey L. Braff, "A Preventative Approach to Using Independent Contractors," *Journal of Accountancy,* September 1997, p. 43.

WAGE AND SALARY PAYMENTS

Tax Consequences to Employees

Employees typically are cash basis taxpayers who recognize wages or salary as income in the year in which payment is actually or constructively received. In terms of cash flow, payments are net of employee payroll tax and income tax withheld by the employer. While payroll tax withholding usually equals the individual's payroll tax liability, the income tax withholding is an approximate number. If the annual withholding exceeds the individual's actual income tax, the Treasury owes the individual a refund. Alternatively, withholding may be less than the actual tax, in which case the individual pays the balance due when she files her Form 1040 or extension request.

Tax Consequences to Employers

The employer's income tax consequences of wage or salary payments depend on the nature of the employee's services. If the employer is an individual and the services are *not* business related, the payment for such services is a nondeductible personal expense. For instance, people who employ private housekeepers, or gardeners, or nannies for their children can't deduct the compensation paid to these household employees. Of course, the fact that employees are performing domestic services does not excuse employers from their payroll tax obligations with respect to the compensation paid.[7]

For sole proprietorships, partnerships, and corporations that hire business employees, the compensation paid is either a deductible expense or a capitalized cost. This distinction depends on the nature of the service and the employer's method of accounting.

Accounting for Compensation Paid	Berring Corporation paid a $90,000 salary to its in-house attorney, an expense that it deducted in the computation of taxable income. It also paid $2,679,000 wages to workers on its production line, a direct labor cost that Berring capitalized to manufactured inventory.

Employers are allowed to deduct compensation expense in the year the compensation is paid and the employee includes the payment in gross income. Accrual-basis employers can deduct accrued compensation expense only if the compensation is paid within two and one-half months after the close of the year.[8]

Reasonable Compensation

The tax law stipulates that only *reasonable* compensation for services rendered is deductible as a business expense. This stipulation is subjective: "Reasonable and true compensation is only such amount as would ordinarily be paid for like services by like enterprises under like circumstances."[9] The IRS generally assumes that compensation resulting from an arm's-length negotiation between employer and employee is reasonable. In other words, the IRS does not challenge compensation determined in the competitive marketplace. The law does limit the compensation *deduction* allowed to publicly held corporations. These corporations can deduct no more than $1 million of the annual compensation paid to their

---

[7] In 2012, household employers are not required to pay or withhold payroll tax unless they pay $1,800 or more in wages to an employee during the year. §3121(a)(7)(B) and (x). Household employers are not required to withhold federal income tax unless the employee requests it and the employer agrees. §3401(a)(3).

[8] See the discussion of compensation accruals in Chapter 6 at footnote 52.

[9] Reg. §1.162-7(a)(3).

principal executive officer and the three other most highly paid officers. This limitation is subject to a major exception: It does not apply to **performance-based compensation** paid solely because the corporate officer reached a performance goal established by a compensation committee consisting of outside members of the board of directors. The terms of the compensation arrangement, including the performance goal, must be disclosed to the shareholders who must approve the arrangement by a majority vote.[10]

Performance-Based Compensation	Susan Pierce is the CEO of Furst Inc., a publicly held corporation. Susan's annual base salary is $975,000. During the first month of each year, Furst's board of directors establishes a performance goal and bonus plan for its corporate officers. Under this year's plan, Susan will receive a $600,000 bonus if annual gross sales exceed 110 percent of last year's gross sales. By year-end, sales were 113 percent of last year's sales, and Furst paid Susan her bonus. Furst can deduct Susan's $975,000 annual salary because it does not exceed $1 million, and it can deduct the $600,000 bonus because it meets the definition of performance-based compensation.

Closely Held Corporations

The payment of compensation by a closely held corporation to an employee who is also a shareholder may not be an arm's-length transaction. To the extent the employee influences or even controls corporate policy in his capacity as a shareholder, salary negotiations occur in a fictitious market.[11] As a result, the IRS looks closely to determine if the compensation is reasonable. If it concludes that the compensation is unreasonably high, it will reclassify the unreasonable portion as a constructive dividend.[12]

Objective 2
List the factors determining reasonable compensation for a shareholder/employee.

Reasonable compensation is based on the facts and circumstances of each particular employer/employee relationship, and the federal courts have heard thousands of cases in which the IRS and a corporate employer disagreed on this issue. In an often-cited decision, the Second Circuit Court of Appeals described five factors relevant to the reasonableness of employee compensation.

1. The shareholder/employee's role in the corporate business, including the number of hours worked and the duties performed.
2. External comparisons with other companies: specifically, compensation paid to the employee relative to compensation paid to comparable employees by unrelated employers in a similar business.
3. The financial condition of the corporate employer, including sales, net income, capital value, and general economic fitness.
4. The employee's degree of control over dividend policy in his or her capacity as shareholder.
5. The internal consistency of the corporation's compensation system throughout the employee ranks.[13]

The appellate court pointed out that no single factor determines the issue and that it must "assess the entire tableau from the perspective of an independent investor—that is, given the dividends and return on equity enjoyed by a disinterested stockholder, would that stockholder

[10] §162(m) and Notice 2007-49, 2007-25 IRB 1429.

[11] See the discussion of fictitious markets involving related parties in Chapter 3.

[12] See the discussion of constructive dividends in Chapter 12.

[13] *Rapco, Inc.* v. *Commissioner,* 85 F.3d 950 (CA-2, 1996). See also *Exacto Spring Corporation* v. *Commissioner,* 196 F.3d 833 (CA-7, 1999) and *E.J. Harrison & Sons, Inc.* v. *Commissioner,* 138 Fed. Appx. 994 (CA-9, 2005).

approve the compensation paid to the employee?"[14] If unrelated shareholders acting in their economic self-interest would agree to the compensation paid to a shareholder/employee, that compensation should be considered reasonable.

$20 Million Man	John Meynard was CEO and controlling shareholder of Menard Inc., the third largest chain of home improvement stores in the country. In 1998, John received total compensation of over $20 million. After the IRS challenged the reasonableness of this compensation, the corporation took its case to court. The Tax Court concluded that only $7 million was reasonable and that the remainder was a nondeductible dividend. The Tax Court's decision emphasized that Lowe's and Home Depot (Menard Inc.'s chief competitors) paid their CEOs only $6.1 million and $2.8 million, respectively, in 1998. The Seventh Circuit Court of Appeals reversed the Tax Court's decision, criticizing it as "arbitrary as well as dizzying." The appellate court was impressed by John's "workaholic, micromanaging ways" and the fact that he worked "12 to 16 hours a day 6 or 7 days a week, taking only 7 days of vacation a year, involving himself in every detail of his firm's operations." Based on this evidence, the court ruled that John was worth every penny of $20 million.[15]

S Corporations

The IRS views the issue of reasonable compensation in an entirely different light when the employment relationship is between an S corporation and its sole shareholder. In this case, the entire corporate income is taxed to the individual who owns the corporation. If the corporation pays the owner a salary as compensation for services rendered as an employee, the corporation's income decreases by the salary deduction, but the owner's income from the business (salary plus corporate income) is unchanged. The only significant tax consequence is the *payroll tax* burden on the salary. Therefore, the owner can minimize this tax cost by having the S corporation pay him an unreasonably low (or even no) salary. The IRS may counter this tax avoidance tactic by treating any cash distributed by the S corporation to its shareholder as a constructive salary payment.[16]

Unreasonably Low Compensation	Mr. Petri is the sole shareholder and CEO of PML Inc., a calendar year S corporation. The IRS recently audited PML's 2009 tax return on which the corporation deducted a $15,000 salary paid to Mr. Petri as CEO. The corporation's taxable income was $741,240, and it distributed $400,000 cash to Mr. Petri as a shareholder. Mr. Petri reported both his salary and his 100 percent share of PML's taxable income on his Form 1040. After comparing Mr. Petri's salary with the salaries paid to CEOs of comparable corporate businesses, the IRS concluded that Mr. Petri's salary should have been $125,000. Consequently, it reclassified $110,000 of Mr. Petri's taxable income from PML as compensation and assessed Social Security and Medicare taxes accordingly.

Family Members as Employees

While the tax law doesn't prohibit closely held businesses from hiring employees who are related to the owners, the compensation paid to these relatives must be reasonable for the services actually performed. Subject to this constraint, business owners can effectively shift income to family members who work in the business.

---

[14] Ibid., p. 955.

[15] *Meynard Inc. v. Comm.*, 560 F.3d 620 (CA-7, 2009).

[16] See *Joseph M. Grey, P.C.*, 119 T.C. 121 (2002), *aff'd*, 93 Fed. Appx. 473 (CA-3, 2004).

Family Members as Employees

Mrs. Young, who owns a sole proprietorship, is in the 35 percent tax bracket. She has two children, ages 14 and 17, who work for her after school and during the summer. The younger child performs clerical chores and runs errands for her mom, while the older child drives a delivery van. Mrs. Young pays her children a reasonable wage based on the actual number of hours worked each week. This year, the younger child earned $3,100, the older child earned $6,350, and the family saved $3,268 income tax.

| Tax savings of business deduction to Mrs. Young ($9,450 wages paid × 35%) | | $3,308 | |

Tax consequences to:		Younger Child	Older Child
Wage income		$ 3,100	$ 6,350
Standard deduction (single)		(3,100)	(5,950)
Taxable income		–0–	$ 400
Tax rate (single)			.10
Tax cost of compensation to children			$ 40

Tax savings to family:	
Mrs. Young's savings	$ 3,308
Older child's cost	(40)
	$ 3,268

The income shift in this example had a second beneficial tax effect. The $9,450 business deduction reduced Mrs. Young's net earnings from self-employment and, therefore, her self-employment tax. However, wages paid to an employer's child under age 18 are not subject to FICA or unemployment tax.[17] Consequently, the wage payments to the two children did not create an additional payroll tax cost for the business.

Foreign Earned Income Exclusion

Before leaving the topic of wages and salaries, we should consider the special case of individuals who are U.S. citizens but who reside and work on an extended basis in another country. These individuals, referred to as **expatriates,** may face a higher cost of living because of their overseas assignment or may incur additional costs such as foreign income taxes. Because of these financial concerns, U.S. firms with international operations may have difficulty staffing their foreign offices. To help U.S. firms compete in the labor market and to encourage them to employ U.S. citizens to work abroad, the tax law allows expatriates to exclude foreign wages or salary from taxable income. This **foreign earned income exclusion** for 2012 is $95,100.[18] Expatriates may not claim a foreign tax credit for any foreign income tax paid on the excluded income.[19]

[17] §3121(b)(3)(A) and §3306(c)(5).
[18] §911(a) and (b). The exclusion is adjusted annually for inflation.
[19] §911(d)(6).

Foreign Earned Income Exclusion	PBG operates a branch office in Portugal, which is managed by Mr. Sims. Although Mr. Sims is a U.S. citizen, he has been a resident of Lisbon since 2003. His 2012 salary from PBG is $135,000, on which he paid $14,280 Portuguese income tax. In preparing his Form 1040, Mr. Sims may exclude $95,100 of his foreign earned income from taxable income. Consequently, only $39,900 of his salary is subject to U.S. tax. He may also claim a foreign tax credit based on the Portuguese income tax attributable to his *taxable* salary.

EMPLOYEE FRINGE BENEFITS

As a general rule, individuals are taxed on any economic benefit received as compensation for services rendered to their employers, even if the benefit does not result in any direct cash flow.[20] However, the tax law allows employees to exclude the value of certain statutorily defined **fringe benefits** from income. These fringe benefits not only escape the income tax but also are exempt from payroll tax. Firms that provide fringe benefits account for the cost of the benefits in the same manner as the base compensation paid. If the salary or wage paid to an employee is currently deductible, the cost of the employee's fringe benefits is also deductible.[21] This section of the chapter describes several important nontaxable fringe benefits and discusses how employers and employees include these benefits in their compensation arrangements to mutual advantage.

Health and Accident Insurance

Objective 3
Identify the most common nontaxable employee fringe benefits.

Employees can exclude the value of health and accident insurance coverage provided by their employers.[22] Hence, premiums that employers pay directly to insurance carriers on behalf of their employees are not taxable to the employees. Similarly, if an employer has a self-insured medical reimbursement plan, participating employees do not recognize the imputed value of their coverage under the plan as income. This fringe benefit has tremendous significance to the U.S. workforce. Millions of employees can't afford private medical insurance and rely on their employers for insurance protection. A worker's decision to accept or reject a job offer may depend on whether the prospective employer provides a comprehensive health and accident insurance plan. The tax law encourages employers to do so by making this form of compensation nontaxable. Such preferential treatment is costly; the Treasury loses about $250 billion of annual income and payroll tax revenue because of the exclusion for employer-provided medical insurance, making it the largest item in the government's tax expenditures budget.

Group Term Life Insurance

Employees can exclude the value of term life insurance coverage provided under a group policy carried by their employers, but only to the extent the coverage does not exceed $50,000. If the coverage exceeds $50,000, the employee is taxed on the cost of the excess. This cost is determined by reference to a uniform premium table provided by the Treasury rather than by reference to the actual insurance premiums paid by the employer.[23]

---

[20] Reg. §1.61-21.

[21] Reg. §1.263A-1(e)(3)(ii)(D).

[22] §106. This exclusion extends to the value of employer-provided long-term-care insurance. §213(d)(1)(D).

[23] Reg. §1.79-3. The employer's actual cost of group term life insurance is a §162 expense. Reg. §1.162-10 and Rev. Rul. 69-478, 1969-2 CB 29.

Group Term Life Insurance	Mr. Kung, a 46-year-old employee of ABC Corporation, has $200,000 life insurance coverage under ABC's group term plan. According to the Treasury's table, the cost of $1,000 of life insurance to a 46-year-old person is 15 cents a month. The annual cost of Mr. Kung's $150,000 excess coverage is $270 (150 × $.15 × 12 months). This amount is a taxable fringe benefit to Mr. Kung, and ABC must report $270 as part of Mr. Kung's compensation on his Form W-2.

Dependent Care Assistance Programs

Employees can exclude amounts paid or incurred by their employers for dependent care assistance.[24] Thus, employers may provide on-site day care for their employees' children (or other dependents) as a nontaxable fringe benefit. Alternatively, employers may contract with a third party to provide dependent care or may reimburse employees directly for their dependent care expenses. The annual exclusion is limited to $5,000 ($2,500 in the case of a separate return filed by a married individual). If the value of employer-provided dependent care exceeds $5,000, the employee must recognize the excess as taxable income.

Other Nontaxable Fringe Benefits

TaxTalk
Beginning in 2009, employer reimbursement of expenses incurred by an employee to purchase, repair, and store a bicycle that the employee regularly rides to work is a nontaxable fringe benefit.

Most firms provide their employees with a variety of fringe benefits. The benefits that a particular firm offers depend on the nature of its business and the composition of its workforce. The list of possible benefits includes employee use of company cars, employer-provided cell phones, on-premise dining facilities, parking and public transportation, moving expense reimbursements, business club memberships, professional dues and subscriptions, and company-sponsored picnics and Christmas parties. Each item on this list (as well as many other employee perks) can qualify as a nontaxable fringe benefit, but only if the item meets the detailed, and sometimes strict, requirements specified in the Internal Revenue Code and Treasury regulations.[25]

Fringe Benefits and Self-Employed Individuals

The tax-exempt status of many employee fringe benefits does not extend to benefits that a self-employed individual provides for himself. As a result, self-employed individuals must spend after-tax dollars to pay for certain commodities that employees can obtain with before-tax dollars (as nontaxable compensation). For example, if a self-employed person pays $750 to purchase a $50,000 life insurance policy to protect her family, the payment is a nondeductible personal expense. The same disadvantage applies to individual partners and shareholders in S corporations. If a partnership has a group term life insurance plan covering both employees and partners, the cost of a partner's insurance is a guaranteed payment that the partner must recognize as taxable income.[26] If an S corporation has a group term life insurance plan, the cost of a shareholder/employee's insurance is taxable compensation instead of a nontaxable fringe benefit.[27]

Self-employed individuals, partners, and S corporation shareholders do receive special consideration with respect to medical and accident insurance for themselves and their families. These taxpayers are allowed an above-the-line deduction for the cost of this insurance.[28]

---

[24] §129.

[25] See §132 and accompanying regulations.

[26] Rev. Rul. 91-26, 1991-1 CB 184.

[27] §1372 prevents any shareholder who owns more than 2 percent of an S corporation's stock from excluding employee fringe benefits from taxable income.

[28] §162(l).

Deduction of Health Insurance Costs	Vernon LLC has 38 employees and five individual members who work for the LLC. The LLC provides a group medical insurance plan that covers both employees and members. The cost of the insurance is a nontaxable fringe benefit to Vernon's employees and taxable compensation to the members. This year, Mrs. George, an LLC member, recognizes the $2,650 cost of her medical insurance as an income item. However, she is allowed an above-the-line deduction of the same amount, so the net effect of this fringe benefit on her AGI is zero.

Compensation Planning with Fringe Benefits

Fringe benefits are an extremely popular form of compensation. One reason is that the employer's cost of providing the benefit is usually less than the benefit's value to the employee. This differential is attributable to the employer's economy of scale: The cost per person of providing a commodity such as health insurance or child care to a large group is less than the cost of the commodity to one individual.

Cost versus Value of Fringe Benefit	Contex Corporation, which has 1,200 employees, maintains a group medical plan with a commercial insurance company. Mr. Liu participates in this plan, and the annual cost of his coverage is $2,400. If Mr. Liu were not a participant, he would pay $3,600 per year for comparable private medical insurance. Contex operates an on-premise day care facility in which employees can enroll their preschool children at no charge. Contex's annual operating cost is $1,750 per child. Mr. Liu's son attends this facility. If the facility were not available, Mr. Liu would pay $2,100 per year to enroll his son in private day care. The aggregate value of these two fringe benefits to Mr. Liu is $5,700. Contex's cost to provide the benefits is only $4,150.

Cafeteria Plans

Because employees have varying financial needs and consumption preferences, each one places a different value on any noncash benefit offered by his or her employer.

Valuing Fringe Benefits	In the preceding example, Mr. Liu placed a $2,100 value on the child care provided by Contex because he is willing to pay $2,100 for this commodity. Ms. Blane, another corporate employee, has no children. Therefore, Ms. Blane places a zero value on employer-provided child care. She would prefer a different fringe benefit or even additional salary from Contex rather than a worthless fringe benefit.

Employers can maximize the aggregate value of their fringe-benefit programs to their employees through a **cafeteria plan.** Under a cafeteria plan, each employee may select noncash benefits from a menu of benefit choices. In lieu of noncash benefits, employees may simply select additional taxable salary.[29] By participating in a cafeteria plan, employees can combine both nontaxable and taxable benefits to result in the greatest after-tax compensation based on their individual needs and preferences.

Negotiating with Nontaxable Fringe Benefits

Employers are aware that employees may enjoy substantial tax savings because of nontaxable fringe benefits. By substituting nontaxable benefits for taxable compensation, employers can capture some portion of this savings for themselves and reduce the after-tax cost of the compensation. The examples that follow demonstrate this important point.

[29] Cafeteria plans are described in §125.

Salary Payment

Leyton Corporation is negotiating a one-year employment contract with Mrs. King, who begins the negotiation by requesting a $200,000 salary. Leyton's marginal tax rate is 35 percent, and Mrs. King's marginal tax rate is 33 percent. The after-tax cost of this salary to Leyton and the after-tax value of this salary to Mrs. King are computed as follows.

	Leyton	Mrs. King
Salary payment	$(200,000)	$200,000
Employer/employee payroll tax	(9,726)	(7,524)
Income tax savings (cost):		
Salary deduction × 35%	70,000	
Payroll tax deduction × 35%	3,404	
Salary income × 33%		(66,000)
After-tax (cost) value	$(136,322)	$126,476

Now assume that Leyton makes a counteroffer to Mrs. King. It will pay a $185,000 salary and provide complete medical and dental insurance coverage for her and her family, free parking in a convenient garage, and membership in its on-premises health spa. Assume that the value of these nontaxable fringe benefits to Mrs. King is $12,000, but their incremental cost to Leyton is only $9,000.[30]

Reduced Salary plus Fringe Benefits

The after-tax cost of the compensation package (salary plus fringe benefits) to Leyton and the after-tax value of this package to Mrs. King are computed as follows.

	Leyton	Mrs. King
Salary payment	$(185,000)	$185,000
Fringe-benefit (cost) value	(9,000)	12,000
Employer/employee payroll tax	(9,508)	(7,306)
Income tax savings (cost):		
Salary deduction × 35%	64,750	
Fringe-benefit deduction × 35%	3,150	
Payroll tax deduction × 35%	3,328	
Salary income × 33%		(61,050)
After-tax (cost) value	$(132,280)	$128,644

The substitution of nontaxable fringe benefits for salary decreased Leyton's after-tax cost by $4,042 and increased Mrs. King's after-tax compensation by $2,168. Thus, both parties to this negotiation benefited from the inclusion of the nontaxable fringe benefits.

EMPLOYEE STOCK OPTIONS

Corporate employers often include stock options as a major component of the compensation package offered to key employees. A **stock option** is the right to purchase the corporation's stock for a stated price (the strike price) for a given period of time. From the employee's

---

[30] Employer-provided parking and on-premises athletic facilities can qualify as nontaxable fringe benefits. §132(f) and (j)(4).

perspective, stock options are an opportunity to acquire equity at a bargain price. From the employer's perspective, stock options are a form of compensation that requires no cash outlay and, in fact, may eventually result in an infusion of capital. In addition, the option gives the employee a financial interest in the corporation's long-term success and a powerful incentive to contribute to that success in every way possible.

Citigroup Stock Options	Citigroup, one of the world's largest banks and a major beneficiary of the U.S. government's bailout of the financial industry, uses stock options to keep its employees happy and hardworking. About 75,000 employees, one-fourth of the company's workforce, have received options that could generate sizeable gains if and when Citigroup's stock price rebounds from its current low. According to the bank's press release, this broad-based options program "links employee rewards to the long-term performance and success of the company."[31]

Objective 4
Describe the tax consequences of stock options.

To analyze the tax consequences of compensatory stock options, consider the case of BRT and its employee, Mr. Bell. In year 1, BRT grants Mr. Bell an option to buy 2,000 shares of BRT stock for a strike price of $30 per share at any time during the next eight years. On the date of grant, BRT stock is selling for $28 per share. Because the strike price exceeds the market price, the option has no readily ascertainable value and Mr. Bell does not recognize income on receipt of the option.[32] The risk that Mr. Bell assumes in accepting the option is that the market price will not climb above $30 per share over the term of the option. In this case, the option is worthless, and Mr. Bell will simply let it lapse.

Mr. Bell's expectation is that the market price of BRT stock will increase over the option period. Suppose that by year 8, the stock is selling at $75 per share. Mr. Bell exercises the option by paying $60,000 cash to BRT for 2,000 shares with a market value of $150,000. Mr. Bell must recognize the $90,000 **bargain element** (excess of market value over cost) as ordinary income in year 8.[33] These results are shown in Exhibit 15.3 in which the vertical axis is BRT stock price and the horizontal axis is the eight-year option period.

The shaded area in Exhibit 15.3 represents the value of Mr. Bell's option, which increased over time as the BRT stock price climbed from $28 to $75. Mr. Bell defers income recognition until he realizes this value by converting the option to actual shares of stock. Mr. Bell's tax basis in his 2,000 shares is $150,000: $60,000 out-of-pocket cost plus $90,000 income recognized on the exercise of the option.

Tax Talk
Forbes *magazine reported that 30 percent of the compensation earned in 2010 by the CEOs of America's 500 biggest corporations consisted of the bargain element from exercised stock options.*

EXHIBIT 15.3
Tax Consequences of Mr. Bell's Stock Option

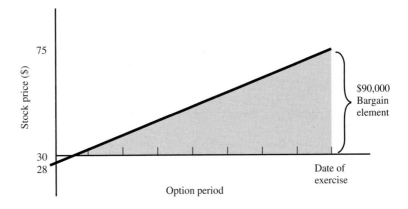

[31] United Press International, Inc., "Citigroup issues employees stock options," November 7, 2009.
[32] Reg. §1.83-7.
[33] Employers must report income from exercise of stock options on their employees' Form W-2.

Note that in year 8, Mr. Bell has *negative* cash flow; he must pay $60,000 for the stock plus both income and payroll tax on $90,000 compensation. Mr. Bell can generate cash by selling some of his BRT shares. This sale will not trigger additional income unless the selling price exceeds Mr. Bell's $75 basis per share. On the other hand, BRT received $60,000 cash as paid-in capital when Mr. Bell exercised his stock option. Moreover, the corporation can deduct the $90,000 bargain element as compensation paid in year 8.[34]

Book/Tax Difference

For financial statement purposes, corporations must record the estimated value of stock options as compensation expense in the year of grant.[35] For tax purposes, the corporation is not allowed a compensation deduction until the year of exercise. This difference in accounting treatment causes a temporary excess of taxable income over book income in the year of grant that reverses in the year of exercise.

Book/Tax Difference from Stock Options	Four years ago, Perino Inc. granted stock options to its employees and expensed their $2,840,000 total estimated value on its income statement. This expense was nondeductible and resulted in a temporary excess of taxable over book income. This year, one of Perino's employees exercised an option and recognized the $103,100 bargain element (excess of market value over option price) as gross income. Perino's $103,100 deduction of the bargain element is a reversal of the original temporary difference.

Incentive Stock Options

The tax law creates a special type of employee stock option called an **incentive stock option (ISO).** The qualification requirements for ISOs are narrow and complex, but the preferential treatment of ISOs as compared to nonqualifying options is straightforward.[36] When an employee exercises an ISO, he does not recognize the bargain element as taxable income.[37] The tax basis in the purchased shares is the employee's out-of-pocket cost, and the employee recognizes no income with respect to these shares unless and until he disposes of them in a taxable transaction. Furthermore, any gain recognized on disposition is capital gain.

Refer back to the facts concerning Mr. Bell's option to purchase 2,000 shares of BRT common stock and assume that the option qualified as an ISO. In year 8, Mr. Bell does not recognize any income when he purchases 2,000 shares worth $150,000 for only $60,000. Suppose that Mr. Bell holds these shares until year 15, when he sells them for $225,000. Mr. Bell's capital gain on sale is $165,000 ($225,000 amount realized − $60,000 basis), $90,000 of which represents the untaxed bargain element on exercise of the option.

ISO versus Nonqualified Option	The following table contrasts Mr. Bell's income tax cost from this sequence of transactions to the tax cost if the stock option had not qualified as an ISO. The table assumes a 35 percent rate on ordinary income and a 15 percent rate on capital gain.

[34] Reg. §1.83-6.

[35] SFAS No. 123 (revised 2004), *Share-Based Payment.*

[36] Incentive stock options are defined in §422(b).

[37] §421(a).

	ISO	Nonqualified Option
Year 8 (exercise of option):		
Ordinary income recognized	–0–	$ 90,000
Tax cost at 35%	**–0–**	**31,500**
Basis in 2,000 shares	$ 60,000	$ 150,000
Year 15 (sale of stock):		
Selling price	$225,000	$ 225,000
Basis	(60,000)	(150,000)
Capital gain recognized	$165,000	$ 75,000
Tax cost at 15%	**$ 24,750**	**$ 11,250**

This table shows the dual advantage of ISOs compared to nonqualified stock options: the extension of the tax-*deferral* period until the year of sale and the *conversion* of the option's bargain element from ordinary income to capital gain. However, individuals who are planning to exercise ISOs must be cautious. The untaxed bargain element is an alternative minimum tax (AMT) adjustment added to taxable income in the computation of alternative minimum taxable income (AMTI).[38] Accordingly, individuals may want to avoid exercising ISOs in a year in which they have any exposure to the AMT.

AMT on ISO	Mrs. Craig plans to exercise an ISO in 2012. Her bargain element (excess of market value over cost) would be $180,000. She estimates that the taxable income on her jointly filed return will be $528,500, and her AMTI (without the bargain element) will be $539,000. Consequently, her regular income tax would be $154,115, her tentative minimum tax would be only $147,420, and she would owe no AMT. If she exercises the ISO, the bargain element would not increase her taxable income. But it would be a tax preference item that would increase her AMTI to $719,000. Her tentative AMT would increase to $197,820, and she would owe $43,705 AMT ($197,820 − $154,115 regular income tax).

A negative feature of ISOs is that employers never receive a tax deduction for the option's bargain element. Consequently, they derive no tax benefit when an employee exercises an ISO. The book/tax difference that originates in the year of grant of an ISO does not reverse in the year of exercise and results in a permanent excess of taxable income over book income.

Corporate Deduction for Stock Options	Refer back to the example concerning Mr. Bell's exercise of his BRT stock option. The following table compares BRT's cash flow consequences of compensating Mr. Bell with an ISO rather than with a nonqualified stock option.

	ISO	Nonqualified Option
Year 8 (Mr. Bell's exercise of option):		
Paid-in capital from issuance of shares	$60,000	$60,000
Deduction for bargain element	–0–	$90,000
BRT's marginal tax rate		.35
Tax savings from deduction	–0–	31,500
Net cash flow in year 8	$60,000	$91,500

Mr. Bell's sale of his stock in year 15 has no effect on BRT.

---

[38] §56(b)(3).

EMPLOYMENT-RELATED EXPENSES

It is not unusual for individuals to incur out-of-pocket expenses relating to their employment. Common examples are union dues, subscriptions to professional or trade journals, uniforms, continuing education courses that maintain or improve job skills, and transportation costs incurred while conducting business for an employer. Employers routinely reimburse employees for employment-related expenses, thereby assuming the economic burden of the expense. In such case, the employee neither reports the cash reimbursement as income nor deducts the expense. The whole expense/reimbursement transaction is a wash without any effect on the employee's taxable income.

The tax consequences of *unreimbursed* employment-related expenses are much less benign. Congress has expressed its belief that individuals should not be allowed to deduct such expenses. If the expenses are truly necessary to the successful performance of an employee's duties, the employer should be willing to provide reimbursement. Acting on this belief, Congress put employment-related expenses into the category of **miscellaneous itemized deductions,** which are deductible only to the extent that their total exceeds 2 percent of AGI.[39] Because of this limitation, many individuals derive no tax benefit from their unreimbursed employment-related expenses.

Unreimbursed Employment-Related Expenses	Ms. Jessup, who is employed by an advertising firm, spent $1,500 to attend a seminar on computer graphics. This unreimbursed employment-related expense is her only miscellaneous itemized deduction for the year. If Ms. Jessup's AGI is $69,400, she can deduct only $112 of the cost of the seminar.

Miscellaneous itemized deductions	$ 1,500
AGI threshold ($69,400 × 2%)	(1,388)
Allowable deduction	$ 112

If Ms. Jessup's AGI equals or exceeds $75,000, her total miscellaneous itemized deductions fall short of the 2 percent AGI threshold. In such case, none of the employment-related expense is deductible, and her *after-tax* cost of the seminar is $1,500.

Moving Expenses

The tax law allows individuals to deduct unreimbursed moving expenses incurred in connection with "the commencement of work by the taxpayer as an employee or as a self-employed individual, at a new principal place of work."[40] **Moving expenses** include the cost of transporting household goods and personal belongings from the individual's former residence to a new residence. The costs of traveling to the new residence (with the exception of the cost of meals en route) also qualify as moving expenses. The moving expense deduction is an above-the-line deduction in the AGI computation.

If an employee receives a moving expense reimbursement from his employer, the reimbursement is nontaxable to the extent of the moving expenses qualifying for the deduction. Any excess reimbursement is taxable compensation to the employee.

---

[39] §67.

[40] §217. Individuals must meet both a distance test and a duration-of-new-employment test to qualify for the deduction.

Moving Expenses	BV Corporation transferred its employee Mr. Carl from its San Diego office to its San Antonio office. Mr. Carl paid $3,800 to the moving company that transported his household goods from his California home to his new home in Texas. He also paid $2,400 to fly his family from California to Texas.
	• If Mr. Carl did not receive any reimbursement from BV, he may deduct $6,200 in the computation of AGI.
	• If Mr. Carl received a $5,000 reimbursement from BV, he may deduct $1,200 in the computation of AGI.
	• If Mr. Carl received a $7,000 reimbursement from BV, he must recognize the $800 excess reimbursement as taxable compensation.

RETIREMENT PLANNING

At some point in their lives, most people confront the need to plan for retirement. Given the life expectancy for the average American, individuals who want to retire by age 65 know that they might live 20 to 30 years after leaving the workforce. They also know that they should take action now to maintain their standard of living during this postemployment period. Specifically, they must invest some portion of their current income in financial assets that will provide future income. In this section of the chapter, we will learn how the tax laws encourage people to save for retirement. By taking advantage of tax-favored retirement plans, individuals can maximize the future value of their investments and enhance their prospects for long-term security.[41]

Retirement Planning Is Top Priority	On the basis of a survey of employee benefit specialists, retirement planning has replaced health care as the top priority for today's labor force. The tidal wave of Baby Boomers approaching retirement age is recognizing the need to evaluate the adequacy of retirement savings. Many firms have initiated investment education programs to help their employees assess their investment options and develop strategies to increase their retirement income. Better still, the value of these retirement planning services is a nontaxable fringe benefit to the employees.[42]

Tax Advantages of Qualified Retirement Plans

Objective 5
Compare the after-tax wealth accumulated in a qualified and a nonqualified retirement plan.

The tax law confers a generous set of advantages on an array of retirement savings plans, described generically as **qualified retirement plans.** While the statutory requirements and the financial and legal structures of the plans vary considerably, they all offer two basic benefits to the individuals who participate.[43]

• Dollars of earned income contributed to the plan (or contributed by an employer on an employee's behalf) are not taxed currently.

---

[41] While many people anticipate that they will receive Social Security benefits during their retirement years, they can't undertake any type of individualized tax planning to increase these benefits. The tax consequences of Social Security are covered in Chapter 17 as part of the discussion of government transfer payments.

[42] Qualified retirement planning services are a nontaxable fringe benefit per §132(a)(7).

[43] In 2001, Congress enacted still another inducement for individuals to save for retirement: a nonrefundable tax credit for low-income taxpayers. The credit equals a percentage of the taxpayer's *elective* contributions to a qualified retirement plan (including a Section 401(k) plan or an IRA). The maximum annual contribution eligible for the credit is $2,000, and the maximum credit percentage is 50 percent. §25B.

- The plan itself is tax exempt, so that the earnings generated by the contributed dollars are not taxed currently.

The effect of these two benefits on the rate at which the contributed dollars grow over time is tremendous. The next example highlights this effect.

Qualified Retirement Plan Contributions	Mr. Quincy and Mrs. Russ, who are both in the 35 percent marginal tax bracket, have decided to contribute $20,000 annual before-tax earned income to a retirement fund. Both funds earn an annual 5 percent rate of return and involve the same financial risk. The only difference is that Mr. Quincy's fund is a qualified retirement plan while Mrs. Russ's fund is not. The following table shows the calculation of the balances in the two funds after 25 years.

	Mr. Quincy	Mrs. Russ
Before-tax annual contribution	$ 20,000	$ 20,000
Income tax cost	–0–	(7,000)
After-tax annual contribution	$ 20,000	$ 13,000
Before-tax rate of return on contributions	.05	.05
After-tax rate of return on contributions	.05	.0325
Fund balance after 25 years	$1,002,269	$505,759

The balance in Mr. Quincy's fund does not represent the disposable wealth available on retirement. The law allows him to *defer* the tax on his retirement savings—not to escape taxation entirely. When Mr. Quincy withdraws money from the fund, the withdrawals are taxable.[44] In contrast, Mrs. Russ's fund balance consists of after-tax dollars that she may withdraw and spend at no further tax cost. The next example provides a final comparison of the two funds.

Qualified Retirement Plan Withdrawals	At the end of 25 years, both Mr. Quincy and Mrs. Russ withdraw the balance from their retirement fund. Assume that Mr. Quincy pays 35 percent tax on the entire withdrawal.

	Mr. Quincy	Mrs. Russ
Fund balance after 25 years	$1,002,269	$505,759
Income tax cost of withdrawal	(350,794)	–0–
After-tax disposable wealth	$ 651,475	$505,759

This comparison of after-tax wealth is dramatic testimony to the power of tax deferral. Moreover, Mr. Quincy can prolong the deferral by liquidating his retirement fund gradually over a number of years rather than in a single lump sum. Depending on the type of plan, he may have the option of receiving the fund balance in the form of an annuity, a series of fixed payments over a specific period of time. In such case, Mr. Quincy will pay tax on the retirement dollars received each year.

---

[44] §402(a) provides that distributions from qualified retirement plans are taxable to the recipient under §72.

The tax law limits the duration of the deferral that people can achieve by investing in qualified retirement plans. Plan participants generally must begin receiving distributions from their plans no later than April 1 of the year following the year in which they reach the age of 70½. The entire interest in the plan must be distributed over a period of years based on the participant's life expectancy and the life expectancy of the designated beneficiary of the plan.[45] Treasury regulations provide life expectancy tables for computing a participant's annual **minimum distribution** from a plan.

Minimum Distribution	Mrs. Ramone participated in a qualified retirement plan for 28 years before retiring eight years ago at age 63. Mr. Ramone is the beneficiary who would receive Mrs. Ramone's interest in the plan if she dies. Because the Ramones have sufficient annual income, they have not withdrawn any funds from the qualified plan. However, Mrs. Ramone reached age 70½ last year, so she must receive a minimum distribution by April 1 of this year. According to Treasury regulations and the Ramones' ages, their distribution period is 26.5 years and their minimum distribution must be 3.77 percent of the plan balance. If the plan balance at the beginning of the year is $319,200, the Ramones must withdraw $12,034 ($319,200 × .0377) and include this distribution in taxable income.

Premature Withdrawals

Tax Talk

According to census data, more than 70 percent of individuals who make premature withdrawals from their qualified retirement plans spend the money, subjecting the withdrawal to the 10 percent penalty.

When Congress decided to allow individuals to defer income tax through participation in qualified plans, the intent was that participants use the plans to save for retirement. To discourage people from withdrawing funds before retirement, the Internal Revenue Code imposes a 10 percent penalty on any **premature withdrawal** from a qualified plan.[46] Generally, a withdrawal is premature unless the participant has reached the age of 59½ by the date of withdrawal. This rule is subject to a number of important exceptions. For instance, the penalty is waived if the owner is totally or permanently disabled; if the owner has reached age 55 and has terminated employment with the plan sponsor; or if the withdrawal is made by the owner's estate or beneficiary after the owner's death.

Premature Withdrawal	Mr. Soo, age 51, withdrew $16,000 cash from his qualified retirement plan to fund an investment in a start-up company. Not only must Mr. Soo include the $16,000 distribution in gross income, but he must also pay a $1,600 premature withdrawal penalty. Now change the facts by assuming that Mr. Soo is age 63. He must include the $16,000 in gross income but he avoids the 10 percent penalty because he has reached the age of 59½.

The 10 percent penalty applies only to the portion of a withdrawal included in the participant's income. Individuals who withdraw funds from a qualified plan can avoid both the income tax and any premature withdrawal penalty by rolling over the funds to *another* qualified plan (including an IRA) within 60 days of the withdrawal.

---

[45] §401(a)(9). In the case of employer-sponsored retirement plans, employees who continue to work after reaching age 70½ may postpone receiving distributions until they retire.

[46] §72(t).

Rollover of Withdrawal	Mrs. Harris, age 48, participated for 14 years in a qualified retirement plan sponsored by her employer, Acton Inc. This year, she resigned from Acton to accept a new job with Zuma Inc. Because of her termination of employment, she received a cash distribution of the $35,000 balance in her Acton plan. Mrs. Harris spent $12,000 to buy a new car and made a **rollover contribution** of the $23,000 remainder to Zuma's qualified retirement plan. Consequently, she recognized only $12,000 of the distribution as taxable income subject to her 25 percent marginal rate. The total tax cost of the withdrawal was $4,200.

Income tax ($12,000 × 25%)	$3,000
Premature withdrawal penalty ($12,000 × 10%)	1,200
Total tax cost	$4,200

TYPES OF QUALIFIED PLANS

Qualified retirement plans fall into three categories.

1. Plans that employers provide for their employees.
2. Plans available to self-employed individuals (Keogh plans).
3. Individual retirement accounts (IRAs) available to any person who recognizes compensation or earned income.

This section of the chapter describes the plans included in each category. As you will observe, qualified plans come in a variety of shapes and sizes. But regardless of the differences in structure or operation, qualified retirement plans share a common characteristic: They all are vehicles for tax-favored savings.

Employer-Provided Plans

Objective 6
Distinguish between defined-benefit and defined-contribution plans.

One of the more common fringe benefits offered to employees is participation in one or more retirement plans sponsored and maintained by their employer. For an **employer-provided plan** to be qualified for federal tax purposes, it must satisfy a formidable list of statutory requirements.[47] These requirements reflect two underlying policy objectives. The first objective is that *employer-provided plans should carry minimum risk for participating employees*. To meet this objective, the law requires that:

- Qualified plans must be written permanent arrangements and must be administered in trust form so that the plan assets are invested by an independent trustee for the exclusive benefit of the employees and their families.
- Qualified plans must be funded; annual contributions made to a plan by an employer on behalf of the employees must consist of cash or other valuable property.
- Employees must have a nonforfeitable (vested) right to 100 percent of their retirement benefits under a qualified plan after no more than six years (defined-contribution plan) or seven years (defined-benefit plan) of service with the employer.

The second objective is that *employer-provided plans should offer benefits in an equitable manner to all participating employees*. Accordingly, plans may not discriminate in favor of officers, owner-employees, or highly compensated employees. In other words, rank-and-file employees must be entitled to participate in qualified retirement plans on essentially the same basis as the chief executive officer.

---

[47] §401 through §415.

Defined-Benefit Plans

Employer-provided plans may take the form of a pension plan under which participating employees are promised a targeted or defined benefit when they retire. Firms make annual contributions to their pension plans based on the actuarially determined cost of funding the future retirement benefits to which the current workforce is entitled.[48] These contributions are deductible payroll expenses, even though the employees do not recognize the contributions as income.[49] For tax purposes, firms must comply with a minimum funding standard for their qualified pension plans.[50] Because of this standard, a firm may be required to make contributions to the retirement trust in years in which it operates at a loss or experiences cash flow difficulties. For this reason, employers should regard employee pension plans as long-term financial obligations.

Funding a Defined-Benefit Plan	BN Inc. provides a qualified defined-benefit plan for its employees. This year, an independent actuary determined that BN must contribute $4.28 million to the retirement trust to fund the future pension benefits to which its workforce is entitled. The contribution does not represent taxable compensation to the employees participating in the plan. However, BN can deduct the $4.28 million contribution on its Form 1120.

The annual pension that employers can provide through a qualified **defined-benefit plan** is limited to the *lesser* of 100 percent of the retiree's average compensation for her three highest compensation years or an inflation-adjusted base amount.[51] In 2012, the base amount is $200,000. Firms wanting to provide more generous pensions must do so through nonqualified retirement plans. The tax consequences of nonqualified plans are discussed later in this section.

Contribution Limit on Defined-Benefit Plan	Mr. Underwood, a corporate officer of BN Inc., currently earns a $190,000 salary and anticipates a salary increase every year until his retirement. He participates in BN's qualified pension plan. Although Mr. Underwood's average compensation for his three highest compensation years is projected to be at least $250,000, BN's 2012 plan contribution on his behalf is limited to the amount necessary to fund an annual pension benefit of only $200,000.

Defined-Contribution Plans

Employer-provided plans may be structured as **defined-contribution plans** under which the retirement trust maintains a separate account for each participating employee. Each year, the employer contributes a specified amount to each account. The yearly contribution for each employee is limited to the *lesser* of 100 percent of annual compensation or an inflation-adjusted base amount.[52] In 2012, this base amount is $50,000. Employers may deduct their yearly contributions even though these contributions are not taxable to the employees.

Contribution Limit on Defined-Contribution Plan	Ms. Lewis, a midlevel manager with JH Corporation, earned a $110,000 salary in 2012 and participates in JH's qualified defined-contribution plan. JH's contribution to Ms. Lewis's plan account is limited to $50,000.

---

[48] In 1974, Congress created the Pension Benefit Guaranty Corporation (PBGC) to insure defined benefit plans and to guarantee that participating employees receive their promised pension, even if the plan is underfunded or is terminated by the employer. Qualified plans must pay annual premiums to the PBGC for such insurance.

[49] Employer contributions to qualified plans are not subject to FICA payroll tax. §3121(a)(5).

[50] §412 contains the minimum funding standards that employers must satisfy every year for qualified defined-benefit plans.

[51] §415(b).

[52] §415(c).

Profit-sharing plans under which firms contribute a percentage of current earnings to a retirement trust are a common type of defined-contribution plan. A firm has no obligation to contribute to the trust in a year in which it operates at a loss. As a result, profit-sharing plans are favored by new companies with volatile earnings and uncertain cash flows. From the employees' perspective, these plans require them to share the risk associated with their employer's business because the retirement savings available to each employee depend on the long-term success of that business.

Profit-Sharing Plan	Solange Inc. has a profit-sharing plan under which it contributes 1.5 percent of annual book income to a qualified retirement plan. The annual contribution is allocated among participating employees in proportion to the base compensation of each employee. In 2011, Solange's book income was $81.3 million, and its profit-sharing contribution was $1.22 million. The contribution was allocated among 93 employees participating in the retirement plan. In 2012, Solange reported a $9.7 million loss on its financial statements and made no contribution to its qualified retirement plan.

Employee stock ownership plans (ESOPs) are a second type of defined-contribution plan that gives corporate employees a vested interest in their employer's long-term financial success. Employer contributions to ESOPs are invested primarily in the employer's own common stock.[53] Consequently, employees who participate in ESOPs become shareholders, and the value of their retirement benefits depends on the market value of their employer's stock. When participants retire, they receive distributions of the stock held in their ESOP accounts. Such distributions represent taxable income only to the extent of the ESOP's aggregate basis in the stock. Any excess of the stock's market value over basis is excluded from the recipient's income.[54]

Participation in an ESOP	Mr. Kemp was employed by BD Inc. for 29 years during which BD made annual contributions to an ESOP on his behalf. Mr. Kemp retired this year and received a lump-sum distribution of the balance in his retirement account: 14,987 shares of BD common stock. The ESOP's aggregate basis in the shares was $79,250, and the market value of the shares at date of distribution was $299,600. Mr. Kemp recognized $79,250 ordinary income because of the distribution and took a $79,250 basis in his BD shares. He will not recognize any of the $220,350 unrealized appreciation in the shares until he sells them.

Tax Talk
On November 1, 2008, General Motors suspended matching payments to its salaried employees' Section 401(k) plans to conserve cash during the current economic downturn.

Section 401(k) plans, also described as *salary reduction plans* or *cash-or-deferred arrangements,* have become the most popular qualified plan. Under these plans, each participating employee defines his or her own contribution by electing to divert some amount of current salary or wage to the employee's retirement account. The compensation diverted to the account is tax deferred to the employee even though it is deductible by the employer.[55] In 2012, the maximum compensation that employees can contribute to a Section 401(k) plan is $17,000.[56] Employers often agree to make additional contributions or even match their employees' elective contributions to Section 401(k) plans.

[53] §409.

[54] §402(e)(4)(B).

[55] This compensation is subject to payroll tax in the year of contribution. §3121(v)(1)(A).

[56] §402(g)(1)(B).

Section 401(k) Plan Contribution	Mrs. Toley, a financial analyst with PW Inc., earned a $92,000 salary in 2012. She elected to contribute the $17,000 maximum to PW's Section 401(k) plan. Consequently, only $75,000 of her salary was taxable. PW's policy is to match each employee's elective contribution up to 5 percent of the employee's salary. So PW contributed $4,600 (5 percent of $92,000) to Mrs. Toley's retirement account, increasing the total tax-deferred contribution to $21,600.

Changing Times for Qualified Plans

Tax Talk

Many states such as Kentucky and Florida that face huge shortfalls in their employee pension funds are considering a switch from traditional pension plans to Section 401(k)-type plans. Unlike private companies, most states are legally barred from changing their retirement plans without the consent of their current employees.

Three decades ago, 40 percent of the U.S. private-sector workforce participated in traditional employer-sponsored pension plans. Today, that percentage is only 14 percent. Over the same 30-year period, the percentage of the workforce participating in defined-contribution plans increased from 17 percent to 41 percent.[57] Clearly, the economic tide is turning in favor of profit-sharing and Section 401(k) plans. One reason is that employers are increasingly leery of the long-term financial commitment represented by pension plans, particularly in light of the increased longevity of retired employees.

A second reason is that participants in traditional pension plans receive the maximum retirement benefit only after working for the company for a long period of time—perhaps 20 or 30 years. A participant who leaves the company before qualifying for a full pension may be entitled to a relatively insignificant cash settlement. In contrast, participants in defined-contribution plans quickly earn a vested right to the entire value of their plan account. Today's workforce is characterized by its mobility. Unlike their grandparents, young employees do not expect to work for the same company for their entire careers. Instead, they expect to move from employer to employer and prefer the portable retirement savings offered by defined-contribution plans.

Nonqualified Deferred-Compensation Plans

Objective 7
Explain why employers use nonqualified deferred-compensation plans.

Qualified retirement plans offer a win-win outcome. Employers can deduct contributions made to the plans on their employees' behalf, while employees defer income recognition until they receive distributions from the plans at retirement. But as we learned in our discussion of pension plans, profit-sharing plans, and Section 401(k) plans, the dollar amount of compensation that employers can offer on a tax-deferred basis is limited. Moreover, because of the nondiscrimination requirements, employers can't be overly selective as to the employees who may participate in a qualified retirement plan. Finally, most employers need professional help to cope with the morass of federal rules and regulations governing qualified plans. Hence, these plans can be expensive to maintain, even for the smallest employer.

These negative aspects of qualified plans have prompted many employers to establish nonqualified retirement plans. Employers use these plans to offer unlimited **deferred compensation** to key employees, such as highly paid corporate executives, without extending the benefits of the plan to other employees. In their simplest form, deferred-compensation plans are nothing more than contractual arrangements under which an employer agrees to pay some portion of the employee's compensation at a specific future date. The arrangement is unfunded: The employer accrues its liability for the deferred compensation but does not set aside any cash or property to secure the liability.

Employees who agree to this arrangement don't recognize their deferred compensation as income because they are not in actual or constructive receipt of any payment.[58] These

---

[57] U.S. Bureau of Labor Statistics, National Compensation Survey, March 2011.
[58] Rev. Rul. 60-31, 1960-1 CB 174. See also §409A.

employees will recognize income in the future year in which their employer makes good on its obligation to pay the deferred compensation. On the employer's side of the arrangement, the accrued liability for deferred compensation is a current expense for financial statement purposes. However, employers are not allowed to deduct deferred compensation until the year of payment when the employee includes the compensation in income.[59]

Deferred Compensation	Mr. Jarvis, age 49 and NY's chief financial officer, received a $300,000 salary in 2012. At its December meeting, NY's board of directors awarded Mr. Jarvis a $150,000 bonus to be paid in three annual installments, beginning in the year he retires at age 60. NY did not set aside any cash or property to fund the deferred compensation but accrued a $150,000 liability on its balance sheet. Mr. Jarvis did not recognize the deferred compensation as 2012 income nor did NY deduct the deferred compensation expense on its 2012 Form 1120. Mr. Jarvis will recognize income and NY will claim a deduction over the three years during which the compensation is actually paid.

Employees who consider saving for retirement through a deferred-compensation plan must weigh the tax advantages against the financial risk inherent in the plan. In the case of an unfunded plan, the employee is an unsecured creditor of the employer with respect to the deferred compensation. If the employer is financially secure, the employee's retirement is equally secure. But if the employer's business should fail and the employer defaults on its liabilities, the employee may discover that her right to deferred compensation has little or no value as a source of retirement income.

Keogh Plans for Self-Employed Individuals

Objective 8
Describe the tax benefit of a Keogh plan to a self-employed individual.

Individuals who earn self-employment income can make annual contributions to a **Keogh plan** (named after the congressman who sponsored the legislation that created this qualified plan).[60] These payments are deductible as an above-the-line deduction in the computation of AGI. Thus, individuals pay no income tax on the business earnings invested in their Keogh plans.[61] Because Keogh plans are qualified retirement plans, the earnings generated by the financial assets held in the plan are tax exempt. Accordingly, sole proprietors and partners can take advantage of Keogh plans to accumulate tax-deferred savings in the same way that employees take advantage of their employer-provided plans.

Like employer-provided plans, Keogh plans must be administered by an independent trustee. Commercial banks, credit unions, brokerage firms, and other financial institutions typically serve as trustees for the prototype Keogh plans they maintain and manage for their individual clients. While Keogh plans can be either defined-benefit or defined-contribution plans, the latter type is more popular. Individuals who own defined-contribution Keogh plans can defer the *lesser* of 20 percent of self-employment income or an inflation-adjusted base amount ($50,000 in 2012) each year.[62] For purposes of computing this limitation, self-employment income is reduced by the deduction for one-half of the individual's self-employment tax.

[59] §404(a)(5). Deferred-compensation plans typically require the employer to accrue interest on its liability to the employee. Employers may not deduct this interest until the year it is actually paid to the employee. *Albertson's Inc.* v. *Commissioner,* 42 F.3d 537 (CA-9, 1994), *cert. denied,* 516 U.S. 807 (1995).

[60] §401(c) and §404(a)(8).

[61] They do, however, pay self-employment tax on this income. *Gale* v. *United States,* 768 F. Supp. 1305 (ND Ill., 1991).

[62] IRS Publication 560, *Retirement Plans for Small Business,* p. 20–21.

Keogh Plan Contribution	Mr. Abeg's sole proprietorship generated $63,000 net profit in 2012 on which he paid self-employment tax. He deducted $4,451 of the SE tax in the computation of AGI. His self-employment income is computed as follows.

Net profit from sole proprietorship	$63,000
SE tax deduction	(4,451)
Self-employment income	$58,549

Mr. Abeg's 2012 contribution to his Keogh plan is limited to the lesser of 20 percent of his self-employment income or $50,000. Therefore, his maximum deductible contribution to the plan is $11,710 (20 percent of $58,549).

Keogh plans have a downside for self-employed individuals who hire employees to work in their business: The plan must provide retirement benefits to such employees on a nondiscriminatory basis. In other words, the owner can't use a Keogh plan to defer tax on her own earnings unless the plan allows her employees to do the same with respect to their compensation. The owner's tax savings from the Keogh plan are eroded by the incremental cost of including employees in the plan. Clearly, the self-employed person with no employees is the ideal candidate for a Keogh plan.[63]

INDIVIDUAL RETIREMENT ACCOUNTS

Objective 9
Describe the tax benefits of IRAs and Roth IRAs.

Every person who earns employee compensation or self-employment income can save for retirement through a tax-favored individual retirement account (IRA). People establish IRAs with commercial banks or other financial institutions that serve as trustee of the account. IRAs are tax-exempt, so that the earnings on the account grow at a before-tax rate of return. When an owner withdraws funds from the account, the tax consequences depend on whether the account is a **traditional IRA** or a **Roth IRA**. In very general terms, withdrawals from traditional IRAs are taxable as ordinary income, so the earnings on the account are *tax-deferred*. Withdrawals from Roth IRAs are nontaxable, so the earnings on the account are *tax-exempt*. The differences between traditional and Roth IRAs are described in detail in this section.

Contribution Limits

In 2012, individuals can contribute up to $5,000 to their IRAs, and those who have reached age 50 by the end of the year can contribute an additional $1,000 *catch-up* contribution. The annual contribution amount cannot exceed 100 percent of the individual's compensation/self-employment income.[64] For married couples filing jointly, this limit is based on their combined compensation/self-employment income.[65]

---

[63] Self-employed individuals can maintain Section 401(k) plans. By making elective contributions to these "solo" or "mini" 401(k) plans in addition to deductible contributions to their Keogh plans, self-employed individuals can defer tax on the maximum annual amount of their self-employment income. See Reg. §1.401(k)-1(a)(6)(i).

[64] §408(a)(1), 408A(c)(2), and §219(b). Contribution amounts are adjusted annually for inflation.

[65] §219(c). Married individuals filing separate returns are subject to special restrictions regarding IRA contributions. However, such individuals who live apart at all times during a taxable year are considered single taxpayers for IRA purposes. §219(g)(4).

IRA Contributions	Mr. Swazey (age 19 and single) earned $3,725 self-employment income. His maximum IRA contribution is $3,725.
	
	    Miss Kwan (age 25 and single) earned $22,050 in wages. Her maximum IRA contribution is $5,000.
	
	    Mr. LaTour (age 36) earned a $47,200 salary and Mrs. LaTour (age 37) earned $4,180 from a part-time job. Because the LaTours file a joint return and their combined compensation exceeds $10,000, they can each contribute the $5,000 maximum to their IRAs.
	
	    Mrs. Dhaliwal (age 64) earned $41,950 self-employment income. Her maximum IRA contribution is $6,000 ($5,000 + $1,000 catch-up contribution).

Individuals can contribute the maximum to their traditional IRAs regardless of their income level. However, the maximum annual contribution to a Roth IRA may be limited based on the contributor's AGI. If AGI exceeds a phaseout threshold, the maximum contribution is reduced by a phaseout percentage. This percentage equals the excess AGI divided by a phaseout range. The 2012 phaseout threshold is $173,000 for married individuals filing jointly and $110,000 for unmarried individuals. The 2012 phaseout range is $10,000 for married individuals filing jointly and $15,000 for unmarried individuals.[66]

Limited Roth IRA Contribution	Mr. Tran (age 40 and single) wants to contribute to a Roth IRA. Because his AGI is $116,670, the amount of his contribution is limited to $2,775.

AGI	$116,670
Phaseout threshold (single)	(110,000)
Excess AGI	$ 6,670

$6,670 ÷ $15,000 = .445 phaseout percentage

Maximum contribution	$5,000
	.445
Contribution phaseout	$2,225
Limited contribution ($5,000 − $2,225)	$2,775

In addition to his $2,775 contribution to a Roth IRA, Mr. Tran can make a $2,225 contribution to a traditional IRA. Thus, his IRA contributions for the year equal the $5,000 maximum.

There is one additional difference between traditional and Roth IRA contributions that deserves mention. Individuals can't contribute to a traditional IRA after reaching age 70½. This age limit on contributions does not apply to Roth IRAs.[67]

Age Limit	Mrs. Shuli, a widow who is age 73, works as a part-time employee. This year, her wages totaled $23,700 and her AGI was $39,900. Mrs. Shuli can't make any contribution to a traditional IRA, but she can contribute up to the $6,000 maximum ($5,000 + $1,000 catch-up contribution) to a Roth IRA.

Deduction of IRA Contributions

Traditional IRAs

Deductibility of contributions to traditional IRAs is governed by a complex web of rules. Such contributions can be fully deductible, partially deductible, or nondeductible; any

[66] §408A(c)(3). Phaseout thresholds are adjusted annually for inflation.

[67] §219(d)(1) and §408A(c)(4).

allowable deduction is above the line in the computation of AGI. Note that any deductible portion of a contribution consists of before-tax dollars, while any nondeductible portion consists of after-tax dollars. Deductibility depends on two factors: the contributor's status as an *active participant* in any other qualified retirement plan and the contributor's AGI.[68]

For individuals who actively participate in an employer-sponsored defined benefit, defined contribution, or Keogh plan, the rules for deducting a contribution to a traditional IRA can be summarized as follows.

- If AGI is below a phaseout threshold, contributions are fully deductible. The 2012 phaseout threshold is $92,000 for married individuals filing jointly and $58,000 for unmarried individuals.[69]
- If AGI exceeds the phaseout threshold, the deduction is reduced by a percentage equal to the excess AGI divided by a phaseout range. The phaseout range is $20,000 for married individuals filing jointly and $10,000 for unmarried individuals.
- The deduction is reduced to zero for married individuals filing jointly with AGI in excess of $112,000 and unmarried individuals with AGI in excess of $68,000.

Deduction for Active Participant

Mr. and Mrs. Howard each made the $5,000 maximum contribution to their traditional IRAs. Both spouses are active participants in their respective employer's profit-sharing plan. Before any deduction for their IRA contributions, the AGI on their joint return is $103,700. Because their excess AGI falls in the phaseout range, their IRA contributions are partially deductible.

AGI before IRA deduction	$ 103,700
Phaseout threshold (MFJ)	(92,000)
Excess AGI	$ 11,700

$11,700 ÷ $20,000 = .585 phaseout percentage

Each spouse's IRA contribution	$5,000
	.585
Deduction phaseout	$2,925

Consequently, Mr. and Mrs. Howard can deduct $2,075 of each IRA contribution, and their AGI is $99,550.

AGI before IRA deduction		$103,700
Each spouse's IRA contribution	$ 5,000	
Deduction phaseout	(2,925)	
Deductible contribution	$ 2,075	
	2	
IRA deduction		(4,150)
AGI		$99,550

---

[68] §219(g).

[69] Phaseout thresholds are adjusted annually for inflation.

For individuals who do *not* actively participate in any other qualified retirement plan, the general rule is that IRA contributions are fully deductible, regardless of the contributor's AGI.

Deduction for Nonparticipant	Mr. Radick, age 48 and single, made a $5,000 contribution to his traditional IRA. Mr. Radick is not an active participant in any other qualified retirement plan. His AGI before any IRA deduction is $364,100. Because his IRA contribution is fully deductible, Mr. Radick's AGI is $359,100.

The general rule is subject to a major exception for a nonparticipant who files a joint return *with a spouse* who is an active participant in a qualified retirement plan. In this case, the nonparticipant's deduction is reduced by a percentage equal to the couple's AGI in excess of a phaseout threshold ($173,000 in 2012) divided by $10,000. Thus, the deduction is reduced to zero when AGI exceeds $183,000.[70]

Deduction for Nonparticipant Spouse	Mr. and Mrs. Dowd (both age 60) each made the $6,000 maximum contribution ($5,000 + $1,000 catch-up contribution) to their traditional IRAs. Mr. Dowd is an active participant in a Keogh plan, but Mrs. Dowd is not an active participant in any other qualified plan. The couple files a joint return.
	• Assume the Dowds' AGI before any IRA deduction is $83,800. This AGI is below the $92,000 phaseout threshold (MFJ) for active participants, so Mr. Dowd's contribution is fully deductible. The AGI is below the $173,000 phaseout threshold for a nonparticipant spouse, so Mrs. Dowd's contribution is fully deductible. The Dowds' AGI is $71,800 ($83,800 − $12,000).
	• Now assume the Dowds' AGI before any IRA deduction is $129,700. This AGI is above the AGI phaseout range (MFJ) for active participants, so Mr. Dowd's contribution is nondeductible. But the AGI is below the $173,000 phaseout threshold for a nonparticipant spouse, so Mrs. Dowd's contribution is fully deductible. The Dowds' AGI is $123,700 ($129,700 − $6,000).
	• Now assume the Dowds' AGI before any IRA deduction is $215,600. This AGI is above the AGI phaseout range (MFJ) for active participants, so Mr. Dowd's contribution is nondeductible. The AGI is also above the AGI phaseout range for a nonparticipant spouse, so Mrs. Dowd's contribution is nondeductible. The Dowds' AGI is $215,600.

Roth IRAs

Contributions to Roth IRAs are subject to one simple rule: Such contributions are not deductible and therefore consist only of after-tax dollars.[71]

Nondeductible Contribution	Mr. and Mrs. Bartlett each made a $2,000 contribution to their Roth IRAs. Regardless of their AGI and whether either spouse actively participates in another qualified retirement plan, their $4,000 contribution is nondeductible on their joint return.

Withdrawals from IRAs

Traditional IRAs

Owners of traditional IRAs must begin withdrawing funds no later than April 1 of the year following the year in which they reach age 70½. Annual withdrawals are subject to the

---

[70] §219(g)(7).

[71] §408A(c)(1).

minimum distribution requirement described on page 455.[72] Any portion of the withdrawal attributable to the owner's nondeductible contributions is a nontaxable return of investment. The remainder of the withdrawal (the portion attributable to deductible contributions and accumulated earnings) is ordinary income. The nontaxable portion of an annual withdrawal is based on the ratio of the owner's unrecovered investment at the beginning of the year to the current year value of the IRA. The current year value is defined as the year-end IRA balance *plus* current year withdrawals.[73]

Traditional IRA Withdrawals	Mr. Potter owns a traditional IRA to which he made $44,000 of contributions, $19,000 of which were nondeductible. In 2011, Mr. Potter retired at age 63 and made a $15,000 withdrawal from his IRA. The account balance at year-end was $73,220. In 2012, he withdrew $17,500 from the IRA. The account balance at year-end was $60,200. (Note that the IRA continued to earn tax-exempt income during both years.) The yearly withdrawals that Mr. Potter must recognize as ordinary income are computed as follows.

		2011		2012
Year-end balance in IRA		$73,220		$60,200
Plus withdrawals during the year		15,000		17,500
Current year value of IRA		$88,220		$77,700
Nondeductible contributions	$19,000		$19,000	
Prior year recoveries	(–0–)		(3,231)	
Unrecovered investment	$19,000		$15,769	
Ratio of unrecovered investment to current year value	.2154		.2029	
Withdrawal during the year		$15,000		$17,500
		.2154		.2029
Nontaxable recovery of investment		$ 3,231		$ 3,551
Ordinary income (withdrawal − nontaxable recovery)		$11,769		$13,949

As Mr. Potter continues to withdraw funds from his IRA, he will treat a portion of each withdrawal as a nontaxable return of investment. By the time he completely liquidates the account, he will have recouped his $19,000 nondeductible contributions on a tax-free basis.

Owners who make withdrawals from their IRAs before reaching age 59½ must pay the 10 percent penalty described earlier in the chapter. However, this penalty is waived in a number of situations. For instance, an individual can withdraw funds from an IRA to pay higher education expenses (tuition, fees, books, supplies, and equipment). An individual who qualifies as a first-time homebuyer can withdraw up to $10,000 to finance the purchase of a home. While some or all of the withdrawal must be included in the owner's taxable income, the taxable portion escapes the premature withdrawal penalty.[74]

[72] §408(a)(6).
[73] §408(d)(2).
[74] §72(t)(2)(E) and (F).

Roth IRAs

Owners of Roth IRAs are not subject to the minimum distribution requirement. Consequently, they don't have to begin withdrawing funds at age 70½ and can allow the account to grow at a tax-free rate until death.[75] When the owner makes a *qualified* withdrawal from a Roth IRA, the entire withdrawal is tax-exempt. Thus, the owner is never taxed on the portion of the withdrawal attributable to accumulated earnings in the account. A withdrawal is qualified only if it occurs after the owner reaches age 59½ *and* after the five-year period beginning with the first year in which the owner contributed to the account.[76]

Roth IRA Withdrawals	This year, Mr. Stone withdrew $14,000 from his Roth IRA to pay for a family vacation. Mr. Stone made the first contribution to this account in 1999. If Mr. Stone is older than 59½, the withdrawal is qualified, and the entire $14,000 is tax-exempt. If Mr. Stone is younger than age 59½, the withdrawal is not qualified. As a result, Mr. Stone must include the taxable portion (attributable to accumulated earnings) in gross income and pay the 10 percent premature withdrawal penalty on the inclusion.

Rollovers to IRAs

Individuals who receive distributions from qualified employer-sponsored plans can avoid income recognition by rolling over the distribution into a traditional IRA. The use of so-called **rollover IRAs** to prolong tax deferral has been a standard planning technique for decades.

Rollover IRA	Mr. Vega, age 49, participated in his corporate employer's Section 401(k) plan for 23 years. This year, he quit his corporate job to go into business for himself. Mr. Vega instructed his former employer to transfer the $148,800 balance in his Section 401(k) account to a new rollover IRA that he opened with a local bank. Mr. Vega does not include any amount of this direct rollover in gross income.

Beginning in 2010, distributions from qualified plans and withdrawals from traditional IRAs can be rolled over into a Roth IRA, *regardless of the income level of the taxpayer.* This new law makes Roth IRAs available to millions of individuals who are precluded from contributing directly to a Roth IRA because their AGI is too high.[77]

Individuals who roll over funds from an employer-sponsored plan or traditional IRA into a Roth IRA are converting a *tax-deferred* investment to a *tax-exempt* investment. Consequently, they must treat this conversion as a taxable event by including the taxable portion of the rollover amount in gross income. Individuals who took advantage of the new law in 2010 enjoyed a one-time benefit: Even though the rollover occurred in 2010, individuals could elect to include one-half of the taxable portion in 2011 gross income and one-half in 2012 gross income.[78]

---

[75] §408A(c)(5).

[76] §408A(d)(1) and (2). First-time homebuyers can make a qualified withdrawal of $10,000 to finance the purchase of a home.

[77] §408A(c)(3)(B) and (C) as effective for taxable years beginning after December 31, 2009.

[78] §408A(d)(3)(A). The amount included in gross income is not subject to any premature withdrawal penalty.

Rollover to *Roth IRA*	Ms. Lenz owned a traditional IRA that she funded entirely with nondeductible contributions. On August 9, 2010, she converted this IRA to a Roth IRA by rolling over the $173,200 balance in the account. The taxable portion of the balance was $97,500. Ms. Lenz elected to include $48,750 in 2011 gross income and $48,750 in 2012 gross income.

As this example demonstrates, individuals who make a rollover into a Roth IRA incur an up-front tax cost. In return, the future earnings on the account are tax-exempt, and the owner is not required to begin liquidating the account at age 70½. Whether a rollover is advantageous depends on the individual's unique financial circumstances. A major consideration is the comparison between the individual's current marginal tax rate and the expected future tax rate on his retirement income.

Current and *Future Rates*	Mr. Kay is age 57 and expects to retire in 10 years. He owns a traditional IRA funded by both deductible and nondeductible contributions. The current account balance is $65,000: $10,200 represents Mr. Kay's after-tax investment (nondeductible contributions) and $54,800 would be taxable upon liquidation of the account. Mr. Kay's current marginal tax rate is 33 percent, and he believes that his marginal rate in retirement will be at least 40 percent. The following table compares Mr. Kay's after-tax retirement income if he maintains the traditional IRA with his income if he rolls the after-tax balance into a Roth IRA.

	Traditional IRA	*Roth IRA*
Pretax current balance	$ 65,000	$ 65,000
Tax cost of rollover ($54,800 × 33%)		(18,084)
After-tax balance	$ 65,000	$ 46,916
Future value of after-tax balance (6% assumed annual growth over 10 years)	$116,405	$ 84,019
Tax cost of withdrawal ([$116,405 − $10,200 nontaxable] × 40%)	(42,482)	
After-tax retirement income	$ 73,923	$ 84,019

If Mr. Kay's assumption about his future tax rate is right, the Roth IRA option results in more retirement income. But what if his assumption is wrong, and his future tax rate proves to be only 28 percent?

	Traditional IRA	*Roth IRA*
Future value of after-tax balance	$116,405	$ 84,019
Tax cost of withdrawal ([$116,405 − $10,200 nontaxable] × 28%)	(29,737)	
After-tax retirement income	$ 86,668	$ 84,019

In this case, Mr. Kay's decision to roll over his traditional IRA into a Roth IRA will ultimately result in less retirement income.

The new rules for rollovers into Roth IRAs certainly complicate tax planning for individual retirement accounts. More than ever before, individuals who plan on saving for retirement through either a traditional or Roth IRA should seek the advice of a tax professional to make a well-informed investment decision.

Conclusion

In Chapter 15, we've explored the tax consequences of compensation arrangements between employer and employee. These arrangements can consist of a mix of cash payments and noncash fringe benefits, many of which are excluded from the recipient's income. Corporate employers frequently include stock options in the compensation packages offered to key employees. By understanding both the economic implications and the tax consequences of the various forms of compensation, employers and employees can negotiate to improve their respective after-tax positions.

No area of the tax law offers a better opportunity for effective long-term planning than qualified retirement plans. The tax deferral available through these plans is one of the surest routes toward wealth maximization. Young adults who are just beginning their careers should take immediate advantage of any qualified retirement plans sponsored by their employers. Entrepreneurs who own their own businesses should consider making regular contributions to a Keogh plan. And every working person, regardless of age, who can afford to save even a few dollars each year toward retirement should open an IRA.

Sources of Book/Tax Differences

Permanent

- Incentive stock options
- Nondeductible compensation

Temporary

- Nonqualified stock options
- Nonqualified deferred compensation

Key Terms

bargain element *453*
cafeteria plan *451*
deferred
  compensation *463*
defined-benefit plan *461*
defined-contribution
  plan *461*
employee *442*
employee stock ownership
  plan (ESOP) *462*
employer-provided
  plan *460*
expatriate *448*

foreign earned income
  exclusion *448*
fringe benefits *449*
incentive stock option
  (ISO) *454*
independent
  contractor *442*
Keogh plan *464*
minimum
  distribution *459*
miscellaneous itemized
  deductions *456*
moving expenses *456*

performance-based
  compensation *446*
premature withdrawal *459*
profit-sharing plan *462*
qualified retirement
  plans *457*
rollover contribution *460*
rollover IRA *470*
Roth IRA *465*
Section 401(k) plan *462*
stock option *452*
traditional IRA *465*

Questions and Problems for Discussion

1. Discuss how the presence of a strong labor union may change the nature of the market in which rank-and-file employees negotiate with their employer.

2. Discuss the difference in the relationship between an employer and employee and a client and an independent contractor.

3. Mr. U accepted an engagement to perform consulting services for MK Company. The engagement will last at least 18 months. Identify any reasons why Mr. U might prefer to be classified as an MK employee rather than as an independent contractor.

4. Discuss the practical reasons why the tax law authorizes the IRS to collect unwithheld employee payroll tax from the employer rather than the employees who were liable for the tax.

5. A reasonable compensation problem for the sole shareholder of a regular corporation is quite different from the reasonable compensation problem for the sole shareholder of an S corporation. What is the difference?

6. Mr. B owns 10 percent of the stock of ABC Inc. and is the corporation's director of marketing. ABC has a medical insurance plan for its employees. This year, it paid $1,400 of premiums to the insurance carrier for Mr. B's coverage. Contrast the treatment of this payment to Mr. B if ABC is a regular corporation or an S corporation.

7. This year, publicly held Corporation DF paid its CEO a $1.4 million salary, only $1 million of which was deductible. It also accrued a $200,000 liability for deferred compensation payable in the year 2016 (when the CEO must retire). To what extent does either transaction result in a difference between DF's book income and taxable income? Is the difference permanent or temporary?

8. Discuss how employees who routinely incur unreimbursed employment-related expenses can maximize the tax benefit of the expenses by bunching them into one year.

9. Mr. Z was recently promoted to an executive position by his corporate employer. The corporation now requires him to entertain clients much more frequently, and Mr. Z expects to incur at least $1,000 out-of-pocket business entertainment expenses each month. The corporation will either reimburse him directly for these expenses or give him a salary bonus at year-end that indirectly covers his annual expenses. Which option should Mr. Z choose and why?

10. Six years ago, Corporation AT granted a stock option to employee N to purchase 1,000 shares of AT stock for $15 per share. At date of grant, AT stock was selling for $14.10 per share. Over the last six years, the market price has steadily declined to $11.80 per share. What are the tax consequences to employee N when the option lapses?

11. Two years ago, Corporation WZ granted a stock option to employee R to purchase 2,500 shares of WZ stock for $30 per share. Since the date of grant, the market price of the stock has risen steadily and reached $31 just days ago. However, the option period is 10 years. Should R exercise the option immediately to minimize the income he must recognize or should he wait for eight more years before exercising the option?

12. Describe the differences between a defined-benefit plan and a defined-contribution plan.

13. How does the fact that employees have a vested right to their benefits reduce the risk of participating in an employer-sponsored qualified retirement plan?

14. How does the fact that an employer-sponsored qualified retirement plan is administered by an independent trustee reduce the employees' risk of participating in the plan?

Application Problems

For the following problems, assume the taxable year is 2012.

1. Greg Company agreed to pay Ms. Bilko $45,000 compensation for services performed for the company.
   a. Compare the income tax consequences to Greg and Ms. Bilko if she is an employee or if she is an independent contractor.
   b. Compare the payroll tax consequences to Greg and Ms. Bilko if she is an employee or if she is an independent contractor.
   c. Compare the income tax *payment* requirements to Ms. Bilko if she is an employee or if she is an independent contractor.

2. Trent Inc. needs an additional worker on a multiyear project. It could hire an employee for a $65,000 annual salary. Alternatively, it could engage an independent contractor for a $72,000 annual fee. If Trent's marginal income tax rate is 34 percent, which option minimizes the after-tax cost of obtaining the worker?

3. Marlo, a publicly held corporation with a 35 percent marginal tax rate, is negotiating a compensation package with its CEO. In each of the following cases, determine Marlo's after-tax cost of the compensation. In making your calculation, ignore the employer payroll tax.

    a. Marlo will pay its CEO a $1,300,000 annual salary.

    b. Marlo will pay its CEO a $900,000 annual salary plus a $500,000 year-end bonus if its gross revenues increase by at least 5 percent for the year. This bonus qualifies as performance-based compensation.

4. Mr. and Mrs. Brock own a bakery. Their marginal tax rate on the bakery's income is 28 percent. The Brocks' 17-year-old daughter Megan works in the bakery after school and on weekends. This year, Megan earned $9,784 of wages, which was her only income. The Brocks claim Megan as a dependent on their tax return.

    a. Compute Megan's income tax this year.

    b. Compute the Brock family's income tax savings from Megan's employment.

5. Mr. and Mrs. Soon are the sole shareholders of SW Inc. For the last three years, SW has employed their son as a sales representative and paid him a $30,000 annual salary. During a recent IRS audit, the revenue agent discovered that the son has never made a sale and spends most of his time playing saxophone in a jazz band. Compute the potential tax cost of this discovery to Mr. and Mrs. Soon under the following assumptions. In making your calculations, ignore any payroll tax implications.

    a. Mr. and Mrs. Soon are in the 35 percent tax bracket, and SW is an S corporation.

    b. Mr. and Mrs. Soon are in the 35 percent tax bracket, and SW is a taxable corporation in the 35 percent tax bracket.

6. Mr. Kim is a U.S. citizen who has been stationed at his employer's Tokyo office for the last six years.

    a. Compute Mr. Kim's AGI if his only income was his $65,000 salary.

    b. Compute Mr. Kim's AGI if his only income for the year was his $169,000 salary.

    c. Under Japanese law, Mr. Kim is a permanent resident and must pay Japanese income tax on his salary. Assuming that the Japanese individual tax rates exceed the U.S. rates, will Mr. Kim owe U.S. tax on any portion of his salary?

7. Mrs. F, age 57, participates in the group-term life insurance plan sponsored by her corporate employer. According to Treasury tables, the cost of $1,000 of life insurance for a 57-year-old person is 43 cents per month. Determine the taxable income that Mrs. F must recognize assuming that:

    a. The plan provides $40,000 coverage.

    b. The plan provides $275,000 coverage.

8. Mrs. ST's corporate employer has a cafeteria plan under which its employees can receive a $3,000 year-end Christmas bonus or enroll in a qualified medical reimbursement plan that pays up to $3,000 of annual medical bills. Mrs. ST is in a 28 percent tax bracket, and her medical bills average $2,300 each year.

    a. Should Mrs. ST choose the cash bonus or the nontaxable fringe benefit? (Ignore any payroll tax implications.)

    b. Does your answer change if Mrs. ST is in the 15 percent tax bracket?

9. Mr. N and Mr. R are employed by HD Inc., which provides its employees with free parking. If the parking were not available, Mr. N would pay $35 a month to a city garage. Mr. R uses public transportation to commute. HD offers a complete family medical plan to its employees in which both Mr. N and Mr. R participate. Mr. N's family consists of five people, while Mr. R is single. Consequently, Mr. N's annual cost of comparable medical insurance would be $9,000, while Mr. R's cost would be just $4,100.

   a. Mr. N has a 28 percent marginal tax rate. How much additional salary would he have to earn to provide himself with parking and medical insurance?

   b. Mr. R has a 35 percent marginal tax rate. How much additional salary would he have to earn to provide himself with parking and medical insurance?

10. Peet Company provides free on-site day care for its employees with preschool children. Determine the pretax value of the care for each of the following employees.

    a. Mrs. U, who has a 33 percent marginal tax rate and who would pay $10,675 annually for day care for her three children.

    b. Mr. Z, who has a 15 percent marginal tax rate and who would pay $3,300 annually for day care for his one child.

11. This year, Gogo Inc. granted a nonqualified stock option to Mrs. Mill to buy 10,000 shares of Gogo stock for $8 per share for five years. At date of grant, Gogo stock was selling on a regional securities market for $7.87 per share. Gogo recorded $26,700 compensation expense for the estimated value of the option.

    a. How much income must Mrs. Mill recognize this year?

    b. Can Gogo deduct the $26,700 expense on this year's tax return?

    c. Assuming a 35 percent tax rate, compute Gogo's deferred tax asset or deferred tax liability (identify which) resulting from the $26,700 compensation expense.

12. Refer to the facts in the preceding problem. Five years after Gogo granted the option to Mrs. Mill, she exercised it on a day when Gogo stock was selling for $10.31 per share.

    a. How much income must Mrs. Mill recognize in the year of exercise?

    b. What is Gogo's tax deduction in the year of exercise?

    c. What is the effect of the exercise on Gogo's book income and deferred taxes?

13. In 2005, BT granted a nonqualified stock option to Ms. P to buy 500 shares of BT stock at $20 per share for five years. At date of grant, BT stock was trading on Nasdaq for $18.62 per share. In 2012, Ms. P exercised the option when BT's stock was trading at $31.40 per share.

    a. How much income did Ms. P recognize in 2005 and 2012 because of the stock option?

    b. Compute Ms. P's basis in the 500 shares.

    c. What are the tax consequences of the stock option to BT in 2005? In 2012?

14. In 2004, BB granted an incentive stock option (ISO) to Mr. Y to buy 8,000 shares of BB stock at $7 per share for 10 years. At date of grant, BB stock was trading on the AMEX for $6.23 per share. In 2012, Mr. Y exercised the option when BB's stock was trading at $22.81 per share.

    a. How much income did Mr. Y recognize in 2004 and 2012 because of the ISO?

    b. Compute Mr. Y's basis in the 8,000 shares.

    c. What are the tax consequences of the stock option to BB in 2004? In 2012?

15. Two years ago, Mrs. EL was granted a stock option from her corporate employer. At date of grant, the stock was selling at $14 per share, and the strike price was $18 per share. This year, Mrs. EL sold the option to an unrelated party for $26,000. How much gain does she recognize on this transaction?

16. In 2005 (year 0), Mrs. L exercised a stock option by paying $100 per share for 225 shares of ABC stock. The market price at date of exercise was $312 per share. In 2012, she sold the 225 shares for $480 per share. Assuming that Mrs. L is in the 35 percent tax bracket, has a 15 percent capital gains rate, and uses a 6 percent discount rate, compute the 2005 NPV of the cash flows from the exercise and sale if:

    a. The stock option was nonqualified.

    b. The stock option was an ISO.

17. Mr. T (a 45-year-old single taxpayer) exercised an ISO and purchased $380,000 worth of his employer's stock for only $113,000. His only other income was his $158,500 salary, and he does not itemize deductions. Compute Mr. T's income tax including any AMT.

18. Ms. C paid $500 of union dues and $619 for small tools used on the job. In each of the following cases, compute her after-tax cost of these employment-related expenses.

    a. Ms. C's employer paid her a $1,119 reimbursement.

    b. Ms. C received no reimbursement. Her AGI is $16,450, she does not itemize deductions, and her marginal tax rate is 10 percent.

    c. Ms. C received no reimbursement. Her AGI is $70,150, she itemizes deductions, and her marginal tax rate is 28 percent.

    d. Ms. C received no reimbursement. Her AGI is $25,300, she itemizes deductions, and her marginal tax rate is 15 percent.

19. Mr. and Mrs. JN moved from Lincoln, Nebraska, to Kansas City, Missouri, so that Mr. JN could take a job with the HM Company. As part of his employment agreement, Mr. JN received a $7,500 moving expense allowance. What is the effect of this $7,500 cash receipt on the couple's AGI assuming that:

    a. Their deductible moving expense was $8,800?

    b. Their deductible moving expense was $6,100?

20. Mr. Tib is employed by RQA Inc. This year, Mr. Tib incurred $3,160 of employment-related entertainment expenses and $4,750 of employment-related moving expenses. Mr. Tib's AGI *before* consideration of these expenses was $61,000, he itemizes deductions, and his marginal tax rate is 25 percent. In each of the following cases, determine Mr. Tib's after-tax cost of the $7,910 total expenses.

    a. RQA reimbursed him for both the entertainment expense and the moving expense.

    b. RQA reimbursed him for $1,500 of the entertainment expense and $4,000 of the moving expense.

    c. RQA did not reimburse him for any of the expenses.

21. Mrs. Kirk withdrew $30,000 from a retirement account and used the money to furnish her new home. Her marginal tax rate is 25 percent. Compute the tax cost of the withdrawal in each of the following cases.

    a. Mrs. Kirk is 56 years old. She withdrew the money from a personal savings account.

    b. Mrs. Kirk is 56 years old. She withdrew the money from her employer-sponsored qualified plan upon her retirement from the company.

    c. Mrs. Kirk is 56 years old. She withdrew the money from her employer-sponsored qualified plan, but she intends to work for the employer for at least 10 more years.

    d. Mrs. Kirk is 61 years old. She withdrew the money from her employer-sponsored qualified plan, but she intends to work for the employer for at least four more years.

22. Mr. Evon, who has participated in his employer's qualified defined-benefit plan for 38 years, retired in June. What is his maximum annual pension benefit assuming that:

    a. His average compensation for his three highest compensation years was $143,890.

    b. His average compensation for his three highest compensation years was $229,300.

23. Mrs. V participates in her employer's qualified profit-sharing plan. What is the maximum contribution to her retirement account, assuming that:

    a. Her annual compensation was $38,200?

    b. Her annual compensation was $180,000?

24. Ms. Jost participates in her employer's Section 401(k) plan, which obligates the employer to contribute 25 cents for every dollar that an employee elects to contribute to the plan. This year, Ms. Jost's salary is $110,000, and she elects to contribute the maximum to her Section 401(k) account.

    a. How much of Ms. Jost's salary is taxable this year?

    b. Compute the total contribution to Ms. Jost's plan.

    c. Compute the employer's deduction for compensation paid to Ms. Jost.

25. Mr. G is the CFO of Petro Inc. This year, his salary was $625,000. Petro paid him $500,000 during the year and accrued an unfunded liability to pay him the $125,000 balance in the year he retires at age 60.

    a. How much compensation income does Mr. G recognize this year?

    b. What is Petro's book expense for Mr. G's current compensation?

    c. What is Petro's tax deduction for Mr. G's current compensation?

    d. Assuming a 35 percent tax rate, compute Petro's deferred tax asset or deferred tax liability (identify which) resulting from the compensation expense.

26. Refer to the facts in the preceding problem. Petro Inc. pays $125,000 deferred compensation to Mr. G in 2016, the year of his retirement.

    a. How much compensation income does Mr. G recognize in 2016?

    b. What is Petro's tax deduction for the payment to Mr. G?

    c. What is the effect of the payment on Petro's book income and deferred taxes?

27. MN's compensation package for its CEO consisted of a $600,000 salary plus $200,000 unfunded deferred compensation. The CEO will receive the $200,000 when he retires in 2018. He is also a participant in MN's qualified pension plan. MN contributed $21,000 to fund a $90,000 annual pension that the CEO will begin to receive in 2018.

    a. Compute MN's financial statement expense for the CEO's compensation.

    b. Compute MN's tax deduction for the CEO's compensation.

    c. Compute the CEO's taxable compensation income.

    d. How much taxable income will the CEO recognize in 2018?

28. Mr. and Mrs. WD had the following income items.

Mr. WD's salary	$105,000
Mrs. WD's earnings from self-employment	50,000

The income tax deduction for Mrs. WD's SE tax was $3,532. Mr. WD contributed the maximum to his Section 401(k) plan, and Mrs. WD contributed the maximum to her Keogh profit-sharing plan. Both spouses contributed $2,750 to their IRAs. Compute their AGI.

29. What is the maximum IRA contribution that Mr. JP can make under each of the following assumptions?

    a. He is age 20 and single. His only income item is $13,200 interest from a trust fund.

    b. He is age 40 and single. His only income item is a $31,900 share of ordinary income from a partnership.

    c. He is age 60 and single. His only income item is $24,200 wages from his job.

    d. He is age 46 and files a joint return with his wife. His sole proprietorship generates a $7,720 loss, and his wife's salary is $43,000.

30. Ms. Calhoun is age 51 and single. What is the maximum contribution that she can make to a Roth IRA if:

    a. Her AGI consists of an $89,400 salary from her employer?

    b. Her AGI consists of an $89,400 salary plus $26,000 interest and dividends from a trust fund?

    c. Her AGI consists of a $116,000 salary plus a $19,250 share of ordinary income from a partnership?

31. Ms. Ray is age 46 and single. Her employer made a $2,895 contribution to her qualified profit-sharing plan account, and she made the maximum contribution to her traditional IRA. Compute her IRA deduction if:

    a. Ms. Ray's $50,000 salary is her only income item.

    b. Ms. Ray's $63,250 salary is her only income item.

    c. Ms. Ray's $63,250 salary and $7,970 dividend income are her only income items.

32. Mr. and Mrs. DM file a joint tax return. Each spouse contributed $3,800 to a traditional IRA. In each of the following cases, compute the deduction for these contributions. The AGI in each case is *before* any deduction.

    a. Neither spouse is an active participant in a qualified retirement plan, and their AGI is $119,400.

    b. Mr. DM is an active participant, but Mrs. DM is not. Their AGI is $119,400.

    c. Both spouses are active participants, and their AGI is $89,200.

    d. Mr. DM is self-employed and does not have a Keogh plan. Mrs. DM is an active participant. Their AGI is $101,400.

33. Mr. GW is self-employed and makes annual contributions to a Keogh plan. Mrs. GW's employer does not offer any type of qualified retirement plan. Each spouse contributes $3,000 to a traditional IRA. In each of the following cases, compute the AGI on their joint return.

    a. AGI before an IRA deduction is $129,000.

    b. AGI before an IRA deduction is $181,100.

34. Mrs. Shin retired in 2011 at age 63 and made her first withdrawal of $20,000 from her traditional IRA. At year-end, the IRA balance was $89,200. In 2012, she withdrew $22,000 from the IRA. At year-end, the account balance was $71,100. Determine how much of each annual withdrawal was taxable assuming that:

    a. Mrs. Shin's contributions to her IRA were deductible.

    b. Mrs. Shin made $26,500 nondeductible contributions to the IRA.

    c. Mrs. Shin made $37,950 nondeductible contributions to the IRA.

35. Mrs. Kwan withdrew the entire $8,000 balance from her Roth IRA this year. Her total contributions to the account were $6,070, and her marginal tax rate is 15 percent. Determine the tax cost of the withdrawal if:

    a. Mrs. Kwan is age 63 and opened the Roth IRA three years ago.

    b. Mrs. Kwan is age 63 and opened the Roth IRA seven years ago.

    c. Mrs. Kwan is age 48 and opened the Roth IRA seven years ago.

36. Mrs. LR, age 64, plans to retire this December. She estimates that the balance in her IRA will be $86,500, which she plans to withdraw to finance the purchase of a condominium. Assuming that her marginal tax rate is 25 percent, compute her after-tax cash from the IRA liquidation assuming that:

    a. The IRA is a Roth IRA which she opened in 1999.

    b. The IRA is a traditional IRA to which she made only deductible contributions.

    c. The IRA is a traditional IRA to which she made $20,400 deductible and $32,600 nondeductible contributions.

37. Ms. Sturm owns a tax-deferred retirement account with a $200,000 current balance. She intends to roll over this balance into a new Roth IRA before the end of the year. Ms. Sturm's current marginal tax rate is 35 percent, but she believes that this rate will increase to 40 percent by the year in which she liquidates the Roth IRA. Compute Ms. Sturm's tax cost of converting her existing retirement account to a Roth IRA and the after-tax rollover if:

    a. The existing account is a Section 401(k) plan funded by Ms. Sturm's elective contributions and her employer's matching contributions.

    b. The existing account is a traditional IRA to which Ms. Sturm made $38,400 of nondeductible contributions.

38. Refer to the facts in the preceding problem. Assume that the $200,000 balance in Ms. Sturm's tax-deferred retirement account or the after-tax rollover to the Roth IRA would grow at a 7 percent rate for 15 years (future value factor 2.76). Compare the amount of Ms. Sturm's future after-tax retirement income from the tax-deferred account with the amount from the Roth IRA under each of the following assumptions.

    a. The tax-deferred account is a Section 401(k) plan, and Ms. Sturm's tax rate at retirement is 40 percent.

    b. The tax-deferred account is a Section 401(k) plan, and Ms. Sturm's tax rate at retirement is 35 percent.

    c. The tax-deferred account is a traditional IRA, and Ms. Sturm's tax rate at retirement is 40 percent.

    d. The tax-deferred account is a traditional IRA, and Ms. Sturm's tax rate at retirement is 35 percent.

Issue Recognition Problems

Identify the tax issue or issues suggested by the following situations and state each issue in the form of a question.

1. Early this year, Mrs. C's employer reassigned her from its Chicago office to its Memphis office. In May, she spent $1,100 on a house-hunting trip to Memphis. She located a new home and moved her family in September. In addition to her direct moving expenses, Mrs. C's employer reimbursed her for the cost of the house-hunting trip.

2. Ms. X is an executive with GG Inc., an international business operation. She flies over 150,000 business miles each year and accumulates considerable frequent-flier points

from the airlines. GG allows its employees to use their frequent-flier points for personal travel. In March, Ms. X used 100,000 points to obtain two first-class round-trip tickets to Paris, which she gave to her daughter as a wedding gift. The value of the tickets was $12,000.

3. Mr. K is a professor at a private university. The university waives the tuition for a faculty member's child who meets the entrance requirements. Mr. K's two children are enrolled in degree programs at the university. If not for the waiver, Mr. K would pay $16,000 annual tuition for each child.

4. Mr. DW has the full-time use of an automobile owned and maintained by his employer. This year, Mr. DW drove this company car 48,000 miles on business and 12,000 for personal reasons. He is not required to report this information to his employer. The employer included the $17,000 imputed value of the full-time use of the car as additional compensation on Mr. DW's Form W-2. Mr. DW's AGI was $196,000.

5. Ms. L is employed at VD's corporate headquarters and often works late hours. The headquarters building is located in a high-crime urban area. As a result, corporate policy is that any employee leaving the premises after 7:00 P.M. must take a cab home rather than walk or use the subway. VD pays the cab fare. However, it does not pay employee commuting expenses under any other circumstances. This year, VD spent $1,080 on cab fare for Ms. L.

6. Mr. G is employed by a closely held corporation that gave him a year-end bonus of 50 shares of stock worth $200 per share. However, Mr. G's ownership of the stock is restricted. If he resigns from his job at any time during the next four years, he forfeits the stock back to the corporation. During this four-year period, he can't sell the stock or pledge it as collateral for a loan. After four years, this restriction lapses, and his ownership of the 50 shares is unrestricted.

7. Mr. and Mrs. SK are both CPAs. Mr. SK is an employee of a national accounting firm, while Mrs. SK operates her own professional practice. Each year, the couple pays approximately $1,300 to subscribe to professional publications and research services that they both read and use in their work.

8. This year, TT Corporation agreed to defer $100,000 compensation owed to Ms. B, the director of research. TT funded its obligation by transferring $100,000 cash to a trust administered by a local bank. TT cannot reclaim these funds. However, the trust fund is subject to the claims of TT's general creditors. Ms. B has no right to the funds unless she works for TT until age 59, the mandatory retirement age.

9. Mr. T and Mr. V founded TV Corporation six years ago and have devoted every waking hour to the corporate business. During the first four years, neither shareholder received any salary. During the last two years, each shareholder received a $400,000 salary, which is about 180 percent of the average salary paid by comparable corporations to their unrelated officers.

10. Ms. J recently moved from Boston to Pittsburgh to take a job with OP Inc. She sold her home in Boston, and OP paid the $14,500 realtor's commission on the sale.

11. Mr. S was fired from his job because of unprofessional conduct. He believed that his reputation in the local business community was damaged and that he should make a new start in a different state. Consequently, he relocated his family to Phoenix and searched for suitable employment, which he had not found by the end of the year. His personal moving expenses totaled $3,820.

12. GHK recently granted a stock option to employee O to purchase 20,000 shares of stock for $11 per share. On the date of grant, GHK stock was selling for $12 on the NYSE.

13. Six years ago, Ms. PL paid $20 per share for 1,000 shares of her employer's stock. This stock is now worth $58 per share. Ms. PL wants to exercise a stock option to buy 1,000 more shares at a strike price of $29 per share. Because she does not have $29,000 cash readily available, she has requested that the corporation allow her to exchange 500 of her original shares (valued at $29,000) for the 1,000 new shares.

14. Corporation J sponsors a qualified profit-sharing plan for its employees. Three years ago, Ms. PQ, a participant in the plan for over 12 years, quit her job and left town without leaving any forwarding address. The corporation has tried to locate Ms. PQ to send a Form W-2 and a final paycheck she failed to collect. So far, its efforts have been unsuccessful.

15. Mr. MC, age 50, is a self-employed writer who published 11 novels in the last 20 years. Each year, he makes the maximum contribution to his Keogh plan. This year, he borrowed $200,000 from the plan to finance the construction of a new home. Under the borrowing agreement, he pays a market interest rate and must repay the debt in five years.

16. Mr. and Mrs. Vishnu are the sole shareholders of VC Enterprises. They are also employed by VC and participate in its qualified pension plan. VC is experiencing cash flow difficulties. To ease the strain, Mr. and Mrs. Vishnu voluntarily forfeited their vested benefits under the plan and instructed the plan administrator to transfer the $219,000 value of such benefits back to VC.

17. Mr. X, age 53, owns a traditional IRA with a $215,000 current balance. Mr. X recently divorced his wife and transferred this IRA to her as part of the property settlement.

Research Problems

1. Curtis Bedford, age 73, is a professor of English at a private university. He holds a tenured position, which represents a lifetime employment contract. The university has offered Curtis a $75,000 lump-sum payment if he will retire from the faculty. If Curtis accepts the payment, he must give up any legal claim against the university for age discrimination and must forfeit all of his privileges as a faculty member. If Curtis accepts the university's offer, will the $75,000 payment represent compensation that is subject to employer and employee payroll (Social Security and Medicare) tax?

2. Helene Toolson, age 67, is an avid collector of historical documents and signatures. Her collection is worth over $300,000 and, by any measure, is an excellent investment. Helene also owns an IRA with First State Bank. She recently learned that a letter written by Thomas Jefferson was available for purchase out of a private collection. As a result, she met with a bank vice president to discuss having her IRA acquire the letter. The vice president determined that state banking laws would not prohibit such an acquisition by an IRA. The asking price of the letter is $32,500. Would the purchase of the letter by her IRA have any adverse tax consequence to Helene?

3. Marion Kline was recently elected mayor of a large midwestern city that furnishes its mayor with an official residence for occupancy during the term of office. The residence (house and gardens) is owned and maintained by the city, and the mayor does not pay any rent. Marion and her family are required to live in the residence so that she can carry out the many social and ceremonial obligations of her office. Many of these obligations occur in the evenings and on weekends. The fair rental value of the mayoral residence is $60,000 annually. Must Marion recognize the value of her employer-provided housing as taxable compensation?

4. Early this year, Scott Lowe, age 54, became dissatisfied with the service he was receiving from the broker who managed his traditional IRA. He requested a distribution of the $48,200 balance in the account and received a check for this amount from the broker on

May 23. Scott planned to roll the distribution over into a new IRA with a different broker. Before he could do so, he received news that his son-in-law had died in a hunting accident. Scott immediately traveled to his daughter's home to console her and his grandchildren. During this period of trauma and confusion, Scott wrote a check for $48,200 to his new broker but failed to instruct the broker to put the money into an IRA. Instead, the broker invested it in a taxable money market account. Scott and his broker did not discover the mistake until late December. Must Scott include the $48,200 withdrawal in his gross income and pay a $4,820 premature withdrawal penalty?

Tax Planning Cases

1. This year, Mr. Joss (age 26 and in the 28 percent marginal tax bracket) accepted a job with BL Inc. He intends to work for only eight years, then start his own business. He has two options for accumulating the money he will need for this business.

   - *Option 1:* He is eligible to participate in BL's Section 401(k) plan and can afford to save $5,000 of his salary each year by diverting it to this plan. The plan earns 10 percent a year. Consequently, his plan balance in eight years will be $57,179 ($5,000 for eight years compounded at 10 percent).

   - *Option 2:* He can take his entire salary in cash, pay income tax, and save $3,600 ($5,000 less $1,400 tax) in an investment fund that earns 10 percent a year. Because the annual earnings are taxable, his savings in the fund will grow at only 7.2 percent a year. Consequently, his fund balance in eight years will be $37,202 ($3,600 for eight years compounded at 7.2 percent).

   Assuming a constant 28 percent tax rate, which option results in the greatest after-tax cash for Mr. Joss to begin his business?

2. Mr. and Mrs. B, ages 64 and 65, are both retired and live on Social Security plus the interest and dividends from several investments. Their taxable income averages $25,000 a year. Mrs. B owns a traditional IRA that she funded entirely with deductible contributions. The couple plans to withdraw $75,000 from the IRA to make some much needed improvements to their home. How should they time the withdrawal (or series of withdrawals) to maximize the cash available from the IRA?

3. Mr. RS is entitled to a $5,200 bonus this year (year 0). His employer gives him two options. He can either receive his $5,200 bonus in cash, or the employer will credit him with $4,500 deferred compensation. Under the deferral option, the employer will accrue 6 percent annual interest on the deferred compensation. Consequently, the employer will pay $8,059 ($4,500 plus compounded interest) to Mr. RS when he retires in year 10. Which option has the greater NPV under each of the following assumptions? In making your calculations, use a 5 percent discount rate.

   a. Mr. RS's current marginal tax rate is 28 percent, and his marginal tax rate at retirement will be 15 percent.

   b. Mr. RS's current marginal tax rate is 28 percent, and his marginal tax rate at retirement will be 28 percent.

4. Ms. P, age 51, plans to save $5,000 this year toward her retirement. She is considering three different investments. First, she could make a nondeductible contribution to a traditional IRA earning 10 percent a year. Second, she could purchase a certificate of deposit paying 10 percent annual interest. Third, she could purchase corporate stock paying a 10 percent annual qualifying dividend. In each case, Ms. P will reinvest her after-tax earnings (each investment will grow at an after-tax rate of return). She anticipates liquidating her investment after 15 years and using the after-tax cash to make a down payment on a condominium.

Determine which investment has the greatest after-tax *future* value. To compute the future value of a sum invested in year 0, use the discount factors in Appendix A. Simply multiply the sum by (1 ÷ discount factor). For example, the future value of $100 invested at 9 percent after five years is $154 [$100 × 1.538 (1 ÷ .650 discount factor)]. In making your computations, assume that Ms. P's marginal tax rate on ordinary income is 20 percent and her preferential rate on qualifying dividends is 10 percent over the 15-year investment period.

Investment and Personal Financial Planning

Learning Objectives

After studying this chapter, you should be able to:

1. Determine the tax consequences of interest and dividend income.

2. Explain how life insurance policies and annuity contracts defer income.

3. Compute gain or loss recognized on security transactions.

4. Compute the tax on short-term and long-term capital gains.

5. Determine the deduction for investment interest expense.

6. Apply the passive activity loss limitation.

7. Compute a taxable gift by applying the annual and lifetime exclusions.

8. Determine a decedent's taxable estate.

Chapter 16 focuses on the tax consequences of investment activities involving the acquisition, holding, and disposition of income-producing property. Individuals engage in investment activities expecting them to be profitable. In financial terms, they expect the investment to yield a positive return on capital. This return can take the form of current income (and cash flow) generated by the property or appreciation in the property's value. This chapter explores the tax consequences of both types of returns. Of course, not every investment is profitable, and Chapter 16 also deals with the tax consequences of investment losses.

Many individuals who accumulate significant wealth through their business and investment activities want their children and grandchildren to benefit from their good fortune. These individuals must develop personal financial planning strategies to achieve this goal in the most cost-effective manner. In the final section of this chapter, we will discover that federal transfer taxes are impediments in this planning process. However, we will also consider some techniques by which people can minimize these taxes and maximize the wealth available to their younger-generation family members.

BUSINESS VERSUS INVESTMENT ACTIVITIES

The tax consequences of investment activities are very different from the tax consequences of business activities. Individuals engage in the two types of activities for the same purpose: to make a profit. The distinction between business and investment activities lies in the extent of the individual's personal involvement in the activity. An individual engaging in a business activity commits time and talent to the activity on a regular basis, and the business profit is partially attributable to this personal involvement.[1] In contrast, an individual engaging in an investment activity takes a passive role as the owner of income-producing property. The profit from the activity is primarily attributable to the invested capital rather than to the owner's personal involvement. For tax purposes, this distinction holds true even when individuals devote substantial time to managing income-producing property. "A taxpayer who merely manages his investments seeking long-term gain is not carrying on a trade or business. This is so irrespective of the extent or continuity of the transactions or the work required in managing the portfolio."[2]

INVESTMENTS IN FINANCIAL ASSETS

Financial assets are legal claims on the production assets owned by a business entity or other organization. Financial assets include equity interests such as common and preferred corporate stock and creditor interests such as savings accounts, certificates of deposit, notes, bonds, and other debt instruments. These types of financial assets are commonly referred to as **securities.** Financial assets are intangible property rights. They have no intrinsic value; their worth depends on the underlying value of the production assets subject to their claim. Financial assets may be publicly traded on an established market or may be privately placed.

Individuals who invest in financial assets can own the assets directly or indirectly through a mutual fund. A **mutual fund** is a diversified portfolio of securities owned and managed by *a regulated investment company (RIC)*. RICs sell shares in their funds to the public—specifically to purchasers wanting to diversify their financial holdings and take advantage of the professional expertise of the fund managers. A mutual fund portfolio can consist of equity stocks, debt instruments, or a combination of both, depending on the investment objectives of the particular fund. Currently, more than 90 million people, about one-half of the households in America, hold over $12 trillion of financial assets in mutual funds, making them the most popular investment vehicle on the market.

Dividend and Interest Income

Objective 1
Determine the tax consequences of interest and dividend income.

Individuals who invest in securities usually expect a return on their investment in the form of dividends or interest. As cash basis taxpayers, individuals recognize dividend or interest income in the year in which they actually or constructively receive payment. Investors in stocks and mutual funds often have a dividend reinvestment option under which their dividends are used to purchase additional shares for their account. Even though shareholders who elect this option receive no cash payments, they are in constructive receipt of the dividends reinvested on their behalf.

---

[1] In capital-intensive businesses, profit is attributable to the assets as well as to the personal involvement of the business owners.
[2] *Moller* v. *United States,* 721 F.2d 810, 814 (CA FC, 1983).

Historically, individual investors recognized both dividends and interest as ordinary income taxed at the regular rates. However, the Jobs and Growth Tax Relief Reconciliation Act of 2003 created a new 15 percent preferential tax rate for qualified dividend income earned by noncorporate (individual) shareholders. In 2008, the preferential rate dropped to zero percent for any qualified dividend income that would be taxed at 15 percent or less under the regular rate structure. **Qualified dividend income** is broadly defined as dividends received from taxable domestic corporations and certain qualified foreign corporations.[3]

Organizations that pay dividends or interest issue annual Forms 1099-DIV (Dividends and Distributions) and Forms 1099-INT (Interest Income) to inform investors of their total payments for the year. The IRS receives copies of these forms and cross-checks to make sure that the payment reported on each form matches the income reported on the investor's Form 1040. Investors must pay careful attention to the detailed information on their Form 1099s to determine the correct tax treatment of their payments. For example, corporations occasionally make cash distributions to their shareholders that are tax-free returns of capital rather than taxable dividends. These distributions, which are identified on Form 1099, are not included in the recipient's gross income but instead reduce the recipient's tax basis in the corporate stock.

Corporate Distributions	Rocko Inc., a New York corporation, distributed $935,700 cash to its shareholders this year. Rocko's tax department determined that only $894,100 (95.55 percent) of the distribution was a dividend paid from corporate earnings. The $41,600 remainder was a return of corporate capital. Mr. Jude Isley received a $44,800 cash distribution from Rocko. According to his Form 1099, only $42,806 (95.55 percent) of his distribution was qualified dividend income, while the $1,994 remainder was a nontaxable reduction in the basis of Mr. Isley's Rocko stock.

Dividend distributions from mutual funds actually represent a flow through of the various types of income generated by the fund's investment portfolio. Consequently, a mutual fund dividend could include a **capital gain distribution** of the net long-term capital gain recognized by the fund on sales of securities. It could also include a **qualified dividend distribution** of the dividends generated by the fund's portfolio of equities. Form 1099s issued by mutual funds must report any capital gain and qualified dividend distributions for the year so that individual investors can benefit from the preferential rates on these types of income.

Mutual Fund Dividend	Stargaze Mutual Fund manages a diversified portfolio consisting of 60 percent stock in taxable domestic corporations, 35 percent corporate bonds, and 5 percent cash. This year, Stargaze received $8 million of dividends and $3.6 million of interest and recognized a $1.9 million net long-term capital gain on security sales. Stargaze distributed a $13.5 million cash dividend to its investors that consisted of an $8 million qualified dividend distribution, a $3.6 ordinary dividend, and a $1.9 million capital gain distribution. Ms. Cindy Jung received a $9,930 cash distribution from Stargaze. According to her Form 1099, $5,884 was a qualified dividend distribution, $2,648 was an ordinary dividend, and $1,398 was a capital gain distribution.

Individuals report interest and dividend income on Schedule B of their Form 1040. Here is a comprehensive example showing how these types of income flow through this schedule.

---

[3] §1(h)(3)(B) and (h)(11).

Mr. and Mrs. *David:* *Schedule B*	Ronald and Janet David, who file a joint return, have a savings account with Midwest Credit Union. They own a $75,000 certificate of deposit with Second Union Bank and a $100,000 bond issued by Tryton Inc. This year, they earned $161 interest on the savings account, $4,712 interest on the CD, and $6,200 interest on the bond. Shortly after year-end, they received a Form 1099-INT from each payor on which their annual interest income was reported. They entered this information on Part I of their Schedule B (shown as Exhibit 16.1). Their $11,073 total interest (line 4) was carried as an income item to page 1, Form 1040.

At the beginning of the year, Mr. and Mrs. David owned 5,122 shares of Prime Growth mutual fund. They elected to reinvest their annual dividends in additional Prime Growth shares. Consequently, they received no cash from the mutual fund during the year. Mr. and Mrs. David received a Form 1099-DIV from Prime Growth containing the following information.

Ordinary dividend	$ 2,316
Qualified dividend distribution	4,775
Capital gain distribution	5,383
Gross distribution	$12,474
Shares owned on January 1	5,122
Additional shares purchased for investor's account	
(198 shares at $63 per share = $12,474)	198
Shares owned on December 31	5,320

Mr. and Mrs. David also own 16,780 shares of Mortimer Industries common stock. At the beginning of the year, their cost basis in these shares was $59,000. During the year, they received cash distributions totaling $19,000 from Mortimer. Their Form 1099-DIV contained the following information.

Qualified dividend income	$17,980
Nontaxable distribution	1,020
Gross distribution	$19,000

Mr. and Mrs. David entered their ordinary and qualified dividends from Prime Growth and Mortimer on Part II, Schedule B. The capital gain distribution was reported on Schedule D for inclusion with their other capital gains and losses. The nontaxable distribution reduced the tax basis in the Mortimer stock to $57,980. Their $25,071 total ordinary dividends (line 6) was carried as an income item to page 1, Form 1040.

Tax-Exempt Interest

The public security markets offer thousands of financial assets that individuals can select to meet their particular investment needs. In making their selection, investors should consider their overall tax situation, as well as any preferential tax characteristics of the assets under consideration. One such characteristic is the tax-exempt status of interest on certain debt instruments.

State and Local Bonds

For federal tax purposes, interest income earned on investments in debt instruments issued by state and local governments, including the District of Columbia, is excluded from income.[4] The interest rate on these tax-exempt bonds is typically lower than the rate on taxable

---

[4] §103. This exclusion extends to any portion of a mutual fund dividend attributable to the fund's investment in tax-exempt bonds.

EXHIBIT 16.1

SCHEDULE B	Interest and Ordinary Dividends	OMB No. 1545-0074
(Form 1040A or 1040)		20**11**
Department of the Treasury Internal Revenue Service (99)	▶ Attach to Form 1040A or 1040. ▶ See instructions on back.	Attachment Sequence No. **08**

Name(s) shown on return	Your social security number
Ronald and Janet David	498 31 1240

Part I

Interest

(See instructions on back and the instructions for Form 1040A, or Form 1040, line 8a.)

Note. If you received a Form 1099-INT, Form 1099-OID, or substitute statement from a brokerage firm, list the firm's name as the payer and enter the total interest shown on that form.

		Amount
1	List name of payer. If any interest is from a seller-financed mortgage and the buyer used the property as a personal residence, see instructions on back and list this interest first. Also, show that buyer's social security number and address ▶	
	Savings account - Midwest Credit Union	161
	Certificate of deposit - Second Union Bank	4,712
	6.2% Tryton Inc. corporate bond	6,200
2	Add the amounts on line 1 . . . . **2**	11,073
3	Excludable interest on series EE and I U.S. savings bonds issued after 1989. Attach Form 8815 . **3**	
4	Subtract line 3 from line 2. Enter the result here and on Form 1040A, or Form 1040, line 8a . . . . ▶ **4**	11,073

Note. If line 4 is over $1,500, you must complete Part III.

Part II

Ordinary Dividends

(See instructions on back and the instructions for Form 1040A, or Form 1040, line 9a.)

Note. If you received a Form 1099-DIV or substitute statement from a brokerage firm, list the firm's name as the payer and enter the ordinary dividends shown on that form.

		Amount
5	List name of payer ▶	
	Prime Growth mutual fund - ordinary dividend	2,316
	Prime Growth mutual fund - qualified dividend distribution	4,775
	Mortimer Industries - qualified dividends	17,980
6	Add the amounts on line 5. Enter the total here and on Form 1040A, or Form 1040, line 9a . . . . ▶ **6**	25,071

Note. If line 6 is over $1,500, you must complete Part III.

Part III

Foreign Accounts and Trusts

(See instructions on back.)

You must complete this part if you **(a)** had over $1,500 of taxable interest or ordinary dividends; **(b)** had a foreign account; or **(c)** received a distribution from, or were a grantor of, or a transferor to, a foreign trust.	Yes	No
7a At any time during 2011, did you have a financial interest in or signature authority over a financial account (such as a bank account, securities account, or brokerage account) located in a foreign country? See instructions		✔
If "Yes," are you required to file Form TD F 90-22.1 to report that financial interest or signature authority? See Form TD F 90-22.1 and its instructions for filing requirements and exceptions to those requirements		
b If you are required to file Form TD F 90-22.1, enter the name of the foreign country where the financial account is located ▶		
8 During 2011, did you receive a distribution from, or were you the grantor of, or transferor to, a foreign trust? If "Yes," you may have to file Form 3520. See instructions on back		✔

For Paperwork Reduction Act Notice, see your tax return instructions.	Cat. No. 17146N	Schedule B (Form 1040A or 1040) 2011

bonds with a comparable degree of risk; investors who purchase tax-exempt bonds pay an implicit tax equal to this rate differential.[5] Moreover, state and local bond interest may be taxed by the state or locality in which the investor resides. Finally, the interest on tax-exempt **private activity bonds** issued by any state or local government after August 7, 1986, is a

---

[5] See the discussion of implicit tax in Chapter 4.

preference item for alternative minimum tax purposes.[6] Because of these variables, even individuals in high marginal tax brackets can't assume that they will benefit by buying tax-exempt bonds until they evaluate the investment on an after-tax basis.

U.S. Debt Obligations

The U.S. government issues a variety of debt instruments for investors. Treasury bills are issued on a discount basis and are payable at a fixed maturity date not exceeding one year from date of issue. Treasury notes have maturity periods ranging from one to 10 years, while Treasury bonds have maturity periods from 10 to 30 years. Both are issued at face value and bear a fixed rate of interest, payable at six-month intervals. **Treasury inflation-protected securities (TIPS)** are long-term debt instruments that pay a fixed rate of interest on a principal amount adjusted semiannually for inflation or deflation based on the Consumer Price Index. **Series EE savings bonds** are long-term debt instruments issued at a discount.

The interest on all these debt instruments is subject to federal income tax. However, the interest is exempt from income tax levied by any state or local government. Because state and local tax rates are generally much lower than federal rates, exemption from such taxes may result in only a modest benefit. Nonetheless, investors should be aware of this preferential state tax characteristic of U.S. debt obligations.

Deferred Interest Income

The tax law offers investors a few narrow opportunities to defer the recognition of interest income. For instance, cash basis taxpayers who purchase short-term debt obligations at a discount do not recognize income until the obligation matures.[7]

Interest Deferral	In July 2012, Mrs. Webb bought a $50,000 U.S. Treasury bill for $48,900; the bill matured 26 weeks after date of issue. She reported no 2012 income from this investment, even though most of the interest on the bill accrued in 2012. When Mrs. Webb redeemed the bill in January 2013 for $50,000, she recognized the entire $1,100 interest income.

Individuals can achieve the same type of deferral if they purchase Series EE savings bonds. Even though these discount bonds have long-term maturity periods, individuals postpone recognition of any interest income until they cash in the bonds. In the unusual case in which an investor prefers to take the discount into annual income on an accrual basis, he may elect to do so by reporting the accrued interest on Schedule B.

Market Discount

Cash basis investors who purchase bonds *in a market transaction* at a price lower than the bond's stated redemption value at maturity are not required to accrue the **market discount** as interest income over the life of the bond.[8] Instead, they recognize the discount as interest in the future year in which they sell the bond or the bond is redeemed.[9]

---

[6] §57(a)(5). The proceeds from private activity bonds are used for nongovernmental purposes, such as industrial development.

[7] See §454 and §1271(a)(3) and (4). Short-term debt obligations have fixed maturity periods of one year or less.

[8] Investors may elect to accrue interest income under §1278(b).

[9] §1276(a)(1). This rule extends to any market discount on state and local bonds. While the periodic interest payments on these bonds are tax exempt, the accrued discount is fully taxable as ordinary income.

Deferral of Market Discount	Mr. Barry bought a publicly traded corporate bond through his broker for $21,300. Although the bond is redeemable at maturity for $25,000, it traded at a discounted price because the stated interest rate (3.5 percent) was below the market rate (4.4 percent). Mr. Barry will include the 3.5 percent interest payments in his annual income but will not include any portion of the market discount. If he holds the bond until maturity, Mr. Barry will recognize the entire $3,700 excess of the $25,000 redemption proceeds over his $21,300 cost basis as ordinary income in the year of redemption.

Original Issue Discount

Investors who purchase *newly issued* corporate debt instruments at a discount can't defer recognition of the interest income represented by the original issue discount. **Original issue discount (OID)** equals the excess of the bond's stated redemption value at maturity (face value) over the issue price. Even cash basis investors must recognize accrued income by amortizing this discount over the life of the bond.[10]

Amortization of OID	Jacks Inc. made a new public offering of 15-year bonds with a stated interest rate of only 1.5 percent of face value. Mr. Barry, our investor in the previous example, bought $50,000 of these bonds for their discounted issue price of $27,000. Mr. Barry's return on his investment consists of the $750 yearly interest payments *plus* the $23,000 difference between his cost and the cash he will collect when the bonds mature. Every year, Jacks sends Mr. Barry the following.
	• Form 1099-INT reporting the $750 interest payment.
	• Form 1099-OID reporting the amortized discount he must recognize as additional interest income.[11]
	Over the 15-year term of the bonds, Mr. Barry will recognize $23,000 OID income with no corresponding cash flow. However, he will not recognize any additional income when he redeems the bonds at maturity for $50,000.

Inflation-Adjusted Debt Instruments

Investors who purchase inflation-adjusted debt instruments (such as TIPS issued by the U.S. government) receive interest payments computed at a fixed rate on an inflation-adjusted principal amount. Investors must include both the interest received and any annual increase in the principal in current income. The tax treatment of the inflation adjustment is similar to the treatment of OID because the adjustment creates taxable income without any corresponding cash flow.[12] In other words, recognition of interest income is accelerated rather than deferred.

Inflation Adjustment	At the beginning of 2012, Mrs. Salina invested $200,000 in TIPS paying 4 percent yearly interest. On the first semiannual interest payment date, the inflation adjustment to principal was 1 percent. Consequently, Mrs. Salina received $4,040 interest ($202,000 adjusted principal × .04 × one-half year). On the second interest payment date, the cumulative inflation adjustment to principal was 2.5 percent, and Mrs. Salina received $4,100 interest ($205,000 adjusted principal × .04 × one-half year). Mrs. Salina's 2012 taxable income from the TIPS totals $13,140 ($8,140 interest payments + $5,000 annual increase in principal).

[10] §1272(a). This income recognition rule does not apply to tax-exempt state and local obligations.

[11] The annual OID income on debt instruments issued after July 1, 1992, is based on the instrument's constant yield to maturity. §1272(a)(3). This calculation results in increasing annual OID income over the life of the instrument. Corporations may take an annual interest deduction for amortized OID. §163(e)(1).

[12] Reg. §1.1275-7.

> Assume that Mrs. Salina holds the TIPS until maturity and receives $233,400 redemption proceeds equal to the inflation-adjusted value of her original $200,000 investment.[13] Because she has recognized the cumulative $33,400 adjustment as interest income over the life of the TIPS, she will not recognize any additional income upon redemption.

Life Insurance Policies and Annuity Contracts

Life Insurance Policies

Objective 2
Explain how life insurance policies and annuity contracts defer income.

A life insurance policy is a legal contract between a purchaser (the owner) and a commercial insurance company. The owner pays a premium or series of premiums for the company's commitment to pay a specific sum of money (death benefit) on the death of the person whose life is insured. The owner has the right to name the beneficiary (the person or organization that will receive the death benefit). An individual purchases insurance on his or her own life primarily to provide financial protection for dependent family members. However, many life insurance contracts offer both protection against premature death and an investment element. The investment element is called the **cash surrender value,** which increases every year that the policy remains in effect. The owner does not recognize this annual increase in value, called the **inside buildup,** as taxable income. If the owner eventually decides that his family no longer needs insurance protection, he may liquidate the policy for its cash surrender value. In this case, the owner recognizes the *excess* cash surrender value over his investment in the policy (total premiums paid) as ordinary income.[14]

Liquidation of Life Insurance Policy	Twenty years ago, Mr. Wilde purchased an insurance policy on his own life. The policy provided a $350,000 death benefit payable to Mr. Wilde's wife and children. To date, Mr. Wilde has paid $38,000 of premiums. Because his wife predeceased him and his children are financially independent, Mr. Wilde liquidated the policy for its $42,800 cash surrender value. The insurance company sent Mr. Wilde a Form 1099-R reporting $4,800 ordinary income ($42,800 − $38,000 aggregate premiums).[15]

The deferral of tax on the inside buildup certainly makes life insurance contracts a tax-preferred investment. The tax consequences are even more favorable if the policy is held until it matures on the death of the insured. In this case, the beneficiary excludes the death benefit from gross income, and the accumulated return on the owner's investment in the life insurance contract escapes tax entirely.[16]

Life Insurance Proceeds	Twenty years ago, Mrs. Muzo purchased an insurance policy on her own life. The policy provided a $350,000 death benefit payable to Mrs. Muzo's children. Mrs. Muzo paid $38,000 of premiums, and the policy's cash surrender value was $42,800. Mrs. Muzo died on May 4 with the policy still in effect. On September 3, her children received $350,000 from the insurance company and excluded the entire payment from their gross income.

---

[13] TIPS provide a *minimum guarantee* feature to protect investors against deflation of the value of their investment: When TIPS mature, investors receive the *greater* of the original principal amount or the inflation-adjusted amount at maturity.

[14] §72(e)(2).

[15] Form 1099-R reports distributions from insurance contracts, annuities, and pension, profit sharing, IRAs, and other retirement plans.

[16] §101.

This highly advantageous tax treatment also applies to **accelerated death benefits:** payments made under the contract to insured individuals who are terminally or chronically ill.[17] Such individuals may be forced to draw against or even liquidate their life insurance policies to pay medical expenses resulting from an extended illness. The tax law alleviates this financial hardship by classifying these premature payments as nontaxable death benefits.

Annuity Contracts

Individuals purchase annuity contracts from commercial insurance companies to provide themselves with a fixed stream of income for a future period of time. The owner pays a premium or series of premiums that the insurance company invests on the owner's behalf. The owner is not taxed on the yearly inside buildup in the value of her investment. Instead, tax is deferred until the owner begins receiving periodic payments under the contract. The portion of each annuity payment representing a distribution of accumulated earnings is taxed as ordinary income, while the portion representing a return of the owner's investment is nontaxable.

Annuity Payments	Mrs. Water purchased an annuity for a $75,000 single premium when she was 51 years old. This year, Mrs. Water reached age 65 and began receiving annuity payments. Under the terms of her contract, she will receive $1,100 per month for the rest of her life. The portion of each payment representing a return of her investment is based on the ratio of that investment to the expected return under the contract.[18] On the basis of life expectancy tables provided in Treasury regulations, Mrs. Water can expect to receive 240 payments ($264,000). Consequently, her exclusion ratio is 28.41 percent.

$$\frac{\$75{,}000 \text{ investment (single premium)}}{\$264{,}000 \text{ expected return}} = .2841$$

Mrs. Water received eight monthly payments totaling $8,800 this year, and her nontaxable return of investment is $2,500.

Total annuity payments received	$8,800
Exclusion ratio	.2841
	$2,500

Mrs. Water must recognize the remaining $6,300 of the total payments as ordinary income.

Each year Mrs. Water will apply the exclusion ratio to determine the nontaxable portion of her total payments until she recovers her entire $75,000 investment. Any additional payments will be fully taxable.[19] If Mrs. Water dies before recovering her investment, the unrecovered portion is allowed as an itemized deduction on her final Form 1040.[20]

---

[17] §101(g). Accelerated death benefits include the proceeds of the sale or assignment of a contract to a *viatical settlement provider,* which is a company licensed to engage in the business of purchasing life insurance contracts from the terminally or chronically ill.

[18] §72(b)(1).

[19] §72(b)(2).

[20] §72(b)(3) and §67(b)(10).

Death of Annuitant	Assume that Mrs. Waters in the previous example collected 203 annuity payments totaling $223,300 before her death. Consequently, she recovered $63,440 of her $75,000 investment ($223,300 × .2841 exclusion ratio) in the annuity contract. Mrs. Water's executor can report her $11,560 unrecovered investment as an itemized deduction on her final Form 1040. This deduction is not classified as a miscellaneous itemized deduction and is not limited by the 2 percent AGI floor.

Nontax Considerations

People buy life insurance policies to protect against dying too soon and annuity contracts to protect against living too long. In addition to their protection element, both assets offer a tax-deferred financial return. However, life insurance policies and annuity contracts may have lower before-tax rates of return and higher transaction costs than investment opportunities that are not tax favored. For instance, life insurance policies have the highest commission charges of any financial product—typically more than 50 percent of the first-year premium paid by the investor. Annuity contracts routinely charge an annual fee and impose early-surrender charges on individuals who liquidate their investment in the contract before the annuity starting date. These nontax costs can outweigh the benefit of tax deferral, particularly for individuals in the lower tax brackets or who aren't prepared to commit to these investments for the long haul.

GAINS AND LOSSES FROM SECURITY TRANSACTIONS

A key principle of federal tax law is that *unrealized* gains and losses are not taxed. Increases or decreases in the value of property over time are not recognized until an external transaction triggers gain or loss realization. Accordingly, individuals who invest in financial assets defer paying tax on any appreciation in value until they dispose of the assets in a taxable transaction. In this section of the chapter, we will examine the tax rules that apply to dispositions of securities. By paying attention to these rules, individuals can control their tax costs and enhance the after-tax return on such investments.

Computing Gains and Losses

Objective 3
Compute gain or loss recognized on security transactions.

Realized gain from the sale of securities equals the excess of the amount realized over the seller's basis in the securities. Realized loss equals the excess of basis over amount realized. Amount realized is the sum of any money plus the fair market value (FMV) of any property received by the seller. If the investor incurred any selling expenses, such as brokerage fees and commissions, these expenses reduce the amount realized on sale. A seller's basis in a security depends on the transaction in which the security was acquired. Securities acquired by purchase have a cost basis including both the price of the securities plus any front-end fees or load charges. Investors who sell securities through a broker receive a Form 1099-B (Proceeds from Broker and Barter Exchange Transactions) reporting both the amount realized on sale and the seller's basis in the securities.

Tracking Security Basis

Individuals should keep careful record of the initial cost of the securities in their investment portfolios and the effect of any subsequent transactions on such basis. For instance, if an investor elects to reinvest dividends in additional shares of stock or a mutual fund, the dividend becomes the cost basis in the new shares. If an investor receives a nontaxable distribution with respect to shares of stock, the basis in the shares must be reduced by this return of capital. Investors who own debt instruments with original issue discount should increase their basis in the securities by the OID income accrued each year. Investors who own inflation-adjusted debt instruments should increase their basis by the annual increase in the principal. Failure to keep track of these common basis adjustments results in overstatement or understatement of gain or loss realized on the eventual disposition of the securities.

Basis Adjustments for Reinvested Dividends	Nine years ago, Ms. Farley paid $25,000 for 3,400 shares of Fastrack mutual fund. She elected to reinvest her dividends in additional shares. As of June 4, Ms. Farley had recognized $19,100 dividend income (without any corresponding cash flow) and acquired 2,816 additional shares. On June 4, she sold all 6,216 shares for $58,000. Her realized gain is computed as follows.

Amount realized on sale		$ 58,000
Adjusted basis:		
Cost of 3,400 shares	$25,000	
Cost of 2,816 shares (reinvested dividends)	19,100	
		(44,100)
Gain realized on sale		$ 13,900

Identifying Basis on Sale

When an investor sells a specific security with an identifiable basis, gain or loss is determined with reference to such basis. However, investment portfolios often contain identical securities acquired at different times and for different prices. If the investor sells some of the securities but can't identify which specific ones were sold, the basis is determined by a first-in, first-out (FIFO) method.[21] In other words, the investor is presumed to have sold the securities with the earliest acquisition date.

Individuals who sell mutual fund shares or shares of stock acquired after 2010 pursuant to a dividend reinvestment plan may also use an average cost basis method for calculating gain or loss.[22] Under the simplest version of this method, the basis of each share equals the aggregate cost of all shares divided by the total number of shares. Mutual funds typically provide average cost basis information on their year-end statements as a service to their investors.

| *Average Basis Method* | At the beginning of the year, Mr. Yao owned 1,000 shares of TNT Mutual Fund with a $52,000 aggregate basis. Every month, he invested $1,000 in the fund. Because of fluctuations in the market price of TNT shares, he acquired a different number of shares with a different cost basis each month. By September, Mr. Yao owned 1,155 shares with a $60,000 aggregate basis. On September 9, he sold 300 shares for $56 per share ($16,800 total price). He can determine his basis in the 300 shares as follows.

$60,000 aggregate basis ÷ 1,155 shares = $51.948 basis per share

300 shares sold × $51.948 basis per share = $15,584

Consequently, Mr. Yao's gain on sale is $1,216 ($16,800 amount realized − $15,584 basis), and his aggregate basis in his 855 remaining shares is $44,416 ($60,000 − $15,584). |
|---|---|

[21] Reg. §1.1012-1(c).
[22] Reg. §1.1012-1(e).

Tax Talk

Darrel Smith had an agreement with his ex-wife Mitzi that she would pay his personal living expenses. When Mitzi reneged on the agreement, Darrel reported his living expenses on his tax return as a bad debt deductible as a capital loss. The district court was unimpressed by Darrel's "novel argument" and disallowed his deduction.

Worthless Securities and Nonbusiness Bad Debts

Securities are capital assets in the hands of individual investors. Therefore, gains and losses realized on security sales are capital gains and losses subject to the special tax rules presented in the next section of the chapter. According to the general statutory definition, capital gains and losses result from the sale or exchange of capital assets.[23] The Internal Revenue Code provides that two other events result in capital loss. If an individual owns a security that becomes worthless, the event is treated as if the individual sold the security on the last day of the year for an amount realized of zero.[24] In other words, the individual recognizes his unrecovered basis in the security as a capital loss. The second event occurs when an individual who loaned money to another party determines that the debt is uncollectible. In such case, the individual recognizes the unpaid balance of the **nonbusiness bad debt** as a capital loss.[25]

Nonbusiness Bad Debt	Two years ago, Mr. Jared loaned $25,000 to PT Partnership in exchange for PT's interest-bearing note. PT has repaid $9,000 of the debt. However, Mr. Jared recently learned that PT is hopelessly insolvent and cannot pay any of its creditors. He can recognize his $16,000 nonbusiness bad debt as a capital loss.

Nontaxable Exchanges of Securities

As a general rule, the exchange of one security for another security is a taxable event. For instance, if an investor exchanges stock in Corporation A for a long-term bond issued by Corporation Z, the investor recognizes the difference between his amount realized (FMV of the bond) and the basis of the stock as capital gain or loss. The tax law does contain several nontaxable exchange provisions applying to security transactions. No gain or loss is recognized on the exchange of one class of common stock for a different class of common stock *in the same corporation.* Similarly, preferred stock can be exchanged for preferred stock *in the same corporation* at no current tax cost.[26] If an investor exchanges stock or securities in one corporation for stock or securities in a different corporation, no gain or loss is recognized only if the exchange is pursuant to a **reorganization** involving the two corporations.[27] In each of these nontaxable exchanges, the investor's basis in his newly acquired security equals the basis of the security surrendered. Because of this substituted basis rule, gain or loss realized on the exchange is merely deferred, not eliminated.[28]

---

[23] §1222.

[24] §165(g).

[25] §166(d). If an individual lends money or extends credit *as part of his business,* any resulting bad debt is a deductible business expense.

[26] §1036.

[27] Reorganizations are a set of very precisely defined transactions in which one corporation acquires another, one corporation divides into two corporations, or one corporation changes its capital structure. Reorganizations are defined in §368.

[28] See the discussion of generic nontaxable exchanges in Chapter 9.

Exchange of Securities	The shareholders of LG Inc. voted to merge their corporation into SM Inc. under Missouri law. Pursuant to the merger, Ms. Gwin exchanged her 813 shares of LG stock for 12,300 shares of SM stock. Her realized gain on the exchange is computed as follows.

Amount realized (FMV of SM stock received)	$ 945,200
Basis in LG stock surrendered	(550,300)
Gain realized on exchange	$ 394,900

If the merger of LG and SM qualifies as a reorganization for federal tax purposes, Ms. Gwin does not recognize any of her realized gain. In this case, the basis in her 12,300 shares of SM stock is $550,300 (basis of LG stock surrendered in the nontaxable exchange). If the merger doesn't qualify as a reorganization, Ms. Gwin must recognize a $394,900 taxable gain on the exchange. In this case, the basis in her 12,300 shares of SM stock is their $945,200 cost (FMV of LG stock surrendered).

TAX CONSEQUENCES OF CAPITAL GAINS AND LOSSES

Individuals who recognize both capital gains and losses during the year can deduct the losses to the extent of the gains. In other words, individuals can combine their capital gains and losses to result in either a net gain or a net loss. A net gain is included in adjusted gross income and may be taxed at a preferential rate. A net loss results in a limited deduction in the AGI computation. Before focusing on these outcomes, we must examine the rules governing the netting of capital gains and losses.

Netting Capital Gains and Losses

Individuals report the sale or other disposition of a capital asset on Form 8949 (new in 2011). Each sale or disposition is classified on Form 8949 as either short-term (Part I) or long-term (Part II).[29]

- **Short-term capital gains or losses** result from the sale or exchange of capital assets owned for one year or less. The capital loss from a nonbusiness bad debt is classified as a short-term loss, regardless of the time period of the debt.
- **Long-term capital gains or losses** result from the sale or exchange of capital assets owned for more than one year. There is a narrow subcategory of long-term gains and losses, described as **28 percent rate gains or losses**, that includes recognized gains and losses from the sale or exchange of **collectibles** (tangible assets such as works of art, antiques, gems, stamps, and coins) and the taxable gain recognized on the sale of qualified small business stock.[30]

The aggregate information from Form 8949 for both short-term and long-term transactions is carried to Schedule D, Form 1040. This information is used to compute *net* short-term and *net* long-term capital gain or loss for the year.

---

[29] See §1222.

[30] §1(h)(5) and (6). When an individual sells or exchanges a collectible held for personal use (rather than as an investment), a realized gain is recognized (taxable) but a realized loss is not recognized (nondeductible). For further discussion, see Chapter 17. Qualified small business stock is discussed on page 503.

Mr. and Mrs. Dixon: Schedule D

In 2011, Mark and Sue made the following four sales of marketable securities.

	Date Acquired	Sales Price	Tax Basis	Gain or Loss
11,812 shares of Oslo Mutual Fund	04/15/11	$28,400	$22,750	$ 5,650
Zephyr corporate bonds	06/22/11	8,340	10,000	(1,660)
2,065 shares of BLP Preferred stock	09/12/02	59,000	67,900	(8,900)
335 shares of Elsco common	07/18/99	71,000	44,200	26,800

Shortly after year-end, the Dixons received a Form 1099-B from their broker reporting the relevant information for the four sales and a Form 1099-DIV from Oslo Mutual Fund reporting that the fund had made a $7,800 capital gain distribution to the Dixons in 2011.

The Dixons reported the details of each sale on Form 8949, then entered the aggregate short-term and long-term information on their Schedule D. They also reported their $7,800 capital gain distribution on line 13 of Schedule D. Page 1 of the Dixons' Schedule D is shown as Exhibit 16.2.

EXHIBIT 16.2

SCHEDULE D (Form 1040)

Department of the Treasury
Internal Revenue Service (99)

Capital Gains and Losses

▶ Attach to Form 1040 or Form 1040NR. ▶ See Instructions for Schedule D (Form 1040).
▶ Use Form 8949 to list your transactions for lines 1, 2, 3, 8, 9, and 10.

OMB No. 1545-0074

2011

Attachment Sequence No. **12**

Name(s) shown on return
Mark and Sue Dixon

Your social security number
512 22 4061

Part I   Short-Term Capital Gains and Losses—Assets Held One Year or Less

Complete Form 8949 before completing line 1, 2, or 3. This form may be easier to complete if you round off cents to whole dollars.	(e) Sales price from Form(s) 8949, line 2, column (e)	(f) Cost or other basis from Form(s) 8949, line 2, column (f)	(g) Adjustments to gain or loss from Form(s) 8949, line 2, column (g)	(h) Gain or (loss) Combine columns (e), (f), and (g)
1 Short-term totals from all Forms 8949 with **box A** checked in **Part I**	36,740	(32,750)		3,990
2 Short-term totals from all Forms 8949 with **box B** checked in **Part I**		( )		
3 Short-term totals from all Forms 8949 with **box C** checked in **Part I**		( )		

4 Short-term gain from Form 6252 and short-term gain or (loss) from Forms 4684, 6781, and 8824 .	**4**	
5 Net short-term gain or (loss) from partnerships, S corporations, estates, and trusts from Schedule(s) K-1	**5**	
6 Short-term capital loss carryover. Enter the amount, if any, from line 8 of your **Capital Loss Carryover Worksheet** in the instructions	**6**	( )
7 **Net short-term capital gain or (loss).** Combine lines 1 through 6 in column (h). If you have any long-term capital gains or losses, go to Part II below. Otherwise, go to Part III on the back . . .	**7**	3,990

Part II   Long-Term Capital Gains and Losses—Assets Held More Than One Year

Complete Form 8949 before completing line 8, 9, or 10. This form may be easier to complete if you round off cents to whole dollars.	(e) Sales price from Form(s) 8949, line 4, column (e)	(f) Cost or other basis from Form(s) 8949, line 4, column (f)	(g) Adjustments to gain or loss from Form(s) 8949, line 4, column (g)	(h) Gain or (loss) Combine columns (e), (f), and (g)
8 Long-term totals from all Forms 8949 with **box A** checked in **Part II**	130,000	(112,100)		17,900
9 Long-term totals from all Forms 8949 with **box B** checked in **Part II**		( )		
10 Long-term totals from all Forms 8949 with **box C** checked in **Part II**		( )		

11 Gain from Form 4797, Part I; long-term gain from Forms 2439 and 6252; and long-term gain or (loss) from Forms 4684, 6781, and 8824	**11**	
12 Net long-term gain or (loss) from partnerships, S corporations, estates, and trusts from Schedule(s) K-1	**12**	
13 Capital gain distributions. See the instructions	**13**	7,800
14 Long-term capital loss carryover. Enter the amount, if any, from line 13 of your **Capital Loss Carryover Worksheet** in the instructions	**14**	( )
15 **Net long-term capital gain or (loss).** Combine lines 8 through 14 in column (h). Then go to Part III on the back	**15**	25,700

For Paperwork Reduction Act Notice, see your tax return instructions.   Cat. No. 11338H   Schedule D (Form 1040) 2011

EXHIBIT 16.2
(*continued*)

Page **2**

Part III	Summary		

16 Combine lines 7 and 15 and enter the result . . . . **16** | **29,690**

> • If line 16 is a **gain**, enter the amount from line 16 on Form 1040, line 13, or Form 1040NR, line 14. Then go to line 17 below.
> • If line 16 is a **loss**, skip lines 17 through 20 below. Then go to line 21. Also be sure to complete line 22.
> • If line 16 is **zero**, skip lines 17 through 21 below and enter -0- on Form 1040, line 13, or Form 1040NR, line 14. Then go to line 22.

17 Are lines 15 and 16 **both** gains?
☑ **Yes.** Go to line 18.
☐ **No.** Skip lines 18 through 21, and go to line 22.

18 Enter the amount, if any, from line 7 of the **28% Rate Gain Worksheet** in the instructions . . ▶ | **18** | **0**

19 Enter the amount, if any, from line 18 of the **Unrecaptured Section 1250 Gain Worksheet** in the instructions . . . . ▶ | **19** | **0**

20 Are lines 18 and 19 **both** zero or blank?
☑ **Yes.** Complete Form 1040 through line 43, or Form 1040NR through line 41. Then complete the **Qualified Dividends and Capital Gain Tax Worksheet** in the instructions for Form 1040, line 44 (or in the instructions for Form 1040NR, line 42). **Do not** complete lines 21 and 22 below.

☐ **No.** Complete Form 1040 through line 43, or Form 1040NR through line 41. Then complete the **Schedule D Tax Worksheet** in the instructions. **Do not** complete lines 21 and 22 below.

21 If line 16 is a loss, enter here and on Form 1040, line 13, or Form 1040NR, line 14, the **smaller** of:

> • The loss on line 16 or
> • ($3,000), or if married filing separately, ($1,500) . . . . | **21** (|)

Note. When figuring which amount is smaller, treat both amounts as positive numbers.

22 Do you have qualified dividends on Form 1040, line 9b, or Form 1040NR, line 10b?

☐ **Yes.** Complete Form 1040 through line 43, or Form 1040NR through line 41. Then complete the **Qualified Dividends and Capital Gain Tax Worksheet** in the instructions for Form 1040, line 44 (or in the instructions for Form 1040NR, line 42).
☐ **No.** Complete the rest of Form 1040 or Form 1040NR.

The short-term and long-term outcomes reported on Part I, line 7, and Part II, line 15, of Schedule D are combined, and the resulting net capital gain or loss is reported on line 16, Part III, Schedule D. If the result is a net gain, such gain is carried to Form 1040, line 13, for inclusion in taxable income for the year. The Dixons' Schedule D reports a $3,990 net short-term capital gain and a $25,700 net long-term gain, which combine to a $29,690 net capital gain includable in their taxable income. Part III of the Dixons' Schedule D is shown as Exhibit 16.2 (continued).

The following examples illustrate two other combinations of short-term and long-term outcomes resulting in a net capital gain.

Total Short-Term Gain	Mr. Boyle's Schedule D reflects a $12,200 net short-term gain and a $4,700 net long-term loss. Because the loss can be deducted (netted) against the gain, he has a $7,500 total short-term capital gain included in taxable income.
Total Long-Term Capital Gain	Ms. Coller's Schedule D reflects an $8,500 net short-term loss and a $20,000 net long-term gain. Because the loss can be deducted (netted) against the gain, she has an $11,500 total long-term capital gain included in taxable income.[31]

[31] If a net long-term capital gain includes any 28 percent rate gain, a short-term capital loss reduces the 28 percent rate gain before other long-term gain.

Preferential Rates on Long-Term Capital Gains

Objective 4
Compute the tax on short-term and long-term capital gains.

If individual taxable income includes capital gain, any short-term portion is taxed at ordinary rates, while any long-term portion is taxed at the following preferential rates.[32]

- A 28 percent rate gain is taxed at a *maximum* rate of 28 percent. Thus, this rate is beneficial only if the ordinary rate that would apply to such gain exceeds 28 percent.
- Other long-term gain is taxed at a 15 percent rate. However, any portion of such gain that would be taxed at 15 percent or less under the ordinary rate structure is taxed at zero percent. This dual rate structure ensures that every individual benefits from the preferential long-term capital gains rate, regardless of his or her marginal rate on ordinary income.

Let's refer back to the preceding three examples to illustrate how these various tax rates apply.

Mr. and Mrs. Dixon: Short-Term and Long-Term Gain	Mr. and Mrs. Dixon's taxable income included $29,690 net capital gain consisting of the following:

Net short-term gain	$ 3,990
Net long-term gain	25,700
Net capital gain	$29,690

The Dixons' marginal rate on ordinary income was 35 percent. Consequently, their $3,990 net short-term gain was taxed at 35 percent, and their $25,700 net long-term gain was taxed at 15 percent.

Short-Term Gain	Mr. Boyle's taxable income includes $7,500 short-term capital gain. This gain is taxed at the ordinary rates that apply to his other income items.

Long-Term Gain	Ms. Coller's taxable income includes $11,500 long-term capital gain. Her marginal rate on ordinary income is 35 percent. Consequently, Ms. Coller's capital gain is taxed at 15 percent. Now change the facts by assuming that Ms. Coller's taxable income is low enough that her marginal ordinary rate is only 15 percent. Consequently, her capital gain is taxed at zero percent. Even though Ms. Coller is in a low tax bracket, she benefits from the preferential capital gain rate, which reduces her tax bill by $1,725 (15 percent of $11,500).

Unrecaptured Section 1250 Gain

Real property used in a business (including rental real estate) and held for more than one year is a Section 1231 asset rather than a capital asset. When an individual sells or exchanges business or rental realty, recognized gain is subject to the Section 1250 partial depreciation recapture rule discussed in Chapter 8. Any additional gain (subject to the Section 1231 netting process) is treated as long-term capital gain. Such long-term gain is taxed according to the following rules.

- Any unrecaptured Section 1250 gain is taxed at a *maximum* rate of 25 percent. **Unrecaptured Section 1250 gain** is defined as Section 1231 gain that would be recaptured as ordinary income under a full depreciation recapture rule.[33]
- Any remaining gain is treated as other long-term capital gain.

[32] §1(h).
[33] §1(h)(6).

Unrecaptured Section 1250 Gain	Mr. Lilley sold two tracts of real estate, Property A and Property B, both of which he held for more than one year. He did not sell any other capital or Section 1231 asset, and his marginal tax rate on ordinary income is 35 percent.

	Property A		Property B	
Sale price		$800,000		$475,000
Original cost	$950,000		$440,000	
Depreciation (straight-line)	(190,000)		(32,000)	
Adjusted basis		(760,000)		(408,000)
Section 1231 gain recognized		$ 40,000		$ 67,000

Because Mr. Lilley used the straight-line method to compute depreciation, the Section 1250 partial recapture rule is inapplicable, and the gain recognized on both sales is Section 1231 gain. However, the $40,000 gain recognized on the sale of Property A is less than the accumulated depreciation. Consequently, the entire gain is classified as unrecaptured Section 1250 gain. The $67,000 gain recognized on the sale of Property B includes only $32,000 unrecaptured 1250 gain (equal to accumulated depreciation). Thus, Mr. Lilley's real estate sales resulted in $72,000 unrecaptured Section 1250 gain (taxed at 25 percent) and $35,000 other long-term capital gain (taxed at 15 percent).[34]

Even simple examples of the various preferential capital gains rates reflect the complexity of this tax rate structure. Individuals who must use the capital gains rates to compute their tax can follow the procedure contained in Part III of Schedule D. Use of this procedure is illustrated in the Comprehensive Schedule D Problem included as Appendix 16–A to this chapter.

Policy Reasons for a Preferential Rate

Capital gains have been taxed at lower rates than ordinary income since 1922. The greatest spread was in the 1950s when the highest marginal rate on ordinary income hovered at 90 percent, and the rate on capital gains was 25 percent. What is the theory justifying a preferential tax rate on capital gains? This tax policy question is relevant in assessing the vertical equity of the income tax system because capital gains are recognized most frequently by high-income individuals who engage in significant investment activities.

Supporters of the preferential rate observe that individuals don't pay tax on capital gain each year as the gain accrues but only in the year in which the gain is realized. This bunching effect could cause the gain to be taxed at a higher rate than if it were taxed in annual increments. Critics of the preferential rate respond that the bunching problem is mitigated by the deferral of tax on the capital gain until the year of realization.

A second argument is that the preferential rate on long-term gains counteracts the effect of inflation. An investor's tax basis in capital assets is not adjusted for changes in the purchasing power of the dollar. If an investor holds an asset for a long time, the dollars realized on sale may exceed the historical basis of the asset, but some or even all the realized gain may be inflationary rather than real. The counterargument is that a preferential rate on all long-term gains, regardless of the duration of the investor's holding period, is a crude solution to this problem. Congress periodically considers indexing the tax basis of assets to reflect changes in the value of the dollar but has backed away from this solution because of the complexity it would add to the tax law.

[34] Net short-term capital loss or net 28 percent rate loss is netted against unrecaptured Section 1250 gain before other long-term gain.

Many economists contend that the preferential rate on capital gains encourages the mobility of capital. Without a tax break on realized gains, individuals owning appreciated assets might be reluctant to liquidate or convert such assets because of the tax cost. This locking-in effect distorts financial decision making and retards the efficiency of the stock and bond markets. A variation on this argument is that the preferential rate reduces the risk of financial investments and thereby increases the supply of venture capital to the economy. A counterargument is that the preferential rate lures wealthy individuals to invest in convoluted tax shelters designed for one purpose: to convert ordinary income into capital gain. As a result, venture capital is diverted from productive investments that could actually bolster the economy.

Capital Loss Limitation

Recall from our discussion on page 497 that an individual's net short-term capital gain or loss is combined with net long-term capital gain or loss to result in a final net capital gain or loss for the year. If the final result is a net gain, some or all of the gain may be taxed at a preferential rate. But what if the final result reported on line 16, Part III, Schedule D is a net loss? In this case, only $3,000 of the net capital loss can be carried to line 13, page 1, Form 1040, to reduce taxable income.[35] The nondeductible portion of the loss is carried forward indefinitely to be combined with the individual's future capital gains and losses. Carryforwards retain their character as short-term or long-term loss.

Net Capital Loss	Ms. Nash sold four blocks of securities this year with the following result.

Short-term capital loss	$ (4,000)
Short-term capital gain	6,100
Long-term capital loss	(11,500)
Long-term capital gain	1,250

She has a $2,100 net short-term gain and a $10,250 net long-term loss that combine to an $8,150 long-term loss. She can deduct $3,000 of this loss in the computation of AGI; the $5,150 nondeductible portion becomes a long-term capital loss carryforward.

The netting of capital gains and losses on Schedule D reflects the basic rule that capital losses are deductible to the extent of capital gains. Thus, the tax savings from a capital loss depend on the amount of capital gain recognized during the year.

Tax Savings from Capital Losses	Refer to the facts in the preceding example. Ms. Nash's capital losses sheltered $6,100 short-term capital gain, $1,250 long-term capital gain, and $3,000 ordinary income from tax. If Ms. Nash's marginal tax rate is 35 percent, the losses saved $3,373 tax.

Tax savings on:	
Short-term gain ($6,100 × 35%)	$2,135
Long-term gain ($1,250 × 15%)	188
Ordinary income ($3,000 × 35%)	1,050
	$3,373

---

[35] §1211(b). If the net capital loss consists of both short-term and long-term loss, the $3,000 deduction is attributed to the short-term loss first. §1212(b).

Ms. Nash's $5,150 capital loss carryforward will save tax in future years to the extent she can deduct it against capital gains or ordinary income.

Capital Loss Carryforward	In the following year, Ms. Nash has only one capital transaction that generates an $1,800 short-term capital gain. Consequently, she has an $1,800 net short-term gain and a $5,150 net long-term loss (her carryforward) that net to a $3,350 long-term loss. She can deduct $3,000 of this loss in computing AGI and carry the $350 nondeductible portion forward to the next year.

In present value terms, the tax savings from a capital loss diminish with each year that the investor must wait to deduct it. The obvious tax planning strategy is for the investor to generate capital gains to absorb the loss as soon as possible. Of course, even without capital gains, individuals can deduct their capital losses at the rate of $3,000 per year. But for investors who suffer large losses, the value of this stream of annual deductions may be negligible.

INVESTMENTS IN SMALL CORPORATE BUSINESSES

Investments in small corporate businesses that are struggling to grow are riskier than investments in well-established corporations with proven track records. To encourage individuals to accept this higher level of risk, the tax law contains two preferential provisions for investments in small corporate businesses.

Qualified Small Business Stock

Individuals who realize capital gain on the sale or exchange of **qualified small business stock** held for more than *five years* may exclude 50 percent of such gain from gross income.[36] The remaining capital gain is classified as 28 percent rate gain. The stock must have been issued after August 10, 1993, and issued directly to the individual in exchange for money, property, or services rendered to the issuing corporation. In other words, individuals can't purchase qualified small business stock from other shareholders.

Congress recently attempted to stimulate investment in the small business sector of the economy by temporarily increasing the 50 percent exclusion rate. The rate jumps to 75 percent for qualified stock acquired after February 17, 2009, and on or before September 27, 2010, and to 100 percent for qualified stock acquired after September 27, 2010, and on or before December 31, 2011. Individuals must still hold the stock for five years to take advantage of the exclusion.[37]

Gain on Qualified Small Business Stock	QB Inc. is a qualified small business corporation. In November 2002, Mrs. Horne contributed $200,000 to QB Inc. in exchange for 1,000 shares of stock. This year, she sold these QB shares for $560,000, realizing a $360,000 long-term capital gain. Mrs. Horne may exclude $180,000 of this gain from gross income. The $180,000 gain included in income is 28 percent rate gain. On November 18, 2011, Mrs. Horne contributed $500,000 to QB Inc. in exchange for 2,500 shares of stock. If Mrs. Horne sells this stock after November 18, 2016, she may exclude 100 percent of her gain from gross income.

[36] §1202. For any tax year, the gain eligible for this exclusion is limited to the *greater* of (1) 10 times the aggregate basis in the stock disposed of during the year or (2) $10 million reduced by eligible gain recognized in prior taxable years.

[37] Under the current version of §57(a)(7), 7 percent of the gain excluded from gross income under §1202 is an AMT preference that must be added to taxable income to compute the individual's AMTI. However, no amount of a 100 percent excluded gain is an AMT preference item.

A qualified small business is a regular corporation with no more than $50 million of gross assets immediately after the qualified stock was issued. The corporation must conduct an active trade or business other than a financial, leasing, real estate, farming, mining, hospitality, or professional service business.[38]

Section 1244 Stock

Individuals who realize a loss on the disposition of **Section 1244 stock** may deduct a limited portion as ordinary, rather than capital, loss. Married couples filing jointly are limited to an annual $100,000 ordinary deduction, while unmarried individuals or married individuals filing separate returns are limited to an annual $50,000 ordinary deduction. Any loss in excess of these limits retains its character as capital loss.[39]

Loss on Section 1244 Stock	Six years ago, Mr. and Mrs. Phipp contributed $200,000 to NW Inc. in exchange for 1,000 shares of stock, which qualified as Section 1244 stock. This year, they sold all 1,000 shares for $30,000. This was their only asset sale. Their salary, interest, and dividend income totaled $319,000, and the AGI on their joint return is $216,000.

Salary, interest, dividends	$ 319,000
Maximum Section 1244 loss	(100,000)
Capital loss deduction	(3,000)
AGI	$ 216,000

Mr. and Mrs. Phipp can carry their $67,000 nondeductible long-term capital loss ($170,000 recognized loss − $100,000 Section 1244 loss − $3,000 deductible capital loss) forward to next year.

As a general rule, the first $1 million of stock issued by a corporation that derives more than 50 percent of its annual gross receipts from the conduct of an active business qualifies as Section 1244 stock.[40] This special character applies only to stock issued directly by the corporation to an individual investor in exchange for money or property. Stock issued for services rendered to the issuing corporation does not qualify as Section 1244 stock. The Section 1244 label has no downside. If the fledgling corporate venture is a success and the investor eventually sells the stock at a gain, that gain is characterized as capital gain. On the other hand, if the investor sells the stock at a loss or if the stock becomes worthless, a significant portion (if not all) of the loss yields an immediate benefit as an above-the-line deduction.

INVESTMENT EXPENSES

Objective 5
Determine the deduction for investment interest expense.

Individuals are allowed to deduct ordinary and necessary expenses paid or incurred for the management, conservation, or maintenance of investment property.[41] Such expenses include the cost of subscriptions to investment publications and newsletters, investment management fees, and the rental of a safety deposit box to hold securities or investment-related

---

[38] See §1202(d) and (e) for the complete definition of a qualified small business.
[39] §1244(a) and (b).
[40] §1244(c).
[41] §212.

documents. The deduction for investment expenses is classified as a miscellaneous itemized deduction and thus often fails to result in any tax benefit.[42]

Investment Expenses	Mrs. Guss owns a portfolio of investment securities. This year, she paid $825 to attend a two-day seminar entitled "Asset Allocation Strategies for the Senior Investor." She also paid a $445 subscription fee to *The Wall Street Journal.* Mrs. Guss itemized deductions and reported her $1,270 total investment expenses as her only miscellaneous deductions. Because her AGI was $65,072, she could not actually deduct any of these expenses.

Miscellaneous itemized deductions	$ 1,270
AGI threshold ($65,072 × 2%)	(1,301)
Allowable deduction	–0–

Investment Interest Expense

An important set of rules governs the deductibility of interest that individuals pay on debt incurred to purchase investment property. If the property is tax-exempt state and local bonds, the interest is nondeductible.[43] The logic of this rule is apparent: Congress doesn't want the tax law to subsidize the purchase of investments yielding nontaxable income. If an individual incurs debt to purchase other investment property, the interest on the debt is an itemized deduction but only to the extent of the debtor's net investment income from any source.[44] The nondeductible portion of the interest expense is carried forward to future taxable years.

Investment Interest Expense	Mr. Guss borrowed $80,000 at 4.5 percent and invested the loan proceeds in a mutual fund that paid a $5,000 dividend. He paid $3,600 of **investment interest expense** for the year. Because his net investment income exceeded $3,600, the entire interest payment is an itemized deduction. Now assume that Mr. Guss used the loan proceeds to purchase common stock in a corporation that did not pay a dividend. His only investment income was $750 interest earned on a savings account. In this case, he can deduct only $750 investment interest expense. The $2,850 nondeductible expense carries forward to next year, when Mr. Guss can deduct it subject to the net investment income limitation.

Net Investment Income

Investment income is generated by property held for investment purposes and includes interest, dividends, annuity payments, and capital gain on the sale of investment assets. **Net investment income** equals total investment income less any expenses (other than interest) directly connected with the production of the income. If an individual recognizes income that is taxed at a preferential rate (qualified dividend income and net long-term capital gain), the tax law offers an interesting choice. The individual may elect to treat such income (or any portion thereof) as investment income, thereby securing a deduction for investment

---

[42] Miscellaneous itemized deductions are allowed only to the extent that their total exceeds 2 percent of AGI. §67.

[43] §265.

[44] §163(d).

interest. But by making this election, the individual forfeits any preferential tax rate on the income.[45] This election prevents investors from enjoying a double benefit. Their dividends and long-term capital gains can increase the investment interest expense deduction or be taxed at a preferential rate, but not both.

Election to Treat Capital Gain as Investment Income	Ms. Small paid $5,000 investment interest this year. She didn't earn any interest, dividend, or other investment income. She did, however, recognize a $6,000 net long-term capital gain from the sale of investment assets. Ms. Small can elect to treat $5,000 of this gain as investment income in order to deduct her investment interest expense. If she makes the election, only $1,000 of the $6,000 long-term capital gain included in taxable income is eligible for the 15 percent preferential rate.

INVESTMENTS IN REAL PROPERTY

As an alternative to financial assets, individuals may put their money into real estate. In this section of the chapter, we will examine the tax consequences of investing in real property.

Undeveloped Land

Individuals who invest in undeveloped land expect a return in the form of appreciation in value because land typically does not generate any significant revenue or cash flow.[46] However, owners may incur out-of-pocket expenses with respect to their land. Real property taxes can be a considerable annual expense; these tax payments are itemized deductions.[47] If the owner financed the purchase of the land through a mortgage, the interest payments are investment interest, deductible to the extent of the owner's net investment income. Instead of treating property taxes and interest as current expenses, the owner may make an annual election to capitalize these carrying charges to the basis of the land.[48] Another important consideration is that undeveloped land may be a very illiquid asset. All in all, land may be a poor investment choice for individuals who want ready access to cash.

Capitalized Interest and Tax	Ms. Jamison recently purchased a 15-acre tract of undeveloped land as a long-term investment. She financed the purchase through a mortgage. This year, she paid $1,780 interest on the mortgage and $492 local property tax on the land. Ms. Jamison took the standard deduction on her income tax return and, therefore, derived no tax benefit from any itemized deductions, including her mortgage interest and property tax. So she elected to capitalize the interest and tax, thereby increasing her basis in the land by $2,272. In any future year in which she itemizes deductions, Ms. Jamison can deduct the mortgage interest and property tax paid during such year instead of making the annual election.

The tax advantage of holding investment land is that appreciation in value is not recognized as income until the owner disposes of the land in a taxable transaction.[49] Moreover, any gain recognized on the sale of land held for at least a year qualifies for a preferential tax rate.

---

[45] §1(h)(2).

[46] Owners might receive revenues from grazing, hunting, mineral, or crop leases.

[47] §164(a)(1).

[48] §266.

[49] Individuals frequently enter into like-kind exchanges of investment real property. See the discussion of these nontaxable exchanges in Chapter 9.

This conclusion, of course, presumes that the land was a capital asset in the owner's hands. Individuals who make periodic sales of land run the risk that the IRS may treat this activity as a business and the land as an inventory asset held primarily for sale to customers. In such case, the gains recognized on the sale are ordinary income rather than capital gain.

The question of whether an individual who sells land is engaging in an investment or a business is subjective; the answer depends on the facts and circumstances of each case. When called on to decide the issue, the federal courts consider the number, frequency, and regularity of the sales and the extent to which the individual actively solicited buyers, either through advertising or a real estate agent. In cases in which the individual added substantial improvements to the land, such as roads and drainage ditches, or subdivided a single tract of land into smaller parcels, the courts have generally agreed with the IRS that the individual engaged in a business.[50]

Rental Real Estate

Developed real estate consists of land with some type of building or structure permanently attached. Individuals who own developed real estate receive rents paid by tenants or lessees who occupy the property. In many respects, a rental real estate activity is treated as a business for tax purposes. The owner recognizes the rents as ordinary income and deducts operating and maintenance expenses.[51] These items are reported on Part I, Schedule E, Form 1040. Consequently, only net profit from the rental activity is included in the owner's AGI. Rental real estate is a Section 1231 asset, and the building component is depreciable property with either a 27.5-year or a 39-year MACRS recovery period. Therefore, the owner can recover his investment in the building through annual depreciation deductions.

Mr. and Mrs. David: Schedule E	Ronald and Janet David own residential real estate that they have leased to the same tenant since 1995. This year, their revenue and expenses were as follows:

Rents received ($2,250 per month)	$27,000
Monthly yard maintenance	1,480
Property and liability insurance	2,880
Interest on mortgage	1,720
Repairs and painting	4,140
Local property tax	2,075
Monthly utilities	2,900
Legal fee for consultation on zoning restriction	675

MACRS depreciation for the year was $6,400. This information is summarized on their Schedule E, shown as Exhibit 16.3. Their $4,730 net income (line 26) was carried as an income item to page 1, Form 1040.

While rental real estate activities have many business characteristics, they actually fall into the special class of *passive activities*.[52] This classification doesn't affect the regular tax consequences of profitable rental activities. But as we will learn in the next section, the classification has major tax consequences for rental activities *operating at a loss*.

[50] See, for example, *Phelan*, T.C. Memo 2004-206, and *Rice*, T.C. Memo 2009-142.
[51] Reg. §1.212-1.
[52] §469(c)(2).

EXHIBIT 16.3

SCHEDULE E (Form 1040) Department of the Treasury Internal Revenue Service (99)	**Supplemental Income and Loss** (From rental real estate, royalties, partnerships, S corporations, estates, trusts, REMICs, etc.) ▶ Attach to Form 1040, 1040NR, or Form 1041. ▶ See separate instructions.	OMB No. 1545-0074 20**11** Attachment Sequence No. **13**

Name(s) shown on return	Your social security number
Ronald and Janet David	498 31 1240

A Did you make any payments in 2011 that would require you to file Form(s) 1099? (see instructions) ☐ Yes ☑ No

B If "Yes," did you or will you file all required Forms 1099? ☐ Yes ☑ No

Part I **Income or Loss From Rental Real Estate and Royalties** **Note.** If you are in the business of renting personal property, use **Schedule C** or **C-EZ** (see instructions). If you are an individual, report farm rental income or loss from **Form 4835** on page 2, line 40.

Caution. For each rental property listed on line 1, check the box in the last column only if you owned that property as a member of a qualified joint venture (QJV) reporting income not subject to self-employment tax.

1	Physical address of each property–street, city, state, zip	Type–from list below	**2**	For each rental real estate property listed, report the number of days rented at fair rental value and days with personal use. See instructions.	Fair Rental Days	Personal Use Days	QJV
A	1412 West Reeder Avenue, Omaha, NE 51102	1	A		365	0	
B			B				
C			C				

Type of Property:
1 Single Family Residence   3 Vacation/Short-Term Rental   5 Land   7 Self-Rental
2 Multi-Family Residence   4 Commercial   6 Royalties   8 Other (describe)

Income:				Properties	
			A	B	C
3a	Merchant card and third party payments. For 2011, enter -0-	**3a**	0		
b	Payments not reported to you on line 3a	**3b**	27,000		
4	Total not including amounts on line 3a that are not income (see instructions)	**4**	27,000		
Expenses:					
5	Advertising	**5**			
6	Auto and travel (see instructions)	**6**			
7	Cleaning and maintenance	**7**	1,480		
8	Commissions.	**8**			
9	Insurance	**9**	2,880		
10	Legal and other professional fees	**10**	675		
11	Management fees	**11**			
12	Mortgage interest paid to banks, etc. (see instructions)	**12**	1,720		
13	Other interest.	**13**			
14	Repairs.	**14**	4,140		
15	Supplies	**15**			
16	Taxes	**16**	2,075		
17	Utilities.	**17**	2,900		
18	Depreciation expense or depletion	**18**	6,400		
19	Other (list) ▶ _____	**19**			
20	Total expenses. Add lines 5 through 19	**20**	22,270		
21	Subtract line 20 from line 4. If result is a (loss), see instructions to find out if you must file **Form 6198** .	**21**	4,730		
22	Deductible rental real estate loss after limitation, if any, on **Form 8582** (see instructions)	**22**	( )	( )	( )

23a	Total of all amounts reported on line 3a for all rental properties	**23a**	0	
b	Total of all amounts reported on line 3a for all royalty properties	**23b**		
c	Total of all amounts reported on line 4 for all rental properties	**23c**	27,000	
d	Total of all amounts reported on line 4 for all royalty properties	**23d**		
e	Total of all amounts reported on line 12 for all properties	**23e**	1,720	
f	Total of all amounts reported on line 18 for all properties	**23f**	6,400	
g	Total of all amounts reported on line 20 for all properties	**23g**	22,270	
24	**Income.** Add positive amounts shown on line 21. **Do not** include any losses	**24**		4,730
25	**Losses.** Add royalty losses from line 21 and rental real estate losses from line 22. Enter total losses here	**25**	(	)
26	**Total rental real estate and royalty income or (loss).** Combine lines 24 and 25. Enter the result here. If Parts II, III, IV, and line 40 on page 2 do not apply to you, also enter this amount on Form 1040, line 17, or Form 1040NR, line 18. Otherwise, include this amount in the total on line 41 on page 2	**26**		4,730

For Paperwork Reduction Act Notice, see your tax return instructions.	Cat. No. 11344L	Schedule E (Form 1040) 2011

INVESTMENTS IN PASSIVE ACTIVITIES

Objective 6
Apply the passive activity loss limitation.

Individuals can own equity interests in business entities without rendering any personal services to the business. Many partners and shareholders have no involvement in the business conducted by their partnership or S corporation. Nevertheless, these owners are allocated a share of business income. Even the owner of a sole proprietorship might choose to leave the business operation entirely in the hands of employees. But regardless of such lack of participation, net profits belong to the proprietor. In these situations, the income to which the partner, shareholder, or sole proprietor is entitled is primarily a return on invested capital. Although such income retains its ordinary business character when reported on the owner's individual tax return, it is economically equivalent to investment income.

If an individual owns an interest in a business but does not materially participate in that business, the interest is a **passive activity** for federal tax purposes. **Material participation** means that the individual is involved in day-to-day operations on a regular, continual, and substantial basis.[53]

Passive Activity	JKL Partnership consists of three equal individual partners. Mr. Jett and Ms. Kyle are general partners who work full-time in JKL's business, while Mr. Lamb is a limited partner who has no personal involvement at all. For the two general partners, their interest in JKL is clearly a business activity. Because Mr. Lamb does not materially participate in the business, his interest in JKL is a passive activity.[54]

The classification of an interest as a passive activity doesn't affect the regular tax consequences of a profitable business interest. Assume that JKL Partnership generated $129,000 business income. Each of the three partners received a Schedule K-1 reporting a $43,000 share of this income. All three included this share as ordinary income on their Form 1040 and paid tax accordingly. The fact that Mr. Lamb's share was passive activity income had no effect on the computation of his regular tax on the income.

Passive Activity Loss Limitation

The classification of business interest as a passive activity has profound tax consequences if the business *operates at a loss.* Specifically, the owner of the passive activity can deduct the loss only to the extent of income generated by other passive activities.[55] Any disallowed loss is carried forward as a suspended passive activity loss. Suspended losses are deductible in any future year to the extent of the owner's passive activity income in that year.[56]

Passive Activity Loss Limitation	Refer to the facts in the preceding example and assume that JKL Partnership generated a $90,000 operating loss. Each partner received a Schedule K-1 reporting a $30,000 share. Mr. Jett and Ms. Kyle, the general partners who work in the business, can deduct their loss in the computation of AGI.[57] Mr. Lamb, the limited partner, is subject to the passive activity loss limitation. If his JKL interest is his only passive activity, he cannot deduct any of his $30,000 loss. If he owns another passive activity that generated income, he can deduct the loss to the extent of such income. Any disallowed loss is carried forward as a suspended passive activity loss. Mr. Lamb can deduct the suspended loss in a future year to the extent he recognizes income from either JKL Partnership or any other passive activity.

[53] §469(c)(1). Reg. §1.496-5T provides several objective tests for determining material participation.

[54] The statute creates a presumption that a *limited* partnership interest is a passive activity. §469(h)(2).

[55] §469(a)(1) and (d)(1).

[56] §469(b).

[57] This statement presumes that the partners have sufficient basis in their partnership interests to absorb their loss. See Chapter 10.

Rental Activities

The definition of passive activity includes any **rental activity** in which revenues are principally derived from the lease of tangible property for an extended period of time.[58] Activities in which revenues are principally derived from the provision of customer services are not rental activities. For instance, the operation of a hotel is a business rather than a rental activity. Similarly, businesses providing short-term use of property such as automobiles, tuxedos, or DVDs are not rental activities. If an individual owns a rental activity, that activity is passive, *regardless of the extent of the owner's participation in the activity.*

As mentioned earlier in the chapter, rental real estate activities are passive activities.[59] Accordingly, individuals who invest in rental real estate can deduct losses only to the extent of their passive activity income. However, the law provides an important exception under which individuals can deduct up to $25,000 annual loss from rental real estate without regard to the passive activity loss limitation.[60] To qualify for the full $25,000 exception, the individual's AGI (before consideration of any rental loss) must not exceed $100,000. If AGI exceeds this threshold, the $25,000 exception is reduced by 50 percent of the excess. Thus, the exception shrinks to zero for taxpayers with AGI over $150,000.

Rental Real Estate Exception	Mr. and Mrs. Ennis own and manage three duplexes that they rent to college students. They do not own any other passive activities. The duplexes generated a $31,000 loss this year. Before deduction of this loss, the couple's AGI was $95,000. Because of the rental real estate exception, they can deduct $25,000 of the rental loss to reduce AGI to $70,000. The $6,000 excess loss is a nondeductible passive activity loss that carries forward to next year.

If Mr. and Mrs. Ennis's AGI before deduction of their rental loss was $141,000, their exception is reduced to $4,500.

AGI before loss	$141,000
AGI threshold	(100,000)
Excess AGI	$ 41,000
	.50
Reduction in $25,000 exception	$ 20,500

Consequently, they can deduct $4,500 of their rental loss to reduce AGI to $136,500. The $26,500 excess loss is a nondeductible passive activity loss that carries forward to next year.

Dispositions of Passive Activities

The passive activity loss limitation is not a *permanent* loss disallowance rule. When an investor disposes of her entire interest in a passive activity in a taxable transaction (generally a sale or exchange), any suspended losses with respect to the interest are fully deductible in

[58] Reg. §1.469-1T(e)(3).

[59] Real estate professionals who devote more than one-half of their work effort each year and at least 750 hours annually to a real property business are engaged in an active business rather than a passive rental activity. A real property business includes the development, redevelopment, construction, reconstruction, acquisition, conversion, rental, operation, management, leasing or brokering of real property. §469(c)(7).

[60] §469(i). The individual must own at least a 10 percent interest in the real estate and must be significantly involved in its management.

the year of disposition. As a result, the investor finally reaps a tax benefit from every dollar of loss disallowed in an earlier year. Of course, in present value terms, the tax savings from the deferred deduction are less than the savings from a deduction in such earlier year.

Deduction of Suspended PAL	Mr. Zhou invested in a limited partnership that generated a substantial business loss in 2006 (year 0). Mr. Zhou couldn't deduct his $48,300 share of this loss because the loss was passive and he had no passive activity income. Nor did he have any passive activity income in 2007 through 2011. Mr. Zhou sold his partnership interest in 2012. Because of this disposition, he was allowed to deduct his $48,300 suspended loss in 2012. If Mr. Zhou was in a 35 percent marginal tax bracket in both 2006 and 2012 and uses a 7 percent discount rate to compute NPV, deferral of the tax savings from the deduction cost him $5,646 in present value terms.

Tax savings from 2006 deduction	
$48,300 \times 35\%$	$ 16,905
PV of tax savings from 2012 deduction	
$48,300 \times 35\% \times .666$ discount factor	(11,259)
Cost of deferral of tax savings	$ 5,646

Planning with Passive Activity Losses

Suppose that Mrs. Queen, a practicing attorney, paid $50,000 to buy stock in an S corporation operating a chain of Mexican restaurants. Because she does not materially participate in the S corporation's business, Mrs. Queen's interest is a passive activity. On her first Schedule K-1, she is allocated a $9,000 ordinary business loss, which reduces the basis in her stock to $41,000.[61] She owns no other passive activities and therefore recognized no passive activity income this year. Consequently, she can't deduct her $9,000 loss in computing AGI. Stated another way, Mrs. Queen's passive activity loss doesn't shelter the income generated by her legal practice (or any other income) from tax.

Sale of the Passive Activity

What are Mrs. Queen's options with respect to her $9,000 suspended loss? Given that the restaurant business apparently is losing money, her best option may be to sell the stock as quickly as possible! Suppose that early in the next year Mrs. Queen finds a buyer who offers $30,000 for her shares. If she sells, she will recognize an $11,000 capital loss *and* can deduct her $9,000 suspended passive activity loss as an ordinary business loss.[62] The total of the two losses ($11,000 capital loss + $9,000 ordinary loss) corresponds to her $20,000 economic loss on this unfortunate investment. The only effect of the passive activity loss limitation was to defer the deduction of the ordinary loss (and the tax benefit therefrom) for one year.

Purchase of a PIG

If Mrs. Queen believes that the restaurant business is a solid long-term investment, her second option is to find a source of passive activity income. Perhaps the restaurant will become

---

[61] §1367(a).

[62] This calculation of loss is based on Mrs. Queen's basis in the stock on January 1 without adjustment for any pro rata share of the corporation's income or loss for the year of sale.

profitable so that Mrs. Queen eventually can deduct her suspended loss against her share of the S corporation's future taxable income. If this possibility is too uncertain, she could invest in a moneymaking passive activity (dubbed a **passive income generator [PIG]** by the financial press). For instance, if she buys an interest in a profitable commercial office building, she can deduct her suspended loss from the S corporation to the extent of her rental income from the PIG.

UNEARNED INCOME MEDICARE CONTRIBUTION TAX

Beginning in 2013, high-income taxpayers with significant investment income will face a new **unearned income Medicare contribution tax,** the revenues from which are earmarked for the Medicare trust funds. This new tax was enacted to complement the existing Medicare taxes imposed on the earned income of employees and self-employed individuals.

The new Medicare tax equals 3.8 percent of the *lesser* of an individual's net investment income or the excess of AGI over a threshold amount.[63] The threshold amount is $250,000 for married individuals filing jointly ($125,000 for married filing separately) and $200,000 for unmarried individuals.

Medicare Tax on Unearned Income	In 2013, Mr. and Mrs. Yuan's net investment income totals $43,000. If the AGI on their joint return is $269,400, their unearned income Medicare contribution tax is $737 (3.8 percent of $19,400 excess AGI). If their AGI is $309,200, their Medicare tax is $1,634 (3.8 percent of $43,000 net investment income).

For purposes of the new Medicare tax, investment income includes taxable interest, dividends, annuities, royalties, and rents. It also includes income from a passive activity (a business in which the individual taxpayer doesn't materially participate) and net taxable gain from the disposition of nonbusiness property. Net investment income is the excess of investment income over any deductions properly allocated to such income.

Net Investment Income	Ms. Dahl's 2013 taxable income includes $8,700 interest and dividends from her portfolio of marketable securities and a $29,000 share of business income from a partnership. Ms. Dahl is a limited partner who doesn't materially participate in the partnership business. Her taxable income also includes an $11,000 net long-term capital gain from the sale of securities. She had no deductions properly allocable to these three income items. Ms. Dahl's net investment income for purposes of the Medicare tax is $48,700.

WEALTH TRANSFER PLANNING

Individuals who engage in successful business and investment activities inevitably accumulate wealth in the process. At some point in their lives, these individuals begin to think about transferring wealth to other parties—usually to their children and grandchildren. The decision to part with property can be intensely personal; the property owner may be more concerned with private family matters than with the financial implications of the decision.

---

[63] §1411. For purposes of this computation, AGI is increased by any §911 foreign earned income exclusion.

However, once the decision is made, most people are eager to adopt financial strategies to maximize the wealth available to younger-generation family members. As we will learn in this final section of Chapter 16, the federal transfer taxes are a primary consideration in the development of such strategies.

The Transfer Tax System

The federal transfer tax system has three components: the gift tax, the estate tax, and the generation-skipping transfer tax (which we will not discuss in this text). Congress enacted the original estate tax in 1916 as a way to redistribute a portion of the private fortunes amassed by society's richest families to the public domain. Historically, only a small percentage of the U.S. population has ever paid a federal transfer tax. Nonetheless, these taxes have always been a political flashpoint. In 2001, Congress took the bold step of prospectively repealing the estate and generation-skipping transfer taxes effective on January 1, 2010. This repeal actually went into effect, but in December 2010, Congress did an about-face by reinstating these two transfer taxes retroactive to the beginning of the year.

The Gift Tax

The gift tax is levied on the transfer of property by an individual during life **(inter vivos transfer)** for which the transferor does not receive adequate consideration in money or money's worth. The amount of the gift equals the property's fair market value.[64] The tax is paid by the **donor** making the gift. Donors are usually motivated by generosity or affection toward the **donee** receiving the gift. In other words, a gift incurs in a personal rather than a business context. Certain transfers are not treated as taxable gifts. Transfers of property to a spouse or to a qualified charity or political organization are not taxable.[65] Similarly, tuition payments to an educational organization or payments of medical expenses on behalf of another person are not taxable.[66]

Nontaxable Transfers	Maria Vargas recently transferred her equity interest in a real estate partnership to her husband Luis. She made a $100,000 donation to her church's building fund and a $50,000 donation to the American Cancer Society. Maria made a $4,500 tuition payment to the University of Oklahoma on behalf of her nephew Robert, and she paid $7,100 of medical expenses incurred by her sister Beth. None of these transfers are subject to federal gift tax.

Objective 7
Compute a taxable gift by applying the annual and lifetime exclusions.

Gift Tax Computation

Every donor can give a *de minimis* amount to any donee that is excluded from the donor's taxable gifts for the year. In 2012, this **annual gift tax exclusion** is $13,000 per donee.[67] The exclusion removes most routine birthday, graduation, wedding, and holiday presents from the gift tax base. Married couples can elect to treat a gift made by either spouse as a gift made equally by both spouses.[68] By making this gift-splitting election, the couple doubles the exclusion for the gift. The first rule of transfer tax planning is that individuals should take full advantage of the annual gift tax exclusion.

---

[64] §2501 and §2512.
[65] §2501(a)(4), §2522, and §2523.
[66] §2503(e).
[67] §2503(b). The annual exclusion is indexed for inflation.
[68] §2513.

Annual Exclusion	Mr. and Mrs. Archer have two adult sons, who are both married, and six unmarried grandchildren. In 2012, Mr. Archer gave $26,000 cash to each of 10 donees (two sons, two daughters-in-law, six grandchildren). Mr. and Mrs. Archer elected to split the gifts, so that each could claim a $13,000 exclusion. As a result, none of the gifts were taxable, and the Archers transferred $260,000 at no tax cost. The couple plans to make this systematic nontaxable transfer of wealth to younger-generation family members every year.

If the value of a gift to a donee exceeds the donor's annual exclusion, the donor has made a taxable gift. The donor must report the gift on Form 709, United States Gift Tax Return, which must be filed with the IRS by April 15 following the calendar year in which the gift was made.[69] However, a donor doesn't owe any tax until the cumulative amount of taxable gifts made during the donor's lifetime exceeds a **lifetime transfer tax exclusion**.[70] The 2010 Tax Relief Act increased the lifetime exclusion from $1 million to $5 million for gifts made after 2010. The tax on the amount of gifts in excess of the lifetime exclusion is computed at a flat 35 percent rate.

Lifetime Exclusion and Tax Computation	Tina Wood made her first taxable gift and filed her first Form 709 in 2007. The value of this gift in excess of the annual exclusion was $850,000. Because this amount was less than the $1 million lifetime exclusion, Tina owed no gift tax in 2007. Tina made a second taxable gift and filed her second Form 709 in 2011. The value of this gift in excess of the annual exclusion was $3,940,000. Because the $4,790,000 cumulative amount of the 2007 and 2011 gifts was less than the $5 million lifetime exclusion, Tina owed no gift tax in 2011. Tina made a third taxable gift and filed her third Form 709 in 2012. The value of the gift in excess of the annual exclusion was $660,000. Because the $5,450,000 cumulative value of the 2007, 2011, and 2012 gifts exceeded the $5 million lifetime exclusion, Tina owes a $157,500 gift tax ($450,000 excess × 35%), which she must pay by the April 15, 2013, filing date of the return.

Income Tax Consequences of Gifts

When a donee receives a gift from a donor, the gift is excluded from the donee's gross income.[71] If the gift includes any noncash property, the donor's adjusted basis in the property carries over to become the donee's basis.[72] Because of this carryover basis rule, unrealized appreciation in the value of the property is shifted from donor to donee.

Carryover Basis	Two years ago, Mr. Solano gave marketable securities with a $15,000 basis and a $43,000 market value to his 25-year-old daughter Eva. Mr. Solano paid no gift tax on this transfer. Eva's carryover basis in the securities was $15,000. This year, Eva sold the securities for $47,000 and recognized a $32,000 capital gain on the sale.

[69] §6075(b)(1).

[70] §2505(a)(1). The exclusion amount is indexed for inflation and is accomplished by a credit offsetting the transfer tax on the exclusion amount.

[71] §102.

[72] §1015 governs the tax basis of gifted property. If the donor pays gift tax, the carryover basis is increased by the tax attributable to the appreciation in the gifted property. If the FMV of gifted property is less than the donor's basis, the donee's basis is limited to FMV, and the donor's unrealized loss in the property disappears. As a result, donors avoid giving away loss property.

A gift of income-producing property (such as marketable securities) shifts the future income from the property (interest, dividends, capital gain) from the donor to the donee. If the donee's marginal tax rate is lower than the donor's, the income shift should result in a tax savings.

Income Shift	Before selling the marketable securities, Eva Solano received $5,100 of qualified dividends. Because her marginal rate on ordinary income was only 15 percent, Eva's preferential rate on the dividend income and capital gain was zero. If her father had received the dividends and recognized the capital gain, he would have paid tax at a 15 percent preferential rate. Consequently, the income shift saved $5,565 tax for the Solano family ($37,100 dividends and capital gain × 15%).

The tax savings from transfers of income-producing property to minor children is severely limited by the kiddie tax rules described in Chapter 14. Recall that the tax on investment income earned by children under the age of 18 is computed by reference to the marginal rate on their parents' return.

Kiddie Tax	Refer to the facts in the previous two examples. Now assume that Eva Solano is only age 14. In this case, Eva's tax on her dividend income and capital gain would be 15 percent (her parents' marginal rate), and the income shift would not save any tax for the Solano family.

While the kiddie tax certainly reduces the potential tax savings from an income shift to children, families can avoid it by transferring assets that yield deferred rather than current income. For instance, children can be given stock in a growth corporation that doesn't pay regular dividends. Similarly, children can be given Series EE savings bonds that won't generate interest income until the year of redemption.

The Estate Tax

Tax Talk
Warren Buffett, billionaire chair of Berkshire Hathaway, wants Congress to maintain the estate tax because "a meaningful estate tax is needed to prevent our democracy from becoming a dynastic plutocracy."

Wealthy individuals who choose not to give away property during life are postponing the inevitable. No one can avoid the final transfer of property that must occur at death. It is this **testamentary transfer** that may be subject to the federal estate tax.

The federal estate tax is levied on the fair market value of a deceased individual's taxable estate.[73] The **taxable estate** includes the decedent's **probate estate,** which consists of the assets bequeathed to individuals or organizations named in the decedent's will. The taxable estate also includes property not included in the probate estate but which transfers by reason of the decedent's death. For example, a decedent may have owned an insurance policy on his own life that pays a death benefit to the beneficiary named in the policy. Similarly, a decedent may have owned an interest in a retirement plan that distributes the plan balance to the beneficiary named in the plan. Both the insurance death benefit and the retirement plan distribution are included in the decedent's taxable estate.[74]

[73] §2001(a) and §2031(a).
[74] §2039 and §2042.

Objective 8
Determine a decedent's taxable estate.

The taxable estate is reduced by the decedent's debts, funeral expenses, and any administrative costs of settling the estate.[75] It is also reduced by testamentary transfers to religious, charitable, educational, government, or other nonprofit organizations.[76] Consequently, a decedent could leave her or his entire fortune to charity and avoid the estate tax altogether. Finally, the taxable estate is reduced by any transfer to a surviving spouse.[77] Because of this **unlimited marital deduction,** the estate tax on the wealth accumulated by a married couple can be deferred until the death of the second spouse.

Taxable Estate

Mr. Webb died on May 3 and was survived by his wife Imelda and two children from a previous marriage. At date of death, Mr. Webb owned property with a $7,270,000 fair market value and had $938,100 of debts. Funeral expenses and legal fees incurred by his estate totaled $94,300. In his will, Mr. Webb left his art collection worth $1,825,000 to the Metropolitan Museum and financial assets and real estate worth $3,000,000 to Imelda. His remaining property transferred in equal shares to his children. Mr. Webb's taxable estate is $1,412,600.

FMV of property transferred at death	$7,270,000
Decedent's debts	(938,100)
Funeral and administrative costs	(94,300)
Net estate	$6,237,600
Charitable bequest	(1,825,000)
Marital deduction	(3,000,000)
Taxable estate	$1,412,600

Estate Tax Computation

Under the revised transfer tax rules included in the 2010 Tax Relief Act, the estates of decedents dying after 2009 are allowed a $5 million transfer tax exclusion from the taxable estate. Any amount of the taxable estate in excess of the allowable exclusion is taxed at a flat 35 percent rate. The $5 million exclusion must be reduced by any lifetime exclusion used by the decedent for gift tax purposes.[78]

Estate Tax Computation

In 2003, 2004, and 2008, Helen Nash made taxable gifts totaling $802,900. She used $802,900 of her lifetime exclusion to reduce the amount on which gift tax was owed to zero. Helen died in 2012, leaving a taxable estate of $9,833,000. The estate tax was computed as follows.

Taxable estate	$9,833,000
Transfer tax exclusion ($5,000,000 − $802,900)	(4,197,100)
Excess taxable estate	5,635,900
Tax rate	.35
Estate tax	$1,972,565

---

[75] §2053.

[76] §2055.

[77] §2056.

[78] §2001(b) and §2010.

Note that every individual, irrespective of marital status, is allowed a $5 million exclusion to reduce the amount of transfers subject to the gift and estate taxes. When a married individual dies, any unused amount of the decedent's exclusion becomes available for use by the surviving spouse. Consequently, a married couple obtains the benefit of a $10 million transfer tax exclusion regardless of the order of their deaths or the amount of wealth transferred by each.[79]

Unused Spousal Exclusion	Ben and Edna Piper, who were married for 22 years, made no taxable gifts during their lifetimes. Ben died on November 9, 2012. His net estate was $7.2 million, half of which he left to Edna and half of which he left to his son from a previous marriage. Because of Ben's $5,000,000 transfer tax exclusion, his estate owed no estate tax.

Net estate	$7,200,000
Marital deduction for transfer to Edna	(3,600,000)
Taxable estate	$3,600,000
Transfer tax exclusion	(3,600,000)
Excess taxable estate	-0-

Benjamin's unused $1,400,000 exclusion increased Edna's transfer tax exclusion to $6,400,000.

Edna Piper survived her husband by 10 years. Upon her death, she left her $11.9 million net estate to various nieces and nephews. Edna's estate tax was computed as follows:

Taxable estate	$11,900,000
Transfer tax exclusion	(6,400,000)
Excess taxable estate	$ 5,500,000
Tax rate	.35
Estate tax	$ 1,925,000

The executor of a decedent's estate must file Form 706, United States Estate Tax Return, and pay any estate tax due within nine months of the date of death. However, the law provides generous extensions of both the filing and payment deadlines.[80]

Income Tax Consequences of Inherited Property

When a beneficiary inherits property from a decedent, the inheritance is excluded from the beneficiary's gross income. If the inheritance includes any noncash property, the beneficiary's basis equals the property's fair market value at date of death.[81] Because of this step-up (or step-down) basis rule, any unrealized appreciation (or depreciation) in the property simply vanishes and is never recognized for income tax purposes.

Stepped-Up Basis	Nancy Carter inherited undeveloped land from her deceased father. The father's basis in the land was $400,000, but its fair market value at the date of his death was $5,250,000. Nancy's basis in the land is $5,250,000.

[79] §2010(c)(2)(B) and (c)(4).
[80] §6075(a) and §6151(a). See §6161(a)(2) and §6166.
[81] §1014.

Conclusion

Millions of individuals work conscientiously to provide financial comfort for their families. They pay close attention to the income tax consequences of their business and investment decisions and implement strategies to minimize income tax cost. Unfortunately, many of these same individuals give little thought to long-range transfer tax planning. They have no idea of the size of the tax bill that would be triggered by their death. Such shortsightedness can have disastrous financial consequences, particularly in cases of unexpected and untimely death.[82] The moral of this story should be clear. People with wealth should consult a tax professional to determine their exposure to the federal transfer tax. In virtually every case, the application of fundamental planning principles can reduce that exposure and guarantee a brighter financial future.

[82] A case in point: When Joe Robbie (former owner of the Miami Dolphins) died, his estate was hit with a $47 million tax bill. The estate had insufficient liquid assets, and the family was forced to sell both the football team and the Dolphins' stadium to raise cash to pay the tax.

Key Terms

accelerated death benefits *493*
annual gift tax exclusion *513*
capital gain distribution *487*
cash surrender value *492*
collectibles *497*
donee *513*
donor *513*
inside buildup *492*
inter vivos transfer *513*
investment interest expense *505*
lifetime transfer tax exclusion *514*
long-term capital gain or loss *497*
market discount *490*

material participation *509*
mutual fund *486*
net investment income *505*
nonbusiness bad debt *496*
original issue discount (OID) *491*
passive activity *509*
passive income generator (PIG) *512*
private activity bonds *489*
probate estate *515*
qualified dividend distribution *487*
qualified dividend income *487*
qualified small business stock *503*
rental activity *510*

reorganization *496*
Section 1244 stock *504*
securities *486*
Series EE savings bonds *490*
short-term capital gain or loss *497*
taxable estate *515*
testamentary transfer *515*
Treasury inflation-protected securities (TIPS) *490*
28 percent rate gain or loss *497*
unearned income Medicare contribution tax *512*
unlimited marital deduction *516*
unrecaptured Section 1250 gain *500*

Questions and Problems for Discussion

1. Contrast the income tax consequences of the yields on the following investments.
   a. U.S. Treasury bonds.
   b. Bonds issued by the State of Illinois.
   c. Bonds issued by a publicly held corporation at their face value.
   d. Bonds issued by a publicly held corporation at a discounted value.
   e. Preferred stock issued by a publicly held corporation.
   f. Shares issued by a mutual fund.

2. Term life insurance has no investment element and no cash surrender value. As a result, a term policy represents pure insurance protection. What are the tax consequences when the owner lets a term policy lapse by discontinuing premium payments?

3. Mrs. SD, age 74, has $50,000 in a certificate of deposit paying 6 percent annual interest. In addition to this interest income, she receives Social Security and a modest pension from her former employer. Her marginal tax rate is 10 percent. Mrs. SD lives independently, but she anticipates that in several years she will need to liquidate the certificate of deposit to buy into an assisted-living retirement home. She recently read a magazine article on the benefits of tax-deferred annuities and wonders if she should transfer her $50,000 savings into an annuity. Discuss whether this tax planning strategy is advisable for Mrs. SD.

4. Ms. Q sadly concluded that a $7,500 debt owed to her by Mr. and Mrs. L is uncollectible. Compare the tax consequences to Ms. Q if the debt arose because she extended credit to Mr. and Mrs. L in a business transaction or if the debt arose because she loaned them money for personal reasons.

5. What is the logic for the presumption that a limited interest in a business partnership is a passive activity?

6. Mrs. K is a shareholder in TK, an S corporation. What fact would be the strongest indicator that she materially participates in TK's business?

7. Discuss the potential effect of the passive activity loss limitation on the market value of *profitable* rental real estate activities.

8. Identify the structural similarity between the investment interest expense limitation, the capital loss limitation, and the passive activity loss limitation.

9. Mr. and Mrs. FB each own 30 percent of the voting common stock of FB Inc. Four unrelated investors each own 10 percent. Based on a recent appraisal, FB's net worth is $10 million. Discuss the *valuation* issue suggested if:

   a. Mr. and Mrs. FB give their combined 60 percent stock interest to their son.

   b. An unrelated investor gives her 10 percent stock interest to her son.

10. Discuss the tax policy rationale behind the unlimited federal estate tax deduction for testamentary transfers to religious, charitable, educational, government, or other nonprofit organizations.

11. Mr. and Mrs. B earn a combined annual salary of $150,000. What *two* basic economic choices do they have with respect to this income (i.e., what can they do with their money)? Now assume that Mr. and Mrs. B own property worth $2 million. What *three* basic economic choices do they have with respect to this wealth?

Application Problems

For the following problems, assume the taxable year is 2012.

1. Ms. S, who has a 33 percent marginal tax rate, owns Benbow Inc. preferred stock in her investment portfolio. Her Form 1099 reported that she earned $19,580 dividend income on her Benbow investment. Compute her tax on this income assuming that:

   a. On the basis of Ms. S's instruction, Benbow made a $19,580 direct deposit into Ms. S's bank account.

   b. On the basis of Ms. S's instruction, Benbow reinvested the dividend in additional Benbow shares.

2. Mr. Lay, who has a 35 percent marginal tax rate, earned a $22,030 dividend on his investment in Rexford Mutual Fund. Compute the tax on this dividend if his Form 1099 reported that:

   a. The entire $22,030 was an ordinary dividend.

   b. $17,540 was an ordinary dividend and $4,490 was a capital gain distribution.

   c. $6,920 was an ordinary dividend, $10,620 was a qualified dividend distribution, and $4,490 was a capital gain distribution.

3. At the beginning of the year, Mr. S paid $15 per share for 620 shares of Carmel common stock. He received cash distributions totaling $840. His Form 1099 reported that $700 was a dividend and $140 was a nontaxable distribution. Compute his basis in his 620 shares at year-end.

4. Mrs. Nunn, who has a 28 percent marginal tax rate, earned $2,690 interest on a debt instrument this year. Compute her *federal* tax on this income assuming that the debt instrument was:

    a. An unsecured note from her son, who borrowed money from his mother to finance the construction of his home.

    b. A certificate of deposit from a federal bank.

    c. A 30-year General Electric bond.

    d. A U.S. Treasury note.

    e. A City of Memphis municipal bond.

5. Refer to the preceding problem and assume that Mrs. Nunn lives in New Jersey, which taxes the interest on bonds issued by state and local jurisdictions outside New Jersey. If Mrs. Nunn's state income tax rate is 7 percent, compute her New Jersey tax on the $2,690 interest assuming that the debt instrument was:

    a. A 30-year General Electric bond.

    b. A U.S. Treasury note.

    c. A City of Memphis municipal bond.

6. Mrs. Z, a resident of Virginia, paid $50,000 for a bond issued by Pennsylvania that paid $3,400 interest this year. Her marginal state income tax rate is 6 percent. Under Virginia law, interest on debt obligations issued by another state is taxable. Mrs. Z can deduct state income tax on her Form 1040, and her marginal federal income tax rate is 35 percent. Compute her after-tax rate of return on the bond.

7. Ms. Pay, who has a 33 percent marginal tax rate, owns HHL Inc. corporate bonds in her investment portfolio. She earned $74,800 interest this year on her HHL bonds. Compute her after-tax cash flow assuming that:

    a. She received two semiannual cash payments of $37,400 each.

    b. She instructed HHL to reinvest her interest payments in additional bonds.

    c. The entire $74,800 represented amortization of OID.

8. Mr. Jolly received the $100,000 face amount on the redemption of a matured corporate bond. How much interest income does he recognize on redemption if:

    a. He purchased the bond from a broker for $93,100?

    b. He purchased the bond from the corporate issuer at its $72,900 original discount price?

9. In 2010, Mrs. Ulm paid $80,000 for a corporate bond with a $100,000 stated redemption value. Based on the bond's yield to maturity, amortization of the $20,000 discount was $1,512 in 2010 and $1,480 in 2011. Mrs. Ulm sold the bond for $84,180 in 2012. What are her tax consequences in each year assuming that:

    a. She bought the newly issued bond from the corporation?

    b. She bought the bond in the public market through her broker?

10. On February 13, Mr. Dega invested $75,000 in TIPS paying 3.5 percent yearly interest. During the year, Mr. Dega received two cash interest payments totaling $2,742. On December 31, the adjusted principal amount of the TIPS was $76,038.

    a. How much interest income from the TIPS does Mr. Dega recognize this year?

    b. What is Mr. Dega's tax basis in his TIPS investment at the beginning of next year?

11. In 2010, Mr. Dale paid $47,600 for 3,400 shares of GKL Mutual Fund and elected to reinvest dividends in additional shares. In 2010 and 2011, he received Form 1099s reporting the following.

	Dividends Reinvested	Shares Purchased	Price per Share	Total Shares Owned
2010	$4,920	312	$15.769	3,712
2011	5,873	340	17.274	4,052

   a. If Mr. Dale sells his 4,052 shares for $18 per share, compute his recognized gain.

   b. If he sells only 800 shares for $18 per share and uses the FIFO method to determine basis, compute his recognized gain.

   c. If he sells only 800 shares for $18 per share and uses the average basis method, compute his recognized gain.

12. Sixteen years ago, Ms. Cole purchased a $500,000 insurance policy on her own life and named her son as sole beneficiary. She has paid $31,280 total premiums to keep this policy in force.

   a. This year, she liquidates the policy for its $38,500 cash surrender value. Does she recognize any income on the liquidation?

   b. Now assume that Ms. Cole is terminally ill. The insurance policy provides that a person with a life expectancy of less than one year can liquidate the policy and receive 80 percent of the death benefit. She does so and receives a $400,000 accelerated death benefit. Does she recognize any income on the liquidation?

13. Fifteen years ago, Mr. F paid $50,000 for a single-premium annuity contract. This year, he began receiving a $1,300 monthly payment that will continue for his life. On the basis of his age, he can expect to receive $312,000. How much of each monthly payment is taxable income to Mr. F?

14. Refer to the facts in the preceding problem. Assume that on January 1, 2023, Mr. F's unrecovered investment in the annuity is $1,875.

   a. How much of his total 2023 annuity payments ($15,600) are taxable?

   b. Assume that he dies in February after receiving only one $1,300 payment. What are the tax consequences on his final Form 1040?

15. Ten years ago, Mr. L paid $8 per share for 1,800 shares of Drago stock. Mr. L learned that Drago is in bankruptcy and can pay only 30 percent of its debt. What are the tax consequences to Mr. L of Drago's bankruptcy?

16. Three years ago, Mrs. B loaned $10,000 to Mr. J in return for his interest-bearing note. She made the loan to enable him to begin his own business. This year, Mr. J informed Mrs. B that his business had failed and that he was unable to repay the debt. Mrs. B decided not to take legal action to enforce the debt. What are her tax consequences of this bad debt?

17. CVF owned 2,000 shares of Jarvis nonvoting common stock with a $225,000 basis. In each of the following cases, determine CVF's recognized gain or loss on the disposition of this stock.

   a. CVF exchanged it for 1,300 shares of Jarvis voting common stock worth $387,000.

   b. CVF exchanged it for U.S. long-term bonds worth $317,500.

   c. CVF exchanged it for 900 shares of Newton common stock worth $280,000. This exchange was not pursuant to a corporate reorganization involving Jarvis and Newton.

   d. CVF exchanged it for 900 shares of Newton common stock worth $280,000. This exchange was pursuant to a corporate reorganization involving Jarvis and Newton.

18. Refer to the preceding problem. For each case, determine CVF's tax basis in the security received in the exchange.

19. Mrs. Beard recognized a $12,290 loss on the sale of corporate stock this year. How much loss can she deduct in each of the following cases?

   a. She had no other capital transactions this year.

   b. She recognized a $3,780 capital gain on the sale of an antique rug and had no other capital transaction this year.

   c. She recognized a $15,610 capital gain on the sale of investment land and had no other capital transaction this year.

20. Mr. Alm earned a $61,850 salary and recognized a $5,600 loss on the sale of corporate stock this year. Compute Mr. Alm's AGI in each of the following cases.

   a. Mr. Alm had no other capital transactions this year.

   b. Mr. Alm recognized a $12,250 capital gain on the sale of mutual fund shares.

   c. Mr. Alm received an $8,000 capital gain distribution from a mutual fund and had a $3,900 capital loss carryforward from a previous year.

21. Mr. and Mrs. Revel had $206,200 AGI before considering capital gains and losses. For each of the following cases, compute their AGI.

   a. On May 8, they recognized a $8,900 short-term capital gain. On June 25, they recognized a $15,000 long-term capital loss.

   b. On February 11, they recognized a $2,100 long-term capital gain. On November 3, they recognized a $1,720 long-term capital loss.

   c. On April 2, they recognized a $5,000 long-term capital loss. On September 30, they recognized a $4,800 short-term capital loss.

   d. On January 12, they recognized a $5,600 short-term capital loss. On July 5, they recognized a $1,500 long-term capital gain.

22. Refer to the preceding problem. Determine which of the four cases results in a capital loss carryforward for Mr. and Mrs. Revel. What is the amount and character of each carryforward?

23. Mr. Fox, a single taxpayer, recognized a $64,000 long-term capital gain, a $14,300 short-term capital gain, and a $12,900 long-term capital loss. Compute Mr. Fox's tax if his taxable income before consideration of his capital transactions is $421,000.

24. Mrs. Cox earned a $313,000 salary and recognized a $29,300 net long-term capital gain this year. Compute the tax on the gain if:

   a. None of the gain is collectibles gain or unrecaptured Section 1250 gain.

   b. $10,000 is collectibles gain.

   c. $15,500 is unrecaptured Section 1250 gain.

   d. $1,700 is collectibles gain and $22,000 is unrecaptured Section 1250 gain.

25. Mr. and Mrs. Scole sold commercial real estate for $685,000. Their adjusted basis at date of sale was $544,700 ($596,600 cost − $51,900 straight-line accumulated depreciation). Compute the Scole's tax on their recognized gain assuming that this sale was their only property disposition this year.

26. In 1995, Ms. Ennis, a head of household, contributed $50,000 in exchange for 500 shares of Seta stock. Seta is a qualified small business. This year, Ms. Ennis sold all 500 shares for $117,400. Her only other capital transaction resulted in an $8,600 long-term capital gain. Her taxable income before consideration of her two capital transactions is $191,000.

   a. Compute her tax for the year.

    b. How would the computation change if Ms. Ennis acquired the Seta stock in 2009 instead of 1995?

27. In 2002, Mr. EF, a single taxpayer, contributed $45,000 in exchange for 500 shares of DB stock. In 2005, he paid $40,000 to another shareholder to purchase 1,000 more DB shares. All DB's stock qualified as Section 1244 stock when it was issued. This year, Mr. EF sold all 1,500 DB shares for $16 per share. His only income item was his $80,000 salary.

    a. Compute Mr. EF's AGI.

    b. How would AGI change if he recognized a $20,000 capital gain on the sale of other securities?

28. Ms. Reid borrowed $50,000 from a broker to purchase Lero Inc. common stock. This year, she paid $3,900 interest on the debt. Compute her itemized deduction for this interest in each of the following cases.

    a. The Lero stock paid a $1,100 dividend this year, and Ms. Reid had no other investment income.

    b. Ms. Reid's only investment income was $690 interest on a certificate of deposit.

    c. Ms. Reid's only investment income was a $4,900 ordinary dividend from her investment in Koal Mutual Fund.

29. Mr. and Mrs. Poe earned $94,900 compensation income and $963 interest this year and recognized a $600 short-term capital gain and a $7,200 long-term capital gain on the sale of securities. They incurred $4,400 investment interest expense and $12,500 other itemized deductions. They have no dependents.

    a. Compute the Poe's tax on a joint return if they do not elect to treat any long-term capital gain as investment income.

    b. Compute the Poe's tax if they elect to treat enough long-term capital gain as investment income to allow them to deduct their investment interest.

30. Mr. Sunn, who is in a 35 percent marginal tax bracket, recognized a $15,000 capital loss in 2012. Compute the tax savings from this loss assuming that:

    a. He also recognized an $18,000 short-term capital gain.

    b. He also recognized an $18,000 long-term capital gain.

    c. He also recognized an $18,000 28 percent rate gain.

    d. He recognized no capital gain in 2012 and doesn't expect to recognize capital gain in 2013 through 2016. Mr. Sunn uses a 5 percent discount rate to compute NPV.

31. Mr. and Mrs. Morris own a grocery store as a sole proprietorship. Their net profit and other relevant items for the year are:

Grocery store net profit	$44,000
Deduction for SE tax	(3,109)
Dividends and interest income	1,080
Loss from a rental house	(6,470)
Loss from a limited partnership interest	(3,400)

Compute Mr. and Mrs. Morris's AGI.

32. Mr. Kelly owns stock in VP and in BL, both of which are S corporations. This year, he had the following income and loss items.

Salary	$ 62,300
Business income from VP	19,000
Business loss from BL	(25,000)

Compute Mr. Kelly's AGI under each of the following assumptions.

a. He materially participates in VP's business but not in BL's business.

b. He materially participates in BL's business but not in VP's business.

c. He materially participates in both corporate businesses.

d. He does not materially participate in either corporate business.

33. Ms. TN owns a one-half interest in an apartment complex, which is her only passive activity. The complex operated at a $53,000 loss this year. In addition to her share of this loss, Ms. TN had the following income items.

Salary	$59,000
Interest and dividends	4,400

a. Compute her AGI.

b. How would AGI change if her salary was $113,400 rather than $59,000?

c. How would AGI change if her salary was $168,250 rather than $59,000?

34. Ms. Adams owns an interest in ABCD Partnership, which is a passive activity. At the beginning of the year, she projects that her share of ABCD's business loss will be $16,000, and that she will have the following additional items.

Net profit from her consulting business	$75,000
Deduction for SE tax	(5,299)
Interest and dividends	1,500

Ms. Adams plans to buy a rental house that should generate $9,500 income this year. Compute her AGI and the tax cost of her projected rent income.

35. Mr. Garza earned an $85,000 salary and recognized a $12,000 loss on a security sale and a $14,000 gain on the sale of a limited partnership interest. His share of the partnership's business income through date of sale was $2,100. (Both the gain and the business income are passive activity income.) Mr. Garza was allocated a $13,900 passive activity loss from an S corporation. Compute his AGI.

36. Mr. Erwin's 2012 marginal tax rate on ordinary income is 35 percent. In 2012, his $958,000 AGI included a $24,900 net long-term capital gain and $37,600 business income from a passive activity.

a. Compute Mr. Erwin's regular tax on the $62,500 investment income from these two sources.

b. Now assume the taxable year is 2013. Compute Mr. Erwin's Medicare contribution tax if the $62,500 is his net investment income for the year. What is Mr. Erwin's marginal tax rate on his long-term capital gain?

37. Mr. Zeplin wants to make a cash gift to each of his five children, to each of their five spouses, and to each of his 13 grandchildren. How much total wealth can he transfer to his descendants without making a taxable gift if:

a. He is an unmarried individual.

b. He is married to Mrs. Zeplin.

38. Mr. Ito, an unmarried individual, made a gift of real estate to his son. Compute the amount subject to the federal gift tax in each of the following situations.

a. The FMV of the real estate was $1,750,000, and the transfer was Mr. Ito's first taxable gift.

    b. The FMV of the real estate was $6,450,000, and the transfer was Mr. Ito's first taxable gift.

    c. The FMV of the real estate was $4,312,000. Two years ago, Mr. Ito made his first taxable gift: marketable securities with a $987,000 FMV *in excess of the annual exclusion.*

39. Connor is the 10-year-old son of Bob and Jane Stevens. This year, Connor earned $5,831 interest from an investment bond portfolio he inherited from his grandfather. Compute Connor's income tax if his parents' marginal tax rate is 28 percent.

40. Mr. JS died on June 19 when the total FMV of his property was $12 million and his debts totaled $789,000. His executor paid $13,000 funeral expenses and $82,600 accounting and legal fees to settle the estate. Mr. JS bequeathed $500,000 to the First Lutheran Church of Milwaukee and $1 million to Western Wisconsin College. He bequeathed his art collection (FMV $2.4 million) to his wife and the residual of his estate to his three children.

    a. Compute Mr. JS's taxable estate.

    b. Compute the estate tax payable by Mr. JS's executor assuming that Mr. JS made no taxable gifts during his lifetime.

    c. Compute the estate tax payable by Mr. JS's executor assuming that Mr. JS made a $915,000 taxable gift in 2011, but paid no gift tax because of his lifetime transfer tax exclusion.

41. Mrs. Wolter owns investment land with a $138,000 basis and a $200,000 FMV. Compute the after-tax sale proceeds in each of the following cases.

    a. She sells the land herself. Her taxable income before considering the long-term gain on sale is $310,000.

    b. She gives a 25 percent interest in the land to each of her four single adult grandchildren (without incurring a gift tax) who immediately sell it. Each grandchild's taxable income before considering the gain on sale is $8,000.

    c. She dies while still owning the land. Her single daughter inherits the land and immediately sells it. The daughter's taxable income before considering the gain on sale is $79,000.

Issue Recognition Problems

Identify the tax issue or issues suggested by the following situations and state each issue in the form of a question.

1. Mr. X invests in Series EE savings bonds. He projects that his sole proprietorship will generate a sizeable loss, and he wants to accelerate income from other sources to offset it. He could elect to recognize $28,000 accrued interest on the savings bonds he now owns. However, he doesn't want to recognize current income on the bonds he will purchase in future years.

2. At the beginning of the year, Ms. A owned 2,900 shares of SBS stock with a basis of $32 per share. SBS paid a 50 percent stock dividend, and Ms. A received 1,450 additional SBS shares. Before this dividend, the market price per share was $90. After the dividend, the price fell to $65.

3. In 1993, Mr. L paid $18,000 for a newly issued BN bond with a $30,000 stated redemption value. He has recognized $6,000 of the original issue discount (OID) as ordinary interest income. This year, BN went bankrupt and informed Mr. L that his bond was worthless.

4. Mr. and Mrs. G paid $53,000 for a corporate bond with a $50,000 stated redemption value. They paid the $3,000 premium because the bond's annual interest rate is higher than the market interest rate.

5. Three years ago, Mrs. B purchased 1,000 shares of NN stock from an unrelated party for $12 per share. After her purchase, the value of the shares steadily declined. Two weeks ago, an unrelated party offered to buy the shares for 30 cents per share. Mrs. B declined the offer and immediately mailed her shares to NN's secretary-treasurer with a note declaring her intention to abandon them.

6. Two years ago, Ms. X loaned $3,500 to her 20-year-old daughter, who used the loan proceeds to buy a used car. This year, the daughter informed her mother that she could not repay the debt.

7. Mr. O was a 25 percent partner in MNOP Partnership, which operated a gift and souvenir shop. He materially participated in the partnership business. Several years ago, Mr. O loaned $10,000 to MNOP in return for a written interest-bearing note. Unfortunately, MNOP went bankrupt before the loan was repaid.

8. This year, Ms. T had a $29,000 capital loss carryforward and a $8,200 suspended passive activity loss carryforward. He died on September 12 and did not recognize any capital gain or passive activity income during the year.

9. Ms. N has $60,000 suspended passive activity losses from her interest in the EZ Limited Partnership. In December, she sold this interest to N Inc., a regular corporation in which she is the sole shareholder.

10. Mr. B has a $7,900 adjusted basis in his limited interest in PKO Partnership. He also has $22,000 suspended passive activity losses from PKO. Mr. B recently sent a letter to PKO's corporate general partner formally abandoning his equity in the partnership.

11. Mr. OG, a 66-year-old divorced individual, has two children with his former wife. He recently married a 45-year-old woman with no property of her own. Therefore, Mr. OG plans to change his will to provide that when he dies, his fortune will be placed in a trust. His new wife will receive the income for as long as she lives, but she has no direct ownership in the trust property. When she dies, Mr. OG's two children will inherit everything.

12. Mr. D died on March 8. His taxable estate includes a traditional IRA with a $140,000 balance. Mr. D's contributions to this IRA were fully deductible. His son is the beneficiary of the IRA.

13. Mrs. AS died on June 1. She and her surviving husband were co-owners of real property with a $200,000 adjusted basis and a $1.6 million FMV. Mr. AS inherited his wife's half of the property.

Research Problems

1. Mrs. Evelyn Baker sued her stockbroker for mismanagement of her account. The broker ultimately settled the case by paying her $250,000. The payment represented the loss in value of Mrs. Baker's stock portfolio attributable to the mismanagement. Because the payment was made with respect to capital assets, Mrs. Baker could report the payment as a $250,000 capital gain (rather than ordinary income) on her Form 1040. Her legal fees for the lawsuit totaled $70,000. Can Mrs. Baker treat the fees as a capital loss by simply offsetting them against the settlement and thereby include only $180,000 net capital gain in her AGI?

2. Todd Zimler, who files a joint income tax return with his wife, Stella, owns 85 percent of the outstanding stock of Zimler Manufacturing. In January of last year, Todd transferred a tract of investment land to the corporation in exchange for 600 shares of nonvoting preferred stock, which qualified as Section 1244 stock. At date of transfer, Todd's basis in the land was $185,000, and the land's FMV was $60,000. The exchange

of land for stock was nontaxable under Section 351. Consequently, Todd recognized no loss and took a $185,000 substituted basis in the 100 shares of stock. In May of this year, Todd sold the 100 shares to an unrelated investor for $62,000. What is the character of Todd's $123,000 recognized loss?

3. Rachel Sanchez is a limited partner in HN Partnership, which operates a souvenir shop, and a member in Jams-n-Jellies LLC, which makes specialty food items and sells them at retail. Rachel has no involvement in the partnership business, but she handles all the advertising for the LLC. The LLC compensates her at the rate of $45 per hour, and she billed the LLC for 592 hours of work during 2012. Rachel's only other income-generating activity is her part-time employment as a librarian.

   Rachel's 2012 Schedule K-1 from HN Partnership reported that her share of ordinary business loss was $3,810. Her 2012 Schedule K-1 from Jams-n-Jellies LLC reported that her share of ordinary business income was $15,082. How much of her share of the partnership loss can Rachel deduct on her 2012 Form 1040?

Tax Planning Cases

1. Ms. K, who is in the 35 percent marginal tax bracket, acquired the following blocks of stock in KDS, a closely held corporation.

July 12, 2001	1,400 shares at $41 per share
December 3, 2005	800 shares at $46 per share
September 30, 2009	2,000 shares at $49 per share*
October 2, 2012	750 shares at $53 per share

   *Qualified small business stock.

   In November 2012, Ms. K agreed to sell 1,000 KDS shares to Mr. N for $60 per share. Which shares should she sell to maximize her after-tax cash from the sale?

2. Ms. EH is the owner and beneficiary of a $150,000 insurance policy on her mother's life. Ms. EH has paid $46,000 premiums, and the policy is fully paid up (no more premiums are due). She needs money and is considering cashing in the policy for its $95,000 cash surrender value. Alternatively, she can borrow $70,000 against the policy from the insurance company. She will pay 5 percent annual interest (a nondeductible personal expense) and repay the loan from the death benefit. Ms. EH's mother is in poor health and should live no more than 10 years. Ms. EH's marginal tax rate is 25 percent. Assuming a 6 percent discount rate, should she cash in the policy or borrow against it?

3. Mr. and Mrs. Prinze are evaluating an investment in undeveloped land. The year 0 cost is $100,000, and they can borrow $60,000 of the purchase price at 8 percent. They will pay interest only in years 1 through 5. The annual property tax on the land will be $1,200 in years 1 through 5. Mr. and Mrs. Prinze project that they can sell the land in year 5 for $160,000 and repay the $60,000 loan from the sales proceeds. They have a 35 percent marginal tax rate and use a 9 percent discount rate to compute NPV. Determine if they should make this investment under the following assumptions.

   a. They have enough net investment income and other itemized deductions so that the $6,000 annual carrying charge (interest plus property tax) is deductible in years 1 through 5.

   b. Because they do not itemize deductions, they elect to capitalize the annual carrying charge to the basis of the land.

4. Mr. and Mrs. U's taxable income is $260,000. Mr. U plans to exercise incentive stock options with a $65,000 bargain element. In addition to this bargain element, the couple has approximately $12,000 positive AMT adjustments and preferences. They want to invest $50,000 excess funds and could purchase either a corporate bond paying 10 percent or a newly issued private activity tax-exempt bond paying 7.5 percent. Both bonds have identical risk. Which investment yields the greater after-tax cash flow?

5. As of November 30, 2012, Ms. B had $12,000 capital losses and no capital gains. She owns 4,900 shares of GG stock with a $15 basis and a $45 FMV per share. Ms. B plans to hold her stock for three more years before selling it and using the proceeds to buy a home. However, she could easily sell 400 shares to trigger a $12,000 capital gain and then immediately repurchase them. If her marginal tax rate is 35 percent, should she implement this strategy?

6. Mrs. Mackey is evaluating two investment opportunities with identical risk. Investment A will generate $7,200 income and cash flow in years 0 through 2. Investment P will generate a $25,000 passive activity loss in years 0 and 1 and no cash flow. In year 2, Investment P will generate $73,000 taxable income and $23,000 cash flow. After three years, both investments will return her initial cash contribution. Mrs. Mackey uses an 8 percent discount rate to compute NPV. Determine the superior investment under each of the following assumptions.

   a. Her marginal tax rate over the investment period is 25 percent, and she owns no other passive activities.

   b. Her marginal tax rate over the investment period is 35 percent, and she owns rental property generating $40,000 annual income.

7. Ms. Barstow purchased a limited interest in Quinnel Partnership in 2012. Her share of the partnership's 2012 business loss was $5,700. Unfortunately, Ms. Barstow could not deduct this loss because she had no passive activity income, so she is carrying it forward into 2013. Quinnel Partnership projects that it will operate at breakeven (no income or loss) for several years. However, Ms. Barstow believes that her partnership interest is a solid long-term investment, and she has no plans to sell it.

   On January 1, 2013, Ms. Barstow must decide between two new investments that are comparable in terms of risk and liquidity. She could invest $100,000 in TNB Limited Partnership, and her share of the partnership's 2013 business income would be $8,000. Alternatively, she could invest $100,000 in a high-yield bond fund that promises a 10 percent return (Ms. Barstow would receive $10,000 interest income in 2013). Which investment would result in a better after-tax return for 2013, assuming that:

   a. Ms. Barstow is in a 25 percent marginal tax bracket?

   b. Ms. Barstow is in a 35 percent marginal tax bracket?

Appendix **16–A**

Comprehensive Schedule D Problem

Martin and Deanna Lowell made the following security sales in 2011.

	Date Acquired	Date Sold	Sales Price	Tax Basis
45 shares Pluto mutual fund	08/03/11	12/30/11	$13,500	$13,100
2,040 shares GG stock	05/14/04	10/06/11	42,400	37,500
13,199 shares MN stock	02/11/02	09/12/11	17,050	21,200
1,782 shares ZT stock	01/08/99	12/29/11	36,900	4,400

- Mrs. Lowell is a limited partner in Cohen LP. Her Schedule K-1 reported a $7,610 share of long-term capital gain.
- The Lowells received a Form 1099 from Pluto mutual fund reporting a $700 long-term capital gain distribution.
- In 2004, Mrs. Lowell loaned $7,500 to her cousin, Cynthia Graetz, who needed the money for a new business venture. Cynthia recently declared personal bankruptcy, and Mrs. Lowell decided not to pursue collection of the $7,500 debt in court.
- The Lowells have a $630 short-term capital loss carryforward and a $2,900 long-term capital loss carryforward.
- The Lowells' taxable income (Form 1040, line 43) is $466,332, which includes $26,200 qualified dividend income (line 9b).

The above information and the calculation of Mr. and Mrs. Lowell's regular tax are shown on the following Form 8949, Schedule D, and Qualified Dividends and Capital Gain Tax Worksheet. (For simplicity of presentation, the required multiple Forms 8949 are condensed into one form.)

Form **8949**

Department of the Treasury
Internal Revenue Service (99)

Sales and Other Dispositions of Capital Assets

▶ See Instructions for Schedule D (Form 1040).
▶ For more information about Form 8949, see *www.irs.gov/form8949*.
▶ Attach to Schedule D to list your transactions for lines 1, 2, 3, 8, 9, and 10.

OMB No. 1545-0074

20**11**

Attachment
Sequence No. **12A**

Name(s) shown on return
Martin and Deanna Lowell

Your social security number
598-65-5150

Part I Short-Term Capital Gains and Losses—Assets Held One Year or Less

Note: You **must** check **one** of the boxes below. Complete a *separate* Form 8949, page 1, for **each** box that is checked.

*Caution. Do not complete column (b) or (g) until you have read the instructions for those columns (see the Instructions for Schedule D (Form 1040)). Columns (b) and (g) do not apply for most transactions and should generally be left blank.

☑ **(A)** Short-term transactions reported on Form 1099-B with basis reported to the IRS ☐ **(B)** Short-term transactions reported on Form 1099-B but basis not reported to the IRS ☑ **(C)** Short-term transactions for which you cannot check box A or B

1	(a) Description of property (Example: 100 sh. XYZ Co.)	(b) Code, if any, for column (g)*	(c) Date acquired (Mo., day, yr.)	(d) Date sold (Mo., day, yr.)	(e) Sales price (see instructions)	(f) Cost or other basis (see instructions)	(g) Adjustments to gain or loss, if any*
	45 shares Pluto mutual fund		08/03/11	12/30/2011	13,500	13,100	
	Nonbusiness bad debt - Cynthia Graetz				0	7,500	
	(statement attached)						

2 Totals. Add the amounts in columns (e) and (f). Also, combine the amounts in column (g). Enter here and include on Schedule D, **line 1** (if **box A** above is checked), **line 2** (if **box B** above is checked), or **line 3** (if **box C** above is checked) . . . . ▶ | **2** | 13,500 | 20,600 | |

For Paperwork Reduction Act Notice, see your tax return instructions.   Cat. No. 37768Z   Form **8949** (2011)

Form 8949 (2011)

Attachment Sequence No. **12A**   Page **2**

Name(s) shown on return. Do not enter name and social security number if shown on other side.

Your social security number

Part II Long-Term Capital Gains and Losses—Assets Held More Than One Year

Note: You **must** check **one** of the boxes below. Complete a *separate* Form 8949, page 2, for **each** box that is checked.

*Caution. Do not complete column (b) or (g) until you have read the instructions for those columns (see the Instructions for Schedule D (Form 1040)). Columns (b) and (g) do not apply for most transactions and should generally be left blank.

☐ **(A)** Long-term transactions reported on Form 1099-B with basis reported to the IRS ☑ **(B)** Long-term transactions reported on Form 1099-B but basis not reported to the IRS ☐ **(C)** Long-term transactions for which you cannot check box A or B

3	(a) Description of property (Example: 100 sh. XYZ Co.)	(b) Code, if any, for column (g)*	(c) Date acquired (Mo., day, yr.)	(d) Date sold (Mo., day, yr.)	(e) Sales price (see instructions)	(f) Cost or other basis (see instructions)	(g) Adjustments to gain or loss, if any*
	2,040 shares GG stock		05/14/04	10/06/11	42,400	37,500	
	13,199 shares MN stock		02/11/02	09/12/11	17,050	21,200	
	1,782 shares ZT stock		01/08/99	12/29/11	36,900	4,400	

4 Totals. Add the amounts in columns (e) and (f). Also, combine the amounts in column (g). Enter here and include on Schedule D, **line 8** (if **box A** above is checked), **line 9** (if **box B** above is checked), or **line 10** (if **box C** above is checked) . . . . ▶ | **4** | 96,350 | 63,100 | |

Form **8949** (2011)

SCHEDULE D
(Form 1040)

Department of the Treasury
Internal Revenue Service (99)

Capital Gains and Losses

▶ Attach to Form 1040 or Form 1040NR. ▶ See Instructions for Schedule D (Form 1040).
▶ Use Form 8949 to list your transactions for lines 1, 2, 3, 8, 9, and 10.

OMB No. 1545-0074

20**11**

Attachment
Sequence No. **12**

Name(s) shown on return

Martin and Deanna Lowell

Your social security number

598-65-5150

Part I Short-Term Capital Gains and Losses—Assets Held One Year or Less

Complete Form 8949 before completing line 1, 2, or 3. This form may be easier to complete if you round off cents to whole dollars.	(e) Sales price from Form(s) 8949, line 2, column (e)	(f) Cost or other basis from Form(s) 8949, line 2, column (f)	(g) Adjustments to gain or loss from Form(s) 8949, line 2, column (g)	(h) Gain or (loss) Combine columns (e), (f), and (g)
1 Short-term totals from all Forms 8949 with **box A** checked in **Part I**	13,500	(20,600)		(7,100)
2 Short-term totals from all Forms 8949 with **box B** checked in **Part I**		( )		
3 Short-term totals from all Forms 8949 with **box C** checked in **Part I**		( )		

4 Short-term gain from Form 6252 and short-term gain or (loss) from Forms 4684, 6781, and 8824 .	**4**	
5 Net short-term gain or (loss) from partnerships, S corporations, estates, and trusts from Schedule(s) K-1	**5**	
6 Short-term capital loss carryover. Enter the amount, if any, from line 8 of your **Capital Loss Carryover Worksheet** in the instructions	**6**	(630)
7 **Net short-term capital gain or (loss).** Combine lines 1 through 6 in column (h). If you have any long-term capital gains or losses, go to Part II below. Otherwise, go to Part III on the back . . .	**7**	(7,730)

Part II Long-Term Capital Gains and Losses—Assets Held More Than One Year

Complete Form 8949 before completing line 8, 9, or 10. This form may be easier to complete if you round off cents to whole dollars.	(e) Sales price from Form(s) 8949, line 4, column (e)	(f) Cost or other basis from Form(s) 8949, line 4, column (f)	(g) Adjustments to gain or loss from Form(s) 8949, line 4, column (g)	(h) Gain or (loss) Combine columns (e), (f), and (g)
8 Long-term totals from all Forms 8949 with **box A** checked in **Part II**	96,350	(63,100)		33,250
9 Long-term totals from all Forms 8949 with **box B** checked in **Part II**		( )		
10 Long-term totals from all Forms 8949 with **box C** checked in **Part II**		( )		

11 Gain from Form 4797, Part I; long-term gain from Forms 2439 and 6252; and long-term gain or (loss) from Forms 4684, 6781, and 8824	**11**	
12 Net long-term gain or (loss) from partnerships, S corporations, estates, and trusts from Schedule(s) K-1	**12**	7,610
13 Capital gain distributions. See the instructions	**13**	700
14 Long-term capital loss carryover. Enter the amount, if any, from line 13 of your **Capital Loss Carryover Worksheet** in the instructions	**14**	(2,900)
15 **Net long-term capital gain or (loss).** Combine lines 8 through 14 in column (h). Then go to Part III on the back	**15**	38,660

For Paperwork Reduction Act Notice, see your tax return instructions.   Cat. No. 11338H   Schedule D (Form 1040) 2011

Schedule D (Form 1040) 2011   Page **2**

Part III   Summary

16   Combine lines 7 and 15 and enter the result . . . . | **16** | 30,930

        • If line 16 is a **gain**, enter the amount from line 16 on Form 1040, line 13, or Form 1040NR, line 14. Then go to line 17 below.

        • If line 16 is a **loss**, skip lines 17 through 20 below. Then go to line 21. Also be sure to complete line 22.

        • If line 16 is **zero**, skip lines 17 through 21 below and enter -0- on Form 1040, line 13, or Form 1040NR, line 14. Then go to line 22.

17   Are lines 15 and 16 **both** gains?
    ☐ **Yes.** Go to line 18.
    ☑ **No.** Skip lines 18 through 21, and go to line 22.

18   Enter the amount, if any, from line 7 of the **28% Rate Gain Worksheet** in the instructions . . ▶ | **18** |

19   Enter the amount, if any, from line 18 of the **Unrecaptured Section 1250 Gain Worksheet** in the instructions . . . . ▶ | **19** |

20   Are lines 18 and 19 **both** zero or blank?
    ☐ **Yes.** Complete Form 1040 through line 43, or Form 1040NR through line 41. Then complete the **Qualified Dividends and Capital Gain Tax Worksheet** in the instructions for Form 1040, line 44 (or in the instructions for Form 1040NR, line 42). **Do not** complete lines 21 and 22 below.

    ☐ **No.** Complete Form 1040 through line 43, or Form 1040NR through line 41. Then complete the **Schedule D Tax Worksheet** in the instructions. **Do not** complete lines 21 and 22 below.

21   If line 16 is a loss, enter here and on Form 1040, line 13, or Form 1040NR, line 14, the **smaller** of:

    • The loss on line 16 or
    • ($3,000), or if married filing separately, ($1,500)   . . . . | **21** (   )

    Note. When figuring which amount is smaller, treat both amounts as positive numbers.

22   Do you have qualified dividends on Form 1040, line 9b, or Form 1040NR, line 10b?

    ☑ **Yes.** Complete Form 1040 through line 43, or Form 1040NR through line 41. Then complete the **Qualified Dividends and Capital Gain Tax Worksheet** in the instructions for Form 1040, line 44 (or in the instructions for Form 1040NR, line 42).
    ☐ **No.** Complete the rest of Form 1040 or Form 1040NR.

Schedule D (Form 1040) 2011

Qualified Dividends and Capital Gain Tax Worksheet–Line 44

1. Enter the amount from Form 1040, line 43 .... 1. <u>466,332</u>
2. Enter the amount from Form 1040, line 9b .... 2. <u>26,200</u>
3. Are you filing Schedule D?
   Yes. Enter the **smaller** of line 15 or 16 of
        Schedule D. If either line 15 or line 16 is
        blank or a loss, enter -0-   } ..... 3. <u>30,930</u>
   No. Enter the amount from Form 1040, line 13
4. Add lines 2 and 3 .... 4. <u>57,130</u>
5. If filing Form 4952, enter any amount
   from line 4g of that form.
   Otherwise, enter -0- 5.   0
6. Subtract line 5 from line 4. If zero or less, enter -0- .... 6.   <u>57,130</u>
7. Subtract line 6 from line 1. If zero or less, enter -0- .... 7. <u>409,202</u>
8. Enter:
      $34,500 if single or married filing separately,
      $69,000 if married filing jointly or qualifying widow(er) } .... 8.   <u>69,000</u>
      $46,250 if head of household.
9. Enter the smaller of line 1 or line 8 .... 9.   <u>69,000</u>
10. Enter the smaller of line 7 or line 9 .... 10.   <u>69,000</u>
11. Subtract line 10 from line 9. This amount is taxed at 0% 11.   0
12. Enter the smaller of line 1 or line 6. .... 12.   <u>57,130</u>
13. Enter the amount from line 11 .... 13.   0
14. Subtract line 13 from line 12. . ... 14.   <u>57,130</u>
15. Multiple line 14 by 15% (.15) .... 15.   <u>8,570</u>
16. Figure the tax on the amount on line 7. Use the Tax Table or
   Tax Computation Worksheet, whichever applies .... 16. <u>113,092</u>
17. Add lines 15 and 16 .... 17. <u>121,662</u>
18. Figure the tax on the amount on line 1. Use the Tax Table or
   Tax Computation Worksheet, whichever applies .... 18. <u>133,088</u>
19. **Tax on all taxable income.** Enter the **smaller** of line 17 or line 18.
   Also include this amount on Form 1040, line 44 .... 19. <u>121,662</u>

Tax Consequences of Personal Activities

Learning Objectives

After studying this chapter, you should be able to:

1. Identify personal receipts that are included in gross income.

2. Describe the tax consequences of divorce settlements.

3. Identify personal expenses and losses that result in itemized deductions.

4. Describe the tax treatment of revenues and expenses from a hobby.

5. Compute the itemized deduction for home mortgage interest.

6. Describe the preferential treatment of gain from the sale of a personal residence.

7. Identify itemized deductions that are limited or disallowed for AMT purposes.

To this point, Part Five has focused on the tax consequences of profit-motivated activities. We learned how to compute taxable income from business, employment, and investment activities and discovered many effective techniques for reducing the tax on such income. Chapter 17 introduces a new topic: the tax consequences of activities in which people engage for personal reasons. The first section of this chapter discusses the taxation of economic benefits that are not derived from business, employment, or investment activities.

The second section of the chapter concentrates on the tax rules for personal expenses or losses and identifies the limited circumstances under which they result in a tax savings. The third section explains the significant tax advantages of home ownership, while the last section integrates the material introduced in Chapter 17 into the alternative minimum tax (AMT) system.

GROSS INCOME FROM WHATEVER SOURCE DERIVED

Section 61 of the Internal Revenue Code states that gross income means all income from whatever source derived. This statement creates a presumption that any receipt of an economic benefit that increases an individual's net worth is subject to income tax. The context in which the receipt occurred or the source of the receipt is irrelevant.[1] The tax law does make exceptions to this inclusive rule, and we will identify a number of them in this chapter. Nevertheless, an individual who receives an economic benefit should assume that it is included in gross income, even if it was derived from a purely personal or private activity.

Property Tax Abatements for Senior Volunteers	More than 50 Massachusetts cities have adopted a state-sponsored program under which senior citizens who perform voluntary civic services receive local property tax abatements of up to $500. The IRS ruled that the amount of the abatements is gross income to the senior citizens for federal tax purposes because no exception to the general rule of inclusion applies to this particular economic benefit.[2]

Restitution for Shooting Victims	The surviving victims and the families of slain victims of the 2007 Virginia Tech shootings are eligible to receive restitution payments from the Hokie Spirit Memorial Fund. Congress passed special legislation to provide that such payments are excluded from the recipient's gross income for federal tax purposes.[3]

Personal Receipts

Objective 1
Identify personal receipts that are included in gross income.

People who receive prizes or awards must include the value of the prize or award in gross income.[4] This general rule applies to awards based on professional achievement or merit such as the Nobel and Pulitzer prizes. It also applies to academic and athletic awards. However, students who are degree candidates at educational institutions may exclude scholarship or fellowship awards to the extent the award pays for tuition, fees, books, supplies, and equipment.[5]

Scholarships	Mary Dillon received a four-year scholarship from the University of Kansas that pays her $12,250 annual tuition (including all fees and books) plus her $10,300 annual room and board. She also received a $2,000 alumni association scholarship that she used to buy her college wardrobe. Mary can exclude the tuition scholarship but must include the $12,300 other scholarship awards in gross income.

Tax Talk
In 2005, the IRS reminded Academy Award nominees that the $100,000 value of the lavish gift bags they received on Oscar night was taxable, and that "there's no special red carpet tax loophole for the stars." The Academy of Motion Picture Arts and Sciences responded by discontinuing its gift-giving practice.

The general rule of taxability also applies to receipts attributable entirely to good luck, such as lottery jackpots, raffle or door prizes, and gambling winnings. The prize or award need not consist of cash; the game show contestant who wins a trip to Paris must include the value of the trip in gross income.[6] Finally, the general rule applies to rewards that people receive for performing a special or noteworthy service.

[1] This presumption applies to receipts derived from unlawful activities such as embezzlement or extortion. Consequently, even illegal income is subject to income tax. *James* v. *United States*, 366 U.S. 213 (1961).
[2] Chief Counsel Advice Memorandum 200227003 (January 15, 2002).
[3] 2007 Virginia Tech Victims Act §1.
[4] §74. The law provides a narrow exception for certain employee achievement awards to the extent the award consists of tangible property worth no more than $1,600. This is called *the gold watch exception*.
[5] §117.
[6] *Reginald Turner*, T.C. Memo 1954-38.

Reward for Whistleblowing	Albert Campbell acted as a whistleblower by suing his former employer, Lockheed Martin, for contract fraud committed against the United States. Lockheed Martin settled the case by paying $37.9 million to the federal government and $8.75 million to Albert in his role as whistleblower. Albert failed to report this payment on his tax return and argued that the payment was simply his share of a nontaxable recovery of federal funds. The courts concluded that the payment was a reward for meritorious service that was clearly includable in Albert's gross income.[7]

The major exception to the rule that personal receipts are taxable applies to gifts and inheritances.[8] Individuals who receive gifts of cash or property from a donor or who inherit cash or property from a decedent don't report the receipt as income on Form 1040. Similarly, life insurance proceeds are nontaxable. The beneficiary of a life insurance policy does not include the death benefit in gross income.[9]

Personal Receipts	This year, Ms. Hardy received the following items.

Birthday gift of cash from her dad	$ 1,500
Set of dishes won at a church raffle (retail value)	600
Pearl ring inherited from her grandmother (appraised FMV)	2,600
Insurance proceeds from a policy on her grandmother's life	50,000

The only item that she must report on her Form 1040 is the $600 raffle prize.

Gift or Compensation Income?	Reverend Lloyd Goodwin received an annual salary plus the use of a parsonage from the church at which he served as pastor. The church held three "special occasion" Sundays each year when the congregation was invited to make anonymous cash contributions to their pastor and his family. For the three tax years in question, the contributions totaled $42,250, and Reverend Goodwin did not report them on his tax return. The IRS concluded that the contributions represented employment compensation and should be included in gross income. Members of the congregation who testified on behalf of Reverend Goodwin described the contributions as gifts made out of "love, respect, and admiration" for him. The court, however, concluded that the contributions were regular payments made by persons to whom Reverend Goodwin provided professional services and, therefore, were taxable compensation rather than nontaxable gifts.[10]

Legal Settlements

Individuals may receive economic benefits under legal agreements or settlements. For instance, a person who suffered an injury or detriment because of the fault of another party may be awarded damages by a court of law. The general rule is that legal damages are gross income unless they represent compensation for physical injury or illness.[11]

Legal Damages	Mr. Kaleb was a candidate for public office when he was accused of being a racist and neo-Nazi in an editorial published in a local newspaper. Mr. Kaleb successfully sued the paper for libel and defamation of character and was awarded $1 million in compensatory damages in a jury trial. Mr. Kaleb must include the $1 million in gross income.

---

[7] *Campbell* v. *Commissioner*, 108 AFTR 2d ¶2011-6420 (CA-11, 2011).

[8] §102.

[9] §101(a).

[10] *Goodwin* v. *Commissioner*, 67 F.3d 149 (CA-8, 1995).

[11] §104(a)(2).

Compensation for Physical Injury	Mrs. Spears was walking along a city sidewalk when she was struck by falling debris from a construction project. She sued the construction company for negligence and was awarded a $300,000 settlement: $100,000 for her physical injuries plus $200,000 punitive damages (damages intended to punish a defendant for extreme misconduct). Mrs. Spears may exclude $100,000 of this settlement from gross income but must report and pay tax on the $200,000 punitive damages.[12]

Divorce

Objective 2
Describe the tax consequences of divorce settlements.

The divorce of a married couple is a personal event that may have profound economic consequences. The divorce decree, which specifies the rights and obligations of the divorcing parties, may require one party to transfer ownership of valuable property to the other. For *income tax* purposes, this transfer is treated as a gift, regardless of any affection or animosity underlying the transfer.[13] As a result, the transferor recognizes no gain or loss on the disposition of the property. The transferee recognizes no gross income on receipt of the property and takes a carryover tax basis from the transferor.

The divorce decree may require one party to pay alimony to the other. Alimony consists of a series of payments by which a person discharges a legal obligation to support an ex-spouse. The recipient must include the alimony in gross income, while the payer is allowed to deduct it above-the-line in computing adjusted gross income (AGI).[14] If the divorcing couple has dependent children, the parent who surrenders custody may be required to pay child support to the custodial parent. Child support payments (in contrast to alimony) are not gross income to the recipient and are nondeductible by the payer. Child support raises the question of which parent can claim the personal exemption and child tax credit for a dependent child. Regardless of the support involved, the custodial parent is entitled to the exemption and credit *unless* he or she signs a written declaration releasing them to the noncustodial parent.[15]

Payments Pursuant to a Divorce	Mr. and Mrs. Watson recently divorced. Under the terms of the divorce decree, Mr. Watson transferred $600,000 worth of marketable securities to Mrs. Watson as a property settlement. His basis in the securities was $319,000. He is also required to pay $1,500 a month to his ex-wife: $900 alimony and $600 child support for their five-year-old daughter, who lives with Mrs. Watson. Mr. Watson did not recognize gain on disposition of the appreciated securities, and Mrs. Watson did not recognize gross income on their receipt. She has a $319,000 basis in the securities. Mrs. Watson includes the $900 monthly alimony payment in her gross income, and Mr. Watson is allowed a corresponding deduction. Mrs. Watson is entitled to claim a personal exemption and child tax credit for the daughter on her Form 1040 unless she releases the exemption and credit to Mr. Watson.

Government Transfer Payments

People who receive need-based payments from a local, state, or federal government agency may exclude the payments from gross income.[16] Consequently, benefits provided through

---

[12] Mrs. Spears's legal fees allocable to the taxable punitive damages are a miscellaneous itemized deduction. See Reg. §1.212-1(k) and *Benci-Woodward,* T.C. Memo 1998-395.

[13] §1041. The transfer is not subject to gift tax.

[14] §71 requires the income inclusion, while §215 and §62(a)(1) allow the deduction. While legal fees paid in connection with a divorce are generally nondeductible, any fee properly attributable to the collection of alimony is a miscellaneous itemized deduction. Reg. §1.262-1(b)(7).

[15] §152(e) and §24(c)(1).

[16] See Rev. Rul. 71-425, 1971-2 CB 76.

public assistance programs such as school lunches, food stamps, and welfare are nontaxable. In contrast, people who are entitled to receive government transfer payments irrespective of any demonstrated economic need must include the payments in gross income. For instance, unemployed workers must pay federal income tax on unemployment compensation received from their state government.[17]

Government Transfer Payments	For the first six months of the year, Mr. Gilly worked as the custodian of an elementary school. When the school was permanently closed, Mr. Gilly lost his job and applied for unemployment benefits from the State of Wisconsin. He received $8,240 unemployment compensation this year. He also applied for help from the federal food assistance program. Based on financial need, Mr. Gilly was eligible to receive $2,050 worth of food stamps. Mr. Gilly must report his $8,240 unemployment compensation on his Form 1040 but may exclude the value of the food stamps from gross income.

Social Security

Individuals who paid employee payroll tax or self-employment tax during their working lives are entitled to receive Social Security and Medicare benefits when they retire. The Social Security system is often described as a safety net that protects the elderly from poverty by providing a guaranteed, if minimal, income during their waning years. Unfortunately, many senior citizens depend on this minimal income to survive. According to Social Security Administration data, Social Security benefits represent more than 90 percent of the income for 35 percent of beneficiaries age 65 and over.

One Leg of the Stool	The Social Security Administration's website cautions that Social Security was never intended to be the sole source of income in retirement and that "a comfortable and stable retirement is based on a three-legged stool of Social Security, private pensions, and savings and investment."

Tax Talk
Kathleen Casey-Kirschling, born at one second after midnight on January 1, 1946, became the first baby boomer to receive a Social Security check. Kathleen is part of the earliest wave of America's "silver tsunami." Over the next two decades, nearly 80 million boomers will become eligible for Social Security, at the rate of more than 10,000 per day.

The question of whether Social Security benefits should be taxable is controversial. One political camp argues that these benefits should be taxed because they are not based on financial need. The opposing camp argues that Social Security benefits should be immune to the income tax. After all, aren't retirees entitled to their benefits because they paid nondeductible employee payroll tax or self-employment tax during their working years? The federal government's complicated approach to taxing Social Security benefits reflects a cautious compromise between these polar positions. In very general terms:

- Married couples with less than $32,000 and single individuals with less than $25,000 of modified AGI do not pay tax on their benefits.
- Married couples with modified AGI between $32,000 and $44,000 and single individuals with modified AGI between $25,000 and $34,000 pay tax on 50 percent of their benefits.
- Married couples with more than $44,000 and single individuals with more than $34,000 of modified AGI pay tax on 85 percent of their benefits.[18]

The complete details of the computation are incorporated into a Social Security Worksheet included as Appendix 17–A to this chapter.

---

[17] §85.

[18] §86. For purposes of this summary, modified AGI includes one-half of any Social Security benefits received and any tax-exempt interest earned during the year.

Social Security	Mr. and Mrs. Dean received $22,800 of Social Security this year. Their only other source of income was Mr. Dean's $18,000 annual pension from his former employer. Because their modified AGI is so low, none of the Deans' Social Security benefit is included in gross income. Mr. and Mrs. Lutz also received $22,800 of Social Security this year. Mr. and Mrs. Lutz earned $79,600 of interest and dividends from their investment portfolio. Because their modified AGI is so high, $19,380 ($22,800 × 85%) of their Social Security benefit is included in gross income.

Gains on Sales of Personal Assets

Individuals who realize gain on the sale of an asset generally must include the gain in gross income, even if the asset was not held for business or investment purposes. The character of gain recognized on the sale of a personal asset depends on whether the asset was a capital or noncapital asset in the hands of the seller. Most personal assets meet the definition of capital asset so that gain recognized on sale is characterized as capital gain. Recall from Chapter 16 that capital gains are taxed at preferential rates. Specifically, long-term capital gain from the sale of collectibles (works of art, antiques, gems, postage stamps, rare coins, and similar tangible personal property) is taxed at a maximum rate of 28 percent, while long-term capital gain from the sale of other personal assets is taxed at 15 percent or zero percent.

Gain on Sale of Collectible	During the last 15 years, Boyd Lovett purchased over 700 bottles of French wine, which he stored in his personal wine cellar. This year, Boyd moved to a small apartment and sold his entire wine collection to a local restaurant for $112,500. Boyd's cost basis in the collection was $73,600. Therefore, he recognized a $38,900 long-term capital gain. Because Boyd's marginal rate on ordinary income was 33 percent, this collectibles gain was taxed at the 28 percent preferential rate, resulting in $10,892 federal income tax ($38,900 × 28%).

A narrow exception to the rule that personal assets are capital assets applies to certain **creative assets:** copyrights; literary or artistic compositions; letters or memoranda; or similar assets. A creative asset is not a capital asset in the hands of the person who created it. In the case of a letter, memorandum, or similar property, the asset is not a capital asset in the hands of the person for whom it was written. Finally, a creative asset is not a capital asset in the hands of a donee who received it as a gift from either the creator or (in the case of letters and memoranda) the person for whom it was written.[19]

A Letter from Michael Jackson	In 1981, Darla Roth wrote a fan letter to Michael Jackson and received a handwritten letter from Michael in return. Darla kept Michael's letter until 2003 when she gave it to her daughter Kathy. This year, Kathy sold the letter on eBay to a collector in Oregon for $55,000. Although the letter is a personal asset, it was not a capital asset to Michael Jackson (its creator), Darla (the person for whom it was written), or Kathy (Darla's donee). Consequently, Kathy's $55,000 gain recognized on sale of the letter is ordinary income. If the collector in Oregon holds the letter as a personal asset, it is a capital asset to the collector.

Most personal assets fall into the category of *consumer durables*—tangible assets that people buy for their private use and enjoyment. Individuals can't recover the cost of these assets through depreciation. Thus, the initial cost basis of consumer durables is not adjusted

---

[19] §1221(a)(3). Individuals who create a musical composition or who receive a musical composition as a gift from the creator can elect to treat the composition as a capital asset.

downward, even though the market value of such goods invariably decreases over time. For this reason, people who sell consumer durables usually realize a loss on the transaction. As we will discuss later in the chapter, these personal losses are nondeductible.

Garage Sale	Emma Pena decided to clean out her basement and attic by selling an accumulation of clothing, books, toys, exercise equipment, and other used household items at a multi-family garage sale. Emma was delighted to clear $1,175 from the sale of these personal assets, even though this amount was substantially less than her original cost. Emma's realized loss on the sale (whatever the amount) is nondeductible.

PERSONAL EXPENSES

The Internal Revenue Code states that no deduction is allowed for personal, living, or family expenses.[20] Accordingly, the everyday costs of managing a household, raising a family, pursuing social or civic interests, and enjoying leisure time do not result in any tax benefit. Even expenses with a tangential connection to a business or employment activity, such as the cost of a professional wardrobe, the daily commute to work, or routine noonday lunches, are inherently personal in nature and thus nondeductible.

Business or Personal Expenses?	Jeffrey Stone operated an appliance repair business out of a shop located about eight miles from his home. On the Schedule C on which he computed business income, he reported several thousand dollars of miscellaneous expenses. The IRS discovered that the miscellaneous expenses included payments for his children's birthday parties, Christmas presents to his nephews, trips to visit Mrs. Stone's parents, family trips to baseball tournaments, a fishing license, subscriptions to *People, Ladies' Home Journal,* and *Family Circle* magazines, and veterinary bills for the family dog and cat. The judge who tried Mr. Stone's case agreed with the IRS that his miscellaneous expenses were clearly nondeductible. "In differentiating between personal and business expenses, there may be some 'grey' areas, but the expenditures here do not fall within those areas, at least not without a Herculean effort of delusion."[21]

The tax law bends the no-deduction rule for three major categories of personal expenses: medical expenses; local, state, and foreign tax payments; and charitable contributions. Individuals who incur such expenses may be allowed an itemized deduction on Schedule A.

Medical Expenses

Objective 3
Identify personal expenses and losses that result in itemized deductions.

Individuals may claim an itemized deduction for the unreimbursed cost of medical care for themselves and their family.[22] Medical care include payments to health care practitioners (doctors, dentists, chiropractors, etc.) and treatment facilities (outpatient clinics, hospitals, and long-term-care facilities), certain travel expenses related to medical treatment, the cost of medical aids (eyeglasses, hearing aids, crutches, wheelchairs, etc.) and prescription drugs. Premiums paid to purchase health, accident, and long-term-care insurance also qualify as medical care expenses.[23]

---

[20] §262.
[21] *Jeffrey C. Stone,* T.C. Memo 1998-437. See also, *Henry J. Langer,* T.C. Memo 2008-255 and *Thomas H. Carver,* T.C. Memo 2009-279.
[22] §213.
[23] Medical insurance reimbursements are excluded from gross income under §105(b).

Medical care doesn't include the cost of cosmetic surgery, unless the surgery is necessary to correct a congenital deformity or damage from a traumatic injury or disfiguring disease. Thus, the costs of procedures intended solely to improve or enhance physical appearance (face lifts, tummy tucks, body piercings, tattoos) are not deductible.

The medical care deduction is limited to the excess of total unreimbursed expenses over 7.5 percent of AGI.

Medical Care Deduction	Mr. and Mrs. Chester incurred $4,400 of medical expenses (including insurance premiums) during the year. They received a $1,800 payment from their insurance company in partial reimbursement of these expenses. If their AGI is $30,000, they are allowed a $350 itemized deduction.

Medical expenses	$ 4,400
Insurance reimbursement	(1,800)
Unreimbursed expenses	$ 2,600
AGI threshold ($30,000 AGI × 7.5%)	(2,250)
Medical care deduction	$ 350

If AGI exceeds $34,667, the 7.5 percent threshold exceeds unreimbursed expenses, and the Chesters have no medical care deduction this year.

Tax Talk
The Tax Court recently ruled that a taxpayer's gender identity disorder (GID) qualified as a disease and the cost of her sex realignment surgery was a deductible medical expense.

As this example demonstrates, the AGI limitation restricts the number of taxpayers who actually receive a tax benefit from their medical expenses. Only those unfortunate families that bear unusually high health care costs receive any tax relief from this particular itemized deduction.

Local, State, and Foreign Tax Payments

Individuals may deduct real or personal property taxes paid on personal assets (such as their home or family automobile).[24] They may elect to deduct *either* state and local sales taxes *or* state and local income taxes (but not both!). This election is particularly beneficial to residents of the seven states that have a sales tax but no individual income tax (Alaska, Florida, Nevada, South Dakota, Texas, Washington, and Wyoming). Individuals who pay income tax to a foreign jurisdiction may either deduct such tax or (as generally is the case) claim a foreign tax credit.[25]

Several common taxes that individuals pay are not deductible for federal income tax purposes. Gift and estate taxes, employee payroll taxes, and employment taxes paid for household employees are all nondeductible personal expenses.[26] Of course, the federal income tax itself is a nondeductible expense. But, interestingly, the tax law authorizes a miscellaneous itemized deduction for "expenses paid or incurred in connection with the determination, collection, or refund of any tax, whether the taxing authority be Federal, State, or municipal."[27] Because of this rule, fees paid to tax practitioners for return

---

[24] §164(a).

[25] §164(b)(5). The election to deduct sales tax currently is effective through 2011 but likely will be extended through 2012. The IRS provides tables that individuals can use to estimate their general sales tax for the year based on AGI.

[26] §275.

[27] Reg. §1.212-1(l). Tax preparation or consultation fees relating to business, rent, or royalty activities are deductible on Schedule C or Schedule E and not as miscellaneous itemized deductions. Rev. Rul. 92-29, 1992-1 CB 20.

preparation and professional advice are deductible. The IRS recently expanded the scope of this deduction to include credit and debit card fees charged for paying federal income taxes electronically.[28]

Taxes and Tax Return Preparation Fee	This year, Ruthie Green paid $2,013 local property tax, $15,119 Louisiana income tax, $2,899 federal gift tax, and $1,240 employer payroll tax on the wages paid to her housekeeper. She also paid $118 Canadian income tax on dividends received from a Canadian corporation. The CPA who prepared Ruthie's various tax returns charged her $3,150. Ruthie reported an itemized deduction for her property tax and state income tax and a *miscellaneous* itemized deduction for the tax preparation fee. She took a foreign tax credit for the Canadian income tax. The federal gift tax and employer payroll tax were nondeductible.

State or Local Income Tax Refunds

Individuals who overpay their state or local income tax in one year will receive a refund of the overpayment in the following year. If the individual deducted the state or local income tax in the year of payment, the tax payment reduced the individual's federal income tax for that year. Consequently, under the tax benefit rule, the individual must include the tax refund in gross income. If the individual did not deduct the tax payment, the refund is excluded from gross income.[29]

State Tax Refund	This year, Mr. and Mrs. Bartino received a $1,418 refund of New York State income tax and a Form 1099-G (Certain Government Payments) documenting the refund. Last year, the Bartinos deducted state income tax on their Schedule A. As a result, they must report the state income tax refund as gross income on line 10 of their Form 1040. If the Bartinos had taken the standard deduction last year, they would have received no federal tax benefit from their state income tax payment, and the refund would be nontaxable.

Tax Talk

An investment banker with a passion for designer dresses and shoes claimed a $48,954 deduction for the value of used clothing donated to charity. A highly skeptical Tax Court reduced the deduction to $8,949.

Charitable Contributions

People who contribute money or property to nonprofit organizations that have been granted tax-exempt status by the IRS can claim the contribution as an itemized deduction.[30] The policy rationale is that this deduction encourages private citizens to support worthy causes that benefit society as a whole. By allowing the charitable contribution deduction, the federal government indirectly subsidizes thousands of social, civic, cultural, religious, scientific, environmental, and educational institutions. This subsidy represents a tax expenditure of over $45 billion annually. There are broad limits on the charitable contribution deduction. In general, the annual deduction for contributions to public charities cannot exceed 50 percent of AGI. Any contribution in excess of such limit is carried forward as an itemized deduction for five years.

[28] IR News Release 2009-37.

[29] The tax benefit of the deduction for state and local taxes is reduced if the taxpayer is in an AMT situation. Individuals can use the State and Local Income Tax Refund Worksheet in the Instructions for Form 1040 to compute the tax benefit attributable to a state tax refund.

[30] §170. Contributions of $250 or more to a single charity must be substantiated by a written acknowledgment from the charity. §170(f)(8).

Charitable Contribution Limitation	In 1996, Hillary Rodham Clinton earned $742,000 royalties from her book *It Takes a Village*, kept $152,000 to pay state and federal tax on the income, and donated the $590,000 remainder to charity. However, because the Clintons' AGI on their joint return was $1,065,101, their charitable contribution deduction was limited to $532,551.

When an individual contributes property to charity, the amount of the deduction depends on the character of the property.[31] If the property is a long-term capital asset to the contributor, the deduction generally equals FMV. As a result, individuals who own highly appreciated capital assets enjoy a significant tax benefit if they give the assets to charity.

Contribution of Appreciated Capital Asset	Mr. Nelke, who is in the 35 percent marginal tax bracket, owns an oil painting that he bought 15 years ago for $50,000. The painting's value was recently appraised at $400,000. If Mr. Nelke gives this painting to the Metropolitan Museum of Art, his itemized deduction is $400,000, and his tax savings are $140,000 (35 percent of $400,000). Most of the savings is attributable to the $350,000 appreciation in the painting's FMV, an unrealized gain on which Mr. Nelke never paid income tax.

If an individual contributes property that is not a capital asset to charity, the deduction is limited to the *lesser* of FMV or the contributor's basis in the property. In this case, the contributor does not enjoy a deduction for any unrealized appreciation in the property.

Contribution of Noncapital Asset	Ms. Holk owns and operates a pet store. She contributed 5,000 bags of cat and dog food from her inventory to the local Society for Prevention of Cruelty to Animals. Her cost basis in the pet food was $6,300, and its FMV (retail) was $9,500. Ms. Holk's itemized deduction for this contribution is limited to $6,300.

Tax Subsidies for Education

The costs incurred by individuals for their own education and the education of their children are nondeductible personal expenses. However, Congress subsidizes the cost of education through a profusion of tax incentives available to low-income and middle-income families. Here is a bullet-point summary of the major education incentives. Students who want more details should refer to IRS Publication 970, *Tax Benefits for Education.*

- Individuals can exclude the interest earned on the redemption of qualified Series EE savings bonds (**education savings bonds**) to the extent of tuition and fees paid to a post-secondary educational institution. This exclusion is phased out for high-income taxpayers.[32]
- Individuals can report **qualified tuition expenses** as an above-the-line deduction.[33] Qualified tuition expenses include tuition and fees paid for postsecondary education. The deduction is limited to $4,000 and is phased out for high-income taxpayers. Currently, the deduction for qualified tuition expenses is not allowed for taxable years after 2011 but likely will be extended for 2012.
- Individuals can report interest paid on **qualified education loans** as an above-the-line deduction.[34] A loan is qualified if the proceeds were used to pay for the cost of postsecondary

[31] See §170(e).
[32] §135.
[33] §222.
[34] §221.

education, such as college tuition, room, and board. This deduction is limited to $2,500 and is phased out for high-income taxpayers.

- Individuals can claim an **American Opportunity Credit** based on the cost of tuition, fees, and course materials paid during the first four years of post-secondary education.[35] The maximum annual credit is $2,500 per eligible student. Alternatively, individuals may claim a **Lifetime Learning Credit** based on 20 percent of their qualified tuition expenses. The maximum annual credit is $2,000. Individuals cannot claim both a deduction and a credit for the same qualified tuition expenses, and both credits are phased out for high-income taxpayers.

- Individuals can contribute a maximum of $2,000 every year to a tax-exempt **Coverdell education savings account** established for a beneficiary (typically a child or grand-child) under the age of 18. Withdrawals from the account are nontaxable to the extent of the beneficiary's elementary, secondary, and higher education expenses. The contribution is phased out for high-income taxpayers.[36]

- Individuals can contribute to tax-exempt **qualified tuition programs** sponsored by states or by private colleges and universities. Distributions from qualified tuition programs are nontaxable to the extent used to pay higher education expenses.[37]

PERSONAL LOSSES

Losses on Sales of Personal Assets

In earlier chapters of this text, we learned that individuals can deduct losses realized on the disposition of business or investment assets. While the capital loss and passive activity loss limitations may defer recognition of such losses to future years, sooner or later the losses reduce AGI and result in a tax savings. If an individual realizes a loss on the disposition of a personal asset, such loss is nondeductible.[38] In many instances, this rule has little economic significance. Suppose a person pays $1,500 for a new refrigerator, uses it for eight years, then sells it to a college student for $200. The $1,300 realized loss ($200 amount realized less $1,500 cost basis) is nondeductible, and the sale of the personal asset is a nonevent for tax purposes.

Nondeductible Personal Loss	Mr. Rooker purchased a membership in a private country club for $20,000. During the last 13 years, he was assessed $7,000 for the cost of capital improvements to the club's swimming pool, tennis courts, and golf course. This year, he sold his membership to an unrelated party for $15,000. The IRS acknowledged that the club membership was a capital asset and that Mr. Rooker realized a $12,000 loss on the sale ($15,000 amount realized – $27,000 original cost plus assessments). However, the IRS ruled that the loss was nondeductible because he held the membership primarily for personal use rather than for investment purposes.[39]

A loss realized on the sale of a personal residence can result in severe economic distress. For many people, their residence is their most valuable asset, and they consider it as a long-term investment. Even so, owner-occupied housing is a personal rather than an investment asset for tax purposes, and a loss on sale is nondeductible.

[35] §25A. The American Opportunity Credit is an expanded version of the Hope Scholarship Credit.

[36] §530.

[37] §529.

[38] Rev. Rul. 54-268, 1954-2 CB 88, and *Wrightsman* v. *United States*, 192 Ct. Cl. 722 (1970).

[39] This example is based on IRS Letter Ruling 8205045.

Loss on Sale of Personal Residence	Mr. and Mrs. Zuma purchased their family home in Colorado Springs for $278,000 in 1995. This year, the Zumas had to relocate to Minnesota. Because of the depressed housing market in their locality, they sold their home for only $250,000. Their $28,000 loss realized on the sale is a nondeductible personal loss.

Casualty and Theft Losses

Individuals can claim an itemized deduction for personal property losses arising from casualty or theft.[40] A casualty is a sudden and unexpected event such as a fire, hurricane, earthquake, automobile accident, or vandalism that damages or destroys property. For tax purposes, the loss is the *lesser* of the tax basis in the property or the decrease in value from the casualty or theft.[41]

Casualty Losses	Mrs. Ober owns a sailboat that was damaged during a recent hurricane. Her basis in the boat is $53,750, but the decrease in value is only $5,000. Accordingly, the casualty loss is $5,000.[42] Mrs. Ober owned a motorcycle that was totally destroyed in a traffic accident. Her basis in the motorcycle was $18,400, and its value immediately before the accident was $20,000. Even though the decrease in value is $20,000, the casualty loss is limited to her $18,400 basis.

A casualty or theft loss is reduced by any insurance proceeds so that only the *unreimbursed* loss is deductible.[43] Furthermore, the loss from each casualty or theft is reduced by a $100 floor. Finally, only the aggregate loss in excess of 10 percent of AGI is deductible.[44]

Casualty Loss Deduction	Mrs. Ober received nothing from her insurance company for the damaged sailboat and $7,600 for the destroyed motorcycle. If she suffered no other casualty or theft losses for the year, her aggregate loss is $15,600.

	Sailboat	*Motorcycle*
Casualty loss	$5,000	$18,400
Insurance proceeds	–0–	(7,600)
Unreimbursed loss	$5,000	$10,800
$100 floor per casualty	(100)	(100)
	$4,900	$10,700

Aggregate loss: $4,900 + $10,700 = $15,600

[40] §165(c)(3).

[41] Reg. §1.165-7(b).

[42] The decrease in value can be determined by independent appraisal or measured by the cost of repairs necessary to restore the property to its original condition. Reg. §1.165-7(a)(2).

[43] If the insurance proceeds exceed the basis of the property, the owner may defer recognition of such gain by replacing the property. See the discussion of involuntary conversions in Chapter 9.

[44] §165(h).

If Mrs. Ober's AGI is $68,000, her itemized deduction for this loss is $8,800. If her AGI is $130,000, her deduction is only $2,600. If her AGI is $200,000, she has no itemized deduction at all.

	AGI		
	$68,000	*$130,000*	*$200,000*
Aggregate casualty loss	$15,600	$ 15,600	$ 15,600
10% AGI threshold	(6,800)	(13,000)	(20,000)
Casualty loss deduction	$ 8,800	$ 2,600	–0–

Hobby and Gambling Losses

Objective 4
Describe the tax treatment of revenues and expenses from a hobby.

Activities in which people engage primarily for personal enjoyment may generate gross income. Consider the case of Dr. Cox, a practicing dentist, who breeds toy poodles as his hobby. Not only does he exhibit his own animals in local and regional dog shows, but he also sells puppies and shows poodles owned by other people. In a good year, Dr. Cox might earn as much as $5,000 from his canine-related activities. His annual expenses, such as dog food, veterinary fees, and travel to shows average $10,000. What are the tax rules concerning his annual **hobby loss**? Because of the inclusive rule for gross income recognition, he must report his annual revenues as "other income" on page 1, Form 1040. He is allowed a deduction for his expenses but only to the extent of his revenues.[45] Moreover, this deduction is a miscellaneous itemized deduction subject to the 2 percent AGI limitation.

Hobby Loss

This year, Dr. Cox's revenues from his dog-breeding activities totaled $4,680, while his related expenses totaled $10,730. His AGI (which includes the $4,680 income) is $181,300. He may report only $4,680 of his dog-breeding expenses as a miscellaneous item on Schedule A. However, if this is his only miscellaneous item, the deduction is limited to $1,054.

Total miscellaneous items	$ 4,680
AGI threshold ($181,300 × 2%)	(3,626)
Miscellaneous itemized deduction	$ 1,054

This is a very unsatisfactory result for Dr. Cox. His hobby expenses exceeded his revenues by $6,050, but his taxable income from the hobby is $3,626 ($4,680 gross income less $1,054 itemized deduction). Furthermore, this result assumes that he can itemize deductions for the year. If he claims the standard deduction, the $4,680 poodle revenue is fully taxable, and he receives no tax benefit at all from the poodle expenses.

The tax consequences would be much more favorable if Dr. Cox could treat his dog-breeding activity as a business. In such case, he would account for revenues and expenses on a Schedule C and could deduct his $6,050 net loss in the computation of AGI. To do so, he must demonstrate that he breeds poodles with the "actual and honest objective" of making a profit rather than for recreation.[46] To this end, he should operate in a businesslike manner by maintaining a separate bank account and proper accounting records. He should actively seek out customers by advertising in the appropriate trade journals and should charge the market rate for his products

[45] §183.
[46] *Ronnen*, 90 T.C. 74, 91 (1988). For recent cases, see *Nora E. Keating*, T.C. Memo 2007-309, and *Whitecavage*, T.C. Memo 2008-203.

and services. Of course, the best way for Dr. Cox to demonstrate a profit motive is to actually make a profit. The tax law establishes a *presumption* that any activity generating net income (gross income over deductible expenses) in three out of five consecutive years is a business. In such case, the IRS must prove that the activity is a hobby, and it rarely tries to do so.

For tax purposes, gambling activities are treated very much like hobbies. Individuals must report their winnings as gross income and may deduct their losses only to the extent of such winnings. The itemized deduction for gambling losses, however, is not categorized as a *miscellaneous* itemized deduction and is not subject to the 2 percent AGI limitation.[47]

Gambling Losses	Mrs. Toomey, a full-time school teacher, loves playing the dollar slot machines in Atlantic City. She keeps a diary in which she records the date, the casino, and her winnings or losses for that day. This year, Mrs. Toomey won a $15,000 jackpot. Because the payout exceeded $1,200, the casino was required to issue a Form W-2G (Certain Gambling Winnings) to Mrs. Toomey and provide a copy to the IRS.[48] According to her diary, Mrs. Toomey won $18,917 (including the $15,000 jackpot) and lost $5,368 during the year. She reported the $18,917 winnings as "other income" on page 1, Form 1040, and the $5,368 loss as an itemized deduction on Schedule A. Now assume that Mrs. Toomey did not win the jackpot. According to her diary, Mrs. Toomey won only $3,917 and lost $5,368 during the year. She must report her $3,917 winnings as other income and can report only $3,917 of her losses as an itemized deduction on Schedule A. In other words, her $1,451 *net* gambling loss is nondeductible.

TAX CONSEQUENCES OF HOME OWNERSHIP

Even though an owner-occupied residence is a personal asset, the Internal Revenue Code contains several preferential rules that can make such residence a fine investment. In fact, one of the greatest economic advantages of home ownership is that the tax law treats owner-occupied real property as a nonproductive personal asset. Consider the relative economic situations of Mr. Hicks and Mr. Gray. Neither individual owns his own home, and each pays $24,000 a year to rent a dwelling. These rent payments are nondeductible personal expenses. This year, each man inherits $300,000. Mr. Hicks uses the money to buy a home, while Mr. Gray invests his money in a financial asset yielding 8 percent a year. What are the cash flow implications of their respective purchases?

Comparative Cash Flows	Mr. Hicks now lives in his own home and no longer pays rent. Consequently, his annual after-tax cash outflow decreases by $24,000. Mr. Gray continues to pay rent but also receives $24,000 income on his investment. If Mr. Gray is in a 28 percent marginal tax bracket, his after-tax cash outflow decreases by only $17,280.

	Mr. Hicks	*Mr. Gray*
Cash outflow before purchase:		
Rent expense	$(24,000)	$(24,000)
Cash outflow after purchase:		
Rent expense	–0–	$(24,000)
Taxable income from investment	–0–	24,000
Tax cost of income	–0–	(6,720)
	–0–	$ (6,720)
Decrease in cash outflow	$(24,000)	$(17,280)

[47] §165(d) and §67(b)(3).
[48] Reg. §7.6041-1(a).

How can the purchase of a personal asset have a better financial result than the purchase of income-producing investment property? Observe that Mr. Hicks's personal residence provides a $24,000 annual benefit—the rent he avoids paying. Economists refer to this benefit as the **imputed income from owner-occupied housing.** The federal tax system has never required homeowners to include such imputed income in their tax base. This preferential treatment creates an economic incentive for people to purchase a home. In our example, both Mr. Hicks and Mr. Gray invested $300,000 in assets yielding an 8 percent before-tax return. Because Mr. Hicks's return consists of nontaxable imputed income, his after-tax return is also 8 percent, making his purchase of a personal residence the superior investment.

Home Mortgage Interest Deduction

Individuals who incur debt to finance a personal expenditure cannot deduct the interest paid on the debt.[49] The major exception to this rule applies to **qualified residence interest,** which individuals may claim as an itemized deduction.[50] This popular home mortgage interest deduction represents a tax expenditure of about $95 billion annually.

Qualified residence interest includes interest paid on both acquisition debt and home equity debt.

Objective 5
Compute the itemized deduction for home mortgage interest.

- **Acquisition debt** is incurred to acquire, construct, or substantially improve a personal residence. Acquisition debt must be secured by the residence and is limited to $1 million ($500,000 for married filing separately).

- **Home equity debt** is any other debt secured by a personal residence to the extent it does not exceed the owner's equity. Home equity debt is limited to $100,000 ($50,000 for married filing separately).

Individuals may take into account the interest paid with respect to their principal residence *and* one other personal residence in computing their deduction for qualified residence interest.[51]

Qualified Residence Interest

Mr. and Mrs. Tabor financed the construction of their home through a mortgage from their local bank. Last year, they took out a second mortgage from another lending institution and used the proceeds to purchase new furniture and to pay for their family vacation.

This year, the average balance of the first mortgage was $600,000, and the average balance of the second mortgage was $140,000. The Tabors paid $52,540 interest on these mortgages, only $49,700 of which is qualified residence interest.[52]

Acquisition debt	$600,000
Home equity debt (limited)	100,000
Qualifying debt	$700,000

$$\frac{\$700,000 \text{ qualifying debt}}{\$740,000 \text{ total debt}} \times \$52,540 \text{ total interest} = \underline{\$49,700}$$

Therefore, Mr. and Mrs. Tabor can claim $49,700 as an itemized deduction. Because they used the proceeds of the home equity debt for personal expenditures, the remainder of the interest payment is nondeductible.

---

[49] §163(h)(1).

[50] §163(h)(3).

[51] §163(h)(4).

[52] IRS Publication 936 *Home Mortgage Interest Deduction* contains a worksheet for computing qualified residence interest when an individual's acquisition or home equity debt exceeds the $1 million or $100,000 limit.

Vacation Homes

Many people own more than one personal residence. In addition to their **principal residence** (the home in which they reside for most of the year and consider their permanent address), they may own a **vacation home** for occasional use. Owners of vacation homes often rent the property to other individuals for some limited period of time. In such case, they can deduct the expenses of maintaining the home (utilities, homeowners insurance, repairs, etc.) allocable to the rental period on a Schedule E.[53] They are also allowed a depreciation deduction based on the number of days of rental usage. The aggregate of these deductions is limited to the gross rents less any mortgage interest or property taxes allocable to the rental period.[54]

| *Vacation Home* | Ms. DeSilva owns a vacation home on Cape Cod. She and her family use the home on weekends and during June and July. During August and September, she rents the home to tourists. This year, this rental activity resulted in the following. |

Rent revenue	$6,400
Mortgage interest and real property tax for August and September[55]	3,505
Maintenance expenses for August and September	3,760
MACRS depreciation for August and September	1,200

Ms. DeSilva reports this rental activity on a Schedule E as follows.

Gross rents	$6,400
Interest and property tax deduction	(3,505)
	$2,895
Deductible maintenance expenses	(2,895)
MACRS depreciation deduction	–0–
Net rental income	–0–

Ms. DeSilva can carry the $865 disallowed maintenance expenses and the $1,200 disallowed depreciation forward and include them in future calculations of her Schedule E deductions.[56] While such deductions may decrease or even eliminate the rental revenue included in Ms. DeSilva's AGI, they can never generate a net rental loss.

Exclusion of Gain on Sale of Principal Residence

Objective 6
Describe the preferential treatment of gain from the sale of a personal residence.

Individuals who realize gain on the sale (or exchange) of a home can exclude the gain from gross income if the home was owned and used as the principal residence for periods aggregating at least two years during the five-year period ending on the date of sale.[57] The exclusion applies to only one sale every two years. The exclusion is limited to $250,000 for each sale. The maximum exclusion is doubled (to $500,000) for a married couple filing jointly if *either* spouse meets the two-out-of-five-year ownership requirement and *both* spouses meet the two-out-of-five-year use requirement for the residence.

[53] §280A(e)(1). If an owner rents a personal residence for less than 15 days during a year, the revenue is nontaxable and the related expenses are nondeductible. §280A(g).

[54] §280A(c)(5).

[55] The mortgage interest allocable to the other 10 months of the year may be deductible as qualified residence interest. Property tax allocable to this 10-month period is an itemized deduction.

[56] §165(c)(5).

[57] §121.

Maximum Exclusion	Mr. and Mrs. Sutton, who file a joint tax return, purchased a principal residence as cotenants in 1983 and have lived there ever since. On October 6, 2010, they realized a $618,000 gain on sale of the residence. Because they met the ownership/use requirement and did not sell another principal residence within the two-year period prior to the sale, they excluded $500,000 of the gain from their 2010 gross income. The $118,000 recognized gain was long-term capital gain taxed at 15 percent.

A person who realizes a gain on sale of a principal residence but fails to meet the ownership/use requirement or violates the two-year/one-sale rule may be eligible for a reduced exclusion. If the person sold the residence because of a change in place of employment, for health reasons, or because of unforeseen circumstances, the allowable exclusion equals the maximum exclusion multiplied by a reduction ratio. The numerator of the ratio equals the *shorter* of (1) the aggregate time period of ownership/use of the residence or (2) the time period between the earlier sale of a residence for which gain was excluded and the current sale. The denominator of the ratio is two years.

Reduced Exclusion	Refer to the facts in the preceding example. Mr. and Mrs. Sutton purchased and moved into a new principal residence on December 13, 2010. In June 2011, Mr. Sutton suffered a major heart attack. To accommodate his physical condition, the couple sold their new residence on August 10, 2011, and moved into an assisted-living apartment. The gain realized on this sale was $15,200. Mr. and Mrs. Sutton owned *and* occupied their new residence for only 240 days and sold it just 308 days after the sale of their former residence. Consequently, they fail the ownership/use requirement *and* violate the two-year/one-sale rule. However, because they sold the new residence for health reasons, they are eligible for a reduced exclusion of $164,384.

$$\$500{,}000 \times \frac{240 \text{ days of ownership/use}}{730 \text{ days (two years)}} = \$164{,}384$$

Consequently, they may exclude the entire $15,200 gain on the second sale from their 2011 gross income.

Unforeseen Circumstances	Eleven months ago, Ralph Small, the single father of two children, purchased a condominium as his family's principal residence. Last week, Ralph became engaged to Gloria Kyle, the single mother of four children. Ralph plans to sell his condominium and purchase a much larger home with enough bedrooms to accommodate the blended family. According to the IRS, Ralph's sale of his condominium before meeting the two-year use/ownership requirement is justified by the "unforeseen circumstance" of his remarriage. Consequently, Ralph is entitled to a reduced exclusion of gain recognized on the condominium sale.[58]

ITEMIZED DEDUCTIONS AS AMT ADJUSTMENTS

Objective 7
Identify itemized deductions that are limited or disallowed for AMT purposes.

Before leaving the topic of personal activities, we should integrate the material introduced in the chapter into the alternative minimum tax (AMT) system. None of the personal income or gain items triggers an AMT adjustment or preference. However, certain personal itemized deductions are limited or disallowed in the computation of alternative minimum taxable income (AMTI).[59]

- Medical expenses are deductible only to the extent they exceed 10 percent of AGI.
- The itemized deduction for tax payments is disallowed.

[58] IRS Letter Ruling 200725018 (June 22, 2007).
[59] §56(b)(1).

- Miscellaneous itemized deductions (including investment and employment-related expenses) are disallowed.
- Qualified residence interest paid on home equity debt is disallowed.

Our last two examples illustrate the computation of these AMT adjustments and their effect on AMT.

AMT Itemized Deductions	Mrs. Keil had $90,700 AGI and the following itemized deductions in 2011.		

Unreimbursed medical expenses	$11,250	
AGI threshold ($90,700 × 7.5%)	(6,803)	$ 4,447
State income tax		4,000
Local property tax on personal residence		3,100
Charitable contributions		5,500
Qualified residence interest:		
Acquisition debt		9,200
Home equity debt		5,800
Miscellaneous itemized deductions	$ 2,600	
AGI threshold ($90,700 × 2%)	(1,814)	786
Itemized deductions		$32,833

In computing her AMTI, Mrs. Keil must make the following *positive* adjustments to taxable income.

Unreimbursed medical expenses	$11,250	
AMT/AGI threshold ($90,700 × 10%)	(9,070)	
	$ 2,180	
Regular medical expense deduction		$ 4,447
AMT medical expense deduction		(2,180)
AMT adjustment for medical expenses		$ 2,267
Disallowed state income tax		4,000
Disallowed local property tax on personal residence		3,100
Disallowed interest on home equity debt		5,800
Disallowed miscellaneous itemized deductions		786
Positive AMT adjustments		$15,953

Computing AMT	Assume that Mrs. Keil is a head of household with two dependent children, ages 18 and 19. Her tentative minimum tax was calculated as follows.

	Regular Tax	Tentative Minimum Tax
AGI	$ 90,700	
Itemized deductions	(32,833)	
Exemption amount ($3,700 × 3)	(11,100)	
Taxable income	$ 46,767	$ 46,767
AMT adjustments for:		
Itemized deductions		15,953
Exemption amount		11,100

AMTI	$ 73,820
Exemption (head of household)	(48,450)
Tax base	$ 25,370
Tax rate	.26
Tentative minimum tax	$ 6,596

Mrs. Keil's total tax is calculated as follows.

Regular tax on $46,767 taxable income	$ 6,459
AMT ($6,596 tentative minimum tax − $6,459)	137
Total tax	$ 6,596

Conclusion

When people engage in personal transactions with no connection to any business, employment, or investment activity, they should be mindful of any tax consequences. Of course, most personal transactions are nonevents for tax purposes. But, occasionally, a personal transaction will have significant tax consequences. If any transaction results in an economic benefit, the individual must consider the prospect that such benefit is taxable. He or she should also determine if the transaction can be structured so that part or all of the benefit escapes taxation. If a transaction involves an expense or loss, the individual might be allowed to deduct some or even the entire expense or loss. Through an awareness of this possibility, the individual can plan to maximize the deduction and minimize his tax bill.

Key Terms

acquisition debt *549*
American Opportunity
   Credit *545*
Coverdell education
   savings account *545*
creative assets *540*
education savings
   bonds *544*
hobby loss *547*
home equity debt *549*

imputed income from
   owner-occupied
   housing *549*
Lifetime Learning
   Credit *545*
principal residence *550*
qualified education
   loan *544*
qualified residence
   interest *549*

qualified tuition
   expenses *544*
qualified tuition
   program *545*
vacation home *550*

Questions and Problems for Discussion

1. Contrast the general rule concerning the recognition of gross income from personal activities with the general rule concerning the deductibility of personal expenses and losses.
2. Discuss the tax policy reasons why gifts and inheritances are not included in gross income.
3. In what way does the tax law give preferential treatment to the divorced spouse with custody of the children?
4. Why are welfare payments from a state social services agency nontaxable to the recipient while state unemployment benefits are taxable?

5. A basic principle of federal tax law is that a return of investment is nontaxable. Discuss the application of this principle to Social Security payments.

6. If an individual purchases property insurance on business equipment, the premiums are deductible, but if that same individual purchases property insurance on his home, the premiums are nondeductible. Can you explain this inconsistent tax treatment?

7. Mr. Cox is a passionate stamp collector. His collection is so valuable that he keeps it in a safety deposit box in a local bank, which charges him $25 a month. Can he deduct this expense?

8. Assume that Congress amended the tax law to limit the itemized deduction for charitable contributions to 5 percent (rather than 50 percent) of AGI. Discuss the incidence of the tax increase represented by this expansion of the tax base.

9. People frequently sell used appliances, old furniture and clothing, books, toys, and other personal goods through an on-line service such as Craigslist or eBay. Should these people recognize the cash proceeds from such sales as gross income?

10. Last year, both the Burton family and the Awad family incurred $8,000 unreimbursed medical expenses. Mr. and Mrs. Burton deducted $6,000 of their expenses, while Mr. and Mrs. Awad were unable to deduct any of their expenses. How do you explain this apparently inequitable result?

11. Wealthy individuals can reduce their taxable estate by donating property to charity either during life or at death. Discuss the reasons why an inter vivos charitable donation is the preferable option for tax planning purposes.

12. Mrs. Leland's profession is dentistry, but she has quite a reputation as a master gardener. Last year she won $990 in prize money from entering her roses in competitions and earned $800 in lecture fees from garden clubs. Because she did not itemize deductions, none of the expenses associated with her hobby were deductible. Should Mrs. Leland pay self-employment tax on her prize money and fees?

13. Discuss the similarities and differences in the structure of the hobby loss rule and the vacation home rule.

Application Problems

1. Marcy Tucker received the following items this year. Determine to what extent each item is included in her AGI.
   a. A $25,000 cash gift from her parents.
   b. A $500 cash award from the local Chamber of Commerce for her winning entry in a contest to name a new public park.
   c. $8,000 alimony from her former husband.
   d. $100,000 cash inheritance from her grandfather.

2. Ms. Queen, age 21, is a full-time college student with an athletic scholarship that provides the following annual benefits.

Tuition payment	$12,800
Fees and books	3,500
Room and board	10,000

Ms. Queen works in the athletic department as a trainer for a $4,200 salary. She also receives a $6,000 annual allowance from her grandmother. Compute Ms. Queen's AGI.

3. Four years ago, Lyle Mercer was injured in a railroad accident and sued the railroad for damages. The jury required the railroad to pay $600,000 compensation for his physical injuries, $150,000 for lost wages during his long recuperation, and $1,000,000 punitive damages. How much of the $1,750,000 settlement is included in Lyle's gross income?

4. Ann Moore receives a $1,000 monthly payment from her former husband Bill. How much of the $12,000 annual receipt is included in Ann's AGI under each of the following assumptions?

    a. The monthly payment is alimony that Bill is required to pay under the Moores' divorce decree.

    b. The monthly payment consists of $600 alimony and $400 child support that Bill is required to pay under the Moores' divorce decree.

    c. The monthly payment is a gift from Bill, who is not legally obligated to pay anything to Ann under their divorce decree.

5. Will and Sandra Emmet were divorced this year. As part of the property settlement, Sandra transferred marketable securities to Will. Her basis in the securities was $89,800, and their FMV was $168,000. Four months after the divorce, Will sold the securities for $175,250.

    a. How much income does Will recognize on receipt of the securities from Sandra?

    b. How much gain does Will recognize on the sale of the securities?

    c. Does Sandra recognize any gain on the transfer of the securities to Will?

6. Mr. Lynch had the following items of financial support this year.

Unemployment compensation	$ 9,279
State welfare payments	4,060
Food stamps	1,948
Proceeds from a life insurance policy on his deceased wife	50,000

   Compute Mr. Lynch's AGI.

7. Mr. and Mrs. Nester had the followings items of financial support this year.

Social Security benefits	$26,890
Dividends and interest	78,600
Pension from Mr. Nester's former employer	28,200
Pension from Mrs. Nester's former employer	34,700

   Both pensions were paid by a qualified defined-benefit plan. Compute Mr. and Mrs. Nester's AGI.

8. Mrs. Small had the followings items of financial support this year.

Social Security benefits	$13,670
Pension from her former employer	10,800
Cash gifts from her grandchildren	12,000

   Mrs. Small's pension was paid by a qualified defined-benefit plan. Compute Mrs. Small's AGI.

9. Ms. Lincoln paid $11,340 of medical expenses this year that were not reimbursed by her insurance provider. Compute the after-tax cost of these expenses assuming that:

    a. Ms. Lincoln does not itemize deductions on her Form 1040.

    b. Ms. Lincoln itemizes deductions, her AGI is $48,300, and her marginal tax rate is 25 percent.

    c. Ms. Lincoln itemizes deductions, her AGI is $127,300, and her marginal tax rate is 28 percent.

10. Mr. and Mrs. Moss have major medical and dental insurance provided by Mrs. Moss's employer. This year, they incurred the following *unreimbursed* expenses:

Routine office visits to doctors and dentists	$940
Emergency room visits	415
Disposable contact lenses for Mr. T	360
Prescription drugs	500

Compute their itemized deduction for medical expenses if AGI is:

    a. $25,000.

    b. $50,000.

11. Mr. Papp paid the following professional fees.

To CPA for preparation of Form 1040	$4,200
To CPA for preparation of federal gift tax return	900
To attorney for drafting Mr. Papp's will	7,800
To attorney for estate tax planning advice	3,000
To attorney for advice concerning custody of Mr. Papp's minor grandson	750
To attorney for settling a dispute concerning a neighbor's barking dog	400

To what extent (if any) can Mr. Papp deduct each of these payments?

12. Mr. Curtis paid the following taxes.

Federal income tax	$50,789
Federal gift tax	285
Federal employer payroll tax for housekeeper	920
Indiana income tax	3,710
Indiana sales tax on consumer goods and services	2,040
Local property tax on:	
Principal residence	4,800
Vacation home	1,800
Two automobiles	900

To what extent (if any) can Mr. Curtis deduct each of these payments?

13. Perry Bell paid $6,438 of state and local property tax this year. Compute the after-tax cost of these payments assuming:

    a. Perry does not itemize deductions on his Form 1040.

    b. Perry itemizes deductions, has a 33 percent marginal tax rate on regular taxable income, and did not pay AMT.

    c. Perry itemizes deductions, has a 25 percent marginal tax rate on regular taxable income, and paid $4,875 AMT.

14. Mary Vale contributed a bronze statuette to a local museum. Mary received the statuette as a gift from her grandmother 35 years ago, and her tax basis was only $200. However, the statue's appraised fair market value at date of contribution was $8,500. Compute Mary's tax savings from the contribution assuming:

    a. Mary does not itemize deductions on her Form 1040.

    b. Mary itemizes deductions and has a 15 percent marginal tax rate.

    c. Mary itemizes deductions and has a 35 percent marginal tax rate.

15. Diane Bauman, a professional artist with AGI in excess of $75,000, made the following donations. Determine to what extent each donation is deductible on her Schedule A.

    a. $2,000 cash to the First Methodist Church of Chicago.

    b. $50 cash to a homeless vagrant.

    c. One of Diane's own oil paintings to the local chapter of Meals on Wheels, a tax-exempt charity. The charity sold the painting for $3,900 at a silent auction.

    d. $10,000 cash to the Democratic political party.

    e. Used household furniture to the Salvation Army. Diane's original cost was $6,800, and the furniture was reasonably worth $1,200.

16. Ms. Prince wants to create a scholarship in honor of her parents at the law school from which she received her degree. She could endow the scholarship with $500,000 cash or with $500,000 worth of marketable securities with a cost basis of $318,000. If her AGI is $1.8 million, compare the after-tax cost of the two endowment options.

17. Mr. and Mrs. Remy have the following *allowable* itemized deductions this year.

Medical expenses	$2,310
State and local taxes	4,019
Casualty loss	8,000
Charitable contributions	2,500
Miscellaneous itemized deductions	337

    Determine the effect on the amount of each deduction if the Remys engage in a transaction generating $20,000 additional AGI on this year's Form 1040.

18. Milt Payner purchased an automobile several years ago for $40,000 and has held it as a personal asset ever since. This year he sold the automobile. Describe the tax consequences of the sale if:

    a. Milt's amount realized on sale was $28,300.

    b. Milt's amount realized on sale was $55,000. The automobile was a classic Thunderbird and was purchased by a vintage car collector in Boston.

19. Conrad Smith, a business executive, is an avid collector of vintage comic books. In February, he sold a 1938 Superman comic for $3,700 that he had purchased six years ago for $625. In December, Conrad sold a 1950 Donald Duck comic for $575 that he had purchased two years ago for $900. What is the effect of these two sales on Conrad's AGI?

20. Mrs. Carr made the following interest payments. Determine the extent to which she can deduct each payment.

    a. $21,000 on a $280,000 mortgage incurred to construct (and secured by) her personal residence.

    b. $3,000 on a $34,000 second mortgage secured by her personal residence. Mrs. Carr used the proceeds to pay off her credit card debt.

  c. $2,290 on credit card debt.

  d. $15,000 on a $200,000 bank loan incurred to purchase inventory for her sole proprietorship.

  e. $1,610 on a bank loan incurred to purchase a car for her son.

  f. $1,750 on a bank loan incurred to purchase mutual fund shares that generated $1,900 dividend income this year.

21. Ms. White has been unlucky this year. On a business trip to Boston, her wallet (which contained $900 cash) was stolen. Her new automobile ($24,000 basis and FMV) was completely destroyed by a fire, and she received only $17,500 from the insurance company. A tornado wiped out a grove of ornamental trees growing near her home. She paid $6,100 to replace the trees and received no insurance reimbursement. Compute Ms. White's casualty loss deduction if her AGI is:

  a. $53,000.

  b. $210,000.

22. A burglar broke into Mr. and Mrs. Vale's home and stole an oil painting purchased 15 years ago for $89,000. This theft was their only property loss, and their AGI was $125,000. Describe the tax consequences of the theft under each of the following circumstances.

  a. The painting was insured for $200,000, which the Vales used to purchase another painting by the same artist.

  b. The painting was insured for $200,000, which the Vales used to purchase marketable securities.

  c. The painting was insured for $50,000, which the Vales used to purchase marketable securities.

  d. The painting was uninsured.

23. Mrs. Hess bakes wedding cakes as a hobby and has developed quite a local reputation for excellence. This year, she sold 29 cakes to family and friends for $200 each and spent a total of $1,700 on ingredients and decorations.

  a. How much taxable income does Mrs. Hess's hobby generate if her AGI before consideration of the hobby revenues and expenses is $33,000 and she does not itemize deductions?

  b. How would your answer change if Mrs. Hess pays enough state and local tax and makes enough charitable contributions to itemize deductions?

24. Mr. Monk is a self-employed computer consultant who earns over $100,000 each year. He also is an enthusiastic artist. This year, he spent $4,900 on oil paints, canvasses, supplies, and lessons at a local studio. Mr. Monk made several trips to the National Gallery in Washington, D.C. to attend lectures on painting technique. His total travel costs were $3,350. Describe the tax treatment of Mr. Monk's painting revenue and expenses under each of the following assumptions.

  a. Mr. Monk earned $13,290 from sales of his paintings. This was the sixth consecutive year that the painting activity generated a profit.

  b. Mr. Monk earned $2,000 from sales of his paintings. The painting activity has never generated a profit.

  c. Mr. Monk earned $2,000 from sales of his paintings. The painting activity also generated a net loss four years ago, but was profitable in each of the past three years.

25. Sandy Assam enjoys betting on horse and dog races. This year, she won $4,308 and lost $6,735 on her gambling activities. If Sandy's marginal tax rate is 25 percent, compute the after-tax cost of her gambling assuming that:

    a. She does itemize deductions.

    b. She does not itemize deductions.

26. Mr. and Mrs. Udall live in a home that Mrs. Udall inherited from her parents. This year, the Udalls took out a first mortgage on the home. Determine their itemized deduction for interest paid on the mortgage in each of the following cases.

    a. The interest payment was $5,830, the average balance of the mortgage was $75,000, and the Udalls used the borrowed funds to buy a recreational vehicle.

    b. The interest payment was $10,506, the average balance of the mortgage was $162,000, and the Udalls used the borrowed funds to pay for their daughter's wedding and honeymoon.

    c. The interest payment was $10,506, the average balance of the mortgage was $162,000, and the Udalls used the borrowed funds to put a new roof on their home.

27. Mr. and Mrs. Kim own a principal residence and a vacation home. Each residence is subject to a mortgage. The mortgage on the principal residence is acquisition debt, while the mortgage on the vacation home is home equity debt. This year, the mortgage holders provided the following information.

	Mortgage Interest Paid	Average Balance of Mortgage
Principal residence	$28,000	$641,800
Vacation home	22,100	340,000

    Compute Mr. and Mrs. Kim's qualified residence interest.

28. Ms. Imo, who is single, purchased her first home in 1991 for $85,000, and sold it in May 2000 for $178,500. She purchased her second home in July 2000 for $385,000 and sold it this year for $700,000.

    a. Compute Ms. Imo's taxable gain on the 2000 sale and on this year's sale.

    b. Compute the tax on her gain this year.

29. On January 12, 2010, Mr. and Mrs. Nixon moved out of their old residence (where they had lived for 22 years) and into a new residence purchased nine days earlier on January 3. They finally sold their old residence on June 7, 2010, for a $278,000 realized gain.

    a. How much gain did they recognize on sale of their old residence?

    b. On February 26, 2012, Mr. and Mrs. Nixon sold their new residence for a $48,000 realized gain and moved into a nearby house with a swimming pool. How much gain did they recognize?

    c. How much gain did they recognize if they sold the new residence because Mrs. Nixon accepted a job in a different state, and the family had to relocate?

30. Mrs. Gomez, a widow, paid $148,000 for her home 20 years ago. She recently sold this home and moved in with her son on a permanent basis. Describe the tax consequences of the sale assuming that her amount realized was:

    a. $140,000.

    b. $262,500.

    c. $467,000.

31. Mr. and Mrs. Boaz file a joint return on which they claim their four children (all over age 14) and Mr. Boaz's mother as dependents. Their AGI is $134,300, and they have the following itemized deductions.

State income tax	$ 7,925
Local real and personal property taxes	5,122
Qualified interest on a home equity loan	4,377
Charitable contributions	5,330
Miscellaneous itemized deductions	769
	$23,523

On the basis of these facts, compute Mr. and Mrs. Boaz's alternative minimum taxable income (AMTI) *before* any exemption amount.

Issue Recognition Problems

Identify the tax issue or issues suggested by the following situations and state each issue in the form of a question.

1. A local radio station offers a $5,000 reward for information leading to the arrest of vandals and other petty criminals. Mr. J received the reward for identifying three people who spray-painted graffiti on a public building.

2. Mr. SA, a real estate broker, just negotiated the sale of a home for a wealthy client. Two days after the sale closed, he received a beautiful leather briefcase from the client with a card reading: "In grateful appreciation of your efforts over the past year."

3. Mr. TL was a contestant on a game show and won a vacuum cleaner with a retail price of $365. Three months later, he sold the unused appliance in a garage sale for $275.

4. The pilots of Skyway Airlines have been on strike for four months. Ms. BG received a $2,700 benefit from her union, the Airline Pilots Association International. The union funded the benefits for Skyway pilots through a solicitation from union members flying for other airlines.

5. Ms. LS, a bartender and aspiring actress, won a statewide beauty pageant and was awarded a $15,000 cash scholarship to further her education and career goals. She used the money to pay for private acting lessons.

6. On a recent scuba dive, Mr. UW located a shipwreck and recovered a Spanish sword inlaid with precious stones. The sword's appraised value is $11,500. Mr. UW mounted the sword over his fireplace.

7. Mrs. OP, age 60, won an age discrimination suit against her former employer. The court awarded her $100,000 in damages for mental anguish and $200,000 for the violation of her civil rights.

8. Zachary and Stella Hernandez divorced this year. The divorce agreement reads "Zachary Hernandez shall pay Stella Hernandez $1,750 every month. This payment is in complete satisfaction of Mr. Hernandez's legal obligation to his former wife and their two children, Tony and Kristen Hernandez." The agreement provides no other information concerning the nature of the monthly payments.

9. Mrs. N, who is a self-employed author, paid $3,200 for a new computer system. She uses the system to write her books, and her two children use it for their schoolwork.

10. Mr. L, who is a member of the Navajo tribe of native Americans, developed severe arthritis this year. He paid $1,100 to a tribal medicine man who performed a series of traditional Navajo healing ceremonies called "sings."

11. Mr. S suffers from severe arthritis. His physician advised him to swim for at least one hour every day in a heated pool. Because such a facility is not conveniently located in his area, he paid $25,000 to build a heated lap pool in his backyard.

12. Mrs. PM's daughter is undergoing physical therapy for injuries sustained in a bike accident. Every two weeks, mother and daughter drive 170 miles to a regional hospital where the daughter is treated. Then they spend the night in a motel before driving home.

13. Mr. R, a CPA who charges $150 per hour for his professional services, keeps the financial records for a local charity. Although he spends at least 10 hours each month at this task, he does not charge the charity a fee for his services.

14. Mr. and Mrs. FP bought $500 worth of Girl Scout cookies from their godchild. Because they don't eat sweets, they gave away every box to various friends and family members.

15. Ms. DS owns a diamond ring worth $12,000 that she has worn on her right hand for 12 years. While washing her hands two days ago, she noticed that the ring was missing. She searched her home, her car, and her place of business but has been unable to locate the ring.

16. Mr. D borrowed $600,000 to purchase 62 acres of undeveloped land and secured the debt with the land. He converted a three-room log cabin on the land to his principal residence. This year, he paid $39,910 interest on the mortgage.

17. For the past 10 years, Mr. Y lived on his sailboat for eight months of the year and spent the other four months in his daughter's home. This year, he realized a $35,200 gain on sale of the boat and moved into his own apartment.

18. Ms. SE paid $155,000 for a house that she occupied as her principal residence until February 1, when she moved out and converted the house to rental property. The appraised FMV of the house was $140,000. She leased the house to tenants who purchased it on November 18. Her realized loss on the sale was $24,700, computed as follows.

Amount realized		$ 125,000
Original cost basis	$155,000	
MACRS depreciation during rental period	(5,300)	
Adjusted basis		(149,700)
		$ (24,700)

19. Mr. and Mrs. AQ purchased their home one year ago. This year, a local government attempted to seize the home because the former residents had failed to pay their property taxes for 12 years. Mr. and Mrs. AQ paid $1,700 to an attorney who resolved the dispute in their favor.

Research Problems

1. Mr. Clark Besson is undergoing extensive chemotherapy treatment for cancer. His oncologist recommended that he ingest marijuana to relieve the painful side effects. However, possession or use of marijuana is illegal in Mr. Besson's state of residence. Therefore, he makes a weekly trip to a neighboring state in which the medically prescribed use of marijuana is legal. Since beginning his treatment, he has spent $2,730 to buy marijuana. Is this a deductible medical expense?

2. Mr. and Mrs. Lukert own a sole proprietorship and have no other source of income. This year, they paid $11,674 Massachusetts income tax, all of which is attributable to their business profit. Can they deduct their state income tax as a business expense on Schedule C, or must they report it as an itemized deduction on Schedule A?

3. Betsy and Larry Lorch own and reside in an apartment in midtown Manhattan. They left the city to avoid the uproar surrounding New Year's Eve and spent a long holiday with Larry's parents in upstate New York. They sublet their apartment to a German couple who wanted to join the throng in Times Square. They paid the Lorches $500 per night ($11,000 total) to stay in the apartment from December 21 through January 11. What are the tax consequences of this rental arrangement?

4. Eighteen months ago, Barry Shelton won a $2 million Maryland state lottery jackpot and chose to receive it as $120,000 annual annuity for the rest of his life. This year his brothers persuaded him to sell the annuity to a financial institution for $1.79 million and invest the sales proceeds in a new family business. How much gain did Barry recognize on sale of his annuity, and is it ordinary income or long-term capital gain?

5. Howard Wilson, a single individual, sold his principal residence in Cleveland eight months ago and excluded his entire $148,000 gain on the sale from gross income. He purchased and moved into a new home in a suburb of Chicago. Shortly thereafter, Howard's 20-year-old son moved in with him. The son was on probation from a prison sentence for drug dealing and assault with a deadly weapon. Howard's neighbors learned about the son's criminal record and have organized protests against the son's presence in the community. Howard has received several verbal and written threats, and his house has been spray-painted with graffiti. The atmosphere has become so hostile that Howard has decided to sell his new home and relocate in a different city. Will he be eligible to exclude any of his gain on this second sale?

Tax Planning Cases

1. Ms. JL is a successful attorney in the 35 percent marginal tax bracket. During the past several years, she provided legal services to her great uncle, who is 78 years old and in failing health. Although the uncle offered to pay for her work, she refused any compensation, requesting instead that her uncle remember her appropriately in his will. The uncle recently added a codicil providing for a $250,000 cash bequest to Ms. JL. The remainder of his estate will pass to his two children and seven grandchildren.

    a. What tax planning objective may Ms. JL have accomplished through her request of her uncle?

    b. Can you identify both the opportunity cost and the risk inherent in her plan?

2. Mr. and Mrs. TB are going through an amicable divorce. Mrs. TB, who is a full-time homemaker, will have custody of their two children, ages 2 and 4. She suggested that Mr. TB pay $4,000 child support each month. He countered by offering to pay $1,600 child support and $3,000 alimony each month if he can claim their two children as dependents. In either case, Mrs. TB will qualify as a head of household. Mr. TB's taxable income averages $150,000, putting him in the 28 percent marginal tax bracket.

    a. Compute Mr. TB's annual after-tax cost and Mrs. TB's annual after-tax cash flow if he pays her $4,000 monthly child support and she claims their children as dependents.

    b. Compute Mr. TB's annual after-tax cost and Mrs. TB's annual after-tax cash flow if she accepts his counterproposal.

3. Mr. and Mrs. JM, ages 68 and 66, always claim the standard deduction on their joint return. They own a local restaurant, the Shoreline Grill, as a sole proprietorship. They are both graduates of State University and make regular donations to their alma mater. Their method for doing so is a bit unusual. At the beginning of each State University home football game, the public address system informs the crowd that the Shoreline Grill will contribute $50 to the athletic scholarship fund for every first down the home

team makes. As a result of this commitment, Mr. and Mrs. JM contributed $4,950 to State University this year. What tax planning objective may they have accomplished by structuring their donation in this manner?

4. Mr. Z, who is in the 33 percent marginal tax bracket and itemizes deductions, recently inherited $30,000. He is considering three alternative uses for this windfall.

   • He could buy shares in a mutual bond fund paying 11 percent interest a year.

   • He could pay off a $30,000 personal debt to a local bank on which he pays $2,350 interest each year.

   • He could pay off $30,000 of the mortgage incurred to buy his home. This principal repayment would decrease his annual home mortgage interest expense by $2,900.

   Compute the annual increase in Mr. Z's after-tax cash flow for each of these three alternatives. Which alternative would you recommend and why?

Comprehensive Problems for Part Five

1. Blake and Valerie Meyer (both age 30) are married with one dependent child (age 5). On the basis of the following information, compute the Meyers' federal income tax (including any AMT) on their joint return.

   • Blake's gross salary from his corporate employer was $70,000, and his Section 401(k) contribution was $6,300.

   • Valerie's salary from GuiTech, an S corporation, was $29,400.

   • Valerie owns 16 percent of GuiTech's outstanding stock. Her pro rata share of GuiTech's ordinary business income was $13,790, her pro rata share of GuiTech's net loss from rental real estate was $8,100, and she received a $12,000 cash distribution from GuiTech.

   • Blake received a $12,000 cash gift from his grandmother.

   • Valerie won $6,400 in the Maryland state lottery.

   • The Meyers received a distribution from their investment in Pawnee Mutual Fund that consisted of a $712 qualifying dividend and a $3,020 long-term capital gain.

   • Blake paid $12,000 alimony to a former spouse.

   • The Meyers paid $14,200 home mortgage interest on acquisition debt and $2,780 property tax on their personal residence.

   • The Meyers paid $7,000 state income tax and $4,200 state and local sales tax.

   • Valerie contributed $1,945 to the First Baptist Church.

2. Mrs. Cora Yank (age 42) is divorced and has full custody of her 10-year-old son, William. From the following information, compute Mrs. Yank's federal income tax (including any AMT) and the amount due with her Form 1040 *or* the refund she should receive.

   • Mrs. Yank works as a medical technician in a Chicago hospital. Her salary was $38,400, from which her employer withheld $3,012 federal income tax and $2,170 employee FICA tax.

   • Several years ago, Mrs. Yank was seriously injured in a traffic accident caused by another driver's negligence. This year, she received a $25,000 settlement from the driver's insurance company: $20,000 as compensation for her physical injuries and $5,000 for lost wages during her convalescent period. Because she was unable to work for the first seven weeks of the year, she collected $1,400 unemployment compensation from the state of Illinois.

   • Mrs. Yank earned $629 interest on a savings account. She contributed $800 to a regular IRA. She is not an active participant in any other qualified retirement plan.

- Mrs. Yank paid $10,800 rent on the apartment in which she and William live. She received $1,600 alimony and $2,350 child support from her former husband.
- Mrs. Yank is covered under her employer's medical reimbursement plan. However, this year's medical bills exceeded her reimbursement limit by $1,630.
- Mrs. Yank paid $2,062 income tax to Illinois.
- Mrs. Yank spent $470 on hospital shoes and uniforms. Her employer did not reimburse her for this expense.
- Mrs. Yank paid $1,300 for after-school child care for William.

3. Tom and Allie Benson (ages 53 and 46) are residents of Fort Worth, Texas, and file a joint federal income tax return. They provide the entire support for their three children, ages 19, 18, and 14. On the basis of the following information, compute Mr. and Mrs. Benson's federal income (including any AMT) and SE tax and the amount due with their Form 1040 *or* the refund they should receive.

- Mr. Benson is an attorney who practices in partnership with 18 other attorneys. His ordinary income was $278,300, and his net earnings from self-employment were $257,010 (92.35 percent of $278,300). The Bensons made estimated tax payments totaling $58,000 to the IRS and a $28,500 contribution to the qualified Keogh plan maintained by the partnership.
- The Bensons earned $10,365 interest income and $13,790 qualified dividend income from their investment portfolio. They also received a $4,218 long-term capital gain distribution from a mutual fund. They have a $9,723 capital loss carryforward from last year.
- The Bensons received a Schedule K-1 from an S corporation in which they own 6 percent of the stock. Their share of the corporation's business loss was $4,930. The S corporation operates a mink farm in Maine.
- Mrs. Benson received a $50,000 cash inheritance from her great aunt.
- The Bensons moved from San Antonio to Fort Worth in April so that Mr. Benson could manage the Fort Worth office. The cost of moving their household goods was $11,260. The law firm reimbursed Mr. Benson for $10,000 of this expense.
- The Bensons paid $33,890 interest on a $573,000 first mortgage and $4,120 interest on a $90,000 second mortgage on their personal residence. They incurred the first mortgage to buy the home and the second mortgage to purchase new furniture.
- The Bensons paid $8,400 real property tax on their home and $2,920 for homeowners insurance.
- The Bensons made $21,980 cash donations to various qualified charities.
- The Bensons paid $1,911 state and local sales tax. (Texas has no individual income tax.)
- The Bensons paid $3,350 to the CPA who prepared their Form 1040.

**CPA Exam
Simulations**

Please visit the text website for the online CPA simulation: mhhe.com/sjones2013.

Frank, age 38, is a single taxpayer and is the sales manager of Standard Co., an auto stereo dealer. Frank's adjusted gross income (AGI) for the year is $67,000. During the year, Frank made a number of interest payments and would like to understand whether these payments are deductible as itemized deductions.

Topics covered in the simulation:

- Mortgage interest on principal residence
- Mortgage points
- Mortgage interest on rental property
- Personal credit card interest
- Interest on late filing of income tax return
- Home equity loan interest

Pike, age 38, is a single taxpayer and is the sales manager of Standard Co., an auto stereo dealer. Pike's adjusted gross income (AGI) for the year is $67,000.

Pike's job is to oversee the sales operations of Standard Co. Pike has a private office at the dealership and is responsible for attracting new customers and retaining current customers. As the sales manager, Pike has the authority to hire and discharge sales personnel.

During the year, Pike suffered several losses and would like to understand whether these losses qualify for a casualty loss deduction on Schedule A.

Topics covered in the simulation:

- Casualty loss definition
- Insurance reimbursements
- Casualty loss AGI limitation

Appendix **17–A**

Social Security Worksheet (Adapted from IRS Publication 915)

1. Social Security benefits received	_____		1. Social Security benefits received	14,400
2. One-half of line 1	_____		2. One-half of line 1	7,200
3. Adjusted gross income (AGI) (without Social Security benefits)	_____		3. Adjusted gross income (AGI) (without Social Security benefits)	43,000
4. Tax-exempt interest income	_____		4. Tax-exempt interest income	600
5. Add lines 2, 3, and 4	_____		5. Add lines 2, 3, and 4	50,800
6. Enter: $32,000 (married filing jointly) $25,000 (single or head of household) –0– (married filing separately)*	_____		6. Enter: $32,000 (married filing jointly) $25,000 (single or head of household) –0– (married filing separately)*	32,000
7. Subtract line 6 from line 5	_____		7. Subtract line 6 from line 5	18,800

If line 7 is zero or less, the Social Security benefits are nontaxable.

If line 7 is zero or less, the Social Security benefits are nontaxable.

8. Enter: $12,000 (married filing jointly) $9,000 (single or head of household) –0– (married filing separately)	_____		8. Enter: $12,000 (married filing jointly) $9,000 (single or head of household) –0– (married filing separately)	12,000
9. Subtract line 8 from line 7. If zero or less, enter zero	_____		9. Subtract line 8 from line 7 If zero or less, enter zero	6,800
10. Enter the lesser of line 7 or line 8	_____		10. Enter the lesser of line 7 or line 8	12,000
11. Enter one-half of line 10	_____		11. Enter one-half of line 10	6,000
12. Enter the lesser of line 2 or line 11	_____		12. Enter the lesser of line 2 or line 11	6,000
13. Multiply line 9 by 85 percent	_____		13. Multiply line 9 by 85 percent	5,780
14. Add line 12 and line 13	_____		14. Add line 12 and line 13	11,780
15. Multiply line 1 by 85 percent	_____		15. Multiply line 1 by 85 percent	12,240
16. Enter the lesser of line 14 or line 15	_____		16. Enter the lesser of line 14 or line 15	11,780

Line 16 is the taxable portion of the Social Security benefits.

Line 16 is the taxable portion of the Social Security benefits.

* Married individuals filing separate returns who live apart at all times during the year are considered single for purposes of this computation.

Example   Mr. and Mrs. PB received $14,400 Social Security benefits this year. The AGI on their joint return before considering these benefits was $43,000, and they received $600 tax-exempt interest. The taxable portion of their Social Security benefits is $11,780.

Part **Six**

The Tax
Compliance Process

18 The Tax Compliance Process

Chapter Eighteen

The Tax Compliance Process

Learning Objectives

After studying this chapter, you should be able to:

1. Determine the filing date and extended filing date for income tax returns.

2. Compute a late-filing and late-payment penalty.

3. Describe the statute of limitations for a tax return.

4. Identify the three types of IRS audits.

5. Discuss the reasons why the IRS imposes a negligence or a civil fraud penalty.

6. Identify the three judicial levels in the tax litigation process.

7. Define the term *transferee liability*.

8. Explain the purpose of the innocent spouse rule.

The federal income, payroll, self-employment, and transfer taxes are all self-assessed taxes. Every person who is required to pay or collect any of these taxes must compute the amount of tax due, file the proper return, and maintain adequate records supporting the calculations presented on the return.[1] As a practical matter, the tax laws are sufficiently complex that the majority of taxpayers engage a tax practitioner to assist in the preparation of their returns. Nevertheless, even taxpayers who rely entirely on professional help are responsible for complying with the law and must bear the consequences of failure to comply.

This final chapter of *Principles of Taxation for Business and Investment Planning* is an overview of the federal tax compliance system. The procedural rules for payment of tax and filing of income tax returns and the IRS's audit process are explained. Your rights as a taxpayer in dealing with the IRS, as well as the penalties the IRS may impose, are described. The chapter ends with a discussion of the judicial process by which both individuals and corporations may challenge the outcome of an IRS audit in federal court.

[1] §6001 and §6011.

FILING AND PAYMENT REQUIREMENTS

Objective 1
Determine the filing date and extended filing date for income tax returns.

Most individuals report income on the basis of a calendar year and are required to file their Form 1040 for the current year by April 15 of the following year. The few individuals who have adopted a fiscal year must file their returns by the 15th day of the fourth month following the close of the taxable year. Corporations, which report on the basis of either a calendar year or a fiscal year, must file their Form 1120 by the 15th day of the third month following the close of their taxable year. As we discussed in earlier chapters, individuals and corporations must pay their income tax periodically over the course of the year, either in the form of withholding (individuals) or quarterly estimated tax payments. Taxpayers that fail to pay their total tax liability during the year must pay the balance due by the filing date of the return for the year.[2]

Both individual and corporate taxpayers may apply for a six-month extension of time to file their income tax return by submitting an application for extension with the IRS by the due date of the return.[3] The extensions are automatic; taxpayers do not have to explain to the IRS why they need additional time to file. An automatic extension of time for filing a return does not extend the time for payment of any tax due. Consequently, taxpayers are required to pay any estimated balance of tax due by the *unextended* due date of the return.

> **Tax Talk**
> *In 1986, the IRS launched a pilot program under which 25,000 individuals filed electronic returns. In 2011, 107 million individuals filed their tax returns electronically!*

Application for Extension

On April 8, 2012, Laurie Crawford submitted an application to extend the filing date of her 2011 Form 1040 from April 15 to October 15, 2012. Laurie estimated that her 2011 tax liability was $62,100. Her 2011 withholding totaled $57,000. Consequently, Laurie paid her $5,100 estimated balance of tax due with her extension application.

Interest Payments

Taxpayers that pay any amount of income tax after the required payment date are charged interest by the federal government. The interest is based on the number of days from the required payment date to the actual payment date.[4] The annual interest rate, referred to as the *underpayment rate*, equals the federal short-term rate plus three percentage points. Interest is compounded daily, and the federal rate is adjusted quarterly.[5]

Interest Charge

On March 29, 2012, Merv Ballow applied for an automatic six-month extension of time to file his 2011 Form 1040. Merv's 2011 withholding totaled $23,750, and he estimated that his 2011 tax liability was only $23,000. Consequently, Merv did not pay any additional tax with his extension application. Merv filed his completed Form 1040 on June 18. Merv's correct tax liability reported on the return was $24,900, so he paid his $1,150 balance of tax due with the return.

Because Merv failed to pay his total 2011 tax by April 15, 2012, the IRS will send him a bill for interest on the $1,150 late payment. The interest period runs from April 16 through June 18. If the federal short-term rate during this period was 1 percent, the IRS will compute the interest charge at a 4 percent annual rate compounded daily.

---

[2] §6072(a) and (b) and §6151(a).

[3] Reg. §1.6081-4T and Reg. §1.6081-3.

[4] §6601(a).

[5] §6621(a)(2) and §6622. The underpayment rate for corporate underpayments exceeding $100,000 equals the federal short-term rate plus five percentage points. §6621(c).

Millions of taxpayers overpay their annual income tax in the form of excess withholding or estimated tax payments. These taxpayers report the overpayment on their tax returns and request a refund from the government. The IRS is not required to pay interest on any income tax overpayment refunded within 45 days after the filing date of the return.[6] As a result, the millions of taxpayers who receive their refunds within this grace period do not earn interest. In the unusual case when the IRS fails to mail a refund check on a timely basis, the government must pay interest to the taxpayer.

The annual overpayment rate for individuals equals the federal short-term rate plus 3 percent, which is the same as the underpayment rate. The overpayment rate for corporations depends on the size of the overpayment. If the corporate overpayment is $10,000 or less, the interest rate equals the short-term rate plus 2 percent. If the overpayment exceeds $10,000, the interest rate equals the short-term rate plus only one-half percent.[7]

Interest on Refunds	Refer to the previous example in which Merv Ballow filed his 2011 Form 1040 on June 18, 2012. Now assume that Merv's correct tax liability reported on the return was only $21,000. Consequently, Merv overpaid his 2011 tax by $2,750 ($23,750 withholding − $21,000 tax liability). If the IRS refunds this overpayment within 45 days after June 18, Merv will not receive any interest from the government. However, if the refund is unusually delayed, Merv will receive his refund plus interest.

Late-Filing and Late-Payment Penalty

Objective 2
Compute a late-filing and late-payment penalty.

A taxpayer who fails to file an income tax return by the required due date and can't provide a good excuse for such failure must pay a **late-filing and late-payment penalty.**[8] This penalty equals 5 percent of the balance of tax due with the return for each month (or portion thereof) that the return is delinquent.

Late-Filing and Late-Payment Penalty	Mr. Toomey failed to request an extension of time to file his 2011 return and didn't file his Form 1040 until July 29, 2012. The return reported a $45,890 tax liability and $42,000 tax withheld by his employer. Mr. Toomey enclosed a check for the $3,890 balance due with his late return. Because the balance due was not paid by April 15, the IRS charged him interest on $3,890 from April 16 through July 28. Because the return was delinquent, the IRS also assessed a $778 late-filing and late-payment penalty ($3,890 × 5% for three full months and a portion of a fourth month).
	The IRS may waive this penalty (but not the interest) if Mr. Toomey can show reasonable cause for his tardiness.

The 5 percent penalty runs for only five months (until the penalty equals 25 percent of the balance due). After five months, the penalty rate drops to one-half percent of the balance due. This reduced penalty can run for an additional 45 months.

---

[6] §6611(e)(1). The filing date is the later of the statutory filing date or the date the return is actually filed.
[7] §6611(a) and §6621(a)(1).
[8] §6651.

Reduced Penalty	Ms. Rojas filed her unextended 2011 Form 1040 on November 22, 2012, and had no reasonable cause for the delinquency. The return showed a $9,094 balance of tax due. The IRS charged Ms. Rojas interest on $9,094 from April 16 through November 21 and assessed a $2,410 late-filing and late-payment penalty.

Penalty for April 16–September 15	
$9,094 × 5% for five months	$2,274
Penalty for September 16–November 21	
$9,094 × .5% for three months	136
Total penalty	$2,410

Reasonable Cause for a Delinquent Return?	David McMahan, an investment broker, engaged James Russell, a tax attorney, to file his individual income tax return. Mr. Russell told his client that he would file the necessary paperwork to extend the filing date of the return. Months later, Mr. McMahan discovered that his attorney had neglected to file the extension request. The IRS assessed a $141,028 late filing and late payment penalty which he contested in court. Mr. McMahan argued that his reliance on a tax professional to file an extension request was reasonable cause for the delinquent return. The court was not persuaded by his argument, observing that a "taxpayer has an affirmative nondelegable duty to ensure that the appropriate forms—whether a tax return or an extension request—are actually filed by the statutory deadline." Consequently, Mr. McMahan was liable for the penalty.[9]

One interesting feature of the late-filing penalty deserves emphasis. The penalty is based on the balance of tax due with a delinquent return. If a taxpayer overpaid his tax, his return will show a refund due instead of a balance due. In this case, the government cannot assess any penalty if such return is filed after the due date. Of course, for as long as the return is delinquent, the government is enjoying an interest-free loan from the taxpayer that it does not repay until the taxpayer finally decides to file.

Return Processing

Tax Talk
The IRS does not usually investigate tax documents with mismatched names and Social Security numbers suggesting illegal immigrant laborers because such cases yield so little revenue.

Each year more than 180 million income tax returns are filed with the IRS by individuals, corporations, partnerships, and fiduciaries. These returns pour into the 10 IRS service centers located throughout the country. The service centers are information-processing facilities where each return is checked for mathematical accuracy and logged into the IRS's computer system. This system cross-checks each return against information returns filed with respect to the taxpayer, such as Form W-2s filed by employers; Form 1099s filed by payers of interest, dividend, rents, or other types of income; and Schedule K-1s filed by partnerships and S corporations. If a return reflects a math error or a discrepancy with an information return, the service center mails a letter to the taxpayer explaining the problem and calculating the additional tax or refund. The service centers are responsible for depositing personal checks or money orders with the U.S. Treasury and for authorizing refund checks to be mailed.

Statute of Limitations

Objective 3
Describe the statute of limitations for a tax return.

Many taxpayers place unjustified significance on the fact that the government cashed their check or mailed their refund. While these events prove that their tax return was processed, they do not mean that the IRS has accepted the accuracy of the return. A **statute of limitations**

---

[9] *McMahan v. Commissioner,* 114 F.3d 366 (CA-2, 1997). For a recent case, see *Louis Greenwald,* T.C. Memo 2011-239.

gives the IRS three years from the later of the statutory due date (April 15th for calendar year individuals) or the date on which the return was actually filed to examine that return for mistakes and to assess any additional tax.[10]

Three-Year Statute of Limitations	Mr. and Mrs. Epps filed their 2011 Form 1040 on March 16, 2012. The IRS has until April 15, 2015, to audit this return and assess any additional tax. Mr. Procter requested an extension of time to file his 2011 return and actually filed the return on August 2, 2012. In his case, the IRS has until August 2, 2015, to audit the return and assess additional tax.

If a taxpayer files a return and omits an amount of gross income exceeding 25 percent of the gross income reported on the return, the normal three-year statute of limitations is extended to six years. If the IRS determines that a return is fraudulent (a concept discussed later in this chapter), the return remains open (subject to audit) indefinitely.

Extended Statute of Limitations	Ms. Yang, a self-employed consultant, failed to include a $13,200 business receipt in the income reported on her 2011 return, which she filed on February 8, 2012. The gross income on the return was $52,000, and the omitted income was more than 25 percent of this income. $13,200 > $13,000 ($52,000 gross income × 25%) Consequently, Ms. Yang's return remains open until April 15, 2018. If the IRS determines that her omission of income constituted fraud, it can audit the return and assess additional tax at any time.

Because of the possibility of audit, taxpayers should keep all supporting paperwork such as receipts and canceled checks for at least three years after the return is filed. Records substantiating the tax basis of property, any legal documents containing tax information (closing statement on a property sale, divorce decree, etc.), and a copy of the return should be retained permanently.

THE AUDIT PROCESS

The IRS selects corporate tax returns for audit primarily on the basis of the size of the business, measured in terms of taxable income and net worth as reported on Form 1120. Individual returns are usually selected by a highly classified computer program that analyzes the contents of each return and assigns a **discriminate function system (DIF) score.** This score theoretically measures the return's potential for generating additional tax revenue on audit. The higher the score, the greater the likelihood that the return contains an error causing an understatement of tax. Obviously, returns with the highest DIF scores are chosen for examination. Although the details of the DIF selection process are a closely guarded secret, tax practitioners assume that highly speculative investment activities, unusually large itemized deductions, and deductions that are prone to manipulation or abuse (travel and entertainment expenses, nonbusiness bad debts, losses generated by a secondary business, etc.) inflate DIF scores. Similarly, high-income returns are much more likely to be selected for audit than returns reflecting modest incomes.

Audit Coverage	According to the 2010 IRS Data Book, the IRS examined 1.58 million of the 143 million individual income tax returns filed for 2009, an audit coverage rate of 1.1 percent. The rate for returns reporting only nonbusiness income totaling less than $200,000 was a mere .5 percent, while the rate for returns reporting income totaling $1,000,000 or more was a substantial 8.4 percent.

[10] §6501.

Types of Audits

Objective 4
Identify the three
types of IRS audits.

Routine audits are conducted by personnel working out of the IRS area offices located throughout the United States. The simplest audit, called a **correspondence examination,** may be handled entirely by telephone or through the mail. More complex audits take place at the IRS office (an **office examination** conducted by a tax auditor) or at the taxpayer's place of business (a **field examination** conducted by a revenue agent). Office audits focus on a few questionable items on a return. Field audits are broader in scope and may involve a complete analysis of the taxpayer's books and records for the year or years under investigation.

Tax Talk
The IRS uses social media tools and platforms to share the latest information on tax changes, initiatives, products, and services. A list of these social media resources, which includes YouTube and Twitter, is available on IRS.gov.

If the IRS requests a personal interview with a taxpayer or if the taxpayer requests an interview during an audit, the IRS must schedule the interview at a reasonable time and a convenient location. Individuals who must deal with the IRS can represent themselves or authorize an attorney, certified public accountant, or enrolled agent to represent them. While attorneys and CPAs are licensed to practice by state boards or agencies, **enrolled agents** receive certification to practice before the IRS by passing an exam on tax law written and administered by the IRS itself.

Assessments of Deficiencies and Interest

Individuals who are notified that they are being audited may panic unnecessarily. Any person who made a good faith effort to comply with the laws in preparing the return and has maintained adequate records has nothing to fear. In a best case scenario, the audit will be concluded with no change in tax, or even with a refund (plus interest) due to the taxpayer. Of course, the return was selected for audit because of its high probability of error. Consequently, the probable outcome is that the IRS will discover that the return contains a mistake that resulted in an understatement of tax. In this case, the taxpayer is assessed a **deficiency** (the additional tax owed), plus interest based on the number of days between the time the return was filed and the date the deficiency is paid.

Corporations may deduct the interest paid on federal income tax deficiencies as a business expense. However, Treasury regulations state that interest paid by an individual on a federal income tax deficiency is nondeductible personal interest "regardless of the source of the income generating the tax liability."[11]

Interest Paid on Tax Deficiency

Maria Cardona owns a sole proprietorship that makes custom-designed patio furniture. This year, Maria received a deficiency notice from the IRS informing her that she owed $42,760 additional income tax for 2010 plus $6,157 interest. The entire deficiency resulted from an understatement of net profit on Maria's Schedule C. Nonetheless, she must treat her $6,157 interest payment as a nondeductible personal expense.

Your Rights as a Taxpayer

In 1989, Congress enacted the **Taxpayer Bill of Rights,** which requires the IRS to deal with every citizen and resident in a fair, professional, prompt, and courteous manner and to provide the technical help needed by taxpayers to comply with the law. The IRS publishes over 100 free information booklets, one of which, IRS Publication 910, *Guide to Free Tax Services,* is a catalog describing the many types of assistance offered. The Taxpayer Bill of Rights ensures personal and financial confidentiality. If the IRS requests information, the taxpayer has the right to know how the information will be used and the nature of any consequences if the taxpayer refuses to provide the information. However, the bill contains an important disclaimer: The IRS can share tax return information with state tax agencies, the Department of Justice, other federal agencies, and foreign governments under tax treaty provisions.

---

[11] Reg. §1.163-9T(b)(2)(i)(A).

In 1996, Congress enacted Taxpayer Bill of Rights 2, which expanded on the 1989 legislation. The IRS Reform and Restructuring Act of 1998 included the massive Taxpayer Bill of Rights 3, described as the "most extensive taxpayer-protective provisions ever enacted in a single setting."[12] The 1998 legislation created the office of National Taxpayer Advocate, the purpose of which is to assist taxpayers in resolving problems and to help taxpayers who suffer hardship because of IRS actions. The National Taxpayer Advocate heads a team of local Taxpayer Advocates who operate independently of the IRS's audit, assessment, and collection functions.

IRS Mission Statement	As part of its ongoing public relations effort, the IRS adopted the following mission statement: "Provide America's taxpayers top-quality service by helping them understand and meet their tax responsibilities and enforce the law with integrity and fairness to all."

Noncompliance Penalties

The Internal Revenue Code attempts to discourage taxpayers from neglecting their legal responsibilities by imposing a variety of penalties. The IRS can assess these penalties, singly or in combination, on any taxpayer who does not make a good faith effort to comply with the tax law. In this section of Chapter 18, we will examine several of the more interesting penalties.

Frivolous Tax Returns

Tax Talk

As a federal judge observed, "Like moths to a flame, some people find themselves irresistibly drawn to the tax protester movement's illusory claim that there is no legal requirement to pay federal income tax. And, like moths, these people sometimes get burned."

The occasional tax protester defies the federal self-assessment system by filing a blatantly incorrect or incomplete return on the basis of a legal argument with absolutely no merit. The IRS can retaliate by imposing a $5,000 penalty for the filing of a frivolous tax return.[13] The IRS is required to publish a list of legal arguments that it considers frivolous. The current list includes 46 such arguments, including: The federal income tax is unconstitutional because the Sixteenth Amendment to the Constitution was not properly ratified; payment of the individual income tax is purely voluntary; and wages, tips, and other compensation received for personal services are not taxable income.[14] In the introduction to this list, the IRS Commissioner cautions people to "remember they are ultimately responsible for what is on their tax return even if some unscrupulous preparers have steered them in the wrong direction. The truth about these frivolous arguments is simple: They don't work."

Frivolous Argument	Norbert Yolandu filed a 2008 Form 1040 on which he entered zeros on every line. Across page 1 of the return, Norbert wrote: "I refuse to pay income tax because of my religious and moral conviction that the war in Iraq is a sin against mankind." He went on to explain that his refusal to pay tax was based on the First Amendment to the United States Constitution that protects his freedom of religion. This legal argument was rejected by the Supreme Court more than 25 years ago, and the IRS has listed it as a frivolous argument.[15] Consequently, the IRS imposed a $5,000 penalty on Mr. Yolandu.

Negligence

Objective 5
Discuss the reasons why the IRS imposes a negligence or a civil fraud penalty.

During the course of an audit, a revenue agent may conclude that the taxpayer failed to make a reasonable attempt to prepare a correct return or intentionally disregarded the tax rules and regulations. In such case, the agent can impose the **negligence** penalty, which equals 20 percent of any tax understatement attributable to the taxpayer's negligent actions.[16]

---

[12] Gerald A. Kafka, "Restructuring and Reforming the IRS and the Code—Congress Takes a Quantum Leap," *Journal of Taxation*, September 1998, p. 134.

[13] §6702.

[14] Notice 2010-33, 2010-17 IRB 609.

[15] *United States* v. *Lee*, 455 U.S. 252 (1982).

[16] §6662.

Negligence	The IRS agent who audited Ms. Purl's Form 1040 discovered three errors that collectively resulted in a $45,000 understatement of her tax. The agent believed that two of the errors reflected a sincere misunderstanding of the law but that the third error was caused by Ms. Purl's flagrant disregard of a clear instruction on the return. The portion of the understatement caused by the third error was $13,000. The agent could impose a $2,600 negligence penalty (20 percent of $13,000). Ms. Purl must pay this penalty *in addition to* the $45,000 deficiency and the interest thereon.

The distinction between an honest mistake and negligence may be unclear. An individual's exposure to the negligence penalty depends on subjective factors such as the complexity of the issue in question, the individual's education and business experience, the existence of supporting documentation, and the individual's degree of cooperation during the audit. Individuals who follow the advice of tax practitioners are much less likely to incur a negligence penalty than individuals who rely on their own judgment, although reliance on professional advice is not a guaranteed defense. When the IRS imposes the negligence penalty and the taxpayer challenges it in court, the IRS has the *burden of production* in the litigation. In other words, the IRS must present a *preponderance of evidence* establishing negligence before the court will sustain the penalty.[17]

An Unlikely Story	Benjamin Smith was a teacher for the New York State Board of Education and a licensed attorney. On his 1992 and 1993 tax returns, he reported $8 gross receipts and deducted $57,938 business expenses in connection with his law practice. When the IRS requested written substantiation of these expenses, Mr. Smith explained that he kept his business records and receipts in a U-Haul trailer. Unfortunately, the trailer had unhitched from his car and had overturned, destroying all its contents. After he failed to provide any evidence of this accident, the IRS disallowed his business deductions and slapped him with a negligence penalty. The Tax Court observed that "petitioner is an attorney. He claims he had been in private practice for several years. Although petitioner contends that he lacks any proficiency with regard to the tax matters, we believe that as a member of the legal profession, he should have recognized the importance of substantiating his expenses. Petitioner was given ample time and opportunity to procure and reconstruct the necessary records. Petitioner chose not to do so." The Tax Court agreed with the IRS that Mr. Smith acted in bad faith in filing his tax returns and was guilty of negligence.[18]

Civil Fraud

The harshest administrative penalty that the IRS may impose is the **civil fraud** penalty, which equals 75 percent of the portion of a tax underpayment attributable to fraud.[19] Fraud can be defined as the intent to cheat the government by deliberately understating tax. Fraud is characterized by the systematic omission of substantial amounts of income from the tax return or by the deduction of nonexistent expenses or losses. Revenue agents often assess a fraud penalty when they discover that a taxpayer keeps two sets of financial records: one for tax purposes and one reflecting the taxpayer's true income. The fact that a taxpayer altered or destroyed business records and documents, concealed assets, or cannot account for large cash receipts or deposits is a strong indication of fraud.

---

[17] §7491(c).

[18] *Benjamin H. Smith,* T.C. Memo 1998-33.

[19] §6663.

Civil Fraud	The IRS agent who audited Mr. Lowe's Form 1040 discovered that he made large monthly cash deposits to a bank account under a fictitious name. He told the agent that he received the cash as a gift from a friend. When asked to reveal the friend's identity, Mr. Lowe became verbally abusive and refused to answer. After further investigation, the agent discovered that the cash represented $62,000 unreported income from Mr. Lowe's lawn service business on which he owed $23,220 federal tax. Because the agent concluded that Mr. Lowe intended to cheat the government by failing to report the income, the IRS assessed a $17,415 fraud penalty (75 percent of $23,220).

Because of the severity of the penalty, the burden of proof in establishing fraud falls on the IRS.[20] To sustain a fraud penalty, the IRS must have more than just a preponderance of evidence; it must show by *clear and convincing evidence* that the fraud occurred.[21]

A Clear Case of Fraud	Mr. Luan Nguyen was the sole shareholder of Hi-Q Personnel, Inc., an employment agency that provided skilled and nonskilled temporary workers to more than 250 clients. Mr. Nguyen offered his workers the choice of being paid by check or in cash. The corporation treated those workers paid by check as employees and paid federal employment tax on their wages. The corporation ignored those workers paid in cash. During the years in question, Hi-Q paid $14,845,019 cash wages on which it failed to pay any employment tax. When the IRS imposed the civil fraud penalty on Mr. Nguyen, he argued that he had to pay his workers in cash to be competitive in the temporary labor market and that he was simply honoring his workers' wishes to maximize their earnings. The Tax Court was unmoved by this argument, concluding that Hi-Q needed to supplement the workers' earnings "either at its own expense or at the expense of the U.S. Treasury." By choosing the latter course, the corporation and its owner committed tax fraud.[22]

Criminal Fraud

Tax Talk
Eighty-six percent of individuals surveyed by the IRS believe that cheating on taxes is wholly unacceptable and that people have a civic duty to honestly pay their taxes.

If a revenue agent uncovers a particularly egregious incident of fraud, the IRS may turn the matter over to its Criminal Investigation office. Criminal Investigation will assign a **special agent** to determine if the government has enough evidence to indict the taxpayer for **criminal fraud,** also known as tax evasion. **Tax evasion** is a felony offense, punishable by severe monetary fines (up to $100,000 in the case of an individual and $500,000 in the case of a corporation) and by imprisonment in a federal penitentiary.[23] A person must be convicted of tax evasion in a court of law, and the prosecution must establish guilt *beyond a reasonable doubt.*[24] If Criminal Investigation decides that the case against the taxpayer does not meet this strict evidential standard and is too weak to prosecute, the IRS may have to settle for the civil fraud penalty.

Celebrity Tax Fraud	The federal government prosecuted actor Wesley Snipes for multiple charges of federal tax evasion, including willful failure to file income tax returns and falsely claiming a $12 million tax refund. The jury acquitted Mr. Snipes of the felony charges but found him guilty of three misdemeanors for which the court sentenced the actor to the maximum three years in prison. Mr. Snipes is now serving his time in a minimum security federal prison in Pennsylvania.

[20] §7454(a).
[21] *McGirl,* T.C. Memo 1996-313.
[22] *Hi-Q Personnel, Inc.,* 132 T.C. 279 (2009).
[23] §7201.
[24] *Bonansinga,* T.C. Memo 1987-586.

Tax Return Preparer Penalties

The Internal Revenue Code imposes penalties on tax return preparers who fail to comply with certain statutory rules of professional conduct.[25] The term **tax return preparer** refers to any person who prepares returns (or who employs other people to prepare returns) for compensation, regardless of whether such person is a licensed attorney, certified public accountant, or enrolled agent. Preparers are required to:

- Sign the tax returns prepared for their clients.
- Include their identifying number on such returns.
- Furnish clients with copies of their completed returns.
- Retain copies of all returns or a list of the names and identifying numbers of all clients.

In addition, preparers are prohibited from endorsing or negotiating tax refund checks. Violation of any of these procedural rules without reasonable cause results in a monetary penalty. For instance, a preparer who fails to sign a tax return may be assessed $50 for each failure. The maximum penalty with respect to returns filed during any calendar year is limited to $25,000.

Tax return preparers must make every effort to prepare accurate returns that report their clients' correct tax. If a preparer takes an unreasonable legal position in preparing a return and that position results in an understatement of the client's tax liability, the IRS may impose a penalty on the preparer. The penalty for an unreasonable position equals the *greater* of $1,000 or 50 percent of the preparer's compensation with respect to the return. A preparer can avoid the penalty by demonstrating that there was a reasonable cause for the understatement and that the preparer was acting in good faith.

If the IRS determines that a tax return preparer willfully understated a client's tax liability or intentionally disregarded the tax law in preparing a return, it can impose a penalty for willful and reckless conduct. This more serious penalty equals the *greater* of $5,000 or 50 percent of the compensation for the return.

Tax Talk

The IRS has started a new preparer tax identification number (PTIN) system, a major step toward the registration and oversight of all paid tax return preparers. Preparers will be required to renew their PTINs every year.

Preparer Penalty	Lionel Mackey is a self-employed enrolled agent who prepared Mr. and Mrs. Boyen's 2010 Form 1040. His fee for the preparation was $6,300. The IRS agent who audited the Boyens' return disallowed a $75,000 itemized deduction, which increased the Boyens' tax liability by $14,475. The agent concluded that Mr. Mackey had no reasonable basis for claiming the deduction and was not acting in good faith by doing so. Consequently, the agent imposed a $3,150 preparer penalty (50 percent of $6,300) on Mr. Mackey. If the agent had concluded that Mr. Mackey's conduct was willful and reckless, his preparer penalty would increase to $5,000.

Clearly, the return preparer penalties are intended to discourage tax return preparers from taking overly aggressive positions on behalf of their clients. Even though the monetary penalties are modest, they can result in adverse publicity that could damage the preparer's professional reputation.

CONTESTING THE RESULT OF AN AUDIT

Taxpayers who disagree with all or any part of the outcome of an audit (including penalties) may appeal the disputed issue to the Appeals Office of the IRS. An appeal leads to an administrative conference between the taxpayer (or more typically, the taxpayer's

---

[25] §6694 through §6696. The American Bar Association and the American Institute of Certified Public Accountants also have standards of professional conduct for their members in tax practice.

representative) and a specially trained IRS appeals officer. The purpose of the conference is to resolve the controversy in a fair and impartial manner. Appeal officers have broad latitude in settling disputes and may negotiate a compromise between the contestants on questionable issues. IRS Publication 5, *Your Appeal Rights and How to Prepare a Protest If You Don't Agree,* explains a taxpayer's appeal rights and the appeals procedure in detail.

Litigation

Trial Court

When a taxpayer and the government fail to resolve their differences in an administrative conference, the taxpayer can take the case to federal court for judicial review. In federal tax matters, one of three trial courts has original jurisdiction. A taxpayer may refuse to pay the deficiency determined by the IRS and file a petition with the **U.S. Tax Court** to hear the case. Alternatively, the taxpayer may pay the deficiency, then immediately sue the government for a refund in either the local **U.S. District Court** or the **U.S. Court of Federal Claims** located in Washington, D.C. The tax litigation process is illustrated in Exhibit 18.1.

The selection of the appropriate judicial forum is an important matter of strategy for the taxpayer's legal counsel. Each of the courts is different in operation, and one may be more advantageous than the others depending on the nature of the controversy. The Tax Court

EXHIBIT 18.1
The Tax Litigation Process

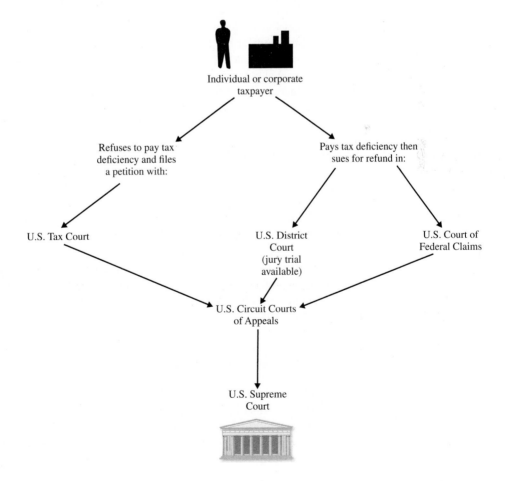

Individual or corporate taxpayer

Refuses to pay tax deficiency and files a petition with:

Pays tax deficiency then sues for refund in:

U.S. Tax Court

U.S. District Court (jury trial available)

U.S. Court of Federal Claims

U.S. Circuit Courts of Appeals

U.S. Supreme Court

adjudicates only federal income, gift, and estate tax issues and is comprised of judges who are acknowledged experts in the tax law. In contrast, judges in the district courts and Court of Federal Claims preside over cases involving many legal issues and typically have no special expertise in the tax area.

Taxpayers who want a jury trial must take their case to district court. In both the Tax Court and Court of Federal Claims, a single judge or a panel of judges tries the case and renders a verdict. If the controversy is one of fact rather than the technical application of the law, the taxpayer's attorney may recommend that the matter be put to a jury in the hope that the jury panel (who, after all, are taxpayers themselves) may be sympathetic. Of course, the viability of this strategy depends on the particular issue at hand. For instance, if the parent of a chronically ill child is arguing that the cost of a nontraditional treatment should qualify as a deductible medical expense, a jury trial seems a wise choice. However, if a businessman is trying to prove that a $750,000 annual salary from his closely held corporation is reasonable compensation, he may be better off pleading his case before a Tax Court judge.

Appellate and Supreme Court

Objective 6
Identify the three judicial levels in the tax litigation process.

The losing party at the trial court level (taxpayer or government) may appeal the verdict to one of 13 **U.S. Circuit Courts of Appeals.** The geographic location of the trial court determines which appellate court has jurisdiction. These courts generally do not review findings of fact by a lower court, but they will consider if the lower court properly applied the relevant law to the facts. After the appellate court has either affirmed or reversed the trial court's decision, the losing party may appeal the case to the **U.S. Supreme Court.** This Court may agree to hear the case *(grant certiorari)* or refuse to hear it *(deny certiorari)*. When the Supreme Court denies certiorari, the decision of the appellate court is final. During an average term, the Supreme Court hears no more than a dozen federal tax cases, which are selected either because the Court believes that the case involves a significant principle of law or because two or more appellate courts have rendered conflicting opinions on the proper resolution of a tax issue.

A Case History: *Lori Williams* v. *United States*

To summarize our discussion of the tax litigation process, consider the sequence of events in which Ms. Lori Williams took her case to the Supreme Court.

Facts of the Case

During Lori Williams's marriage to Jerrold Rabin, he failed to pay $41,000 of federal employment tax related to his business. The government assessed a deficiency for the unpaid tax against Mr. Rabin and placed a lien on all his property, including the personal residence jointly owned with his wife. However, just one month before the lien was recorded, Mr. Rabin transferred his interest in the residence to Lori Williams as part of a divorce settlement. Nine months later, she contracted to sell the residence. Although Ms. Williams was not personally liable for her former husband's $41,000 tax deficiency, she paid it under protest. Her payment was the only way to remove the government's lien on the residence so that she could convey clear title to the purchasers.

Trial Court Decision

After paying her former husband's tax bill, Ms. Williams filed a claim for refund, arguing that the government had "erroneously or illegally assessed or collected" the tax. The IRS refused to even consider her claim, responding that Ms. Williams could not seek a refund of tax assessed against another person, even though she paid the tax. Ms. Williams then brought suit against the United States for her refund in district court.[26] The district court accepted the government's argument and held that Ms. Williams lacked standing to seek a refund. In making its decision, the district court relied on precedent established in decisions by the Fifth and Seventh Circuit Courts of Appeals.[27]

Lori Williams's Appeal

Lori Williams appealed the trial court's verdict to the Ninth Circuit Court of Appeals. This court analyzed a very similar case decided in the taxpayer's favor by the Fourth Circuit Court.[28] The Ninth Circuit Court was persuaded by the Fourth Circuit Court's reasoning and decided that Lori Williams had the right to seek a refund, thereby reversing the district court's verdict.[29]

The Government's Appeal

Now it was the government's turn to appeal the case to the Supreme Court, which granted certiorari to resolve the conflict among the appellate courts. In a decision in which six justices concurred and three justices dissented, the Court affirmed the Ninth Circuit Court's decision by holding that any person who pays a tax has the right to seek a refund of such tax.[30] Justice Ruth Bader Ginsburg, writing for the majority, concluded that federal statute does not expressly restrict refund claims to those persons against which the tax was assessed. Ms. Williams had no realistic alternative to paying the tax assessed against her former husband if she ever wanted to sell the residence. Congress did not intend to leave people in Ms. Williams's predicament without legal remedy, and equity demands that the IRS consider her claim.

Making the Legal System More Taxpayer Friendly

While every taxpayer who disagrees with the IRS has a right to his day in court, many people are reluctant to bear the emotional and financial cost of litigation. To make the legal system more accessible to the average person, Congress established a **Small Tax Case Division** of the Tax Court.[31] A taxpayer who is disputing a deficiency of $50,000 or less may request an informal hearing presided over by an officer of the court. The filing fee for such hearing is only $60, and the taxpayer may plead his own case without an attorney. After the presiding officer has heard the taxpayer's side of the story and rendered judgment, the matter is settled—neither taxpayer nor government may appeal the case to any other court.

Taxpayers who win their tax case may be entitled to recover litigation expenses from the government.[32] Such expenses include court costs, attorney fees, fees paid to expert witnesses, and payments for technical studies, analyses, tests, and reports necessary for the preparation of the taxpayer's case. Taxpayers are reimbursed for these expenses unless the IRS can convince the court that its position in the case was substantially justified. If the IRS failed to follow any of its own published rules, regulations, and procedures

---

[26] *Lori Rabin Williams* v. *United States,* Civil No. 91-5286 WMB (DC CA, September 2, 1992).

[27] *Snodgrass* v. *United States,* 834 F.2d 537 (CA-5, 1987) and *Busse* v. *United States,* 542 F.2d 421 (CA-7, 1976).

[28] *Martin* v. *United States*, 895 F.2d 992 (CA-4, 1990).

[29] *Williams* v. *United States,* 24 F.3d 1143 (CA-9, 1994).

[30] *United States* v. *Williams*, 514 U.S. 527 (1995).

[31] §7463.

[32] §7430. Taxpayers may also be entitled to recover reasonable administrative costs incurred when dealing with the IRS.

during the taxpayer's audit, the legal presumption is that the IRS's position was unjustified. Another factor that the courts consider is whether the IRS pursued the litigation to harass or embarrass the taxpayer or for political reasons.

Recovery of Litigation Expenses	St. David's Health Care System is a nonprofit corporation that provides medical services to the public. The IRS challenged St. David's charitable purpose and attempted to revoke its tax-exempt status, and the corporation fought the revocation in court. The Texas district court sided with the corporation by concluding that "there is absolutely no issue as to whether St. David's has a charitable purpose, and any argument to the contrary appears at least mildly disingenuous."[33] The court then ordered the federal government to pay the corporation's $950,000 of litigation expenses because the IRS's position in the case was not substantially justified.

The existence of the Small Tax Case Division and the right of taxpayers to recover litigation costs reflect congressional sympathy for individuals who sincerely believe that they are right and the IRS is wrong. On the other hand, Congress has little tolerance for people who waste federal time and money by initiating foolish lawsuits against the IRS. The Internal Revenue Code authorizes the Tax Court to impose a monetary penalty up to $25,000 on a taxpayer who takes a frivolous or groundless position before the court or institutes a case primarily for delay.[34]

A Frivolous Lawsuit	During 2005, Daniel Callahan worked as an assistant supervisor for the Midwest College of Oriental Medicine in Racine, Wisconsin. He is a well-educated man, holding college degrees in economics, industrial relations, and nutrition. However, Mr. Callahan failed to file a 2005 federal income tax return or pay any tax for that year. In 2008, the IRS notified Mr. Callahan that he owed a $2,261 tax deficiency plus $837 of penalties for 2005. In response, Mr. Callahan petitioned the Tax Court to hear his case. Mr. Callahan argued that he didn't have to pay federal income tax because he is a citizen of the "Republic of Wisconsin" and not a citizen of the United States. He also argued that the exchange of his "time and talents" for money from his employer was a nontaxable transaction. The Tax Court concluded that these arguments were moot, irrelevant, and without merit. Not only did the court require Mr. Callahan to pay the approximately $3,000 of unpaid tax plus penalties, but it imposed an additional $3,000 penalty for wasting the court's time.[35]

Tax Talk

According to the IRS, the mayor of Oakland, California, owes $239,000 in back taxes to the federal government. The IRS recently placed a lien on all of the mayor's personal assets in an attempt to satisfy the deficiency.

IRS Collection Procedures

Taxpayers who have exhausted every avenue of appeal must finally pay their tax deficiency (including interest and penalties) to the government. The IRS is authorized to collect the deficiency by whatever means necessary, including seizing the taxpayer's assets and selling them at auction, levying bank accounts, and garnishing the taxpayer's salary or wage. A taxpayer who lacks the current resources to pay a tax bill may request an **installment agreement** that provides for monthly payments over a reasonable period of time. The IRS must approve an installment agreement for an *individual* if the tax owed is not more than $10,000, the agreement requires full payment within three years, and the IRS determines that the individual is financially unable to make immediate

---

[33] *St. David's Health Care System Inc. v. United States,* 90 AFTR 2d 2002-6878 (DC TX, 2002).

[34] §6673.

[35] *Daniel G. Callahan,* T.C. Memo 2010-201.

payment.[36] If a taxpayer's financial condition is so bad that it is unlikely that a tax bill will ever be paid in full, the IRS may accept the taxpayer's **offer in compromise** to settle the bill for a lesser amount.[37] The government's goal in accepting the settlement is to collect the most feasible amount at the earliest possible time and at the least cost to the government.

Objective 7
Define the term *transferee liability*.

A question sometimes arises as to which person is legally responsible for the payment of a federal tax deficiency. If the taxpayer is a corporation, the deficiency must be satisfied with corporate assets; shareholders are not liable for their corporation's unpaid taxes. A major exception to this limited shareholder liability arises when the corporation no longer exists. In this case, the shareholders have **transferee liability** for the corporation's unsatisfied debts, including federal taxes, to the extent of the value of any assets received on liquidation of the corporation.[38]

Transferee Liability	Ms. Morgan owned 30 percent of the stock of KLM, which was dissolved under state law in 2010. Ms. Morgan received a $55,000 cash distribution from KLM in complete liquidation of her equity interest. The IRS audited KLM's tax returns for 2008, 2009, and 2010, and determined that it underpaid its income tax by $114,800. The IRS can assess $55,000 of this deficiency against Ms. Morgan.

The Innocent Spouse Rule

Objective 8
Explain the purpose of the innocent spouse rule.

When individuals sign their Form 1040s, they become liable for any tax deficiency with respect to that return. In the case of a joint return, both husband and wife must sign, thereby becoming jointly and severally liable.[39] As a result, the IRS may assess either person for the entire deficiency determined on subsequent audit of the return. Occasionally this rule can work a real hardship on a person who is liable for unpaid taxes on a joint return that he or she signed without any knowledge of the information on the return. Such a person may be relieved of liability under the **innocent spouse rule**.[40] Such relief is dependent on three conditions:

1. The deficiency must be attributable to erroneous items (such as omitted income or bogus deductions) of the person's spouse.
2. The person must establish that in signing the return he or she did not know, and had no reason to know, that the return understated the correct tax.
3. Taking into account all the facts and circumstances, it is inequitable to hold the person liable for the deficiency.

One factor that the courts weigh very heavily in analyzing the third condition is whether the person significantly benefited, directly or indirectly, from any income omitted from the return. If a court concludes that a significant benefit existed, innocent spouse relief is denied, even if the person was ignorant of the omission. Normal spousal support is not considered a significant benefit, but an unusually lavish or extravagant lifestyle may indicate that both spouses enjoyed the omitted income. Another factor that the courts consider is whether the person seeking relief has been deserted by or is divorced from his or her spouse.

[36] §6159.
[37] §7122.
[38] §6901.
[39] §6013(d)(3).
[40] §6015.

Innocent Spouse Relief	Kathleen and Joe Alioto were married for 20 years before his death at age 82. Kathleen, who was 30 years younger than her husband, was Joe's second wife. Joe was an antitrust attorney who served for eight years as mayor of San Francisco. During their marriage, Mrs. Alioto "attended to" Mayor Alioto, kept their home, and raised their two children. Mayor Alioto did not want his wife to work outside the home, and he never discussed finances or business matters with her. Mrs. Alioto reasonably believed that her husband was a successful lawyer with substantial earning capacity, a man of wealth, and a "man who was on top of everything and who was in control." After Mayor Alioto's death in 1998, Mrs. Alioto was stunned to learn that his creditors had filed claims in excess of $74 million against his estate. The IRS's claim for unpaid federal tax totaled $4,239,834. Mrs. Alioto struggled for eight years to settle her husband's debts while working to support her family before she petitioned the Tax Court for relief from the $1,998,551 balance of unpaid federal tax. At the date of trial, Mrs. Alioto was 64 years old and had $7,000 in a savings account, $99,000 deposited in retirement plans, and did not own a car. The Tax Court concluded that further payment of the unpaid tax would represent a substantial hardship for Mrs. Alioto and that she was entitled to relief as an innocent spouse.[41]

Conclusion

Chapter 18 has provided a brief summary of the tax compliance process. After reading this chapter, you should have a much better sense of the rights and responsibilities of corporate and individual taxpayers. You should be aware that noncompliance with the tax laws can result in monetary penalties and, in extreme cases, criminal prosecution. Finally, you should understand the roles played by the IRS and the federal courts in administering our nation's tax laws. The information contained in this chapter, which culminates our study of the federal tax system, should serve you in good stead in your role as a taxpaying citizen or resident of the United States.

[41] *Kathleen S. Alioto*, T.C. Memo 2008-185.

Key Terms

civil fraud *576*
correspondence
  examination *574*
criminal fraud *577*
deficiency *574*
discriminate function
  system (DIF)
  score *573*
enrolled agent *574*
field examination *574*
innocent spouse
  rule *583*

installment
  agreement *582*
late-filing and late-payment
  penalty *571*
negligence *575*
offer in compromise *583*
office examination *574*
Small Tax Case
  Division *581*
special agent *577*
statute of limitations *572*
tax evasion *577*

tax return preparer *578*
Taxpayer Bill of
  Rights *574*
transferee liability *583*
U.S. Circuit Courts of
  Appeals *580*
U.S. Court of Federal
  Claims *579*
U.S. District Court *579*
U.S. Supreme
  Court *580*
U.S. Tax Court *579*

Questions and Problems for Discussion

1. Discuss the policy reasons for a statute of limitations for tax returns.
2. Historically, about 1 percent of Form 1040s are audited. Why does a Form 1040 reflecting $31,000 AGI and a standard deduction have much *less* than a 1 percent chance

while a Form 1040 reflecting $912,800 AGI and $214,790 itemized deductions has a much *greater* than 1 percent chance of audit?

3. Which has the greater chance of audit: a Form 1040 with $200,000 AGI, all of which is salary income, or a Form 1040 with $200,000 AGI, all of which is net profit from a sole proprietorship?

4. Mrs. NM received a letter from the IRS asking her to submit written substantiation of a $1,500 charitable contribution deduction. Discuss the probable tax consequences to Mrs. NM if:

   a. She sends the IRS copies of her canceled check for $1,500 made out to the charitable organization and the thank-you letter in which the organization acknowledged her contribution.

   b. She ignores the IRS request because she has no substantiation.

5. Is it easier for the IRS to determine that an individual omitted an income item from a return or overstated deductions?

6. Vitronix Corporation's net worth exceeds $160 million, its stock is publicly traded, and a national CPA firm audits its financial statements. Wilson Corporation's net worth also exceeds $160 million. However, it is closely held by members of the Wilson family. Discuss the reasons that the IRS might choose to audit Wilson Corporation rather than Vitronix Corporation.

7. NK and CS are both closely held corporations. NK's tax returns for the last five years reflect average taxable income of $90 million. CS's tax returns for the same period reflect average taxable income of $90,000. Discuss the reasons that the IRS might choose to audit NK rather than CS.

8. During an IRS audit, Ms. H provided the revenue agent with a meticulous set of records substantiating every number on the return. The agent actually complimented her on the quality of her preparation. Nevertheless, Ms. H did make an error in her favor. When she received formal notification that she owed an additional $4,350 tax, she was dismayed that the IRS also billed her for $920 interest on the deficiency. She doesn't understand why she must pay interest when she obviously made a good faith effort to comply with the tax law. Can you explain why?

9. Discuss the burden of proof as it relates to the penalties for:

   a. Negligence.

   b. Civil fraud.

   c. Criminal fraud.

10. During a field examination of GNT's income tax returns for 2008 and 2009, the revenue agent discovered that the treasurer had systematically omitted substantial income items and inflated deductions to minimize the corporation's tax. The agent suspects that the treasurer adopted this deliberate course of action as early as 1998. Can the IRS initiate an audit of GNT's tax returns all the way back to 1998? Explain briefly.

11. Mr. JY, a commercial artist, engaged Mr. DE, a local attorney, to prepare his income tax return. Mr. JY provided the attorney with his check register, deposit slips, receipts, and pertinent financial documents, and read through the completed return before signing it. This year, the return was selected for audit. The IRS agent discovered that Mr. DE incorrectly deducted certain of Mr. JY's personal living expenses. Consequently, the tax was understated by $8,900. The agent decided that the deduction was based on an unreasonable legal position.

    a. Is Mr. JY liable for payment of the $8,900 tax deficiency plus interest?

    b. Could the IRS impose a negligence penalty on Mr. JY?

    c. Could Mr. DE be penalized because of the error made in preparing Mr. JY's income tax return?

    d. Would your answer to the preceding questions change if Mr. DE were Mr. JY's brother-in-law, who prepared the return as a favor rather than for compensation?

12. Mr. NG is an enrolled agent in tax practice. Last year, the IRS imposed a $1,000 preparer penalty on him, and he immediately hired an attorney to contest the penalty. Mr. NG's legal fee was $7,900. Was he acting irrationally by spending so much money to avoid the penalty?

13. Mr. and Mrs. BL filed a joint tax return reporting $24,000 AGI. During the year, Mr. BL was extremely ill and was hospitalized for four months. Mrs. BL, desperate for funds to pay her husband's medical bills, took a night job as a bartender. She earned approximately $7,000 in tips, none of which she reported on the return. Mr. BL had no idea his wife had gone to such lengths on his behalf. After auditing this return, the IRS notified Mr. BL that he owed a $1,100 deficiency plus interest because of the unreported tip income. Can he avoid liability as an innocent spouse? Explain your conclusion.

14. Mrs. QE has decided to contest a $28,650 tax deficiency. She understands that she can initiate the litigation in district court or the Tax Court. Identify any reasons why she might prefer one trial court over the other.

Application Problems

1. Percy Wilson is a calendar year taxpayer. What is the unextended due date of Percy Wilson's 2012 federal income tax return if:

    a. Percy Wilson Inc. is a corporation.

    b. Mr. Percy Wilson is an individual.

2. Mr. and Mrs. Boyd Knevel use a fiscal year ending July 31 as the taxable year for filing their joint Form 1040.

    a. What is the last date on which the Knevels can apply for an automatic extension of time to file their return for fiscal year ending July 31, 2012?

    b. Assuming that the Knevels make a timely application, what is the extended due date for the return?

3. Mr. and Mrs. Pratt failed to apply for an extension of time to file their 2011 Form 1040 and did not mail it to the IRS until May 29, 2012. Assuming the Pratts had no excuse for filing a delinquent return, compute their late-filing and late-payment penalty if:

    a. The return showed a $19,758 balance of tax due.

    b. The return showed a $7,098 refund due.

4. Mr. Hall prepared and signed last year's tax return on April 3. However, he forgot to mail the return until the morning of April 18. He enclosed his check for the $3,612 balance of tax due with the return. Compute his late-filing and late-payment penalty.

5. Ms. Cross did not request an extension of time to file last year's income tax return and did not mail the completed return to the IRS until August 8. She enclosed a check for $2,380, the correct balance of tax due with the return.

    a. Assuming that Ms. Cross cannot show reasonable cause for filing a delinquent return, compute the late-filing and late-payment penalty.

    b. How would your answer change if she did not mail her return until November 21?

6. Mr. Davis filed a delinquent tax return on July 27. The return reflected $3,700 total tax, $4,000 withholding, and a $300 refund due. Compute his late-filing penalty.

7. LZ Corporation uses a fiscal year ending November 30. The controller filed LZ's Form 1120 for the year ending November 30, 2011, on December 23, 2011.

    a. What is the last day on which the IRS may assess additional tax for this fiscal year?

    b. How would your answer change if LZ's return was timely filed on its extended due date of August 15, 2012?

8. Mrs. Fugate, who is divorced, failed to include $28,000 alimony on her 2011 Form 1040. The only income she reported was her $78,000 salary. She filed her return on January 19, 2012.

    a. What is the last date on which the IRS can assess additional tax for 2011?

    b. Would your answer change if Mrs. Fugate also reported $37,500 dividend income on her Form 1040?

9. Collin Products received notice of a $21,000 income tax deficiency plus $4,300 interest. The deficiency related to an incorrect method of accounting for business inventory. Compute the after-tax cost of the $4,300 interest payment assuming that:

    a. Collin Products is a corporate taxpayer with a 35 percent marginal tax rate.

    b. Collin Products is a sole proprietorship owned by Leslie Collin. Leslie's marginal tax rate on her Form 1040 is 35 percent.

10. A revenue agent determined that Ms. Owen understated her tax by $48,100 and concluded that $9,200 was caused by her inadequate record keeping while the remainder was caused by her misapplication of a complex rule of law. Compute the negligence penalty that the revenue agent can impose on Ms. Owen.

11. Mr. Stanhope has an MBA degree from Stanford University and has been in business for himself for 18 years. The revenue agent who audited his Form 1040 discovered a glaring error resulting in a $16,200 understatement of tax. When the agent questioned him about the error, Mr. Stanhope just shrugged his shoulders and offered no logical explanation.

    a. If the error resulted from Mr. Stanhope's intentional disregard of a tax rule, compute the negligence penalty.

    b. Should the fact of Mr. Stanhope's education and business experience influence the agent's decision to impose the negligence penalty?

12. The revenue agent who audited Ms. Hsui's Form 1040 discovered that she had claimed a $15,250 deduction that was not allowed by the tax law. The improper deduction reduced Ms. Hsui's tax by $5,033. Her total tax deficiency for the year under audit was $6,490.

    a. Compute the penalty that the agent can impose if he concludes that the improper deduction was due to Ms. Hsui's negligence in preparing her tax return.

    b. Compute the penalty that the agent can impose if he concludes that the improper deduction represented Ms. Hsui's deliberate attempt to cheat the government by underpaying her tax.

13. During the audit of Mr. and Mrs. Jessel's 2009 and 2010 tax returns, the revenue agent learned that they kept two sets of books for their sole proprietorship. A comparison of the two revealed that Mr. and Mrs. Jessel earned over $80,000 unreported income. The tax deficiency on the unreported income was $32,000.

    a. Compute the civil fraud penalty the IRS may impose.

    b. Describe the procedural steps the IRS must take to charge the couple with criminal fraud.

  c. Why might the IRS decide to impose a civil fraud penalty on Mr. and Mrs. Jessel but not charge them with criminal fraud?

14. Mr. and Mrs. Lear filed their 2010 Form 1040 on April 1, 2011. On November 11, 2012, they received a notice of deficiency in which the IRS assessed $19,044 of additional 2010 income tax. Compute the amount that the Lears owe the federal government assuming:

  a. The federal *annual* interest rate throughout the 18-month period between April 15, 2011, and the assessment date was 3 percent per annum. Ignore the effect of interest compounding.

  b. The IRS agent who audited the return imposed a negligence penalty on the entire deficiency.

  c. The IRS agent who audited the return imposed a civil fraud penalty on the entire deficiency.

15. The IRS assessed a $32,800 income tax deficiency plus $4,015 interest against Mr. and Mrs. Reczyk because of an alleged understatement of investment income. They refused to pay and took their case to the U.S. Tax Court. The Reczyks incurred $7,829 attorney fees and other costs of the litigation. Determine their after-tax cost assuming that:

  a. They won their case, and the IRS failed to demonstrate that its position was substantially justified.

  b. They won their case, but the IRS convinced the court that its position was substantially justified.

  c. They lost their case.

16. Ms. Barth is a professional tax return preparer. Three years ago, she prepared the Form 1120 for Denver Inc. Her fee for the preparation was $14,850. Upon audit of the return, the IRS disallowed a $112,000 deduction, which increased the corporation's tax liability by $39,200. Compute Ms. Barth's preparer penalty if the IRS concludes that:

  a. Ms. Barth had no reasonable legal basis for claiming the deduction and was not acting in good faith by doing so.

  b. Ms. Barth intentionally disregarded the tax law by claiming the deduction in a willful attempt to understate Denver's tax.

  c. How would your answers to *a.* and *b.* change if Ms. Barth's preparation fee was only $8,200?

17. Two years ago, Lodi Inc.'s shareholders voted to dissolve the corporation. Pursuant to the dissolution, Lodi sold all its assets, paid off its outstanding debts, and distributed $789,000 remaining cash to its shareholders in complete liquidation of their equity. This year, the IRS determined that Lodi underpaid its corporate income tax for its last three years. The tax deficiency totaled $1.4 million.

  a. To what extent can the IRS collect the deficiency from the former Lodi shareholders?

  b. MN Partnership was a 5 percent Lodi shareholder. How much tax can the IRS collect from MN partnership?

Issue Recognition Problems

Identify the tax issue or issues suggested by the following situations and state each issue in the form of a question.

1. On April 3, Mr. and Mrs. BR traveled to Japan. They made the trip because their son, who lives in Tokyo, was injured in an accident and needed their care. After nursing

their son back to health, they returned home on June 11. On June 17, Mrs. BR mailed their delinquent Form 1040 and remitted the $18,262 balance of tax due with the return.

2. On July 2, Mrs. N received a notice assessing a $10,861 tax deficiency plus $1,900 interest (computed through the date the IRS mailed the notice). She was short of funds, so she did not pay her tax bill within 10 days as required by the notice. Instead, she waited until September 29 to mail a check for $12,761 to the IRS.

3. On April 13, Mr. LP applied for an automatic extension of time to file his Form 1040. He estimated that the balance of tax due was $3,800, which he paid with the extension request. He filed his return on June 20. The actual balance of tax due was $6,900, so he paid an additional $3,100 with the return.

4. Mr. B, a self-employed consultant, charged a client a $15,000 fee plus $3,900 reimbursable business expenses. The client paid the $18,900 bill and sent a Form 1099 reporting $18,900 income. When Mr. B prepared his Schedule C, he simply reported $15,000 income from the client. He did not report the $3,900 reimbursement or deduct the expenses.

5. Mrs. LK died on February 12 and left her entire estate (including her marketable securities) to her son. After the end of the year, the son received 14 Form 1099s showing his mother's name and Social Security number. These 1099s reported $29,788 dividend income that the son simply reported on his Form 1040.

6. Mr. T has not paid income tax or filed a tax return for the last eight years. He believes that the IRS can no longer assess any back taxes for the first five of those years.

7. KP, a calendar year corporation, filed its 2008 return on March 8, 2009. On February 19, 2012, it filed an amended 2008 return reflecting $2.61 million *less* taxable income than the original return and requesting a $913,000 tax refund.

8. Corporation N, a calendar year taxpayer, incurred a net operating loss in 2011 that it carried back as a deduction against 2009 income. Corporation N's treasurer filed a claim for a $712,600 refund of 2009 tax and expects to receive a check from the government any day now.

9. Mr. MK died and left all his property to his only grandson. After the estate was settled, the grandson received his $942,000 inheritance. Nine months later, the IRS audited Mr. MK's final Form 1040 and discovered that he underpaid his income tax by $18,450.

Research Problems

1. Using an electronic tax library that contains IRS publications, determine the purpose of Publication 334, Publication 504, and Publication 907.

2. Locate information on the procedure by which an individual taxpayer can request a photocopy of a prior-year federal income tax return. What is the number of the form to request a photocopy? Does the IRS charge a fee for this service? How many days will it take to receive the copy from the IRS?

3. Using an electronic tax library, locate a recent judicial decision involving taxpayer negligence and a different decision involving taxpayer fraud. Describe the actions of the taxpayers that resulted in these penalties.

Tax Planning Cases

1. Mr. JR's tax situation for the year is very complicated. He engaged in several high-dollar investment transactions involving unresolved tax issues. He has instructed his accountant to take the most aggressive position possible with respect to these transactions. Mr. JR also wants to take a home office deduction for one of his business activities.

The deduction would be only $1,293. Can you suggest any strategic reason why he should forgo the home office deduction?

2. The IRS recently assessed a $290,800 income tax deficiency on CMP Corporation. The deficiency is attributable to a complicated accounting issue involving CMP's investment in a controlled foreign corporation. CMP plans to contest the deficiency in court. CMP is located in the Third Circuit. Neither the local district court, the Tax Court, nor the Third Circuit Court of Appeals has considered the accounting issue. The Court of Federal Claims and the Eighth Circuit Court of Appeals have decided the issue in favor of the government. However, the Ninth and Tenth Circuit Courts of Appeals have decided the identical issue in favor of the taxpayer. Discuss CMP's litigation strategy in selecting a trial court.

Appendixes

A Present Value of $1

B Present Value of Annuity of $1

C 2012 Income Tax Rates

Appendix A

Present Value of $1

Periods	3%	4%	5%	6%	7%	8%	9%
1	.971	.962	.952	.943	.935	.926	.917
2	.943	.925	.907	.890	.873	.857	.842
3	.915	.889	.864	.840	.816	.794	.772
4	.888	.855	.823	.792	.763	.735	.708
5	.863	.822	.784	.747	.713	.681	.650
6	.837	.790	.746	.705	.666	.630	.596
7	.813	.760	.711	.665	.623	.583	.547
8	.789	.731	.677	.627	.582	.540	.502
9	.766	.703	.645	.592	.544	.500	.460
10	.744	.676	.614	.558	.508	.463	.422
11	.722	.650	.585	.527	.475	.429	.388
12	.701	.625	.557	.497	.444	.397	.356
13	.681	.601	.530	.469	.415	.368	.326
14	.661	.577	.505	.442	.388	.340	.299
15	.642	.555	.481	.417	.362	.315	.275
16	.623	.534	.458	.394	.339	.292	.252
17	.605	.513	.436	.371	.317	.270	.231
18	.587	.494	.416	.350	.296	.250	.212
19	.570	.475	.396	.331	.277	.232	.194
20	.554	.456	.377	.312	.258	.215	.178

Periods	10%	11%	12%	13%	14%	15%	20%
1	.909	.901	.893	.885	.877	.870	.833
2	.826	.812	.797	.783	.769	.756	.694
3	.751	.731	.712	.693	.675	.658	.579
4	.683	.659	.636	.613	.592	.572	.482
5	.621	.593	.567	.543	.519	.497	.402
6	.564	.535	.507	.480	.456	.432	.335
7	.513	.482	.452	.425	.400	.376	.279
8	.467	.434	.404	.376	.351	.327	.233
9	.424	.391	.361	.333	.308	.284	.194
10	.386	.352	.322	.295	.270	.247	.162
11	.350	.317	.287	.261	.237	.215	.135
12	.319	.286	.257	.231	.208	.187	.112
13	.290	.258	.229	.204	.182	.163	.093
14	.263	.232	.205	.181	.160	.141	.078
15	.239	.209	.183	.160	.140	.123	.065
16	.218	.188	.163	.141	.123	.107	.054
17	.198	.170	.146	.125	.108	.093	.045
18	.180	.153	.130	.111	.095	.081	.038
19	.164	.138	.116	.098	.083	.070	.031
20	.149	.124	.104	.087	.073	.061	.026

Appendix B

Present Value of Annuity of $1

Periods	3%	4%	5%	6%	7%	8%	9%
1	.971	.962	.952	.943	.935	.926	.917
2	1.913	1.886	1.859	1.833	1.808	1.783	1.759
3	2.829	2.775	2.723	2.673	2.624	2.577	2.531
4	3.717	3.630	3.546	3.465	3.387	3.312	3.240
5	4.580	4.452	4.329	4.212	4.100	3.993	3.890
6	5.417	5.242	5.076	4.917	4.767	4.623	4.486
7	6.230	6.002	5.786	5.582	5.389	5.206	5.033
8	7.020	6.733	6.463	6.210	5.971	5.747	5.535
9	7.786	7.435	7.108	6.802	6.515	6.247	5.995
10	8.530	8.111	7.722	7.360	7.024	6.710	6.418
11	9.253	8.760	8.306	7.887	7.499	7.139	6.805
12	9.954	9.385	8.863	8.384	7.943	7.536	7.161
13	10.635	9.986	9.394	8.853	8.358	7.904	7.487
14	11.296	10.563	9.899	9.295	8.745	8.244	7.786
15	11.938	11.118	10.380	9.712	9.108	8.559	8.061
16	12.561	11.652	10.838	10.106	9.447	8.851	8.313
17	13.166	12.166	11.274	10.477	9.763	9.122	8.544
18	13.754	12.659	11.690	10.828	10.059	9.372	8.756
19	14.324	13.134	12.085	11.158	10.336	9.604	8.950
20	14.877	13.590	12.462	11.470	10.594	9.818	9.129

Periods	10%	11%	12%	13%	14%	15%	20%
1	.909	.901	.893	.885	.877	.870	.833
2	1.736	1.713	1.690	1.668	1.647	1.626	1.528
3	2.487	2.444	2.402	2.361	2.322	2.283	2.106
4	3.170	3.102	3.037	2.974	2.914	2.855	2.589
5	3.791	3.696	3.605	3.517	3.433	3.352	2.991
6	4.355	4.231	4.111	3.998	3.889	3.784	3.326
7	4.868	4.712	4.564	4.423	4.288	4.160	3.605
8	5.335	5.146	4.968	4.799	4.639	4.487	3.837
9	5.759	5.537	5.328	5.132	4.946	4.772	4.031
10	6.145	5.889	5.650	5.426	5.216	5.019	4.192
11	6.495	6.207	5.938	5.687	5.453	5.234	4.327
12	6.814	6.492	6.194	5.918	5.660	5.421	4.439
13	7.103	6.750	6.424	6.122	5.842	5.583	4.533
14	7.367	6.982	6.628	6.302	6.002	5.724	4.611
15	7.606	7.191	6.811	6.462	6.142	5.847	4.675
16	7.824	7.379	6.974	6.604	6.265	5.954	4.730
17	8.022	7.549	7.120	6.729	6.373	6.047	4.775
18	8.201	7.702	7.250	6.840	6.467	6.128	4.812
19	8.365	7.839	7.366	6.938	6.550	6.198	4.843
20	8.514	7.963	7.469	7.025	6.623	6.259	4.870

Appendix C

2012 Income Tax Rates

INDIVIDUAL TAX RATE SCHEDULES

Married Filing Jointly and Surviving Spouse

If taxable income is:	The tax is:
Not over $17,400	10% of taxable income
Over $17,400 but not over $70,700	$1,740.00 + 15% of the excess over $17,400
Over $70,700 but not over $142,700	$9,735.00 + 25% of the excess over $70,700
Over $142,700 but not over $217,450	$27,735.00 + 28% of the excess over $142,700
Over $217,450 but not over $388,350	$48,665.00 + 33% of the excess over $217,450
Over $388,350	$105,062.00 + 35% of the excess over $388,350

Married Filing Separately

If taxable income is:	The tax is:
Not over $8,700	10% of taxable income
Over $8,700 but not over $35,350	$870.00 + 15% of the excess over $8,700
Over $35,350 but not over $71,350	$4,867.50 + 25% of the excess over $35,350
Over $71,350 but not over $108,725	$13,867.50 + 28% of the excess over $71,350
Over $108,725 but not over $194,175	$24,332.50 + 33% of the excess over $108,725
Over $194,175	$52,531.00 + 35% of the excess over $194,175

Heads of Household

If taxable income is:	The tax is:
Not over $12,400	10% of taxable income
Over $12,400 but not over $47,350	$1,240.00 + 15% of the excess over $12,400
Over $47,350 but not over $122,300	$6,482.50 + 25% of the excess over $47,350
Over $122,300 but not over $198,050	$25,220.00 + 28% of the excess over $122,300
Over $198,050 but not over $388,350	$46,430.00 + 33% of the excess over $198,050
Over $388,350	$109,229.00 + 35% of the excess over $388,350

Single

If taxable income is:	The tax is:
Not over $8,700	10% of taxable income
Over $8,700 but not over $35,350	$870.00 + 15% of the excess over $8,700
Over $35,350 but not over $85,650	$4,867.50 + 25% of the excess over $35,350
Over $85,650 but not over $178,650	$17,442.50 + 28% of the excess over $85,650
Over $178,650 but not over $388,350	$43,482.50 + 33% of the excess over $178,650
Over $388,350	$112,683.50 + 35% of the excess over $388,350

CORPORATE TAX RATES

If taxable income is:	The tax is:
Not over $50,000	15% of taxable income
Over $50,000 but not over $75,000	$7,500 + 25% of the excess over $50,000
Over $75,000 but not over $100,000	$13,750 + 34% of the excess over $75,000
Over $100,000 but not over $335,000	$22,250 + 39% of the excess over $100,000
Over $335,000 but not over $10,000,000	$113,900 + 34% of the excess over $335,000
Over $10,000,000 but not over $15,000,000	$3,400,000 + 35% of the excess over $10,000,000
Over $15,000,000 but not over $18,333,333	$5,150,000 + 38% of the excess over $15,000,000
Over $18,333,333	$6,416,667 + 35% of the excess over $18,333,333

Visit the *Principles of Taxation for Business and Investment Planning* Online Learning Center at www.mhhe.com/sjones2013.

Glossary

abandonment loss The unrecovered basis in an abandoned asset. Abandonment losses with respect to business assets are ordinary deductions.

abatement A property tax exemption granted by a government for a limited period of time.

ability to pay Economic resources under a person's control from which he or she can pay tax.

above-the-line deduction An allowable deduction for an individual taxpayer that can be subtracted from total income to compute AGI.

accelerated death benefits Payments made under a life insurance contract to insured individuals who are terminally or chronically ill.

accrual method of accounting An overall method of accounting under which revenues are realized in the year the earnings process is complete and expenses are matched against revenues in the year the liability for the expense is incurred.

accumulated earnings tax A penalty tax levied on corporations accumulating income beyond the reasonable needs of the business to avoid paying dividends to their shareholders. The tax is levied in addition to the regular income tax.

ACE adjustment An adjustment to regular taxable income in the computation of corporate AMTI. The adjustment equals 75 percent of adjusted current earnings in excess of AMTI computed before the adjustment.

acquisition debt Debt incurred to acquire, construct, or substantially improve a personal residence. The debt must be secured by the residence and is limited to $1 million ($500,000 for married filing separately).

activity-based tax A tax imposed on the results of an ongoing activity in which persons or organizations engage.

ad valorem tax A tax based on the value of property.

adjusted basis The initial tax basis of an asset reduced by cost recovery deductions allowable with respect to the basis.

adjusted gross income (AGI) Total income less adjustments as computed on page 1, Form 1040. AGI is an intermediate step in the calculation of individual taxable income.

affiliated corporation For purposes of the tax rules governing worthless securities, any 80 percent or more controlled domestic subsidiary that has always derived more than 90 percent of annual gross receipts from the conduct of an active business.

affiliated group A parent corporation and its 80 percent or more controlled subsidiaries.

all-events test The test for determining if an accrued expense is deductible. The test is satisfied if the liability on which the accrued expense is based is fixed, the amount of the liability is determinable with reasonable accuracy, and economic performance with respect to the liability has occurred.

allowance method The GAAP method for computing bad debt expense. The expense is based on the estimated losses from current year receivables.

alternative minimum tax (AMT) A second federal tax system parallel to the regular tax system. Congress enacted the AMT to ensure that every individual and corporation pays at least a minimal tax every year.

alternative minimum taxable income (AMTI) The tax base for the AMT: regular taxable income increased or decreased by AMT adjustments and increased by AMT tax preferences.

American Opportunity Credit An individual tax credit based on the cost of tuition, fees, and course materials paid during the first four years of post-secondary education.

amortization The ratable deduction of the capitalized cost of an intangible asset over its determinable life.

amount realized The sum of any money plus the fair market value of any property received by a seller on the sale or exchange of property.

AMT adjustments Increases or decreases to regular taxable income in the computation of AMTI.

annual gift tax exclusion The annual amount that a donor can give to each donee that is excluded from taxable gifts.

annualized income The taxable income reported on a short-period return mathematically inflated to reflect 12 months of business operations.

annuity A cash flow consisting of a constant dollar amount for a specific number of time periods.

apportionment A method of dividing a firm's taxable income among the various states with jurisdiction to tax the firm's business activities.

arm's-length transaction A transaction occurring between unrelated parties who are dealing in their own self-interest.

assignment of income doctrine Income must be taxed to the entity that renders the service or owns the capital with respect to which the income is paid.

average rate The tax rate determined by dividing total tax liability by the total tax base.

bargain element The excess of fair market value over cost of stock acquired on exercise of a stock option.

bonus depreciation Accelerated deduction in the year placed in service of 50 percent of the cost of qualified tangible personal property.

boot   Cash or other nonqualifying property included as part of a nontaxable exchange.

bracket   The portion of a tax base subject to a given percentage rate in a graduated rate structure.

bunching   A tax planning technique to concentrate itemized deductions into one year so that the total exceeds the standard deduction for the year.

business purpose doctrine   A transaction should not be effective for tax purposes unless it is intended to achieve a genuine and independent business purpose other than tax avoidance.

buy-sell agreement   A binding agreement that restricts the conditions and terms under which shareholders may dispose of corporate stock.

cafeteria plan   A compensation plan under which employees may choose among two or more benefits, including both cash and noncash items.

calendar year   The 12-month period from January 1 through December 31.

capital asset   Any asset that does not fall into one of eight statutory categories of noncapital assets. Most business assets (accounts receivable, supplies, inventories, tangible personalty, realty, and purchased intangibles) are noncapital assets.

capital gain distribution   A distribution of long-term capital gain recognized by a mutual fund to investors in the fund.

capital gain or loss   Gain or loss realized on the sale or exchange of a capital asset. Capital gain may be eligible for a preferential tax rate.

capitalization   An accounting requirement that an expenditure be charged to a balance sheet account rather than against the firm's current income.

carryover basis   The basis of transferred property in the hands of the recipient equal to the basis of the property in the hands of the transferor.

cash method of accounting   An overall method of accounting under which revenue is accounted for when payment is received and expenses are accounted for when payment is made.

cash surrender value   The amount paid to the owner of a life insurance policy on the liquidation of the policy.

centralized management   A legal characteristic of the corporate form of business: Corporations are managed by a board of directors appointed by and acting on behalf of the shareholders.

child credit   A credit based on the number of the taxpayer's dependent children under age 17.

Citator   A resource used to determine the status of tax judicial decisions, Revenue Rulings, and Revenue Procedures.

civil fraud   The intention to cheat the government by deliberately understating tax liability.

closely held corporations   Corporations privately owned by a relatively small number of shareholders.

collectibles   Tangible capital assets such as works of art, antiques, gems, stamps, and coins.

Commerce Clause   Article 1 of the U.S. Constitution that grants the federal government the power to regulate interstate commerce.

consolidated tax return   A single Form 1120 reporting the combined results of the operations of an affiliated group of corporations.

constructive dividend   A distribution by a corporation to a shareholder that the corporation classifies as salary, interest, rent, or some other type of payment but that the IRS classifies as a dividend.

constructive receipt   The point at which a taxpayer has unrestricted access to and control of income, even if the income item is not in the taxpayer's actual possession.

controlled foreign corporation (CFC)   A foreign corporation in which U.S. shareholders own more than 50 percent of the voting power or stock value.

controlled group   A brother-sister group of corporations owned by the same individual shareholders or a parent-subsidiary group of corporations.

convenience   The second standard for a good tax. A tax should be convenient for the government to administer and for people to pay.

correspondence examination   The simplest type of audit that can be handled entirely by telephone or through the mail.

cost basis   The purchase price of an asset including any sales tax paid by the purchaser and any incidental costs related to getting the asset in place and into production.

cost depletion   The method for recovering the capitalized cost of an exhaustible natural resource. Cost depletion equals unrecovered basis in the resource (mine or well) multiplied by the ratio of units of production sold during the year to the estimated total units of production at the beginning of the year.

cost of goods sold   The capitalized cost of inventory sold during the taxable year and subtracted from gross receipts in the computation of gross income.

Coverdell education savings account   An investment account through which individuals can save for education expenses on a tax-exempt basis.

creative assets   Copyrights; literary, musical, or artistic compositions; letters or memoranda; or similar assets.

criminal fraud   A felony offense involving the willful attempt to evade or defeat any federal tax.

cross-crediting   Crediting the excess foreign tax paid in high-tax jurisdictions against the excess limitation attributable to income earned in low-tax jurisdictions.

Cumulative Bulletin (CB) Semiannual compilation of weekly Internal Revenue Bulletins.

declining marginal utility of income The theory that the financial importance associated with each dollar of income diminishes as total income increases.

deduction An offset or subtraction in the calculation of taxable income.

deemed paid foreign tax credit A credit available to U.S. corporations that receive dividends from a foreign subsidiary. The credit is based on foreign income tax paid by the subsidiary.

deferred compensation A nonqualified plan under which an employer promises to pay a portion of an employee's current compensation in a future year.

deferred tax asset The excess of tax payable over tax expense per books resulting from a temporary difference between book income and taxable income.

deferred tax liability The excess of tax expense per books over tax payable resulting from a temporary difference between book income and taxable income.

deficiency An underpayment of tax determined on audit and assessed by the IRS.

defined-benefit plan A qualified plan under which participants are promised a targeted benefit, usually in the form of a pension, when they retire.

defined-contribution plan A qualified plan under which an annual contribution is made to each participant's retirement account.

dependent A member of a taxpayer's family or household who receives more than half of his or her financial support from the taxpayer.

dependent care credit A credit based on the taxpayer's cost of caring for dependents either under age 13 or physically or mentally incapable of caring for themselves.

depreciation The systematic deduction of the capitalized cost of tangible property over a specific period of time.

depreciation recapture Recapture computed with reference to depreciation or amortization deductions claimed with respect to property surrendered in a sale or exchange.

direct write-off method The method for determining a bad debt deduction required by the tax law. Only receivables that are written off as uncollectible during the year are deductible.

discount rate The rate of interest used to calculate the present value of future cash flows.

discriminate function system (DIF) score A numeric score assigned to individual tax returns that measures the return's potential for generating additional tax on audit.

distributive share A partner's share of any item of income, gain, deduction, loss, or credit recognized by the partnership. Distributive shares are usually expressed as a percentage and specified in the partnership agreement.

dividends-received deduction A corporate deduction equal to a percentage of dividend income received from other taxable domestic corporations.

domestic production activities deduction A tax preference deduction for U.S. manufacturers equal to a percentage of net income from a qualified domestic production activity.

donee An individual or organization that receives a gift.

donor An individual who makes a gift.

dynamic forecast A projection of revenue gain or loss resulting from a tax rate change that assumes that the change will affect the tax base.

earmarked tax A tax that generates revenues for a designated project or program rather than for the government's general fund.

earned income credit A refundable income tax credit that offsets the impact of the payroll tax on low-income workers.

economic performance The third requirement of the all-events test.

economic substance doctrine A transaction that doesn't change the taxpayer's economic situation except by the tax savings from the transaction should be disregarded for tax purposes.

education savings bonds Qualified Series EE savings bonds that can be redeemed tax-free to pay for certain education expenses.

efficiency The third standard for a good tax. Classical economic theory holds that an efficient tax is neutral and has no effect on economic behavior. In contrast, Keynesian theory holds that an efficient tax is a fiscal policy tool by which the government can affect economic behavior.

employee An individual who performs services for compensation and who works under the direction and control of an employer.

employee payroll tax The FICA tax (Social Security and Medicare tax) levied on employees who receive compensation during the year.

employee stock ownership plan (ESOP) A qualified defined contribution plan in which contributions are invested primarily in the corporate employer's common stock.

employer identification number A number assigned to an employer by the IRS to identify the employer for employment tax purposes.

employer payroll tax The FICA tax (Social Security and Medicare tax) levied on employers that pay compensation during the year.

employer-provided plan A retirement plan sponsored and maintained by an employer for the benefit of the employees.

employment tax A tax based on wages, salaries, and self-employment income. Federal employment taxes are earmarked to fund Social Security and Medicare.

enrolled agent A tax practitioner certified by the IRS to represent clients in IRS proceedings.

estimated tax payments Quarterly installment payments of estimated current year tax liability required of both corporate and individual taxpayers.

event- or transaction-based tax A tax imposed on the occurrence of a certain event or transaction.

excess foreign tax credit Foreign tax paid or accrued during the year but not credited against U.S. tax because of the foreign tax credit limitation.

excess Social Security tax withholding credit An overpayment of employee Social Security tax allowed as a credit against income tax.

excise tax A tax levied on the retail sale of specific goods or services. An excise tax may be in addition to or instead of a general sales tax.

exemption amount A dollar amount allowed as a deduction from AGI for each taxpayer and dependent. The dollar amount is indexed annually for inflation.

expansion costs Costs of enlarging the scope of operations of an existing business.

expatriate An individual who is a U.S. citizen and resides and works for an extended period in a foreign country.

explicit tax An actual tax liability paid directly to the taxing jurisdiction.

field examination An audit conducted by a revenue agent at the taxpayer's place of business.

FIFO The inventory costing convention under which the first goods manufactured or purchased are assumed to be the first goods sold.

filing status A classification for individual taxpayers reflecting marital and family situation and determining the rate schedule for the computation of tax liability.

firm A generic business organization. Firms include sole proprietorships, partnerships, limited liability companies, Subchapter S and regular corporations, and any other type of arrangement through which people carry on a profit-motivated activity.

fiscal year Any 12-month period ending on the last day of any month except December.

flat rate A single percentage that applies to the entire tax base.

foreign earned income exclusion An annual amount of foreign source earned income on which expatriates are not required to pay federal income tax.

foreign source income Taxable income attributable to a U.S. firm's business activities carried on in a foreign jurisdiction.

foreign tax credit A credit against U.S. tax based on foreign income tax paid or accrued during the year.

free transferability A legal characteristic of the corporate form of business: Shareholders can buy and sell corporate stock with maximum convenience and minimal transaction cost.

fringe benefits Any economic benefit subject to valuation received by an employee as additional compensation.

general business credit The aggregate of numerous different tax credits available to business enterprises.

general partnership A partnership in which all the partners have unlimited personal liability for the debts incurred by the partnership.

generally accepted accounting principles (GAAP) The set of accounting rules developed by the Financial Accounting Standards Board (FASB) and adhered to by the public accounting profession.

going-concern value Value attributable to the synergism of business assets working in coordination.

goodwill Value created by the expectancy that customers will continue to patronize a business.

graduated rates Multiple percentages that apply to specified brackets of the tax base.

gross income Realized increases in wealth from whatever source derived. In the business context, gross profit from sales of goods, performance of services, and investments of capital.

gross profit percentage The ratio of gain realized to total contract price in an installment sale.

guaranteed payment A distribution from a partnership to a partner to compensate the partner for ongoing services performed for the partnership.

half-year convention Property placed in service on any day of the taxable year is treated as placed in service halfway through the year for MACRS purposes.

head of household Filing status for an unmarried individual who maintains a home for a child or dependent family member.

hobby loss Excess of expenses over revenue from a personal activity not engaged in for profit.

home equity debt Debt secured by a personal residence to the extent the debt does not exceed the owner's equity in the residence. Home equity debt is limited to $100,000 ($50,000 for married filing separately).

horizontal equity One aspect of the fourth standard of a good tax: A tax is fair if persons with the same ability to pay (as measured by the tax base) owe the same tax.

hybrid method of accounting An overall method of accounting that combines the accrual method for purchases and sales of inventory and the cash method for all other transactions.

implicit tax The reduction in before-tax rate of return that investors are willing to accept because of the tax-favored characteristics of an investment.

imputed income from owner-occupied housing   The nontaxable economic benefit (fair rental value) derived by the owner of a home.

incentive stock option (ISO)   A qualified stock option for federal tax purposes. Individuals do not recognize the bargain element as income on the exercise of an ISO.

incidence   The ultimate economic burden represented by a tax.

income effect   A behavioral response to an income tax rate increase: Taxpayers engage in more income-producing activities to maintain their level of disposable income.

income tax   A tax imposed on the periodic increases in wealth resulting from a person's economic activities.

income tax return preparer   Any person who prepares returns (or who employs other people to prepare returns) for compensation and who is subject to tax return preparer penalties.

income tax treaty   A bilateral agreement between the governments of two countries defining and limiting each country's respective tax jurisdiction.

independent contractor   A self-employed individual who performs services for compensation and who retains control over the manner in which the services are performed.

innocent spouse rule   The rule of law under which a person who filed a joint return with a spouse is not held liable for any deficiency of tax with respect to the return.

inside buildup   Annual increase in value of a life insurance or annuity contract.

installment agreement   An agreement with the IRS under which a taxpayer can make monthly payments to settle a tax deficiency over a reasonable period of time.

installment sale method   A method of accounting for gains realized on the sale of property when some part of the amount realized consists of the buyer's note. Under the installment sale method, gain recognition is linked to the seller's receipt of cash over the life of the note.

intangible drilling and development costs (IDC) Expenses such as wages, fuel, repairs to drilling equipment, hauling, and supplies associated with locating and preparing oil and gas wells for production. IDC are deductible for federal tax purposes.

inter vivos transfer   A transfer of property occurring during the life of the property owner.

Internal Revenue Bulletin (IRB)   The IRS's weekly publication containing revenue rulings and revenue procedures.

Internal Revenue Code of 1986   The compilation of statutory tax laws written and enacted by the Congress of the United States.

Internal Revenue Service (IRS)   The subdivision of the U.S. Treasury Department responsible for the enforcement of the federal tax laws and the collection of federal taxes.

investment interest expense   Interest paid by an individual on debt incurred to purchase or carry investment property.

involuntary conversion   The receipt of insurance or condemnation proceeds with respect to property destroyed by theft or casualty or taken by eminent domain.

itemized deduction   An allowable deduction for an individual taxpayer that cannot be subtracted in the calculation of AGI.

joint and several liability   Each spouse on a joint tax return is individually liable for the entire tax for the year.

joint return   A return filed by husband and wife reflecting their combined activities for the year.

jurisdiction   The right of a government to levy tax on a specific person or organization.

Keogh plan   A qualified retirement plan for self-employed individuals.

key-person life insurance policies   Insurance purchased by a firm on the life of a high-level employee. The firm is the beneficiary of the policy.

kiddie tax   The tax on a child's unearned income based on the child's parents' marginal rate.

late-filing and late-payment penalty   The penalty imposed on taxpayers who fail to file their returns and pay the balance of tax due on a timely basis.

leasehold costs   Up-front costs incurred to acquire a lease on tangible business property.

leasehold improvements   Physical improvements made by a lessee to leased real property.

leverage   The use of borrowed funds to create tax basis.

lifetime transfer tax exclusion   The $5 million cumulative amount of transfers that an individual can make without incurring federal transfer tax.

Lifetime Learning Credit   An individual tax credit based on 20 percent of the cost of tuition, fees, and course materials.

LIFO   The inventory costing convention under which the last goods manufactured or purchased are assumed to be the first goods sold.

like-kind property   Qualifying business or investment property that can be exchanged on a nontaxable basis.

limited liability   A legal characteristic of the corporate form of business: Corporate shareholders are not personally liable for the unpaid debts of the corporation.

limited liability company (LLC)   A form of unincorporated business organization in which the members have limited liability for business debt. LLCs are generally treated as partnerships for federal tax purposes.

limited liability partnership (LLP)   A partnership in which the general partners are not personally liable for malpractice-related claims arising from the professional misconduct of another general partner.

limited partnership   A partnership in which one or more partners are liable for partnership debt only to the extent of their capital contributions to the partnership. Limited partnerships must have at least one general partner.

long-term capital gain or loss   Gain or loss resulting from the sale or exchange of a capital asset owned for more than one year.

marginal rate   The tax rate that applies to the next dollar of taxable income.

market   A forum for commercial interaction between two or more parties for the purpose of exchanging goods or services.

market discount   The excess of a bond's stated redemption value over the price paid for the bond in a market transaction.

material participation   An owner's regular, continual, and substantial involvement in the day-to-day operation of an active business.

method of accounting   A consistent system for determining the point in time at which items of income and deduction are recognized for tax purposes.

midmonth convention   Property placed in service on any day of a month is treated as placed in service at the midpoint of the month for MACRS purposes.

midquarter convention   Property placed in service on any day of a quarter is treated as placed in service at the midpoint of the quarter for MACRS purposes.

minimum distribution   The annual withdrawal an individual must make from a qualified retirement plan beginning no later than April 1 of the year following the year in which he reaches age 70½.

minimum tax credit   AMT liability carried forward indefinitely as a credit against future regular tax liability.

miscellaneous itemized deductions   Itemized deductions that are deductible only to the extent their total exceeds 2 percent of AGI.

Modified Accelerated Cost Recovery System (MACRS)   The statutory and regulatory rules governing the computation of depreciation for tax purposes.

moving expenses   The cost of transporting household goods and personal belongings and travel costs incurred in connection with an employment-related move. Moving expenses are an adjustment in computing AGI.

mutual fund   A diversified portfolio of securities owned and managed by a regulated investment company.

negative externality   An undesirable by-product of the free enterprise system.

negligence   Failure to make a prudent attempt to comply with the tax law or the intentional disregard of tax rules and regulations.

net capital gain   The excess of current year capital gains over capital losses.

net capital loss   The excess of current year capital losses over capital gains.

net cash flow   The difference between cash received and cash disbursed.

net investment income   Income from investment assets reduced by expenses directly related to the production of investment income.

net long-term gain or loss   Aggregate gain or loss from the sale or exchange of capital assets owned for more than a year.

net operating loss (NOL)   An excess of allowable deductions over gross income.

net present value (NPV)   The sum of the present values of all cash inflows and outflows relating to a transaction.

net short-term gain or loss   Aggregate gain or loss from the sale or exchange of capital assets owned for a year or less.

nexus   The degree of contact between a business and a state necessary to establish the state's jurisdiction to tax the business.

NOL carryback   A net operating loss allowed as a deduction in the two years prior to the year of loss.

NOL carryforward   A net operating loss allowed as a deduction in the 20 years following the year of loss.

nonbusiness bad debt   An uncollectible debt held by an individual creditor that is unrelated to the individual's business.

nonprofit corporation   A corporation formed for philanthropic purposes and, as a result, exempt from the federal income tax.

nonrecaptured Section 1231 loss   A net Section 1231 loss recognized in any of the five preceding taxable years that has not caused recharacterization of Section 1231 gain as ordinary income.

nonrecourse debt   A debt secured by specific collateral for which the debtor is not personally liable.

nontaxable exchange   A transaction resulting in realized gain or loss that is not recognized (in whole or part) in the current year.

offer in compromise   A negotiated settlement with the IRS in which the taxpayer pays less than the entire deficiency.

office examination   An audit conducted by a tax auditor at an IRS district office.

ordinary gain or loss   Any realized gain or loss that is not a capital gain or loss.

ordinary income   Any income that is not capital gain. Ordinary income is taxed at the regular individual or corporate tax rates.

organizational costs Expenditures incurred in connection with the formation of a partnership or corporate entity.

original issue discount (OID) The excess of a bond's stated redemption value over the issue price.

outbound transaction A transaction by which a U.S. firm engages in business in a foreign jurisdiction.

partnership An unincorporated association of two or more persons to conduct business as co-owners.

passenger automobiles Four-wheeled vehicles manufactured primarily for use on public roads with an unloaded gross vehicle weight of 6,000 pounds or less.

passive activity An individual's interest in (1) an active business in which the individual does not materially participate or (2) a rental activity.

passive income generator (PIG) An interest in a profitable passive activity.

passthrough entities Business entities that are not taxable entities. The income, gains, deductions, and losses recognized by a passthrough entity are reported by the entity's owners and taxed only once at the owner level.

payment liabilities Accrued liabilities for which economic performance does not occur until payment is made.

percentage depletion An annual deduction based on the gross income generated by a depletable property multiplied by a statutory depletion rate.

performance-based compensation Compensation paid solely because the recipient employee attained a performance goal established by a compensation committee of outside members of the corporate board of directors.

permanent difference A difference between financial statement income and taxable income that does not reverse over time.

permanent establishment A fixed location at which a firm carries on its regular commercial activities. For income tax treaty purposes, a country has no jurisdiction to tax a foreign business entity unless the entity maintains a permanent establishment in the country.

personal holding company A corporation owned by a small number of individuals that receives taxable income consisting primarily of nonbusiness income such as dividends, interest, rents, and royalties.

personal holding company tax A penalty tax levied on personal holding companies in addition to the regular corporate income tax.

personal service corporations Closely held corporations owned by individuals who perform services in the fields of health, law, engineering, architecture, accounting, actuarial science, performing arts, or consulting for the corporation's clientele. Personal service corporations are subject to a flat 35 percent tax rate.

personalty Any asset that is not realty.

premature withdrawal A withdrawal from a qualified retirement plan made before the individual reaches age 59½.

prepaid income Payment for goods and services made in advance of the provision of the goods or performance of the services.

primary authorities Statutory, administrative, and judicial authority.

principal residence The home in which an individual resides for most of the year and considers his permanent address.

private activity bonds Tax-exempt bonds issued by state or local governments for nongovernmental purposes such as industrial development.

private letter ruling (PLR) The IRS's written response to a taxpayer's inquiry as to how the tax law applies to a proposed transaction.

private market A market in which the parties deal directly with each other and can customize the terms of their agreement to meet their respective objectives.

probate estate Property owned by a decedent and disposed of according to the terms of a valid will or state intestacy laws.

profit-sharing plan A defined-contribution plan under which an employer regularly contributes a percentage of current earnings to the employee's retirement accounts.

progressive rate structure A graduated rate structure with rates that increase as the base increases.

property similar or related in service or use Qualifying replacement property in a nontaxable involuntary conversion.

proportionate rate structure A rate structure with a single, or flat, rate.

pro rata share A shareholder's share of any item of income, gain, deduction, loss, or credit recognized by an S corporation. Pro rata shares are based on the number of shares of outstanding stock owned by the shareholders.

public market A market in which the parties deal indirectly through an intermediary such as a broker or a financial institution.

publicly held corporations Corporations with outstanding stock traded on an established securities market.

qualified dividend distribution A distribution of qualified dividend income received by a mutual fund to investors in the fund.

qualified dividend income Dividends received from taxable domestic corporations and certain qualified foreign corporations eligible for a preferential individual tax rate.

qualified education loan Any debt incurred to pay higher education expenses.

qualified residence interest Interest paid on acquisition debt or home equity debt allowed as an itemized deduction.

qualified retirement plans   Retirement plans that meet certain statutory requirements and that allow participants to save for retirement on a tax-deferred basis.

qualified small business stock   Stock in a corporate business that meets certain statutory requirements. Individuals who recognize gain on the sale of qualified small business stock may be eligible to exclude 50 percent of the gain from income.

qualified tuition expenses   Tuition and fees required for enrollment in a post-secondary educational institution.

qualified tuition program   A savings program sponsored by a state or private educational institution in which individuals can invest to pay future college expenses.

qualifying child   A child (or specified family member) who has the same principal residence as the taxpayer, who does not provide more than one-half of his or her own financial support, and who is less than 19 years old or a student less than 24 years old.

qualifying property   The specific property eligible for a particular nontaxable exchange.

qualifying relative   A specified family member or member of the taxpayer's household who receives more than one-half of his or her financial support from the taxpayer and whose annual gross income is less than the exemption amount.

real property tax   A tax levied on the ownership of realty and based on the property's assessed market value.

realization   Income is taken into account when the earnings process with respect to the income is complete and an event or transaction occurs that provides an objective measurement of the income.

realized gain or loss   The positive or negative difference between the amount realized on the disposition of property and the adjusted basis of the property.

realty   Land and whatever is erected or growing on the land or permanently affixed to it.

recapture   Recharacterization of Section 1231 or capital gain as ordinary income.

recognition   Inclusion of an item of income or deduction in the computation of taxable income.

recognized gain or loss   Realized gain or loss taken into account for tax purposes in the current year.

recourse debt   A debt for which the debtor is personally liable.

recovery period   The number of years prescribed by statute over which the basis of tangible business property is depreciated under MACRS.

recurring item exception   An exception to the economic performance requirement under which a liability is considered incurred in a taxable year in which it meets the first two requirements of the all-events test and economic performance occurs within 8½ months after year-end.

regressive rate structure   A graduated rate structure with rates that decrease as the base increases.

rehabilitation credit   A business credit equal to a percentage of the cost of rehabilitating commercial buildings placed in service before 1936 or certified historic structures.

related party transaction   A transaction between parties who share a common economic interest or objective and who may not be dealing at arm's length.

rental activity   An activity where payments are principally for the use of tangible property for an extended period of time. Rental activities are passive activities.

reorganization   A statutorily defined transaction in which one corporation acquires another, one corporation divides into two corporations, or a corporation changes its capital structure.

research and experimental expenditures   A preferential deduction for costs of basic research designed to encourage businesses to conduct such research.

revenue   Total tax collected by the government and available for public use.

revenue procedure   An IRS pronouncement advising taxpayers how to comply with IRS procedural or administrative matters.

revenue ruling   An IRS pronouncement explaining how the IRS applies the tax law to a particular set of facts.

rollover contribution   A distribution from one qualified plan contributed to another qualified plan within 60 days.

rollover IRA   An IRA created to receive a distribution from another qualified retirement plan.

Roth IRA   An investment account through which individuals with compensation or earned income can save for retirement on a tax-exempt basis.

safe-harbor estimate   Estimated current year tax payments based on the preceding year's tax liability that protect the taxpayer from the underpayment penalty.

sales tax   A general tax levied on the retail sale of goods and services.

secondary authorities   Textbooks, treatises, professional journals, and commercial tax services.

section   Numerically labeled subdivision of the Internal Revenue Code. Each section contains an operational, definitional, or procedural rule relating to one of the federal taxes.

Section 179 election   The election under which firms can expense a limited dollar amount of the cost of tangible personalty placed in service during the taxable year.

Section 401(k) plan   A defined-contribution plan under which employees elect to contribute a portion of current year compensation to an employer-provided retirement plan.

Section 1231 asset   Real or depreciable property used in a trade or business (including rental real estate) and intangible business assets subject to amortization held by the owner for more than one year.

Section 1244 stock   The first $1 million of stock issued by a corporation for cash or property. Some portion of the loss on the disposition of Section 1244 stock is ordinary to individual investors.

Section 1245 recapture   Full recapture of depreciation or amortization allowed for tangible personalty or purchased intangibles.

Section 1250 recapture   Recapture of excess accelerated depreciation over straight-line depreciation allowed for buildings placed in service before 1987.

securities   Financial instruments including equity interests in business organizations and creditor interests such as savings accounts, notes, and bonds.

self-employment (SE) tax   Employment tax levied on an individual's net earnings from self-employment.

seller-financed sale   A sale transaction in which the seller accepts the purchaser's debt obligation as part of the sale price.

separate return   A return filed by a married individual reflecting his or her independent activity and tax liability for the year. The tax liability is based on the married filing separately rate schedule.

separately stated item   An item of income, gain, deduction, or loss recognized by a passthrough entity that retains its character as it flows through to the owners. Separately stated items are not included in the computation of the entity's ordinary business income or loss.

Series EE savings bonds   Long-term debt instruments issued by the U.S. government at a discount.

short-period return   A tax return for a taxable year consisting of less than 12 months.

short-term capital gain or loss   Gain or loss resulting from the sale or exchange of a capital asset owned for one year or less.

single taxpayer   An unmarried individual who is neither a surviving spouse nor a head of household.

Small Tax Case Division   A division of the U.S. Tax Court that holds informal hearings of disputes involving tax deficiencies of $50,000 or less.

sole proprietorship   An unincorporated business owned by one individual.

special agent   A revenue agent who handles criminal fraud investigations.

specific identification method   An accounting method under which cost of goods sold includes the actual cost of specific items of inventory sold during the year.

standard deduction   A deduction from AGI based on filing status. The standard deduction amounts are indexed annually for inflation.

start-up expenditures   Up-front costs of investigating the creation or purchase of a business and the routine expenses incurred during the preoperating phase of a business.

static forecast   A projection of revenue gain or loss resulting from a tax rate change that assumes that the change will have no effect on the tax base.

statute of limitations   The statutory limit on the time period after a tax return is filed during which the IRS can audit the return and assess additional tax.

step transaction doctrine   The IRS can collapse a series of intermediate transactions into a single transaction to determine the tax consequences of the arrangement in its entirety.

stock option   The right to purchase corporate stock for a stated price (the strike price) for a given period of time.

subchapter S corporation   A corporation with a subchapter S election in effect. The corporation is a passthrough entity for federal tax purposes and does not pay federal income tax.

subpart F income   A category of foreign source income earned by a CFC constructively distributed to U.S. shareholders in the year earned. Conceptually, subpart F income is artificial income in that it has no commercial or economic connection to the country in which the CFC is incorporated.

substance over form doctrine   The IRS can look through the legal formalities to determine the economic substance (if any) of a transaction and to base the tax consequences on the substance instead of the form.

substituted basis   The basis of qualifying property received in a nontaxable exchange determined by reference to the basis of the property surrendered in the exchange.

substitution effect   A behavioral response to an income tax rate increase: Taxpayers engage in fewer income-producing activities and more non-income-producing activities.

sufficiency   The first standard for a good tax. A tax should generate enough revenue to pay for the public goods and services provided by the government levying the tax.

supply-side economic theory   A decrease in the highest income tax rates should stimulate economic growth and ultimately result in an increase in government revenues.

surtax   In the corporate context, the extra 5 percent or 3 percent tax imposed to recoup the benefit of the progressive corporate tax rates.

surviving spouse   Filing status that permits a widow or widower to use the married filing jointly rate schedule for two taxable years following the death of a spouse.

tax   A payment to support the cost of government. A tax is nonpenal but compulsory and is not directly related to any specific benefit provided by the government.

tax assessor   An elected or appointed government official responsible for deriving the value of realty located within a taxing jurisdiction.

tax avoidance   The implementation of legal strategies for reducing taxes.

tax base   An item, occurrence, transaction, or activity with respect to which a tax is levied. Tax bases are usually expressed in monetary terms.

tax basis   A taxpayer's investment in any asset or property right and the measure of unrecovered dollars represented by the asset.

tax benefit rule   The recovery of an amount deducted in an earlier year must be included in gross income in the year of recovery.

tax cost   An increase in tax liability for any period resulting from a transaction.

tax credit   A direct reduction in tax liability.

tax evasion   The willful and deliberate attempt to defraud the government by understating a tax liability through illegal means. Also see *Criminal fraud.*

Tax Expenditures Budget   Part of the federal budget that quantifies the annual revenue loss attributable to each major tax preference.

tax haven   A foreign jurisdiction with minimal or no income tax.

tax law   The body of legal authority consisting of statutory laws, administrative pronouncements, and judicial decisions.

tax planning   The structuring of transactions to reduce tax costs or increase tax savings to maximize net present value.

tax policy   A government's attitude, objectives, and actions with respect to its tax system.

tax preferences   In the general context, provisions included in the federal tax law as incentives to encourage certain behaviors or as subsidies for certain activities; in AMT context, specific items added to regular taxable income in the computation of AMTI.

tax return preparer   Any person who prepares returns (or who employs other people to prepare returns) for compensation, regardless of whether such person is a licensed attorney, certified public accountant, or enrolled agent.

tax savings   A decrease in tax liability for any period resulting from a transaction.

taxable estate   The aggregate fair market value of property owned by a decedent or transferred because of the decedent's death reduced by allowable deductions.

taxable income   Gross income minus allowable deductions for the taxable year.

taxpayer   Any person or organization required by law to pay tax to a governmental authority.

Taxpayer Bill of Rights   Part of the federal law requiring the IRS to deal with every citizen and resident in a fair, professional, prompt, and courteous manner.

technical advice memorandum (TAM)   The IRS position on a disputed item in a tax return.

temporary difference   A difference between financial statement income and taxable income that reverses over time.

tentative minimum tax   AMTI in excess of the exemption multiplied by the AMT rates. Any excess of tentative minimum tax over regular tax is the AMT for the year.

testamentary transfer   A transfer of property occurring on the death of the property owner.

thin capitalization   A corporate capital structure with a high ratio of debt to equity.

time value of money   A dollar available today is worth more than a dollar available tomorrow because the current dollar can be invested to start earning interest immediately.

total income   The sum of the income items recognized by an individual during the year and listed on page 1, Form 1040.

traditional IRA   An investment account through which individuals with compensation or earned income can save for retirement on a tax-deferred basis.

transfer price   In the international area, the price at which goods or services are exchanged between controlled corporations operating in different taxing jurisdictions.

transfer tax   A tax levied on the transfer of wealth by gift or at death and based on the market value of the transferred assets.

transferee liability   Liability of a recipient of property (transferee) for the unpaid tax of the transferor of the property.

Treasury inflation-protected securities (TIPS)   Long-term U.S. debt instruments with a fixed interest rate on an inflation-adjusted principal amount.

Treasury regulation   The official interpretation of a statutory tax rule written and published by the U.S. Treasury.

20 percent recapture   Twenty percent of the excess of Section 1245 recapture over Section 1250 recapture for buildings owned by corporations.

28 percent rate gain or loss   Long-term capital gain or loss from the sale or exchange of collectibles or qualified small business stock.

underpayment penalty   The penalty imposed by the Internal Revenue Code on both individuals and corporations that fail to make required estimated payments of current tax on a timely basis.

unearned income Medicare contribution tax   A 3.8 percent tax on an individual taxpayer's net investment income, the revenues from which are earmarked for the Medicare trust funds.

unemployment tax   A tax levied by both the federal and state governments on compensation paid by employers to their employees. Unemployment taxes are earmarked to fund the national unemployment insurance program.

uniform capitalization (unicap) rules   The set of tax rules governing the type of current expenditures that must be capitalized to inventory.

Uniform Division of Income for Tax Purposes Act (UDITPA)   A model act describing a recommended method for apportioning a firm's taxable income among multiple state jurisdictions.

U.S. Circuit Courts of Appeals   Thirteen federal courts that hear appeals of trial court decisions.

U.S. Court of Federal Claims   A federal trial court located in Washington, D.C., in which taxpayers can sue the government for a refund of tax.

U.S. District Courts   Federal trial courts in which taxpayers can sue the government for a refund of tax.

U.S. Supreme Court   The highest federal court. The Supreme Court hears appeals of circuit court decisions.

U.S. Tax Court   A federal court that tries only federal income, gift, and estate tax cases.

unlimited life   A legal characteristic of the corporate form of business: A corporation's legal existence is not affected by changes in the identity of its shareholders.

unlimited marital deduction   A deduction in the computation of a decedent's taxable estate equal to the value of property transferred to the decedent's surviving spouse.

unrecaptured Section 1250 gain   Section 1231 gain on the sale of business realty that would be recaptured as ordinary income under the full recapture rule.

use tax   A tax levied on the ownership, possession, or consumption of goods if the owner did not pay the jurisdiction's sales tax when the goods were purchased.

vacation home   A personal residence other than the owner's principal residence.

value-added tax (VAT)   A tax levied on firms engaged in any phase of the production or manufacture of goods and based on the incremental value added by the firm to the goods.

vertical equity   One aspect of the fourth standard of a good tax: A tax is fair if persons with a greater ability to pay (as measured by the tax base) owe more tax than persons with a lesser ability to pay.

wash sale   A sale of marketable securities if the seller reacquires substantially the same securities within 30 days after (or 30 days before) the sale.

withholding tax   A tax on dividends paid to foreign shareholders that is withheld by the corporation paying the dividend.

Index

Page numbers followed by n refer to notes.

Abandonment loss, 222
Abatement, 7–8
Ability to pay, 32
Above-the-line deductions, 410
Academy Award gift bags, 536
Accelerated death benefits, 493
Accelerated depreciation, 218
Accounting method; *see* Method of accounting
Accounting principles; *see* Generally accepted accounting principles (GAAP)
Accounts receivable, 208, 212
    factoring of, 213
Accrual method of accounting, 129–139
    business bad debts, 138–139
    expenses and, 130
    prepaid income, 133–134
    related party accruals, 137–138
    revenues and, 129
Accrued expenses
    all-events test, 134–135
    fixed and determinable liability, 134
    liability not fixed and determinable, 134–135
    provision of property to taxpayer, 135
    provision of services by taxpayer, 135
    provision of services to taxpayer, 135
Accumulated earnings tax, 359
ACE (adjusted current earnings) adjustment, 323–324
Acquisition debt, 549
Active participant, 467
Activity-based tax, 6
Ad valorem tax, 7
Adjusted basis, 162–163
Adjusted current earnings (ACE), 323–324
Adjusted gross income (AGI), 410
Adjustments, 410
Administrative authority, 15–16
Advertising costs, 161
Affiliated corporation, 223
Affiliated group, 310–311
After-tax cost, leveraged purchase, 164
Agricultural business, 272n
AICPA Core Competency Framework, 93
Albertson's Inc. v. Commissioner, 464n
Alimony, 538
All-events test, 134–135
Allowance method, 138
Alternative Minimum Tax (AMT), 321–326
    AMT exemption, 427
    AMT trap, 429

calculation of, 324–325
computing of, 428–429
individual taxpayers and, 427–429
Alternative Minimum Tax (AMT) adjustments, 322–324
    depreciation adjustment, 322–323
    excess percentage depletion, 323
    itemized deductions as, 549–551
    NOL adjustment, 324
Alternative Minimum Tax (AMT) exemption, 321–326
Alternative Minimum Taxable Income (AMTI), 322–325, 549–551
American Express Company, 123
American Express Company v. United States, 123n
American Jobs Creation Act of 2004, 125, 318, 381n, 414
American Opportunity Credit, 545
American Recovery and Reinvestment Act of 2009, 30
Americans for Fair Taxation, 12
Amortization, 178
    intangible assets, 178–182
    leasehold costs and improvement, 180
    lump-sum purchase example, 182
    organizational and startup costs, 178–179
    purchased intangibles, 180–181
Amount realized, 201
    relief of debt as, 202
AMT trap, 429
Annual gift tax exclusion, 513
Annual vs. lifetime horizontal equity, 33
Annualized, 121
Annualized income, 120–122
Annuity, 49
    present value of, 49, 594
Annuity contracts, 493–494
Apportionment, 374–376
Apportionment formulas, 375–376
Arkansas Best Corp. v. Commissioner, 211n
Arm's-length transaction, 60–61, 137, 355–356
Asbestos replacement, 160
ASC 845, Nonmonetary Transactions, 245n
Asset(s); *see also* Depreciation; Financial asset(s); Intangible asset
    after-tax cost of, 158–162
    brand equity as, 161
    capital asset, 78, 208–209, 211–212
    dispositions of noncapital assets, 212–220
    noncapital asset, 212

personal asset, 540–541, 545–548
    tangible business asset, 166–177
    wasting assets, 167
Asset disposition, book/tax differences, 201
Asset sales, 163n
Assignment of income doctrine, 73
Audit process, 573–578
    assessments of deficiencies and interests, 574
    civil fraud, 576–577
    contesting the result of, 578–584
    criminal fraud, 577
    negligence, 575–576
    noncompliance penalties, 575–577
    tax return preparer penalties, 578
    types of audits, 574
    your rights as taxpayer, 574–575
Audit risk, 55–56
Average rate, 36
Awards, 536

Bad debts, 138–139, 496
Bargain element, 453
Barry, Dave, 14
Basis recovery, realized gain/loss and, 202–203
Bismarck, Otto von, 14
Bittker, Boris I., 357n
Blum, Walter J., 35n
Bonus depreciation, 176
Book/tax differences
    asset disposition, 201
    capital loss, 211
    conservatism and, 130
    depreciation, 167
    domestic production activities, 319
    employee stock options, 454
    foreign operations, 392
    goodwill, 181
    income measurement, 130
    nondeductible expenses, 128
    nontaxable exchange, 245–246
    origins of, 130–131
    permanent vs. temporary differences, 130–139, 144, 330
    reversal of temporary differences, 131
    Schedule M-1 reconciliation, 315–316
    Schedule M-3 reconciliation, 315
    sources of, 144, 185, 225, 256, 393, 472
    tax expense vs. tax payable, 315n
    Unicap and cost of goods sold, 165–166

Boot, 244–245
Brackets, 5
Braff, Jeffrey L., 444n
Branch operations, 383
Brand equity asset, 161
Brand names, 180
Brealey, Richard A., 48n, 328n
Bribes, 124
Brookings Institution, 22
Buffett, Warren, 515
Bunching itemized deductions, 414–415
Burden of production, 576
Burden of proof, 55n
Burke, Edmund, 38
Bush, George W., 15, 27
Business accounts receivable and supplies,
        213–214
Business activities, 486; *see also*
        International business operations;
        Nontaxable exchanges; Transactions
    book/tax differences, 130–137, 144
    method of accounting, 122–125
    net operating loss (NOL), 139–143
    property dispositions, 199–225
    taxable income, 118
    taxable year, 119–121
Business assets, dispositions of, 275
Business bad debts, 138–139
Business decisions
    structuring transactions to reduce taxes,
        57–62
    tax avoidance, 70
    tax legal doctrines and, 83–84
Business entities; *see* Business organizations
Business expansion, 179
Business expenditures; *see also* Cost
        recovery methods; Depreciation;
        Tax basis
    capital expenditures as subsidies, 160–161
    deductible expense vs. capitalized cost,
        157–161
    repairs and cleanup costs, 159–160
    tax treatment summary, 184
    travel and entertainment, 124
Business inventories, 212
Business organizations; *see also*
        Corporation(s); International business
        operations; Passthrough entities
    categories of, 271–272
    choice of entity, 345
    corporations, 252–254, 309–312
    family partnerships, 348–351
    formations of, 252–255
    jurisdictional issues in taxation, 371–393
    limited liability companies, 290–291
    partnerships, 254–255, 279–291, 351–354
    sole proprietorships, 272–279
    subchapter S corporations, 291–298,
        351–354

Business profit, as taxable income, 118–119
Business purpose doctrine, 83
Business start-up, 179
Buy-sell agreement, 310, 351

C corporations, 272, 309, 309n
Cafeteria plan, 451
Calendar year, 119
Cancellation-of-debt income, 224n
Capital asset, 78, 208
    defined, 208–209, 211–212
Capital cost, 158
Capital-intensive businesses, 486n
Capital expenditures, preferential rules as
        subsidies, 160–161
Capital gain, 78, 208, 497–503
    preferential rates for individuals, 211, 420
    tax character of, 208–212
Capital gains distribution, 487
Capital improvements, 159
Capital loss, 199, 208
    book/tax differences for, 211
    fully deductible loss, 209
    limitation of, 209–211, 502–503
    loss carrybacks/carryforwards, 210
    nondeductible capital loss, 210
    partially deductible loss, 209
    tax character of, 208–212
Capital loss limitation, 209–211, 502–503
Capitalism, 29
Capitalization, 158
Capitalized cleanup costs, 160
*Carmichael v. Southern Coal &
        Coke Co.*, 4n
Carryover basis, 254
Cash disbursements, 278
Cash flow
    cash method of accounting and, 125–129
    current deduction vs. capitalized cost,
        158–159
    from NOL carryback, 139–143
    quantifying, 48
    taxes and, 51–57
Cash method of accounting, 125–129
    cash flows and, 126
    constructive receipt, 126–127
    for expenses, 125
    hybrid method, 128
    income and cash flows, 126
    limitations on use of, 129
    merchandise inventories, 128
    noncash receipts, 126
    prepaid expenses, 127–128
    prepaid insurance, 125
    prepaid interest, 127–128
    for revenues, 125
    small service business exception, 128
    year-end tax planning, 129
Cash-or-deferred arrangements, 462

Cash surrender value, 492
Casualties and thefts, 224–225, 546–547
Casualty losses, 546–547
CCH Federal Tax Service, 100
Centralized management, 310
Character variable, 77–80
    conversion constraints, 79
    implicit taxes, 79–80
    ordinary income vs. capital gains, 78
    preferential rates, 78–79
Charitable contributions, 284n, 312,
        543–544, 543n
Checkpoint online tax research service, 100
Child credit, 424
Child support payments, 538
Citator, 102
Civil fraud, 576–577
Cleanup costs, 159–160
Clear and convincing evidence, 577
Closely held corporation, 310, 318, 354–361
    compensation, 446–447
    constructive dividends, 354–356
    controlled corporate groups, 360–361
    getting cash out of, 354–357
    penalty tax on corporate accumulations,
        358–360
    as tax shelters, 357–358
    thin capitalization, 356–357
Cohen, Edwin S., 422
Collectibles, 497, 497n, 540
Commerce Clause, 373
Commercial activity tax (CAT), 377
Commercial building, MACRS depreciation
        for, 172
Commercial tax services, 99–100
Commissioner v. Culbertson, 348n
Commissioner v. Danielson, 83n
Commissioner v. Glenshaw Glass Co., 118n
*Commissioner v. Lincoln Savings & Loan
        Assn.*, 158n
Commissioner v. Newman, 70n
Commissioner v. Tufts, 224n
Commodity derivative financial instrument,
        208, 212
Company, 271
Compensation, 277; *see also* Fringe benefits
    cash disbursements, 278
    closely held corporation, 446–447
    employee vs. independent contractor,
        442–444
    employee stock options, 452–455
    employment-related expenses, 456–457
    foreign earned income exclusion,
        448–449
    fringe benefits, 449–452
    incentive stock option (ISO), 454–455
    performance-based compensation, 446
    reasonable compensation, 445–448
    S corporation, 447

stock options, 452–455
  unreasonable compensation, 355
  wage and salary payments, 445–449
Compensation accruals, 136–137
Computer software, 181n
Condemned property, 251
Congressional Budget Office, 23
Conservatism, 130
Consolidated corporate returns, 383n
Consolidated tax return, 311
Constructive dividend, 354–356
Constructive receipt, 126–127
Consumer durables, 540
Consumption tax, 9
Contribution limits, individual retirement
      accounts, 465–466
Controlled corporate groups, 360–361
Controlled foreign corporation (CFC),
      388–390
  subpart F income, 389–390
  transfer pricing and Section 482, 391–392
  U.S. investment of earnings, 390
Controlled group, 360–361
Controlling interest, 137n
Convenience, good tax as, 28
Copyright, 178, 181, 208, 212
Corporate accumulations
  accumulated earning tax, 359
  penalty taxes on, 358–360
  personal holding company tax, 359–360
Corporate distributions, 487
Corporate formations, 252–254
Corporate income taxes, 9–10
Corporate rate structure, 71n
Corporate reorganizations, 496, 496n
Corporate tax shelter, 357–358
  current environment, 358
  decline of, 357–358
Corporate taxable income; *see also*
      Alternative minimum tax; Tax credit
  computation of, 312–316
  dividends-received deduction, 314–315
  reconciling book/taxable income,
      315–316
  regular corporate tax, 316–319
Corporation(s); *see also* Closely held
      corporation; Subchapter S
      corporation
  affiliated groups, 310–311
  alternative minimum tax, 321–326
  book and taxable income reconciliation,
      316
  characteristics of, 310–311
  closely held corporation, 354–361
  corporate tax incidence, 329
  dividends-received deduction, 314–315
  double taxation, 328–329
  legal characteristics of, 310–312
  nonprofit corporations, 312

payment and filing requirements, 326–327
  personal service corporation, 318
  profit distribution to investors, 327–329
  regular corporate tax, 316–319
  tax credits, 319–321
  taxable income computation, 312–315
  as taxpayers, 4, 309, 329
  twenty (20) percent recapture rule,
      219–220
Correspondence examination, 574
Cost basis, 163–164
  assets exchanged for note, 163
  assets exchanged for property, 163
  assets exchanged for services, 163
  leveraged cost basis, 163–164
Cost depletion, 182–183
  percentage depletion, 183–184
Cost of goods sold, 165–166
  allocating costs, 166
  formula for, 165
  Unicap rules, 165–166
Cost recovery, 164
Cost recovery deductions, 119
Cost recovery methods, 164
  amortization, 178–182
  cost of goods sold, 165–166
  depletion, 182–184
  depreciation, 166–176
Coverdell education savings account, 545
Crane v. Commissioner, 163n
Creative assets, 540
Credit card payments, 430
Criminal fraud, 577
Cross-crediting, 381–382
Cumulative Bulletins (CBs), 15
Cyberspace, taxes in, 374

Debt financing, 163, 328, 356, 356n
Debt income, discharge of, 118
Debt obligations, 22–23, 203, 490
Decision making; *see also* Net present value;
      Tax planning; Transactions; Wealth
      transfer planning
  financial risk and, 50
  net present value and, 48–51
  taxes and cash flows, 51–57
  uncertainty of tax consequences, 55–57
  wealth maximization and, 47
Declining balance method, 167–168
Declining marginal utility of income, 35
Deductible cleanup costs, 160
Deductible expense, 157–161
  all-events test, 134–135
  preferential capital expenditures as
      subsidies, 160–161
Deduction, 52, 119
  IRA contributions, 466–468
Deduction shift, 72–73
Deemed paid foreign tax credit, 385–386

Deferred compensation, 463–464
Deferred interest income, 490–492
Deferred tax asset, 132
Deferred tax liability, 132
Deferred taxes, 132–133
Deficiency, 574
Deficit spending, 23
Defined-benefit plan, 461
Defined-contribution plan, 461–463
Dependent, 415
Dependent care assistance programs, 450
Dependent care credit, 425
Depreciation, 166–177
  accelerated depreciation, 218
  appreciating assets and, 173
  bonus depreciation, 176
  book and tax concepts of, 166–167
  book/tax difference, 167
  conventions for, 168–169
  half-year convention, 168, 171
  MACRS framework, 167–173
  methods for, 167–168
  midmonth convention, 169
  midquarter convention, 169
  passenger automobiles, 173–174
  purchase vs. leasing decision, 177
  recovery deductions under
      2008/2009/2010 Acts, 176
  straight-line, 168, 218
  tangible business assets and, 166–177
Depreciation adjustment, 322–323
Depreciation methods, 167–168; *see also*
      MACRS (Modified Accelerated Cost
      Recovery System)
Depreciation passenger automobiles, 174n
  Section 179 expensing election, 174–175
Depreciation recapture, 216–220
  Section 1231 assets, 216–220
Direct costs, 165
Direct write-off method, 138
Disallowed losses, related party sales,
      206–207
Discount rate, 48, 50
Discriminate function system (DIF) score,
      573
Disposable bag tax, 30
Distributive justice, tax policy and, 36–37
Distributive share, 284
Dividend income, 486–488
Dividends-received deduction, 314–315, 384n
Divorce, 538, 583
Domestic manufacturing facilities, 125
Domestic production activities deduction,
      125, 318
Domestic subsidiaries, 383
Donee, 513
Donor, 513
Double taxation, 272, 328–329, 354
  passthrough entities and, 347–348

Double-weighted scale factor, 376
Duplicative taxation, 12
Dynamic forecast, 23–24

E-file program, 327n
Earmarked tax, 6
Earned income credit, 425–426
    refund of, 425–426
Echols v. Commissioner, 222n
Economic Growth and Tax Relief
        Reconciliation Act of 2001, 15, 27
Economic nexus, 374
Economic performance, 135
Economic Recovery Tax Act, 27
Economic Stimulus Act of 2008, 176
Education IRA, 544–545
Education savings bonds, 544
Efficiency standard for good tax, 28–31
    classical standard, 29
    neutral effect of tax, 29, 31
    taxes as fiscal policy, 29–30
*E.J. Harrison & Sons, Inc. v.
        Commissioner*, 446n
Electronic Federal Tax Payment System
        (EFTPS), 327n
Embezzlement, 536n
Employee(s), 442; *see also* Compensation;
        Fringe benefits
    compensation transaction, 442
    cost of, 57
    family members as, 447–448
    income tax withholding, 277–278
    independent contractor vs., 442–444
    tax consequences of, 442–443
    wage and salary payments, 445
    worker classification, 442–444
Employee compensation, 277–278
Employee fringe benefits, 449–452
Employee payroll tax, 276–277
Employee stock options, 452–455
    book/tax difference, 454
    incentive stock options (ISO), 454–455
Employee stock ownership plan (ESOP), 462
Employer, wage and salary payments, 445
Employer identification number, 276
Employer payroll tax, 276
Employer-provided parking, 452n
Employer-provided retirement plans,
        460–464
Employment Act of 1946, 30
Employment-related expenses, 456–457
    moving expenses, 456–457
Employment taxes, 11, 276–278
    employer's tax consequences, 278
    income tax withholding, 277–278
    sole proprietorships, 276–278
    unemployment and FICA tax, 276–277
Employment transaction, after-tax cost of, 57
Enrolled agent, 574

Entity variable, 70–73
    deduction shifting, 72–73
    income shifting, 72
Environmental clean up costs, 159–160
Environmental pollution, 30
Equity, disguised equity, 356
Estate of Emerson Winkler, 349n
Estate tax, 6, 515–517
    estate tax computation, 516–517
    inherited property, 517
    unused spousal exclusion, 517
Estimated tax payments, 430
Ethics, tax avoidance and, 70
Eustice, James S., 357n
Event or transaction-based tax, 6
*Exacto Spring Corporation v.
        Commissioner*, 446n
Excess foreign tax credit, 381
Excess payroll tax withholding, 426
Excess percentage depletion, 323
Excess Section 179 property limitation, 175
Excise tax, 6, 9
Exemption amount, 415
Expansion costs, 179
Expatriate, 448
Expenses; *see also* Cost of goods sold;
        Personal expenses
    accrual method for, 130
    capital expenditures as subsidies, 160–161
    deductible expense vs. capitalized cost,
        158–161
    graphic design costs, 161
    handicapped/elderly accessibility
        modifications, 160
    repairs and cleanup costs, 159–160
    research and experimental
        expenditures, 160
    Section 179 expensing election, 174–175
    self-created patent, 161
    tax basis, 161–164
    tax treatment summary, 184
    travel and entertainment, 124
Explicit tax, 80
Extended statute of limitations, 573
Extension, 570
Extortion, 536n
Extraterritorial value, 375

Fair market value, 163n
    MACRS and, 172–173
Fairness standard for good tax, 32–38
    ability to pay, 32
    distributive justice, 36–37
    horizontal equity, 32–33
    perception of inequity, 37–38
    vertical equity, 33–34
Family partnership, 348–351
    compensation for services, 350
    income shifting and restrictions, 348–350

    nontax considerations, 350–351
    transactions costs, 350
Farmers, 161
Federal debt, 23
Federal gift tax, 350n
Federal Insurance Contribution Act (FICA),
        276–277
Federal payroll taxes, 62n
Federal Tax Coordinator 2d, 100–101
Federal tax law; *see also* Internal Revenue
        Code
    administrative authority, 15–16
    judicial authority, 16
    limited liability company and, 290–291
    sources of, 14–16
    statutory authority, 15
Federal taxes, 10–11
    employment/unemployment taxes, 11
    fiscal year 2010 revenues, 11
    income tax, history of, 10–11
    other taxes, 11
    transfer taxes, 11
Fellowships, 536
FICA payroll tax, 276–277
Field examination, 574
FIFO (first-in, first-out), 166, 495
Fifteen (15) year amortization rule, 181n
Filing and payment requirements, 570–573
Filing status, 408–409
Financial Accounting Standards Board
        (FASB), 129n
Financial asset(s); *see also* Passive activities;
        Security transactions
    deferred interest income, 490–492
    dividend and interest income, 486–488
    investment in, 486–494
    life insurance and annuities, 492–494
    qualified small business stock, 503–504
    Section 1244 stock, 504
    tax-exempt interest, 488–490
Financial risk, 50
Financial statements, income tax expense, 131
Fines, 4
Firm, 271
First-in, first-out (FIFO), 166, 495
Fiscal policies, 29–30
    taxes as instrument of, 29–30
Fiscal year, 119–120
Flat rate, 5
Foreclosures, 224
Foreign earned income exclusion, 448–449
Foreign jurisdictions, taxes of, 12
Foreign partnerships, 383
Foreign source income, 380
Foreign subsidiaries, 384–386
Foreign tax credit, 119n, 379–382
    cross-crediting, 381–382
    excess credit carrybacks/carryforwards, 381
    limitation on annual credit, 380–382

Foreign tax payments, 542–543
Form 709 (U.S. Gift Tax Return), 514
Form 1040 (U.S. Individual Income Tax
    Return), 272–276, 284, 409–412,
    443, 487, 570
  innocent spouse rule, 583–584
  taxable income computation, 409–418
Form 1065 (U.S. Partnership Return of
    Income), 281–282
Form 1099, 572
Form 1099-B (Proceeds from Broker and
    Barter Exchange Transactions), 494
Form 1099-DIV (Dividends and
    Distributions), 487–488
Form 1099-INT (Interest Income),
    487–488
Form 1099-MISC (Miscellaneous
    Income), 443
Form 1099-R, 492, 492n
Form 1120 (U.S. Corporation Income Tax
    Return), 312, 315, 316, 326–327, 570
Form 1120S (U.S. Income Tax Return for an
    S Corporation), 291–293
Form 1139 (Corporation Application for
    Tentative Refund), 140n
Form 4686 (Application for Automatic
    Extension of Time to File U.S.
    Individual Tax Return), 431
Form 8829, 276
Form W-2 (Wage and Tax Statement), 278,
    284, 295, 442–443, 572
Form W-4 (Employee's Withholding
    Allowance Certificate), 275, 427n
Formations of business entities, 252–255
Free transferability, 310
Friedman, 374n
Fringe benefits, 449–452
  cafeteria plans, 451
  compensation planning with, 451–452
  dependent care assistance programs, 450
  employer-provided retirement plans,
    460–464
  group term life insurance, 449–450
  health and accident insurance, 449, 451
  negotiation with nontaxable benefits,
    451–452
  nontaxable benefits, 450
  qualified retirement plans, 457–465
  Section 401k plans, 462–463
  self-employed individuals, 450–451
  valuing, 451
Frivolous tax returns, 575
Full recapture rule, 217–218

Gale v. United States, 464n
Gambling
  losses, 547–548
  as nontax revenue, 13
  winnings, 536

Gates, William H., Sr., 513
*General Bancshares Corp. v.
    Commissioner*, 159n
General business credit, 320
General partner's risk, 280n
General partnership, 280
*General Theory of Employment, Interest and
    Money, The* (Keynes), 29n
Generally accepted accounting principles
    (GAAP), 129
  conservatism, 130
  depreciation, 166–176
  income measurement, 130–139
  realization principle, 129
  reconciling book and taxable income,
    315–316
*Geoffrey, Inc. v. South Carolina Tax
    Commission*, 374n
Gift tax, 350, 350n, 513–515
  annual exclusion, 514
  computation and payment, 513–514
  lifetime exclusion, 514
Gifts, income tax consequences of,
    514–515
Ginsburg, Ruth Bader, 581
Glaxo, 122
Global tax costs, 77
Globalization, 378–379
Going-concern value, 180, 212n
Gold watch exception, 536n
Good tax standards, 22, 38
  convenience, 28
  efficiency, 28–31
  fairness, 32–38
  sufficiency, 22–27
Goodwill, 180, 212n, 247
  book/tax difference for, 181
Goodwin v. Commissioner, 537n
Government transfer payments, 538–540
Graduated rate, 5
Graduated tax, 5
Graphic design costs, 161
Grassley, Charles, 124
Gregory v. Helvering, 83n
Gross compensation, 277
Gross income, 118
  defined, 118
  divorce settlements and, 538
  from whatever source derived, 535–541
  government transfer payments, 538–540
  legal settlements, 537–538
  personal receipts, 536–537
  sales/exchanges of personal assets,
    540–541
Gross profit percentage, 204
Gross receipts taxes, 377–378
Group term life insurance, 449–450
Groups, 279n
Guaranteed payment, 284

Haiti earthquake charitable donations, 76
Half-year convention, 168, 171
Hand, Learned, 70
Handicapped/elderly accessibility
    modifications, 160
Hazardous Substance Superfund, 6
Head of household, 409
Head (per capita) tax, 5n
Health and accident insurance, 449, 451
Health and fitness facilities, 452n
Hedging transaction properties, 208, 212
Hellerstein, Jerome, 8n, 10n
Hellerstein, Walter, 8n, 10n
*Helvering v. Alabama Asphaltic Limestone
    Co.*, 84n
Helvering v. Horst, 73n
Higher education expenses, 544–545
Historic preservation, 30–31, 321
Hobby loss, 547–548
Holmes, Oliver Wendell, 22
Home equity debt, 549
Home mortgage interest deduction, 549
Home office deduction
  legal requirements of, 275–276
  principle place of business, 276
  sole proprietorship, 275
Home ownership
  exclusion of gain realized on sale,
    550–551
  mortgage interest deduction, 549
  principal residence, 550–551
  tax consequences of, 548–551
  vacation homes, 550
HOPE scholarship credit, 545n
Horizontal equity, 32–33
  annual vs. lifetime horizontal equity, 33
  tax preferences and, 33
  taxable income and ability to pay, 32–33
Houghton, 374n
Household employers/employees, 445n
Hurricane Katrina, special tax law, 75
Hybrid method of accounting, 128

Illegal income, 536n
Implicit tax, 79–80
Imputed income from owner-occupied
    housing, 549
Inbound transactions, 379n
Incentive stock option (ISO), 454–455
Incident, defined, 4
Income, prepaid income, 133–134
Income apportionment, 374–376
Income effect, 25
Income measurement
  all-events test, 134
  arm's-length transaction, 137
  bad debts, 138–139
  book income vs. taxable income, 130–131
  book/tax differences, 120–131

Income measurement—*Cont.*
  deferred taxes, 132–133
  economic performance, 134
  managers' bias, 128
  permanent vs. temporary differences, 130–139
  prepaid income, 133–134
  prepaid rent, 133
  reversal of temporary book/tax difference, 131
  tax expense per books, 131
  tax policy objectives, 123–125
Income recognition, 122
Income shifting, 72, 448
  among family members, 348–351
  assignment of income doctrine, 73
  constraints on, 73
  passthrough entities and, 348–351
Income tax, 6
  as activity based tax, 6
  corporate, 9–10
  history of, 10–11
  personal, 9
  planning maxims, 69
  rate structures, 34–36
Income tax cost, 51–52
Income tax incident, 4
Income tax planning
  character variable, 70, 77–80
  constraints on conversion, 79
  deduction shifting, 72–73
  developing strategies, 80–84
  entity variable, 70–73
  implicit taxes, 79–80
  income deferral, 75–76
  income shifting and constraints, 73
  jurisdiction variable, 70
  preferential rates, 78–79
  tax avoidance, 70
  tax legal doctrines, 83–84
  time period variable, 70
  variables which make it possible, 70
Income tax rate
  behavior responses to changes in, 25–27
  2011 individual tax rate schedules, 595
Income tax return preparer, 578
Income tax savings, 52
Income tax treaty, 378
Income tax withholding, 277–278
Independent contractor, 57–58, 57n, 442–444
  tax consequences of, 442–443
  worker classification controversy, 443–444
Indirect costs, 165
Individual capital losses, 209n
Individual Income Tax Returns Publication 1304 (Complete Report), 413n
Individual net operating loss, 273

Individual retirement account (IRA), 465–471
  age limit, 466
  catch up contributions, 465
  contribution limits, 465–466
  deduction of contributions, 466–468
  education IRA, 545
  rollovers to, 470–471
  Roth IRAs, 465, 468
  self-employed individuals, 465n
  withdrawals from, 75, 468–470
Individual tax credits, 424–426
  child credit, 424
  dependent care credit, 425
  earned income credit, 425–426
  excess payroll tax withholding, 426
Individual tax rate schedules, 419
Individual taxpayer; *see also* Personal activities; Wealth transfer planning
  alternative minimum tax, 427–429
  credit card tax payments, 430
  dependent requirements, 415
  filing status, 408–409
  itemized deduction, 410–415
  marriage penalty, 421–422
  married individuals, 408–409
  payment and filing requirements, 429–431
  standard deduction, 410–415
  surviving spouse, 408–409
  tax credits, 424–426
  tax liability computation, 419–424
  taxable income
    adjusted gross income calculation, 410
    computation, 409–418
    exemption amount, 415–418
    formula for, 418
    standard/itemized deductions, 410–415
  unmarried individuals, 409
Indopco Inc. v. Commissioner, 158n
Inflation-adjusted debt instrument, 491–492
Inflationary gains, 203
Inheritance, 537
Inherited property
  income tax consequences of, 517
  stepped-up basis, 517
Injury/illness compensation, 537
Innocent spouse rule, 583–584
Inside buildup, 492
Installment agreement, 582
Installment sale method, 204–205
  inventory and, 205
  seller's basis in purchaser's note, 205–206
Intangible assets, 8n
  amortization, 189
  amortization and, 178–182
  determinable life, 178
  indeterminable life, 178
  purchased intangibles, 180–181

Intangible drilling and development costs (IDC), 161
Intangible personalty, 248
Inter vivos transfers, 513
Interest expense, sole proprietorship, 275
Interest income, 486–488
Interest payments, income tax due, 570
Internal Revenue Bulletins (IRBs), 15
Internal Revenue Code, 10, 15n, 380n
  capital asset, defined by exception, 208
  deductible expenses, 158
  on gross income, 200
  health and accident insurance, 449
  higher education tax subsidies, 544–545
  income shifting restrictions, 348–350
  nontaxable exchanges, 246
  partnership reporting requirements, 281–283
  personal expenses, 541–545
  qualified retirement plans, 457–465
  related parties, defined, 206
  Section(s), 15
  Section 1, 71
  Section 11, 71
  Section 61, 535–536
  Section 274, 124n
  Section 460, 122
  Section 482, 122–123, 391–392
  Section 1231 assets, 214–216, 500
  Section 1244 stock, 504
  stable/unstable tax provisions, 56
  tax breaks, 30–31
  worthless securities, 223
Internal Revenue Code of 1954, 10
Internal Revenue Code of 1986, 10–11, 15, 97
Internal Revenue Service (IRS), 15–16, 28; *see also* Tax compliance process
  capital costs, 158–159
  collection procedures, 582–583
  depreciation tables, 170–172
    mid-quarter convention, 195–197
    nonresidential real property, 172
    residential real property, 172
  e-file program, 327n
  mission statement, 575
  private letter ruling (PLF), 56
  Publication 5 (*Appeal Rights and How to Prepare a Protest if You Don't Agree*), 579
  Publication 463 (*Travel, Entertainment, Gift and Car Expenses*), 174
  Publication 560 (*Retirement Plans for Small Business*), 464n
  Publication 910 (*Guide to Free Tax Service*), 574
  Publication 936 (*Home Mortgage Interest Deduction*), 549n
  Publication 970 (*Tax Benefits for Higher Education*), 544

on reasonable compensation, 445–446

Reform and Restructuring Act of 1998, 55n, 575

regional Appeals Office, 578–579

return processing, 572–573

Tax Trails (interactive questions/ answers), 97

worker classification controversy, 443–444

International business operations; *see also* Organizational forms

controlled foreign corporations, 388–390

deemed paid foreign tax credit, 385

foreign tax credit, 379–382

income tax treaties, 378

organizational forms of, 383–386

Section 482 adjustment, 391

subpart F income, 389–390

tax consequences of, 12–13, 378–379

tax deferral on foreign source income, 386–392

transfer pricing, 391–392

U.S. jurisdiction to tax global income, 379

Internet sales, 14, 374

Internet Tax Freedom Act, 374

Interstate Transit Lines v. Commissioner, 158n

Inventory, 208, 212

allocating costs, 166

cost of goods sold and, 165–166

costing convention, 166

installment sale of, 205

uniform capitalization (Unicap) rules, 165–166

Investment activities

business activities vs., 486

deferred interest income, 490–492

dividend and interest income, 486–492

financial assets, 486–494

interest expense, 504–506

investment expenses, 504–506

life insurance and annuities, 492–494

net investment income, 505–506

nontax considerations, 494

passive activities, 508–512

qualified small business stock, 503–504

real property, 506–508

rental activities, 507–508

Section 1244 stock, 504

security transactions, 494–497

small corporate businesses, 503–504

state and local bonds, 488–490

Investment expenses, 504–506

Investment interest expense, 505–505

Involuntary conversion, 251–252, 252n

gain recognized on, 251

IRA; *see* Individual retirement account (IRA)

IRS; *see* Internal Revenue Service (IRS)

Itemized deduction, 372n, 410–415

as AMT adjustments, 551–553

bunching, 414–415

James v. United States, 536n

Jobs and Growth Tax Relief Reconciliation Act of 2003, 354, 358, 421, 487

Johnson & Johnson, 180

Joint return, 408

Joint and several liability, 408

Joint ventures, 279n

Judicial authority, 16

Jurisdiction, 4–5; *see also* Taxing jurisdiction

Jurisdiction variable, 70, 77

Kafka, Gerald A., 575n

Kalven, Harry, Jr., 35n

Kemp, Jack, 38

Keogh plan, 464–465

Key-person life insurance policies, 124–125

Keynes, John Maynard, 29–30, 29n

Keyword searching, tax research, 101–102

Kickbacks, 122

Kiddie tax, 423–424, 515

KPMG's Total Tax Index, 77

Kuhl v. Garner, 280n

Laissez-faire system, 29

Land sales, 212–213

Late-filing and late-payment penalty, 571–572

Law of Federal Income Taxation (Mertens), 100

Leasehold costs, 180

Leasehold improvements, 180

Leasing, 177

Legal settlements, 537–538

Legalized gambling, 13, 22

Legislative regulations, 15n

Leverage, 164

Leveraged cost basis, 163–164

Liberty Loan Corp. v. U.S., 391n

Life insurance policies, 124–125, 492–493

Lifetime Learning Credit, 545

Lifetime transfer tax exclusion, 514

LIFO (last-in, first-out), 166

Like-kind exchanges, 246–250, 506n

mortgaged properties, 249–250

Like-kind personality with boot given, 247

Like-kind property/realty, 246–249, 251n

Limited liability, 310

Limited liability company (LLC), 271–272, 290–291, 351–353

Limited liability partnership (LLP), 280, 352–353

Limited partnership, 280, 509n

Limited standard deduction for dependent, 413

Lobbying expenses, 124

Local property tax, 32

Local tax payments, 542–543

Local taxation, 7–8, 372–378

Long, Russell, 32

Long-term capital gains or losses, 78n, 497–502

Loss carrybacks/carryforward, 210

Loss recapture, Section 1231 assets, 214–216

Lotteries, 13, 536

Lucas v. American Code Co., 138n

Lucas v. Earl, 73n

Lump-sum purchase, 182

McCain, John and Cindy, 409

McMahan v. Commissioner, 572n

McNamee v. Treasury, 290

MACRS (Modified Accelerated Cost Recovery System), 167–173

commercial buildings, 172

depreciation conventions, 168–169, 320–321

depreciation methods, 167–168

examples of, 170

IRS depreciation tables, 170–172

passenger automobiles, 173–174, 174n

purchase vs. leasing decision, 177

recovery periods, 167–168

Mail order purchases, self-assessment tax responsibility, 9, 14

Managers; *see* Decision making

Marginal rate, 36

Marginal rate uncertainty, 56

Marginal tax rate

child's unearned income, 423–424

constant vs. changing rate, 52–53

individual rate, 422–423

significance of, 52–53

Market, 58

Market discount, 490–491

Market transaction, 490

Marriage penalty, 421–422

Married individuals, 408–409

Martin v. United States, 581n

Material participation, 509

Medical expenses, 541–542

Medicare, 6, 11, 27, 276

Medicare benefits, 539

Merchandise inventories, 128

Method of accounting, 122–125; *see also* Book/tax differences

accrual method, 129–139

cash method, 125–129

to shift income, 123

Meynard Inc. v. Commissioner, 447n

Midmonth convention, 169

Midquarter convention/convention tables, 169, 195–197

Mills Estate, Inc. v. Commissioner, 159n
Mineral exploration and extraction, 182
Minimum distribution, 459
Minimum tax credit, 325–326
Miscellaneous itemized deductions, 456,
　505n, 538n
Modified Accelerated Cost Recovery System
　(MACRS), 167–173
Moller v. United States, 486n
*Moorman Manufacturing Co. v. Bair,
　Director of Revenue of Iowa*, 376n
Mortgaged properties, like-kind exchanges,
　249–250
Moving expenses, 456–457
Municipal bonds, 79–80, 124
Musgrave, Peggy, 25n
Musgrave, Richard, 25n
Mutual fund, 486
Mutual fund dividend, 487
Myers, Stewart C., 48n, 328n

NASDAQ, 310
National Commission on Economic Growth
　and Tax Reform, 11n
National Conference of Uniform State Laws,
　375
National debt, 23
National Gambling Impact Study
　Commission, 13
National Park Service, 321
National sales tax, 12
National Taxpayer Advocate, 575
Natural resources, depletion of, 182–184
Negative externalities, 30
Negligence, 575–576
Net capital loss, 209
Net cash flow, 48
Net compensation, 277
Net debt relief as boot, 250
Net investment income, 505–506
Net operating loss (NOL), 139–143
　accounting for carryback/carryforward, 143
　average tax rate, 140
　excess deductions problem, 140
　giving up an NOL carryback, 142
　NOL deduction, 140–141, 273, 324
　　determining value of, 141–142
Net present value (NPV), 48
　concept of present value, 48–50
　depreciation and, 177
　different tax rates over time, 54–55
　different tax treatments across
　　transactions, 54
　example of, 51, 53–55
　net cash flow and, 48
　NOL carryforward, 142
　optimal business decision and, 58
　purchase vs. leasing decision, 177
　quantifying cash flows, 48

　risk and, 50
　role in decision making, 48–51
　tax costs and savings, 51–52
　uncertainty of tax consequences, 55–57
Net profits, 119
New York Stock Exchange, 310
Nexus, 373–374
　economic nexus, 374
　Internet sales, 374
　physical presence vs. economic nexus,
　　373–374
　U.S. Constitution, Article 1, 373
NOL carryback, 140–141, 143
NOL carryforward, 140
　accounting for, 143
　net present value (NPV) of, 142
Nonbusiness bad debt, 496
Noncapital assets, 212
　dispositions of, 212–220
　sale of, 212–220
Noncash receipts, 126
Nondeductible expenses, 124, 130
Nondeductible penalties, 124
Nonfamily partnerships, 349n
Nonprofit corporations, 312
Nonqualified deferred-compensation plans,
　463–464
Nonrecaptured Section 1231 loss, 216
Nonrecourse debt, 224
Nonrefundable fringe benefit, 457n
Nonresident aliens, 408n
　U.S. jurisdiction, 5
Nonresidential realty, 218n
Nontax revenue, legalized gambling, 13
Nontaxable exchanges, 241–255, 496–497
　book/tax differences from, 245
　boot effect, 244–245
　characteristics of, 246
　corporate formations, 252–254
　formations of business entities, 252–255
　involuntary conversion, 251–252, 252n
　like-kind exchanges, 246–250
　mortgaged properties, 249–250
　neutrality of tax law, 241–242
　partnership formations, 254–255
　qualifying property, 242–243
　substituted basis rule, 243–244
　tax-free exchanges of assets, 242–246
　wash sales, 255
Nontaxable fringe benefits, 59n, 450–451
　moving expenses, 456–457
　negotiating with, 451–452
Nonwasting assets, 167
Note receivable basis, 205
　installment sale method, 206
NPV; *see* Net present value (NPV)

Obama administration, 27, 30
Offer in compromise, 583

Office examination, 574
Oil and gas producers, 161, 182–184
O'Meara, Daniel P., 444n
Operating cycle, choice of taxable year and,
　119–120
Operating expenses, 119
Ordinary gain or loss, 208
Ordinary income, 78, 420
Organizational costs, 178–179
Organizational forms
　branch operations, 383
　domestic subsidiaries, 383
　entity variable and, 71–73
　foreign partnerships, 383
　foreign subsidiaries, 384–386
Original issue discount (OID), 491
Out of state purchases, self-assessment tax
　responsibility, 9, 14
Outbound transactions, 379

Package design, 161
Parent-subsidiary controlled groups,
　360–361
Partial recapture rule for realty, 218
Partnership, 71, 179n, 271–272, 279
　basis limitation on loss deductions,
　　288–290
　cost of formation and operation,
　　351–353
　distributive shares and cash flows, 284
　example of, 286–287
　flexibility of income/loss sharing, 352
　formation and type of, 254–255,
　　279–281
　guaranteed payments, 284
　income shifting and, 348–351
　limited liability companies, 290–291
　loss deductions, 288–290
　owner liability, 352–353
　partnership basis adjustments, 287–290
　partnership debt, 281n
　planning example, 353–354
　reporting requirements, 281
　S corporation vs., 351–354
　self-employment income, 285–286
　self-employment tax, 352
　tax basis in, 280–281
　tax consequences to partners, 284–287
Partnership formation, 254–255, 279–281
　transactions costs, 350
Passenger automobiles, 173–174
　defined, 173
　limited depreciation for, 173–174
Passive activities, 508–512
　disposition of, 510–511
　loss limitation, 353n, 509–511
　planning strategies with, 511–512
　purchase of a PIG, 511–512
　sale of, 511

Passive income generator (PIG), 511–512

Passthrough entities, 71, 281, 291
   avoiding double tax, 347–348
   income shifting
      among family, 348–351
      statutory restrictions, 348–350
   partnership vs. S corporation, 351–354
   start-up losses, maximizing tax benefit of, 346–347
   tax planning with, 346–351
   transactions costs, 350

Patents, 178, 181, 212

Paulson, Henry, 425

Payment liabilities, 135–136

Paymer v. Commissioner, 83n

Payroll factor, 375

Pearlstein, Steven, 31n

Penalties, 4

Pension Benefit Guaranty Corporation (PBGC), 461n

Per capita tax, 5n

Percentage of completion method, 122

Percentage depletion, 183–184, 323

Performance-based compensation, 446

Period costs, 165

Permanent difference, 130–131

Permanent establishment, 378

Person, defined, 4

Personal activities; *see also* Home ownership; Investment activities
   government transfer payments, 538–540
   gross income from whatever source, 535–541
   home ownership, 548–551
   itemized deductions as AMT adjustments, 551–553
   legal settlements, 537–538
   personal expenses, 541–545
   personal losses, 545–548
   personal receipts, 536–537
   sales/exchanges of personal assets, 540–541
   tax consequences of, 535–553

Personal assets
   losses on sales/exchanges of, 545–548
   sales/exchanges of, 540–541

Personal expenses, 541–545
   charitable contributions, 543–544, 543n
   higher education tax subsidies, 544–545
   itemized deductions as AMT adjustments, 551–553
   local, state, and foreign tax payments, 542–543
   medical expenses, 541–542
   personal losses, 545–548

Personal holding company, 359–360

Personal holding company tax, 359–360

Personal income taxes; *see* Individual taxpayer

Personal losses
   casualty and theft losses, 546–547
   hobby and gambling losses, 547–548
   on sales/exchanges of personal assets, 545–548

Personal property taxes, 8
   business tangibles, 8
   household tangibles, 8
   intangibles, 8

Personal receipts, 536–537

Personal service corporation, 129, 318, 359n

Personal services, 252

Personalty, defined, 8

Phi Delta Theta Fraternity v. Commissioner, 312n

Pollack, Sheldon D., 23n

Pollock v. Farmers' Loan and Trust Company, 10

Pools, 279n

Preferential capital gains rate
   long-term gains, 497–502
   policy reasons for, 501–502

Preferential rate structure, 211

Premature withdrawal, 459–460

Prepaid expenses, 127–128

Prepaid income, 133–134

Prepaid income for services, 134

Prepaid interest, 127–128

Prepaid rent, 133

Prepaid service income, 134

Preponderance of evidence, 576

Present value; *see also* Net present value (NPV)
   annuities, 49
   concept of, 48–50
   issue of risk, 50
   mathematical derivation of, 49

Present value tables, 50, 593

President's Council of Economic Advisors, 30

Primary authorities, 97–99
   sample citations to, 98–99

Principal residence, 550–551

Private activity bonds, 489

Private letter ruling (PLR), 56, 97

Private market, 58–60

Prizes, 536

Pro rata share, 295

Probate estate, 515

Product costs, 165

Profit-sharing plan, 462

Progressive rate structure, 35, 37

Property, 252–253, 346n

Property acquisitions; *see* Business expenditure; Home ownership

Property dispositions, 199–225; *see also* Capital gain; Capital loss; Nontaxable exchanges
   abandonment and worthlessness, 222–223

business accounts receivable and supplies, 213–214
   casualties and thefts, 224–225
   comprehensive example of, 220–222
   corporations and twenty percent recapture, 219–220
   deferring gains/accelerating losses, 201
   disallowed losses on related party sales, 206–208
   donation of appreciated property, 544
   foreclosures, 224
   inflationary gains, 203
   installment sale method, 204–205
   inventory, 212–213
   land sales, 212–213
   noncapital assets, 212–220
   offset of gain by previously disallowed loss, 207
   other types, 222–225
   realization and recognition of gains/losses, 200–201
   sales and exchanges, 201–203
   Section 1231 assets, 214–220
      depreciation recapture, 216–220
      full recapture rule, 217–218
      loss recapture, 215–216
      partial recapture rule for realty, 218
   seller-financed sales, 203–206
   tax consequences (summary), 222
   tax-free recovery of basis and cash flow, 202–203
   taxation of capital gains, 211

Property factor, 375

Property similar or related in service or use, 251

Property tax, 7–8, 32

Property tax abatements, 7
   for senior volunteers, 536

Property tax incident, 4

Property tax rates, 7–8

Proportionate rate structure, 34–35, 37

Public goods, 23n

Public market, 61

Publicly held corporation, 310

Purchase versus leasing decision, 177

Purchased goodwill, 212n

Purchased intangibles, 180–181, 212n

Purchaser's note, seller's basis in, 205–206

Qualified dividend distribution, 487

Qualified dividend income, 487

Qualified education loan, 544

Qualified intermediaries, 249

Qualified residence interest, 549, 549n

Qualified retirement plans, 457–465
   changing times for, 463
   employee stock ownership plans (ESOPs), 462
   employer-provided plans, 460–464

Qualified retirement plans—*Cont.*
 individual retirement accounts, 465–471
 Keogh plan, 464–465
 minimum distribution, 459
 premature withdrawals, 459–460
 profit-sharing plans, 462
 tax advantages of, 457–459
 types of plans, 460–465
Qualified small business stock, 503–504
Qualified tuition expenses/programs,
 544–545
Qualified tuition programs, 545
Qualifying child, 415–417
Qualifying property, 242
 nontaxable exchanges, 242–246
Qualifying relative, 417
Quill Corporation v. North Dakota, 14n

R. J. Reynolds Tobacco Company, 161
Rabin, Jerrold, 580
*Rainbow Tax Service, Inc. v.
 Commissioner*, 318n
Rapco, Inc. v. Commissioner, 446n
Ratable inclusion method deduction, 123
Reagan administration and Reaganomics, 27
Real estate professionals, 510n
Real estate sales, 212–213
Real property, 208, 500; *see also* Home
 ownership
 defined, 7
 investment activities, 506–508
 rental real estate, 507–508
 undeveloped land, 506–507
Real property taxes, 5, 7
Realization principle, 129, 200, 494
Realized gain or loss, 200
 basis recovery and, 202–203
Realty, defined, 7
Reasonable compensation, 355n, 445–446
Reasonable doubt, 577
Recapture, 215
Recapture rules, summary for Section 1231
 asset, 220
Recognition, 122
Recognized gain or loss, 200
Recourse debt, 224
Recovery Act (2009), 176
Recovery of bad debt, 139
Recovery period, 167–168
Recurring item exception, 136
Refunds, 571
Regressive rate structure, 34
Regressive sales tax rates, 34
Regressive taxes, 34
Regulated investment company (RIC), 486
Rehabilitation credit, 320–321
Related party accruals, 137–138
Related party transaction, 61–62
 disallowed losses, 206–208
Rent payments, 356

Rental activity, 507, 510
Rental real estate, 208, 507–508
Reorganization, 496
Repairs and cleanup costs, 159–160
Research and experimental expenditures, 160
Research memo, 106–108
Resident, 378n
Resident aliens, 408n
Residual value, 163n, 166n
Restitution payments, 536
Retail sales tax, 8–9, 13–14, 34
Retirement planning, 457–460; *see also*
 Qualified retirement plans
 premature withdrawals, 459–460
 qualified retirement plans, 460–465
Return processing, 572–573
Revenue Act of 1913, 10
Revenue procedures, 15, 97
Revenue rulings, 15, 97
Revenues, 5
 accrual method for, 129
 cash method for, 125
 rulings and revenue procedures, 15
Revised Uniform Limited Partnership Act, 279
Revised Uniform Partnership Act, 279
Risk, 50
Robbie, Joe, 518
Rollover contribution, 460
Rollover IRAs, 470–471
Roth IRAs, 465–466, 468
 rollover to, 471
 withdrawals from, 470

S corporation; *see* Subchapter S corporation
Safe-harbor estimates, 430
Safe-harbor provision, 32
*St. David's Health Care System Inc. v.
 United States*, 582n
Salary payments, 45
 S corporation, 295–297
Salary reduction plans, 462
Sales and exchanges of property, 201–203
Sales factor, 375
Sales tax, 6, 8–9
 expansion to services, 13–14
 Internet purchases, 14
Sales tax exemption, 9n
Salvage value, 166n
Sawhill, Isabel V., 27n
Schedule A (Itemized Deductions), 416
Schedule B, 487–489
Schedule C (Profit or Loss From Business),
 272–276, 410, 443
Schedule D (Capital Gains and Losses),
 497–500, 502
 comprehensive problem, 529–533
Schedule E (Supplemental Income and
 Loss), 284, 508, 550
Schedule F (Profit or Loss From
 Farming), 272n

Schedule K, 282–283
Schedule K-1 (Shareholder's Share of
 Income, Credits, Deductions, etc.),
 284–289, 295–298
Schedule M-1, 315–316
Schedule M-3, 315, 341–344
Scholarships, 536
Scholes, Myron S., 80n
Secondary authorities, 97, 99–100
Section(s), 15
Section 1, 71
Section 11, 71
Section 61, 535–536
Section 179 expensing election, 174–175
Section 274, 124n
Section 401(k) plans, 462–463
Section 460, 122
Section 482, transfer pricing and, 122–123,
 391–392
Section 1231 asset, 200, 214–220, 500
 depreciation recapture, 216–220
 loss recapture, 215–216
 net gain/loss, 214–216
 partial recapture rule for realty, 218
 summary of recapture rules, 220
Section 1231 netting process, 222
Section 1244 stock, 504
Section 1245 recapture, 217
Section 1250 recapture, 218
Section 7491(a), 55n
Securities, 205, 486
Securities and Exchange Commission
 (SEC), 129
Securities markets, 205n
Security transactions
 basis on sale, 495
 capital gains and losses, 494–497
 capital loss limitation, 502–503
 long-term gains, 497–500
 nonbusiness bad debt, 496
 nontaxable exchanges, 496–497
 tracking security basis, 494–495
 worthless securities, 496
Self-created asset, 161
Self-created patents, 161, 212
Self-employed independent contractor, 442
Self-employed individuals, 278n, 465n; *see
 also* Home office deduction, Sole
 proprietorship
 fringe benefits and, 450–451
 health insurance deduction, 451
 Keogh plan, 464–465
 partnership income, 283–286
Self-employment tax (SE), 276–277,
 284n, 352
 limited liability company and, 290–291
Seller-financed sales, 203–206
Separate returns, 409
Separately stated items, 282–283
Series EE savings bonds, 490, 544

SFAS No. 142, *Goodwill and other Intangible Assets*, 181n
Shareholder expenses, 356
Sheppard, Lee, 374n
Short-period return, 120–122
    annualizing income on, 120–122
Short-term capital gains or losses, 497–499
Short-term debt obligations, 490n
Simons, Henry, 36n
Single taxpayer, 409
Sixteenth Amendment, 10–11
Small business exception, 128
Small Business Jobs Act of 2010, 176
Small Tax Case Division, 581–582
Smith, Adam, 22n, 29, 35
Smith, Benjamin H., 570
Snodgrass v. United States, 581n
Social problems, taxes and behavior
    modification, 30–31
Social Psychological Services, Inc., 356n
Social Security, 6, 11, 23, 27, 276, 278, 457n
Social Security benefits, 539
Social Security worksheet, 566
Sole proprietorship, 71, 272–279
    cash flow implications, 273–274
    dispositions of business assets, 275
    employment taxes, 276–279
    home office deduction, 275–276
    individual net operating loss, 273
    interest expense, 275
    Schedule C overview, 272–276
    self-employment tax, 278–279
Special agent, 577
Special interest groups, 14
Specialized state and local tax (SALT), 372
Specific identification method, 166
Standard deduction, 410–415
Standard Federal Tax Reporter, 100
Standards of processional conduct, 578
Start-up expenditures, 178–179, 279n
Start-up losses, 346–347
State and local bonds, 488–490
State lotteries, 13
State tax payments, 542–543
State taxation, 8–10, 372–378
    apportionment of business income,
        374–376
    constitutional restrictions on, 372–374
    corporate income taxes, 9–10
    excise tax, 9
    personal income taxes, 9
    physical presence vs. economic nexus,
        372–374
    sales tax, 8–9
    tax planning implications, 376–377
    use tax, 9
Static forecast, 23–24
Statute of limitations, 572–573
Statutory authority, Federal tax law, 15
Statutory law, 15n

Step transaction doctrine, 83–84
Stewart, Potter, 6
Stock; *see* Security transaction
Stock option, 452–455
Straight-line depreciation, 168, 218
Subchapter K, 350
Subchapter S corporation, 71, 269–270,
        289–296, 309n
    adjusting basis of stock, 295–296
    basis limitation on loss deductions,
        295–296
    basis restoration, 296
    compensation, 449
    cost of formation and operation, 349–351
    election of, 294
    eligible corporations, 293–295
    flexibility of income/loss sharing, 350
    fringe benefits, 449–450
    gain on debt repayment, 298
    income shifting and, 346–348
    nondeductible loss, 297
    owner liability, 350–351
    partnership vs., 351–354
    payments to shareholders/employees,
        295–297
    planning example, 353–354
    salary payments, 295–297
    Subchapter K vs., 350
    tax basis in, 294–295
    tax consequences to shareholders,
        295–297
Subpart F income, 387–389
Substance over form doctrine, 83
Substituted basis rule, 243–244
Substitution effect, 25–27
Sufficiency, good tax and, 22–27
Sunset provision, 15
Supplies, 208, 213–214
    selling unwanted, 214
Supply-side economic theory, 27
Surtax, 317
Surviving spouse, 408
Swig Investment Co. v. United States, 159n
Syndicates, 279n

Tangible business assets, recovery periods
    for, 168
Tangible personalty, 247
Tangible property, 8n
Tax, defined, 4
Tax assessors, 7
Tax avoidance, 70
Tax base, 5
Tax basis, 161
    basis, cost recovery, and cash flow,
        162–163
    critical role of, 161–164
    defined, 161
Tax benefit rule, 139
Tax brackets, 5

Tax breaks, to subsidize targeted activities,
        30–31
Tax compliance process, 569–584
    audit process, 573–578
    contesting audit result, 578–584
    criminal fraud, 577
    filing and payment requirements, 570–573
    innocent spouse rule, 583–584
    IRS collection procedures, 582–583
    late-filing and late-payment penalty,
        571–572
    making a taxpayer friendly system, 581–582
    noncompliance penalties, 575–577
    return processing, 572–573
    statute of limitations, 572–573
    tax return preparer penalties, 578
    Taxpayer Bill of Rights, 574
    Williams v. United States case history,
        580–581
Tax cost, 51–52
Tax credits, 317–319
    deduction vs. credit, 317
    domestic manufacturers, 316–317
    general business credit, 318
    for individuals, 424–426
    preferential tax rate, 318
    rehabilitation credit, 318–319
Tax-deferred, 463, 468
Tax evasion, 70, 577
Tax-exempt, 463, 468
Tax-exempt interest, 130, 486–488
Tax-exempt status, 7, 312
Tax expenditure, 31n
Tax Expenditures Budget, 31–32
Tax expense per books, 131
Tax expenses vs. tax payable, 132–133
Tax filing date, 570
Tax gap, 275, 278
Tax haven, 388
Tax law, 14
    tax preferences, 124–125
Tax law doctrines, 83–84
    business purpose doctrine, 83
    step transaction doctrine, 83–84
    substance over form doctrine, 83
Tax law uncertainty, 56
Tax litigation process, 579–580
    making system taxpayer friendly, 581–582
    trial court, 579–580
    Williams v. United States case history,
        580–581
Tax loopholes, 321
Tax Management Portfolios, 100
Tax neutrality, 31
Tax planning, 69; *see also* Income tax
        planning; MACRS; Wealth transfer
        planning
    business managers and, 16
    capital gains and losses, 211
    cash method and, 129

Tax planning—*Cont.*
 closely held corporations, 354–361
 compensation planning with fringe
  benefits, 451–452
 defined, 69
 developing strategies for, 80–84
 driver of, 70
 flexibility factor, 82
 income tax planning maxims, 69, 80–81
 international business operations, 378–379
 multilateral planning, 82
 net present value (NPV) in decision
  making, 48–51
 passthrough entities, 346–351
 realization principle and, 200–201
 state and local taxation, 376–377
 strategic considerations, 81–82
 tax legal doctrines, 83–84
 tax savings vs. additional costs, 82
Tax policy
 behavior modification by, 30–31
 defined, 21
 distributive justice and, 36–37
 income effect and, 25
 increasing tax revenues, 23
 as instrument of fiscal policy, 29–30
 marginal and average tax rates, 36
 normative standards of, 21
 objectives of, 123–125
 perception of inequality, 38
 standards for a good tax, 22, 38
  convenience, 28
  efficiency, 28–31
  fairness, 32–38
  sufficiency, 22–27
 static vs. dynamic forecasting, 23–24
 substitution effect and, 25–27
 supply side economics and, 27
 tax preferences, 31, 124–125, 322–323
 taxable income and ability to pay, 32–33
Tax preferences, 31, 124–125, 322–323
 horizontal equity and, 32–33
Tax rate differential, 71
Tax rates
 entity variable and, 71
 individual tax rate schedules, 419
Tax Reform Act of 1986, 27
Tax refund, 431
Tax Relief Act (2010), 514
Tax research, 84, 93–108
 developing research skills, 93–95
 keyword searching, 101–102
 primary authorities, 97–99
 secondary authorities, 99–100
 table of contents for, 101
 topical index for, 101
Tax research process, 94–108
 analyzing authority, 103–105
 communicating conclusions, 106–108
 fact finding, 95–96

 issue identification, 96–97
 locating authoritative sources, 97–103
 repeating steps of, 105–106
Tax return preparer, 578
Tax revenue, 6, 23
Tax savings, 52
Tax services, 318
Tax services (commercial), 99–100
Tax shelters, decline of, 357–358
Tax shield, 52n
Tax subsidies, higher education expenses,
 544–545
Taxable estate, 515–516
Taxable exchange, property for stock, 253
Taxable income, 118–119
 corporate, 312–316
 federal definition, 10
 from business operation, 118
Taxable income limitation, 175
Taxable year, 119–122, 119n
 changing a taxable year, 120
 choice of, 118–120
 short-period return, annualizing income,
  120–122
TaxAlmanac, 102
Taxes and taxation, 3; *see also* Individual
 taxpayer; Partnership, Sole
 proprietorship; Subchapter S
 corporation
 base, rate, and revenue (formula)
  relationship, 5
 basic terminology of, 4–6
 cash flows and, 51–52
 dynamic nature of, 13–14
 earmarked taxes, 6
 federal taxes, 10–11
 foreign taxes, 12, 542–543
 inflationary gains, 203
 jurisdictional competition, 12–13
 local taxation, 7–8, 372–378
 marginal tax rate, 52–53
 nature of tax environment, 6–7
 pervasive nature of, 6–13
 political process and, 14
 special interest groups, 14
 sufficiency standard for, 22–27
 tax base changes, 13–14
 uncertainty of tax consequences, 55–57
Taxing jurisdiction, 371–374
 competition among, 12–13
 controlled foreign corporations (CFC),
  388–390
 defined, 4–5
 foreign source income, tax deferral on,
  386–392
 foreign taxes, 12
 increasing tax revenues, 23
 nonresident aliens, 5
 state and local taxation, 7–10, 372–378
 U.S. and global income, 379

Taxpayer, defined, 4
Taxpayer Bill of Rights, 574–575
Taxpayer negligence and fraud, 62n
Technical advice memorandum (TAM), 97
Temporary book/tax accounting differences,
 131, 144, 166, 185, 225, 256,
 392–393, 472
Tentative minimum tax, 325
Testamentary transfer, 515
Theft losses, 546–547
Thin capitalization, 356–357
Thor Power Tool Co. vs. Commissioner, 130n
Three-martini lunch, 124
Three-party exchanges, 249
Three-year statute of limitations, 53
Time period variable, 73–76
 opportunity costs and income deferral,
  75–76
 rate changes and income deferral, 76
Time value of money, 48, 50
Total income, 410
Traditional IRA, 465–466
 deduction of contributions, 466–468
 withdrawals from, 468–469
Transaction-based tax, 6
Transaction costs, 350
Transactional markets, 58–62
Transactions
 arm's-length presumption, 60–61
 private market transactions, 58–60
 public market transactions, 61
 related party transactions, 61–62
 structuring to reduce taxes, 57–62
 tax consequences of
  character variable, 77–80
  entity variable, 71–73
  jurisdiction variable, 77
  time-period variable, 73–76
Transfer price, 391–392
 global proportion, 392
Transfer tax system, 513
Transfer taxes, 11
Transferee liability, 583
Treasury bills, 490
Treasury inflation-protected securities
 (TIPS), 490–491
Treasury regulations, 15, 97
Trial court, 579–580
Twenty (20) percent recapture rule,
 219–220
Twenty-eight (28) percent rate gain or
 loss, 497

Undeliverable refund checks, 430
Underpayment penalty, 326
Underpayment rate, 570
Undeveloped land, 504–505
Unearned income Medicare contribution
 tax, 512
Unemployment tax, 11, 276–277

Uniform capitalization (Unicap) rules, 165–166
Uniform Division of Income for Tax Purposes Act (UPITPA), 375
Unincorporated business organization, 279n
U.S. Circuit Courts of Appeals, 98, 580
U.S. Constitution, Sixteenth Amendment, 10–11
U.S. Court of Federal Claims, 98, 579
U.S. debt obligations, 490
U.S. Department of the Interior, 320
U.S. Department of Treasury, 15, 378n
U.S. District Court, 98, 579
U.S. Patent Office, 70
U.S. production activities deduction, 125, 318–319
U.S. Supreme Court, 98, 580
   assignment of income doctrine, 73
   on income tax deduction, 158
   on national income tax, 10
   on taxpayer's benefits, 4
   on use tax of mail-order companies, 14
U.S. Tax Court, 98, 579
United States Tax Reporter, 100

United States v. Bisceglia, 6n
United States v. General Dynamics Corp., 134n
Unlimited life, 310
Unlimited marital deduction, 516
Unmarried individuals, 409
Unreasonable compensation, 355, 446–447
Unreasonably low compensation, 447
Unrecaptured Section 1250 gain, 500–501
Use tax, 8–9
Useful life, 167

Vacation home, 550
Value-added tax (VAT), 12
Vertical equity, 33–36
Viatical settlement provider, 493n

Wage base, 23
Walter v. United States, 127n
Wash sale, 255
Wasting assets, 167
Wealth distribution, 37n
Wealth maximization, 47
Wealth of Nations (Smith), 22n, 29, 35

Wealth transfer planning, 512–517
   annual exclusion, 514
   gift tax, 513–515
   income shift, 515
   kiddie tax, 515
   transfer tax system, 513
Welch v. Helvering, 127n
Wetzler, James W., 70
Williams, Lori, 580–581
Williams v. United States case history, 580–581
Withholding amount, 429n
Withholding tax, 384
Wolff, Edward N., 37n
Wolfson, Mark A., 80n
Worker classification
   business vs. IRS, 443–444
   tax consequences of, 442–443
Worker, Homeownership, and Business Assistance Act of 2009, 140n
Worthless securities, 496
Wrightsman v. United States, 543n

Zero tax basis, 162